THEATRE PROFILES 10

THEATRE PROFILES 10

THE ILLUSTRATED REFERENCE GUIDE TO AMERICA'S NONPROFIT PROFESSIONAL THEATRE

EDITED BY STEVEN SAMUELS

THEATRE COMMUNICATIONS GROUP
NEW YORK • 1992

TCG gratefully acknowledges public funds from the National Endowment for the Arts, the New York State Council on the Arts and the New York City Department of Cultural Affairs in addition to the generous support of the following foundations and corporations: Alcoa Foundation, Ameritech Foundation, ARCO Foundation, AT&T Foundation, Citibank, N.A., Consolidated Edison Company of New York, Council of Literary Magazines and Presses, Nathan Cummings Foundation, Dayton Hudson Foundation, Exxon Corporation, Ford Foundation, James Irvine Foundation, Jerome Foundation, Andrew W. Mellon Foundation, Metropolitan Life Foundation, National Broadcasting Company, Pew Charitable Trusts, Philip Morris Companies, Scherman Foundation, Shubert Foundation, Lila Wallace-Reader's Digest Fund.

TCG would like to thank the following staff members and individuals who helped with the massive job of preparing this volume: Stephanie Coen, Gretchen Griffin, M. Elizabeth Osborn, Gillian Richards, Regina Raiford, Dora Serafini, and Scott Sonneborn.

Text design and composition by Peter Lukic
Cover design by The Sarabande Press

ISBN 1-55936-040-2

First Edition, March 1992

On the cover: The Shakespeare Theatre at the Folger. Stacy Keach in *Richard III*. Photo by Joan Marcus.

Frontis: Ping Chong and Company. Johanna Melamed, John Fleming, Jeannie Hutchins and Ric Oquita in *Elephant Memories*. Photo by Carol Rosegg/Marth Swope Associates.

CONTENTS

FOREWORD

By Peter Zeisler and Lindy Zesch

When Theatre Communications Group was founded in 1961, it offered services to 16 theatres—virtually the total pool of nonprofit professional companies then operating in the United States. Among them were the Alley Theatre of Houston, Arena Stage of Washington, D.C., the Barter Theatre of Abingdon, Va., the Cleveland Play House, the Goodman Theatre of Chicago and the predecessors of the Milwaukee Repertory Theater and the Mark Taper Forum of Los Angeles.

These companies pioneered a new way of making theatre in an institutional setting. Organizations specifically established for educational and charitable purposes, they eschewed the project-oriented ethos of the New York-based commercial theatre, which reached out to the rest of the nation only through touring "road shows." The result, as can be seen in the Theatre Chronology beginning on page 166, was a true explosion of theatrical activity across the country throughout the Sixties and Seventies, spurred by support from private foundations (most notably the Ford and Rockefeller Foundations) and later by the growth of government support following the birth of the National Endowment for the Arts and the advent of the state arts agency movement.

TCG itself, founded by the Ford Foundation in the belief that "the theatre in America is a cultural rather than a commercial resource," has grown along with the field and today encompasses the diverse group of 229 constituent theatres that appears in this book. These theatres are located in major metropolitan centers, rural communities, urban neighborhoods and suburbs. They engage in work from a wide-ranging repertoire that includes classics; modern plays and musicals; new plays, adaptations and translations by American and international writers; experimental, multi-media and performance art works. They are based in every corner of the country—in more than 150 towns and cities across the United States, representing forty two states as well as the District of Columbia. In 1989-90, these theatres collectively presented more than 50,000 performances of 2,500 productions at home and on tour, attracting an attendance of some twenty million. Taken together, they represent a truly American theatre that speaks through art to the concerns of culturally diverse audiences throughout the country.

Yet despite such growth and achievement, the nonprofit professional theatre entered the 1990s facing many challenges and obstacles to its continued growth. An increasingly worsening economy has led to declining growth rates in support from private foundations, corporations and individuals, while deep cuts in government funding have produced not only losses in dollars, but signify a disturbing erosion of support for the arts among the American people. In 1990, under fierce attack from conservatives in Congress, as well as from lobbyists representing the religious right, the National Endowment for the Arts fought for its life to defend freedom of expression and to protect the right to government funding even for controversial art. The debate continues and shows no sign of abatement, and the future of government leadership in the arts remains severely threatened. In the face of these developments, fourteen TCG theatres have closed their doors over the past two seasons.

The rapid growth in the nonprofit theatre movement has also provided America's theatres with a new set of internal challenges. While the talent pool of artists has continually expanded since the Sixties in tandem with the opportunities afforded by the burgeoning national theatre movement, more lucrative new opportunities in film and television have begun to lure those artists away from the theatre, resulting in an ominous talent drain. Rapidly changing demographics have opened up new opportunities to embrace diverse cultures within American society, requiring new ways of attracting audiences, and new organizational structures.

But perhaps the most significant development faced by the nonprofit professional theatre is the fact that virtually the entire generation of founders—those pioneering individuals so inspired by the idea of creating a new theatre for America—has now passed the torch on to those who grew up with the movement already in place. An era has all but ended. In 1991, Zelda Fichandler retired from Arena Stage after forty years at its helm. Lloyd Richards completed his tenure as artistic director of the Yale Repertory Theatre. William Ball, founder and former artistic director of the American Conservatory Theater—one of the few institutions to succeed in creating a repertory theatre coupled with a professional conservatory—died. And, as we write this, it is just a few weeks since the theatre community lost its most dedicated fighter—Joseph Papp, founder of the New York Shakespeare Festival. The vision shared by these and other trailblazing individuals demonstrated that America had the talent and ability to create an indigenous theatre, and one that could flourish not only in a single theatre capital but throughout the land; that it is possible to provide a home for artists to practice their art with the freedom to experiment and explore—and to have the right to fail. As a result, virtually all new American dramatic work is nurtured within the nonprofit theatre today.

The legacy of those who spearheaded this theatre revolution will remain forever part of the theatre. But that spirit and drive that characterizes revolutions will and must be replaced by other attributes and concerns as we move into the future. The inheritors of the mantle of the pioneers will have to work hard to overcome the obstacles of the Nineties, not only to survive, but to flourish in the approaching new century. Happily, there is no shortage of talent to replace the generation of theatre founders.

Among the promising trends that will help them along the road is an encouraging receptiveness to international exchange as the world has opened up; festivals, for instance, have now been established in some of our major cities, where artists can see the work of their peers from countries and cultures around the globe. That exposure has enriched and broadened the horizons of America's theatre artists. Other promising signs include the design of new buildings and the development of alternative and site-specific theatre spaces, expansions of seasons and growth in audiences in spite of the flagging economy. Artists are increasingly working in collaborative ways, sometimes crossing disciplines within the theatre and outside—thereby enriching their work.

As TCG celebrates thirty years of service to the American theatre, the *Theatre Profiles* series is in its tenth volume—reflecting twenty years of American theatre activity. Taken as a set, these ten volumes record an extraordinary body of work and pay tribute to the theatre artists, administrators, trustees and audiences who comprise the nonprofit professional theatre nationwide, who have traveled together on the remarkable journey through the movement's first three decades.

November 22, 1991

HIGHLIGHTS 1961-1991

Thirty Years in the American Theatre

Although the early Sixties were a turning point in the American theatre, the seeds of three alternatives to Broadway's commercial activities had been planted prior to 1960. The Off Broadway movement, which had been established with the success of several companies including an early nonprofit theatre—Circle in the Square (founded 1951)—faced escalating costs, prompting the rise of what inevitably became known as Off-*Off* Broadway. This energetic offshoot encompassed the efforts of such pioneering groups as The Living Theatre (1951) and Caffe Cino (1958). Elsewhere in the U.S., what was coming to be known as the "regional theatre movement" had taken hold in such cities as Cleveland (The Cleveland Play House, 1915), Chicago (Goodman Theatre, 1925), Abingdon, Va. (Robert Porterfield's Barter Theatre, 1933), Houston (Alley Theatre, 1947), Dallas (Margo Jones's Theatre 47, 1947), Washington, D.C. (Arena Stage, 1950) and San Francisco (Actors Workshop, 1952).

In addition to these regional or resident theatres, a number of Shakespeare festivals dotted the American landscape, including the Oregon Shakespeare Festival in Ashland (1935), Old Globe Theatre in San Diego (1937), New York Shakespeare Festival (1954) and American Shakespeare Theatre in Stratford, Conn. (1955). It was from these roots—the early regional companies along with a vital Off-Off Broadway movement—that the full-fledged non-commercial theatre sprang, spreading, through the Seventies, to the furthest reaches of the nation.

1961—The Living Theatre presents Kenneth Brown's *The Brig*, following its influential 1959 production of Jack Gelber's *The Connection*. Tennessee Williams's last widely acclaimed play, *Night of the Iguana*, appears on Broadway. The Judson Poets' Theatre, under the direction of Al Carmines, opens in lower Manhattan's Judson Church. The Bread and Puppet Theatre is born in New York with a production of *Totentanz*. Ford Foundation trustees appropriate an initial $9 million to begin "strengthening the position of resident theatre in the U.S." along with $244,000 for the establishment of Theatre Communications Group. In addition, Ford vice president for the humanities and arts W. McNeil Lowry engages Danny Newman, through TCG, as a subscription consultant, sparking enormous audience growth throughout the nation.

1962—Edward Albee's *Who's Afraid of Virginia Woolf?* opens on Broadway, directed by Alan Schneider. New York Shakespeare Festival's 2,300-seat, open-air Delacorte Theatre opens in Central Park. Arthur Kopit's *Oh Dad Poor Dad . . .* premieres Off Broadway. Ellen Stewart creates Cafe La Mama Off-Off Broadway, beginning with Tennessee Williams's *One Arm*. The Great Lakes Shakespeare Festival opens in Cleveland.

1963—The Guthrie Theater, the first institutional theatre in the U.S. built solely with community support and dedicated to a classical repertoire, opens in Minneapolis with *Hamlet*. Joseph Chaikin, along with Peter Feldman and a group of artists, founds the Open Theater in New York. The Seattle Repertory Theatre and Center Stage in Baltimore begin operations. Gilbert Moses and John O'Neal open the Free Southern Theatre at Mississippi's Tougaloo College, in response to the Civil Rights movement.

1964—The first two plays of budding playwright Sam Shepard, *Cowboy* and *Rock Garden*, are produced at New York's Theatre Genesis. The Lincoln Center Repertory Theatre is established with Elia Kazan and Robert Whitehead at the helm. The Phoenix and APA theatres merge, and for four years produce plays in repertory on Broadway. The recently founded American Place Theatre opens Off Broadway with a production of Robert Lowell's *The Old Glory*. Adrian Hall founds Trinity Repertory Company (originally Trinity Square Repertory Company) in Providence. Among other theatres to begin operation are Actors Theatre of Louisville and Hartford Stage Company. Ming Cho Lee designs sets for a production of *Electra* in Central Park, forging a new, sculptural design style. The Living Theatre begins two decades of exile in Europe and South America.

1965—San Francisco's American Conservatory Theatre, the first company to operate a professional conservatory, opens under the artistic direction of William Ball. Luis Valdez founds El Teatro Campesino to entertain California's striking farm workers. Robert Kalfin founds the Chelsea Theater Center in Manhattan. The O'Neill Theater Center holds its first National Playwrights' Conference in Waterford, Conn. President Lyndon B. Johnson signs legislation creating the National Endowment for the Arts. Long Wharf Theatre opens in New Haven.

1966—The Twentieth Century Fund publishes the first book to study in depth the subject of economics and the arts, *Performing Arts—The Economic Dilemma*, by William J. Baumol and William G. Bowen. The NEA receives its first funds from Congress: $2.5

million to be spread among all the arts throughout the country. Robert Brustein establishes the Yale Repertory Theatre, to operate in conjunction with the Yale School of Drama. Jules lrving and Herbert Blau bring members of their Actors Workshop from San Francisco to found a new company at New York's Lincoln Center. Megan Terry's *Viet Rock* is born out of an Open Theater workshop. Ronald Ribman's *Journey of the Fifth Horse*, featuring Dustin Hoffman, premieres at the American Place Theatre. The first League of Resident Theatres contract comes into being.

1967—Sir Tyrone Guthrie directs the *Oresteia* at the Guthrie, with designs by Tanya Moiseiwitsch. John Houseman's Theatre Group, in residence at UCLA since 1959, is invited to move into the Los Angeles Music Center and becomes the Mark Taper Forum; Gordon Davidson is appointed artistic director. Barbara Garson's *MacBird* is first performed at New York's Village Gate. Edward Albee's *A Delicate Balance* wins the Pulitzer Prize for Drama. The New York Shakespeare Festival moves into its new facility, the Public Theater on Lafayette Street, opening with the rock musical *Hair*. Richard Schechner founds The Performance Group in New York along Grotowski-inspired lines. The San Francisco Mime Troupe (founded in 1959 by Ronnie Davis) comes to national prominence with a cross-country tour of anti-war scenarios. Douglas Turner Ward, Robert Hooks and Gerald S. Krone found the Negro Ensemble Company in New York, opening with Peter Weiss's *Song of the Lusitanian Bogey*. Eugene Lee designs his first set for Trinity Repertory Company, *The Threepenny Opera*, beginning a long association with the theatre and with director Adrian Hall. A group of theatre artists, psychologists and social scientists found the National Theatre of the Deaf. Joe Cino commits suicide and Caffe Cino closes its doors.

1968—The Open Theater presents Jean-Claude van Itallie's *The Serpent*, and The Performance Group opens *Dionysus in 69*. The Living Theatre returns to the U.S. briefly to present *Paradise Now* and *Frankenstein* at the Yale Repertory Theatre and the Brooklyn Academy of Music. *Hair* brings Broadway its first nude scene. The Arena Stage production of *The Great White Hope* opens on Broadway, winning the Pulitzer. Richard Foreman founds the Ontological-Hysteric Theater.

1969—Gilbert Moses directs the Chelsea Theater Center production of Amiri Baraka's *Slave Ship* at the Brooklyn Academy of Music, with an elaborate environment designed by Eugene Lee. Robert Wilson founds the Byrd Hoffman School of Byrds. Marshall W. Mason, Lanford Wilson and colleagues found Circle Repertory Company in New York. Gerald Freedman's production of *The Taming of the Shrew* at the New York Shakespeare Festival uses American farce techniques inspired by Chaplin, Keaton and the like. Romanian director Andrei Serban arrives in the U.S. and begins directing at La Mama. Broadway's ANTA Theatre hosts the first showcase of work from the nation's resident theatres, including the American Conservatory Theatre, the American Shakespeare Theatre, Trinity Repertory Company and the National Theatre of the Deaf.

1970—A collective of performing artists founds Mabou Mines, and Lee Breuer presents the first of his "Animations." Daniel Berrigan's *The Trial of the Catonsville Nine*, directed by Gordon Davidson, premieres at the Mark Taper Forum. Andre Gregory and his Manhattan Project premiere their landmark *Alice in Wonderland* in New York.

1971—Peter Brook and the Royal Shakespeare Company return to New York with their *Midsummer Night's Dream*. The Negro Ensemble Company produces *The River Niger* and takes it on tour. David Rabe's *The Basic Training of Pavlo Hummel* premieres at the New York Shakespeare Festival. Playwrights Horizons, dedicated to new work, is founded by Robert Moss in New York City. Lyn Austin founds the Music-Theatre Group/Lenox Arts Center in Massachusetts to nurture dynamic collaborations among music and theatre artists. The Rockefeller Foundation launches its Fellowships for American Playwrights program.

1972—In collaboration with composer Elizabeth Swados, Andrei Serban directs his adaptation of *Medea* at La Mama, the first play in a classical trilogy that will later be presented collectively as *Fragments of a Trilogy*. John Houseman and Margot Harley found The Acting Company, a national touring theatre, with members of the first graduating class of the Juilliard School's Drama Division. A bill of four Beckett plays including *Krapp's Last Tape* and *Happy Days* opens at Lincoln Center, directed by Alan Schneider and featuring Hume Cronyn and Jessica Tandy. A Richard Foreman/Stanley Silverman collaboration entitled *Dr. Selavy's Magic Theatre* bows at Music-Theatre Group.

1973—Joseph Papp assumes direction of theatre at Lincoln Center. The Ridiculous Theatrical Company, founded by Charles Ludlam in 1967, presents *Camille* with Ludlam in the title role. *Candide*, directed by Hal Prince, premieres at the Chelsea Theater Center. Adrian Hall and Richard Cumming's *Feasting with Panthers* premieres at Trinity Repertory Company and is then televised nationally in the first season of WNET's "Theatre in America" series. Arena Stage is chosen by the U.S. State Department to be the first American company to tour the Soviet Union, and they take *Our Town* and *Inherit the Wind*. The Open Theater disbands. TCG publishes the inaugural edition of *Theatre Profiles*, covering 89 theatres.

1974—*A Chorus Line* debuts at the New York Shakespeare Festival's Public Theater, after a long workshop period (later going on to Broadway and the 1976 Pulitzer). Liviu Ciulei directs his first play in the U.S., Buchner's *Leonce and Lena*, at Arena Stage. Miguel Pinero's *Short Eyes* opens at the Theatre at the Riverside Church. The Yale Repertory Theatre produces a musical version of Aristophanes' *The Frogs* in the university swimming pool.

1975—Edward Albee wins his second Pulitzer for *Seascape*. The New Federal

Theatre production of Ntozake Shange's *For Colored Girls...* opens, then moves to the New York Shakespeare Festival. Gregory Mosher directs the world premiere of David Mamet's *American Buffalo* at the Goodman's Stage 2 in Chicago. The Los Angeles Actors' Theatre is founded by Ralph Waite. Richard Foreman directs *The Threepenny Opera* at Lincoln Center. Mabou Mines adapts and produces two Beckett works, *Cascando* and *The Lost Ones*, featuring music by Philip Glass.

1976—Robert Wilson's *Einstein on the Beach* premieres at France's Avignon Festival, and is subsequently produced at the Metropolitan Opera in New York. Lynne Meadow stages David Rudkin's *Ashes* at the Manhattan Theatre Club. *Annie* premieres at the Goodspeed Opera House in Connecticut. David Rabe's *Streamers* premieres at Long Wharf Theatre, directed by Mike Nichols. Fired after a controversial season at Trinity, Adrian Hall in turn fires his board of trustees and remains at the helm. Actors Theatre of Louisville, under the artistic direction of Jon Jory, presents its first Festival of New American Plays. The Alaska Repertory Theatre is founded and is the 50th state's first professional performing arts institution. TCG holds its first National Conference at Yale University, bringing the national nonprofit theatre community together for the first time.

1977—Richard Maltby, Jr. directs his Fats Waller revue, *Ain't Misbehavin'*, at Manhattan Theatre Club. Christopher Durang's *A History of the American Film* enjoys a triple opening at Arena Stage, the Mark Taper Forum and Hartford Stage Company. Michael Cristofer's *The Shadow Box*, born at the Mark Taper, wins the Pulitzer after a run on Broadway. Andrei Serban's production of Chekhov's *The Cherry Orchard* opens at Lincoln Center.

1978—The Oregon Shakespeare Festival completes the entire Shakespeare canon for the second time (having completed it once in 1959). The American Place Theatre inaugurates its Women's Project. Ernest Thompson's *On Golden Pond* bows at the Hudson Guild Theatre. D.L. Coburn's *The Gin Game*, which had premiered at American Theatre Arts in Los Angeles in a different production, wins the Pulitzer. *Zoot Suit* by Luis Valdez is produced at the Mark Taper. Sam Shepard's *Buried Child*, directed by Robert Woodruff, premieres at the Magic Theatre in San Francisco, forging an alliance between the writer, the director and the theatre. (The play will go on to net the Pulitzer the following season.) Arthur Kopit's *Wings* is produced at the Yale Repertory Theatre and moves on to Broadway.

1979—Mark Medoff's *Children of a Lesser God* premieres at the Mark Taper Forum under Gordon Davidson's direction. John Hirsch is hired by the Seattle Repertory Theatre as consulting artistic director. The BAM Theater Company, dedicated to a "company approach to the classics," opens at the Brooklyn Academy of Music under the direction of David Jones, but survives only two seasons. Lloyd Richards is appointed to head both the Yale Repertory Theatre and Yale School of Drama, and institutes a new play festival entitled Winterfest. Robert Brustein founds the American Repertory Theatre at Harvard University.

1980—Richmond Crinkley and an artistic directorate take over operation of the theatre at Lincoln Center and produce one season. Wilford Leach breathes new energy into Gilbert and Sullivan's *Pirates of Penzance*, and it soon transfers from the New York Shakespeare Festival's Delacorte Theater to Broadway. The Yale Repertory Theatre's production of Athol Fugard's *A Lesson from Aloes*, directed by the playwright, begins Fugard's fruitful association with Lloyd Richards and the theatre. Lanford Wilson's *Talley's Folly*, which originated at his theatrical "home base," Circle Repertory Company, under Marshall W. Mason's direction, wins the Pulitzer. The Denver Center Theatre Company is founded as a component of the Denver Center for the Performing Arts.

1981—Liviu Ciulei is appointed artistic director of the Guthrie and opens with an acclaimed production of *The Tempest*. The Phoenix Theatre closes after a number of moves around New York City. Tennessee Williams turns to the noncommercial theatre to premiere his *Something Cloudy, Something Clear* at New York's Cocteau Repertory, and his *A House Not Meant to Stand* at the Goodman Theatre. Charles Fuller's *A Soldier's Play* opens at the Negro Ensemble Company, going on to win the Pulitzer for 1982 and tour extensively. The Wooster Group's *Route 1 & 9* opens at New York's Performing Garage to a flurry of controversy over what some feel is its racist content. Bill Irwin brings his *The Regard of Flight* to the American Place Theatre after its appearance at the New Theatre Festival in Baltimore, introducing the "new vaudeville" movement.

1982—The Eureka Theatre Company in San Francisco commissions Emily Mann to write a play that is to become *Execution of Justice*. *Torch Song Trilogy*, born sequentially at La Mama, lands on Broadway. *Little Shop of Horrors*, the Howard Ashman/Alan Menken musical based on a low-budget horror film, opens at New York's WPA Theatre.

1983—The Brooklyn Academy of Music holds its first Next Wave Festival, featuring Lee Breuer's *Gospel at Colonus* and *The Photographer*, a collaboration of David Gordon, JoAnne Akalaitis and Philip Glass. Marsha Norman's *'night, Mother*, first produced at the American Repertory Theatre, wins the Pulitzer. *In the Belly of the Beast*, adapted by Adrian Hall from Jack Henry Abbott's book, opens at Trinity Repertory Company. The Theatre Project Company of St. Louis stirs up the community and jeopardizes its state funding with a production of *Sister Mary Ignatius...* which some brand "antiCatholic." *Sunday in the Park with George* begins life as a workshop production at Playwrights Horizons. Mabou Mines and Interart Theatre collaborate on a production of Franz Xaver Kroetz's *Through the Leaves*. Alan Schneider directs his last play in America, Pinter's *Other Places*, at the Manhattan Theatre Club. *The Ballad of Soapy Smith* by Michael Weller opens the Seattle Repertory Theatre's new Bagley Wright Theatre complex. Two productions from Chicago's Steppenwolf

Theatre Company, *True West* and *And a Nightingale Sang...*, introduce New York audiences to the energetic "Steppenwolf style."

1984—The Goodman Theatre production of David Mamet's *Glengarry Glen Ross*, directed by Gregory Mosher, transfers to Broadway and wins the Pulitzer, while its production of *Hurlyburly*, directed by Mike Nichols, travels from the Goodman to Off Broadway and Broadway. Berkeley Repertory Theatre, under newly appointed artistic director Sharon Ott, produces *Kingdom Come*, a drama about Norwegian pioneers in the Midwest, using black, Hispanic and Asian-American actors. Robert Wilson produces his first fullscale work in this country since *Einstein on the Beach*, *The CIVIL warS*, at the American Repertory Theatre. The first Olympic Arts Festival is held in Los Angeles, presenting such international artists as Ariane Mnouchkine's Theatre du Soleil, Pina Bausch's Wuppertaler Tanztheater, Tadashi Suzuki's SCOT Theatre and Giorgio Strehler's Piccolo Teatro. James Reston Jr.'s *Jonestown Express* premieres at Trinity Repertory Company. Peter Sellars is appointed artistic director of the American National Theatre at the Kennedy Center. Milwaukee Repertory Theater artistic director John Dillon stages *Death of a Salesman* in Japan with an all-Japanese cast. After several visa denials, Dario Fo is finally permitted into the U.S., not to perform but to attend the Broadway opening of his *Accidental Death of an Anarchist*, which originated at Arena Stage. *Garden of Earthly Delights* by Martha Clarke and Richard Peaslee premieres at Music-Theatre Group/Lenox Arts Center. *American Theatre*, a national monthly magazine, begins publication.

1985—The new Los Angeles Theatre Center opens its four-theatre performing arts facility, and the Alabama Shakespeare Festival's new $21.5 million theatre begins operation in Montgomery. Former Goodman artistic director Gregory Mosher is appointed artistic director and Bernard Gersten managing director of the new Lincoln Center Theater. Liviu Ciulei resigns from The Guthrie, directing *A Midsummer Night's Dream* as his final production. He is succeeded by Garland Wright. *Big River*, the Roger Miller/William Hauptman musical developed at American Repertory Theatre and the La Jolla Playhouse, moves to Broadway in a production staged by Des McAnuff, salvaging an indifferent commercial season and sweeping the Tonys. Wooster Group member Spalding Gray continues his exploration of the autobiographical monologue with his most ambitious work, *Swimming to Cambodia*, taking it on national and international tour after performances in New York. Circle Repertory Company tours Japan with two productions, launching a ten-year project initiated by the Japan-United States Friendship Commission. The Joyce Theater inaugurates an annual American Theatre Exchange, inviting the Mark Taper Forum, the Yale Repertory Theatre and the Alley Theatre to bring productions to New York.

1986—After 20 years as general director of the company he founded, William Ball resigns from San Francisco's American Conservatory Theater and founding member/executive director Edward Hastings is appointed artistic director. Former Wisdom Bridge artistic director Robert Falls and Frank Galati are appointed artistic director and associate director, respectively, of Chicago's Goodman Theatre. Michael Kahn directs *Romeo and Juliet* for his inaugural production as artistic director of the Shakespeare Theatre at the Folger in Washington, D.C. The First National Hispanic Theatre Conference, a gathering of more than 150 Hispanic theatre organizations in the United States and Puerto Rico, convenes in San Antonio, Texas. INTAR Hispanic American Arts Center in New York celebrates its 20th anniversary with five specially commissioned plays. The First National Symposium on Non-Traditional Casting convenes in New York with over 500 in attendance. Lee Blessing's *A Walk in the Woods* is produced at Yale Repertory Theatre after having been developed at the O'Neill Theater Center's National Playwrights Conference, held annually in Waterford, Conn. The New York Shakespeare Festival brings attention to the AIDS crisis with its production of Larry Kramer's *The Normal Heart*. Crossroads Theatre Company in New Brunswick, N.J. premieres George C. Wolfe's *The Colored Museum* directed by company co-founder/co-artistic director L. Kenneth Richardson. Ping Chong's Fiji Company and Meredith Monk present *The Games* at the Brooklyn Academy of Music. Euripides' *Alcestis*, adapted and translated by Robert Wilson, is produced by the American Repertory Theatre in Cambridge, Massachusetts.

1987—August Wilson's *Fences*, originally produced at Yale Repertory Theatre and various other resident theatres across the country, arrives on Broadway and goes on to win the Pulitzer Prize. Exiled Soviet director Yuri Lyubimov makes his American debut at Washington, D.C.'s Arena Stage with an adaptation of Dostoevsky's *Crime and Punishment*. Peter Brook's nine-hour production of *The Mahabharata* is presented at the Los Angeles Festival and the Brooklyn Academy of Music's Next Wave Festival. Chicago's International Theatre Festival debuts. New York's Lincoln Center Theater presents Mbongeni Ngema's *Sarafina!*, a South African musical about Township school children. Alfred Uhry's *Driving Miss Daisy* premieres at New York's Playwrights Horizons, and goes on to win the 1988 Pulitzer Prize, receive national and international stage productions and become a successful film. Marshall W. Mason resigns from New York's Circle Repertory Company, where he is succeeded by co-founder Tanya Berezin. Garland Wright begins his tenure as artistic director of the Guthrie Theater in Minneapolis with *The Misanthrope*. New York Shakespeare Festival producer Joseph Papp announces an ambitious six-year plan to present all 36 Shakespeare plays with foremost American actors in leading roles.

1988—*The Artistic Home*, a landmark report on the series of nationwide meetings with artistic directors convened as part of TCG's National Artistic Agenda Project, is published.

The Milwaukee Repertory Theater, Washington D.C.'s Arena Stage, Berkeley Repertory Theatre and StageWest of Springfield, Mass. bring acclaimed Japanese director Tadashi Suzuki to America to adapt and direct *The Tale of Lear* using actors from each theatre who had studied with Sukuzi in Japan. Three artistic directors—Mark Lamos of Hartford Stage Company, Nagle Jackson of the McCarter Theatre in Princeton, N.J. and Theodore Mann of New York's Circle in the Square—become the first Americans to direct Soviet companies in Soviet theatres. The First New York International Festival of the Arts, offering some 350 events in all arts disciplines, is held in New York City. Eugene O'Neill's centenary is celebrated with commemorative productions in theatres across the country, including Yale Repertory Theatre's productions of *Ah, Wilderness!* and *Long Day's Journey into Night* starring Jason Robards and Colleen Dewhurst. Chicago's Steppenwolf Company mounts the premiere stage version of John Steinbeck's *The Grapes of Wrath*, adapted and directed by Frank Galati. Founder Gregory A. Falls resigns as artistic director of A Contemporary Theatre in Seattle, where he is succeeded by Jeff Steitzer. David Henry Hwang's *M. Butterfly* opens on Broadway.

1989—PepsiCo's Summerfare, held annually at the State University of New York in Purchase, marks its 10th and final season with "Perestroika on Stage," hosting the Anatoly Vasiliev Theatre Company and Pushkin Theatre from the Soviet Union and Poland's Stary Theatre Company. Founding artistic director Mako resigns from East West Players in Los Angeles, the country's oldest Asian-American theatre, and Nobu McCarthy is named to succeed him. Theatre de la Jeune Lune in Minneapolis marks the 200th birthday of the French Revolution and its own 10th anniversary with the epic production, *1789—The French Revolution*. Cornerstone Theater, founded in 1986, mounts a controversial, racially mixed production of *Romeo and Juliet* in Port Gibson, Miss., employing actors from both the company and the community. *New Music*, an ambitious trilogy of plays by Reynolds Price, debuts at the Cleveland Play House under the guidance of recently appointed artistic director Josephine Abady. David Feldshuh's historical drama *Miss Evers' Boys* debuts at Baltimore's Center Stage. John Hirsch directs *Coriolanus* for the Old Globe Theatre in San Diego. The Hartford Stage Company presents Ibsen's complete *Peer Gynt* in a two-part, five-hour production. Wendy Wasserstein's *The Heidi Chronicles*, developed at Seattle Repertory Theatre and New York's Playwrights Horizons before moving to Broadway, is awarded the Pulitzer Prize. Adrian Hall, the first person to serve simultaneously as artistic head of two major institutions, steps down as head of the Dallas Theater Center and Trinity Repertory Company in Providence, R.I. Nikos Psacharopoulos, founder and artistic director of the Williamstown Theatre Festival since 1955, dies and is succeeded by Peter Hunt. Martin L. Platt, founder and artistic director of the Alabama Shakespeare Festival, resigns after 17 years and is succeeded by Kent Thompson. Gregory Boyd becomes artistic director of Houston's Alley Theatre and is succeeded at StageWest in Springfield, Mass. by Eric Hill. Vaclav Havel, banned in his native country since 1969 but sustained in this country at the New York Shakespeare Festival and Philadelphia's Wilma Theater, is elected President of Czechoslovakia.

1990—Sparked by exhibits of work by the late photographer Robert Mapplethorpe and visual artist Andres Serrano, Senator Jesse Helms and other conservative legislators and religious groups launch a campaign against federal funding of controversial art that threatens to cripple the National Endowment for the Arts and sets off an explosion of debate among artists and professionals across the country. August Wilson is awarded his second Pulitzer Prize for *The Piano Lesson*. John Guare's *Six Degrees of Separation* premieres at New York's Lincoln Center Theater. Director and actor Kenny Leon is appointed artistic director of Atlanta's Alliance Theatre Company. Boston's Huntington Theatre presents the premiere of *O Pioneers!*, adapted by Darrah Cloud from Willa Cather, which is later filmed for television's *Great Performances*. Julie Taymor and Elliot Goldenthal adapt Horacio Quiroga's *Juan Darien* for the Music-Theatre Group. Michael Greif—appointed with David Greenspan, George C. Wolfe and artistic associate JoAnne Akalaitis to a new artistic collective at the New York Shakespeare Festival—revives Sophie Treadwell's little-known 1928 feminist drama, *Machinal*. Playwright and director Emily Mann succeeds Nagle Jackson as artistic director of the McCarter Theatre in Princeton, N.J. Mary B. Robinson opens her debut season as artistic director of the Philadelphia Drama Guild with Athol Fugard's *Boesman and Lena*. Tony Kushner's two-part epic *Angels in America* is commissioned and produced by San Francisco's Eureka Theatre. Productions by Ingmar Bergman, Tadeusz Kantor's Cricot 2 company and the State Theatre of Lithuania enliven the second New York International Festival of the Arts. The New York Shakespeare Festival production of *A Chorus Line* ends the longest run in Broadway history after 6,137 performances. New York's Chelsea Stage, founded as the Hudson Guild Theatre in 1896, closes.

USING THIS BOOK

All the theatres included in *Theatre Profiles 10* are constituents of Theatre Communications Group, the national organization for the nonprofit professional theatre. Information was requested in the spring and summer of 1991. The text of this volume is based on the materials submitted by the 229 theatres included. The following notes provide a guide to the elements of the book.

Personnel

Each theatre's current artistic and managerial leaders are included. This information was updated through November 1, 1991. If there had been a change in the artistic leadership of the theatre within the past two seasons, the former artistic head is noted following the artistic statement, with an indication of the season(s) for which he or she was responsible.

Contact Information

The mailing address of each organization is included, which is not necessarily the address of the theatre. Where two telephone numbers are listed, the first is for the administrative or business "(bus.)" office and the second for the box office "(b.o.)."

Founding Date and Founders

The founding date represents the beginning of public performances, or in a few cases the conceptual or legal establishment of the organization. The names of all founders are listed under the date.

Season

The season information is included as a general guide to the annual performance dates of each theatre. The months listed indicate the opening and closing of each theatre's season. "Year-round" designates companies that perform continuously throughout the year; "variable" indicates irregular or varying schedules.

Facilities

The facilities are the theatre space(s) in which each company regularly performs. The seating capacity and type of stage are included for each facility. The name of the space is provided if it differs from the organization's name. The information is current as of July 1991 and doesn't necessarily indicate the performance venues of the seasons highlighted in the book. The following terminology is used in describing each facility:

PROSCENIUM: The traditional, picture-window stage separated from the auditorium by a proscenium arch, so that the audience views the action from a single "fourth wall" perspective.

THRUST: All types of facilities wherein the stage juts into the audience and is thereby surrounded on three sides. A "modified thrust" or "modified proscenium" protrudes less, often utilizing a fan-shaped apron on which action can take place.

Theatre de la Jeune Lune. Steven Epp and Felicity Jones in *Crusoe, Friday and the Island of Hope*. Photo: Donna Mulcahy.

ARENA: Also called "theatre-in-the-round." The audience completely surrounds the stage.

FLEXIBLE: All types of theatre space which can be altered or converted from one category to another.

CABARET: A simple performance platform, with the audience usually seated at tables.

Finances

Operating expenses are included to provide a general sense of the overall size of each theatre's operation. Most often the financial figures are from calendar year 1990 or fiscal year 1990-91, the most recent year available at the time information was gathered for *Theatre Profiles*.

Actors' Equity Association Contracts

The following AEA abbreviations are used:

BAT:	Bay Area Theatre contract
CAT:	Chicago Area Theatre contract
COST:	Council on Stock Theatres contract
CORST:	Council on Resident Stock Theatres contract
LORT:	League of Resident Theatres contract
SPT:	Small Professional Theatre contract
TYA:	Theatre for Young Audiences contract
U/RTA:	University/Resident Theatre Association contract

The letters enclosed in parentheses following the contract abbreviations designate the contract type, based on the size of theatre and scale of payment. Please note that members of the League of Resident Theatres (LORT) also operate under agreements with the Society of Stage Directors and Choreographers (SSDC) and United Scenic Artists (USA), which are referenced to the LORT Equity contracts. For more specific information on these contracts, please contact the unions directly.

Artistic Director's Statement

All artistic heads were invited to submit a statement describing the artistic philosophy governing the work at their respective institutions from their personal perspectives. While all have been edited for style, every attempt has been made to retain the individuality of each statement.

Production Lists

Productions from the 1989-90 and the 1990-91 seasons (1990 and 1991 for theatres with summer operations) are listed, most often in the chronological order in which they were produced. The title of each production is immediately followed by the name of the playwright and, where applicable, the adapter, translator and/or source of literary adaptation if such information was provided by the theatre. In the case of musicals, all composers, librettists and lyricists are included. The director and set, costume and lighting designers follow, designated by a letter in parentheses directly preceding the name—(D), (S), (C), (L). Choreographers, sound/video designers and musical directors are not included due to space limitations.

Photographs

A photograph from one of each theatre's listed productions accompanies each entry. The photos help convey the range and diversity of production activity and were generally selected for clarity of image from those submitted for possible inclusion by the theatre. Actors' names are included in the caption when there are five or fewer actors pictured.

Regional Index

A geographical, state-by-state listing of every theatre is included to readily identify theatres by region.

Theatre Chronology

The "time line" history of the founding of the nonprofit professional theatres included in this volume is intended to demonstrate the growth pattern of the decentralized nonprofit professional theatre movement in the United States.

Name/Title Indices

Playwrights, composers, artistic and management heads, directors, designers and founders appear in the index of names. For convenience, a separate index includes titles of all dramatic works listed in this book.

THEATRES

Academy Theatre
A Contemporary Theatre
The Acting Company
Actors Theatre of Louisville
Alabama Shakespeare Festival
Alley Theatre
Alliance Theatre Company
American Conservatory Theater
The American Place Theatre
American Repertory Theatre
American Stage
American Stage Festival
American Theatre Company
American Theatre Works
Arden Theatre Company
Arena Stage
Arizona Theatre Company
The Arkansas Arts Center Children's Theatre
Arkansas Repertory Theatre
ArtReach Touring Theatre
Asolo Center for the Performing Arts
A Traveling Jewish Theatre
Attic Theatre
Baltimore Theatre Project
Barter Theatre
The Bathhouse Theatre
Berkeley Repertory Theatre
Berkshire Theatre Festival
Bilingual Foundation of the Arts
Blackfriars Theatre
Bloomsburg Theatre Ensemble
BoarsHead: Michigan Public Theater
The Body Politic Theatre
Boston Post Road Stage Company
Bristol Riverside Theatre
Caldwell Theatre Company
California Shakespeare Festival
California Theatre Center
Capital Repertory Company
The CAST Theatre
Center Stage
Center Theater
The Children's Theatre Company
Childsplay, Inc.
Child's Play Touring Theatre
Cincinnati Playhouse in the Park
Circle Repertory Company
City Theatre Company
Clarence Brown Theatre Company
The Cleveland Play House
Cornerstone Theater Company
The Coterie
Court Theatre
The Cricket Theatre
Crossroads Theatre Company
CSC Repertory Ltd.-The Classic Stage Company
Cumberland County Playhouse
Dallas Theater Center
Delaware Theatre Company
Dell'Arte Players Company
Denver Center Theatre Company
Detroit Repertory Theatre
East West Players
El Teatro Campesino
Emmy Gifford Children's Theater
The Empty Space Theatre
Ensemble Studio Theatre
Eureka Theatre Company
First Stage Milwaukee
Florida Studio Theatre
Ford's Theatre
Free Street Theater
Fulton Opera House
George Street Playhouse
Germinal Stage Denver
GeVa Theatre
Gloucester Stage Company
Goodman Theatre
Goodspeed Opera House
Great American History Theatre
Great Lakes Theater Festival
Grove Shakespeare Festival
The Guthrie Theater
Hartford Stage Company
Hippodrome State Theatre
Honolulu Theatre for Youth
Horse Cave Theatre
Huntington Theatre Company
Illinois Theatre Center
Illusion Theater
The Independent Eye
Indiana Repertory Theatre
INTAR Hispanic American Arts Center
Intiman Theatre Company
Irondale Ensemble Project
Jean Cocteau Repertory
Jewish Repertory Theatre
Jomandi Productions, Inc.
La Jolla Playhouse
Lamb's Players Theatre
L. A. Theatre Works
Lincoln Center Theater
Live Oak Theatre
Living Stage Theatre Company
Long Wharf Theatre
Los Angeles Theatre Center
Mabou Mines
Madison Repertory Theatre
Magic Theatre
Manhattan Theatre Club
Marin Theatre Company
Mark Taper Forum
McCarter Theatre Center for the Performing Arts
Meadow Brook Theatre
Merrimack Repertory Theatre
Mill Mountain Theatre
Milwaukee Public Theatre
Milwaukee Repertory Theater
Missouri Repertory Theatre
Mixed Blood Theatre Company
Music-Theatre Group
National Jewish Theater
Nebraska Theatre Caravan
New American Theater
New Dramatists
New Federal Theatre
New Jersey Shakespeare Festival
New Mexico Repertory Theatre
New Repertory Theatre, Inc.
New Stage Theatre
New York Shakespeare Festival
New York State Theatre Institute
New York Theatre Workshop
Northlight Theatre
Oakland Ensemble Theatre
Odyssey Theatre Ensemble
The Old Creamery Theatre Company
Old Globe Theatre
Omaha Magic Theatre
Ontological-Hysteric Theater
The Open Eye: New Stagings
Oregon Shakespeare Festival
Organic Theater Company
Pan Asian Repertory Theatre
PCPA Theaterfest
Pegasus Players
Pennsylvania Stage Company
The Penumbra Theatre Company
The People's Light and Theatre Company
Periwinkle National Theatre for Young Audiences
Perseverance Theatre
Philadelphia Drama Guild
Philadelphia Festival Theatre for New Plays
The Philadelphia Theatre Company
Ping Chong and Company
Pioneer Theatre Company
Pittsburgh Public Theater
Players Theatre Columbus
Playhouse on the Square
PlayMakers Repertory Company
The Playwrights' Center
Playwrights Horizons
Portland Repertory Theater
Portland Stage Company
Remains Theatre
Repertorio Español
The Repertory Theatre of St. Louis
River Arts Repertory
Riverside Theatre
The Road Company
Roadside Theater
Roundabout Theatre Company
Round House Theatre
Sacramento Theatre Company
The Salt Lake Acting Company
San Diego Repertory Theatre
San Jose Repertory Theatre
Seattle Children's Theatre
Seattle Group Theatre
Seattle Repertory Theatre
Second Stage Theatre
Seven Stages
Shakespeare Repertory
The Shakespeare Theatre at the Folger
Snowmass/Aspen Repertory Theatre

Society Hill Playhouse
Source Theatre Company
South Coast Repertory
Stage One: The Louisville Children's Theatre
Stages Repertory Theatre
Stage West
StageWest
Steppenwolf Theatre Company
St. Louis Black Repertory Company
The Street Theater
Studio Arena Theatre
The Studio Theatre
Syracuse Stage
Tacoma Actors Guild
Tennessee Repertory Theatre
The Theater at Monmouth
The Theatre Club of the Palm Beaches
Theatre de la Jeune Lune
Theatre for a New Audience
Theater for the New City
Theatre in the Square
Theatre IV
Theatre Rhinoceros
TheatreVirginia
TheatreWorks
Theatreworks/USA
Theatre X
Theatrical Outfit
Three Rivers Shakespeare Festival
Touchstone Theatre
Trinity Repertory Company
Unicorn Theatre
Victory Gardens Theater
Vineyard Theatre
Virginia Stage Company
White River Theatre Festival
Williamstown Theatre Festival
The Wilma Theater
Wisdom Bridge Theatre
The Women's Project and Productions
The Wooster Group
Worcester Foothills Theatre Company
Yale Repertory Theatre
Young Playwrights Festival

New Mexico Repertory Theatre. Scott MacDonald and Meg Judson in *Man and Superman*. Photo: Murrae Haynes.

THEATRE PROFILES 10

Berkeley Repertory Theatre. Charles Dean and Morgan Strickland in *The Illusion*. Photo: Ken Friedman.

Academy Theatre

FRANK WITTOW
Producing Artistic Director

LORENNE FEY
Managing Director

Box 191306
Atlanta, GA 31119
(404) 365-8088

FOUNDED 1956
Frank Wittow

SEASON
Sept.-June

FACILITIES
7 Stages Performing Arts Center's Back Door Theatre
Seating Capacity: 75
Stage: flexible

FINANCES
July 1, 1990-June 30, 1991
Expenses: $277,600

CONTRACTS
AEA letter of agreement

The Academy Theatre is a professional company whose mission is to serve the community through interdependent programs: touring original, issue-oriented Theatre for Youth plays with themes of family, peer pressure, addiction and the environment throughout the Southeast; presenting and developing new plays by local and regional playwrights through classes, readings and a New Play Series that strives to provide Atlanta's audiences with fresh, stimulating theatrical experiences; facilitating Human Service Programs with disenfranchised populations, such as inner-city youth, developmentally disabled adults and incarcerated adolescents, that give participants an avenue to express creatively the issues that are relevant to their lives; and training a professional ensemble of actors, directors, playwrights and facilitators to fulfill the social and artistic needs of our community.

—*Frank Wittow*

PRODUCTIONS 1989-90

The Crucible, Arthur Miller; (D) Frank Wittow; (S) Guy Tuttle; (C) Judy Winograd; (L) Margaret Tucker

A Christmas Carol, adapt: Michael Wainstein, from Charles Dickens; (D) Michael Wainstein; (S) Gary Jennings; (C) Gary Jennings; (L) Margaret Tucker

Pantomime, Derek Walcott; (D) Peter Hackett; (S) Elena Zlotescu; (C) Elena Zlotescu; (L) Timothy M. Chew

New Play Program:

Antioch, Randal Jackson; (D) Haynes Brooke

Single Room Occupancy, Stephen Peace; (D) Haynes Brooke

Theatre for Youth:

The Fleas in the Cheese, Barbara Lebow; (D) Frank Wittow; (S) Stephen Bartlow

The Only Light For Miles, Bill Johns and Michael Maschinot; music and lyrics: Bill Johns and Michael Maschinot; (D) Holly Stevenson; (S) Stephen Bartlow

Masks, company-developed; (D) Judith Shotwell; (S) Stephen Bartlow

PRODUCTIONS 1990-91

Trains, Barbara Lebow; (D) Barbara Lebow; (S) Michael Halpern; (C) Anita Beaty; (L) R. Scott Preston

Kafkaphony, Frank Wittow; (D) Frank Wittow; (S) Elliott Berman; (L) Gregg Wallace

Housebreaking, Dennis Camilleri; (D) Frank Wittow; (S) Elliott Berman; (L) Gregg Wallace

Walkin' Ta Heaven, Stephen Peace; (D) Frank Wittow; (S) Elliott Berman; (L) Gregg Wallace

"I Want To Be...", company-developed; (D) Barbara Lebow

Choices, company-developed; (D) Michael Maschinot, Charles Reed, Malcolm Spears and Pamela Wright

Theatre for Youth:

The Fleas in the Cheese, Barbara Lebow; (D) Frank Wittow; (S) Stephen Bartlow

Me in the Galaxy, The Galaxy in Me, Barbara Lebow; (D) Frank Wittow; (S) James Halpern

Masks, company-developed; (D) Judith Shotwell; (S) Stephen Bartlow

Images, company-developed; (D) Frank Wittow; (S) James Halpern

Academy Theatre. Thomas Byrd and Haynes Brooke in *Trains*. Photo: Alan David.

A Contemporary Theatre

JEFF STEITZER
Artistic Director

SUSAN T. MORITZ
Managing Director

PHIL SHERMER
Producing Director

Box 19400
Seattle, WA 98109
(206) 285-3220 (bus.)
(206) 285-5110 (b.o.)

FOUNDED 1965
Gregory A. Falls

SEASON
May-Dec.

FACILITIES
Mainstage
Seating Capacity: 449
Stage: thrust

FINANCES
Jan. 1, 1990-Dec. 31, 1990
Expenses: $2,356,216

CONTRACTS
AEA LORT (C) and TYA

A Contemporary Theatre is dedicated to offering our audiences the most provocative, engaging and theatrical contemporary plays available—in productions that represent the most vibrant collaborations among actors, directors and designers that we can assemble. At ACT, the playwright is the predominant point of focus, with a new priority on generating work by commissioning writers whose efforts we want to support on a long-term basis. ACT vigorously seeks out dramatists with lively, unique voices: playwrights whose work examines issues that are socially pertinent to our audience; whose writing appeals to the head, heart and soul; and whose aesthetic is informed by the imaginative possibilities that can occur only on the stage. Our professional theatre for young audiences, the Young ACT Company, is one year younger than our main stage. It has produced more than 30 plays, half of which were original scripts, performed for hundreds of thousands of young people throughout Washington State.

—*Jeff Steitzer*

PRODUCTIONS 1989

The Downside, Richard Dresser; (D) Jeff Steitzer; (S) Scott Weldin; (C) Rose Pederson; (L) Rick Paulsen

Breaking the Silence, Stephen Poliakoff; (D) David Ira Goldstein; (S) Karen Gjelsteen; (C) Sally Richardson; (L) Rick Paulsen

A Walk in the Woods, Lee Blessing; (D) Jeff Steitzer; (S) Bill Forrester; (C) Susan Haas; (L) Rick Paulsen

Red Noses, Peter Barnes; (D) Jeff Steitzer and David Ira Goldstein; (S) Scott Weldin; (C) Michael Sommers and Susan Haas; (L) Rick Paulsen

A Contemporary Theatre. Mark Drusch, Allen Galli, Michael Santo and Peter Silbert in *An American Comedy*. Photo: Chris Bennion.

Happenstance, Steven Dietz; book adapt: Steven Dietz; music and lyrics: Eric Bain Peltoniemi; (D) Steven Dietz; (S) Shelley Henze Schermer; (C) Frances Kenny; (L) Rick Paulsen
Woman in Mind, Alan Ayckbourn; (D) David Ira Goldstein; (S) Bill Forrester; (C) Rose Pederson; (L) Rick Paulsen
A Christmas Carol, adapt: Gregory A. Falls, from Charles Dickens; (D) Jeff Steitzer; (S) Bill Forrester; (C) Nanrose Buchman; (L) Jody Briggs

PRODUCTIONS 1990

Juggling & Cheap Theatrics, The Flying Karamazov Brothers; (D) The Flying Karamazov Brothers; (L) Peter Dansky
An American Comedy, Richard Nelson; (D) Jeff Steitzer; (S) Bill Forrester; (C) Jazmin Mercer; (L) Rick Paulsen
Lloyd's Prayer, Kevin Kling; (D) David Ira Goldstein; (S) Shelley Henze Schermer; (C) Rose Pederson; (L) Phil Schermer
A Normal Life, adapt: Erik Brogger, from Delmore Schwartz; (D) Mary B. Robinson; (S) Kent Dorsey; (C) Mimi Maxmen; (L) Kent Dorsey
The Falcon, adapt: Greg Palmer; (D) David Ira Goldstein; (S) Jeffrey A. Frkonja; (C) Nana Gerasimova; (L) Kent Dorsey
Born in the RSA, Barney Simon and original cast; (D) Barney Simon; (S) Michael S. Philippi; (C) Susan Hilferty; (L) Michael S. Philippi
Four Our Fathers, Jon Klein; (D) Jeff Steitzer; (S) Karen Gjelsteen; (C) Laura Crow; (L) Rick Paulsen
Hapgood, Tom Stoppard; (D) David Ira Goldstein; (S) Scott Weldin; (C) Rose Pederson; (L) Rick Paulsen
A Christmas Carol, adapt: Gregory A. Falls, from Charles Dickens; (D) Jeff Steitzer; (S) Bill Forrester; (C) Nanrose Buchman; (L) Jody Briggs

The Acting Company

ZELDA FICHANDLER
Artistic Director

MARGOT HARLEY
Executive Producer

JOHN MILLER-STEPHANY
Associate Producer

Box 898, Times Square Station
New York, NY 10108
(212) 564-3510

FOUNDED 1972
John Houseman, Margot Harley

SEASON
variable

FINANCES
July 1, 1990-June 30, 1991
Expenses: $2,900,000

CONTRACTS
AEA LORT (B) and (C)

Made up of a mix of young actors who have just completed their conservatory training and experienced professionals, the Acting Company has gathered itself around the idea of an ensemble that trains and performs and teaches together. The company regards the actor as the center of the theatre art: the greater the expressivity of the actor's instrument, and of the ensemble as a whole, the more profound the experience of the audience. In a country that has not significantly valued or provided for the development of the actor or supported the educative power of the theatre, the Acting Company fills an important niche. In the 1991-92 season, the 17-member company will play in 52 cities and towns in 22 states on a stage especially designed to be carried from place to place. The actors and designers comprise an ethnic mosaic which reflects the audiences to whom the work is geared. In becoming the Acting Company's artistic director this year, I hope to fulfill and extend the vision of Margot Harley and the late John Houseman, who founded the company in 1972.

—*Zelda Fichandler*

Note: Zelda Fichandler joined The Acting Company as artistic director beginning with the 1991-92 season.

PRODUCTIONS 1989-90

Romeo and Juliet, William Shakespeare; (D) Leon Rubin; (S) Derek McLane; (C) Martin Pakledinaz; (L) Stephen Strawbridge

PRODUCTIONS 1990-91

Romeo and Juliet, William Shakespeare; (D) Leon Rubin; (S) Derek McLane; (C) Martin Pakledinaz; (L) Stephen Strawbridge
Two Gentlemen of Verona, William Shakespeare; (D) Charles Newell; (S) Derek McLane; (C) Catherine Zuber; (L) Marcus Dilliard
Five by Tenn, Tennessee Williams; (D) Michael Kahn; (S) Derek McLane; (C) Ann Hould-Ward; (L) Dennis Parichy

Actors Theatre of Louisville

JON JORY
Producing Director

ALEXANDER SPEER
Executive Director

MARILEE HEBERT-SLATER
Associate Director

316-320 West Main St.
Louisville, KY 40202-4218
(502) 584-1265 (bus.)
(502) 584-1205 (b.o.)

FOUNDED 1964
Ewel Cornett, Richard Block

SEASON
Sept.-June

FACILITIES
Pamela Brown Auditorium
Seating Capacity: 637
Stage: thrust

Victor Jory Theatre
Seating Capacity: 159
Stage: thrust

Downstairs at Actors
Seating Capacity: 100
Stage: cabaret

The Acting Company. Rainn Wilson and Jeffrey Guyton in *The Two Gentlemen of Verona*. Photo: Irene Haupt.

FINANCES
June 1, 1990-May 31, 1991
Expenses: $4,800,000

CONTRACTS
AEA LORT (B) and (D)

Actors Theatre of Louisville has four primary areas of emphasis which constitute an artistic policy. Central to our aesthetic is the discovery and development of a new generation of American playwrights. In the last 19 years, Actors Theatre has produced the work of more than 200 new writers. The Humana Festival of New American Plays is our major outlet for this work, strongly backed by a commissioning program. Our second area of emphasis is an interdisciplinary approach to the classical theatre, combining lectures, discussions, films and plays through the annual Classics in Context Festival. Working under a different umbrella theme each year, this festival provides new insights into the classical repertoire, both for our company and our resident audience. The Bingham Signature Shakespeare Series supplements programming by presenting one of the Bard's masterworks each season. In addition, since 1980, Actors Theatre has performed by invitation in festivals and theatres in 14 countries.

—Jon Jory

PRODUCTIONS 1989-90

Classics in Context Festival:
The Seagull, Anton Chekhov; trans: Michael Frayn; (D) Jon Jory; (S) David Jenkins; (C) Lewis D. Rampino; (L) Pat Collins
Children of the Sun, adapt: Zirka Derlycia and Aaron Levin, from Maxim Gorky; trans: Zirka Derlycia; (D) Gloria Muzio; (S) David Jenkins; (C) Lewis D. Rampino; (L) Pat Collins
Anton, Himself, Karen Sunde; (D) Frazier W. Marsh; (S) Paul Owen; (C) Lewis D. Rampino; (L) Ralph Dressler
Cinzano, Liudmila Petrushevskaya; (D) Roman Kozak; (S) Valery Firsov; (C) Victor Platonov; (L) Victor Platonov

Sing Hallelujah!, conceived: Worth Gardner and Donald Lawrence; (D) Worth Gardner; (S) Paul Owen; (C) Hollis Jenkins-Evans; (L) Ralph Dressler
A Christmas Carol, adapt: Barbara Field, from Charles Dickens; (D) Frazier W. Marsh; (S) Paul Owen; (C) Lewis D. Rampino; (L) Ralph Dressler
The Gift of the Magi, adapt, music and lyrics: Peter Ekstrom, from O. Henry; (D) Bob Krakower; (S) Paul Owen; (C) Hollis Jenkins-Evans; (L) Ralph Dressler
The Immigrant, Mark Harelik; (D) Ray Fry; (S) Paul Owen; (C) Lewis D. Rampino; (L) Ralph Dressler
Frankie and Johnny in the Clair de Lune, Terrence McNally; (D) Frazier W. Marsh; (S) Paul Owen; (C) Lewis D. Rampino; (L) Ralph Dressler
Oil City Symphony, Mike Craver, Mark Hardwick, Debra Monk and Mary Murfitt; (D) Larry Forde; (S) Paul Owen; (C) Hollis Jenkins-Evans; (L) Ralph Dressler

Humana Festival of New American Plays:
The Pink Studio, Jane Anderson; (D) Steve Schachter; (S) Paul Owen; (C) Michael Krass; (L) Victor En Yu Tan
Vital Signs, Jane Martin; (D) Jon Jory; (S) Paul Owen; (C) Michael Krass; (L) Victor En Yu Tan
In Darkest America, Joyce Carol Oates; (D) Steven Albrezzi; (S) Paul Owen; (C) Michael Krass; (L) Victor En Yu Tan
Zara Spook and Other Lures, Joan Ackermann-Blount; (D) Kyle Donnelly; (S) Paul Owen; (C) Lewis D. Rampino; (L) Ralph Dressler
The Swan, Elizabeth Egloff; (D) Evan Yionoulis; (S) Paul Owen; (C) Lewis D. Rampino; (L) Ralph Dressler
Infinity's House, Ellen McLaughlin; (D) Jackson Phippin; (S) Paul Owen; (C) Lewis D. Rampino; (L) Ralph Dressler
2, Romulus Linney; (D) Thomas Allan Bullard; (S) Paul Owen; (C) Lewis D. Rampino; (L) Ralph Dressler

The Boys Next Door, Tom Griffin; (D) Frazier W. Marsh; (S) Paul Owen; (C) Lewis D. Rampino; (L) Ralph Dressler
As You Like It, William Shakespeare; (D) Jon Jory; (S) John Lee Beatty; (C) John Lee Beatty; (L) Pat Collins

PRODUCTIONS 1990-91

Classics in Context Festival:
The Three Cuckolds, adapt: Bill Irwin with Michael Greif, from Leon Katz; (D) Jon Jory; (S) John Conklin; (C) Marcia Dixcy; (L) Victor En Yu Tan
Pigeon Show, conceived: Ronlin Foreman; (L) Mark Quinn

The Trip To Bountiful, Horton Foote; (D) Ray Fry; (S) Paul Owen; (C) Lewis D. Rampino; (L) Karl E. Haas
A Christmas Carol, adapt: Jon Jory and Marcia Dixcy, from Charles Dickens; (D) Frazier W. Marsh; (S) Elmon Webb and Virginia Dancy; (C) Lewis D. Rampino; (L) Karl E. Haas
The Gift of the Magi, adapt, music and lyrics: Peter Ekstrom, from O. Henry; (D) Bob Krakower; (S) Paul Owen; (C) Hollis Jenkins-Evans; (L) Matt Reinert
Treasure Island, adapt: Ara Watson, from Robert Louis Stevenson; (D) Barbara Damashek; (S) Paul Owen; (C) David Murin; (L) Karl E. Haas
Speed-the-Plow, David Mamet; (D) Bob Krakower; (S) Paul Owen; (C) Hollis Jenkins-Evans; (L) Karl E. Haas
The Cocktail Hour, A.R. Gurney, Jr.; (D) Frazier W. Marsh; (S) Paul Owen; (C) Hollis Jenkins-Evans; (L) Karl E. Haas

Humana Festival of New American Plays:
A Passenger Train of Sixty-One Coaches, Paul Walker; (D) Paul Walker; (S) Paul Owen; (C) Marcia Dixcy; (L) Mary Louise Geiger
Down the Road, Lee Blessing; (D) Jeanne Blake; (S) Paul Owen; (C) Hollis Jenkins-Evans; (L) Mary Louise Geiger
Night-Side, Shem Bitterman; (D) Frazier W. Marsh; (S) Paul Owen; (C) Hollis Jenkins-Evans; (L) Mary Louise Geiger
Cementville, Jane Martin; (D) Jon Jory; (S) Paul Owen; (C) Marcia Dixcy; (L) Karl E. Haas
A Piece of My Heart, Shirley Lauro; (D) Allen R. Belknap; (S) Paul Owen; (C) Michael Krass; (L) Karl E. Haas
The Death of Zukasky, Richard Strand; (D) Nagle Jackson; (S) Paul Owen; (C) Michael Krass; (L) Karl E. Haas
In the Eye of the Hurricane, Eduardo Machado; (D) Anne Bogart; (S) Paul Owen; (C) Michael Krass; (L) Karl E. Haas

Other People's Money, Jerry Sterner; (D) Larry Carpenter; (S) Paul Owen; (C) David Murin; (L) Karl E. Haas
King Lear, William Shakespeare; (D) Jon Jory; (S) Hugh Landwehr; (C) Paul Tazewell; (L) Robert Wierzel

Actors Theatre of Louisville. Madeleine Sherwood and Beth Dixon in *In Darkest America*. Photo: Richard Trigg.

Alabama Shakespeare Festival

KENT THOMPSON
Artistic Director

E. TIMOTHY LANGAN
Managing Director

1 Festival Drive
Montgomery, AL 36117
(205) 272-1640 (bus.)
(205) 277-BARD (b.o.)

FOUNDED 1972
Martin L. Platt

SEASON
Nov.-Aug.

FACILITIES
Festival Stage
Seating Capacity: 750
Stage: proscenium

The Octagon
Seating Capacity: 225
Stage: flexible

FINANCES
Oct. 1, 1989-Sept. 30, 1990
Expenses: $4,661,221

CONTRACTS
AEA LORT (C) and (D)

The Alabama Shakespeare Festival is committed first and foremost to artistic excellence in the production and performance of classics and outstanding contemporary plays, with the works of Shakespeare forming the core of our repertoire. We believe this aim is best achieved through a commitment to a company of resident artists and through producing in repertory. ASF is by far the largest arts organization in Alabama, demanding a progressive arts leadership; therefore, the theatre is now pursuing a more passionate, socially aware artistry. Without undermining our principal commitment to Shakespeare, we have changed our focus to include plays which deal with our own culture and society—American classics and plays about black and Southern issues. In a community with a noted civil rights history, ASF has begun to address its minority audiences, with aggressive nontraditional casting and hiring, and with greater diversity in play selection.

—*Kent Thompson*

PRODUCTIONS 1989-90

All God's Dangers, adapt: Theodore Rosengarten, Michael Hadley and Jennifer Hadley, from Theodore Rosengarten; (D) William Partlan; (S) G.W. Mercier; (C) G.W. Mercier; (L) Tina Charney
A Christmas Carol, adapt: John Jakes, from Charles Dickens; (D) John Briggs; (S) David Crank; (C) Alan Armstrong; (L) Karen Spahn
Crimes of the Heart, Beth Henley; (D) Robert Hall; (S) Joseph Varga; (C) Stanley Poole; (L) Michael Rourke
Macbeth, William Shakespeare; (D) David McClendon; (S) Kent Dorsey; (C) Alan Armstrong; (L) F. Mitchell Dana
Cat on a Hot Tin Roof, Tennessee Williams; (D) William Gregg; (S) Joseph Varga; (C) Mark Hughes; (L) Michael Rourke
Twelfth Night, William Shakespeare; (D) Kent Thompson; (S) G.W. Mercier; (C) G.W. Mercier; (L) F. Mitchell Dana
Noises Off, Michael Frayn; (D) Charles Abbott; (S) Charles S. Kading; (C) Mark Hughes; (L) Michael Rourke
Tartuffe, Moliere, trans: Richard Wilbur; (D) Kent Thompson; (S) David Crank; (C) Marjorie McCown; (L) F. Mitchell Dana
Major Barbara, George Bernard Shaw; (D) Will York; (S) Charles Caldwell; (C) Kristine Kearney; (L) Michael Rourke
Measure for Measure, William Shakespeare; (D) Gavin Cameron-Webb; (S) Harry Feiner; (C) Colleen Muscha; (L) F. Mitchell Dana
The Immigrant, Mark Harelik; (D) Kent Thompson; (S) Charles Caldwell; (C) Stanley Poole; (L) Michael Rourke

PRODUCTIONS 1990-91

A Christmas Carol, adapt: John Jakes, from Charles Dickens; (D) John Briggs; (S) David Crank; (C) Alan Armstrong; (L) Michael Rourke
Season's Greetings, Alan Ayckbourn; (D) Gavin Cameron-Webb; (S) Charles Caldwell; (C) Charles Caldwell; (L) William H. Grant, III
Julius Caesar, William Shakespeare; (D) Gavin Cameron-Webb; (S) Charles Caldwell; (C) Gail Brassard; (L) F. Mitchell Dana
Fences, August Wilson; (D) Thomas Allan Bullard; (S) David Crank; (C) Alvin Perry; (L) William H. Grant, III
All's Well That Ends Well, William Shakespeare; (D) Libby Appel; (S) William Bloodgood; (C) Elizabeth Novak; (L) Michael Rourke
Two Gentlemen of Verona, William Shakespeare; (D) Kent Thompson; (S) G.W. Mercier; (C) G.W. Mercier; (L) F. Mitchell Dana
I'm Not Rappaport, Herb Gardner; (D) Peter Hackett; (S) Jefferson D. Sage; (C) Mark Hughes; (L) Michael Rourke
Inherit the Wind, Jerome Lawrence and Robert E. Lee; (D) Kent Thompson; (S) Michael Anania; (C) Jeanne Button; (L) F. Mitchell Dana
The Cherry Orchard, Anton Chekhov; trans: Elisaveta Lavrova; (D) Kent Thompson; (S) Charles McClennahan; (C) Kristine Kearney; (L) Michael Rourke
The Rivals, Richard Brinsley Sheridan; (D) Kyle Donnelly; (S) Charles Caldwell; (C) Alan Armstrong; (L) F. Mitchell Dana

Alabama Shakespeare Festival. Laurie Birmingham and Philip Pleasants in *Tartuffe*. Photo: Scarsbrook/ASF.

Alley Theatre

GREGORY BOYD
Artistic Director

MICHAEL WILSON
Associate Director

615 Texas Ave.
Houston, TX 77002
(713) 228-9341 (bus.)
(713) 228-8421 (b.o.)

FOUNDED 1947
Nina Vance

SEASON
Jan.-Dec.

FACILITIES
Large Stage
Seating Capacity: 824
Stage: thrust

Hugo V. Neuhaus
Seating Capacity: 296
Stage: arena

Alley Theatre. Glen Allen Pruett, Steve Phillips, Harold Suggs and Peter Robinson in *Measure for Measure*. Photo: Peter Yenne.

FINANCES
July 1, 1990-June 30, 1991
Expenses: $5,300,000

CONTRACTS
AEA LORT (B) and (C)

The Alley Theatre, one of America's oldest not-for-profit resident theatres, produces a year-round repertoire of new plays, reinterpretations of classic plays, and new music-theatre works. Alley productions have been seen throughout the United States as well as internationally. In 1989, under the artistic direction of Gregory Boyd, the Alley added to its mission the intent to create for leading theatre artists from around the world a home where they can develop their work. The theatre is committed to an extended family of artists, some in residence, others with an ongoing relationship with the Alley over several seasons. The Alley is also dedicated to extensive training, educational and outreach programs including sponsoring of multicultural, community-based productions, English-as-a-second-language playwriting projects, the Rockwell Fund Studio, an extensive professional internship program, the Shakespeare tour of southeastern Texas middle and high schools, student matinees, preperformance discussions, symposiums and lectures.

—*Gregory Boyd*

PRODUCTIONS 1989-90

Measure for Measure, William Shakespeare; (D) Gregory Boyd; (S) Peter David Gould; (C) V. Jane Suttell; (L) Robert Jared

A Christmas Carol, adapt: Gregory Boyd, from Charles Dickens; (D) James Martin; (S) Jay Michael Jagim; (C) V. Jane Suttell; (L) Robert Jared

Fences, August Wilson; (D) Claude Purdy; (S) Vicki Smith; (C) Constanza Romero; (L) Don Darnutzer

Who's Afraid of Virginia Woolf?, Edward Albee; (D) Edward Albee; (S) Jay Michael Jagim; (C) Ainslie G. Bruneau; (L) Robert P. Hill

Private Lives, Noel Coward; (D) Vivian Matalon; (S) David Potts; (C) David Loveless; (L) Robert Jared

Road to Nirvana, Arthur Kopit; (D) James Simpson; (S) Jay Michael Jagim; (C) Ainslie G. Bruneau; (L) Robert P. Hill

The Three Sisters, Anton Chekhov; adapt: Gregory Boyd; trans: Nicholas Fersen; (D) Gregory Boyd; (S) Peter David Gould; (C) V. Jane Suttell; (L) Robert Jared

Act of Passion, adapt: John Tyson, from Charles Dickens; (D) John Tyson; (S) Jay Michael Jagim; (C) Ainslie G. Bruneau; (L) Christina Giannelli

Jekyll and Hyde, book adapt and lyrics: Leslie Bricusse, from Robert Louis Stevenson; music: Frank Wildhorn; (D) Gregory Boyd; (S) Peter David Gould; (C) V. Jane Suttell; (L) Robert Jared

Speed-the-Plow, David Mamet; (D) Jack Stehlin; (S) Jay Michael Jagim; (C) Ainslie G. Bruneau; (L) John E. Ore

PRODUCTIONS 1990-91

The King Stag, Carlo Gozzi; trans: Albert Bermel; music: Elliot Goldenthal; (D) Andrei Serban; (S) Michael Yeargan; (C) Julie Taymor; (L) John Ambrosone

T Bone N Weasel, Jon Klein; (D) Sidney Berger; (S) Jay Michael Jagim; (C) Claremarie Verheyen; (L) Christina Giannelli

As You Like It, William Shakespeare; music: John Dickson; (D) Gregory Boyd; (S) Derek McLane; (C) Judith Anne Dolan; (L) Howell Binkley

A Christmas Carol, adapt: Michael Wilson, from Charles Dickens; music: John Dickson; (D) Michael Wilson; (S) Jay Michael Jagim; (C) Ainslie G. Bruneau; (L) Howell Binkley

The Czar of Rock & Roll, book: Lewis Black; music and lyrics: Rusty Magee; (D) Rand Foerster; (S) Jay Michael Jagim; (C) Deborah Rosenberg; (L) Christina Giannelli

Joe Turner's Come and Gone, August Wilson; (D) Claude Purdy; (S) Scott Bradley; (C) Ainslie G. Bruneau; (L) Phil Monat

Harvey, Mary Chase; (D) David Wheeler; (S) Jay Michael Jagim; (C) Ainslie G. Bruneau; (L) Christina Giannelli

Ohio Impromptu and ***Krapp's Last Tape***, Samuel Beckett; (D) Edward Albee; (S) Jay Michael Jagim; (C) Ainslie G. Bruneau; (L) John Gow

Other People's Money, Jerry Sterner; (D) Michael Wilson; (S) Jay Michael Jagim; (C) Ainslie G. Bruneau; (L) Christina Giannelli

Svengali, book adapt: Gregory Boyd, from George Du Maurier; music: Frank Wildhorn; lyrics: John Bettis, Gregory Boyd and Frank Wildhorn; (D) Gregory Boyd; (S) Jerome Sirlin; (C) V. Jane Suttell; (L) Howell Binkley

When We Dead Awaken, Henrik Ibsen; adapt: Robert Wilson; trans: Robert Brustein; songs by Charles Honi Coles; (D) Robert Wilson; (S) Robert Wilson and John Conklin; (C) John Conklin; (L) Stephen Strawbridge and Robert Wilson

The Boys Next Door, Tom Griffin; (D) David Wheeler; (S) Jay Michael Jagim; (C) Ainslie G. Bruneau; (L) Christina Giannelli

Alliance Theatre Company

KENNY LEON
Artistic Director

EDITH H. LOVE
Managing Director

Robert W. Woodruff Arts Center
1280 Peachtree St. NE
Atlanta, GA 30309
(404) 898-1132 (bus.)
(404) 892-2414 (b.o.)

FOUNDED 1968
Atlanta Arts Alliance

SEASON
Sept.-May

FACILITIES
Memorial Arts Building
Alliance Theatre
Seating Capacity: 784
Stage: proscenium

Studio Theatre
Seating Capacity: 200
Stage: flexible

14th Street Playhouse
Mainstage
Seating Capacity: 374
Stage: proscenium

Second Stage
Seating Capacity: 200
Stage: flexible

Stage 3
Seating Capacity: 75
Stage: flexible

FINANCES
Aug. 1, 1990-July 31, 1991
Expenses: $6,215,000

CONTRACTS
AEA LORT (B), (D) and TYA

As we approach the 21st century, it is imperative that the American theatre address those problems that face us as diverse people living in an increasingly shrinking world. Through the nurturing of artists, we are committed to touching the lives of the total community, regardless of race, creed, physical handicap, geographical barriers or economic status. The Alliance Theatre is dedicated to producing exciting,

Alliance Theatre Company. Nicholas Strouse and Carol Harris in *Broadway Bound*. Photo: Frank Teeple.

entertaining and evocative programs for a culturally diverse audience with a strong bond to our community.

—*Kenny Leon*

Note: During the 1989-90 season, Robert J. Farley served as artistic director.

PRODUCTIONS 1989-90

Southern Cross, Jon Klein; (D) Robert J. Farley; (S) Victor Becker; (C) Pamela Scofield; (L) Jim Sale
Annie Get Your Gun, book: Herbert Fields and Dorothy Fields; music and lyrics: Irving Berlin; (D) Fran Soeder; (S) James Leonard Joy; (C) Mariann Verheyen; (L) Marcia Madeira
Fences, August Wilson; (D) Kenny Leon; (S) Michael Olich; (C) Susan E. Mickey; (L) Ann G. Wrightson
Gal Baby, Sandra Deer; (D) Kenny Leon; (S) Michael Olich; (C) Susan E. Mickey; (L) Ann G. Wrightson
The Cocktail Hour, A.R. Gurney, Jr.; (D) Dan Bonnell; (S) David Potts; (C) Jeff Cone; (L) Liz Lee
I Do! I Do!, book and lyrics: Tom Jones; music: Harvey Schmidt; (D) Fran Soeder; (S) Dex Edwards; (C) Jeff Cone; (L) Liz Lee
Driving Miss Daisy, Alfred Uhry; (D) Robert J. Farley; (S) Michael Stauffer; (C) Michael Stauffer; (L) Michael Stauffer
Measure for Measure, adapt: Skip Foster, from William Shakespeare; (D) Skip Foster; (S) Victor Becker; (C) Susan E. Mickey; (L) Liz Lee
The Voice of the Prairie, John Olive; (D) Fontaine Syer; (S) Dex Edwards; (C) Jeff Cone; (L) P. Hamilton Shinn
Cobb, Lee Blessing; (D) Lloyd Richards; (S) Rob Greenberg; (C) Joel O. Thayer; (L) Ashley York Kennedy
The Adventures of Marco Polo, Skip Foster; (D) Skip Foster; (S) Victor Becker; (C) Susan E. Mickey; (L) Liz Lee
Merlin!, Larry Larson and Eddie Levi Lee; (D) Larry Larson; (S) Dex Edwards; (C) Jeff Cone; (L) Liz Lee

PRODUCTIONS 1990-91

Miss Evers' Boys, David Feldshuh; (D) Kenny Leon; (S) Michael Olich; (C) Susan E. Mickey; (L) Robert Peterson
A Christmas Carol, adapt: Sandra Deer, from Charles Dickens; (D) Fontaine Syer; (S) John Paoletti and Mary Griswold; (C) John Paoletti and Mary Griswold; (L) Geoffrey Bushor
The Seagull, Anton Chekhov; trans: Jean-Claude van Itallie; (D) Irene Lewis; (S) Christopher Barreca; (C) Catherine Zuber; (L) Pat Collins
Broadway Bound, Neil Simon; (D) Charlie Hensley; (S) Rob Odorisio; (C) Jeff Cone; (L) Liz Lee
Ma Rainey's Black Bottom, August Wilson; (D) Dwight Andrews; (S) Michael Olich; (C) Susan E. Mickey; (L) Ann G. Wrightson
3-Point Shot, adapt: Sandra Deer, from David Field; (D) Chris Coleman; (S) Dex Edwards; (C) Jeff Cone; (L) Robert Peterson
The Velveteen Rabbit, adapt: John Stephens, from Margery Williams; (D) John Stephens; (S) Dex Edwards; (C) Stephanie Kaskel; (L) Liz Lee

American Conservatory Theater

EDWARD HASTINGS
Artistic Director

JOHN SULLIVAN
Managing Director

450 Geary St.
San Francisco, CA 94102
(415) 749-2200 (bus.)
(415) 749-2228 (b.o.)

FOUNDED 1965
William Ball

SEASON
Oct.-May

FACILITIES
Geary Theatre*
Seating Capacity: 1,396
Stage: proscenium

Playroom
Seating Capacity: 49
Stage: flexible

FINANCES
June 1, 1989-May 31, 1990
Expenses: $10,400,000

CONTRACTS
AEA LORT (A)

**A.C.T. presently operates in various theatres as a result of the October 17, 1989 earthquake damage to the Geary Theatre. The theatres include: The Orpheum, P.G. & E. Theatre, Stage Door, Palace of Fine Arts and the Herbst Theatre.*

The American Conservatory Theatre of San Francisco is a national center for the theatre arts, dedicated to the revelation of the truths of human experience through

American Conservatory Theater. Sydney Walker and Peter Donat in *The Imaginary Invalid*. Photo: Harry Wade.

the exploration of the dramatic literature of all ages and nations. We affirm the principle that the growth of individual creativity is the essential component of cultural progress, and that this growth and its expression in the theatre reach their fullest realization when repertory performance and professional training are concurrent and inseparable. We advocate the inherent right of the company member to participate in the formation of institutional policy, and are committed to the development of artists and audiences from all sectors of the ethnically diverse community that we serve.

—Edward Hastings

PRODUCTIONS 1989-90

Right Mind, book and lyrics: George Coates; music: Marc Ream; (D) George Coates; image process coordinator: Charles Rose

A Tale of Two Cities, adapt: Nagle Jackson, from Charles Dickens; (D) Sabin Epstein; (S) Ralph Funicello; (C) Robert Fletcher; (L) Derek Duarte

A Christmas Carol, adapt: Dennis Powers and Laird Williamson, from Charles Dickens; (D) Laird Williamson; (S) Robert Blackman; (C) Robert Morgan; (L) Derek Duarte

Almost Like Being In Love, conceived: Paul Blake; book and lyrics: Alan Jay Lerner; music: Frederick Loewe; (D) Paul Blake; (L) Derek Duarte

Judevine, David Budbill; (D) Edward Hastings; (S) Joel Fontaine; (C) Warren Travis; (L) Derek Duarte

Twelfth Night, William Shakespeare; (D) John C. Fletcher; (S) Richard R. Goodwin; (C) Beaver Bauer; (L) Derek Duarte

Hapgood, Tom Stoppard; (D) Joy Carlin; (S) Ralph Funicello; (C) Terence Tam Soon; (L) Derek Duarte

The Imaginary Invalid, Moliere; trans: Laird Williamson and M. Xantrailles; (D) Laird Williamson; (S) Gerard Howland; (C) Gerard Howland; (L) Derek Duarte

Burn This, Lanford Wilson; (D) Albert Takazauckas; (S) Ralph Funicello; (C) Sandra Woodall; (L) Derek Duarte

PRODUCTIONS 1990-91

Saturday, Sunday and Monday, Eduardo De Filippo; trans: James Keller and Albert Takazauckas; (D) Albert Takazauckas; (S) John Wilson; (C) Sandra Woodall; (L) Derek Duarte

The Gospel at Colonus, adapt: Lee Breuer, from Sophocles; music: Bob Telson; lyrics: Lee Breuer and Bob Telson; (D) Lee Breuer; (S) Alison Yerxa; (C) Ghretta Hynd; (L) Derek Duarte

A Christmas Carol, adapt: Dennis Powers and Laird Williamson, from Charles Dickens; (D) Laird Williamson; (S) Robert Blackman; (C) Robert Morgan; (L) Derek Duarte

Food and Shelter, Jane Anderson; (D) Joy Carlin; (S) Gerard Howland; (C) Gerard Howland; (L) Derek Duarte

1918, Horton Foote; (D) Sabin Epstein; (S) Edward Burbridge;- (C) Cathleen Edwards; (L) Derek Duarte

Hamlet, William Shakespeare; (D) John C. Fletcher; (S) Kate Edmunds; (C) Jeffrey Struckman; (L) Robert Jared

Dark Sun, Lisette Lecat Ross; (D) Edward Hastings; (S) Joel Fontaine; (C) Karin Simonson Kopischke; (L) Derek Duarte

The Marriage of Figaro, book adapt and trans: Joan Holden, from Pierre-Augustin de Beaumarchais; music: Stephen LeGrand and Eric Drew Feldman; lyrics: Joan Holden and Stephen LeGrand; (D) Richard E.T. White; (S) Kent Dorsey; (C) Michael Olich; (L) Derek Duarte

The American Place Theatre

WYNN HANDMAN
Director

DARA HERSHMAN
General Manager

111 West 46th St.
New York, NY 10036
(212) 840-2960 (bus.)
(212) 840-3074 (b.o.)

FOUNDED 1963
Michael Tolan, Myrna Loy, Sidney Lanier, Wynn Handman

SEASON
Sept.-June

The American Place Theatre. Tim Johnson and Elizabeth Van Dyke in *Zora Neale Hurston*. Photo: Martha Holmes.

FACILITIES
Mainstage
Seating Capacity: 299
Stage: thrust

Subplot Cafe
Seating Capacity: 74
Stage: flexible

First Floor Theatre
Seating Capacity: 74
Stage: flexible

FINANCES
July 1, 1990-June 30, 1991
Expenses: $925,000

CONTRACTS
AEA Production, Mini and Cabaret

The American Place Theatre is currently in its 27th season of producing new American plays by living American writers. Its continuing purpose is to be a force for the advancement of theatre by actively responding to the contemporary theatre's needs. Toward that end, the American Place provides talented writers with a creative environment free of commercial considerations. Our innovative, original programming opens the way for increased public awareness and enrichment of the mainstream of the nation's theatre. In order to promote and encourage new work of various genres with differing production needs, the American Place has several ongoing programs in addition to its Venture Plays Series. These include The American Humorists' Series, JUBILEE! Festival Celebrating Ethnic America, the experimental First Floor Theatre Series, and INTER-PLAY, our Arts-in-Education initiative.

—Wynn Handman

PRODUCTIONS 1989-90

Zora Neale Hurston, Laurence Holder; (D) Wynn Handman; (S) Terence Chandler; (L) Shirley Prendergast

Neddy, Jeffrey Hatcher; (D) Amy Saltz; (S) G.W. Mercier; (C) G.W. Mercier; (L) Frances Aronson

Ground People, Leslie Lee; (D) Walter Dallas; (S) Charles McClennahan; (C) Beth Ribblett; (L) Shirley Prendergast

Bobo's Birthday, Catherine Butterfield; (D) Stephen Stout; (S) Andrew J. Meyer; (L) Andrew J. Meyer

The Consuming Passions of Lydia E. Pinkham and Rev.

Sylvester Graham, Margery Cohen; (D) Wynn Handman; (S) Andrew J. Meyer; (L) Andrew J. Meyer

PRODUCTIONS 1990-91

Calvin Trillin's Words, No Music, Calvin Trillin; (D) Wynn Handman; (S) Bill Stabile; (L) Andrew J. Meyer

I Stand Before You Naked, Joyce Carol Oates; (D) Wynn Handman; (S) Bill Stabile; consultant: Sally J. Lesser; (L) Andrew J. Meyer

Mambo Mouth, John Leguizamo; (D) Peter Askin; (S) Philipp Jung; (L) Graeme F. McDonnell

Midnight Carnival, creators: Rob Faust and Wynn Handman; (D) Rob Faust and Wynn Handman; (S) Bill Stabile; (C) Faustwork Mask Theater; (L) Shirley Prendergast

The Mask Man, Faustwork Mask Theater; (D) Rob Faust; (S) Faustwork Mask Theater; (C) Faustwork Mask Theater; (L) Shirley Prendergast

Struck Dumb, Jean-Claude van Itallie and Joseph Chaikin; (D) Nancy Gabor; (S) Woods Mackintosh; (C) Mary Brecht; (L) Beverly Emmons

The War in Heaven, Sam Shepard and Joseph Chaikin; (D) Nancy Gabor; (S) Woods Mackintosh; (C) Mary Brecht; (L) Beverly Emmons

States of Shock, Sam Shepard; (D) Bill Hart; (S) Bill Stabile; (C) Gabriel Berry; (L) Pat Dignan and Anne Militello

American Repertory Theatre

ROBERT BRUSTEIN
Artistic Director

ROBERT J. ORCHARD
Managing Director

Loeb Drama Center
64 Brattle St.
Cambridge, MA 02138
(617) 495-2668 (bus.)
(617) 547-8300 (b.o.)

FOUNDED 1979
Robert Brustein

SEASON
Jan.-Dec.; mainstage Nov.-July

FACILITIES
Loeb Drama Center
Seating Capacity: 556
Stage: flexible

Hasty Pudding Theatre
Seating Capacity: 353
Stage: proscenium

FINANCES
Aug. 1, 1990-July 31, 1991
Expenses: $5,549,000

CONTRACTS
AEA LORT (B)

The American Repertory Theatre, founded as a professional producing organization and a theatrical training conservatory, is one of a very few companies in this country with a resident acting ensemble performing in rotating repertory. The company has presented 83 productions, including more than 40 premieres, new translations and adaptations. Our productions, which have increasingly involved artists of national and international stature from a wide variety of disciplines, generally fall into three distinct categories: newly interpreted classical productions, new American plays and neglected works of the past, frequently involving music. ART has toured extensively within this country (including an appearance at the 1984 Olympic Arts Festival in Los Angeles) and abroad, including performances in Tokyo, Madrid, Avignon, Paris, Venice, Edinburgh, Tel Aviv, Belgrade, London and Amsterdam. In 1987, the American Repertory Theatre Institute for Advanced Theatre Training at Harvard began formal instruction under the direction of Richard Riddell. ART received the 1985 Jujamcyn Award and a special Tony Award in 1986 for continued excellence in resident theatre.

—Robert Brustein

PRODUCTIONS 1989-90

The Bald Soprano and ***The Chairs***, Eugene Ionesco; trans: Donald Watson; (D) Andrei Belgrader; (S) Anita Stewart; (C) Candice Donnelly; (L) Stephen Strawbridge

Twelfth Night, William Shakespeare; (D) Andrei Serban; (S) Derek McLane; (C) Catherine Zuber; (L) Howell Binkley

American Repertory Theatre. Christopher Lloyd and Thomas Derrah in *Power Failure*. Photo: Richard Feldman.

Major Barbara, George Bernard Shaw; (D) Michael Engler; (S) Philipp Jung; (C) Catherine Zuber; (L) James F. Ingalls

The Father, August Strindberg; adapt: Robert Brustein; (D) Robert Brustein; (S) Derek McLane; (C) Dunya Ramicova; (L) Richard Riddell

The Caucasian Chalk Circle, Bertolt Brecht, trans: Ralph Manheim; (D) Slobodan Unkovski; (S) Meta Hocevar; (C) Catherine Zuber; (L) Richard Riddell

Road To Nirvana, Arthur Kopit; (D) Michael Bloom; (S) Scott Bradley; (C) Ellen McCartney; (L) Peter West

The Lost Boys, Allan Knee; (D) Jerome Kilty; (S) Scott Bradley; (C) Karen Eister; (L) John Ambrosone

The Island of Anyplace, Charles Marz; music: Barry Rocklin; lyrics: Charles Marz; (D) Thomas Derrah; (S) Scott Bradley; (C) Scott Bradley; (L) John Ambrosone

PRODUCTIONS 1990-91

The Homecoming, Harold Pinter; (D) David Wheeler; (S) Derek McLane; (C) Catherine Zuber; (L) Frances Aronson

Once In A Lifetime, George S. Kaufman and Moss Hart; (D) Anne Bogart; (S) Loy Arcenas; (C) Catherine Zuber; (L) James F. Ingalls

When We Dead Awaken, Henrik Ibsen; adapt: Robert Wilson; trans: Robert Brustein; (D) Robert Wilson; (S) John Conklin and Robert Wilson; (C) John Conklin; (L) Stephen Strawbridge and Robert Wilson

King Lear, William Shakespeare; (D) Adrian Hall; (S) Eugene Lee; (C) Catherine Zuber; (L) Natasha Katz

Power Failure, Larry Gelbart; (D) Michael Engler; (S) Philipp Jung; (C) Candice Donnelly; (L) Natasha Katz

The King Stag, Carlo Gozzi; trans: Albert Bermel; (D) Andrei Serban; (S) Michael Yeargan; (C) Julie Taymor; (L) John Ambrosone

Rameau's Nephew, Denis Diderot; adapt: Andrei Belgrader and Shelley Berc; (D) Andrei Belgrader; (S) Anita Stewart; (C) Candice Donnelly; (L) Robert Wierzel

The Writing Game, David Lodge; (D) Michael Bloom; (S) Bill Clarke; (C) Ellen McCartney; (L) Richard Riddell

Steel, book and lyrics: Derek Walcott; music: Galt MacDermot; (D) Derek Walcott and Robert Scanlan; (S) Richard Montgomery; (C) Catherine Zuber; (L) Richard Riddell

American Stage

VICTORIA L. HOLLOWAY
Artistic Director

JOHN BERGLUND
Producing Director

Box 1560
St. Petersburg, FL 33731
(813) 823-1600 (bus.)
(813) 822-8814 (b.o.)

FOUNDED 1979
Bobbie Seifer-Paul, Richard Hopkins

SEASON
Oct.-Aug.

FACILITIES
Mainstage
Seating Capacity: 120
Stage: thrust

Deman's Landing
Seating Capacity: 1,500
Stage: flexible

Tampa Bay Performing Arts Center
Seating Capacity: 1,000
Stage: proscenium

FINANCES
Oct. 1, 1989-Sept. 30, 1990
Expenses: $835,764

CONTRACTS
AEA SPT, TYA and letter of agreement

American Stage, St. Petersburg's professional theatre ensemble, is mandated as a nonprofit arts agency to provide theatre, educational and outreach programs to the citizens of west central Florida. This mission has always been implicit in the theatre's operation and serves as a reference point for all major decisions made by our staff of artists. Artistic excellence, expanded community service and the creation of new programs for new audiences define the theatre's intent in fulfilling its mission: to produce alive, challenging and enriching theatre, and to prosper as a cultural institution which represents and influences the life of its community through the art of professional theatre. For the past decade, we have sought the perfect union between personal artistic expression and realistic programming. We have responded on the one hand to our artistic needs and on the other hand to the needs of our community. The balance between the two has insured our success.

—Victoria L. Holloway

American Stage. Jennifer Lanier, Barry Press and Pete Bauer in *Rebel Armies Deep Into Chad*. Photo: Joe Walles.

PRODUCTIONS 1989-90

Stage Blood, Charles Ludlam; (D) Bruce Siddons; (S) Barton Lee; (C) Abby Lillethun; (L) Joseph Oshry
The Boys Next Door, Tom Griffin; (D) Victoria L. Holloway; (S) Jimmy Humphries; (C) Joanne L. Johnson; (L) Richard Sharkey
Serenading Louie, Lanford Wilson; (D) Judy Braha; (S) Jeffrey Dean; (C) Kathy Foley; (L) Richard Sharkey
Oldtimers Game, Lee Blessing; (D) John Berglund; (S) Richard Sharkey; (C) Joanne L. Johnson; (L) Richard Sharkey
Twelfth Night, William Shakespeare; (D) Victoria L. Holloway; (S) Keven Lock; (C) Mark Hughes; (L) Richard Sharkey
Rebel Armies Deep Into Chad, Mark Lee; (D) Victoria L. Holloway; (S) Barton Lee; (C) Peter Massey; (L) Joseph Oshry
The Early Girl, Caroline Kava; (D) Victoria L. Holloway; (S) Barton Lee; (C) Hugh Slack; (L) Richard Sharkey
Cinderella—The True Story, book adapt: Victoria L. Holloway, from Charles Perrault; music and lyrics: Lee Ahlin; (D) Victoria L. Holloway; (S) Jeffrey Dean; (C) Susan Kelly
The Cricket in Times Square, book adapt: Victoria L. Holloway, from George Selden; music and lyrics: Lee Ahlin; (D) Victoria L. Holloway; (S) Barton Lee; (C) Susan Kelly
Billy Bishop Goes to War, John Gray and Eric Peterson; (D) Cathey Sawyer; (S) Richard Crowell; (C) Deborah Thompson; (L) Richard Crowell

PRODUCTIONS 1990-91

Billy Bishop Goes to War, John Gray and Eric Peterson; (D) Cathey Sawyer; (S) Richard Crowell; (C) Deborah Thompson; (L) Richard Crowell
Steel Magnolias, Robert Harling; (D) Victoria L. Holloway; (S) Allen D. Cornell; (C) Rosemary Bengele; (L) Richard Crowell
Death of a Salesman, Arthur Miller; (D) Cathey Sawyer; (S) Richard Crowell; (C) Deborah Thompson; (L) Richard Crowell
Two Rooms, Lee Blessing; (D) John Berglund; (S) Barton Lee; (C) John Huls; (L) Richard Crowell
The Glass Menagerie, Tennessee Williams; (D) Victoria L. Holloway; (S) Barton Lee; (C) David Malcolm Bewley; (L) Richard Crowell
A Midsummer Night's Dream, William Shakespeare; (D) Victoria L. Holloway; (S) Keven Lock; (C) David Malcolm Bewley; (L) Richard Crowell
Boy Meets Girl, Bella Spewack and Samuel Spewack; (D) John Berglund and Victoria L. Holloway; (S) Barton Lee; (C) David Malcolm Bewley; (L) Richard Crowell
The Artificial Jungle, Charles Ludlam; (D) Cathey Sawyer; (S) Richard Crowell; (C) Peter Massey; (L) Richard Crowell
The Cricket in Times Square, book adapt: Victoria L. Holloway, from George Selden; music and lyrics: Lee Ahlin; (D) Victoria L. Holloway; (S) Barton Lee; (C) Susan Kelly

American Stage Festival

RICHARD ROSE
Producing Director

AUSTIN TICHENOR
Associate Producing Director

Box 225
Milford, NH 03055-0225
(603) 673-4005 (bus.)
(603) 673-7515 (b.o.)

FOUNDED 1975
Terry C. Lorden

SEASON
May-Sept.

FACILITIES
American Stage Festival
Seating Capacity: 496
Stage: proscenium

FINANCES
Nov. 1, 1989-Oct. 31, 1990
Expenses: $789,697

CONTRACTS
AEA LORT (D)

The artistic mission of the American Stage Festival is to expand the spectrum of theatre art by presenting rewarding and challenging theatrical material, with particular attention to pieces that reflect the concerns of southern New Hampshire; to invigorate audiences with work that is emotionally fulfilling and intellectually stimulating; to discover, develop and produce new theatrical works; to further the education of young theatre artists by serving as a bridge between training programs and the "real world"; to entertain and educate the young people of our area through the performances and workshops of our Young Company; to further enrich our audiences through the presentation of works from the entire realm of live performance, including dance and music; and, finally, to raise our standards and those of our audience so that the limits of regional resources do not limit expectation or imagination.

—Richard Rose

PRODUCTIONS 1989-90

A Current Christmas Carol, adapt: Austin Tichenor, from

American Stage Festival. Joy Franz, William Parry, Karyn Quackenbush and Bjorn Johnson in *Cole Porter's Malibu*.

Charles Dickens; (D) Richard Rose; (S) Gary English; (C) Amanda Aldridge; (L) Kendall Smith

Graceland, Donald Steele; (D) Austin Tichenor; (S) Charles Morgan; (C) Dianne Tyree; (L) Sid Bennett

Almost Like Being In Love, conceived: Paul Blake; book and lyrics: Alan Jay Lerner; music: Frederick Loewe, et al; (D) Richard Rose; (S) Charles Morgan; (C) Dianne Tyree; (L) Sid Bennett

Cyrano de Bergerac, Edmond Rostand; trans: Richard Rose; (D) Austin Tichenor; (S) Charles Morgan; (C) Dawna Gregory; (L) Kendall Smith

A Little Night Music, book: Hugh Wheeler; music and lyrics: Stephen Sondheim; (D) Richard Rose; (S) Gary English; (C) Amanda Aldridge; (L) Kendall Smith

Bus Stop, William Inge; (D) Robert Walsh; (S) Alison Ford; (C) Scott Pegg; (L) David Lockner

Frankenstein, Austin Tichenor, from Mary Shelley; (D) Richard Rose; (S) Charles Morgan; (C) Amanda Aldridge; (L) Kendall Smith

Young Company:

The Prince and the Pauper, adapt: Eve Muson, from Mark Twain; (D) Denise Ryan; (S) Charles Morgan; (C) Ginny Sassan; (L) Karalee Dawn

Rapunzel, adapt: Jacques LaMarre, from The Brothers Grimm; (D) Scott Pegg; (S) Scott Pegg; (C) Ginny Sassan; (L) Karalee Dawn

Snow White and the Seven Dwarfs, adapt: Denise Ryan, from The Brothers Grimm; (D) Jennifer Brown; (S) Jennifer Brown; (C) Ginny Sassan; (L) Karalee Dawn

Pee Wee Parker Mystery: Who Stole the Cookies from the Cookie Jar?, Austin Tichenor; (D) Michael Bernard; (S) Michael Bernard; (C) Ginny Sassan; (L) Jonathan Knight

The Magnificent Mega-Man and Me, John Tichenor; (D) John Tichenor; (S) John Tichenor; (C) Ginny Sassan; (L) Karalee Dawn

Casey at the Bat, adapt: John Tichenor, from Ernest Lawrence Thayer; (D) Katherine Potts; (S) Katherine Potts; (C) Ginny Sassan; (L) Karalee Dawn

Jack and the Beanstalk, adapt: Michael Bernard and Denise Ryan; (D) Jennifer Brown; (S) Jennifer Brown; (C) Ginny Sassan; (L) Karalee Dawn

The Wind in the Willows, book adapt and lyrics: Blanche Risteen, from Kenneth Grahame; music: Dan Strange-Murphy; (D) Denise Ryan; (S) Denise Ryan; (C) Ginny Sassan; (L) Karalee Dawn

Puss in Boots, adapt: Brett Tolman, from Charles Perrault; (D) Russel Lees; (S) Andy Lomeau; (C) Ginny Sassan; (L) Karalee Dawn

The Tempest, adapt: Denise Ryan, from William Shakespeare; (D) Austin Tichenor; (S) Andy Lomeau; (C) Ginny Sassan; (L) Karalee Dawn

PRODUCTIONS 1990-91

Table Manners, Alan Ayckbourn; (D) Robert Walsh; (S) Charles Morgan; (C) Kevin Pothier; (L) Dave Brown

Cole Porter's Malibu, conceived: Judy Brown; book: Jerome Chodorov; music and lyrics: Cole Porter; (D) Richard Rose; (S) Charles Morgan; (C) Amanda Aldridge; (L) Kendall Smith

Educating Rita, Willy Russell; (D) Austin Tichenor; (S) Alison Ford; (C) Amanda Aldridge; (L) Christopher Ackerlind

Kuru, Josh Manheimer; (D) Richard Rose; (S) Clifton Taylor; (C) Mary Meyers; (L) Clifton Taylor

Jesus Christ Superstar, music: Andrew Lloyd Webber; lyrics: Tim Rice; (D) Austin Tichenor; (S) Charles Morgan; (C) Amanda Aldridge; (L) Kendall Smith

Young Company:

The Twelve Dancing Princesses, adapt: John Tichenor, from The Brothers Grimm; (D) John Tichenor; (S) Kristine Dornbusch; (C) Bridget Savadge; (L) Karalee Dawn

The Arabian Nights, adapt: Jonathan Knight; (D) Blair Hundertmark; (S) Kristine Dornbusch; (C) Bridget Savadge; (L) Blair Hundertmark

Pecos Bill, adapt: John Tichenor; (D) Barbara Bosch; (S) Kristine Dornbusch; (C) Bridget Savadge; (L) Karalee Dawn

The Frog Prince, adapt: John Tichenor, from The Brothers Grimm; (D) Jonathan Knight; (S) Kristine Dornbusch; (C) Bridget Savadge; (L) Jonathan Knight

Goldilocks and the Three Bears, adapt: David Letwin; (D) Margarett Perry; (S) Kristine Dornbusch; (C) Bridget Savadge; (L) Karalee Dawn

Stone Soup, book adapt and lyrics: Austin Tichenor; music: Andrew Howard; (D) John Tichenor; (S) Kristine Dornbusch; (C) Bridget Savadge; (L) Karalee Dawn

Captain Whoopee Show, John Tichenor; (D) Blair Hundertmark; (S) Kristine Dornbusch; (C) Bridget Savadge; (L) Karalee Dawn

The Pied Piper of Hamelin, adapt: Jacques LaMarre, from The Brothers Grimm; (D) John Tichenor; (S) Kristine Dornbusch; (C) Bridget Savadge; (L) Karalee Dawn

The Comedy of Errors, adapt: Richard Rose, from William Shakespeare; (D) Richard Rose; (S) Kristine Dornbusch; (C) Bridget Savadge; (L) Karalee Dawn

American Theatre Company

KITTY ROBERTS
Producing Artistic Director

LISA SWIGGART
Manager

Box 1265
Tulsa, OK 74101
(918) 747-9494

FOUNDED 1970
Kitty Roberts

SEASON
Jan.-Dec.

FACILITIES
John Williams Theatre
Seating Capacity: 429
Stage: proscenium

The Brady Theatre
Seating Capacity: 1,200
Stage: proscenium

Studio I
Seating Capacity: 293
Stage: flexible

FINANCES
Jan. 1, 1990-Dec. 31, 1990
Expenses: $330,000

CONTRACTS
AEA Guest Artist

Oklahoma's pioneer spirit arises from a life shared together at the edge of recent American history—the forced resettlement of Native Americans from 1820 on, the land rush by European settlers in 1889, statehood in 1907, the oil boom from 1912 to 1920, the Dustbowl depression of the 1930s, the expansion of military bases during World War II, the energy crisis and oil embargo of 1973. As Oklahoma's only resident professional theatre company, the American Theatre Company can persuade Oklahomans that their frontier viewpoint is mirrored in the traditions of world drama, and that their frontier voices can be expressed in a unique dramatic idiom. Therefore, our goal is to play a leading role in shaping a common public vision for the economic, political, educational, religious and artistic life of

Oklahoma. ATC presents six mainstage and two summer productions, and conducts an ongoing statewide education program.

—*Kitty Roberts*

PRODUCTIONS 1989-90

The Passion of Dracula, adapt: Bob Hall and David Richmond, from Bram Stoker; (D) Randy Blair; (S) Richard Ellis; (C) Jo Wimer and Pam Curtis; (L) Richard Wilson

A Christmas Carol, book adapt: Robert Odle, from Charles Dickens; music: Richard Averill; lyrics: Richard Averill and Robert Odle (D) Randy Blair; (S) Richard Ellis; (C) Jo Wimer and Pam Curtis; (L) Richard Wilson

Fences, August Wilson; (D) Tyrone Wilkerson; (S) Richard Ellis; (C) Randy Blair; (L) Richard Wilson

The Boys Next Door, Tom Griffin; (D) Randy Blair; (S) Richard Ellis; (C) Pam Curtis; (L) Richard Wilson

The Immigrant, Mark Harelik; (D) David Valla; (S) Warren Houtz; (C) Randy Blair; (L) Warren Houtz

Treasure Island, book adapt: Robert Odle, from Robert Louis Stevenson; music: Richard Averill; lyrics: Richard Averill, Robert Odle and Kerry Hauger; (D) Erick Devine; (S) Richard Ellis; (C) Randy Blair; (L) Charles Gilroy

Eddie and The Ecclectics, music and lyrics: various; (D) Randy Wimer; (S) Richard Ellis; (C) Jo Wimer; (L) Larry McKinney

Dandelion, Judith Martin; (D) Lori Bryant; (S) student cast; (C) student cast; (L) Thad Strassberger

PRODUCTIONS 1990-91

The Mystery of Irma Vep, Charles Ludlam; (D) Lori Bryant; (S) Ricky Green Newkirk; (C) Randy Blair; (L) Richard Wilson

A Christmas Carol, book adapt: Robert Odle, from Charles Dickens; music: Richard Averill; lyrics: Richard Averill and Robert Odle; (D) Randy Blair and Lori Bryant; (S) Richard Ellis; (C) Jo Wimer and Pam Curtis; (L) Richard Wilson

Driving Miss Daisy, Alfred Uhry; (D) Randy Blair; (S) Richard Ellis; (C) Pam Curtis; (L) Richard Wilson

Temptation, Vaclav Havel; trans: Marie Winn; (D) Lori Byrant

The Heidi Chronicles, Wendy Wasserstein; (D) Tyrone Wilkerson; (S) Richard Ellis; (C) Randy Blair; (L) Richard Wilson

Harvey, Mary Chase; (D) David Valla; (S) Richard Ellis; (C) Randy Blair; (L) Richard Wilson

Eddie and The Ecclectics, music and lyrics: various; (D) John Nicholas; (S) Tad Townes; (C) Jo Wimer; (L) Larry McKinney

Tom Sawyer, book adapt: Fred Graves and Vern Stefanic, from Mark Twain; music: Doug Smith; lyrics: Fred Graves, Vern Stefanic and Doug Smith; (D) Erick Devine and Fred Graves; (S) Gerald Graham; (C) Randy Blair; (L) Richard Wilson

A Shakespeare Summer, adapt: Rena Cook, from William Shakespeare; (D) Rena Cook; (S) student cast; (C) student cast; (L) Thad Strassberger

I Didn't Know That, Louis Moloney, Johnny Saldana, Joyce Chambers Selber and Rachel Winfree; (D) Lori Bryant; (S) student cast; (C) student cast; (L) Thad Strassberger

American Theatre Company. Robert Bowie in *Harvey*.

American Theatre Works. Harley Venton, Jennie Moreau, Eric Swanson and Micheal Liani in *Advice from a Caterpillar*. Photo: Wm. John Aupperlee.

American Theatre Works

JILL CHARLES
Artistic Director

JOHN NASSIVERA
Producing Director

Box 519
Dorset, VT 05251
(802) 867-2223 (bus.)
(802) 867-5777 (b.o.)

FOUNDED 1976
John Nassivera, Jill Charles

SEASON
June-Sept.

FACILITIES
The Dorset Playhouse
Seating Capacity: 218
Stage: proscenium

FINANCES
Jan. 1, 1990-Dec. 31, 1990
Expenses: $370,000

CONTRACTS
AEA SPT

American Theatre Works, Inc. produces the Dorset Theatre Festival at the Dorset Playhouse, a season of five or six contemporary American and British plays as well as revivals of American classics and at least one new play. Over the past 16 seasons, the company has built up a pool of New York-based directors, designers, technicians and actors to draw from, and new talent is added each year. The educational arm of American Theatre Works serves the theatre profession in two ways: through its outstanding apprentice program, offering Actors' Equity membership credit and a focus on career development, and through publication of two annual employment resources, *Summer Theatre Directory* and *Regional Theatre Directory*, as well as the *Directory of Theatre Training Programs*. Also, from September through May, American Theatre Works operates the Dorset Colony, a resident artists' colony, offering writers (particularly playwrights) a retreat for intensive periods of work.

—*Jill Charles*

PRODUCTIONS 1989

Educating Rita, Willy Russell; (D) Mark Ramont; (S) Wm. John Aupperlee; (C) Eric Hansen; (L) Jeffrey A. Bernstein

The 1940's Radio Hour, Walton Jones; (D) Jill Charles; (S) Wm. John Aupperlee; (C) Judy Kahn; (L) Jeffrey A. Bernstein

Wait Until Dark, Frederick Knott; (D) John Morrison; (S) Wm. John Aupperlee; (C) Eric Hansen; (L) Jeffrey A. Bernstein

"Master Harold"...and the boys, Athol Fugard; (D) Mark Ramont; (S) Wm. John Aupperlee; (C) Eric Hansen; (L) Jeffrey A. Bernstein

Crimes of the Heart, Beth Henley; (D) Jill Charles; (S) Wm. John Aupperlee; (C) Eric Hansen; (L) Jeffrey A. Bernstein

PRODUCTIONS 1990

The Increased Difficulty of Concentration, Vaclav Havel; (D) John Morrison; (S) Wm. John

Aupperlee; (C) Eric Hansen; (L) Jeffrey A. Bernstein

Side by Side by Sondheim, music: Stephen Sondheim and collaborators; lyrics: Stephen Sondheim; (D) Jill Charles; (S) Wm. John Aupperlee; (C) Eric Hansen; (L) C. Barrack Evans

Les Liaisons Dangereuses, Christopher Hampton, from Choderlos de Laclos; (D) John Morrison; (S) Wm. John Aupperlee; (C) Eric Hansen; (L) Jeffrey A. Bernstein

Driving Miss Daisy, Alfred Uhry; (D) Mark Ramont; (S) Wm. John Aupperlee; (C) Eric Hansen; (L) Jeffrey A. Bernstein

Advice from a Caterpillar, Douglas Carter Beane; (D) Edgar Lansbury; (S) Wm. John Aupperlee; (C) Eric Hansen; (L) Jeffrey A. Bernstein

Arden Theatre Company

TERRENCE J. NOLEN
Producing Artistic Director

AARON POSNER
Artistic Director

Box 801
Philadelphia, PA 19105
(215) 829-8900

FOUNDED 1988
Terrence J. Nolen, Aaron Posner, Amy L. Murphy

SEASON
Sept.-May

FACILITIES
St. Stephen's Alley
Seating Capacity: 150-175
Stage: flexible

FINANCES
June 1, 1990-May 31, 1991
Expenses: $310,410

CONTRACTS
AEA letter of agreement

The Arden Theatre Company is dedicated to bringing to life the greatest stories by the greatest storytellers of all time. Since the greatest stories touch some essential part of the human experience, the *story itself* remains the primary focus of all our productions. The Arden will draw from any source which is inherently dramatic and theatrical—fiction, nonfiction, poetry, music and drama: Adapting nondramatic writings to the stage is an important aspect of our work. These new texts create fascinating challenges which force us to create new theatrical language, establish new conventions, and continually reinvent and rediscover theatrical possibilities. The Arden stages works for the diverse Philadelphia community that arouse, provoke, illuminate and inspire. All our programs aim to enrich the lives of those living throughout our diverse community. Our commitment is *here*, with local students, actors, authors, artists and audiences.

—Terrence J. Nolen, Aaron Posner

PRODUCTIONS 1989-90

The Sneeze, adapt and trans: Michael Frayn, from Anton Chekhov; (D) Aaron Posner; (S) James F. Pyne, Jr.; (C) Marla Jurglanis; (L) Curt Senie

As You Like It, William Shakespeare; (D) Aaron Posner; (S) Tina Krovetz; (C) Victoria Pero; (L) Whitney Quesenbery

Godspell, book: John Michael Tebelak; music and lyrics: Stephen Schwartz; (D) Terrence J. Nolen; (S) James F. Pyne, Jr.; (C) Marla Jurglanis; (L) Whitney Quesenbery

The Invisible Man, adapt: Terrence J. Nolen, from H.G. Wells; (D) Terrence J. Nolen; (S) Wesley Maloney-Truitt; (C) Janus Stefanowicz; (L) Ellen M. Owens

Philadelphia Phiction, adapt: Deborah Block, Terrence J. Nolen and Aaron Posner, from writings by various Philadelphia writers; (D) Deborah Block, Terrence J. Nolen and Aaron Posner; (S) Melinda Oblinger and Meg Hyatt; (C) Jilline Ringle; (L) Ellen M. Owens

PRODUCTIONS 1990-91

As You Like It, William Shakespeare; (D) Aaron Posner; (S) Tina Krovetz; (C) Jilline Ringle; (L) Whitney Quesenbery

The Girl With the Silver Eyes, adapt: Terrence J. Nolen, from Dashiell Hammett; (D) Terrence J. Nolen; (S) Daniel Jackson; (C) Max Wilson; (L) Curt Senie

Arden Theatre Company. David Stein Azen and Tom McCarthy in *The Girl With the Silver Eyes*. Photo: Mary D'Anella.

Appalachian Ebeneezer, book adapt: Cheyney Ryan and Randi Douglas, from Charles Dickens; music: Linda Danielson; (D) Aaron Posner; (S) Lynne Porter; (C) Linda Roethke; (L) Whitney Quesenbery

Hamlet, William Shakespeare; (D) Aaron Posner; (S) Daniel Jackson; (C) Michele Osherow; (L) Ellen M. Owens

Working, adapt: Stephen Schwartz and Nina Faso, from Studs Terkel; various composers and lyricists; (D) Terrence J. Nolen; (S) Lynne Porter; (C) Chryss Hionis; (L) Ellen M. Owens

Arena Stage

DOUGLAS C. WAGER
Artistic Director

STEPHEN RICHARD
Executive Director

6th and Maine Ave. SW
Washington, DC 20024
(202) 554-9066 (bus.)
(202) 488-3300 (b.o.)

FOUNDED 1950
Edward Mangum, Zelda Fichandler, Thomas C. Fichandler

SEASON
Sept.-June

FACILITIES
The Arena
Seating Capacity: 818
Stage: arena

The Kreeger Theater
Seating Capacity: 514
Stage: thrust

The Old Vat Room
Seating Capacity: 180
Stage: flexible

FINANCES
July 1, 1990-June 30, 1991
Expenses: $9,206,000

CONTRACTS
AEA LORT (B+) and (D)

Arena Stage enters its fifth decade, under new leadership, dedicated to its founding belief that true artistic excellence is achieved by means of a resident ensemble of actors, artists, craftspeople and administrators who collaborate in an evolutionary process from play to play, season after season. We are committted to enriching the imaginative and spiritual life of our audience. Our repertoire provides our community with an aggressively eclectic mix of classics and new works, musicals and culturally diverse offerings. The actor inhabits the epicenter of our work as a living instrument of human expressivity. Arena has expanded and reemphasized its longstanding commitment to encourage participation by people of color in every aspect of the theatre's life by establishing a comprehensive cultural diversity program which includes the Allen Lee Hughes Fellows Program for the training of ethnically diverse young people in artistic, technical and administrative areas. We seek to create a vibrant emotional and intellectual theatrical landscape that, through storytelling, probes the infinite mystery of the human experience.

—Douglas C. Wager

Note: During the 1989-90 and 1990-91 seasons, Zelda Fichandler served as producing director.

PRODUCTIONS 1989-90

On The Way Home, Stephen Wade; (D) Milton Kramer

A Midsummer Night's Dream, William Shakespeare; (D) Liviu Ciulei; (S) Liviu Ciulei; (C) Smaranda Branescu; (L) Allen Lee Hughes

The Glass Menagerie, Tennessee Williams; (D) Tazewell Thompson; (S) Loy Arcenas; (C) Marjorie Slaiman; (L) Nancy Schertler

The Man Who Came to Dinner, George S. Kaufman and Moss Hart; (D) Douglas C. Wager; (S) Adrianne Lobel; (C) Marjorie Slaiman; (L) Nancy Schertler

Stand-Up Tragedy, Bill Cain; (D) Max Mayer; (S) Andrew Jackness; (C) Paul Tazewell; (L) Donald Holder

Merrily We Roll Along, book adapt: George Furth, from George S. Kaufman and Moss Hart; music and lyrics: Stephen Sondheim; (D) Douglas C. Wager; (S) Douglas Stein; (C) Ann Hould-Ward; (L) Allen Lee Hughes

A Doll House, Henrik Ibsen; trans: Gerry Bamman and Irene B. Berman; (D) Zelda Fichandler; (S) Douglas Stein; (C) Marjorie Slaiman; (L) Nancy Schertler

Conquest of the South Pole, Manfred Karge; adapt: Silas Jones and Laurence Maslon; (D) Paul Walker; (S) David M. Glenn; (C) Betty Siegel; (L) Christopher V. Lewton

Fences, August Wilson; (D) Tazewell Thompson; (S) Loy Arcenas; (C) Marjorie Slaiman; (L) Nancy Schertler

Juno and the Paycock, Sean O'Casey; (D) Joe Dowling; (S) F. Hallinan Flood; (C) Marjorie Slaiman; (L) Allen Lee Hughes

PRODUCTIONS 1990-91

On The Way Home, Stephen Wade; (D) Milton Kramer

Closer Than Ever, conceived: Steven Scott Smith; music: David Shire; lyrics: Richard Maltby, Jr.; (D) Richard Maltby, Jr.; (S) Philipp Jung; (C) Jess Goldstein; (L) Joshua Starbuck

The Caucasian Chalk Circle, Bertolt Brecht; trans: Ralph Manheim; (D) Tazewell Thompson; (S) Loy Arcenas; (C) Paul Tazewell; (L) Nancy Schertler

Cerceau, Viktor Slavkin; trans: Fritz Brun and Laurence Maslon; (D) Liviu Ciulei; (S) Liviu Ciulei; (C) Marjorie Slaiman; (L) Nancy Schertler

Our Town, Thornton Wilder; (D) Douglas C. Wager; (S) Thomas Lynch; (C) Marjorie Slaiman; (L) Allen Lee Hughes

From The Mississippi Delta, Dr. Endesha Ida Mae Holland; (D) Jonathan Wilson; (S) Michael S. Philippi; (C) Jeffrey Kelly; (L) Chris Phillips

Before It Hits Home, Cheryl West; (D) Tazewell Thompson; (S) Douglas Stein; (C) Helen Qizhi Huang; (L) Nancy Schertler

Born Guilty, adapt: Ari Roth, from Peter Sichrovsky; (D) Zelda Fichandler; (S) Douglas Stein; (C) Noel Borden; (L) Nancy Schertler

Pygmalion, George Bernard Shaw; (D) Douglas C. Wager; (S) Michael Yeargan; (C) Barbra Kravitz; (L) Mark McCullough

My Children! My Africa!, Athol Fugard; (D) Max Mayer; (S) David M. Glenn; (C) Crystal Walker; (L) Christopher Townsend

She Stoops To Conquer, Oliver Goldsmith; (D) Joe Dowling; (S) F. Hallinan Flood; (C) Marjorie Slaiman; (L) Allen Lee Hughes

Vivisections From the Blown Mind, Alonzo D. Lamont, Jr.; (D) Clinton Turner Davis; (S) Michael Franklin-White; (C) Betty Siegel; (L) Christopher V. Lewton

Two Gentlemen of Verona, William Shakespeare; (D) Charles Newell; (S) Derek McLane; (C) Catherine Zuber; (L) Marcus Dilliard

The Seagull, Anton Chekhov; trans: Jean-Claude van Itallie; (D) Douglas C. Wager; (S) Ming Cho Lee; (C) Marjorie Slaiman; (L) Arden Fingerhut

Arena Stage. Ruby Dee and Jonathan Earl Peck in *The Glass Menagerie*. Photo: Joan Marcus.

Arizona Theatre Company

ROBERT ALPAUGH
Managing Director

Box 1631
Tucson, AZ 85702
(602) 884-8210 (bus.)
(602) 622-2823 (b.o.)

1040 East Osborn Road
Phoenix, AZ 85014
(602) 234-2892 (bus.)
(602) 279-0534 (b.o.)

FOUNDED 1967
Sandy Rosenthal

SEASON
Oct.-June

FACILITIES
Temple of Music and Art
Seating Capacity: 603
Stage: proscenium

Herberger Theater Center
Seating Capacity: 790
Stage: proscenium

FINANCES
July 1, 1989-June 30, 1990
Expenses: $2,388,612

CONTRACTS
AEA LORT (C)

The Arizona Theatre Company celebrates its 25th anniversary during the 1991-92 season. For the first time in 11 years, the theatre is changing its artistic leadership. Change is inevitable and can be a

Arizona Theatre Company. Gary Briggle and George Morfogen in *Amadeus*. Photo: Tim Fuller.

catalyst for self-evaluation, redefinition and evolution. We have a strong legacy upon which to build—now it is time to consider new directions and new journeys. ATC continues to be challenged by its two-city operation: Tucson remains the loyal old guard, while Phoenix offers many new opportunities. Evaluating "who" each market is and what "his or her" tastes are, is an ongoing dialogue among our staff. The future holds many uncertainties; some things, however, never vary—ATC will always produce an eclectic repertoire, including the classics and contemporary work. ATC has initiated two new programs, the New Play Reading Series and the New Play/Guest Artist Project, evidence of our commitment to developing and nurturing new work. Our home in the heart of the Sonoran Desert provides a unique haven for experimentation and creativity.

—Robert Alpaugh

Note: During the 1989-90 and 1990-91 seasons, Gary Gisselman served as artistic director.

PRODUCTIONS 1989-90

Quilters, book adapt: Molly Newman and Barbara Damashek, from Patricia Cooper and Norma Bradley Allen; music and lyrics: Barbara Damashek; (D) Gary Gisselman; (S) Greg Lucas; (C) Jared Aswegan; (L) Don Darnutzer

The Cocktail Hour, A.R. Gurney, Jr.; (D) Richard Russell Ramos; (S) Tom Butsch; (C) David Kay Mickelsen; (L) Tracy Odishaw

The Boys Next Door, Tom Griffin; (D) David Ira Goldstein; (S) Greg Lucas; (C) David Kay Mickelsen; (L) Don Darnutzer

The Importance of Being Earnest, Oscar Wilde; (D) Gary Gisselman; (S) Greg Lucas; (C) David Kay Mickelsen; (L) Don Darnutzer

Fences, August Wilson; (D) Claude Purdy; (S) Vicki Smith; (C) Constanza Romero; (L) Don Darnutzer

The Road to Mecca, Athol Fugard; (D) Gary Gisselman; (S) Greg Lucas; (C) David Kay Mickelsen; (L) Tracy Odishaw

PRODUCTIONS 1990-91

Amadeus, Peter Shaffer; (D) Gary Gisselman; (S) Greg Lucas; (C) David Kay Mickelsen; (L) Don Darnutzer

Loot, Joe Orton; (D) Gary Gisselman; (S) Greg Lucas; (C) David Kay Mickelsen; (L) Don Darnutzer

The Price, Arthur Miller; (D) Matthew Wiener; (S) Michael Miller; (C) Sigrid Insull; (L) Don Darnutzer

The Holy Terror, Simon Gray; (D) Simon Gray; (S) David Jenkins; (C) David Murin; (L) Dennis Parichy

The School for Wives, Moliere; trans: Richard Wilbur; (D) Gary Gisselman; (S) Greg Lucas; (C) Sigrid Insull; (L) Don Darnutzer

Other People's Money, Jerry Sterner; (D) David Ira Goldstein; (S) Jeff Thomson; (C) David Kay Mickelsen; (L) Tracy Odishaw

The Arkansas Arts Center Children's Theatre

BRADLEY D. ANDERSON
Artistic Director

P. J. POWERS
Theatre Administrative Manager

Box 2137
Little Rock, AR 72203
(501) 372-4000

FOUNDED 1963
Museum of Fine Arts, The Junior League of Little Rock, The Fine Arts Club

SEASON
Sept.-May

FACILITIES
The Arkansas Arts Center Theatre
Seating Capacity: 389
Stage: proscenium

The Arkansas Arts Center Theatre Studio
Seating Capacity: 200
Stage: flexible

FINANCES
July 1, 1989-June 30, 1990
Expenses: $422,224

The Arkansas Arts Center Children's Theatre exists to provide high-quality theatre experiences for young people and their families. We provide a master/apprentice education where children work alongside professional actors, all sharing in the common goal of excellence. Our best work can be experienced on at least three distict levels: For the young child there is simply a great story and lots of sensory pleasure; the older child enjoys more of the subtleties in the language and in the art form; adults appreciate the more sophisticated humor or irony and see the symbolism that moves beyond the immediate story itself to the world at large. A dedicated ensemble of actors, directors and designers produce a mainstage season, three touring productions and an experimental lab studio, and teach in an intensive summer theatre academy that brings children into direct working contact with the creative process. We attempt to educate young audiences through artistic observations of the human condition, while trying to heighten the quality of theatre experiences for children.

—Bradley D. Anderson

PRODUCTIONS 1989-90

The Adventures of a Bear Called Paddington, Alfred Bradley and Michael Bond; music: Lori Loree; lyrics: Michael Bond; (D) Debbie Weber; (S) James E. Lyden; (C) Jeff Kinard; (L) James E. Lyden

The Hunchback of Notre-Dame, book adapt and lyrics: Alan Keith Smith, from Victor Hugo; music: Lori Loree; (D) Bradley D. Anderson; (S) Alan Keith Smith; (C) Jeff Kinard; (L) James E. Lyden

The Velveteen Rabbit, adapt: Thomas W. Olson, from Margery Williams; (D) Alan Keith Smith; (S) James E. Lyden; (C) Jeff Kinard; (L) James E. Lyden

Rumpelstiltskin, book adapt and lyrics: Alan Keith Smith, from The Brothers Grimm; music: Lori Loree; (D) Bradley D. Anderson; (S) James E. Lyden; (C) Jeff Kinard; (L) Alan Keith Smith

Pollyanna, adapt: Alan Keith Smith, from Eleanor H. Porter; (D) Bradley D. Anderson;

The Arkansas Arts Center Children's Theatre. Susan Frampton and Tony Owens in *Snow-White and Rose-Red*. Photo: Dixie Knight.

(S) Alan Keith Smith; (C) Jeff Kinard; (L) James E. Lyden

The Odyssey, adapt: Alan Keith Smith, from Homer; (D) Alan Keith Smith; (S) James E. Lyden; (C) Jeff Kinard; (L) James E. Lyden

Jack and the Beanstalk, book adapt and lyrics: Burton Curtis and Rich Geddes; music: Lori Loree; (D) Bradley D. Anderson; (S) Jim Brewi; (C) Burton Curtis and Rich Geddes

The Elves and the Shoemaker, adapt: Alan Keith Smith, from The Brothers Grimm; (D) D.J. Ladd; (S) Jim Brewi; (C) Melanie Taylor

Rootabaga Stories, adapt: Debbie Weber, from Carl Sandburg; (D) Debbie Weber; (S) Jim Brewi; (C) Melanie Taylor

The Mall, book and lyrics: P.J. Powers; music: Lori Loree; (D) Debbie Weber; (S) James E. Lyden; (C) Jeff Kinard; (L) Alan Keith Smith

PRODUCTIONS 1990-91

James and the Giant Peach, adapt: Alan Keith Smith, from Roald Dahl; (D) Bradley D. Anderson; (S) Alan Keith Smith; (C) Jeff Kinard; (L) James E. Lyden

Little Women, adapt: Sandra Deer, from Louisa May Alcott; (D) Alan Keith Smith; (S) James E. Lyden; (C) Jeff Kinard; (L) Kathy Gray

Snow-White and Rose-Red, adapt: Alan Keith Smith, from The Brothers Grimm; (D) Bradley D. Anderson; (S) James E. Lyden; (C) Jeff Kinard; (L) James E. Lyden

Babar the Elephant, adapt: Thomas W. Olson, from Jean de Brunhoff; (D) Debbie Weber; (S) James E. Lyden; (C) Jeff Kinard; (L) Kathy Gray

Young Alexis and Rasputin, book and lyrics: Alan Keith Smith; music: Lori Loree; (D) Bradley D. Anderson; (S) James E. Lyden; (C) Jeff Kinard; (L) Alan Keith Smith

The Hobbit, adapt: Alan Keith Smith, from J.R.R. Tolkien; (D) Alan Keith Smith; (S) Alan Keith Smith; (C) Jeff Kinard; (L) James E. Lyden

Johnny Appleseed, Bradley D. Anderson; (D) Bradley D. Anderson; (S) Jim Brewi; (C) Jeff Kinard

Hansel and Gretel, adapt: P.J. Powers, from The Brothers Grimm; (D) Debbie Weber; (S) Jim Brewi; (C) Jeff Kinard

Red Badge of Courage, adapt: Thomas W. Olson, from Stephen Crane; (D) Bradley D. Anderson; (S) Richard J. Sillen, Jr.

Arkansas Repertory Theatre

CLIFF FANNIN BAKER
Producing Artistic Director

Box 110
Little Rock, AR 72203
(501) 378-0445 (bus.)
(501) 378-0405 (b.o.)

FOUNDED 1976
Cliff Fannin Baker

SEASON
Sept.-June

FACILITIES
MainStage Theatre
Seating Capacity: 354
Stage: proscenium

SecondStage Theatre
Seating Capacity: 99
Stage: flexible

FINANCES
July 1, 1989-June 30, 1990
Expenses: $1,122,111

CONTRACTS
AEA letter of agreement

Arkansas Rep's 16th season is hallmarked by the diversity of our audiences and our outreach goals, while exhibiting a prevailing interest in contemporary scripts and American playwrights. Our mission at The Rep has remained a constant: to provoke, educate and entertain our audiences while providing meaningful experiences for the professional artistic company. The Rep is still best described as "emerging." We moved into a new performing arts center in 1988 and we operate under a letter of agreement with Actors' Equity Association. Our subscription base has doubled in the past few years, our company is growing and our programming is challenging both artists and audiences. We are proud of the theatre's regional reputation and local impact. Our programs include an eight-play mainstage season, selected second-stage productions, play readings and "Talkbacks," a professional intern program, a 14-year-old arts-in-education program and a six-state regional tour.

—*Cliff Fannin Baker*

PRODUCTIONS 1989-90

Broadway Bound, Neil Simon; (D) Cliff Fannin Baker; (S) Mike Nichols; (C) Don Bolinger; (L) Kathy Gray

A Midsummer Night's Dream, William Shakespeare; (D) Elfin Frederick Vogel; (S) Mike Nichols; (C) Mark Hughes; (L) David Neville

Guys and Dolls, book adapt: Jo Swerling and Abe Burrows, from Damon Runyon; music and lyrics: Frank Loesser; (D) Cliff Fannin Baker; (S) Mike Nichols; (C) Mark Hughes; (L) Kathy Gray

Little Lulu in a Tight Orange Dress, John G. Moynihan; (D) Cliff Fannin Baker; (S) Mike Nichols; (C) Connie Fails; (L) Crickette Brendel

The Mystery of Irma Vep, Charles Ludlam; (D) Mark DeMichele; (S) Mike Nichols; (C) Rosemary Bengele; (L) Kathy Gray

I'm Not Rappaport, Herb Gardner; (D) Frank Bonner; (S) Jeff Thomson; (C) Don Bolinger; (L) David Neville

Arkansas Repertory Theatre. Kathryn Newbrough, Judy Blue and Sally Edmundson in *Homefires*. Photo: Deann Shields-Marley.

Orphans, Lyle Kessler; (D) Cliff Fannin Baker; (S) Mike Nichols; (C) Don Bolinger; (L) Kathy Gray
Evita, music: Andrew Lloyd Webber; lyrics: Tim Rice; (D) Cliff Fannin Baker; (S) Don Yanik; (C) Mark Hughes; (L) David Neville
Lady Day at Emerson's Bar and Grill, Lanie Robertson; (D) Brad Mooy; (S) Richard Grace; (C) Don Bolinger; (L) William Young
Road, Jim Cartwright; (D) Brad Mooy; (S) Brian Hemesath and Sean Devine; (C) Jonna McElrath; (L) Brian Hemesath and Sean Devine
Boy's Play, Jack Heifner; (D) Cliff Fannin Baker; (S) Mike Nichols; (C) Don Bolinger; (L) Crickette Brendel

PRODUCTIONS 1990-91

Nunsense, book, music and lyrics: Dan Goggin; (D) Fred D. Klaisner; (S) Mike Nichols; (C) Marilyn Powers; (L) Crickette Brendel
The Importance of Being Earnest, Oscar Wilde; (D) Cliff Fannin Baker; (S) Mike Nichols; (C) Mark Hughes; (L) Crickette Brendel
Driving Miss Daisy, Alfred Uhry; (D) Cliff Fannin Baker; (S) Mike Nichols; (C) Marilyn Powers; (L) Kathy Gray
The Boys Next Door, Tom Griffin; (D) Cliff Fannin Baker; (S) Mike Nichols; (C) Marilyn Powers; (L) Crickette Brendel
The Dining Room, A.R. Gurney, Jr.; (D) Robert Graham Small; (S) Mike Nichols; (C) Mark Hughes; (L) Tony Nye
Laughing Wild, Christopher Durang; (D) Cliff Fannin Baker; (S) Don Yanik; (C) Don Yanik; (L) Crickette Brendel
Homefires, Jack Heifner; (D) Cliff Fannin Baker; (S) Jeff Thomson; (C) Mark Hughes; (L) David Neville
Oil City Symphony, Mike Craver, Mark Hardwick, Debra Monk and Mary Murfitt; music: Debra Monk and Mary Murfitt; lyrics: Mike Craver and Mark Hardwick; (D) Mike Craver and Mark Hardwick; (S) Mike Nichols; (C) Marilyn Powers; (L) Crickette Brendel

ArtReach Touring Theatre

KATHRYN SCHULTZ MILLER
Artistic Director

ANDI SCHROLUCKE
Business Manager

3074 Madison Road
Cincinnati, OH 45209
(513) 871-2300

FOUNDED 1976
Kathryn Schultz Miller, Barry I. Miller

SEASON
Jan.-Dec.

FINANCES
July 1, 1990-June 30, 1991
Expenses: $444,282

ArtReach's artistic mission is simple and clear: to present intelligent well-crafted work that touches the hearts and minds of our young audiences. We emphasize carefully structured plots with fully developed characters that offer our actors the opportunity to express themselves fully. Each script must inspire thought and understanding, whether it be the consideration of Washington Irving's poetic language or greater awareness of American history as seen in *Welcome Home*, our play about a Vietnam-veteran father. We are looking foward to introducing our audiences to the complexities of our multicultural society in the upcoming plays *Young Cherokee* and *The Trail of Tears*. We have found that the youngest child will respond in a surprisingly mature way to serious subjects presented with an honesty that respects the child's ability to watch, listen, learn and think. These are the kinds of experiences that contribute to the intellectual sensitivity he or she will carry through life. This is a responsibility we take very seriously.

—*Kathryn Schultz Miller*

ArtReach Touring Theatre. Shelley Weisheit and Ralph Scott in *The Legend of Sleepy Hollow*. Photo: Barry Miller.

PRODUCTIONS 1989-90

The Legend of Sleepy Hollow, adapt: Kathryn Schultz Miller, from Washington Irving; (D) Dahn Schwarz and Kathryn Schultz Miller; (S) Dahn Schwarz; (C) Kathie Brookfield; (L) Ron Shaw
Welcome Home, Kathryn Schultz Miller; (D) Dahn Schwarz and Kathryn Schultz Miller; (S) Barry I. Miller; (C) Kathie Brookfield; (L) Ron Shaw
Beauty and the Beast, Kathryn Schultz Miller; (D) Dahn Schwarz; (S) Dahn Schwarz; (C) Kathie Brookfield; (L) Ron Shaw
Red Badge of Courage, adapt: Kathryn Schultz Miller, from Stephen Crane; (D) Dahn Schwarz; (S) Kathryn Schultz Miller; (C) Kathie Brookfield; (L) Ron Shaw

PRODUCTIONS 1990-91

The Sword in the Stone, Kathryn Schultz Miller; (D) Dahn Schwarz and Kathryn Schultz Miller; (S) Dahn Schwarz; (C) Kathie Brookfield; (L) Ron Shaw
The Knights of the Roundtable, Kathryn Schultz Miller; (D) Dahn Schwarz and Kathryn Schultz Miller; (S) Dahn Schwarz; (C) Kathie Brookfield; (L) Ron Shaw
The Legend of Sleepy Hollow, adapt: Kathryn Schultz Miller, from Washington Irving; (D) Dahn Schwarz; (S) Dahn Schwarz; (C) Kathie Brookfield; (L) Ron Shaw
Welcome Home, Kathryn Schultz Miller; (D) Dahn Schwarz; (S) Barry I. Miller; (C) Kathie Brookfield; (L) Ron Shaw
Beauty and the Beast, Kathryn Schultz Miller; (D) Shelley Weisheit; (S) Shelley Weisheit; (C) Kathie Brookfield; (L) Ron Shaw
Red Badge of Courage, adapt: Kathryn Schultz Miller, from Stephen Crane; (D) Shelley Weisheit; (S) Kathryn Schultz Miller; (C) Kathie Brookfield; (L) Ron Shaw

Asolo Center for the Performing Arts

MARGARET BOOKER
Artistic Director

LEE WARNER
Executive Director

5555 North Tamiami Trail
Sarasota, FL 34243
(813) 351-9010 (bus.)
(813) 351-8000 (b.o.)

FOUNDED 1960
Eberle Thomas, Robert Strane, Richard G. Fallon, Arthur Dorlag

SEASON
Oct.-July

FACILITIES
Mainstage
Seating Capacity: 499
Stage: proscenium

Second Stage
Seating Capacity: 175
Stage: flexible

Bette Oliver Theatre
Seating Capacity: 138
Stage: flexible

FINANCES
Sept. 1, 1990-June 30, 1991
Expenses: $4,091,905

CONTRACTS
AEA LORT (C) and TYA

The Asolo Theatre Company is the primary component of the Asolo Center for the Performing Arts, which also houses the MFA Conservatory of Professional Actor Training and the MFA Conservatory of Motion Picture, Television and Recording Arts, both administered by Florida State University. The Asolo Theatre Company, which produces both mainstage and touring programs, is Florida's oldest and largest nonprofit professional theatre. It is committed to presenting the classics with freshness and new vision, and to premiering new plays with dedication and respect for the playwright's art.

—*Margaret Booker*

Note: During the 1989-90 season, John Ulmer served as artistic director.

PRODUCTIONS 1989-90

A Walk in the Woods, Lee Blessing; (D) John Gulley; (S) Jeffrey Dean; (C) Howard Tsvi Kaplan; (L) Martin Petlock
Blithe Spirit, Noel Coward; (D) Fred Chappell; (S) Keven Lock; (C) Joy Breckenridge; (L) Pat Simmons
Man and Superman, George Bernard Shaw; (D) John Gulley; (S) Kenneth Kurtz; (C) Howard Tsvi Kaplan; (L) Martin Petlock
Eastern Standard, Richard Greenberg; (D) Garry Allen Breul; (S) Keven Lock; (C) Sharon Sobel; (L) Martin Petlock
70, Girls, 70, book: Fred Ebb and Norman L. Martin; music: John Kander; lyrics: Fred Ebb; (D) John Ulmer and Rob Marshall; (S) John Ezell; (C) Howard Tsvi Kaplan; (L) Martin Petlock
Talking Pictures, Horton Foote; (D) John Ulmer; (S) John Ezell; (C) Howard Tsvi Kaplan; (L) Martin Petlock
Steel Magnolias, Robert Harling; (D) John Gulley; (S) Jeffrey Dean; (C) Sharon Sobel; (L) Joseph Oshry
Quarry, Ronald Bazarini; (D) Garry Allen Breul; (S) Keven Lock; (C) Howard Tsvi Kaplan; (L) Martin Petlock
The Mystery of Irma Vep, Charles Ludlam; (D) John Briggs; (S) Bennet Averyt; (C) Howard Tsvi Kaplan; (L) Martin Petlock

PRODUCTIONS 1990-91

The Cocktail Hour, A. R. Gurney, Jr.; (D) Jamie Brown; (S) Keven Lock; (C) Vicki S. Holden; (L) Martin Petlock
Driving Miss Daisy, Alfred Uhry; (D) John Gulley; (S) Jeffrey Dean; (C) Howard Tsvi Kaplan; (L) Martin Petlock
A Tale of Two Cities, adapt: Larry Carpenter, from Charles Dickens; (D) Larry Arrick; (S) Keven Lock; (C) Howard Tsvi Kaplan; (L) Martin Petlock
Only Kidding, Jim Geoghan; (D) Larry Arrick; (S) Jeffrey Dean; (C) Howard Tsvi Kaplan; (L) Martin Petlock
Other People's Money, Jerry Sterner; (D) William Gregg; (S) Keven Lock; (C) Howard Tsvi Kaplan; (L) Martin Petlock
"Master Harold"...and the boys, Athol Fugard; (D) Jamie Brown; (S) Lewis Folden, recreated by Keven Lock; (C) Rebecca Keightley; (L) Phil Monat
Bedroom Farce, Alan Ayckbourn; (D) John Going; (S) Keven Lock; (C) Howard Tsvi Kaplan; (L) Martin Petlock
The Heidi Chronicles, Wendy Wasserstein; (D) Amy Saltz; (S) Michael Miller; (C) Howard Tsvi Kaplan; (L) Ann G. Wrightson

Asolo Center for the Performing Arts. Murray Rubinstein and Susan Knight in *The Heidi Chronicles*. Photo: Lawrence C. Vaughn.

A Traveling Jewish Theatre

COREY FISCHER, NAOMI NEWMAN, ALBERT GREENBERG, HELEN STOLTZFUS
Artistic Ensemble

ANNA BECKER
Managing Director

Box 421985
San Francisco, CA 94142
(415) 861-4880

FOUNDED 1978
Corey Fischer, Naomi Newman, Albert Greenberg

SEASON
variable

FACILITIES
New Performance Gallery
Seating Capacity: 200
Stage: proscenium

Eureka Theatre
Seating Capacity: 200
Stage: flexible

Climate Theatre
Seating Capacity: 80
Stage: proscenium

FINANCES
July 1, 1990-June 30, 1991
Expenses: $350,000

CONTRACTS
AEA letter of agreement

A Traveling Jewish Theatre was born out of a desire to create a contemporary theatre that would give form to streams of visionary experience that run through Jewish history, culture and imagination. Since its founding, the company has created nine original works that cross boundaries of time, place, style and theme. Our concerns have ranged from the legends of Hasidism to the assassination of Trotsky, from the world of the Yiddish poets and the experience of exile, to women's wisdom and the nature of healing. We have used music, masks, puppets, bare stages, naked faces, English, Yiddish, Hebrew, Ladino, silence and sound in various combinations as tools to

A Traveling Jewish Theatre. Albert Greenberg and Helen Stoltzfus in *Heart of the World.* Photo: John Stamets.

share what we feel needs to be shared. Now celebrating our 13th season, we have performed in Oslo, New York, Berlin, Chicago, Jerusalem, Prague and more than 60 other cities in the United States, Canada, Europe and Israel.

—*Albert Greenberg*

PRODUCTIONS 1989-90

Heart of the World, Martha Boesing, Albert Greenberg and Helen Stoltzfus; (D) Martha Boesing; (S) Allan Droyan and Bruce Hasson; (C) Martha Boesing; (L) Jim Quinn

The Orphan King: Warsaw Is Mine, Gary Aylesworth; (D) Naomi Newman; (S) Nancy McNally; (C) Nancy McNally; (L) David Welle

Snake Talk: Urgent Messages From the Mother, Naomi Newman and Martha Boesing; (D) Martha Boesing; (S) Joelle Chartier-Serban; (L) Joelle Chartier-Serban

Dybbuk, S. Ansky; adapt and trans: Bruce Myers; (D) Mark Samuels; (S) Mark Samuels; (C) Eliza Chugg

PRODUCTIONS 1990-91

Heart of the World, Martha Boesing, Albert Greenberg and Helen Stoltzfus; (D) Martha Boesing; (S) Allan Droyan and Bruce Hasson; (C) Martha Boesing; (L) Jim Quinn

Last Yiddish Poet, Corey Fischer, Albert Greenberg and Naomi Newman; (D) Naomi Newman; (C) Jane Pollack; (L) Jim Quinn

Snake Talk: Urgent Messages From the Mother, Naomi Newman and Martha Boesing; (D) Martha Boesing; (S) Joelle Chartier-Serban; (L) Joelle Chartier-Serban

Attic Theatre

LAVINIA MOYER
Artistic Director

JAMES J. MORAN
Managing Director

2990 West Grand Blvd., Suite 308
Detroit, MI 48202
(313) 875-8285 (bus.)
(313) 875-8284 (b.o.)

FOUNDED 1975
Nancy Shayne, Lavinia Moyer, James J. Moran, Herbert Ferrer, Divina Cook, Curtis Armstrong

SEASON
Jan.-Dec.

FACILITIES
New Center Theatre
Seating Capacity: 299
Stage: proscenium

FINANCES
Sept. 1, 1990-Aug. 31, 1991
Expenses: $1,300,000

CONTRACTS
AEA SPT

The Attic Theatre offers contemporary American works, regional and world premieres, and the classics—focusing on themes and issues that give voice to matters of concern to our region. Our special educational and outreach programs make a strong impact on our urban community: artist residencies in the schools, student matinees with study guides and postperformance discussions, internships for gifted students and in-service teacher training; a senior-citizen touring company that serves both old and young; and master classes and workshops for the ensemble and the public. Our Writers' Unit, which serves playwrights developing new theatre pieces, was recently recognized by a Rockefeller Foundation playwright fellowship grant. Our artistic rationale is based on a professionally trained ensemble engaging both audience and artist in theatre that is challenging, innovative and compelling.

—*Lavinia Moyer*

PRODUCTIONS 1989-90

The Mystery of Irma Vep, Charles Ludlam; (D) Jack Reuler; (S) Robert Fuecker; (C) Anne Ruben; (L) Paul Epton

Burn This, Lanford Wilson; (D) Lavinia Moyer; (S) Eric M. Johnson; (C) Catherine M. Woerner; (L) Thomas Schraeder

Sand Mountain, Romulus Linney; (D) Patricia Ansuini; (S) Eric M. Johnson; (C) Melinda Pacha; (L) Paul Epton

A Shayna Maidel, Barbara Lebow; (D) Samuel Pollack; (S) Rolfe Bergsman; (C) Catherine M. Woerner; (L) Reid Downey

Hamlet, William Shakespeare; (D) Gordon Reinhart; (S) Eric M. Johnson; (C) Sharon Sprague; (L) Loren Brame

Coda, Bill Harris; (D) Woodie King, Jr.; (S) Felix E. Cochren; (C) Felix E. Cochren; (L) Paul Epton

Songbook, book: Monty Norman and Julian More; music: Monty Norman; lyrics: Julian More; (D) James Baird; (S) Sharon Yesh; (C) Catherine M. Woerner; (L) James Latzel

Hot Snow, Laurence Holder; (D) Patricia Ansuini; (S) Eric M. Johnson; (C) Catherine M. Woerner; (L) Paul Epton

PRODUCTIONS 1990-91

Billy Bishop Goes to War, John Gray and Eric Peterson; (D) Richard Klautsch; (S) Eric M. Johnson; (C) Catherine M. Woerner; (L) Paul Epton

Frankie and Johnny in the Clair de Lune, Terrence McNally; (D) Lavinia Moyer; (S) Peter Beudert; (C) Catherine M. Woerner; (L) Paul Epton

Teibele and her Demon, Isaac Bashevis Singer and Eve

Attic Theatre. Tim Rhoze and Wayne David Parker in *Teibele and her Demon.* Photo: John Sobczak.

Friedman; (D) Blair Vaughn Anderson; (S) Eric M. Johnson; (C) Mary Copenhagen; (L) Kendall Smith

A Doll House, Henrik Ibsen; trans: Gerry Bamman and Irene B. Berman; (D) Eric M. Johnson; (S) Melinda Pacha; (C) Edith Leavis Bookstein; (L) Reid Downey

Three Ways Home, Casey Kurtti; (D) Patricia Ansuini; (S) Eric M. Johnson; (C) Catherine M. Woerner; (L) Paul Epton

Conversations with an Irish Rascal, Kathleen Kennedy and David O. Frazier; (D) Dinah Lynch; (S) Eric M. Johnson; (C) Catherine M. Woerner; (L) Paul Epton

Baltimore Theatre Project

Formerly Theatre Project

PHILIP ARNOULT
Artistic Director

ROBERT P. MROZEK
General Manager

45 West Preston St.
Baltimore, MD 21201
(301) 539-3091 (bus.)
(301) 752-8558 (b.o.)

FOUNDED 1971
Philip Arnoult

SEASON
Sept.-July

FACILITIES
Theatre Project
Seating Capacity: 157
Stage: flexible

FINANCES
July 1, 1990-June 30, 1991
Expenses: $465,000

I travel to many theatres each year to find work to bring to Theatre Project. I look for work that is small and young—rooted in its own culture, but not bound by it—with a fullness that breaks through the boundaries of language, race and politics. My commitment to these companies is very personal, and it is as much a commitment to an artistic vision as to a particular production. My role as dramaturg, helping a visiting company fine-tune a work for its American audiences, is a precious one. In my travels everywhere, I see wondrous permutations of the American avant-garde. What is most gratifying is the openness in our selves and in our theatres to presenting these visions, wherever they come from. I have a kind of romantic belief that this special grace will help keep the planet sane.

—*Philip Arnoult*

PRODUCTIONS 1989-90

Maybe This Is Heaven, Robert Shields; (D) Robert Shields

The Escape or L'Evasion, Dominique Abel and Fiona Gordon; (D) Dominique Abel and Fiona Gordon

Jack Benny!, book, music and lyrics: John Moran; (D) Bob McGrath

Dream Bardo, company-developed; (D) Bruce Paul Reik; (S) Emma Elizabeth Downing; (C) Emma Elizabeth Downing

Anna on Anna, adapt: Adrian Mitchell and Illona Linthwaite, from Anna Wickham; (D) Cordelia Monsey

The Serpent's Fall, Sarah Cathcart; (D) Sarah Cathcart

From the Ashes, company-developed; (D) Robert Smythe, Patricia Blanchet, Darko Tresnjak and Annemarie B. Quigly

Radio Sing Sing, company-developed; (D) Robert Smythe, Patricia Blanchet, Darko Tresnjak and Annemarie B. Quigly

Zig Zag Zelda, Drury Pifer; (D) Drury Pifer, with Ceal Phelan and Peter DeLaurier

Waiters, choreographer: Terry Beck

PRODUCTIONS 1990-91

Ah Cabaret, Ah Cabaret!, company-developed (Theatre Buffo of USSR); (D) Isaak Schtokbant

It's Not a Movie, company-developed; (D) Nava Zukerman and the company

The Pleasure Raiders, company-developed (Impossible Industrial Action Theatre); (D) Kirby Malone and Tony Tsendeas; (S) the company; (C) the company; (L) the company

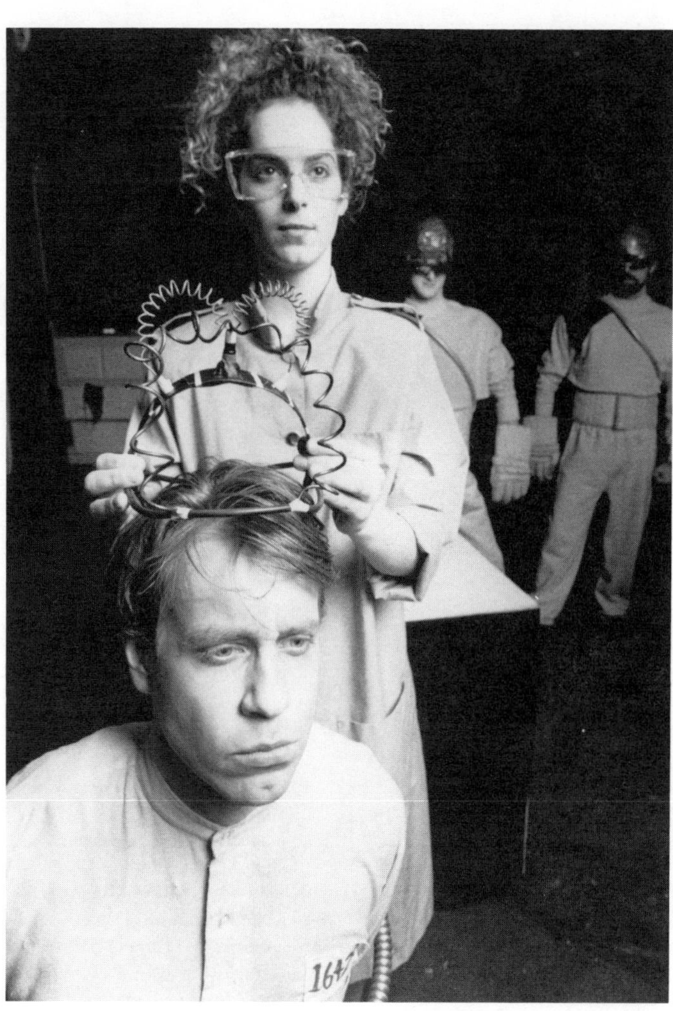

Baltimore Theatre Project. Kathryn E. Cole and Robb Bauer in *The Pleasure Raiders*. Photo: Tim Ford.

The Orange Earth, Adam Small; (D) Seven Stages company

Dead Marilyn, Peter Stack; music: Curtis Webster; (D) Peter Stack; (C) Liz Tee

Stories from Here: The House and The Fish, House: Neill Bogan and Janie Geiser; Fish: Russell Banks; adapt: company-developed (Jottay Theatre); (D) the company; (S) the company; (C) the company; (L) the company

Whosis, company-developed (Figures of Speech Theatre); (D) Michael Rafkin; (S) the company; (C) the company; (L) the company

Shakespeare: Dreams of Power and Passion, adapt: Paul Alexander, from William Shakespeare; (D) Paul Alexander

Magic Voices, adapt: Damian Popchristov; (D) Damian Popchristov

Honey Chil' Milk, Donald Byrd and company; music: Paul Mathews; (D) Donald Byrd

Candide, adapt: William Pope L. and Sara Zielinska, from Voltaire; (D) Jim Calder

Home Family God Country Flag, company-developed (Ninth Street Theatre); (D) Joanne Schultz and the company

Invitations to Heaven, Eric Bass and the Sandglass Theatre; (D) Eric Bass

A Fresh of Breath Air, book and lyrics: Dale Stein; music: Charles Goldbeck and Dale Stein; (D) Christopher Ashley; (S) Russell Metheny; (C) Sharon Lynch; (L) Jeff Guzik

Memories, Dreams & Illusions, company-developed (Diablomundo of Argentina); (D) the company; (S) the company; (C) the company; (L) the company

Barter Theatre

REX PARTINGTON
Artistic Director/Producer

Box 867
Abingdon, VA 24210
(703) 628-2281 (bus.)
(800) 368-3240 (b.o.)

FOUNDED 1933
Robert Porterfield

SEASON
Apr.-Nov.

FACILITIES
Barter Theatre
Seating Capacity: 394
Stage: proscenium

Barter Playhouse
Seating Capacity: 150
Stage: thrust

FINANCES
Nov. 1, 1989-Oct. 31, 1990
Expenses: $987,530

CONTRACTS
AEA LORT (D)

Barter is the oldest, longest-running professional repertory theatre in the U.S. It is our desire that the plays we produce, in addition to entertaining our patrons, will give them something to think about. We do not intend that each play must impart a profound message; but we do feel the productions we present, whether they are classical or contemporary or brand-new, should be provocative. They should reflect and comment on the times and on the human race. As a pioneer of regional theatre, we are dedicated to quality—whether it's on our mainstage Barter Theatre, in the Playhouse, on our Youth Stage or in our touring productions. Our diversified audiences can expect to see the finest in classical and contemporary comedy and drama as well as worthwhile new plays.

—Rex Partington

PRODUCTIONS 1990

Treasure Island, adapt: Rex Partington, from Robert Louis Stevenson; (D) Rex Partington; (S) Rex Partington; (C) Pamela Hale; (L) Tony Partington
Brighton Beach Memoirs, Neil Simon; (D) Ken Costigan; (S) Daniel Ettinger; (C) Pamela Hale; (L) Christopher Green
All My Sons, Arthur Miller; (D) Ken Costigan; (S) Daniel Ettinger; (C) Pamela Hale; (L) Daniel Ettinger
Pump Boys and Dinettes, John Foley, Mark Hardwick, Debra Monk, Cass Morgan, John Schimmel and Jim Wann; (D) Jason Edwards; (S) Daniel Gray and Yoshimi Hamana; (C) Pamela Hale; (L) Christopher Green
Wait Until Dark, Frederick Knott; (D) Ken Costigan; (S) Daniel Ettinger; (C) Pamela Hale; (L) Tony Partington
The Foreigner, Larry Shue; (D) Geoffrey Hitch; (S) Daniel Ettinger; (C) Pamela Hale; (L) Tony Partington
Monteith and Rand, John Monteith and Suzanne Rand; (D) Bill Russell; (L) Tony Partington
Steel Magnolias, Robert Harling; (D) Dorothy Robinson; (S) Daniel Gray; (C) Karen Brewster; (L) Tony Partington
A Journey Through the Mind...Edgar Allan Poe, Will Stutts; (D) Terrance Pace; (S) Stephen A. Keever; (C) Sandra-Christine; (L) Christopher Green
Jonathan Frid's Shakespearean Odyssey, adapt: Jonathan Frid, from William Shakespeare; (D) Jonathan Frid; (L) Christopher Green
Good Evening, Peter Cook and Dudley Moore; (D) William Van Keyser; (S) Greg Owens; (C) Pamela Hale; (L) Christopher Green
Robin Hood, Cathryn Pisarski; (D) Christopher Armbrister; (C) Jennifer Bengston
Rapunzel and Rumpelstiltskin, N. Sherie Douglas and Victor Armbrister, from The Brothers Grimm; (D) Christopher Armbrister; (C) Jennifer Bengston; (L) Rema Keen

PRODUCTIONS 1991

Scapin, Moliere; adapt: Rex Partington; (D) Rex Partington; (S) Bennet Averyt; (C) Pamela Hale; (L) Tony Partington
Greater Tuna, Jaston Williams, Joe Sears and Ed Howard; (D) Trip Plymale; (S) Daniel Gray; (C) Karen Brewster; (L) Christopher Green
Arsenic and Old Lace, Joseph Kesselring; (D) Ken Costigan; (S) Kevin Joseph Roach; (C) Pamela Hale; (L) Christopher Green
Oil City Symphony, Mike Craver, Mark Hardwick, Debra Monk and Mary Murfitt; (D) Larry Forde; (L) William Sauerbrey
Steel Magnolias, Robert Harling; (D) Dorothy Robinson; (S) Daniel Gray; (C) Karen Brewster and Pamela Hale; (L) Christopher Green
Stage Struck, Simon Gray; (D) Ken Costigan; (S) Kevin Joseph Roach; (C) Pamela Hale; (L) William Sauerbrey
The Diary of Anne Frank, adapt: Frances Goodrich and Albert Hackett, from Anne Frank; (D) Ken Costigan; (C) Pamela Hale; (L) Tony Partington
Charlotte's Web, adapt: Joseph Robinette, from E.B. White; (D) John Hardy; (S) Daniel Gray; (C) Jennifer Bengston; (L) John Hardy
American Tall Tales, John Hardy; (D) John Hardy; (S) Scott Nagel and Daniel Gray; (C) Jennifer Bengston; (L) John Hardy

Barter Theatre. Jason Edwards, Dixie Partington and Stephen Gabis in *Arsenic and Old Lace*. Photo: Bill Adams.

The Bathhouse Theatre

ARNE ZASLOVE
Artistic Director

STEVEN LERIAN
Managing Director

7312 West Greenlake Drive N
Seattle, WA 98103
(206) 524-3608 (bus.)
(206) 524-9108 (b.o.)

FOUNDED 1980
Arne Zaslove, Mary-Claire Burke

SEASON
Jan.-Dec.

FACILITIES
Bathhouse Theatre
Seating Capacity: 174
Stage: thrust

Moore Theatre
Seating Capacity: 1,000
Stage: proscenium

Broadway Performance Hall
Seating Capacity: 295
Stage: proscenium

FINANCES
Jan. 1, 1990-Dec. 31, 1990
Expenses: $765,855

CONTRACTS
AEA SPT

Storytelling has, throughout time, been a method of self-examination and self-revelation. The community is purged of its ills by the shaman/actor/artist/healer. At the Bathhouse, we see ourselves as

The Bathouse Theatre. Randy Hoffmeyer and Tina Marie Goff in *King Oedipus*. Photo: Fred Andrews.

being in a position to create change: to change the awareness of individuals so that they assume responsibility for making the earth safer, healthier and more balanced. The cornerstone of our approach is the performing ensemble, in the classical European tradition. Through that medium, we explore material that asks the fundamental questions and touches the human spirit directly—sometimes in classics of world stage literature, sometimes in pieces we have woven together ourselves from elements of popular American culture. Theatre must regulate and reflect, monitor and maintain a healthy balance. Theatre can improve the weather of the soul.

—*Arne Zaslove*

PRODUCTIONS 1990

U.S.A., Paul Shyre and John Dos Passos; (D) Jack Clay; (S) Rollin Thomas; (C) Sarah Campbell; (L) Judy Wolcott

The Play's the Thing, Ferenc Molnar; trans: P.G. Wodehouse; (D) Ted D'Arms; (S) Rollin Thomas; (C) Sarah Campbell; (L) Judy Wolcott

Macbeth, William Shakespeare; (D) Arne Zaslove; (S) Ronald Fedoruk; (C) Sarah Campbell; (L) Judy Wolcott

Buckskin to Satin, company-developed; (D) Arne Zaslove; (S) Shelley Henze Schermer; (C) Sarah Campbell; (L) Judy Wolcott

Dybbuk adapt and trans: Bruce Myers, from S. Ansky; (D) Arne Zaslove; (S) Ronald Fedoruk; (C) Sarah Campbell; (L) Phil Schermer

And a Nightingale Sang, C.P. Taylor; (D) Mark Samuels; (S) Jeffrey A. Frkonja; (C) Sarah Campbell; (L) Phil Schermer

The Big Broadcast on Broadway, company-developed; (D) Arne Zaslove; (S) Shelley Henze Schermer; (C) Shauna Frazier; (L) Judy Wolcott

PRODUCTIONS 1991

Buckskin to Satin, company-developed; (D) Arne Zaslove; (S) Shelley Henze Schermer; (C) Sarah Campbell; (L) Judy Wolcott

King Oedipus, adapt: W.B. Yeats, from Sophocles; music: Robert Davidson; (D) Arne Zaslove; (S) Kathryn Rathke; (C) Shauna Frazier; (L) Meg Fox

Sherlock's Last Case, Charles Marowitz; (D) Ted D'Arms; (S) Bill Forrester; (C) Daniel Cole; (L) Judy Wolcott

Uncle Vanya, Anton Chekhov; adapt: Zoltan Schmidt; trans: Roger Downey and Zoltan Schmidt; (D) Zoltan Schmidt; (S) Ronald Fedoruk; (C) Sarah Campbell; (L) Ronald Fedoruk

Black Stage Views, company-developed; (D) Arne Zaslove; (S) Shelley Henze Schermer; (C) Daniel Cole; (L) Judy Wolcott

The Merchant of Venice, William Shakespeare; (D) Arne Zaslove; (S) Kathryn Rathke; (C) Martha Mattus; (L) Judy Wolcott

Three Men on a Horse, George Abbott and John Cecil Holm; (D) Michael Griggs; (S) Jeffrey A. Frkonja; (C) Jeanne Arnold; (L) Judy Wolcott

The Big Broadcast on Broadway, company-developed; (D) Arne Zaslove; (S) Shelley Henze Schermer; (C) Martha Mattus; (L) Judy Wolcott

Berkeley Repertory Theatre

SHARON OTT
Artistic Director

SUSAN MEDAK
Managing Director

ANTHONY TACCONE
Associate Artistic Director

2025 Addison St.
Berkeley, CA 94704
(510) 841-6108 (bus.)
(510) 845-4700 (b.o.)

FOUNDED 1968
Michael W. Leibert

SEASON
Sept.-Aug.

FACILITIES
Mark Taper Mainstage
Seating Capacity: 401
Stage: flexible

FINANCES
Sept. 1, 1990-Aug. 31, 1991
Expenses: $3,750,000

CONTRACTS
AEA LORT (B)

Berkeley Repertory Theatre is dedicated to an ensemble of first-rate artists—including actors, playwrights, directors, artisans and designers. We intend the theatre to be a place where plays are created, not just produced, communicating a distinct attitude about the world of the play and about the world around us. Our repertoire includes plays chosen from the major classical and contemporary dramatic literatures, specifically works that emphasize the cultural richness that makes American art so dynamic and vital. We will involve dramatists, either as playwrights-in-residence or on commission, in the development of original pieces. It is our intention to view the works of the past through the eyes of the present; even when a play is chosen from the classical repertoire, it will be given the focus and attention of a new play. We will also research and produce classical works that are outside the Anglo-European repertoire. As a regional resource, we will continue to expand our TEAM program for young audiences, augmenting the

Berkeley Repertory Theatre. Kelvin Han Yee and Stan Egi in *Fish Head Soup*. Photo: Ken Friedman.

Student Matinee Program and school touring productions.

—*Sharon Ott*

PRODUCTIONS 1989-90

Lulu, Frank Wedekind; adapt and trans: Roger Downey; (D) Sharon Ott; (S) John Arnone; (C) Deborah Dryden; (L) Jennifer Tipton

Reckless, Craig Lucas; (D) Richard E.T. White; (S) Kate Edmunds; (C) Sam Fleming; (L) Michael S. Philippi

The Winter's Tale, William Shakespeare; (D) Sharon Ott; (S) Kate Edmunds; (C) Elsa Ward; (L) Dan Kotlowitz

The Speed of Darkness, Steve Tesich; (D) Anthony Taccone; (S) Rob Greenberg; (C) Barbara Bush; (L) Peter Kaczorowski

Man and Superman, George Bernard Shaw; (D) Irene Lewis; (S) Christopher Barreca; (C) Candice Donnelly; (L) Ken Tabachnick

Born in the RSA, Barney Simon and original cast; (D) Barney Simon; (S) Michael S. Philippi; (C) Susan Hilferty; (L) Michael S. Philippi

The Virgin Molly, Quincy Long; (D) Anthony Taccone; (S) Kate Edmunds; (C) Susan Snowden; (L) David K.H. Elliott

Each Day Dies With Sleep, Jose Rivera; (D) Roberta Levitow; (S) Tom Kamm; (C) Tina Cantu Navarro; (L) Robert Wierzel

PRODUCTIONS 1990-91

Fuente Ovejuna, Lope de Vega; adapt and trans: Adrian Mitchell; (D) Sharon Ott; (S) Kate Edmunds; (C) Deborah Dryden; (L) Peter Maradudin

Life During Wartime, Keith Reddin; (D) Anthony Taccone; (S) Kent Dorsey; (C) Christine Dougherty; (L) Kent Dorsey

Who's Afraid of Virginia Woolf?, Edward Albee; (D) Richard Seyd; (S) David Jon Hoffman; (C) Susan Snowden; (L) Jack Carpenter

Our Country's Good, Timberlake Wertenbaker, from Thomas Keneally; (D) Anthony Taccone; (S) John Wilson; (C) Cathleen Edwards; (L) Ashley York Kennedy

The Illusion, Tony Kushner, from Pierre Corneille; (D) Sharon Ott; (S) Christopher Barreca; (C) Susan Hilferty; (L) Stephen Strawbridge

Fish Head Soup, Philip Kan Gotanda; (D) Oskar Eustis; (S) Kent Dorsey; (C) Lydia Tanji; (L) Kent Dorsey

Vid, John O'Keefe; (D) John O'Keefe; (L) Joel Giguere and Kent Dorsey

Berkshire Theatre Festival

RICHARD DUNLAP
Artistic Director

CHUCK STILL
Managing Director

Box 797
Stockbridge, MA 01262
(413) 298-5536 (bus.)
(413) 298-5576 (b.o.)

FOUNDED 1928
Three Arts Society

SEASON
June-Aug.

FACILITIES
Mainstage
Seating Capacity: 427
Stage: proscenium

Unicorn Theatre
Seating Capacity: 100
Stage: thrust

Children's Theatre
Seating Capacity: 100
Stage: arena (tent)

FINANCES
Sept. 1, 1990-Aug. 31, 1991
Expenses: $1,027,839

CONTRACTS
AEA LORT (B)

From its inception, the Berkshire Theatre Festival's mission has been threefold: to present thought-provoking professional entertainment to its audiences; to offer established and emerging actors, designers and playwrights the opportunity to work in a relaxed and supportive environment; and to provide quality educational programs to aspiring theatre artists. To that end, BTF supports three stages: our Playhouse, presenting Equity productions of well-known works as well as new plays by established playwrights; the Unicorn Theatre where new and experimental works are performed by a non-Equity company of recent graduates from professional acting programs; and the Children's Theatre in the tent where our acting interns perform in plays by local students enrolled in our Young American Playwrights Program. In recent years, the complementary nature of our professional work and training programs has been exemplified by young actors who have progressed through the ranks of our education programs to the Unicorn Company, and then to star on the main stage.

—*Richard Dunlap*

PRODUCTIONS 1990

She Loves Me, book: Joe Masteroff; music: Jerry Bock; lyrics: Sheldon Harnick; (D) Kent Paul; (S) Jane Clark; (C) David Murin; (L) Kenneth Posner

Breaking Legs, Tom Dulack; (D) John Tillinger; (S) James Noone; (C) David C. Woolard; (L) Arden Fingerhut

The Road to Mecca, Athol Fugard; (D) Gordon Edelstein; (S) Hugh Landwehr; (C) Candice Donnelly; (L) Arden Fingerhut

The Hasty Heart, John Patrick; (D) Richard Dunlap; (S) David Gallo; (C) Helen C. Ju; (L) Kenneth Posner

The Caucasian Chalk Circle, Bertolt Brecht; trans: Ralph Manheim and John Willett; (D) Michael Greif; (S) David Gallo; (C) Danielle Hollywood; (L) Kenneth Posner

Sincerity Forever, Mac Wellman; (D) Richard Caliban; (S) James Youmans; (C) Mary Myers; (L) Kenneth Posner

Come and Go and other plays, Samuel Beckett; (D) Kim Rubinstein; (S) David Gallo; (C) Danielle Hollywood; (L) Kenneth Posner

PRODUCTIONS 1991

Kiss Me Kate, book and lyrics: Samuel Spewack; music: Cole Porter; (D) Kent Paul; (S) John Falabella; (C) David Murin; (L) Phil Monat

Trains, Barbara Lebow; (D) Richard Dunlap; (S) Ed Wittstein; (C) Helen C. Ju; (L) Kenneth Posner

The Real Thing, Tom Stoppard; (D) Larry Carpenter; (S) James Noone; (C) Gail Brassard; (L) Kenneth Posner

California Suite, Neil Simon; (D) Richard Dunlap; (S) David Gallo; (C) David C. Woolard; (L) Kenneth Posner

A Slap in the Farce and ***A Matter of Wife and Death***, Eugene Labiche; (D) Gregory Abbels and Tom Simpson; (S) Judy Gailen; (C) Barbara Beccio; (L) Geoff Korf

Derek, Edward Bond; and ***Outside the Door***, Wolfgang Borchert; trans: Douglas Langworthy; (D) Elizabeth Margid; (S) Geoff Korf and Nephelie Andonyadis; (C) Geoff Korf and Nephelie Andonyadis; (L) Geoff Korf and Nephelie Andonyadis

Sarita, Maria Irene Fornes; (D) Kim Rubinstein; (S) David Gallo; (C) Nephelie Andonyadis; (L) Jeanne Koenig

Berkshire Theatre Festival. *Sincerity Forever*. Photo: Walter Scott.

Bilingual Foundation of the Arts. *Divinas Palabras.* Photo: Margarita Galban.

Bilingual Foundation of the Arts

MARGARITA GALBAN
Artistic Director

CARMEN ZAPATA
President/Producing Director

JIM PAYNE
Managing Director

421 North Ave. 19
Los Angeles, CA 90031
(213) 225-4044

FOUNDED 1973
Margarita Galban, Estela Scarlata, Carmen Zapata

SEASON
Jan.-Dec.

FACILITIES
Little Theatre
Seating Capacity: 99
Stage: arena

FINANCES
Jan. 1, 1990-Dec. 31, 1990
Expenses: $514,690

CONTRACTS
AEA 99-seat Theatre Plan

The Bilingual Foundation of the Arts creates theatre for both Hispanic and non-Hispanic communities. Each of these communities varies widely. To serve them all, BFA must have an artistic philosophy that can best be characterized by three words: pluralism, diversity and eclecticism. BFA's Theatre Teatro meets this challenge by presenting diverse material drawn from our rich Hispanic heritage, performed in English one night and Spanish the next. We present the classics from the Golden Age of Spain, contemporary Latin American plays and new plays by Hispanic Americans. In 1991 BFA will present a workshop of a new American opera, *Lorca, Child of the Moon*, and *Los de Abajo*, a new adaptation of Mariano Azuela's classic novel. BFA has represented the U.S. in Spain's foremost festival, Encuentro de 3 Continentes, and at Festival Iberoamericano in Colombia. Our Theatre for Children (Teatro Para Los Ninos) has played to more than 750,000 underprivileged elementary school children, building future audiences. The success of this program led to a new program, Teatro Para Los Jovenes (for at-risk youth) that will tour schools in L.A. and surrounding countries.

—*Margarita Galban*

PRODUCTIONS 1989-90

Divinas Palabras, Ramon del Valle-Inclan; trans: Edwin Williams; (D) Xavier Rojas; (S) Estela Scarlata; (C) Estela Scarlata and Alejandra Flores; (L) Robert Fromer

Cupo Limitado, Tomas Urtusastegui; trans: Margarita Stocker; (D) Margarita Galban; (S) Estela Scarlata; (C) Estela Scarlata and Ernie Fimbres; (L) Robert Fromer

La Nonna, Roberto M. Cossa; trans: Raul Moncada; (D) Margarita Galban; (S) Estela Scarlata; (C) Estela Scarlata and Alejandra Flores; (L) Robert Fromer

PRODUCTIONS 1990-91

Dona Rosita la Soltera, Federico Garcia Lorca; trans: Michael Dewell and Carmen Zapata; (D) Margarita Galban; (S) Estela Scarlata; (C) Richard D. Smart; (L) Robert Fromer

Made in Lanus, Nelly Fernandez Tiscornia; trans: Margarita Stocker; (D) Margarita Galban; (S) Estela Scarlata; (C) Julie Ann-Agosto; (L) Robert Fromer

Women Without Men, Edward Gallardo; trans: Margarita Stocker; (D) Charles Bazaldua; (S) Estela Scarlata; (C) Julie Ann-Agosto; (L) Robert Fromer

Blackfriars Theatre

Formerly The Bowery Theatre

RALPH ELIAS
Artistic Director

TODD BLAKESLEY
Managing Director

Box 126957
San Diego, CA 92112-6957
(619) 232-4088

FOUNDED 1982
Kim McCallum, Lisa Rigdon

SEASON
Jan.-Dec.

FACILITIES
Kingston Playhouse
Seating Capacity: 78
Stage: proscenium

FINANCES
July 1, 1990-June 30, 1991
Expenses: $278,000

CONTRACTS
AEA SPT

Blackfriars Theatre (formerly The Bowery Theatre) seeks to present plays that explore the human condition by exposing conflicts and characters that have an archetypal or mythic dimension, even when this dimension exists beneath the surface of a contemporary, seemingly "mundane" setting or premise. We are particularly interested in the nature and origins of American consciousness. The salient characteristic of our productions is the immediacy of contact between actor and audience experienced in our small, intimate playhouse. We select scripts which we feel can be enhanced by presentation in our space, and we regard our "smallness" as an impetus to honest performance and innovative staging rather than as a limitation. We focus on the soundness and integrity of the actor's process as the key to achieving the highly detailed performance which transports an audience. Our Community Collaborations Program provides administrative and technical support

Blackfriars Theatre. Robert Larsen, Erin Garrett and Burnham Joiner in *Laughing Buddha Wholistik Radio Theatre.* Photo: Ken Jacques.

in co-productions with emerging multicultural and educational organizations.

—Ralph Elias

PRODUCTIONS 1989-90

Italian American Reconciliation, John Patrick Shanley; (D) Ralph Elias; (S) Eric Hansen; (C) Kelly Fuller; (L) J.A. Roth
What the Butler Saw, Joe Orton; (D) Eugene Kallman; (S) Eric Hansen; (C) Stacey Rae; (L) J.A. Roth
Teibele and Her Demon, Isaac Bashevis Singer and Eve Friedman; (D) Ralph Elias; (S) Beeb Salzer; (C) Beeb Salzer; (L) Beeb Salzer
Jesse & The Bandit Queen, David Freeman; (D) Ollie Nash; (S) John Blunt and Ralph Elias; (C) Dione Lebhar; (L) Kris Sabel

PRODUCTIONS 1990-91

The Glass Menagerie, Tennessee Williams; (D) Ralph Elias; (S) John Blunt; (C) Dione Lebhar; (L) Kevin Sussman
Speed-the-Plow, David Mamet; (D) Frank Dwyer; (S) Ralph Elias; (C) Dione Lebhar; (L) J.A. Roth
Hauntings, Gordon Cox; (D) Scott M. Rubsam; (S) Beeb Salzer; (C) Sharone Mendes-Nassi; (L) Louis Tury
The Shakespeare Club, Adam Stein; (D) Victor Smith-Kervia; (S) Beeb Salzer; (C) Sharone Mendes-Nassi; (L) Louis Tury
For My Very Dust Is Laughing, Aaron Thomas; (D) Nonnie Vishner; (S) Beeb Salzer; (C) Sharone Mendes-Nassi; (L) Louis Tury
Also Known As..., Rachel Balko; (D) Deborah Falb; (S) Beeb Salzer; (C) Sharone Mendes-Nassi; (L) Louis Tury
When Reality Refuses to Cooperate, Robert Sayles; (D) Nonnie Vishner; (S) Beeb Salzer; (C) Sharone Mendes-Nassi; (L) Louis Tury
Laughing Buddha Wholistik Radio Theatre, Todd Blakesley and Burnham Joiner; (D) Linda Vickerman, Helen Lehman and Todd Blakesley; (S) Todd Blakesley; (C) Linda Vickerman and Helen Lehman; (L) Roger Henderson

Bloomsburg Theatre Ensemble

LEIGH STRIMBECK
Ensemble Director

STEPHEN COPPICK
Administrative Director

Box 66
Bloomsburg, PA 17815
(717) 784-5530 (bus.)
(717) 784-8181 (b.o.)

FOUNDED 1978
Ensemble

SEASON
Oct.-June

FACILITIES
Alvina Krause Theatre
Seating Capacity: 369
Stage: proscenium

FINANCES
Sept. 1, 1990-Aug. 31, 1991
Expenses: $463,516

The Bloomsburg Theatre Ensemble is a resident body of artists taking responsiblility for its collective artistic destiny. The ensemble as a whole selects its season and directors, determines its membership and elects its leadership. Its repertoire is deliberately eclectic, and encompasses many cultures and styles in order to provide its rural audience with a forum for the investigation of our own particularly American privileges and challenges. The ensemble remains in a rural region because it needs a home where dialogue with an audience is possible, and where its impact on the community is positive and demonstrable. BTE's five-play season is presented in the Alvina Krause Theatre, named for the acting teacher who was the guiding spirit behind the founding of the company. The annual Theatre in the Classroom tour brings original, group-created pieces to schools statewide, and the BTE Theatre School offers classes for all age groups.

—Leigh Strimbeck

PRODUCTIONS 1989-90

Company, book: George Furth; music and lyrics: Stephen Sondheim; (D) Dan Kirsch; (S) Jim Bazewicz; (C) P. Chelsea Harriman; (L) Richard Latta
A Christmas Carol, adapt: Whit MacLaughlin, from Charles Dickens; (D) Laurie McCants; (S) Jim Bazewicz; (C) Jane Alois Stein; (L) Bob Steineck
About Face, Dario Fo; trans: Ron Jenkins; (D) Martin Shell; (S) Peter Waldron; (C) Judy Kahn; (L) Doug Cox
Sea Marks, Gardner McKay; (D) Leigh Strimbeck; (S) Robert Katkowsky; (C) S.Q. Campbell; (L) Bruce Auerbach
King Lear, William Shakespeare; (D) Gerard Stropnicky; (S) Jim Bazewicz; (C) John C. Rager; (L) Richard Latta
Flywheel, Shyster, and Flywheel, adapt: Gerard Stropnicky and Martin Shell, from The Marx Brothers; (D) David Moreland; (S) David Moreland; (C) Lisa Mandle; (L) Gerard Stropnicky
Echoes of Tomorrow, company-developed; (D) Rand Whipple and David Moreland

PRODUCTIONS 1990-91

The House of Blue Leaves, John Guare; (D) Gail Garrisan; (S) Jim Bazewicz; (C) Hillarie Blumenthal; (L) A.C. Hickox
A Child's Christmas in Wales, adapt: Jeremy Brooks and Adrian Mitchell, from Dylan Thomas; (D) Rand Whipple; (S) Barbara Cohig; (C) Rebecca Ermisch; (L) Scott Zielinski
Candida, George Bernard Shaw; (D) Gerard Stropnicky; (S) Jim Bazewicz; (C) David Smith; (L) A.C. Hickox
Out Cry, Tennessee Williams; (D) Conrad Bishop; (S) Robert A. Nelson; (C) S.Q. Campbell; (L) Richard Latta
Land of the Rising Sun, company-developed; (D) A. Elizabeth Dowd and James Goode
13 rue de L'Amour, Georges Feydeau; trans: Mawby Green and Ed Feilbert; (D) Martin Shell; (S) John C. Rager; (C) David Smith; (L) Richard Latta
Along the Susquehanna, company-developed; (D) A. Elizabeth Dowd
The Voice of the Prairie, John Olive; (D) Leigh Strimbeck; (S) Robert Katkowsky; (C) David Smith; (L) Patrick Northway

BoarsHead: Michigan Public Theater

JOHN PEAKES
Artistic Director

JUDITH GENTRY
Managing Director

Bloomsburg Theatre Ensemble. Rand Whipple, David Moreland and Leigh Strimbeck in *13 rue de L'Amour*. Photo: Marlin Wagner.

BoarsHead: Michigan Public Theater. Michael John Page and Gary Andrews in *Not About Heroes*. Photo: Connie Peakes.

425 South Grand Ave.
Lansing, MI 48933
(517) 484-7800 (bus.)
(517) 484-7805 (b.o.)

FOUNDED 1970
Richard Thomsen, John Peakes

SEASON
Oct.-Apr.

FACILITIES
Seating Capacity: 249
Stage: thrust

FINANCES
June 1, 1989-May 31, 1990
Expenses: $517,331

CONTRACTS
AEA SPT

BoarsHead: Michigan Public Theater is a center for theatre in our region. Our goal is the presentation of high-standard professional theatre chosen from the classic and modern repertoires. BoarsHead has a strong commitment to the staging of new plays, and the support of emerging playwrights is manifest in its seasons. The resident company remains dedicated to the idea of an expanding theatre, reaching into both the community and the state. Plays tour statewide, new pieces are developed by area writers, and designs are commissioned from area artists. The effort to involve new audiences is central. The theatre exists for the company as well, providing time and space for artists' individual growth and development. Our focus remains the audience. Productions must be accessible, must address the concerns of the time and then, hopefully, remain with our audiences beyond the moment.

—John Peakes

PRODUCTIONS 1989-90

Educating Rita, Willy Russell; (D) Kyle Euckert; (S) Kyle Euckert; (C) Charlotte Deardorff; (L) James Peters
A Streetcar Named Desire, Tennessee Williams; (D) John Peakes; (S) Kyle Euckert; (C) Maria Valencia; (L) James Peters
The Lion in Winter, James Goldman; (D) Judith Gentry; (S) Kyle Euckert; (C) Lisa Molyneux; (L) James Peters
Not About Heroes, Stephen MacDonald; (D) Judith Gentry; (S) Kyle Euckert; (C) Lisa Molyneux; (L) James Peters
The Voice of the Prairie, John Olive; (D) Jonathan Gillespie; (S) Kyle Euckert; (C) Lisa Molyneux; (L) James Peters
Painting Churches, Tina Howe; (D) Laural Merlington; (S) Kyle Euckert; (C) Lisa Molyneux; (L) James Peters
Steel Magnolias, Robert Harling; (D) John Peakes; (S) Kyle Euckert; (C) Lisa Molyneux; (L) James Peters

PRODUCTIONS 1990-91

Mass Appeal, Bill C. Davis; (D) Kyle Euckert; (S) Kyle Euckert; (C) Lisa Molyneux; (L) James Peters
King Lear, William Shakespeare; (D) Douglas Campbell; (S) Kyle Euckert; (C) Lisa Molyneux; (L) James Peters
Under Milk Wood, Dylan Thomas; (D) John Peakes; (S) Kyle Euckert; (C) Lisa Molyneux; (L) James Peters
Big Sister, Little Brother and Dumbarton Oaks, Richard Thomsen; (D) Laural Merlington; (S) Tim Stapleton; (C) Lisa Molyneux; (L) James Peters
Vikings, Stephen Metcalfe; (D) Judith Gentry; (S) Gordon Phetteplace; (C) Lisa Molyneux; (L) Rick Knapp
Two Rooms, Lee Blessing; (D) John Peakes; (S) Richard W. Lindsay, Jr.; (C) Lisa Molyneux; (L) Richard W. Lindsay, Jr.
Driving Miss Daisy, Alfred Uhry; (D) Judith Gentry; (S) Gary Decker; (C) Lisa Molyneux; (L) Rick Knapp

The Body Politic Theatre

ALBERT PERTALION
Artistic Director

2261 North Lincoln Ave.
Chicago, IL 60614-6297
(312) 348-7901 (bus.)
(312) 871-3000 (b.o.)

FOUNDED 1966
James Shiflett, Paul Sills

SEASON
Sept.-June

FACILITIES
Seating Capacity: 192
Stage: thrust

FINANCES
Aug. 1, 1990-July 31, 1991
Expenses: $400,000

CONTRACTS
AEA CAT

The Body Politic Theatre is an ensemble dedicated to presenting the work of playwrights who cherish the richness of our language and the resilience of the human spirit. We present a five-play subscription season on the main stage. This season seeks to balance a classic, a new script and three shows which speak to our muscular city. In addition, our new studio performing space will soon house experimental works, the Discovery Project of staged readings and guest appearances by small professional groups seeking a performance venue. A recently formed partnership with Roosevelt University lays the foundation for an exciting new phase of development: a family series. Ensemble members serve on the faculty of the university, and internships with the professional company prepare Roosevelt graduates for a career in the theatre.

—Albert Pertalion

Note: During the 1989-90 season, Pauline Brailsford served as artistic director.

PRODUCTIONS 1989-90

Cowardy Custard, devised: Gerald Frow, Alan Strachan and Wendy Toye, from Noel Coward;

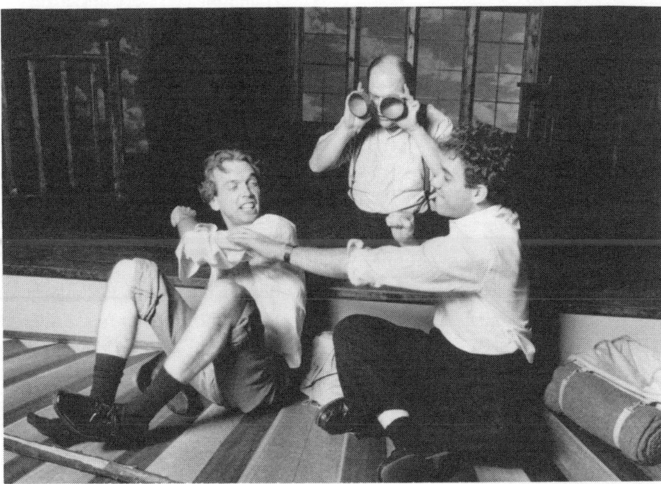

The Body Politic Theatre. Donald Brearley, Larry Brandenburg and James McCance in *Artist Descending a Staircase*.

music and lyrics: Noel Coward; (D) Peter Amster; (S) Jeff Bauer; (C) Lynn Sandberg; (L) Barbara Reeder

The Importance of Being Earnest, Oscar Wilde; (D) Pauline Brailsford; (S) Kent Goetz; (C) Andrew Vincent; (L) Michael Rourke

September in the Rain, John Godber; (D) Pauline Brailsford; (S) Kristofer Eitrheim; (C) Lynn Sandberg; (L) David Gipson

Hello and Goodbye, Athol Fugard; (D) Albert Pertalion; (S) Arthur Ridley; (C) Arthur Ridley; (L) David Gipson

Wenceslas Square, Larry Shue; (D) Tom Mula; (S) Brian Traynor; (C) Kerry Fleming; (L) Michael Rourke

PRODUCTIONS 1990-91

Artist Descending a Staircase, Tom Stoppard; (D) Joseph Sadowski; (S) Kent Goetz; (C) Andrew Vincent; (L) Mark P. Radziejeski

The Lion in Winter, James Goldman; (D) Richard S. Kordos; (S) Katherine Ross; (C) Nancy Missimi; (L) Kenneth Moore

The Belle of Amherst, William Luce; (D) Albert Pertalion; (S) Arthur Ridley; (C) Arthur Ridley; (L) Kenneth Moore

Talley's Folly, Lanford Wilson; (D) Albert Pertalion; (S) Kristofer Eitrheim; (L) Kenneth Moore

Hi-Hat Hattie!, Larry Parr; (D) Albert Pertalion; (S) Kristofer Eitrheim; (C) Claudia Boddy; (L) Kenneth Moore

The Little Humpback Horse, adapt: Virginia Smith; (D) Viacheslav V. Dolgachov; (S) Brian Traynor; (C) Claudia Boddy; (L) Kenneth Moore

Boston Post Road Stage Company

DOUGLAS MOSER
Artistic Director

MARILYN HERSEY
Executive Director

25 Powers Court
Westport, CT 06880
(203) 227-1290 (bus.)
(203) 227-1072 (b.o.)

FOUNDED 1984
Rob LaGamba, Ellen LaGamba

SEASON
Oct.-June

FACILITIES
Westport Playhouse
Seating Capacity: 190
Stage: thrust

FINANCES
July 1, 1990-June 30, 1991
Expenses: $450,000

CONTRACTS
AEA letter of agreement

The Boston Post Road Stage Company was conceived to provide artistic opportunities to the vast number of theatrical artists living in the area and to create theatre that is relevant to today's culture. Producing an eclectic mix of plays including Off Broadway revivals, rediscovered classics and original scripts, the Stage Company chooses plays that reflect on the personal and the intimate. In an era in which the survival of theatre in general is of the utmost importance, the Stage Company seeks uplifting works that challenge audiences while entertaining. The choices and approaches to the work are often unpredictable and surprising, supporting the Stage Company's reputation as "Off Broadway in Connecticut."

—*Douglas Moser*

PRODUCTIONS 1989-90

Trixie True, Teen Detective, book, music and lyrics: Kelly Hamilton; (D) Bert Bernardi; (S) Warren Karp; (C) Jose M. Rivera; (L) Hugh Hallinan

The Boys Next Door, Tom Griffin; (D) Douglas Moser; (S) David Goetsch; (C) Jon S. Jordan; (L) John F. Carr

The Mistress of the Inn, adapt: Helen Lohmann, from Carlo Goldoni; (D) Burry Fredrik; (S) John King, Jr.; (C) Blanche Blakeny; (L) Hugh Hallinan

Frankie and Johnny in the Clair de Lune, Terrence McNally; (D) Douglas Moser; (S) David Goetsch; (C) Jon S. Jordan; (L) John F. Carr

The Ice Cream Sunday, Frank Salisbury; (D) Burry Fredrik; (S) Bob Phillips; (C) Helen Conlon; (L) Craig Kennedy

The Mystery of Irma Vep, Charles Ludlam; (D) Douglas Moser; (S) David Goetsch; (C) Blanche Blakeny; (L) Mimi Jordan Sherin

PRODUCTIONS 1990-91

Songs of Innocence, G. Brent Darnell; (D) Douglas Moser; (S) David Goetsch; (C) Jon S. Jordan; (L) Jim Sale

Sister Mary Ignatius Explains It All For You and ***The Actor's Nightmare***, Christopher Durang; (D) Bert Bernardi; (S) Richard Chambers; (C) Blanche Blakeny; (L) Lisa Myers

Closer Than Ever, conceived: Steven Scott Smith; music: David Shire; lyrics: Richard Maltby, Jr.; (D) Burry Fredrik; (S) Burry Fredrik; (C) Jon S. Jordan; (L) Tracy Lee Wilson

Burn This, Lanford Wilson; (D) Douglas Moser; (S) John F. Carr; (C) Jon S. Jordan; (L) Mimi Jordan Sherin

Kingdom of Earth, Tennessee Williams; (D) James Luse; (S) John King, Jr.; (C) Jon S. Jordan; (L) Tracy Lee Wilson

Okiboji, Conrad Bishop and Elizabeth Fuller; (D) Burry Fredrik; (S) David Goetsch; (C) Melissa Rowe; (L) Gary Marde

Boston Post Road Stage Company. Daniel Nathan Specter and Jo Twiss in *Kingdom of Earth*. Photo: Lawrence Merz.

Bristol Riverside Theatre

SUSAN D. ATKINSON
Producing Artistic Director

Box 1250
Bristol, PA 19007
(215) 785-6664 (bus.)
(215) 788-7827 (b.o.)

FOUNDED 1987
Susan D. Atkinson, Robert K. O'Neill

SEASON
Sept.-May

FACILITIES
Mainstage
Seating Capacity: 302
Stage: proscenium

Showroom
Seating Capacity: 80
Stage: flexible

Bristol Riverside Theatre. Bryant Lanier, Barbara McCulloh in *Murder in a Nutshell*. Photo: Milt Klein.

FINANCES
Sept. 1, 1990-Aug. 31, 1991
Expenses: $500,000

CONTRACTS
AEA letter of agreement

Bristol Riverside Theatre is a professional, nonprofit regional theatre company dedicated to the development of new plays and playwrights, and to freshly interpreting vintage plays, musicals and classics. Ideally, the manner in which we develop a new play or reexamine an overlooked work from the past is to: 1) give the work a staged reading and determine the necessary period of time to make appropriate revisions, so that 2) a workshop production can be given, and 3) if that is successful, further develop the work so that the fullest possible artistic merit can be shared with our audience in a mainstage production. Our primary concern is maintaining artistic integrity and pursuing excellence in our efforts to affirm the rich cultural heritage of Bucks County and the entire region, the legacy of American theatre, the betterment of the quality of life and the sharing of high-quality, affordable entertainment.

—Susan D. Atkinson

PRODUCTIONS 1989-90

Sally Blane...Girl Detective, book: Helen Sneed and Peter Webb; music and lyrics: David Levy and Leslie Eberhard; (D) Neal Kenyon; (S) Bob Barnett; (C) Beverly Bullock; (L) Scott Pinkney
The Glass Menagerie, Tennessee Williams; (D) Susan D. Atkinson; (S) Nels Anderson; (C) Bradford Wood and Gregory Poplyk; (L) John Culbert
Mass Appeal, Bill C. Davis; (D) Susan D. Atkinson; (S) Don Ricklin and Catherine Gruetzke; (C) Claudia Wolf; (L) Jerry Jonas
I'm Not Rappaport, Herb Gardner; (D) Mierley Davis; (S) George Passage; (C) Bradford Wood and Gregory Poplyk; (L) Jerry Jonas
The Roar of the Greasepaint, The Smell of the Crowd, book, music and lyrics: Anthony Newley and Leslie Bricusse; (D) Edward Earle; (S) George Passage; (C) Bradford Wood and Gregory Poplyk; (L) Jerry Jonas

PRODUCTIONS 1990-91

Irma La Douce, adapt and trans: Julian More, David Heneker and Monty Norman, from Alexandre Brefort; music: Marguerite Monnot; lyrics: Julian More, David Heneker and Monty Norman; (D) Susan D. Atkinson; (S) Bart Healy; (C) Bradford Wood and Gregory Poplyk; (L) Dean Seabrook
Malice Aforethought, Erik Jendresen; (D) Frederick Rolf; (S) Bart Healy; (C) Bradford Wood and Gregory Poplyk; (L) Dean Seabrook
Murder in a Nutshell, LaRue Watts; (D) Susan D. Atkinson; (S) Bart Healy; (C) Bradford Wood and Gregory Poplyk; (L) Dean Seabrook
The Lion in Winter, James Goldman; (D) Stuart Vaughan; (S) David Gordon; (C) Bradford Wood and Gregory Poplyk; (L) Dean Seabrook
Moby Dick, book adapt: Doug Katsaros and Mark St. Germain, from Herman Melville; music: Doug Katsaros; lyrics: Mark St. Germain; (D) Susan D. Atkinson; (S) David Gordon; (C) Bradford Wood and Gregory Poplyk; (L) Dean Seabrook

Caldwell Theatre Company

MICHAEL HALL
Artistic/Managing Director

Box 277
Boca Raton, FL 33429
(407) 241-7380 (bus.)
(407) 241-7432 (b.o.)

FOUNDED 1975
Michael Hall, Frank Bennett

SEASON
Aug.-May

FACILITIES
Mainstage
Seating Capacity: 305
Stage: proscenium

FINANCES
Oct. 1, 1990-Sept. 30, 1991
Expenses: $1,725,000

CONTRACTS
AEA LORT (C)

The Caldwell Theatre Company, a state theatre of Florida, was founded as an ensemble group that has two goals: to produce socially relevant contemporary plays, and to revive American and European classics from 1890-1940, while striving to develop the Caldwell as an alternative to the commercial houses in the surrounding Ft. Lauderdale–Palm Beach area. Each spring, Caldwell's annual Mizner Festival highlights plays, musical cabarets and events that relate to the 1920s and '30s—the period when architect Addison Mizner introduced a style of living that made Boca Raton famous. Caldwell's other programs include theatre for schools, a touring musical cabaret and master classes for professional actors.

—Michael Hall

PRODUCTIONS 1989-90

Bus Stop, William Inge; (D) Michael Hall; (S) Rick Rasmussen; (C) Bridget Bartlett; (L) Mary Jo Dondlinger
The Perfect Party, A.R. Gurney, Jr.; (D) Michael Hall; (S) Frank Bennett; (C) Bridget Bartlett; (L) Mary Jo Dondlinger
Angel Street, Patrick Hamilton; (D) Michael Hall; (S) Frank Bennett; (C) Bridget Bartlett; (L) Mary Jo Dondlinger
Les Liaisons Dangereuses, Christopher Hampton, from Choderlos de Laclos; (D) Michael Hall; (S) James Morgan; (C) Bridget Bartlett; (L) Mary Jo Dondlinger
Hay Fever, Noel Coward; (D) Michael Hall; (S) Frank Bennett; (C) Bridget Bartlett; (L) Mary Jo Dondlinger
The Taffettas, book: Rick Lewis; music and lyrics: various; (D) Michael Hall; (S) James Morgan; (C) Bridget Bartlett; (L) Mary Jo Dondlinger
Bent, Martin Sherman; (D) Michael Hall; (S) James Morgan; (C) Bridget Bartlett; (L) Mary Jo Dondlinger

PRODUCTIONS 1990-91

The Rainmaker, N. Richard Nash; (D) Kenneth Kay; (S) Frank Bennett; (C) Bridget Bartlett; (L) Russ Swift
The Heidi Chronicles, Wendy Wasserstein; (D) Michael Hall; (S) James Morgan; (C) Bridget Bartlett; (L) Kenneth Posner
See How They Run, Philip King; (D) Michael Hall; (S) Frank Bennett; (C) Bridget Bartlett;

Caldwell Theatre Company. Amanda Naughton and Beth Fowler in *The Royal Family*. Photo: Paul Perone.

(L) Mary Jo Dondlinger
Other People's Money, Jerry Sterner; (D) Kenneth Kay; (S) James Morgan; (C) Bridget Bartlett; (L) Mary Jo Dondlinger
The Royal Family, George S. Kaufman and Edna Ferber; (D) Michael Hall; (S) Frank Bennett; (C) Bridget Bartlett; (L) Mary Jo Dondlinger
Songs from the Silver Screen, various composers and lyricists; (D) James Morgan; (S) James Morgan; (C) Bridget Bartlett; (L) Chip Latimer

California Shakespeare Festival

Formerly Berkeley Shakespeare Festival

MICHAEL ADDISON
Artistic Director

MARCIA O'DEA
Managing Director

Box 1032
Berkeley, CA 94701
(510) 548-3422 (bus.)
(510) 525-8844 (b.o.)

FOUNDED 1974
Mikel Clifford, Bay Area actors

SEASON
June-Nov.

FACILITIES
Lt. G. H. Bruns III Memorial Amphitheatre
Seating Capacity: 550
Stage: thrust

FINANCES
Jan. 1, 1989-Dec. 31, 1990
Expenses: $1,300,000

CONTRACTS
AEA LORT (D)

The California Shakespeare Festival (formerly Berkeley Shakespeare Festival) enters its 19th season with a renewed commitment to productions that are conceived in vividly contemporary terms but rooted in a rigorous exploration of Shakespeare's texts and the Renaissance milieu. We continue to draw on a core of artists who have been at the center of the work for the last decade, but also seek out new artists each season to reinvigorate our process. The season now includes four productions in repertory in our new 550-seat outdoor amphitheatre, and a fall tour throughout California and the West. The rigors of playing in repertory, performing outdoors and touring extensively all demand particularly resilient artists, creatively adaptive to the shifting realities of the moment and the energies of the event. We embrace this as a theatre company, convinced that our artistic reflexes and vision are always brought into focus by one constant: direct and immediate contact with our audience.

—Michael Addison

PRODUCTIONS 1990

The Merry Wives of Windsor, William Shakespeare; (D) Julian Lopez-Morillas; (S) Michael R. Cook; (C) Gail Russell; (L) Kurt Landisman
Othello, William Shakespeare; (D) Michael Addison; (S) Eric E. Sinkkonen; (C) Nancy Jo Smith; (L) Kurt Landisman
Cymbeline, William Shakespeare; (D) Laird Williamson; (S) Laird Williamson; (C) Warren Travis; (L) Kurt Landisman
Twelfth Night, William Shakespeare; (D) Richard E.T. White; (S) Ariel; (C) Barbara Bush; (L) Kurt Landisman

PRODUCTIONS 1991

A Midsummer Night's Dream, William Shakespeare; (D) Richard Seyd; (S) Barbara Mesney; (C) Sandra Woodall; (L) Kurt Landisman
King Lear, William Shakespeare; (D) Michael Addison; (S) Jeff Hunt; (C) Warren Travis; (L) Kurt Landisman
All's Well That Ends Well, William Shakespeare; (D) Julian Lopez-Morillas; (S) Eric E. Sinkkonen; (C) Gail Russell; (L) Kurt Landisman
Antony and Cleopatra, William Shakespeare; (D) Nagle Jackson; (S) Michael R. Cook; (C) Barbara Bush; (L) Kurt Landisman

California Theatre Center

GAYLE CORNELISON
General Director

Box 2007
Sunnyvale, CA 94087
(408) 245-2979 (bus.)
(408) 245-2978 (b.o.)

FOUNDED 1976
Gayle Cornelison

SEASON
Sept.-Aug.

California Shakespeare Festival. Lura Dolas in *The Merry Wives of Windsor*. Photo: David Allen.

FACILITIES
Sunnyvale Performing Arts Center
Seating Capacity: 200
Stage: proscenium

FINANCES
July 1, 1989-June 30, 1990
Expenses: $885,000

CONTRACTS
AEA Guest Artist

The California Theatre Center is a company with three major programs: a resident company that performs primarily for students and families from October to May; a resident company that performs primarily for adults in the summer; and touring companies that perform regionally, nationally and internationally. The performing artist is the focal point of CTC. Since our society fails to recognize the value of performers, it is essential that their worth be fully appreciated in our theatre. We attempt to provide the performing artist with the best possible environment so that he or she can be as creative as possible. At CTC we believe it is important for us to think of excellence as a process rather than a product. Our company strives toward the goal of outstanding theatre. As we grow and mature our concern is with the future, not the past. What we are attempting in the present is always far more exciting than our past successes. We are passionately driven by our search for excellence.

—*Gayle Cornelison*

PRODUCTIONS 1989-90

Beach of Dreams, Graziano Melano; (D) Mary Hall Surface; (S) Paul Vallerga; (C) Jane Lambert; (L) Paul Vallerga

The Ugly Duckling, book adapt and lyrics: Gayle Cornelison, from Hans Christian Andersen; music: Brian Bennett; (D) Will Huddleston; (S) Brian Alan Reed; (C) Colleen Troy Lewis; (L) Brian Alan Reed

Caterina, James Keller; (D) Albert Takazauckas; (S) Joel Fontaine; (C) Jane Lambert; (L) Brian Alan Reed

Rapunzel and the Witch, adapt: Shannon Edwards and Gayle Cornelison, from The Brothers Grimm; (D) Mary Gibboney; (S) Paul Vallerga; (C) Jane Lambert

Santa's Secret, Clayton Doherty and Mary Gibboney, conceived: Shannon Edwards; (D) Shannon Edwards; (S) Brian Alan Reed; (C) Colleen Troy Lewis; (L) Brian Alan Reed

A Christmas Carol, adapt: Mary Hall Surface, from Charles Dickens; (D) Gayle Cornelison; (S) Brian Alan Reed; (C) Jane Lambert; (L) Patricia McGeary

A Holiday of Times Past, Gayle Cornelison; (D) Gayle Cornelison; (S) Paul Vallerga; (C) Colleen Troy Lewis; (L) Paul Vallerga

The Princess and the Pea, adapt: Gayle Cornelison, from Hans Christian Andersen; (D) Gayle Cornelison; (S) Brian Alan Reed; (C) Jane Lambert; (L) Brian Alan Reed

The Mixed Blessings, Mary Hall Surface; (D) Graham Whitehead; (S) Brian Alan Reed; (C) Colleen Troy Lewis; (L) Brian Alan Reed

Jack and the Beanstalk, Gayle Cornelison; (D) Russell Blackwood; (S) Tom Hurd; (C) Jane Lambert; (L) Paul Vallerga

Apollo: To The Moon, Mary Hall Surface; (D) Mary Hall Surface; (S) Kevin Reese; (C) Mary Hall Surface; (L) Kevin Reese

Amelia Earhart: Flights of Fancy, Will Huddleston; (D) Shannon Edwards; (S) Paul Vallerga; (C) Colleen Troy Lewis; (L) Paul Vallerga

The Secret Garden, adapt: Thomas W. Olson, from Frances Hodgson Burnett; (D) Will Huddleston; (S) Paul Vallerga; (C) Jane Lambert; (L) Paul Vallerga

Hansel and Gretel, adapt: Gayle Cornelison, from The Brothers Grimm; (D) Scott Williams; (S) Brian Alan Reed; (C) Colleen Troy Lewis; (L) Brian Alan Reed

The Contrast, adapt: James Keller, from Royall Tyler; (D) Albert Takazauckas; (S) Paul Vallerga; (C) Jane Lambert; (L) Brian Grove

The Matchmaker, Thornton Wilder; (D) Gayle Cornelison; (S) Paul Vallerga; (C) Jane Lambert; (L) Brian Grove

Star-Spangled Girl, Neil Simon; (D) Will Huddleston; (S) Paul Vallerga; (C) Colleen Troy Lewis; (L) Brian Grove

The Male Animal, James Thurber and Elliot Nugent; (D) Andrew J. Traister; (S) Paul Vallerga; (C) Colleen Troy Lewis; (L) Brian Grove

PRODUCTIONS 1990-91

Troubled Waters, Brian Kral; (D) Clayton Doherty; (S) Patricia McGeary; (C) Rosita Ganitsky; (L) Paul Vallerga

California Theatre Center. Allison Rowley and Domenique Lozano in *The Ugly Duckling*. Photo: Marcia Lepler.

Androcles and the Lion, adapt: Aurand Harris; (D) Will Huddleston; (S) Paul Vallerga; (C) Jane Lambert; (L) Paul Vallerga

The Princess and the Pea, adapt: Gayle Cornelison, from Hans Christian Andersen; (D) Gayle Cornelison; (S) Michael R. Cook; (C) Jane Lambert; (L) Paul Vallerga

Undine, book adapt and lyrics: James Keller; music: Andras Ranki; (D) Albert Takazauckas; (S) John Wilson; (C) Jane Lambert; (L) Kurt Landisman

The Elves and the Shoemaker, adapt: Gayle Cornelison, from The Brothers Grimm; (D) Lynne A. Pace; (S) Paul Vallerga; (C) Jane Lambert; (L) Paul Vallerga

A Christmas Carol, adapt: Mary Hall Surface, from Charles Dickens; (D) Gayle Cornelison; (S) Paul Vallerga and Michael Cook; (C) Jane Lambert; (L) Paul Vallerga

The Ugly Duckling, book adapt and lyrics: Gayle Cornelison, from Hans Christian Andersen; music: Brian Bennett; (D) Will Huddleston; (S) Michael Cook; (C) Colleen Troy Lewis; (L) Bill M. Rupel

The Time Machine, adapt: Gayle Cornelison, from H.G. Wells; (D) Will Huddleston; (S) Paul Vallerga; (C) Jane Lambert; (L) Bill M. Rupel

Cinderella, adapt: Gayle Cornelison; (D) Alexander Mikhailov; (S) Alexander Mikhailov and Paul Vallerga; (C) Colleen Troy Lewis; (L) Bill M. Rupel

Maggie Magalita, Wendy Kesselman; (D) Paul Gaffney; (S) Paul Vallerga; (C) Jane Lambert; (L) Bill M. Rupel

Imagine, Clayton Doherty; (D) Clayton Doherty; (S) Clayton Doherty; (C) Clayton Doherty; (L) Clayton Doherty

King of the Golden River, adapt: James Still, from John Ruskin; (D) Will Huddleston; (S) Paul Vallerga; (C) Colleen Troy Lewis; (L) Bill M. Rupel

Mr. Fix-It, Lars Vik; (D) Fritjof Fomlesen; (S) Lars Vik and Hans Ellison Patterson; (C) Lars Vik; (L) Hans Ellison Patterson

The Sleeping Beauty, adapt: Gayle Cornelison, from The Brothers Grimm; (D) Sam Bevridge;

(S) Paul Vallerga; (C) Jane Lambert; (L) Bill M. Rupel

The Lion in Winter, James Goldman; (D) Tom Ramirez; (S) Jerald Enos; (C) Jane Lambert; (L) Bill M. Rupel

The Miracle Worker, William Gibson; (D) Bill James; (S) Jerald Enos; (C) Debbie Owens; (L) Bill M. Rupel

The Tempest, William Shakespeare; (D) Jerald Enos; (S) Jerald Enos; (C) Jane Lambert; (L) Bill M. Rupel

A Midsummer Night's Dream, William Shakespeare; (D) Will Huddleston; (S) Paul Vallerga; (C) Debbie Owens; (L) Bill M. Rupel

Capital Repertory Company

BRUCE BOUCHARD
Artistic Director

ROBERT HOLLEY
Managing Director

Box 399
Albany, NY 12201-0399
(518) 462-4531 (bus.)
(518) 462-4534 (b.o.)

Capital Repertory Company. Tom Riis Farrell in *Laughing Wild*. Photo: M. Desiderio/Schuyler.

FOUNDED 1980
Michael Van Landingham, Oakley Hall, III

SEASON
Oct.-June

FACILITIES
Market Theatre
Seating Capacity: 254
Stage: thrust

FINANCES
July 1, 1990-June 30, 1991
Expenses: $1,300,000

CONTRACTS
AEA LORT (D)

The worlds we make onstage are reflective of and instructive to the world in which we live. As the very act of looking at artwork *is* the *act* of education, we seek to turn the unconscious and mysterious inside out, in works of intellectual and emotional integrity. Our aim is to inspire re-vision of our selves and our community. Our work is contemporary: We present premieres, second productions of new works and texts largely unfamiliar to our audience. Our productions of modern and traditional classics highlight aspects of these plays which address current conditions and beg reexamination of both the factual shape of history and the human event of history-making. As we enter our second decade, we point with pride to a long-term association with a body of artists who return to Capital Rep as "artistic home" to stretch and refine their craft.

—*Bruce Bouchard*

PRODUCTIONS 1989-90

Shakin' the Mess Outta Misery, Shay Youngblood; (D) Glenda Dickerson; (S) Charles McClennahan; (C) Felix E. Cochren; (L) Shirley Prendergast

Twelfth Night, William Shakespeare; (D) Rene Buch; (S) Robert Weber Federico; (C) Robert Weber Federico; (L) Robert Weber Federico

The Sea Horse, Edward J. Moore; (D) Bruce Bouchard; (S) Andi Lyons; (C) Lynda L. Salsbury; (L) Andi Lyons

Crossing Delancey, Susan Sandler; (D) D. Lynn Meyers; (S) Joseph P. Tilford; (C) Rebecca Senske; (L) Spencer Mosse

Burn This, Lanford Wilson; (D) Bruce Bouchard; (S) Rick Dennis; (C) Martha Hally; (L) Brian MacDevitt

Private Lives, Noel Coward; (D) Michael J. Hume; (S) James Noone; (C) Lynda L. Salsbury; (L) David Yergan

PRODUCTIONS 1990-91

The Scandalous Adventures of Sir Toby Trollope, Ron House and Alan Sherman; (D) Stephen Rothman; (S) Joseph Varga; (C) Lynda L. Salsbury; (L) Betsy Adams

The Cherry Orchard, Anton Chekhov; trans: Alex Szogyi; (D) Rene Buch; (S) Robert Weber Federico; (C) Robert Weber Federico; (L) Robert Weber Federico

Other People's Money, Jerry Sterner; (D) Bruce Bouchard; (S) Rick Dennis; (C) Michael Krass; (L) Jackie Manassee

Laughing Wild, Christopher Durang; (D) Michael J. Hume; (S) Donald Eastman; (C) Lynda L. Salsbury; (L) David Yergan

The Belmont Avenue Social Club, Bruce Graham; (D) James J. Christy; (S) James Wolk; (C) Vickie Esposito; (L) Curt Senie

Fences, August Wilson; (D) Seret Scott; (S) Donald Eastman; (C) Lynda L. Salsbury; (L) William H. Grant, III

The CAST Theatre

DIANA GIBSON
Artistic Director

ANDY DALEY
Production Manager

804 North El Centro
Hollywood, CA 90038
(213) 462-9872 (bus.)
(213) 462-0265 (b.o.)

FOUNDED 1974
Ted Schmitt

SEASON
Jan.-Dec.

FACILITIES
The CAST Theatre
Seating Capacity: 65
Stage: proscenium

The CAST-at-The-Circle
Seating Capacity: 99
Stage: proscenium

FINANCES
Oct. 1, 1989-Sept. 30, 1990
Expenses: $235,050

CONTRACTS
AEA 99-seat Theatre Plan

The CAST Theatre generates new American plays and serves emerging American playwrights by developing their original scripts. CAST plays illuminate the human condition—particularly relationships and the indomitability of the human spirit. The CAST is one of the most playwright-accessible, high-profile, intimate, professional theatres in southern California and is a supportive, embracing, award-winning environment for new works that illuminate the wide variety of experiences in our diverse cultural landscape. Musicals are a theatrical form in which the CAST also excels. In the past 10 years, of 203 works presented, 129 were world premieres and 38 were musicals. The CAST uses an intensive three-step process to develop material. First, scripts are screened by the literary staff; some then pass into our Foundry Series of public readings. Selected scripts may then move into the third step, the Safe Harbor—staged, script-in-hand, work-in-progress, nonreviewed

The CAST Theatre. Gloria Mann, David Steen, Gene Lithgow and Mark Ruffalo in *Avenue A*. Photo: Ed Krieger.

presentations that lead ultimately to a mainstage production.

—*Ted Schmitt*

Note: During the 1989-90 season, Ted Schmitt served as artistic director.

PRODUCTIONS 1989-90

Conspicuous Consumption, Shawn Schepps; (D) Toby Reisz; (S) Andy Daley; (C) Kitty Murphy

Night Owls, Suzanne Lummis; (D) Deborah LaVine; (S) Robert Smith; (C) Kitty Murphy; (L) Robert Smith

Zombie Attack!, Justin Tanner and Andy Daley; (D) Justin Tanner and Andy Daley; (S) Andy Daley; (C) Maro Hakopian; (L) Dana J. Kilgore

Place, Robert Hummer; (D) Robert Hummer; (S) Robert Hummer; (C) Molly Cleator; (L) Erica Bradbury

Happytime X-Mas, Justin Tanner; (D) Justin Tanner; (S) Andy Daley; (L) Dana J. Kilgore

I Hate!, Michael Sargent; (D) Michael Sargent; (S) Courtenay Marvin; (C) Courtenay Marvin; (L) Sekia Billman

Canaan Land, Maurice Noel; (D) Joe Mays; (S) Andy Daley

Ruby Ruby Sam Sam, Stan Edleman; (D) Lee Garlington; (S) Andy Daley; (L) Kathi O'Donohue

Faultline, John Heaner; (D) Harvey Perr; (S) Andy Daley; (L) Erica Bradbury

Tremor Cordis, Joel K. Murray; (D) Mick Collins; (S) Andy Daley; (L) Laura Carter

My Crime, Michael Sargent; (D) Michael Sargent; (S) Eric Hansen; (C) Eric Hansen

PRODUCTIONS 1990-91

Zombie Attack!, Justin Tanner and Andy Daley; (D) Justin Tanner and Andy Daley; (S) Andy Daley; (C) Maro Hakopian; (L) Dana J. Kilgore

Babes, book: Bill Sawyer; music and lyrics: Brian Shucker; (D) Michael Michetti; (S) Andy Daley; (C) Scott Lane

Party Mix, Justin Tanner; (D) Justin Tanner; (S) Andy Daley

Masked Angel, Bruce Dale; (D) Paul Warner; (S) Steve Nelson; (C) Natacha Beyeler; (L) Ellen Lundquist

Love or Something Out on Highway 97, Connie Monaghan; (D) John DiFusco

Better Days, Richard Dresser; (D) Lisa James; (S) Andy Daley; (C) Vicki Sanchez; (L) Ilya Mindlin

Avenue A, David Steen; (D) Jim Holmes; (S) Andy Daley; (C) Patricia Wilson; (L) Ken Booth

B-Sides, Angelo Masino; (D) Andrew De Angelo; (S) Andy Daley

Center Stage

IRENE LEWIS
Acting Artistic Director

PETER W. CULMAN
Managing Director

700 North Calvert St.
Baltimore, MD 21202
(301) 685-3200 (bus.)
(301) 332-0033 (b.o.)

FOUNDED 1963
Community Arts Committee

SEASON
Oct.-June

FACILITIES
The Pearlstone Theater
Seating Capacity: 541
Stage: thrust

The Head Theater
Seating Capacity: 150-350
Stage: flexible

FINANCES
July 1, 1990-June 30, 1991
Expenses: $3,995,000

CONTRACTS
AEA LORT (B) and (C)

As the acting artistic director of Center Stage, I am interested in investigating the spirit of the great works of dramatic literature through highly theatrical productions of the classics, supplemented by daring and innovative new voices in contemporary playwriting. I hope to enlist a diverse and inquisitive audience that embraces works that are literate, intellectually challenging, bold and often disturbing. Happily, Center Stage is one theatre with two performance spaces, allowing us to suit the project to the venue, the idea to the space. Its endowment enables us to remain aggressive (even in this difficult climate) in the area of artist compensation and the commissioning of new projects. This flexibility offers some welcome relief from the situation in which the demands of traditional season selection (e.g., balanced subscription offerings) become *de facto* artistic policy.

—*Irene Lewis*

Note: During the 1989-90 and 1990-91 seasons, Stan Wojewodski, Jr. served as artistic director.

PRODUCTIONS 1989-90

Man and Superman, George Bernard Shaw; (D) Stan Wojewodski, Jr.; (S) Derek McLane; (C) Catherine Zuber; (L) Stephen Strawbridge

Miss Evers' Boys, David Feldshuh; (D) Irene Lewis; (S) Douglas Stein; (C) Catherine Zuber; (L) Pat Collins

The Film Society, Jon Robin Baitz; (D) Jackson Phippin; (S) Derek McLane; (C) Catherine Zuber; (L) Stephen Strawbridge

An Enemy of the People, Henrik Ibsen; trans: Rick Davis and Brian Johnston; (D) Stan Wojewodski, Jr.; (S) Christopher Barreca; (C) Marina Draghici; (L) Stephen Strawbridge

All's Well That Ends Well, William Shakespeare; (D) Stan Wojewodski, Jr.; (S) Derek McLane; (C) Catherine Zuber; (L) Robert Wierzel

The Making of Americans, book adapt: Leon Katz, from Gertrude Stein; music: Al Carmines; (D) Lawrence Kornfeld; (S) Marina Draghici; (C) Marina Draghici; (L) Clay Shirky

Center Stage. *The Heliotrope Bouquet by Scott Joplin & Louis Chauvin*. Photo: Richard Anderson.

Beckett: Short Works, Samuel Beckett; (D) Cheryl Faver and Jackson Phippin; (S) Marina Draghici; (C) Catherine Zuber; (L) Clay Shirky

PRODUCTIONS 1990-91

Ma Rainey's Black Bottom, August Wilson; (D) L. Kenneth Richardson; (S) Donald Eastman; (C) Mary Mease Warren; (L) Christopher Akerlind
O Pioneers!, book adapt and lyrics: Darrah Cloud, from Willa Cather; music: Kim D. Sherman; (D) Stan Wojewodski, Jr.; (S) Derek McLane; (C) Catherine Zuber; (L) Robert Wierzel
Candida, George Bernard Shaw; (D) Rick Davis; (S) Craig Clipper; (C) Mary Mease Warren; (L) Dennis Parichy
The Heliotrope Bouquet by Scott Joplin & Louis Chauvin, Eric Overmyer; (D) Stan Wojewodski, Jr.; (S) Christopher Barreca; (C) Catherine Zuber; (L) Richard Pilbrow
Twelfth Night, William Shakespeare; (D) Irene Lewis; (S) John Conklin; (C) Catherine Zuber; (L) Stephen Strawbridge
The Mystery of Irma Vep, Charles Ludlam; (D) Stan Wojewodski, Jr.; (S) Hugh Landwehr; (C) Robert Wojewodski; (L) Robert Wierzel

Center Theater

DAN LaMORTE
Artistic Director

RJ COLEMAN
General Manager

1346 West Devon Ave.
Chicago, IL 60660
(312) 508-0200 (bus.)
(312) 508-5422 (b.o.)

FOUNDED 1984
Dan LaMorte, Dale Calandra, Marc Vann, Carole Gutierrez, Eileen Manganaro

SEASON
Sept.-July

FACILITIES
Mainstage
Seating Capacity: 99
Stage: thrust

Studio
Seating Capacity: 30
Stage: flexible

FINANCES
Sept. 1, 1990-Aug. 31, 1991
Expenses: $294,450

CONTRACTS
AEA CAT

The Training Center for the Working Actor was developed to create a coherent and unified lifelong approach to the art and science of acting—Center Theater was born out of this dedication. Our repertory company presents both new and established material in a deliberately bold, imaginative manner, and explores all the elements of production to realize the potential of every individual work. Each is dealt with specifically—discovering the play's quality, molding it, designing it with concept and color, bringing it to life for the "first time." Our theatre and training program focus on the actor and the acting process to create exciting and risky theatre. The dream is to build an ensemble of talent—actors, directors, designers, writers—capable of bringing theatre to levels that are truthful and rare, so that risks can be taken to inspire artists and audiences alike.

—Dan LaMorte

PRODUCTIONS 1989-90

Hotel Universe, Philip Barry; (D) Dale Calandra; (S) Rob Hamilton; (C) Lynn Sandberg; (L) Chris Phillips
My Three Angels, Samuel Spewack and Bella Spewack; (D) Dan LaMorte; (S) Rob Hamilton; (C) Renee Starr-Liepins; (L) Chris Phillips
Lysistrata 2411 A.D., adapt: Dale Calandra and company, from Aristophanes; (D) Dale Calandra; (S) Rob Hamilton; (C) Rob Hamilton; (L) Chris Phillips
Fulfilled, Dan LaMorte; (D) Randi Jennifer Collins-Hard; (S) Sheryl Nieman; (C) J. Kevin Draves; (L) Richard G. Tatum
14 Times, Elizabeth Shepherd; (D) Dan LaMorte; (S) Sheryl Nieman; (C) J. Kevin Draves; (L) Richard G. Tatum
Just Call Me Bill, Charles Morgan; (D) Dan LaMorte; (S) Sheryl Nieman; (C) J. Kevin Draves; (L) Richard G. Tatum

Center Theater. Suzanne Carney and John McCormack in *Another Antigone*. Photo: Joanne Carney.

PRODUCTIONS 1990-91

Rum and Coke, Keith Reddin; (D) Dan LaMorte; (S) Rob Hamilton; (C) Lynn Sandberg; (L) Chris Phillips
The Lucky Spot, Beth Henley; (D) Norma Saldivar; (S) John Murbach; (C) Renee Starr-Liepins; (L) Chris Phillips
Two Gentlemen of Verona, William Shakespeare; (D) Dan LaMorte and Kathy Scambiatterra; (S) Richard Mahaney and Sheryl Nieman; (C) Lynn Sandberg; (L) Chris Phillips
The Black Tulip, book adapt and lyrics: Tracy Friedman, from Alexandre Dumas pere; music: Brian Lasser; (D) Dan LaMorte and Tracy Friedman; (S) Sheryl Nieman; (C) Ginger Driscoll; (L) Chris Phillips
First Comes Love..., Elizabeth Shepherd; (D) Dan LaMorte; (S) Richard Mahaney; (C) Kate Wester; (L) Kelly Heligas
Another Antigone, A.R. Gurney, Jr.; (D) John Carlile; (S) Richard Mahaney; (C) Mark Hughes; (L) Kelly Heligas

The Children's Theatre Company

JON CRANNEY
Artistic Director

GARY GISSELMAN
WENDY LEHR
Associate Artistic Directors

2400 Third Ave. S
Minneapolis, MN 55404
(612) 874-0500 (bus.)
(612) 874-0400 (b.o.)

FOUNDED 1961
Beth Linnerson

SEASON
Sept.-June

FACILITIES
Mainstage
Seating Capacity: 746
Stage: proscenium

Studio Theatre
Seating Capacity: 150
Stage: flexible

O'Shaughnessy Auditorium
Seating Capacity: 1,500
Stage: proscenium

FINANCES
July 1, 1990-June 30, 1991
Expenses: $4,900,486

CONTRACTS
AEA Guest Artist

The Children's Theatre Company is dedicated to the creation and presentation of new adaptations and original plays for young people and families, inspired by classic and contemporary sources. A rotating repertory season of seven mainstage productions is comprised of full-scale musicals, children's classics and literary dramas, created by its resident artists and artisans (80 full-time staff), who are complemented by numerous guest artists. National touring and international cultural exchanges enhance CTC's understanding of and its influence within the world theatre community. CTC also provides classroom/workshop training for children and adolescents, as well as intern-apprentice positions for young adults, culminating in appropriate performance opportunities with CTC's resident company. To maintain an artistic sanctuary and wellspring that is resourceful, responsive and responsible, and to provide an honest, reverent, relevant and challenging artistic experience for the young and youthful artist and audience is the legacy and continuing quest of the Children's Theatre Company.

—Jon Cranney

PRODUCTIONS 1989-90

Coyote Discovers America, book: Jim Lenfesty; music: Michael Sommers; lyrics: Michael Sommers and David Simmons; (D) Jon Cranney; (S) Stephan Olson; (C) David Kay Mickelsen; (L) Michael Murnane

The Story of Babar, the Little Elephant, adapt: Thomas W. Olson, from Jean de Brunhoff; (D) Myron Johnson; (S) Robert Braun; (C) Barry Robison; (L) Michael Murnane

Raggedy Ann and Andy, adapt: Constance Congdon, from Johnny Gruelle; (D) Myron Johnson; (S) William Schroder; (C) William Schroder; (L) Barry Browning

Cinderella, adapt: John B. Davidson, from Charles Perrault; (D) David Ira Goldstein; (S) Edward Haynes; (C) Gene Davis Buck; (L) Barry Browning

Tomie de Paola's Mother Goose, adapt: Constance Congdon, from Tomie de Paola; (D) Myron Johnson; (S) Steven Kennedy; (C) Tomie de Paola; (L) Barry Browning

Nancy Drew, adapt: Marisha Chamberlain; (D) Alan Shorter; (S) Hugh Landwehr; (C) William Schroder; (L) Barry Browning

The Hobbit, adapt: Thomas W. Olson, from J.R.R. Tolkien; (D) Jon Cranney; (S) Tom Butsch; (C) William Schroder; (L) Duane Schuler

PRODUCTIONS 1990-91

Madeline's Rescue, adapt: Constance Congdon, from Ludwig Bemelmans; music: Mel Marvin; lyrics: Constance Congdon; (D) Jon Cranney; (S) Ann Sheffield; (C) Ann Sheffield; (L) Stephen Strawbridge

Oliver Twist, adapt: Frederick Gaines, from Charles Dickens; (D) Gary Gisselman; (S) Michael C. Smith; (C) David Kay Mickelsen; (L) Stephen Strawbridge

Pippi Longstocking, book adapt: Thomas W. Olson and Truda Stockenstrom, from Astrid Lindgren; music: Roberta Carlson; lyrics: Roberta Carlson and Thomas W. Olson; (D) Brian Russell; (S) Don Yunker; (C) Marsha Wiest-Hines; (L) Charles D. Craun

Peter Pan, adapt: Frederick Gaines, from James M. Barrie; (D) Robert Lanchester; (S) Peter Harrison; (C) William Schroder; (L) Dawn Chiang

Cinderella, adapt: John B. Davidson, from Charles Perrault; (D) Wendy Lehr; (S) Edward Haynes; (C) Gene Davis Buck; (L) Barry Browning

Lyle the Crocodile, adapt: Kevin Kling, from Bernard Waber; music: Michael Koerner; lyrics: Kevin Kling; (D) David Ira Goldstein; (S) William Bloodgood; (C) Michael Olich; (L) Michael Murnane

A Midsummer Night's Dream, William Shakespeare; adapt: Constance Congdon; (D) Jon Cranney; (S) William Schroder; (C) William Schroder; (L) Michael Murnane

Pinocchio, adapt: Timothy Mason, from Carlo Collodi; (D) Wendy Lehr; (S) Steven Kennedy; (C) Ricia Birturk; (L) Don Darnutzer

he Children's Theatre Company. Katherine Ferrand, Libby Winters and Vance Holmes in *Madeline's Rescue*. Photo: Giannetti.

Childsplay, Inc.

DAVID SAAR
Artistic Director

GARY BACAL
Managing Director

Box 517
Tempe, AZ 85280
(602) 350-8101 (bus.)
(602) 350-8112 (b.o.)

FOUNDED 1977
David Saar

SEASON
Sept.-May

FACILITIES
Tempe Performing Arts Center
Seating Capacity: 300
Stage: flexible

Herberger Theater Center
Seating Capacity: 300
Stage: proscenium

Scottsdale Center for the Arts
Seating Capacity: 800
Stage: proscenium

FINANCES
July 1, 1990-June 30, 1991
Expenses: $415,764

Childsplay was founded by a group of artists who were in love with the process of theatre, and convinced that it could make a difference in the lives of young people. We exist to: create theatre so strikingly original in form or content, or both, that it instills in young people an eduring awe, love and respect for the medium. In so doing we work to preserve imagination and wonder, those hallmarks of childhood which are the keys to our future. It is vital that our audiences be exposed to theatre which entertains, but also challenges and provokes, providing insights which can impact and influence "real-life" problems and possibilities. Our search for material leads us to new interpretations of classic literature, ongoing commissions of new works by regional, national and international playwrights, and company-developed explorations.

—David Saar

PRODUCTIONS 1989-90

Embroidered Yarns, book: Monica Long Ross; music and lyrics: Alan Ruch; (D) Mark DeMichele; (S) John Stark; (C) Rebecca Akins; (L) Jon Gentry

The Bear That Wasn't, adapt: Erin Cressida Wilson, from Frank Tashlin; (D) David Saar; (S) Jeff Thomson; (C) Rebecca Powell; (L) Luetta Newnam

The Velveteen Rabbit, adapt: Brian Clark, from Margery Williams; music: Alan Ruch; (D) David Saar; (S) Jeff Thomson; (C) Rebecca Akins; (L) Marc Riske

Just So Stories, adapt: Larry Pressgrove, from Rudyard Kipling; music: Ross Care; (D) Larry Pressgrove; (S) John Stark;

Childsplay, Inc. Sandra Bussey-Smith, Lillie Richardson and Jon Gentry in *Embroidered Yarns*. Photo: Renata Golden.

(C) Rebecca Powell; (L) Tom Semans

The Masquerade of Life/La Mascarada de la Vida, book: Mary Hall Surface; music and lyrics: Zarco Guerrero and Allen Lea; (D) David Saar; (S) Jeff Thomson; (C) Rebecca Akins; (L) Marc Riske

PRODUCTIONS 1990-91

Just So Stories, adapt: Larry Pressgrove, from Rudyard Kipling; (D) Larry Pressgrove; (S) John Stark; (C) Rebecca Powell; (L) Tom Semans

Ama and the White Crane, Maureen A. O'Toole; (D) David Saar; (S) Jeff Thomson; (C) Pam Robertson; (L) Marc Riske

The Masquerade of Life/La Mascarada de la Vida, book: Mary Hall Surface; music and lyrics: Zarco Guerrero and Allen Lea; (D) David Saar; (S) Jeff Thomson; (C) Rebecca Akins; (L) Marc Riske

The Velveteen Rabbit, adapt: Brian Clark, from Margery Williams; music: Alan Ruch; (D) David Saar; (S) Jeff Thomson; (C) Rebecca Akins; (L) Marc Riske

Mr. Jones Lives Alone, Monica Long Ross; (D) Monica Long Ross; (S) Ronn Stanley; (C) Ronn Stanley; (L) Jere Luisi

Through the Looking Glass, book adapt: Ross Care, from Lewis Carroll; music: Ross Care; additional lyrics: Charles Leayman; (D) Michael Barnard; (S) Jeff Thomson; (C) Rebecca Akins; (L) Luetta Newnam

Child's Play Touring Theatre

VICTOR PODAGROSI
Artistic Director

JUNE PODAGROSI
Executive Director

2650 West Belden Ave.
2nd Floor, Chicago IL 60647
(312) 235-8911

FOUNDED 1979
June Podagrosi, Victor Podagrosi

SEASON
Jan.-Dec.

FINANCES
Sept. 30, 1990-Aug. 31, 1991
Expenses: $488,000

Child's Play Touring Theatre is a professional theatre for young audiences, dedicated to performing stories and poems written by children. Every year we present works by hundreds of young poets, essayists, and short-story writers, discovering exciting theatre in their imaginations. As the raw material for theatre, we find literature written by children to be technically demanding and artistically satisfying. Children create delightfully bizarre characters and unusual plot twists; their writing can also display startling candor and sharp insight when they address social issues and private concerns. We believe that every theatre dedicated to serving children has a part in shaping the audiences of the future. Child's Play takes that goal one step further—we're working to inspire the artists of the future. As writers, children have a unique voice that should be heard. Child's Play Touring Theatre provides a stage where that voice can be shared, examined and treasured.

—*Victor Podagrosi*

PRODUCTIONS 1989-90

Write On!, company-developed; (D) Victor Podagrosi; (S) Richard Harris and Michael Thomas; (C) Deborah Miller and Christine Birt

New Voices, company-developed; (D) Victor Podagrosi; (S) Richard Harris and Michael Thomas; (C) Deborah Miller and Christine Birt

Animal Tales & Dinosaur Scales, company-developed; (D) Victor Podagrosi; (S) Richard Harris and Michael Thomas; (C) Deborah Miller and Christine Birt

The Christmas That Almost Wasn't, company-developed; (D) Victor Podagrosi; (S) Richard Harris and Michael Thomas; (C) Deborah Miller

Fun!, company-developed; (D) Victor Podagrosi; (S) Richard Harris and Michael Thomas; (C) Deborah Miller and Christine Birt

Writing Is...Child's Play, company-developed; (D) Victor Podagrosi

PRODUCTIONS 1990-91

New Voices, company-developed; (D) Victor Podagrosi; (S) Michael Thomas and Jeff Richmond; (C) Deborah Miller

Me, a Scientist?, company-developed; (D) Victor Podagrosi; (S) Michael Thomas

Do the Write Thing, company-developed; (D) Victor Podagrosi; (S) Michael Thomas and Jeff Richmond; (C) Deborah Miller

The Christmas That Almost Wasn't, company-developed; (D) Victor Podagrosi; (S) Michael Thomas; (C) Deborah Miller

Tales 'N Scales, company-developed; (D) Victor Podagrosi; (S) Michael Thomas and Jeff Richmond; (C) Deborah Miller

Writing Is...Child's Play, company-developed; (D) Victor Podagrosi

Cincinnati Playhouse in the Park

KATHLEEN NORRIS
Managing Director

Box 6537
Cincinnati, OH 45206
(513) 345-2242 (bus.)
(513) 421-3888 (b.o.)

FOUNDED 1960
Community Members

Child's Play Touring Theatre. Vee Ringo, Renee Lockett-Lawson and Steve Emerson in *Do the Write Thing*.

Cincinnati Playhouse in the Park. Renoly Santiago, Charles Sanchez, Enrique Munoz, Keith Robert Bennett and Trevor Jackson in *Stand-Up Tragedy*. Photo: Sandy Underwood.

SEASON
Sept.-Aug.

FACILITIES
Robert S. Marx Theatre
Seating Capacity: 629
Stage: thrust

Thompson Shelterhouse Theatre
Seating Capacity: 220
Stage: thrust

FINANCES
Sept. 1, 1990-Aug. 31, 1991
Expenses: $3,952,915

CONTRACTS
AEA LORT (B) and (D)

Cincinnati Playhouse is dedicated to creating an enlivening interchange between artists and audience through presentation of a diverse range of classics and new works. Plans are now underway to further expand and diversify programming through an occasional series of dance, performance art, play and poetry readings, and special events. The annual Lois and Richard Rosenthal New Play Prize provides special support to emerging playwrights and complements a 10-play season that is deliberately eclectic. The Playhouse intern company has its own performance schedule for schools in a three-state region and for adult audiences, as well as taking smaller roles in mainstage productions. The Playhouse feels a special responsibility to ensure adventurous theatre of the highest standard for the broadest audience. It is a responsibility we can approach joyously, for the work we do and the experience we seek to share create new energies each time.

—*Kathleen Norris*

Note: During the 1989-90 and 1990-91 seasons, Worth Gardner served as artistic director.

PRODUCTIONS 1989-90

Les Liaisons Dangereuses, Christopher Hampton, from Choderlos de Laclos; (D) Jonathan Eaton; (S) Paul Shortt; (C) Eduardo Sicangco; (L) James H. Gage
Pump Boys and Dinettes, John Foley, Mark Hardwick, Debra Monk, Cass Morgan, John Schimmel and Jim Wann; (D) William S. Morris; (S) Jay Depenbrock; (C) Jo Wimer; (L) Kirk Bookman
Treasure Island, adapt: Ara Watson, from Robert Louis Stevenson; (D) Worth Gardner; (S) Paul Shortt; (C) D. Bartlett Blair; (L) Kirk Bookma
¿De Donde?, Mary Gallagher; (D) Sam Blackwell; (S) Jay Depenbrock; (C) Laura Crow; (L) Kirk Bookman
Fences, August Wilson; (D) Luther Goins; (S) Patricia Woodbridge; (C) Muriel Stockdale; (L) Kirk Bookman
Frankie and Johnny in the Clair de Lune, Terrence McNally; (D) Sam Blackwell; (S) Joseph P. Tilford; (C) Jo Wimer; (L) Kirk Bookman
The Boys Next Door, Tom Griffin; (D) Worth Gardner; (S) Paul Shortt; (C) D. Bartlett Blair; (L) Kirk Bookman
Fanshen, David Hare, from William Hinton; (D) Sam Blackwell; (S) Linda Carmichael Rose; (C) D. Bartlett Blair; (L) Kirk Bookman
How the Other Half Loves, Alan Ayckbourn; (D) David Gately; (S) Eduardo Sicangco; (C) Eduardo Sicangco; (L) Kirk Bookman
Club, The Flying Karamazov Brothers; (D) The Flying Karamazov Brothers; (L) Peter Dansky

PRODUCTIONS 1990-91

Loot, Joe Orton; (D) Margaret Booker; (S) Patricia Woodbridge; (C) D. Bartlett Blair; (L) Kirk Bookman
Burn This, Lanford Wilson; (D) Jay E. Raphael; (S) Joseph P. Tilford; (C) Cindy Witherspoon; (L) Kirk Bookman
The Wizard of Oz, book adapt: Frank Gabrielson, from L. Frank Baum; music and lyrics: Harold Arlen and E.Y. Harburg; additional music: Worth Gardner; (D) Worth Gardner; (S) Paul Shortt; (C) Paul Shortt; (L) Kirk Bookman
Educating Rita, Willy Russell; (D) Dorothy Robinson; (S) Jay Depenbrock; (C) Jo Wimer; (L) Kirk Bookman
A Shayna Maidel, Barbara Lebow; (D) Charles Richter; (S) Joseph P. Tilford; (C) Eduardo Sicangco; (L) Kirk Bookman
Stand-Up Tragedy, Bill Cain; (D) Jay E. Raphael; (S) Linda Carmichael Rose; (C) Fay Conway; (L) Kirk Bookman
Other People's Money, Jerry Sterner; (D) Worth Gardner; (S) Eduardo Sicangco; (C) Eduardo Sicangco; (L) Kirk Bookman
Lost Electra, Bruce E. Rodgers; (D) Margaret Booker; (S) Joseph P. Tilford; (C) Scott Chambliss; (L) Kirk Bookman
The Mesmerist, Ara Watson; (D) Worth Gardner; (S) Marjorie Bradley Kellogg; (C) Laura Crow; (L) Kirk Bookman
The Mystery of Irma Vep, Charles Ludlam; (D) David Holgrieve; (S) Jay Depenbrock; (C) Martha Hally; (L) James Fulton

Circle Repertory Company

TANYA BEREZIN
Artistic Director

TERRENCE DWYER
Managing Director

161 Ave. of the Americas
New York, NY 10013
(212) 691-3210 (bus.)
(212) 924-7100 (b.o.)

FOUNDED 1969
Lanford Wilson, Robert Thirkield, Marshall W. Mason, Tanya Berezin

SEASON
Sept.-June

FACILITIES
Circle Repertory Theatre
Seating Capacity: 160
Stage: flexible

FINANCES
July 1, 1990-June 30, 1991
Expenses: $1,809,466

CONTRACTS
AEA Off Broadway

Circle Repertory Company comprises a family of more than 200 theatre artists who share a commitment to excellence and a vision of truth and humanity in the theatre. Now in its third decade, Circle Rep has become a national resource of new plays, producing more than 100 that have subsequently been presented at scores of professional theatres in all 50 states and many foreign countries. Dedicated to developing American works for the stage, Circle Rep continues to expand its definition of a lyric realistic style to include a multiplicity of American voices and world visions. Our developmental process, which includes a writers and directors lab, as well as three series of staged readings, allows us to challenge our mature theatre artists to explore new areas of their art while proceeding with an active search for new talent. It is this collaboration by an ensemble of artists to create a vibrant and vital theatrical experience that has become the source of growth and creative achievement for the company over the last two decades.

—*Tanya Berezin*

PRODUCTIONS 1989-90

Beside Herself, Joe Pintauro; (D) John Bishop; (S) John Lee Beatty; (C) Ann Emonts; (L) Dennis Parichy

Sunshine, William Mastrosimone; (D) Marshall W. Mason; (S) David Potts; (C) Susan Lyall; (L) Dennis Parichy

Imagining Brad, Peter Hedges; (D) Joe Mantello; (S) Loy Arcenas; (C) Laura Cunningham; (L) Dennis Parichy

Prelude to a Kiss, Craig Lucas; (D) Norman Rene; (S) Loy Arcenas; (C) Walker Hicklin; (L) Debra J. Kletter

Each Day Dies With Sleep, Jose Rivera; (D) Roberta Levitow; (S) Tom Kamm; (C) Tina Cantu Navarro; (L) Robert Wierzel

PRODUCTIONS 1990-91

The Colorado Catechism, Vincent J. Cardinal; (D) Mark Ramont; (S) James Youmans; (C) David C. Woolard; (L) Pat Dignan

Love Diatribe, Harry Kondoleon; (D) Jorge Cacheiro; (S) G.W. Mercier; (C) Walker Hicklin; (L) Dennis Parichy

Road to Nirvana, Arthur Kopit; (D) James Simpson; (S) Andrew Jackness; (C) Ann Roth; (L) Scott Zielinski

Walking the Dead, Keith Curran; (D) Mark Ramont; (S) Tom Kamm; (C) Toni-Leslie James; (L) Kenneth Posner

The Balcony Scene, Wil Calhoun; (D) Michael Warren Powell; (S) Kevin Joseph Roach; (C) Thomas L. Keller; (L) Dennis Parichy

Circle Repertory Company. Barnard Hughes, Mary-Louise Parker, Debra Monk and Alec Baldwin in *Prelude to a Kiss*. Photo: Bob Marshak.

City Theatre Company

MARC MASTERSON
Producing Director

CHARLES HARRINGTON
General Manager

57 South 13th St.
Pittsburgh, PA 15203
(412) 431-4400 (bus.)
(412) 431-4900 (b.o.)

FOUNDED 1973
City of Pittsburgh

City Theatre Company. Iva Jean Saraceni and Morgan Lund in *Le Bourgeois Avant-Garde*. Photo: Sue Ellen Fitzsimmons.

SEASON
Oct.-Aug.

FACILITIES
City Theatre
Seating Capacity: 275
Stage: flexible

Hartwood Acres Summer Theatre
Seating Capacity: 275
Stage: thrust

FINANCES
July 1, 1990-June 30, 1991
Expenses: $550,000

CONTRACTS
AEA SPT

City Theatre is interested in developing new American plays, and in producing works of substance which deal with ideas relevant to contemporary values and cultures. The company has developed an ongoing relationship with a loosely defined ensemble of actors, directors and designers over the last 11 years. For its 1991-92 season, City Theatre moves into a new facility in Pittsburgh's South Side neighborhood, taking a major step toward greater fulfillment of its mission. City Theatre produces programming for all ages and socioeconomic backgrounds. It is founded in deep respect for the artist, as well as the audience, and attempts to join the needs of both through the art form. City Theatre's programs include a five-play subscription series; an active new script development program including workshops, staged readings and full productions of new plays; the Playworks street theatre program, which commissions new scripts each year for performances for inner-city youth; and a summer season at Hartwood Acres Park in Allegheny County.

—*Marc Masterson*

PRODUCTIONS 1989-90

American Buffalo, David Mamet; (D) Richard Keitel; (S) Tony Ferrieri; (C) Peter Harrigan; (L) Tom Morgan

The Colored Museum, George C. Wolfe; (D) Clinton Turner Davis; (S) William O'Donnell; (C) Peter Harrigan; (L) William O'Donnell

Harry and Claire, Jaime Meyer; (D) Scott T. Cummings; (S) Tony

Ferrieri; (C) Lorraine Venberg; (L) Bob Steineck

Incommunicado, Tom Dulack; (D) Jed Allen Harris; (S) Henry Heymann; (C) Peter Harrigan; (L) Jean-Pierre Nutini

Cole, book: Alan Strachan and Benny Green; music and lyrics: Cole Porter; (D) Tome Cousin; (S) Tony Ferrieri; (C) Sue O'Neill; (L) Bob Steineck

T Bone N Weasel, Jon Klein; (D) Marc Masterson; (S) Tony Ferrieri; (C) Sue O'Neill; (L) Joel P. Blanchard

PRODUCTIONS 1990-91

Daytrips, Jo Carson; (D) Susan Chapek; (S) William O'Donnell; (C) Lorraine Venberg; (L) William O'Donnell

Le Bourgeois Avant-Garde, Charles Ludlam; (D) Marc Masterson and Jed Allen Harris; (S) Tony Ferrieri; (C) Robert C.T. Steele; (L) Emanuel Treeson

Steel Kiss, Robin Fulford; (D) Jed Allen Harris; (S) Tony Ferrieri; (C) Melinda S. Miller; (L) R C Baker

Seeking Wild, Christopher Durang; (D) Jed Allen Harris; (S) Tony Ferrieri; (C) Melinda S. Miller; (L) R C Baker

The Road to Mecca, Athol Fugard; (D) Larry John Meyers; (S) Charles McCarry; (C) Lorraine Venberg; (L) William O'Donnell

Theatre-Sports, conceived: Keith Johnstone; (D) Tim Carryer and Babs Bailey; (S) Tony Ferrieri; (C) Melinda S. Miller; (L) Bob Steineck

Clarence Brown Theatre Company

THOMAS P. COOKE
Artistic Director

MARGARET FERGUSON
General Manager

206 McClung Tower
Knoxville, TN 37996
(615) 974-6011 (bus.)
(615) 974-5161 (b.o.)

FOUNDED 1974
Anthony Quayle, Ralph G. Allen

SEASON
Sept.-June

FACILITIES
Clarence Brown Theatre
Seating Capacity: 600
Stage: proscenium

Clarence Brown Theatre Lab
Seating Capacity: 125
Stage: thrust

Carousel Theatre
Seating Capacity: 350
Stage: flexible

FINANCES
July 1, 1990-June 30, 1991
Expenses: $622,700

CONTRACTS
AEA LORT (D)

The Clarence Brown Theatre Company is the professional component of the theatre program of the University of Tennessee and is intended to provide the university community and the American southeast region with theatre of the highest caliber. The company has a distinguished tradition of presenting the finest professional theatre and is committed to the development of new plays. It has brought to regional audiences such performances as Anthony Quayle in *Macbeth*, Simon Ward in Isherwood's *A Meeting by the River*, and Zoe Caldwell and Dame Judith Anderson in *Medea*. Duing the past two seasons, the company has participated in the development of an International Theatre Research Center at UT.

—*Thomas P. Cooke*

PRODUCTIONS 1989-90

Camille, adapt: Pam Gems, from Alexandre Dumas fils; music: James Brimer; (D) Albert J. Harris; (S) Anita Stewart; (C) Johann Stegmeir; (L) Marcus Dilliard

Crimes of the Heart, Beth Henley; (D) Marcia Mary Cook; (C) Chrissanna Diamanti; (L) Julie Booth

Heathen Valley, Romulus Linney; (D) Thomas P. Cooke; (S) Robert Cothran; (C) Marianne Custer; (L) L.J. DeCuir

The Winter's Tale, William Shakespeare; (D) Maurice Daniels; (S) Margo McNerney; (C) Bill Black; (L) John Horner

A Christmas Carol, adapt: Albert J. Harris, from Charles Dickens; (D) Thomas P. Cooke and Albert J. Harris; (S) Robert Cothran; (C) Bill Black; (L) John Horner

On Golden Pond, Ernest Thompson; (D) Robert Mashburn; (S) Robert Cothran; (C) Marianne Custer; (L) John Horner

Nine, adapt: Mario Fratti; book: Arthur Kopit; music and lyrics: Maury Yeston; (D) Albert J. Harris; (S) William J. Windsor; (C) Bill Black; (L) Julie Booth

PRODUCTIONS 1990-91

Steel Magnolias, Robert Harling; (D) Robert Mashburn; (S) Marianne Custer; (C) Marianne Custer; (L) L.J. DeCuir

To Kill a Mockingbird, adapt: Christopher Sergel, from Harper Lee; (D) Albert J. Harris; (S) Jim Moran; (C) Bill Black; (L) Julie Booth

A Christmas Carol, adapt: Albert J. Harris, from Charles Dickens; (D) Thomas P. Cooke and Albert J. Harris; (S) Robert Cothran; (C) Bill Black; (L) John Horner

Mr. Roosevelt's Train Never Got Here, Albert J. Harris; (D) Thomas P. Cooke; (S) Jim Moran; (C) Bill Black; (L) L.J. DeCuir

Blood Wedding, Federico Garcia Lorca; trans: David Johnston; (D) Gerard Mulgrew; (S) Robert Cothran; (C) Marianne Custer; (L) John Horner

The Skin of our Teeth, Thornton Wilder; (D) Robert Mashburn; (S) Jim Moran; (C) Chrissanna Diamanti; (L) Julie Booth

Into the Woods, book: James Lapine; music and lyrics: Stephen Sondheim; (D) Albert J. Harris; (S) Robert Cothran; (C) Bill Black; (L) John Horner

Clarence Brown Theatre Company. Samuel Washington and Robert Mashburn in *A Christmas Carol*. Photo: University of Tennessee

The Cleveland Play House

JOSEPHINE R. ABADY
Artistic Director

DEAN R. GLADDEN
Managing Director

Box 1989
Cleveland, OH 44106
(216) 795-7010 (bus.)
(216) 795-7000 (b.o.)

FOUNDED 1915
Raymond O'Neill

SEASON
Oct.-June

FACILITIES
Kenyon C. Bolton Theatre
Seating Capacity: 612
Stage: proscenium

Francis E. Drury Theatre
Seating Capacity: 503
Stage: proscenium

Charles S. Brooks Theatre
Seating Capacity: 159
Stage: proscenium

FINANCES
July 1, 1990-June 30, 1991
Expenses: $6,221,653

CONTRACTS
AEA LORT (C) and AEA TYA

The Cleveland Play House is experiencing a renaissance. With emphasis on new works and new ways of presenting the classics, and with our concentration on American works, more than half of our resources are allocated to new plays. The Play House is a cultural leader in the revitalization of its surrounding neighborhood. But physical recovery is only one part of the solution—theatre begins and ends with people. One of our strongest imperatives is to offer work that appeals to all segments of our community, strengthening the bonds with our supporters while reaching out to new and lost audiences. Our obligation to the artists who work here is to provide them with an environment that fosters creativity and experimentation, participation and commitment, and an audience that is ready to be an active partner in creating theatre. For as we sit together in the dark—laughing, crying and experiencing live performance—we discover the best that we are as human beings.

—Josephine R. Abady

The Cleveland Play House. Marlo Thomas and Chiara Peacock in *The Effect of Gamma Rays on Man-in-the-Moon Marigolds*. Photo: Roger Mastroianni.

PRODUCTIONS 1989-90

Stem of a Briar, Beddow Hatch; (D) Larry Arrick; (S) David Potts; (C) Deborah Shaw; (L) Richard Winkler

New Music (***August Snow***, ***Night Dance*** and ***Better Days***), Reynolds Price; (D) David Esbjornson (*August Snow* and *Night Dance*); (D) Josephine R. Abady (*Better Days*); (S) Dan Conway; (C) C.L. Hundley; (L) John Hastings

The Man Who Came to Dinner, George S. Kaufman and Moss Hart; (D) Roger T. Danforth; (S) Dan Conway; (C) C.L. Hundley; (L) John Hastings

Only Kidding, Jim Geoghan; (D) Larry Arrick; (S) Karen Schultz; (C) Patricia E. Doherty; (L) Dennis Parichy

Fences, August Wilson; (D) Tazewell Thompson; (S) Dan Conway; (C) C.L. Hundley; (L) John Hastings

Mama Drama, Leslie Ayvazian, Donna Daley, Christine Farrell and Ann Sachs; (D) John David Lutz; (S) Dan Conway; (C) C.L. Hundley; (L) John Hastings

The Cocktail Party, A.R. Gurney, Jr.; (D) Margaret Booker; (S) Ken Foy; (C) John Carver Sullivan; (L) Norbert U. Kolb

The March on Russia, David Storey; (D) Josephine R. Abady; (S) Marjorie Bradley Kellogg; (C) Linda Fisher; (L) Marc B. Weiss

PRODUCTIONS 1990-91

Heart's Desire, book adapt: Stuart Dybek, Beverly Lowry, Armistead Maupin and Treva Silverman; music and lyrics: Glen Roven; (D) Jack Hofsiss; (S) Kevin Rigdon; (C) Michael Krass; (L) Beverly Emmons

The Effect of Gamma Rays on Man-in-the-Moon Marigolds, Paul Zindel; (D) Larry Arrick; (S) David Potts; (C) C.L. Hundley; (L) Ann G. Wrightson

Harvey, Mary Chase; (D) Melvin Bernhardt; (S) Steven Rubin; (C) Steven Rubin; (L) Marc B. Weiss

Bravo, Caruso!, William Luce; (D) Peter Mark Schifter; (S) David Potts; (C) C.L. Hundley; (L) Ann G. Wrightson

Say Zebra, Sherry Coman; (D) Michael Breault; (S) David Potts; (C) C.L. Hundley; (L) Richard Winkler

By the Pool, Stewart Conn; (D) Josephine R. Abady; (S) David Potts; (C) C.L. Hundley; (L) Richard Winkler

You Touched Me!, Tennessee Williams and Donald Windham; (D) Josephine R. Abady; (S) David Potts; (C) C.L. Hundley; (L) Marc B. Weiss

Abyssinia, book adapt: James Racheff and Ted Kociolek, from Joyce Carol Thomas; music: Ted Kociolek; lyrics: James Racheff; (D) Tazewell Thompson; (S) Donald Eastman; (C) Paul Tazewell; (L) Allen Lee Hughes

Frankie and Johnny in the Clair de Lune, Terrence McNally; (D) Lee Costello; (S) Norbert U. Kolb; (C) Mimi Maxmen; (L) Norbert U. Kolb

Cornerstone Theater Company

BILL RAUCH
Artistic Director

ALISON CAREY
Founding Director

General Delivery
Norcatur, KS 67653
(913) 693-4334

FOUNDED 1986
Alison Carey, Bill Rauch

SEASON
Jan.-Dec.

FINANCES
July 1, 1990-June 30, 1991
Expenses: $537,750

Cornerstone Theater Company works alone as a professional ensemble, and in collaboration with ethnically and economically diverse communities across the United States. All of our productions are epic interactions between specific noncontemporary works of dramatic literature and specific American

Cornerstone Theater Company. Ashby Semple, Trina Darby and Wanda Daniels in *Three Sisters From West Virginia*. Photo: Benajah Cobb.

communities: Moliere's disintegrating and combative families in the Kansas farmland, Shakespeare's civil strife in the segregated streets of Mississippi, Aeschylus's ancient rituals on the modern American Indian reservation. By writing local concerns into the script, by sewing local color into the costumes, by rehearsing local actors into the roles, we work to open people's minds and hearts to plays which have been traditionally closed to them. We work to help build new, inclusive American theatre. Company members are: Amy Brenneman, Timothy Banker, James Bundy, Alison Carey, Benajah Cobb, Peter Howard, Mary-Ann Greanier, Lynn Jeffries, Christopher Moore, Sabrina Peck, Bill Rauch, David Reiffel and Ashby Semple.

—Bill Rauch

PRODUCTIONS 1989-90

Three Sisters from West Virginia, adapt: company; trans: Maria M. Belaeff-Ianovsky, from Anton Chekhov; music and lyrics: David Feiffel; (D) Bill Rauch; (S) Lynn Jeffries; (C) Lynn Jeffries; (L) Mary-Ann Greanier

The Video Store Owner's Significant Other, adapt: company and Dyann Simile; trans: James Graham-Lujan and Richard L. O'Connell, from Federico Garcia Lorca; (D) Bill Rauch; (S) Lynn Jeffries; (C) Lynn Jeffries; (L) Mary-Ann Greanier

Pier Gynt, adapt: company; trans: Rolf Fjelde, from Henrik Ibsen; music and lyrics: David Reiffel; (D) Bill Rauch; (S) Benajah Cobb; (C) Lynn Jeffries; (L) Mary-Ann Greanier

A Midsummer Night's Dream, William Shakespeare; (D) Bill Rauch; (S) Lynn Jeffries; (C) Lynn Jeffries; (L) Benajah Cobb and David Reiffel

I Can't Pay the Rent, company-developed; music and lyrics: David Reiffel; (D) Bill Rauch; (S) Lynn Jeffries; (C) Lynn Jeffries; (L) Mary-Ann Greanier

PRODUCTIONS 1990-91

The Video Store Owner's Significant Other, adapt: company and Dyann Simile; trans: James Graham-Lujan and Richard L. O'Connell, from Federico Garcia Lorca; music and lyrics: David Reiffel; (D) Bill Rauch; (S) Lynn Jeffries; (C) Lynn Jeffries; (L) Mary-Ann Greanier

The Winter's Tale: An Interstate Adventure, adapt: company, from William Shakespeare; music and lyrics: David Reiffel; (D) Bill Rauch; (S) Lynn Jeffries; (C) Lynn Jeffries and Jeanne E. Amis; (L) Mary-Ann Greanier

The Coterie

JEFF CHURCH
Artistic Director

KIMBERLY A. INGELS
Executive Director

2450 Grand Ave.
Kansas City, MO 64108
(816) 474-6785 (bus.)
(816) 474-6552 (b.o.)

FOUNDED 1979
Judith Yeckel, Vicky Lee

SEASON
Jan.-Dec.

FACILITIES
Seating Capacity: 220-234
Stage: flexible

FINANCES
Jan. 1, 1990-Dec. 31, 1990
Expenses: $398,072

The Coterie is a professional theatre dedicated to presenting theatre for all ages that educates as well as entertains. By producing a wide range of material, be it classic or contemporary, original scripts or adaptations of classic works of literature, we strive to break through existing stereotypes of what children want or can comprehend—to present material which challenges traditional views of theatre for young audiences and which opens lines of communication among races, sexes and generations.

—Jeff Church

Note: During the 1990 season, Pamela Sterling served as artistic director.

PRODUCTIONS 1990

Animal Farm, book adapt: Peter Hall, from George Orwell; music: Richard Peaslee; lyrics: Adrian Mitchell; (D) Ross Freese; (S) Bruce Hermans; (C) Shelly McKnight; (L) Randy Winder

Most Valuable Player, Mary Hall Surface and California Theatre Center; (D) Pamela Sterling; (S) Gary Mosby; (C) Joel B. Hoy; (L) Art Kent

The Ugly Duckling, book adapt: Pamela Sterling, from Hans Christian Andersen; music and lyrics: Chris Limber; (D) Linda Ade Brand; (S) Laura L. Burkhart; (C) Wendy Harms; (L) Art Kent

Laughter in the Rafters, Jay Cady, Leslie Seifert-Cady, Peter Nicolaus and Carol Comer; (S) Laura L. Burkhart; (C) Wendy Harms; (L) Art Kent

The Adventures of Nate the Great, adapt: Pamela Sterling, from Marjorie Weinman Sharmat; (D) Brad Shaw; (S) Laura L. Burkhart; (C) Brad Shaw; (L) Art Kent

Doors, Suzan Zeder; (D) Lisa Cordes; (S) Atif Rome; (C) Joel B. Hoy; (L) Greg Westfall

Winnie the Pooh, adapt: Kristen Sergel, from A.A. Milne; (D) Linda Ade Brand; (S) Laura L. Burkhart; (C) Catherine Hirner; (L) Greg Westfall

The Coterie. Matthew Rapport, Annie Kellogg, Susan Parker and Daniel Barnett in *Amber Waves*. Photo: Kimberly Ingels.

PRODUCTIONS 1991

Amber Waves, James Still; (D) Lisa Cordes; (S) Laura L. Burkhart; (C) Joel B. Hoy; (L) Greg Westfall

Amelia Lives, Laura Annawyn Shamas; (D) Jeff Church; (S) Brad Shaw; (C) Brad Shaw; (L) Art Kent

Dinosaurus, Edward Mast and Lenore Bensinger; (D) Jeff Church; (S) Laura L. Burkhart; (C) Laura L. Burkhart; (L) Art Kent

Charlotte's Web, adapt: Josephine Robinette, from E.B. White; (D) Jeff Church; (S) Laura L. Burkhart; (C) Mary Traylor; (L) Art Kent

The Secret Garden, adapt: Pamela Sterling, from Frances Hodgson Burnett; (D) Ross Freese; (S) Howard Jones; (C) Gayla Voss; (L) Art Kent

A Woman Called Truth, Sandra Fenichel Asher; (D) Brad Shaw; (S) Brad Shaw; (C) Brad Shaw; (L) Greg Westfall

Winnie the Pooh, adapt: Kristen Sergel, from A.A. Milne; (D) Linda Ade Brand; (S) Laura L. Burkhart; (C) Brad Shaw; (L) Greg Westfall

Dennis: The Musical, book adapt: Ernest Chambers, from Hank Ketcham; music: Doug Katsaros; lyrics: Richard Engquist and Ernest Chambers; (D) Jeff Church; (S) Howard Jones; (C) Gayla Voss; (L) Rob Murphy

Court Theatre

NICHOLAS RUDALL
Executive Director

SANDRA KARUSCHAK
Managing Director

5535 South Ellis Ave.
Chicago, IL 60637
(312) 702-7005 (bus.)
(312) 753-4472 (b.o.)

FOUNDED 1955
Nicholas Rudall

SEASON
Sept.-June

FACILITIES
Abelson Auditorium
Seating Capacity: 251
Stage: thrust

FINANCES
July 1, 1990-June 30, 1991
Expenses: $1,192,461

CONTRACTS
AEA CAT

Court Theatre presents a repertoire of breadth and diversity—both cultural and theatrical. We recreate the masterworks of the classics and bring to life the significant works of other cultures. While maintaining a lively base of Shaw, Shakespeare and other major authors, Court has also produced such works as Mustapha Matura's *Playboy of the West Indies*, Caryl Churchill's *Serious Money*, Wole Soyinka's *The Lion and the Jewel* and Lope de Vega's *Fuente Ovejuna*. Court is embarking on a plan to expand the limits of theatrical design through the creative use of symbolic and metaphoric elements. For 10 years Court has been offering an extensive education and outreach program for students and adults. Each season the high school matinee program serves 5,000 students from schools ranging from Chicago's inner city to metropolitan-area suburbs.

—Nicholas Rudall

PRODUCTIONS 1989-90

Serious Money, Caryl Churchill; (D) Terry McCabe; (S) John Culbert; (C) Renee Starr-Liepins; (L) John Culbert

Paradise Hotel, Georges Feydeau; trans: Nicholas Rudall; (D) Kyle Donnelly; (S) Jeff Bauer; (C) Claudia Boddy; (L) Rita Pietraszek

Ghosts, Henrik Ibsen; trans: Nicholas Rudall; (D) Bernard Hopkins; (S) Richard Isackes; (C) Jessica Hahn; (L) Ron Greene

The Beggar's Opera, John Gay; (D) Richard Russell Ramos; (S) Jeff Bauer; (C) Jeff Bauer; (L) Rita Pietraszek

A Chorus of Disapproval, Alan Ayckbourn; (D) Richard Russell Ramos; (S) Jeff Bauer; (C) Jeff Bauer; (L) Rita Pietraszek

PRODUCTIONS 1990-91

Candida, George Bernard Shaw; (D) Nicholas Rudall; (S) John Culbert; (C) Nanette Acosta; (L) John Culbert

The Lion and the Jewel, Wole Soyinka; (D) Jonathan Wilson; (S) Jeff Bauer; (C) Jeff Bauer; (L) Rita Pietraszek

Brief Lives, adapt: Patrick Garland, from John Aubrey; (D) Nicholas Rudall; (S) Jeff Bauer; (C) Jeff Bauer; (L) Ron Greene

What the Butler Saw, Joe Orton; (D) Jacques Cartier; (S) Richard Isackes; (C) Renee Starr-Liepins; (L) Todd Hensley

Fuente Ovejuna, adapt and trans: Adrian Mitchell, from Lope de Vega; (D) Richard E.T. White; (S) Linda Buchanan; (C) Linda Buchanan; (L) Michael S. Philippi

The Caucasian Chalk Circle, Bertolt Brecht; trans: Ralph Manheim; (D) Jeff Steitzer; (S) Mary Griswold and John Paoletti; (C) Mary Griswold and John Paoletti; (L) Rita Pietraszek

Court Theatre. *Serious Money*. Photo: David Sutton.

The Cricket Theatre

WILLIAM PARTLAN
Artistic Director

STEVEN KRAHNKE
General Manager

1407 Nicollet Ave. S
Minneapolis, MN 55403
(612) 871-3763 (bus.)
(612) 871-2244 (b.o.)

FOUNDED 1971
William Semans

SEASON
Sept.-July

FACILITIES
Seating Capacity: 213
Stage: proscenium

Upstairs
Seating Capacity: 99
Stage: flexible

FINANCES
July 1, 1990-June 30, 1991
Expenses: $475,000

CONTRACTS
AEA SPT

The Cricket is a playwright-oriented producing theatre. I believe our playwrights are among our most important visionaries; they create imagined worlds which contain people, a language and a code of interaction all their own. I look for inventively peopled theatrical worlds; for intensively interactive plays with muscular language. As theatre artists, we explore the boundaries of these worlds with the writers and together we give them a theatrical life which reaches for resonance in our audiences' lives. The Cricket provides developmental and production resources for a number of local, national and international playwrights in our new, intimate theatre facility. We do not employ a full-time company but hire the best artists and technicians available to create the world of each project. The Cricket has emerged from economic hard times as a leaner, more flexible organization—attempting to create a vital theatrical proving ground for theatre artists.

—William Partlan

PRODUCTIONS 1989-90

Two Rooms, Lee Blessing; (D) Jeanne Blake; (S) Rick Polenek; (C) Anne Ruben; (L) Tina Charney

Reckless, Craig Lucas; (D) William Partlan; (S) Jack Barkla; (C) Nayna Ramey; (L) Tina Charney

Birdsend, Keith Huff; (D) William Partlan; (S) G.W. Mercier; (C) G.W. Mercier; (L) Tina Charney

Zig Zag Zelda, Drury Pifer; (D) Kent Stephens; (S) Lori Sullivan; (C) Sandra Schulte; (L) Frederic Desbois

Tomfoolery, conceived: Cameron Mackintosh and Robin Ray; music and lyrics: Tom Lehrer; (D) William Partlan; (S) Nayna Ramey; (C) Rich Hamson; (L) Tina Charney

PRODUCTIONS 1990-91

Drinking in America, Eric Bogosian; (D) William Partlan; (S) Steven Krahnke; (C) Katherine Kohl; (L) Tina Charney

About Time, Tom Cole; (D) George C. White; (S) Nayna Ramey; (C) Katherine Kohl; (L) Tina Charney

Marvin's Room, Scott McPherson; (D) William Partlan; (S) Robert Klingelhoefer; (C) Nayna Ramey; (L) Tina Charney

Ready for the River, Neal Bell; (D) William Partlan; (S) Robert Klingelhoefer; (C) Nayna Ramey; (L) Tina Charney

Closer Than Ever, conceived: Steven Scott Smith; music: David Shire; lyrics: Richard Maltby, Jr.; (D) Randy Winkler; (S) Nayna Ramey; (C) Beth Sanders; (L) Tina Charney

The Cricket Theatre. J.C. Cutler, Steven Hendrickson and Alice Haining in *Birdsend*. Photo: Glenn Morehouse Olson.

Crossroads Theatre Company. Reggie Montgomery, Betty K. Bynum and Tico Wells in *Spunk*. Photo: Eddie Birch.

Crossroads Theatre Company

RICARDO KHAN
Producing Artistic Director

ANDRE ROBINSON, JR.
Managing Director

7 Livingston Ave.
New Brunswick, NJ 08901
(908) 249-5581 (bus.)
(908) 249-5560 or 249-5561 (b.o.)

FOUNDED 1978
Ricardo Khan, L. Kenneth Richardson

SEASON
Sept.-June

FACILITIES
Mainstage
Seating Capacity: 264
Stage: thrust

FINANCES
July 1, 1989-June 30, 1990
Expenses: $1,974,286

CONTRACTS
AEA LORT (D)

We exist in a society that persists in perpetuating images on screen and stage that depict black people in socially limited, culturally deprived and spiritually debilitating ways. This fact has reinforced the sense of despair felt by so many black artists—those who can, through their art and the media, help correct these social misperceptions. Artists are among the most powerful of truth messengers and must, therefore, be encouraged to sing above the confusing sounds of despair and cause art to resound with a power that renews. This is why at Crossroads, we choose not to design seasons of plays but of people. Our associate artists program supports African-American writers, directors, actors and designers, asking them, "What have you always dreamed of working on, but for some reason never could?" By providing a "safe haven" for artists like George C. Wolfe, Mbongeni Ngema, Sandra Reaves-Phillips, Denise Nicholas and Leslie Lee, we have produced significant contributions to world theatre and spawned a new generation of black innovators.

—Ricardo Khan

PRODUCTIONS 1989-90

Sheila's Day, Duma Ndlovu; (D) Richard Gant and Mbongeni Ngema; (S) Lloyd Harris; (C) Toni-Leslie James; (L) Victor En Yu Tan

Spunk, George C. Wolfe, from Zora Neale Hurston; (D) George C. Wolfe; (S) Loy Arcenas; (C) Toni-Leslie James; (L) Donald Holder

And Further Mo', Vernel Bagneris; (D) Vernel Bagneris and Ricardo Khan; (S) Charles McClennahan; (C) Joann Clevenger; (L) Shirley Prendergast

Black Eagles, Leslie Lee; (D) Ricardo Khan; (S) Charles McClennahan; (C) Beth Ribblett; (L) Shirley Prendergast

Genesis: A Festival of New Voices, various playwrights; various directors; (S) Gary Kechely; (L) Shirley Prendergast

Tod, the Boy, Tod, Talvin Wilks; (D) Ken Johnson; (S) Lloyd Harris; (C) Toni-Leslie James; (L) William H. Grant, III

PRODUCTIONS 1990-91

The Beautiful LaSalles, Michael Dinwiddie; (D) Ellyn Long Marshal; (S) Felix E. Cochren; (C) Toni-Leslie James;

(L) Christian Epps
Bongi's Journey, Welcome Msomi and Thuli Dumakude; (D) Welcome Msomi and Ricardo Khan; (S) Felix E. Cochren; (C) Beth Ribblett; (L) William H. Grant, III
Buses, Denise Nicholas; (D) Shirley Jo Finney; (S) Peter Harrison; (C) Celia Bryant; (L) Sandra Ross
Genesis: A Festival of New Voices, various playwrights; various directors; (S) Gary Kechely; (L) Dan Hochstine and Ebun Pyne Bailey
The Mother Project, Sydne Mahone and The Women of Sangoma; (D) Sydne Mahone; (S) Gary Kechely and Alice Baldwin; (C) Anita Ellis; (L) Robin Miller
Paul Robeson, Phillip Hayes Dean; music: Ernie Scott; (D) Harold Scott; (L) Shirley Prendergast

CSC Repertory Ltd.-The Classic Stage Company

CAREY PERLOFF
Artistic Director

PATRICIA TAYLOR
Managing Director

136 East 13th St.
New York, NY 10003
(212) 477-5808 (bus.)
(212) 677-4210 (b.o.)

FOUNDED 1967
Christopher Martin

SEASON
Oct.-June

FACILITIES
Seating Capacity: 180
Stage: flexible

FINANCES
July 1, 1990-June 30, 1991
Expenses: $726,883

CONTRACTS
AEA letter of agreement

CSC Repertory-The Classic Stage Company, exists to rediscover and reinterpret the rich international classical repertoire often ignored in the American theatre and to find vivid new ways to bring the classics to the contemporary stage. Located in the East Village, one of the hottest visual and performing arts communities in America, CSC is committed to visually evocative productions of plays from every culture—from Sophocles to Pinter to Chekhov to Ezra Pound—plays that exhibit rich language, theatricality and depth of subject matter. We actively commission American playwrights to create new translations and adaptations of classic plays, which we develop in our Sneak Previews of New and Undiscovered Classics reading series. CSC seeks out imaginative artists from every race, background, gender and genre, and makes extensive use of live music and dance in production. The Conservatory at CSC trains young actors in classical theatre, and our City Stages for City Students program brings free productions to New York City students.

—Carey Perloff

CSC Repertory Ltd.-The Classic Stage Company. Richard Ziman, John Turturro and David Patrick Kelly in *The Resistible Rise of Arturo Ui*. Photo: Paula Court.

PRODUCTIONS 1989-90

Mountain Language and ***The Birthday Party***, Harold Pinter; (D) Carey Perloff; (S) Loy Arce; (C) Gabriel Berry; (L) Beverly Emmons
Heart of a Dog, adapt: Deloss Brown, from Mikhail Bulgakov; (D) Robert Lanchester; (S) Tom Kamm; (C) Jane Eliot; (L) Mary Louise Geiger
Tower of Evil, Alexandre Dumas pere; trans: Michael Feingold; (D) Carey Perloff; (S) Donald Eastman; (C) Gabriel Berry; (L) Frances Aronson

PRODUCTIONS 1990-91

Happy Days, Samuel Beckett; (D) Carey Perloff; (S) Donald Eastman; (C) Julie Weiss; (L) Frances Aronson
The Learned Ladies, Moliere; trans: Freyda Thomas; (D) Richard Seyd; (S) Richard Hoover; (C) Beaver Bauer; (L) Mary Louise Geiger
The Resistible Rise of Arturo Ui, Bertolt Brecht; trans: Ralph Manheim; (D) Carey Perloff; (S) Douglas Stein; (C) Donna Zakowska; (L) Stephen Strawbridge

Cumberland County Playhouse

JIM CRABTREE
Producing Director

KATHY VANLANDINGHAM
Staff & Financial Manager

Box 484
Crossville, TN 38557
(615) 484-2300 (bus.)
(615) 484-5000 (b.o.)

FOUNDED 1965
Margaret Keyes Harrison, Moses Dorton, Paul Crabtree

SEASON
Mar.-Dec.

FACILITIES
Cumberland County Playhouse
Seating Capacity: 478
Stage: proscenium

Theater-in-the-Woods
Seating Capacity: 199
Stage: arena

Adventure Theater
Seating Capacity: 200-300
Stage: flexible

FINANCES
Jan. 1, 1990-Dec. 31, 1990
Expenses: $794,084

CONTRACTS
AEA Guest Artist

Our home is a town of 6,500 in a rural Appalachian county within two hours of Knoxville and Chattanooga, to which we draw more than 75,000 patrons a year. We embrace the idea that the arts can be an indigenous part of rural America, not just an imported commodity. Our Fairfield Living History Series presents new plays and musicals rooted in Tennessee history. Playhouse-in-the-Schools puts company members in classrooms as teachers for the curriculum we're developing with local educators. Mainstage productions and shows for young audiences tour to rural schools and communities. Since 1980 we have presented a dozen world premieres, mostly of works relating to our home region. Our resident company is from Tennessee and the Southeast, and they're joined by guest artists and a strong volunteer corps. During 1992 we will begin a major expansion, including a black-box theatre, classrooms, and production and administrative space.

—Jim Crabtree

PRODUCTIONS 1990

Man of La Mancha, book adapt: Dale Wasserman, from Miguel de Cervantes; music: Mitch Leigh; lyrics: Joe Darion; (D) Jim Crabtree; (S) Jim Crabtree and John Partyka; (C) Mary Crabtree; (L) John Partyka
See How They Run, Philip King; (D) Mary Crabtree; (S) Martha Hill; (C) Renee Garrett; (L) John Partyka
Anastasia, Marcelle Maurette; adapt: Guy Bolton; (D) Abigail Crabtree; (S) Ron Keller;

Cumberland County Playhouse. *Wings Over Appalachia.*

(C) Brenda Schwab; (L) Steve Woos

Tennessee, USA!, book, music and lyrics: Paul Crabtree; (D) Abigail Crabtree; (S) Brian Jackins, Nathan Kwame Braun and Jim Crabtree; (C) Mary Crabtree; (L) John Partyka

Wings Over Appalachia, book: Jim Crabtree and Billy Edd Wheeler; music: Dennis Davenport and Billy Edd Wheeler; lyrics: Billy Edd Wheeler; (D) Jim Crabtree; (S) Jim Crabtree; (C) Renee Garrett; (L) Stephen Shaw

Noah's Flood, book adapt, music and lyrics: Benjamin Britten; (D) Jim Crabtree; (S) Leonard Harman; (C) Renee Garrett; (L) John Partyka

Hans Christian Andersen, adapt: John Fearnley, Beverly Cross and Tommy Steele, from original screenplay; music and lyrics: Frank Loesser; (D) Mary Crabtree; (S) Leonard Harman; (C) Brenda Schwab; (L) Stephen Shaw

Peter Pan, book: James M. Barrie; music: Mark Charlap; lyrics: Carolyn Leigh; (D) Jim Crabtree and Ginger Hulbert; (S) Joseph Varga; (C) Mary Crabtree; (L) John Partyka

PRODUCTIONS 1991

Inherit the Wind, Jerome Lawrence and Robert E. Lee; (D) Jim Crabtree; (S) Leonard Harman; (C) Mary Crabtree; (L) John Partyka

Charlotte's Web, book adapt: Joseph Robinette, from E.B. White; music and lyrics: Charles Strouse; (D) Mary Crabtree; (S) John Partyka; (C) Renee Garrett; (L) John Partyka

Evita, book and lyrics: Tim Rice; music: Andrew Lloyd Webber; (D) Jim Crabtree; (S) Leonard Harman; (C) Terry Schwab; (L) Stephen Shaw

Shenandoah, book: James Lee Barrett, Peter Udell and Philip Rose; music: Gary Geld; lyrics: Peter Udell; (D) Abigail Crabtree; (S) John Partyka; (C) Mary Crabtree and Renee Garrett; (L) John Partyka

Tomorrow Songs, conceived: Abigail Crabtree and Dennis Davenport; (D) Abigail Crabtree; (S) John Partyka; (C) Renee Garrett and Terry Schwab; (L) Stephen Shaw

Driving Miss Daisy, Alfred Uhry; (D) Jim Crabtree; (S) Leonard Harman; (C) Mary Crabtree; (L) Leonard Harman

The Wizard of Oz, book adapt: John Kane, from L. Frank Baum; (D) Jim Crabtree; (S) Leonard Harman; (C) Mary Crabtree; (L) Stephen Shaw

The Best Christmas Pageant Ever, Barbara Robinson

Dallas Theater Center

JEFF WEST
Managing Director

3636 Turtle Creek Blvd.
Dallas, TX 75219-5598
(214) 526-8210 (bus.)
(214) 526-8857 (b.o.)

FOUNDED 1959
Robert D. Stecker, Sr., Beatrice Handel, Paul Baker, Dallas Citizens

SEASON
Sept.-May

FACILITIES
Kalita Humphreys Theater
Seating Capacity: 466
Stage: thrust

Arts District Theater
Seating Capacity: 500
Stage: flexible

In the Basement
Seating Capacity: 150
Stage: flexible

FINANCES
July 1, 1990-June 30, 1991
Expenses: $3,729,955

CONTRACTS
AEA LORT (C) and (D)

The most important thing an institution can offer the artist is an environment in which to flower, so certain requirements become immediately apparent. I firmly believe that the notion of stability, of company, is critical to the act of creation. History teaches that meaningful, deeply personal art arises out of a fertile community of ideas, and only rarely out of isolation. In a world that overwhelmingly prefers to reward the individual over the efforts of a group, this notion of a collective places profound demands on all concerned: the commitment over time of actors, designers and directors; the willingness of our board to finance an enterprise that may not always be economically "efficient"; the active desire of a very diverse community to come together in the meeting place that is the theatre to examine the roots of who we are. The theatre is one of the last strongholds of direct, unmediated human contact. I want the Dallas Theatre Center to continue to bend our collective imagination to creating an intimate dialogue with the audience, the community. Fashionable entertainment is no longer enough.

—*Ken Bryant*

Note: During the 1989-90 season, Ken Bryant served as artistic director.

Dallas Theater Center. Sean Hennigan and Nance Williamson in *Temptation.* Photo: Carl Davis.

PRODUCTIONS 1989-90

Romeo and Juliet, William Shakespeare; (D) Ken Bryant; (S) Eugene Lee; (C) Donna M. Kress; (L) Natasha Katz
Once in a Lifetime, George S. Kaufman and Moss Hart; (D) Larry Sloan; (S) Andrew Jackness; (C) Donna M. Kress; (L) Russell H. Champa
A Christmas Carol, book adapt: Adrian Hall and Richard Cumming, from Charles Dickens; music and lyrics: Richard Cumming; (D) Adrian Hall; (S) Eugene Lee; (C) Donna M. Kress; (L) Eugene Lee
Prologue to All the King's Men, adapt: Adrian Hall, from Robert Penn Warren; (D) Adrian Hall; (S) Eugene Lee; (C) Donna M. Kress; (L) Eugene Lee
Temptation, Vaclav Havel; trans: Marie Winn; (D) Ljubisa Georgievski; (S) Eugene Lee; (C) Donna M. Kress; (L) Natasha Katz
Buried Child, Sam Shepard; (D) Ken Bryant; (S) Eugene Lee; (C) Donna M. Kress; (L) Eugene Lee
Zero Positive, Harry Kondoleon; (D) Chris Coleman; (S) Michael McGarty; (C) Tom Jaekels; (L) Russell H. Champa
The Secret Rapture, David Hare; (D) Ken Bryant; (S) Eugene Lee; (C) Donna M. Kress; (L) Roger Morgan
A Flea in Her Ear, Georges Feydeau; trans: Barnett Shaw; (D) Itamar Kubovy; (S) Eugene Lee; (C) Donna M. Kress; (L) Eugene Lee

PRODUCTIONS 1990-91

The Inspector General, Nikolai Gogol; trans: Betsy Hulick; (D) company in honor of Ken Bryant; (S) Eugene Lee; (C) Donna M. Kress; (L) Russell H. Champa
A Christmas Carol, book adapt: Adrian Hall and Richard Cumming, from Charles Dickens; music and lyrics: Richard Cumming; (D) Allen McCalla; (S) E. David Cosier, Jr.; (C) Donna M. Kress; (L) Russell H. Champa
All My Sons, Arthur Miller; (D) Lou Salerni; (S) Eugene Lee; (C) Leila Heise; (L) Monique L'Heureux
As You Like It, William Shakespeare; (D) David McClendon; (S) E. David Cosier, Jr.; (C) Donna M. Kress; (L) Natasha Katz
My Children! My Africa!, Athol Fugard; (D) Clinton Turner Davis; (S) Charles McClennahan; (C) Donna M. Kress; (L) William H. Grant, III
Abundance, Beth Henley; (D) John Henry Davis; (S) Philipp Jung; (C) Donna M. Kress; (L) Frances Aronson
Other People's Money, Jerry Sterner; (D) Charles Towers; (S) E. David Cosier, Jr.; (C) Donna M. Kress; (L) Linda Blase
His Unconquerable Enemy, adapt: Bill Bolender, from W.C. Morrow; (D) Bill Bolender; (S) Tristan Wilson; (C) Donna M. Kress; (L) Russell H. Champa

Delaware Theatre Company

CLEVELAND MORRIS
Artistic Director

DAVID EDELMAN
Managing Director

200 Water St.
Wilmington, DE 19801
(302) 594-1104 (bus.)
(302) 594-1100 (b.o.)

FOUNDED 1979
Cleveland Morris, Peter DeLaurier

SEASON
Oct.-Apr.

FACILITIES
Seating Capacity: 389
Stage: proscenium

FINANCES
July 1, 1990-June 30, 1991
Expenses: $1,074,000

CONTRACTS
AEA letter of agreement

The Delaware Theatre Company is the state's only professional theatre. We seek to offer an encompassing, diverse examination of the art of theatre through our annual programs that mix well-known classics with unknown new plays, as well as lesser-known vintage plays with familiar contemporary works. In all cases, we seek plays of lasting social and literary value, worthy of thoughtful consideration by both artist and viewer, and produced in a style designed to strengthen the force of the playwright's language and vision. Our presentations are produced in a boldly modern facility that opened in November 1985, located on Wilmington's historic riverfront. The theatre company offers a wide variety of ancillary and educational programs in an effort to assist the general public in finding the art of theatre an ongoing and joyful addition to their lives and community.

—*Cleveland Morris*

Delaware Theatre Company. David C. Wyeth, Lawrence Laravela, Will Stutts, Drew Hanson and Kit Jones in *To Kill a Mockingbird*. Photo: Richard C. Carter.

PRODUCTIONS 1989-90

Tartuffe, Moliere; trans: Richard Wilbur; (D) Cleveland Morris; (S) Eric Schaeffer; (C) Marla Jurglanis; (L) Bruce K. Morriss
Tomfoolery, conceived: Cameron Mackintosh and Robin Ray; music and lyrics: Tom Lehrer; (D) Derek Walshonak; (S) Eric Schaeffer; (C) Marla Jurglanis; (L) Bruce K. Morriss
Benefactors, Michael Frayn; (D) Cleveland Morris; (S) Eric Schaeffer; (C) Marla Jurglanis; (L) Bruce K. Morriss
Memoir, John Murrell; (D) Jamie Brown; (S) Lewis Folden; (C) Marla Jurglanis; (L) Scott Pinkney
Fences, August Wilson; (D) Clinton Turner Davis; (S) Charles McClennahan; (C) Alvin Perry; (L) Bruce K. Morriss

PRODUCTIONS 1990-91

To Kill a Mockingbird, adapt: Christopher Sergel, from Harper Lee; (D) Cleveland Morris; (S) Eric Schaeffer; (C) Marla Jurglanis; (L) Bruce K. Morriss
Oil City Symphony, Mike Craver, Mark Hardwick, Debra Monk and Mary Murfitt; (D) Maureen Heffernan; (S) Sarah Baptist; (C) Kathleen Egan; (L) Bruce K. Morriss
A Shayna Maidel, Barbara Lebow; (D) Alex Dmitriev; (S) Lewis Folden; (C) Marla Jurglanis; (L) Bruce K. Morriss
A Walk in the Woods, Lee Blessing; (D) Terence Lamude; (S) Eric Schaeffer; (C) Marla Jurglanis; (L) Bruce K. Morriss
What the Butler Saw, Joe Orton; (D) Maureen Heffernan; (S) Daniel Gray; (C) Marla Jurglanis; (L) Bruce K. Morriss
Ain't Misbehavin', conceived: Murray Horwitz and Richard Maltby, Jr.; music and lyrics: Fats Waller, et al; (D) Derek Walshonak; (S) Eric Schaeffer; (C) Marla Jurglanis; (L) Bruce K. Morriss

Dell'Arte Players Company

MICHAEL FIELDS
JOAN SCHIRLE
Co-Artistic Directors

BOBBI RICCA
Administrative Director

Box 816
Blue Lake, CA 95525
(707) 668-5663

FOUNDED 1971
Jael Weisman, Alain Schons, Joan Schirle, Carlo Mazzone-Clementi, Jane Hill, Michael Fields, Jon Paul Cook

SEASON
Jan.-Dec. touring

FACILITIES
Dell'Arte Studio
Seating Capacity: 100
Stage: flexible

Dell'Arte Amphitheatre
Seating Capacity: 250
Stage: thrust

FINANCES
Oct. 1, 1990-Sept. 30, 1991
Expenses: $254,197

CONTRACTS
AEA letter of agreement

The Dell'Arte Players Company is a rurally based touring theatre ensemble which performs nationally and internationally. The four core-company artists share 14 years of collaborative work on original theatre pieces. Our nonurban point of view and themes for many of our major works come from the California north coast where we live. The creative focus of our original work is on strong textual values expressed in a highly physical performance style; the integration of acting, text, music, movement and content is a primary goal of our ensemble process. Our unique style has brought invitations to perform with regional repertory theatres in large-scale works such as Peter Barnes's *Red Noses*. We also do extended teaching residencies and extensive outreach in our rural region. Our commitment to influencing theatre through traditional popular forms is also reflected in the training we offer at the Dell'Arte School of Physical Theatre. As recognition of our work grows, we move closer toward our vision of becoming an international center for the exploration and development of physical theatre traditions and their relationship to contemporary forms.

—Michael Fields

PRODUCTIONS 1989-90

Slapstick, company-developed; (D) Jael Weisman; (S) Alain Schons; (C) Nancy Jo Smith; (L) Michael Foster

Animal Nation, book and lyrics: Steve Friedman; music: Gina Leishman; (D) Sam Woodhouse and Jael Weisman; (S) Victoria Petrovich; (C) Nancy Jo Smith; (L) Peter Nordyke

Little Lotta Crabtree's Incredible Adventure, Jane Hill; (D) Michael Fields; (S) Michael Foster; (C) Jane Hill; (L) Michael Foster

Malpractice, adapt: company, from Moliere; (D) Jael Weisman; (S) Andy Stacklin; (C) Mimi Mace; (L) Michael Foster

Dell'Arte Players Company. Michael Fields, Joan Schirle and Donald Forrest in *Slapstick*. Photo: Wyn Tucker.

PRODUCTIONS 1990-91

Beautiful Swimmers, Lynne Abels; (D) Jane Hill; (S) Tom Roscoe; (C) Jane Hill; (L) Michael Foster

Slapstick, company-developed; (D) Jael Weisman; (S) Alain Schons; (C) Nancy Jo Smith; (L) Michael Foster

Journey of the Ten Moons, Jane Hill and David Ferney; (D) Michael Fields; (S) Michael Foster; (C) Jane Hill and Lene Jelle; (L) Michael Foster

Malpractice, adapt: company, from Moliere; (D) Jael Weisman; (S) Andy Stacklin; (C) Mimi Mace; (L) Michael Foster

Denver Center Theatre Company

DONOVAN MARLEY
Artistic Director

KEVIN C. MAIFELD
Executive Director

BARBARA E. SELLERS
Producing Director

1050 13th St.
Denver, CO 80204
(303) 893-4000 (bus.)
(303) 893-4100 (b.o.)

FOUNDED 1980
Donald R. Seawell

SEASON
Sept.-June

FACILITIES
The Stage
Seating Capacity: 550
Stage: thrust

The Space
Seating Capacity: 450
Stage: arena

The Source
Seating Capacity: 154
Stage: thrust

The Ricketson
Seating Capacity: 195
Stage: proscenium

FINANCES
July 1, 1990-June 30, 1991
Expenses: $4,806,800

CONTRACTS
AEA LORT (C) and (D), and TYA

The Denver Center Theatre Company is a resident ensemble committed to the long-range development of a production style unique to this Rocky Mountain company. Central to this search is the operation of a theatre conservatory that clarifies and unifies the work of our professional artists through ongoing training. Our mature artists pursue company continuity through the selection and training of young artists to sustain the ideals, disciplines and traditions of the company. A vigorous play development program is designed to search for playwrights to give the ensemble a regional voice with global perspective. One-third to one-half of each season is comprised of world premieres. The remainder of an 11-production season examines world classics from a contemporary perspective, and explores both the major works of preeminent American playwrights and lost or obscure works that deserve to be reintroduced into the American repertoire.

—Donovan Marley

PRODUCTIONS 1989-90

Saint Joan, George Bernard Shaw; (D) Laird Williamson; (S) Andrew V. Yelusich; (C) Andrew V. Yelusich; (L) Daniel L. Murray

Desire Under the Elms, Eugene O'Neill; (D) Donovan Marley; (S) Richard L. Hay; (C) Andrew V. Yelusich; (L) Charles MacLeod

A Little Night Music, book: Hugh Wheeler; music and lyrics: Stephen Sondheim; (D) Bruce K. Sevy; (S) Vicki Smith; (C) Frances Kenny; (L) Peter Maradudin

Three Men on a Horse, John Cecil Holm and George Abbott; (D) Randal Myler; (S) Andrew Carter; (C) Patricia Ann Whitelock; (L) Daniel L. Murray

Henry IV, Parts 1 and 2, adapt: Dakin Matthews, from William Shakespeare; (D) Dakin Matthews; (S) Michael Ganio; (C) Sarah Nash Gates; (L) Charles MacLeod

Fences, August Wilson; (D) Israel Hicks; (S) John Dexter;

Denver Center Theatre Company. Mathew Vipond, Michael Ian Schwartz and Chelsea Altman in *Junk Bonds*. Photo: P. Switzer.

(C) Andrew V. Yelusich; (L) Daniel L. Murray

The Adventures of Huckleberry Finn, adapt: Randal Myler, from Mark Twain; (D) Randal Myler; (S) Andrew V. Yelusich; (C) Andrew V. Yelusich; (L) Charles MacLeod

The Road to Mecca, Athol Fugard; (D) Frank Georgianna; (S) Pavel Dobrusky; (C) Pavel Dobrusky; (L) Pavel Dobrusky

Ready for the River, Neal Bell; (D) Gitta Honegger; (S) Andrew V. Yelusich; (C) Andrew V. Yelusich; (L) Daniel L. Murray

Mine Alone, Conrad Bishop and Elizabeth Fuller; (D) Frank Georgianna; (S) Carolyn Leslie Ross; (C) Patricia Ann Whitelock; (L) Peter Maradudin

Animal Fair, book, music and lyrics: Clark Gesner; (D) Steve Stettler; (S) Richard L. Hay; (C) Janet S. Morris; (L) Charles MacLeod

Soundbite, Gary Leon Hill; (D) Donovan Marley; (S) Andrew V. Yelusich; (C) Andrew V. Yelusich; (L) Daniel L. Murray

PRODUCTIONS 1990-91

The Man Who Came to Dinner, George S. Kaufman and Moss Hart; (D) Donovan Marley; (S) Bill Curley; (C) Andrew V. Yelusich; (L) Charles MacLeod

A Christmas Carol, adapt: Dennis Powers and Laird Williamson, from Charles Dickens; (D) Laird Williamson; (S) Robert Blackman; (C) Andrew V. Yelusich; (L) Charles MacLeod

Joe Turner's Come and Gone, August Wilson; (D) Israel Hicks; (S) Andrew V. Yelusich; (C) Andrew V. Yelusich; (L) Charles MacLeod

The American Clock, Arthur Miller; (D) Randal Myler; (S) Vicki Smith; (C) Patricia Ann Whitelock; (L) Don Darnutzer

Twelfth Night, William Shakespeare; (D) Laird Williamson; (S) Vicki Smith; (C) Andrew V. Yelusich; (L) Don Darnutzer

Miss Julie, August Strindberg; adapt: Romulus Linney; trans: David Reed; (D) Donovan Marley; (S) Richard L. Hay; (C) Andrew V. Yelusich; (L) Charles MacLeod

Okiboji, Conrad Bishop and Elizabeth Fuller; (D) Frank Georgianna; (S) Richard L. Hay; (C) Laura Love; (L) Charles MacLeod

New Business, Tom Williams; (D) Steven Dietz; (S) Richard L. Hay; (C) Janet S. Morris; (L) Charles MacLeod

Junk Bonds, Thomas Babe; (D) Anthony Powell; (S) Andrew V. Yelusich; (C) Andrew V. Yelusich; (L) Daniel L. Murray

Back to the Blanket, Gary Leon Hill; (D) Roberta Levitow; (S) Pavel Dobrusky; (C) Pavel Dobrusky; (L) Pavel Dobrusky

Detroit Repertory Theatre

BRUCE E. MILLAN
Artistic Director

13103 Woodrow Wilson Ave.
Detroit, MI 48238
(313) 868-1347

FOUNDED 1957
Bruce E. Millan, Barbara Busby, T. O. Andrus

SEASON
Nov.-June

FACILITIES
Seating Capacity: 196
Stage: proscenium

FINANCES
Jan. 1, 1990-Dec. 31, 1990
Expenses: $331,348

CONTRACTS
AEA SPT

The Detroit Repertory's purpose over the past 33 years has been to build a first-class professional theatre by assembling a resident company of theatre artists recruited from among local professionals in the field; to seed new plays and bring worthwhile forgotten plays back to life; to expand the creative possibilities of theatre by increasing the opportunities for participation of all artists regardless of their ethnic or racial origins or gender; to reach out to initiate the uninitiated; to build a theatre operation that is "close to the people" by acting as a catalyst for the revitalization of the neighborhood in which the theatre resides; and to attract audiences reflecting the cultural and ethnic diversity of southeastern Michigan.

—Bruce E. Millan

PRODUCTIONS 1989-90

Blood Relations, Sharon Pollack; (D) Yolanda Fleischer; (S) Bruce

Detroit Repertory Theatre. Jennifer Jones, Christina E. Monique Brown and Allen T. Sheffield in *Fences*. Photo: Bruce Millan.

E. Millan; (C) B.J. Essen; (L) Kenneth R. Hewitt, Jr.

Fences, August Wilson; (D) Reuben Yabuku; (S) Robert Katkowsky; (C) B.J. Essen; (L) Kenneth R. Hewitt, Jr.

Bullpen, Steven Kluger; (D) Bruce E. Millan; (S) Bruce E. Millan; (C) B.J. Essen; (L) Kenneth R. Hewitt, Jr.

Disability: A Comedy, Ron Whyte; (D) William Boswell; (S) Robert Katkowsky; (C) B.J. Essen; (L) Kenneth R. Hewitt, Jr.

PRODUCTIONS 1990-91

Cotton Patch Gospel, book: Tom Key and Russell Treyz, from Clarence Jordan; music: Harry Chapin; (D) Bruce E. Millan; (S) Bruce E. Millan; (C) B.J. Essen; (L) Kenneth R. Hewitt, Jr.

Joe Turner's Come and Gone, August Wilson; (D) Woodie King, Jr.; (S) Bruce E. Millan and Dick Smith; (C) B.J. Essen; (L) Kenneth R. Hewitt, Jr.

Daytrips, Jo Carson; (D) Barbara Busby; (S) Monika Essen; (C) B.J. Essen; (L) Kenneth R. Hewitt, Jr.

Lover's Cove, Frederick St. John; (D) William Boswell; (S) Robert Katkowsky; (C) B.J. Essen; (L) Kenneth R. Hewitt, Jr.

East West Players

NOBU MCCARTHY
Artistic Director

CHARMEEN WING
Managing Director

4424 Santa Monica Blvd.
Los Angeles, CA 90029
(213) 666-1929 (bus.)
(213) 660-0366 (b.o.)

FOUNDED 1965
Beulah Quo, Mako, Yet Lock, Pat Li, Guy Lee, June Kim, James Hong, Rae Creevey

SEASON
Oct.-July

FACILITIES
Seating Capacity: 99
Stage: flexible

FINANCES
July 1, 1990-June 30, 1991
Expenses: $350,000

CONTRACTS
AEA 99-seat Theatre Plan

As the country's oldest Asian-American theatre, East West Players is dedicated to the development of new works by Asian-American playwrights, and to the presentation of original plays, musicals and the classics. Our theatre aims to provide a professional, as well as creative, environment in which actors, directors, designers and technicians can develop their craft. Our professional theatre training program, advanced acting workshop and a newly formed writers workshop nurture the young artists of tomorrow and allow working theatre artists a place to explore their art form. Beyond the work on our main stage and in our workshops, East West Players' underlying goal is to serve its community by presenting creative bilingual projects that are multicultural, socially relevant, often provocative and ultimately enlightening. Future plans are being developed to organize national and international touring productions to broaden our audiences and share with them Asian-American theatre.

—Nobu McCarthy

PRODUCTIONS 1989-90

Company, book: George Furth; music and lyrics: Stephen Sondheim; (D) Paul Hough; (S) Rae Creevey; (C) Dori Quan and G. Shuzuko Herrera; (L) Rae Creevey

The Chairman's Wife, Wakako Yamauchi; (D) Nobu McCarthy; (S) Gronk; (C) Terence Tam Soon; (L) Rae Creevey

Performance Anxiety, Vernon Takeshita; (D) Alberto Isaac; (S) Steven La Ponsie; (C) Lydia Tanji; (L) Rae Creevey

Come Back, Little Sheba, William Inge; (D) Tom Atha; (S) Gronk; (C) Terence Tam Soon; (L) Rae Creevey

PRODUCTIONS 1990-91

Songs of Harmony, Karen Huie; (D) Heidi Helen Davis; (S) Rae Creevey; (C) Dori Quan; (L) Rae Creevey

Doughball, Perry Miyake; (D) Patricia S. Yasutake; (S) Rae Creevey; (C) Diane J. Winesburg; (L) Rae Creevey

Hedda Gabler, Henrik Ibsen; trans: Michael Meyer; (D) Dorothy Lyman; (S) Gronk and Steven La Ponsie; (C) Terence Tam Soon; (L) Jose Lopez

Canton Jazz Club, book: Dom Wagwili; music: Nathan Wang and Joel Iwataki; lyrics: Tim Dang; (D) Tim Dang; (S) Gronk; (C) Terence Tam Soon; (L) Jose Lopez

East West Players. Steven Vincent Leigh and Jude Narita in *Hedda Gabler*. Photo: Shane Sato.

El Teatro Campesino

LUIS VALDEZ
Artistic Director

PHILLIP ESPARZA
Producer/Administrative Director

Box 1240
San Juan Bautista, CA 95045
(408) 623-2444

FOUNDED 1965
Luis Valdez

SEASON
Variable

FACILITIES
ETC Playhouse
Seating Capacity: 150
Stage: flexible

Mission San Juan Bautista
Seating Capacity: 300
Stage: arena

FINANCES
Oct. 1, 1989-Sept. 30, 1990
Expenses: $800,000

CONTRACTS
AEA SPT

Now into its 25th-anniversary season, El Teatro Campesino continues to explore the curative, affirmative power of live perfomance on actors and audiences alike, through its global vision of society. We remain acutely aware of the role of theatre as a creator of community, in the firm belief that the future belongs to those who can imagine it. We thus imagine an America born of the worldwide cultural fusion of our times, and see as our aesthetic and social purpose the creation of theatre that illuminates that inevitable future. To achieve this purpose, our evolving complex in San Juan Bautista continues to function as a research-and-development center, a place to explore the evolution of new works, new images, and new ideas. Our aim is to maintain a dynamic crossroads for talent: a place where children can work with adults, teenagers with senior citizens, professionals with nonprofessionals, Latino/Hispanics with Anglos, Asians, blacks, and Native Americans. Once works are refined in San Juan Bautista, the more successful plays and productions are produced professionally in larger urban venues. Our productions of *Corridos!*, *La Pastorela*, *Simply Maria* and *I Don't Have to Show You No Stinking Badges* are examples of this process. Our theatre work is simple, direct, complex and profound, but it works. In the heart, el corazon, of a way of life.

—*Luis Valdez*

PRODUCTIONS 1989-90

Food for the Dead and ***Simply Maria***, Josefina Lopez; (D) Amy Gonzalez; (S) Joe Cardinalli; (C) Michael Pacciorini; (L) Lisa Larice

La Pastorela, adapt: Luis Valdez, from medieval shepherd's play; (D) Tony Curiel; (S) Victoria Petrovich; (C) Marilyn Abad; (L) Rick Larsen

I Don't Have to Show You No Stinking Badges, Luis Valdez; (D) Luis Valdez; (S) Joe Cardinalli; (C) Sylvia Vega-Vasquez; (L) Russell Pyle

Culture Clash, Herbert Siguenza, Ricardo Salinas and Richard Montoya; (D) Tony Curiel; (S) Herbert Siguenza; (L) Jim Cave

Simply Maria, Josefina Lopez; and ***Soldado Razo***, Luis Valdez; (D) Marilyn Abad; (S) Joe Cardinalli; (C) Niessa Bauder; (L) Lisa Larice

PRODUCTIONS 1990-91

La Virgen del Tepeyac, adapt: Luis Valdez; (D) Rosa Maria Escalante; (S) Victoria Petrovich; (C) Niessa Bauder; (L) Rick Larsen

Greater Tuna, adapt: Jennifer Proctor, Francine Torres, Joseph Velasco and David Calvillo, from Jaston Williams, Joe Sears and Ed Howard; (D) Joseph Velasco; (S) Jim Cave; (C) Michael Pacciorini; (L) Jim Cave

El Teatro Campesino. Andres Gutierrez, Anahuac Valdez and Lakin Valdez in *Soldado Razo*. Photo: Allen McEwen.

Emmy Gifford Children's Theater

JAMES LARSON
Artistic Director

MARK HOEGER
Executive Director

3504 Center St.
Omaha, NE 68105
(402) 345-4852 (bus.)
(402) 345-4849 (b.o.)

FOUNDED 1949
19 child advocacy agencies, Emmy Gifford

SEASON
Sept.-May

FACILITIES
Seating Capacity: 525
Stage: proscenium

FINANCES
June 1, 1990-May 31, 1991
Expenses: $910,000

CONTRACTS
AEA Guest Artist

At the Emmy Gifford Children's Theater we believe that children's theatre is an exciting and suitable performance mode for experimentation. Children have different psychological and aesthetic needs from those of adults, primarily because a child's cerebral design is synaptically more active. For children, fantasy and anitrealism are the norm. Thus, artists in children's theatre have startling freedom in the theatrical choices they can make to break out of the straightjacket of stultifying, ossified realism—the traditional theoretical and formal style out of which most U.S. theatre artists have developed.

—*James Larson*

Emmy Gifford Children's Theater. Laura Marr and Michael Wilhelm in *The Ugly Duckling*. Photo: J. Keller.

PRODUCTIONS 1989-90

Raggedy Ann and Andy, adapt: Patricia Thackray, from Johnny Gruelle; (D) James Larson; (S) Steve Wheeldon; (C) Sherri Geerdes; (L) Steve Wheeldon

Frankenstein, adapt: Gail Erwin, from Mary Shelley; (D) Robert Urbinati; (S) Larry Kaushansky; (C) Sherri Geerdes; (L) Steve Wheeldon

The Best Christmas Pageant Ever, adapt: Barbara Robinson; (D) James Larson; (S) Larry Kaushansky; (C) Sherri Geerdes; (L) Steve Wheeldon

The Snow Queen, adapt: Megan Terry, from Hans Christian Andersen; (D) James Larson; (S) Steve Wheeldon; (C) Sherri Geerdes; (L) Steve Wheeldon

Tales of a Fourth Grade Nothing, adapt: Bruce Mason, from Judy Blume; (D) Mark Hoeger; (S) Steve Wheeldon; (C) Sherri Geerdes; (L) Steve Wheeldon

The Secret Garden, adapt: Laura Amy Schlitz, from Frances Hodgson Burnett; (D) Robert Urbinati; (S) Emmy Gifford; (C) Sherri Geerdes; (L) Steve Wheeldon

Ticket to Toyland, Karen Abbott; (D) Roberta Larson; (S) Steve Wheeldon; (C) Ruth Ciemnoczolowski; (L) Steve Wheeldon

PRODUCTIONS 1990-91

The Ugly Duckling, Gail Erwin, from Hans Christian Andersen; (D) James Larson; (S) Larry Kaushansky; (C) Sherri Geerdes; (L) Tim Osteen

The Chicago Gypsies, V. Glasgow Koste; (D) Robert Urbinati; (S) Lonn Atwood; (C) Sherri Geerdes; (L) Steve Wheeldon

Madeline, adapt: James Still, from Ludwig Bemelmans; (D) James Larson; (S) Larry Kaushansky;

(C) Sherri Geerdes; (L) Tim Osteen

The Cricket in Times Square, adapt: Donald Winslow, from George Selden; (D) Mark Hoeger; (S) Dana Westring; (C) Sherri Geerdes; (L) Tim Osteen

The Divorce Express, Gail Erwin, from Paula Danziger; (D) Roberta Larson; (S) Lonn Atwood; (C) Sherri Geerdes; (L) Tim Osteen

Curious George, adapt: Douglas Marr, from Margaret Rey and H.A. Rey; (D) Cindy Phaneuf; (S) Steve Wheeldon; (C) Sherri Geerdes; (L) Steve Wheeldon

Jack Frost, adapt: James Still; (D) Kevin Ehrhart; (S) Steve Wheeldon; (C) Kenda Slavin; (L) Tim Osteen

The Empty Space Theatre

KURT BEATTIE
Artistic Director

MELISSA HINES
Managing Director

Box 1748
Seattle, WA 98111-1748
(206) 587-3737 (bus.)
(206) 467-6000 (b.o.)

FOUNDED 1970
M. Burke Walker, James Royce, Julian Schembri, Charles Younger

SEASON
Oct.-Aug.

FACILITIES
Seating Capacity: 150
Stage: proscenium

FINANCES
Oct. 1, 1989-Sept. 30, 1990
Expenses: $716,635

CONTRACTS
AEA letter of agreement

The Empty Space Theatre is an association of theatre workers devoted to the exploration of cutting-edge works and unusual classics and to the development of gifted artists. Our traditional offbeat eclecticism, which in past years matched such wildly different works as *Ronnie B'wana, Jungle Guide* by Shallat and Engerman with *Woyzeck* by Georg Buchner, will bring together the anonymously authored *Arden of Faversham* and George Walker's *Love and Anger* during our 1991-92 season. In addition to our ongoing commitment to new plays and new playwrights, plus a deepening commitment to a multicultural theatre, we are creating an ensemble of distinguished actors who will mount productions of plays of their own choosing for a portion of our season. The Empty Space moves into its third decade of existence with artistic optimism, vigor and a will to embrace the most challenging ambitions of its artists.

—*Kurt Beattie*

Note: During the 1989-90 season, M. Burke Walker served as artistic director.

PRODUCTIONS 1989-90

Laughing Wild, Christopher Durang; (D) M. Burke Walker; (S) Peggy McDonald; (C) Paul Chi-Ming Louey; (L) Brian R. Duea

Etta Jenks, Marlane Meyer; (D) M. Burke Walker; (S) Peggy McDonald; (C) Anne Thaxter Watson; (L) Michael Wellborn

Speed-the-Plow, David Mamet; (D) David Ira Goldstein; (S) Don Yanick; (C) Rose Pederson; (L) Brian R. Duea

Tales of the Lost Formicans, Constance Congdon; (D) Nikki Appino; (S) Nina Moser; (C) Sarah Campbell; (L) Meg Fox

Smokey Joe's Cafe, conceived: M. Burke Walker; music and lyrics: Jerry Leiber and Mike Stoller; (D) M. Burke Walker; (S) Bill Forrester; (C) Jazmin Mercer; (L) Darren McCroom

PRODUCTIONS 1990-91

Virtus, Gregg Loughridge; (D) Gregg Loughridge; (S) Michael Olich; (C) Frances Kenny; (L) Meg Fox

Reckless, Craig Lucas; (D) M. Burke Walker; (S) Bill Forrester; (C) Frances Kenny; (L) Rick Paulsen

My Civilization, Paul Zaloom; (D) Donny Osman; (L) William Shipley Schaffner

Unkle Tomm's Kabin: A Deconstruction of the Novel by Harriet Beecher Stowe, Rick Rankin, J.T. Stewart and ensemble; (D) Susan Finque; (S) Karen Gjelsteen; (C) Paul Chi-Ming Louey; (L) Patty Matthieu

Jar the Floor, Cheryl West; (D) Gilbert McCauley; (S) Don Yanick; (C) Sarah Campbell; (L) Brian R. Duea

The Empty Space Theatre. Tawnya Pettiford-Wates, Frankie Trevino, Marcus Khalfani Rolland, Laurie Thomas and Kurt Beattie in *Unkle Tomm's Kabin*. Photo: Chris Bennion.

Ensemble Studio Theatre

CURT DEMPSTER
Artistic Director

DOMINICK BALLETTA
Managing Director

549 West 52nd St.
New York, NY 10019
(212) 247-4982 (bus.)
(212) 247-3405 (b.o.)

FOUNDED 1971
Curt Dempster

SEASON
Oct.-June

FACILITIES
Seating Capacity: 99
Stage: flexible

FINANCES
July 1, 1989-June 30, 1990
Expenses: $728,706

CONTRACTS
AEA Mini and letter of agreement

Founded in 1971, the Ensemble Studio Theatre remains dedicated to its original mission of nurturing theatre artists, with particular focus on the development and introduction of new American plays by emerging and established playwrights. The Ensemble has been an ecological cause—not just theatre, but a daily challenge to create new plays and keep them alive in an increasingly uncertain environment. The emphasis is on process—whether in the writing of a play or in the creation of a role—rather than product. All the works produced on the Ensemble's main stage are world premieres and have gone through several stages of development including readings, staged readings and workshops. The need of the individual work determines the method and manner of its development. The Ensemble's impact continues to be felt through our annual Marathon festival of new one-act plays and through the more than 360 productions across the country of full-length plays first developed at the Ensemble.

—Curt Dempster

PRODUCTIONS 1989-90

Briar Patch, Deborah Pryor; (D) Lisa Peterson; (S) David Birn; (C) Michael Krass; (L) Greg MacPherson

Sedalia Run, Katherine Long; (D) Mary B. Robinson

Harry Black, J. Dakota Powell; (D) Christopher A. Smith

Marathon '90 Series:

Match Point, Frank D. Gilroy; (D) Billy Hopkins; (S) Paul Wosnek; (C) David E. Sawaryn; (L) Greg MacPherson

Captive, Paul Weitz; (D) Susann Brinkley; (S) Paul Wosnek; (C) David E. Sawaryn; (L) Greg MacPherson

The Second Coming, Bill Bozzone; (D) Donato D'Albis; (S) Paul Wosnek; (C) David E. Sawaryn; (L) Greg MacPherson

Two War Scenes, David Mamet; (D) W.H. Macy; (S) Paul Wosnek; (C) David E. Sawaryn; (L) Greg MacPherson

Hamlet, Shel Silverstein; (D) Curt Dempster; (S) Mark Fitzgibbons; (C) Lauren Press; (L) Greg MacPherson

The Eclipse, Joyce Carol Oates; (D) Curt Dempster; (S) Mark Fitzgibbons; (C) Lauren Press; (L) Greg MacPherson

Eulogy for Mister Hamm, book, music and lyrics: Michael John LaChiusa; (D) Kirsten Sanderson; (S) Mark Fitzgibbons; (C) Lauren Press; (L) Greg MacPherson

The Stalwarts, OyamO; (D) Jack Gelber; (S) Mark Fitzgibbons; (C) Lauren Press; (L) Greg MacPherson

Mere Mortals, David Ives; (D) Jason McConnell Buzas; (S) Linda Gehring Balmuth; (C) Leslie McGovern; (L) Greg MacPherson

Death and the Maiden, Susan Kim; (D) Lisa Peterson; (S) Linda Gehring Balmuth; (C) Leslie McGovern; (L) Greg MacPherson

Tonight We Love, Romulus Linney; (D) John Stix; (S) Linda Gehring Balmuth; (C) Leslie McGovern; (L) Greg MacPherson

Stay Away a Little Closer, John Ford Noonan; (D) William Roudebush; (S) Linda Gehring Balmuth; (C) Leslie McGovern; (L) Greg MacPherson

Ensemble Studio Theatre. Melvin Van Peebles in *Kickin the Science*. Photo: Richard Wright.

PRODUCTIONS 1990-91

Go To Ground, Stuart Spencer; (D) Matthew Penn; (S) Sharon Sprague; (C) Lee Robin; (L) Greg MacPherson

Kickin the Science, Melvin Van Peebles; (D) Curt Dempster

Marathon '91 Series:

Where Were You When It Went Down?, David Mamet; (D) Billy Hopkins; (S) Ann Waugh; (L) Greg MacPherson

Naomi in the Living Room, Christopher Durang; (D) Christopher Durang; (S) Ann Waugh; (L) Greg MacPherson

Intimacy, Raymond Carver; adapt: Harris Yulin; (D) Harris Yulin; (S) Ann Waugh; (L) Greg MacPherson

You Can't Trust the Male, Randy Noojin; (D) Melodie Somers; (S) Ann Waugh; (L) Greg MacPherson

A Way With Words, Frank D. Gilroy; (D) Christopher A. Smith; (S) Ann Waugh; (L) Greg MacPherson

Practice, Leslie Ayvazian; (D) Elinor Renfield; (S) David Gallo; (C) David E. Sawaryn; (L) Greg MacPherson

Face Divided, Edward Allan Baker; (D) Risa Bramon Garcia; (S) David Gallo; (C) David E. Sawaryn; (L) Greg MacPherson

Rapid Eye Movement, Susan Kim; (D) Margaret Mancinelli; (S) David Gallo; (C) David E. Sawaryn; (L) Greg MacPherson

Over Texas, book, music and lyrics: Michael John LaChiusa; (D) Kirsten Sanderson; (S) David Gallo; (C) David E. Sawaryn; (L) Greg MacPherson

Can Can, Romulus Linney; (D) David Shookhoff; (S) David Gallo; (C) David E. Sawaryn; (L) Greg MacPherson

The World at Absolute Zero, Sherry Kramer; (D) Jason McConnell Buzas; (S) Ann Waugh; (C) Patricia Sarnaturo; (L) Greg MacPherson

Big Al, Bryan Goluboff; (D) Peter Maloney; (S) Ann Waugh; (C) Patricia Sarnaturo; (L) Greg MacPherson

The Last Yankee, Arthur Miller; (D) Gordon Edelstein; (S) Ann Waugh; (C) Patricia Sarnaturo; (L) Greg MacPherson

Salaam, Huey Newton, Salaam, Ed Bullins; (D) Woodie King, Jr.; (S) Ann Waugh; (C) Patricia Sarnaturo; (L) Greg MacPherson

Eureka Theatre Company

DEBRA J. BALLINGER
Producing Artistic Director

ALBERT HASSON
General Manager

2730 16th St.
San Francisco, CA 94103
(415) 558-9811 (bus.)
(415) 558-9898 (b.o.)

FOUNDED 1972
Robert Woodruff, Chris Silva

SEASON
Sept.-June

FACILITIES
Seating Capacity: 200
Stage: flexible

FINANCES
July 1, 1990-June 30, 1991
Expenses: $675,000

CONTRACTS
AEA BAT

Since its inception, the Eureka Theatre Company has been committed to producing plays that dig deeply into political and social concerns affecting contemporary life. Our productions question oppressive social structures, expose complacency, entertain, and reflect the cultural and ethnic diversity of

Eureka Theatre Company. 'Harry Waters, Jr. and Stephen Spinella in *Millennium Approaches*, Part I of *Angels in America*. Photo: Katy Raddatz.

our community. The Eureka has produced more than 70 premieres in the past 20 years. Our repertoire has included plays by Dario Fo, Caryl Churchill, Athol Fugard, Philip Kan Gotanda, Milcha Sanchez-Scott, Cherrie Moraga, Tony Kushner, Cassandra Medley and George C. Wolfe. Commissioned works have included Emily Mann's *Execution of Justice*, Amlin Gray's *Ubu Unchained* and, most recently, Tony Kushner's two-part epic, *Angels in America*. As we enter our third decade, we will continue to commission and develop new plays, as well as adding new music-theatre works and plays from international dramatic literature to our repertoire. Our School Adoption Program establishes a year-long relationship with groups of multicultural teens from three local high schools, and we work closely with many community and activist organizations to build ties and share both resources and audiences.

—*Debra J. Ballinger*

Note: During the 1989-90 season, Suzanne Bennett served as artistic director.

PRODUCTIONS 1989-90

Tales of the Lost Formicans, Constance Congdon; (D) Julie Hebert; (S) John Wilson; (C) Fumiko Bielefeldt; (L) Novella Smith

Heart of the World, Martha Boesing, Albert Greenberg and Helen Stoltzfus; (D) Martha Boesing; (S) Allan Droyan; (L) Jim Quinn

Pick Up Ax, Anthony Clarvoe; (D) Susan Marsden; (S) David Jon Hoffman; (C) Cassandra Carpenter; (L) Jack Carpenter

Ma Rose, Cassandra Medley; (D) Suzanne Bennett; (S) Pamela S. Peniston; (C) Allison Connor; (L) Jim Quinn

Roots in Water, Richard Nelson; (D) Amy Gonzalez; (S) Kate Edmunds; (C) Sandra Woodall; (L) Ellen Shireman

Solo Journeys, Part One: Doug Beale—Atlanta 1983, Kent Whipple; ***Part Two: From the Outside Looking In: On the Road—San Francisco 1990***, Anna Deavere Smith; (D) Suzanne Bennett; (S) Antonia R. Sheller; (C) Jayne Serba; (L) Dede Moyse

PRODUCTIONS 1990-91

Mensch Meier, Franz Xaver Kroetz; trans: Roger Downey; (D) Paul Hellyer; (S) Shevra Tait; (C) Nancy Jo Smith; (L) James Brentano

Shadow of a Man, Cherrie Moraga; (D) Maria Irene Fornes; (S) Maria Irene Fornes; (C) Gail Russell; (L) Timothy Wessling

The Mystery of Irma Vep, Charles Ludlam; (D) Suzanne Bennett; (S) Dawn Swiderski; (C) Sandra Woodall; (L) Michael Foster

Angels in America, Tony Kushner; (D) David Esbjornson; (S) Tom Kamm; (C) Sandra Woodall; (L) Jack Carpenter and Jim Cave

First Stage Milwaukee

ROB GOODMAN
Producer/Artistic Director

JOHN HEDGES
Managing Director

929 North Water St.
Milwaukee, WI 53202
(414) 273-7121 (bus.)
(414) 273-7206 (b.o.)

FOUNDED 1987
Archie Sarazin

SEASON
Oct.-May

FACILITIES
Todd Wehr Theater
Seating Capacity: 500
Stage: thrust

FINANCES
July 1, 1990-June 30, 1991
Expenses: $554,500

CONTRACTS
AEA TYA

First Stage Milwaukee is a theatre whose audience is young people: children, adolescents, teenagers, young adults. As a theatre for young people we are dedicated to producing works, both new and classic, which explore the world through the eyes of youth. At any given age, our world is full of mystery, wonder, joy, tragedy, and all the complexities of human relationships and experiences. First Stage Milwaukee chooses material that explores and exposes these complexities, enabling young people to understand, experience or perhaps simply acknowledge them in ways that will impact their daily lives. To this end the company uses a broad range of children's and world literature, including scripted plays and new adaptations. We believe theatre is full of possibilities

First Stage Milwaukee. David Ansay in *The Velveteen Rabbit*. Photo: Richard Brodzeller.

for today's young people as it takes them beyond the ordinary into worlds that engage the imagination, stimulate the mind and deeply touch the heart.

—Rob Goodman

PRODUCTIONS 1989-90

Tales of Peter Rabbit, adapt: K.A. Kern, from Beatrix Potter; (D) Rob Goodman; (S) Pat Doty; (C) Les Searing; (L) Robert Zenoni
Of Mice and Men, John Steinbeck; (D) Rob Goodman; (S) David B. Justin; (C) Ellen M. Kozak; (L) Robert Zenoni
To Kill a Mockingbird, adapt: K.A. Kern, from Harper Lee; (D) Tom Blair; (S) David B. Justin; (C) Ellen M. Kozak; (L) Spencer Mosse
Tales of a Fourth Grade Nothing, adapt: Bruce Mason, from Judy Blume; (D) Rob Goodman; (S) Pat Doty; (C) Ellen M. Kozak; (L) Robert Zenoni

PRODUCTIONS 1990-91

The Velveteen Rabbit, adapt: Thomas W. Olson, from Margery Williams; (D) Rob Goodman; (S) Pat Doty; (C) Dawna Gregory; (L) Robert Zenoni
The Best Christmas Pageant Ever, adapt: Barbara Robinson; (D) Michael LaGue; (S) Tom Colwin; (C) Therese Donarski; (L) Spencer Mosse
Dr. Jekyll and Mr. Hyde, adapt: K.A. Kern and Mark Weil, from Robert Louis Stevenson; (D) Mark Weil; (S) Danila Korogodski; (C) Danila Korogodski; (L) Robert Zenoni
My Emperor's New Clothes, Larry Shue, from Hans Christian Andersen; (D) Jon Kretzu; (S) Danila Korogodski; (C) Danila Korogodski; (L) Robert Zenoni
Play to Win, book: Carles Cleveland and James de Jongh; music: Jimi Foster; lyrics: Carles Cleveland, James de Jongh and Jimi Foster; (D) Bruce Butler; (S) Tom Barnes; (C) Linda Geley; (L) Robert Zenoni

Florida Studio Theatre

RICHARD HOPKINS
Artistic Director

JOHN JACOBSEN
General Manager

1241 North Palm Ave.
Sarasota, FL 34236
(813) 366-9017 (bus.)
(813) 366-9796 (b.o.)

FOUNDED 1973
Jon Spelman

SEASON
Nov.-June

FACILITIES
Seating Capacity: 165
Stage: thrust

FINANCES
July 1, 1989-June 30, 1990
Expenses: $498,000

CONTRACTS
AEA SPT

In the 1990s Florida Studio Theatre has firmly established itself as a resident contemporary theatre presenting alternative, thought-provoking work, and as a home for new works in its region. FST executes four primary programs: the mainstage season of four plays dedicated to contemporary writers, which serves 4000 subscribers annually; a New Play Development program, which culminates in the spring with a five-week event consisting of three festivals in one—the Children's Playwrights Festival, the Florida Playwrights Festival and the National Playwrights Festival; an educational program serving the area's avocational needs in addition to a training program for child and adult theatre students from around the country; and the Cabaret Club, which produces traditional and nontraditional cabaret work in a dinner-and-drink setting. The philosophy and driving vision of FST are best summed up in the words of James Joyce: "I go for the millionth time to forge in the smithy of my soul the uncreated conscience of the human race."

—Richard Hopkins

PRODUCTIONS 1989-90

Nite Club Confidential, book: Dennis Deal; music and lyrics: Dennis Deal and Albert Evans; (D) Richard Hopkins; (S) Keven Lock; (C) Vicky Small; (L) Paul D. Romance
Lies and Legends, music and lyrics: Harry Chapin; (D) Ted Papas; (S) Jeffrey Dean; (C) Vicky Small; (L) Paul D. Romance
Invictus, Laurie H. Hutzler; (D) Richard Hopkins; (S) Jeffrey Dean; (C) Marcella Beckwith; (L) Paul D. Romance
The Good Doctor, Neil Simon; (D) Richard Hopkins; (S) Jeffrey Dean; (C) Jimm Halliday; (L) Paul D. Romance
Drinking in America, Eric Bogosian; (D) Mark Hunter; (S) Jeffrey Dean; (C) Mark Hunter; (L) Paul D. Romance

PRODUCTIONS 1990-91

Hi-Hat Hattie!, Larry Parr; various composers and lyricists; (D) Richard Hopkins; (S) Jeffrey Dean; (C) Marcella Beckwith; (L) Paul D. Romance
Alfred Stieglitz Loves O'Keeffe, Lanie Robertson; (D) Carolyn Michel; (S) Jeffrey Dean; (C) Marcella Beckwith; (L) Paul D. Romance
Death By Misadventure, Michael Shaffer; (D) Richard Hopkins; (S) Jeffrey Dean; (C) Marcella Beckwith; (L) Paul D. Romance
Dynamic Products, Ron House; (D) Stephen Rothman; (S) Jeffrey Dean; (C) Marcella Beckwith and Thomas Preziosi; (L) Paul D. Romance
One Foot in Scarsdale, Jack Fournier; (D) Steve Ramay; (S) Jeffrey Dean; (C) Vicky Small; (L) Paul D. Romance

Ford's Theatre

FRANKIE HEWITT
Executive Producer

MICHAEL GENNARO
Managing Director

511 Tenth St. NW
Washington, DC 20004
(202) 638-2941 (bus.)
(202) 347-4833 (b.o.)

Florida Studio Theatre. Douglas Jones and Kate Hurd in *Alfred Steiglitz Loves O'Keeffe*. Photo: Betsy Reed.

Ford's Theatre. Scott Whitehurst, Brian Evaret Chandler and David Rainey in *Black Eagles.*

FOUNDED 1968
Frankie Hewitt

SEASON
Oct.-July

FACILITIES
Seating Capacity: 699
Stage: proscenium

FINANCES
Oct. 1, 1989-Sept. 30, 1990
Expenses: $4,474,577

CONTRACTS
AEA Special Production

Ford's Theatre presents plays that reflect America's joyous spirit and unique heritage. Accordingly, our productions often focus on the lives of influential and treasured Americans like Will Rogers (*Will Rogers USA*), Eleanor Roosevelt (*Eleanor*), Harry S. Truman (*Give 'Em Hell Harry*) and Martin Luther King, Jr. (*I Have a Dream*). Foremost in Ford's artistic mission is the creation, nurturing and performance of new musicals, a truly American art form. *Don't Bother Me I Can't Cope, Your Arms Too Short to Box with God, The Amen Corner* and other outstanding musical productions began as world premieres at Ford's Theatre. Many continued to Broadway engagements and national tours. Ford's Theatre has fostered relationships with many of our country's most innovative theatres. This healthy creative interaction has made a national forum for the work of many talented artists. Companies that have shared Ford's stage are Long Wharf Theatre, Crossroads Theatre Company and the Negro Ensemble Company.

—Frankie Hewitt

PRODUCTIONS 1989-90

Don't Let This Dream Go, book: Queen Esther Marrow; music featured by: Mahalia Jackson; lyrics: Queen Esther Marrow and Reginald Royal; (D) Robert Kalfin; (S) Fred Kolo; (C) Andrew B. Marlay; (L) Fred Kolo
A Christmas Carol, adapt: David H. Bell, from Charles Dickens; (D) David H. Bell; (S) Daniel Proett; (C) D. Polly Kendrick; (L) David Kissel
Sheila's Day, Duma Ndlovu; (D) Mbongeni Ngema; (S) Charles McClennahan; (C) Toni-Leslie James; (L) William H. Grant, III
Woody Guthrie's American Song, book: Peter Glazer; music and lyrics: Woody Guthrie; (D) Peter Glazer; (S) Philipp Jung; (C) Deborah Shaw; (L) David Noling
Grandma Moses, An American Primitive, Stephen Pouliot; (D) Howard Dallin; (S) Michael C. Beery; (C) Stephanie Schoelzel; (L) Duane Schuler

PRODUCTIONS 1990-91

Mountain, Douglas Scott; (D) John Henry Davis; (S) Philipp Jung; (C) David C. Woolard; (L) F. Mitchell Dana
A Christmas Carol, adapt: David H. Bell, from Charles Dickens; (D) David H. Bell; (S) Daniel Proett; (C) D. Polly Kendrick; (L) David Kissel
Black Eagles, Leslie Lee; (D) Ricardo Khan; (S) Charles McClennahan; (C) Beth Ribblett; (L) Shirley Prendergast
Forever Plaid, Stuart Ross; (D) Stuart Ross; (S) Neil Peter Jampolis; (C) Debra Stein; (L) Jane Reisman

Free Street Theater

DAVID SCHEIN
Artistic Director

CARROL McCARREN
General Manager

441 West North Ave.
Chicago, IL 60610
(312) 642-1234

FOUNDED 1969
Patrick Henry, Perry Baer

SEASON
Jan.-Dec. touring

FINANCES
Apr. 1, 1990-Mar. 31, 1991
Expenses: $513,000

CONTRACTS
AEA letter of agreement

Free Street Theatre is an outreach organization dedicated to developing new audiences and participants for the performing arts. We pursue this goal by creating original performance material based on the experiences of the people we seek to engage. Frequently, performers are drawn from the community that has inspired the work—such as an inner-city neighborhood (*Project!*), or the community of the elderly (the Free Street Too company). Their experiences are interpreted through music, dance and theatre by Free Street's artistic staff. The resultant performance pieces are unique documentaries of aspects of the contemporary American condition which speak both to and for the community. Some of our companies operate on Actors' Equity contracts, others do not; but all maintain the highest standards. Although the surroundings and trappings may be low-rent, our endeavor is to make the experience high art.

—David Schein

Note: During the 1989-90 and 1990-91 seasons, Donald Douglas served as acting artistic director.

Free Street Theater. *Project!* Photo: R. Aberman.

PRODUCTIONS 1989-90

Project!, Patrick Henry, Tricia Alexander and Doug Lofstrom; (D) Donald Douglass; (S) Rob Hamilton; (L) Marc Shellist
Reflections, Patrick Henry, Jim Rossow, Tricia Alexander and Ron Bieganski; (D) Tricia Alexander
Two Soldiers, book and lyrics: Doug Lofstrom and Al Day; music: Doug Lofstrom; (D) Jeff Berkson; (S) Bill Dicker; (C) J. Magowski; (L) Ken Bowen
When the Drum Speaks, adapt: Patrick Henry and Jim Rossow; (D) Donald Douglass

PRODUCTIONS 1990-91

Project!, Patrick Henry, Tricia Alexander and Doug Lofstrom; (D) Donald Douglass; (S) Rob Hamilton; (L) Marc Shellist
Reflections, Patrick Henry, Jim Rossow, Tricia Alexander and Ron Bieganski; (D) David Schein
When the Drum Speaks, adapt: Patrick Henry and Jim Rossow; (D) Donald Douglass
Images, book: Donald Douglass; music: Doug Lofstrom; lyrics: Donald Douglass and Tricia Alexander; (D) Donald Douglass; (S) Donald Douglass
Club Date, book and music: Doug Lofstrom; lyrics: Tricia Alexander; (D) David Schein

Fulton Opera House

KATHLEEN A. COLLINS
Artistic Director

DEIDRE W. SIMMONS
Executive Director

Box 1865
Lancaster, PA 17603
(717) 394-7133 (bus.)
(717) 397-7425 (b.o.)

FOUNDED 1963
Fulton Opera House Foundation

SEASON
Oct.-May

FACILITIES
Seating Capacity: 909
Stage: proscenium

FINANCES
Oct. 1, 1989-Sept. 30, 1990
Expenses: $848,454

CONTRACTS
AEA letter of agreement

The Fulton Opera House, a magnificent National Historic Landmark, houses a theatre company producing contemporary American plays. By concentrating on works that explore powerful social issues, we are striving to create theatre that breathes new life into these venerable old bricks. Our educational outreach programs include classes for children and a touring production that reaches more than 30,000 young people annually. We are gathering a company of artists committed to building a vital and challenging regional theatre here in the midst of this conservative, nonmetropolitan community.

—*Kathleen A. Collins*

PRODUCTIONS 1989-90

Dracula, adapt: Hamilton Deane and John L. Balderston, from Bram Stoker; (D) Kathleen A. Collins; (S) Robert Klingelhoefer; (C) Virginia M. West; (L) Bill Simmons
Hans Christian Andersen, book adapt: John Fearnley, Beverly Cross and Tommy Steele, from original screenplay; music and lyrics: Frank Loesser; (D) Carol M. Tanzman; (S) Robert Klingelhoefer; (C) Gabriel Berry; (L) Bill Simmons
A Shayna Maidel, Barbara Lebow; (D) Margaret Booker; (S) Robert Klingelhoefer; (C) Beth Dunkelberger; (L) Bill Simmons
The Elephant Man, Bernard Pomerance; (D) Kathleen A. Collins; (S) Robert Klingelhoefer; (C) Beth Dunkelberger; (L) Bill Simmons
Cracker Barrel, Barry Kornhauser; (D) Kathleen A. Collins; (S) Robert Klingelhoefer; (C) Gabriel Berry; (L) Peter Smith

PRODUCTIONS 1990-91

Frankenstein, adapt: Robert N. Sandberg, from Mary Shelley; (D) Kathleen A. Collins; (S) Robert Klingelhoefer; (C) Beth Dunkelberger; (L) Bill Simmons
The Secret Garden, adapt: Pamela Sterling, from Frances Hodgson Burnett; (D) John Going; (S) Robert Klingelhoefer; (C) Marla Jurglanis; (L) Bill Simmons
The Road to Mecca, Athol Fugard; (D) Kathleen A. Collins; (S) Robert Klingelhoefer; (C) Chib Gratz; (L) Bill Simmons
Other People's Money, Jerry Sterner; (D) Kathleen A. Collins; (S) Robert Klingelhoefer; (C) Chib Gratz; (L) Bill Simmons
The Nose, Elizabeth Egloff, from Nikolai Gogol; (D) Barry Kornhauser; (S) Robert Klingelhoefer; (C) Beth Dunkelberger; (L) Bill Simmons

George Street Playhouse

GREGORY S. HURST
Producing Artistic Director

DIANE CLAUSSEN
Managing Director

9 Livingston Ave.
New Brunswick, NJ 08901
(908) 846-2895 (bus.)
(908) 246-7469 (b.o.)

FOUNDED 1974
John Herochik, Eric Krebs

SEASON
Sept.-June

FACILITIES
George 367
Seating Capacity: 367
Stage: thrust

George 99
Seating Capacity: 99
Stage: flexible

State Theatre
Seating Capacity: 1800
Stage: proscenium

FINANCES
July 1, 1990-June 30, 1991
Expenses: $1,948,970

CONTRACTS
AEA LORT (C)

We are imagining regional theatre at its best: an art form that

Fulton Opera House. Jon Krupp in *The Elephant Man*. Photo: A. Jack Leonard.

George Street Playhouse. Beth Fowler, Mark Shannon and Barbara Gulan in *Greetings*. Photo: Miguel Pagliere.

illuminates great moments in our lives. We choose plays which reveal the truth within those great moments. Our focus on developing new plays and musicals is balanced by innovative productions of classic and contemporary plays by world-class playwrights. We seek plays that transcend their own time and possess vivid characterizations, imaginative metaphors, universality, color and intensity. Our investment in new plays by playwrights who speak to the concerns and experience of all humankind earns for our stage the commitment of the finest actors including Ellen Barkin, Len Cariou, John Cullum, Celeste Holm, Anne Jackson, Audra Lindley, Estelle Parsons, Eli Wallach and James Whitmore. The playhouse is collaborating on a range of projects with a select group of theatres, individuals and artists who share our dedication to excellence. Our Outreach Touring Company presents five issue-oriented plays to more than 60,000 students statewide.

—*Gregory S. Hurst*

PRODUCTIONS 1989-90

Les Liaisons Dangereuses, Christopher Hampton, from Choderlos de Laclos; (D) Gregory S. Hurst; (S) Atkin Pace; (C) Barbara Forbes; (L) Donald Holder

Brighton Beach Memoirs, Neil Simon; (D) Susan Kerner; (S) Deborah Jasien; (C) Barbara Forbes; (L) Donald Holder

Broadway Bound, Neil Simon; (D) Wendy Liscow; (S) Deborah Jasien; (C) Barbara Forbes; (L) Donald Holder

Mountain, Douglas Scott; (D) John Henry Davis; (S) Philipp Jung; (C) Barbara Forbes; (L) Donald Holder

Johnny Pye and the Foolkiller, book adapt: Mark St. Germain, from Stephen Vincent Benet; music: Randy Courts; lyrics: Mark St. Germain and Randy Courts; (D) Paul Lazarus; (S) William Barclay; (C) Mary L. Hayes; (L) Donald Holder

Jekyll and Hyde, book adapt: Leonora Thuna, from Robert Louis Stevenson; music: Norman Sachs; lyrics: Mel Mandel; (D) Gregory S. Hurst; (S) Deborah Jasien; (C) Barbara Forbes; (L) Donald Holder

Handy Dandy, William Gibson; (D) Tony Giordano; (S) Deborah Jasien; (C) Barbara Forbes; (L) Donald Holder

Feast of Fools, Geoff Hoyle; (D) Anthony Taccone; (S) Scott Weldin; (L) David Lincecum

PRODUCTIONS 1990-91

Greetings, Tom Dudzick; (D) Gregory S. Hurst; (S) Atkin Pace; (C) Barbara Forbes; (L) Donald Holder

Driving Miss Daisy, Alfred Uhry; (D) Susan Kerner; (S) Deborah Jasien; (C) Barbara Forbes; (L) Harry Feiner

Oil City Symphony, Mike Craver, Mark Hardwick, Debra Monk and Mary Murfitt; (D) Wendy Liscow; (S) James Medved; (C) Deborah Jasien and Barbara S. Reich; (L) David Lincecum

Pendragon, Laurie H. Hutzler; (D) Wendy Liscow; (S) Deborah Jasien; (C) Barbara Forbes; (L) David Neville

Sparky and the Fitz, Craig Volk; (D) Stephen Rothman; (S) Deborah Jasien; (C) Barbara Forbes; (L) Donald Holder

Forgiving Typhoid Mary, Mark St. Germain; (D) Gregory S. Hurst; (S) Atkin Pace; (C) Barbara Forbes; (L) Donald Holder

The Root, Gary Richards; (D) Matthew Penn; (S) Deborah Jasien; (C) Barbara Forbes; (L) Donald Holder

Germinal Stage Denver

ED BAIERLEIN
Director/Manager

2450 West 44th Ave.
Denver, CO 80211
(303) 455-7108

FOUNDED 1974
Ed Baierlein, Ginger Valone, Sallie Diamond, Jack McKnight

SEASON
Oct.-Aug.

FACILITIES
Seating Capacity: 100
Stage: thrust

FINANCES
Sept. 1, 1989-Aug. 31, 1990
Expenses: $100,360

Germinal Stage Denver is the vestigial tail of regional theatres, an independent neighborhood filling station striving mightily against the u-pump-its, washing your windshields whether you like it or not. We're an actors' theatre, semi-rough, minimalist when we can afford it, still vaguely postmodern, but backpedalling forward to modern, advancing back to ritual, or lateralling to shamelessly theatrical in moments of weakness. Denver lacks therapists skilled at dealing with the hit-flop mentality. Support groups are forming slowly. Goals for the next two years:
1) development of guerilla tactics against political correctness (e.g. pro-cannibalism theme session); 2) consequent cultivation of private patronage sources. Outlook: dismal to bleak.

—*Ed Baierlein*

PRODUCTIONS 1989-90

Major Barbara, George Bernard Shaw; (D) Ed Baierlein; (S) Ed Baierlein; (C) Sallie Diamond; (L) Stephen R. Kramer

Exit The King, Eugene Ionesco;

Germinal Stage Denver. *Exit The King*. Photo: Strack Edwards.

trans: Donald Watson; (D) Ed Baierlein; (S) Ed Baierlein; (C) Sallie Diamond; (L) Ed Baierlein

A View from the Bridge, Arthur Miller; (D) Laura Cuetara; (S) Ed Baierlein; (C) Sallie Diamond; (L) Stephen R. Kramer

Private Lives, Noel Coward; (D) Ed Baierlein; (S) Ed Baierlein; (C) Heather Doyle; (L) Ed Baierlein

The Birthday Party, Harold Pinter; (D) Ed Baierlein; (S) Ed Baierlein; (C) Sallie Diamond; (L) Ed Baierlein

PRODUCTIONS 1990-91

Arms and the Man, George Bernard Shaw; (D) Ed Baierlein; (S) Ed Baierlein; (C) Sallie Diamond; (L) Ed Baierlein

The White Whore and the Bit Player, Tom Eyen; (D) Ed Baierlein; (S) Stephen R. Kramer; (C) Carol L. Timblin; (L) Stephen R. Kramer

Woyzeck, Georg Buchner; trans: Stephen R. Kramer; (D) Stephen R. Kramer; (S) Stephen R. Kramer; (C) Carol L. Timblin; (L) Stephen R. Kramer

What the Butler Saw, Joe Orton; (D) Ed Baierlein; (S) Ed Baierlein; (C) Sallie Diamond; (L) Ed Baierlein

The Learned Ladies, Moliere; trans: Richard Wilbur; (D) Laura Cuetara; (S) Laura Cuetara; (C) Paula M. Harvey; (L) Ed Baierlein

The Gin Game, D.L. Coburn; (D) Ed Baierlein; (S) Stephen R. Kramer; (C) Sallie Diamond; (L) Stephen R. Kramer

GeVa Theatre

HOWARD J. MILLMAN
Producing Artistic Director

CHRISTOPHER F. KAWOLSKY
Managing Director

ANTHONY ZERBE
Associate Artistic Director

75 Woodbury Blvd.
Rochester, NY 14607
(716) 232-1366 (bus.)
(716) 232-GEVA (b.o.)

FOUNDED 1972
William Selden, Cynthia Mason Selden

SEASON
Sept.-June

FACILITIES
Richard Pine Theatre
Seating Capacity: 552
Stage: thrust

FINANCES
July 1, 1990-June 30, 1991
Expenses: $3,438,628

CONTRACTS
AEA LORT (B)

GeVa Theatre presents a distinctive variety of theatre experience including the classics of the world and American stage, revivals, musicals, contemporary dramas and comedies. GeVa has a specific commitment to the American playwright, to the production of new plays and to the implementation of those projects that reflect new vision and direction on the part of theatre artists. Associate artistic director Anthony Zerbe has specific responsibility for the production of new plays for the main stage. The French Roast Festival, a staged reading series, works with playwrights in developing that work. GeVa has also completed its first year of a new theatre-in-education program designed by the theatre in collaboration with the Rochester City School District. The theatre's ancillary programming enhances the community's knowledge of the process of theatre and includes a noontime lecture series, interpreted performances for the hearing-impaired, discussion forums with artists and audience, play support teams, tours of the renovated landmark theatre facility, and an extensive volunteer program. Free-to-the-public outreach efforts include availability of staff for workshops and lectures, and the loan of the theatre's costumes and props.

—Howard J. Millman

PRODUCTIONS 1989-90

Peccadillo, Garson Kanin; (D) Stephen Rothman; (S) Joseph Varga; (C) Shigeru Yaji; (L) Betsy Adams

Frankie and Johnny in the Clair de Lune, Terrence McNally; (D) Howard J. Millman; (S) Bob Barnett; (L) Phil Monat

Ma Rainey's Black Bottom, August Wilson; (D) Claude Purdy; (S) James Sandefur; (C) Constanza Romero; (L) Phil Monat

Groucho: A Life in Revue, Arthur Marx; (D) Howard J. Millman; (S) Michael Hotopp; (L) Michael Hotopp

A Streetcar Named Desire, Tennessee Williams; (D) Gus Kaikkonen; (S) James Fenhagen; (C) Constanza Romero; (L) F. Mitchell Dana

Oh, the Innocents, Ari Roth; (D) Joe Mantello; (S) Marjorie Bradley Kellogg; (C) Susan E. Mickey; (L) Kirk Bookman

Forgiving Typhoid Mary, Mark St. Germain; (D) Anthony Zerbe; (S) Marjorie Bradley Kellogg; (C) Susan E. Mickey; (L) Kirk Bookman

Adult Fiction, Brian Richard Mori; (D) Craig Belknap; (S) Marjorie Bradley Kellogg; (C) Susan E. Mickey; (L) Kirk Bookman

A Christmas Carol, adapt: Eberle Thomas, from Charles Dickens; (D) Barbara Redmond; (S) Bob Barnett; (C) Pamela Scofield; (L) Nic Minetor

GeVa Theatre. Les Marsden and Amelia Prentice in *Groucho: A Life in Revue*. Photo: Gelfand-Piper.

PRODUCTIONS 1990-91

Jane Eyre, book adapt and lyrics: Ted Davis, from Charlotte Bronte; music: David Clark; (D) Ted Davis; (S) Bob Barnett; (C) Pamela Scofield; (L) F. Mitchell Dana

Driving Miss Daisy, Alfred Uhry; (D) William Gregg; (S) James Fenhagen; (C) Susan E. Mickey; (L) F. Mitchell Dana

A Stone Carver, William Mastrosimone; (D) Howard J. Millman; (S) Marjorie Bradley Kellogg; (C) James B. Greco; (L) Kirk Bookman

Man of La Mancha, book adapt: Dale Wasserman, from Miguel de Cervantes; music: Mitch Leigh; lyrics: Joe Darion; (D) Howard J. Millman; (S) Bob Barnett; (C) Pamela Scofield; (L) Kirk Bookman

A Raisin in the Sun, Lorraine Hansberry; (D) Woodie King, Jr.; (S) Felix E. Cochren; (C) Judy Dearing; (L) Robert Christen

The Closer, Willy Holtzman; (D) Anthony Zerbe; (S) James

Fenhagen; (C) Susan E. Mickey; (L) Phil Monat

Life in the Trees, Catherine Butterfield; (D) Louis Scheeder; (S) James Fenhagen; (C) Susan E. Mickey; (L) Phil Monat

Pitz & Joe, Dominique Cieri; (D) Gus Kaikkonen; (S) James Fenhagen; (C) Susan E. Mickey; (L) Phil Monat

A Christmas Carol, adapt: Eberle Thomas, from Charles Dickens; (D) Barbara Redmond; (S) Bob Barnett; (C) Pamela Scofield; (L) Nic Minetor

Gloucester Stage Company

ISRAEL HOROVITZ
Artistic Director

MARY JOHN BOYLAN
Business Director

267 East Main St.
Gloucester, MA 01930
(508) 281-4099

FOUNDED 1979
Israel Horovitz, Geoffrey Richon, Alden Blodgett

SEASON
May-Sept.

FACILITIES
Gorton Theatre
Seating Capacity: 150
Stage: flexible

FINANCES
Jan. 1, 1990-Dec. 31, 1990
Expenses: $243,099

CONTRACTS
AEA SPT

The Gloucester Stage Company exists primarily to produce new American and British stage writing that relates thematically to life as it is lived in Gloucester, Massachusetts. The company also embraces actor and director-oriented projects that relate specifically to the Gloucester community. The theatre is especially disposed to linkage with other nonprofit theatres in the development of new work, with a firm dedication to a continuing creative process in the completion of a play prior to its New York City premiere. Further, Gloucester Stage is dedicated to the development and training of future professionals in every aspect of theatre production, and to providing a continuing educational resource to the residents of Cape Ann and the north-of-Boston area.

—Israel Horovitz

PRODUCTIONS 1990

Happy Days, Samuel Beckett; (D) Patrick Swanson; (S) Whitney White; (C) Jane Alois Stein; (L) Whitney White

Hard Times, adapt: Stephen Jeffreys, from Charles Dickens; (D) Grey Cattell Johnson; (S) Whitney White; (C) Jane Alois Stein; (L) Whitney White

Strong-Man's Weak Child, Israel Horovitz; (D) Israel Horovitz; (S) Jay C. McLauchlan; (C) Janet Irving; (L) John Ambrosone

Shirley Valentine, Willy Russell; (D) Patrick Swanson; (S) Patrick Carey; (C) Janet Irving; (L) Kim McManus

PRODUCTIONS 1991

The Dance, Jay O'Callahan; (D) Richard McElvain; (S) Jay C. McLauchlan; (C) Jay O'Callahan; (L) Kim McManus

The Primary English Class, Israel Horovitz; (D) Robert Walsh; (S) James Fallon; (C) Jane Alois Stein; (L) Whitney White

Talking Heads, Alan Bennett; (D) Patrick Swanson; (S) James Fallon; (C) Jane Alois Stein; (L) Whitney White

A Streetcar Named Desire, Tennessee Williams; (D) Sidney Montz; (S) Eric Levenson; (C) Jane Alois Stein; (L) Eric Levenson

Gloucester Stage Company. Paula Phim in *Happy Days*. Photo: Clark S. Cinchan.

Goodman Theatre

ROBERT FALLS
Artistic Director

ROCHE SCHULFER
Producing Director

FRANK GALATI
MICHAEL MAGGIO
Associate Directors

200 South Columbus Drive
Chicago, IL 60603
(312) 443-3811 (bus.)
(312) 443-3800 (b.o.)

FOUNDED 1925
Art Institute of Chicago

SEASON
Sept.-July

FACILITIES
Goodman Mainstage
Seating Capacity: 683
Stage: proscenium

Goodman Studio Theatre
Seating Capacity: 135
Stage: proscenium

FINANCES
July 1, 1990-June 30, 1991
Expenses: $6,240,800

CONTRACTS
AEA LORT (B+) and (D)

The Goodman is Chicago's largest and oldest nonprofit theatre, and we take advantage of its great resources to produce classic and contemporary works of size—large in both imagination and physical scale. Our goal is to infuse the classics with the energy usually reserved for new works, and to treat new plays with the care and reverence usually given to the classics. Working with associate directors Frank Galati and Michael Maggio, I intend to continue our efforts on the Goodman five-play mainstage series. At the same time, we aim to expand our artistic scope, and our audience's, by using our Studio Theatre to introduce new plays and leading theatre artists whose work is rarely seen in Chicago. We will continue to expand auxiliary programming to accompany each production, encouraging our audience into active participation in the theatrical process. We also seek to develop younger audiences through our program of free student matinees and close collaboration with the public school system.

—Robert Falls

PRODUCTIONS 1989-90

The Misanthrope, Moliere; adapt: Neil Bartlett; (D) Robert Falls; (S) George Tsypin; (C) Susan Hilferty; (L) James F. Ingalls

The Winter's Tale, William Shakespeare; (D) Frank Galati; (S) John Conklin; (C) Virgil Johnson; (L) Jennifer Tipton

'Tis Pity She's a Whore, John

Goodman Theatre. Brian Dennehy and Jerome Kilty in *The Iceman Cometh.*

Ford; (D) JoAnne Akalaitis; (S) John Conklin; (C) Gabriel Berry; (L) Pat Collins

Uncle Vanya, Anton Chekhov; adapt: David Mamet; trans: Vlada Chernomordik; (D) Michael Maggio; (S) Linda Buchanan; (C) Nan Cibula-Jenkins; (L) James F. Ingalls

The Gospel at Colonus, adapt: Lee Breuer, from Sophocles; music: Bob Telson; lyrics: Lee Breuer and Bob Telson; (D) Lee Breuer; (S) Alison Yerxa; (C) Ghretta Hynd; (L) Robert Christen

The Meeting, Jeff Stetson; (D) Chuck Smith; (S) Tim Oien; (C) Glenn Billings; (L) Tim Oien

Marvin's Room, Scott McPherson; (D) David Petrarca; (S) Linda Buchanan; (C) Claudia Boddy; (L) Robert Christen

Elliot Loves, Jules Feiffer; (D) Mike Nichols; (S) Tony Walton; (C) Ann Roth; (L) Paul Gallo

PRODUCTIONS 1990-91

The Iceman Cometh, Eugene O'Neill; (D) Robert Falls; (S) John Conklin; (C) Merrily Murray-Walsh; (L) James F. Ingalls

Joe Turner's Come and Gone, August Wilson; (D) Jonathan Wilson; (S) Michael S. Philippi; (C) Claudia Boddy; (L) Robert Christen

A Midsummer Night's Dream, William Shakespeare; (D) Michael Maggio and Steve Scott; (S) John Conklin; (C) Susan Hilferty; (L) Pat Collins

The Visit, Friedrich Durrenmatt; adapt: Maurice Valency; (D) David Petrarca; (S) Paul Steinberg; (C) Virgil Johnson; (L) James F. Ingalls

Book of the Night, book, music and lyrics: Louis Rosen and Thom Bishop; (D) Robert Falls; (S) Michael S. Philippi; (C) Gabriel Berry; (L) James F. Ingalls

Terrors of Pleasure and ***Monster in a Box***, Spalding Gray; (D) Renee Shafransky

From the Mississippi Delta, Dr. Endesha Ida Mae Holland; (D) Jonathan Wilson; (S) Michael S. Philippi; (C) Jeffrey Kelly; (L) Chris Phillips

Deep in a Dream of You, David Cale; (D) David Petrarca; (S) Linda Buchanan; (C) Linda Buchanan; (L) Linda Buchanan

Goodspeed Opera House

MICHAEL P. PRICE
Executive Director

SUE FROST
Associate Producer

Box A, Goodspeed Landing
East Haddam, CT 06423
(203) 873-8664 (bus.)
(203) 873-8668 (b.o.)

FOUNDED 1963
Goodspeed Opera House Foundation

SEASON
Apr.-Dec.

FACILITIES
Goodspeed Opera House
Seating Capacity: 398
Stage: proscenium

Goodspeed-at-Chester/The Norma Terris Theatre
Seating Capacity: 200
Stage: proscenium

CONTRACTS
AEA LORT (B+) and (D)

The Goodspeed Opera House is dedicated to the heritage, preservation and development of the musical theatre. Producing both classical and contemporary musicals, the Opera House has sent 12 productions to Broadway, including *Annie*, *Shenandoah* and *Man of La Mancha*. The Goodspeed was awarded a special Tony Award in 1980 for its significant contributions to this important art form. Goodspeed's second stage, Goodspeed-at-Chester/The Norma Terris Theatre, provides an intimate performing space exclusively for new works of musical theatre. Here, writers and creative staff have a rare opportunity to develop a "musical-in-progress" before an audience. Goodspeed operates the Library of the Musical Theatre, a resource center which houses performance and archival materials, and publishes *Show Music* magazine, a national publication on the musical theatre. Both are part of Goodspeed's continuing commitment to the musical theatre.

—*Michael P. Price*

PRODUCTIONS 1989-90

A Connecticut Yankee, book adapt: Herbert Fields, from Mark Twain; music: Richard Rodgers; lyrics: Lorenz Hart; (D) Thomas Gruenewald; (S) Clarke Dunham; (C) Dean Brown; (L) Craig Miller

Madame Sherry, book and lyrics: Otto Harbach; music: Karl Hoschna; (D) Martin Connor; (S) Eduardo Sicangco; (C) Jose Lengson; (L) Kirk Bookman

Oh, Kay!, book adapt: James Racheff, from Guy Bolton and P.G. Wodehouse; music: George Gershwin; lyrics: Ira Gershwin; (D) Martin Connor; (S) Kenneth Foy; (C) Judy Dearing; (L) Craig Miller

A Fine and Private Place, book adapt and lyrics: Erik Haagensen, from Peter S. Beagle; music: Richard Isen; (D) Robert Kalfin; (S) Fred Kolo; (L) Fred Kolo

The Real Life Story of Johnny de Facto, book, music and lyrics: Douglas Post; (D) Andre Ernotte; (S) William Barclay; (C) Roslyn Brunner; (L) Phil Monat

Goodspeed Opera House. Spiro Malas and Sophie Hayden in *The Most Happy Fella*. Photo: Diane Sobolewski.

PRODUCTIONS 1990-91

The Chocolate Soldier, book adapt: Larry Carpenter, from Stanislaus Stange; music: Oscar Straus; lyrics: Ted Drachman; (D) Larry Carpenter; (S) James Leonard Joy; (C) John Falabella; (L) Craig Miller

Pal Joey, book: John O'Hara; music: Richard Rodgers; lyrics: Lorenz Hart; (D) Dan Siretta; (S) Kenneth Foy; (C) Jose Lengson; (L) Kirk Bookman

Bells Are Ringing, book and lyrics: Betty Comden and Adolph Green; music: Jule Styne; (D) Sue Lawless; (S) James Noone; (C) Bradford Wood and Gregory Poplyk; (L) Kirk Bookman

The Most Happy Fella, book, music and lyrics: Frank Loesser; (D) Gerald Gutierrez; (S) John Lee Beatty; (C) Jess Goldstein; (L) Craig Miller

Annie 2, book: Thomas Meehan; music: Charles Strouse; lyrics: Martin Charnin; (D) Martin Charnin; (S) Evelyn Sakash; (C) Theoni V. Aldredge; (L) Ken Billington

Blanco!, book: Willy Holtzman; music and lyrics: Skip Kennon; (D) Joe Billone; (S) Linda Hacker; (C) Thom J. Peterson; (L) John Hastings

Arthur: The Musical, book adapt and lyrics: Marta Kauffman and David Crane, from original screenplay; music: Michael Skloff; (D) Joe Billone; (S) Linda Hacker; (C) Emily L. Ockenfels; (L) John Hastings

Great American History Theatre

Formerly Great North American History Theatre

LYNN LOHR
LANCE S. BELVILLE
Co-Artistic Directors

THOMAS H. BERGER
General Manager

30 East 10th St.
St. Paul, MN 55101
(612) 292-4323

FOUNDED 1978
Lynn Lohr, Lance S. Belville

SEASON
Sept.-June

FACILITIES
Crawford Livingston Theatre
Seating Capacity: 595
Stage: thrust

FINANCES
July 1, 1989-June 30, 1990
Expenses: $525,100

CONTRACTS
AEA Guest Artist

The Great American History Theatre exists to develop world premieres that connect with audiences and speak to their lives. The theatre uses history, folklore, social issues, narratives and oral histories as the launching platforms for the imaginations of playwrights. The theatre focuses first on the untold stories of the Midwest but also offers its audiences a window to other people and other times and places: Brazil, Ireland, Sweden and the Southwest. The theatre seeks offbeat, surreal stagings and likes to transform airplane hangars or forts into theatres, or its own performing space into a speakeasy or an open-pit mine/union hall. Touring nationally with companies as large as 15, the theatre also is at home in rural communities, burrowing in with long-term research/writing/production workshops.

—Lynn Lohr, Lance S. Belville

PRODUCTIONS 1989-90

A Time on Earth, Vilhelm Moberg; trans: Roger McKnight and Jay Lutz; (D) Vicky Boone; (S) Chris Johnson; (C) Chris Johnson; (L) Chris Johnson

The Immigrant, Mark Harelik; (D) Ron Peluso; (S) Chris Johnson; (C) Frederick Rogers; (L) Chris Johnson

December Mornings, adapt: Peg Sheldrick, from Truman Capote; (D) Lynn Musgrave; (S) Chris Johnson; (C) Frederick Rogers; (L) Chris Johnson

A Servants' Christmas, John Fenn; (D) Dennis Lickteig; (S) Steve Griffith; (C) Frederick Rogers; (L) Thomas H. Berger

Nina! The Musical, book: Lance S. Belville; music and lyrics: John Van Orman; (D) Lynn Lohr; (S) Chris Johnson; (C) Dawn D'Hanson; (L) Chris Johnson

Mesabi Red, book: Lance S. Belville; music and lyrics: Charlie Maguire and Jim Miller; (D) Ron Peluso; (S) Chris Johnson; (C) Thomas H. Berger; (L) Chris Johnson

Homegrown Heroes, Lance S. Belville, Ta-Coumba T. Aitkin, Grant Richey and Lynn Nankivil; (D) Leah Lowe, Vance Holmes, Grant Richey, Lance S. Belville; (S) Thomas H. Berger; (C) Thomas H. Berger; (L) Chris Johnson

Great American History Theatre. Rod Pierce, Tony Denman and Jan Lee in *Mesabi Red*. Photo: Gerald Gustafson.

PRODUCTIONS 1990-91

Last Hooch at the Hollyhocks, Lance S. Belville; various composers and lyricists; (D) Lynn Lohr and Michael Ellison; (S) Chris Johnson; (C) Mary Alden, Joan Gerten and Brigitte Heaney; (L) Chris Johnson

Exile from Main Street: A Portrait of Sinclair Lewis, Lance S. Belville; (D) Don T. Maseng; (S) Don T. Maseng; (C) Stephen Meredink; (L) Thomas H. Berger

Tree of Memory II, Tony Bouza, Susan Vass, David Hawley, Craig Wright and Lance S. Belville; (D) Phil Bratnober, Don T. Maseng and Michael Ellison; (S) Chris Johnson; (C) Mary Alden, Joan Gerten and Brigitte Heaney; (L) Chris Johnson

A Servants' Christmas, John Fenn; (D) Leah Lowe; (S) Steve Griffith; (C) Mary Alden, Joan Gerten and Brigitte Heaney; (L) Chris Johnson

Mesabi Red, book: Lance S. Belville; music and lyrics: Charlie Maguire and Jim Miller; (D) Michael Ellison; (S) Chris Johnson; (C) Mary Alden, Joan Gerten and Brigitte Heaney; (L) Chris Johnson

Selkirk Avenue, Bruce McManus;

Great Lakes Theater Festival. Brian Keeler and Nan Martin in *Dividing the Estate*. Photo: Roger Mastroianni.

(D) Don T. Maseng; (S) Chris Johnson; (C) Mary Alden, Joan Gerten and Brigitte Heaney; (L) Chris Johnson

A Couple of Blaguards, Frank McCourt and Malachy McCourt; (D) Ron Peluso; (S) Thomas H. Berger; (C) Mary Alden, Joan Gerten and Brigitte Heaney; (L) Chris Johnson

Great Lakes Theater Festival

GERALD FREEDMAN
Artistic Director

MARY BILL
Managing Director

1501 Euclid Ave., Suite 250
Cleveland, OH 44115
(216) 241-5490 (bus.)
(216) 241-6000 (b.o.)

FOUNDED 1962
Community members

SEASON
Oct.-May

FACILITIES
Ohio Theatre
Seating Capacity: 643
Stage: proscenium

FINANCES
Feb. 1, 1990-Jan. 31, 1991
Expenses: $3,162,793

CONTRACTS
AEA LORT (B)

Though the Great Lakes Theatre Festival continues to uphold the mandate for classical theatre that launched it, we have been challenging our perception of what that responsibility means. We are interested in the whole spectrum of American plays—not only the acknowledged great works, but the culturally significant plays and musicals that placed Broadway in the mainstream of American entertainment from the 1920s through the 1950s. And we are interested in pursuing the special resonance that comes from seeing world classics side by side with new plays. With regard to performance style, I am drawn to actors adept at both classic drama and musicals. I find a kinship between doing Shakespeare, for example, and musical theatre. The presentational styles—the soliloquies in one form, the songs in the other—each require a high-energy performance level that forms a visceral relationship with an audience and that is very much my signature.

—*Gerald Freedman*

PRODUCTIONS 1989-90

King Lear, William Shakespeare; (D) Gerald Freedman; (S) John Ezell; (C) Robert Wojewodski; (L) Thomas R. Skelton

A Delicate Balance, Edward Albee; (D) Amy Saltz; (S) G.W. Mercier; (C) Alfred Kohout; (L) Joseph A. Futral

PRODUCTIONS 1990-91

The Lady from Maxim's, Georges Feydeau; trans: John Mortimer; (D) Gerald Freedman; (S) John Ezell; (C) James Scott; (L) Mary Jo Dondlinger

Dividing the Estate, Horton Foote; (D) Gerald Freedman; (S) John Ezell; (C) Alfred Kohout; (L) Mary Jo Dondlinger

La Ronde, Arthur Schnitzler; trans: John Barton; (D) Victoria Bussert; (S) G.W. Mercier; (C) Alfred Kohout; (L) Mary Jo Dondlinger

A Christmas Carol, adapt: Gerald Freedman, from Charles Dickens; (D) Gerald Freedman and Victoria Bussert; (S) John Ezell and Gene Emerson Friedman; (C) James Scott; (L) Mary Jo Dondlinger

Grove Shakespeare Festival

JULES AARON
Acting Artistic Director

BARBARA G. HAMMERMAN
Managing Director/Executive Vice President

12852 Main St.
Garden Grove, CA 92640
(714) 636-7213

FOUNDED 1979
The City of Garden Grove

SEASON
May-Dec.

FACILITIES
Gem Theatre
Seating Capacity: 172
Stage: proscenium

Festival Amphitheatre
Seating Capacity: 550
Stage: thrust

FINANCES
Jan. 1, 1990-Dec. 31, 1990
Expenses: $714,000

CONTRACTS
AEA SPT and letter of agreement

The Grove Shakespeare Festival utilizes the plays of Shakespeare as its cornerstone program, presenting works that challenge both the artists and the audience by addressing our mutual experiences, beliefs and concerns. In our theatre, whose inspiration is launched by the playwright, the text is the principal source for artistic exploration and vision. The festival strives to provide the finest examples of dramatic literature from both the classical and contemporary theatre. With two working stages, the festival produces five-to-eight productions each season for the central Orange County area, attracting new directors, actors and designers from the Los Angeles basin. While remaining true to the text, we make every effort to explore the written work with an eye for contemporary, yet

Grove Shakespeare Festival. Elizabeth Norment and Gary Armagnac in *Much Ado About Nothing*. Photo: Patrick O'Donnell.

meaningful, insights into our complex and challenging world.

—*Jules Aaron*

Note: During the 1989-90 and 1990-91 seasons, Thomas F. Bradac served as artistic director.

PRODUCTIONS 1990

Twelfth Night, William Shakespeare; (D) Thomas F. Bradac; (S) Tony Maggi; (C) Laura Deremer; (L) Liz Stillwell
The Miser, Moliere; adapt: Miles Malleson; (D) Deborah LaVine; (S) Don Llewellyn; (C) Laura Deremer; (L) Doc Ballard
Much Ado About Nothing, William Shakespeare; (D) Jules Aaron; (S) D. Martyn Bookwalter; (C) Lyndall L. Otto; (L) David Palmer
As You Like It, William Shakespeare; (D) Thomas F. Bradac; (S) D. Martyn Bookwalter; (C) Lyndall L. Otto; (L) David Palmer
Othello, William Shakespeare; (D) David Herman; (S) D. Martyn Bookwalter; (C) Lyndall L. Otto; (L) David Palmer
The Importance of Being Earnest, Oscar Wilde; (D) Jules Aaron; (S) Gil Morales; (C) Martha Ferrara; (L) Rex Heuschkel
A Child's Christmas in Wales, Jeremy Brooks and Adrian Mitchell, from Dylan Thomas; (D) Thomas F. Bradac; (S) Gil Morales; (C) Laura Deremer; (L) David M. Darwin

PRODUCTIONS 1991

Les Liaisons Dangereuses, Christopher Hampton, from Choderlos de Laclos; (D) Thomas F. Bradac; (S) E. Scott Shaffer; (C) Karen Weller; (L) Liz Stillwell
The Merchant of Venice, William Shakespeare; (D) Thomas F. Bradac; (S) Don Llewellyn; (C) Lyndall L. Otto; (L) David Palmer
Tomfoolery, conceived: Cameron Mackintosh and Robin Ray; music and lyrics: Tom Lehrer; (D) Cyrus Parker
Measure for Measure, William Shakespeare; (D) Jules Aaron; (S) Don Llewellyn; (C) Lyndall L. Otto; (L) David Palmer
Our Town, Thornton Wilder; (D) Carl Reggiardo
The Taming of the Shrew, William Shakespeare; (D) Thomas F. Bradac; (S) Don Llewellyn; (C) Lyndall L. Otto; (L) David Palmer
A Child's Christmas in Wales, Jeremy Brooks and Adrian Mitchell, from Dylan Thomas; (D) Bud Leslie

The Guthrie Theater

GARLAND WRIGHT
Artistic Director

EDWARD A. MARTENSON
Executive Director

725 Vineland Place
Minneapolis, MN 55403
(612) 347-1100 (bus.)
(612) 377-2224 (b.o.)

FOUNDED 1963
Tyrone Guthrie, Peter Zeisler, Oliver Rea

SEASON
June-Feb.

FACILITIES
Seating Capacity: 1,441
Stage: thrust

FINANCES
Apr. 1, 1990-Mar. 31, 1991
Expenses: $9,935,981

CONTRACTS
AEA LORT (A)

Theatre is not a place or a thing, but an act—an interchange that has consequence. It is the means by which actors and audiences choose together to examine and participate in the world—to recognize it, to experience it and, ultimately, to understand it. Theatre reflects the complexity of our reality and, although it is perhaps better at illuminating questions than providing answers, its questioning spirit gives testimony to the seriousness with which it seeks to contribute to the human endeavor. We at the Guthrie firmly commit our efforts to artistic excellence at every level, to the greatest plays of the world repertoire, to the actor as the central communicator of the ideas and the poetry within those plays, and to the imagination and its transforming power.

—*Garland Wright*

The Guthrie Theater. Ruth Maleczech and Jesse Borrego in *The Screens*.

PRODUCTIONS 1989-90

Harvey, Mary Chase; (D) Douglas Hughes; (S) Hugh Landwehr; (C) Linda Fisher; (L) Marcus Dilliard
Uncle Vanya, Anton Chekhov; trans: Jean-Claude van Itallie; (D) Garland Wright; (S) Douglas Stein; (C) Martin Pakledinaz; (L) Marcus Dilliard
The Duchess of Malfi, John Webster; (D) Michael Kahn; (S) Derek McLane; (C) Martin Pakledinaz; (L) Frances Aronson
Volpone, Ben Jonson; (D) Stan Wojewodski, Jr.; (S) Christopher Barreca; (C) Catherine Zuber; (L) Stephen Strawbridge
The Screens, Jean Genet; trans: Paul Schmidt; (D) JoAnne Akalaitis; (S) George Tsypin; (C) Eiko Ishioka; (L) Jennifer Tipton
A Christmas Carol, adapt: Barbara Field, from Charles Dickens; (D) Richard Ooms; (C) Jack Edwards; (L) Marcus Dilliard
Candide, book adapt: Hugh Wheeler; music: Leonard Bernstein; lyrics: Richard Wilbur; additional lyrics: Stephen Sondheim and John LaTouche; (D) Garland Wright; (S) John Arnone; (C) David C. Woolard; (L) Marcus Dilliard

PRODUCTIONS 1990-91

Richard II, William Shakespeare; (D) Garland Wright and Charles Newell; (S) Douglas Stein; (C) Ann Hould-Ward; (L) Marcus Dilliard
Henry IV, Parts 1 and 2, William Shakespeare; (D) Garland Wright and Charles Newell; (S) Douglas Stein; (C) Ann Hould-Ward; (L) Marcus Dilliard
Henry V, William Shakespeare; (D) Garland Wright and Charles Newell; (S) Douglas Stein; (C) Ann Hould-Ward; (L) Marcus Dilliard
The Skin of Our Teeth, Thornton Wilder; (D) Robert Woodruff; (S) Douglas Stein; (C) Susan Hilferty; (L) Rob Murphy
The Front Page, Ben Hecht and Charles MacArthur; (D) Douglas Hughes; (S) Hugh Landwehr; (C) Michael Olich; (L) Marcus Dilliard
A Christmas Carol, adapt: Barbara Field, from Charles Dickens; (D) Richard Ooms; (C) Jack Edwards; (L) Marcus Dilliard
Medea, Euripides; trans: Philip Vellacott; (D) Garland Wright; (S) Douglas Stein; (C) Susan Hilferty; (L) Jennifer Tipton

Hartford Stage Company

MARK LAMOS
Artistic Director

DAVID HAWKANSON
Managing Director

50 Church St.
Hartford, CT 06103
(203) 525-5601 (bus.)
(203) 527-5151 (b.o.)

FOUNDED 1964
Jacques Cartier

SEASON
Oct.-June

FACILITIES
John W. Huntington Theatre
Seating Capacity: 489
Stage: thrust

FINANCES
July 1, 1990-June 30, 1991
Expenses: $3,600,000

CONTRACTS
AEA LORT (B)

The work at Hartford Stage reflects the desire to explore every possible kind of theatrical style, whether through new plays, commissioned translations of old plays or adaptations of theatrical works. Our work is centered on the production of texts from the past—primarily works by Shakespeare, but also plays by Schnitzler, Shaw, Moliere and Ibsen. Occasionally plays from the recent past are also revived, and fully half of each season is devoted to world premieres or to second productions of new plays by U.S. writers.

—*Mark Lamos*

PRODUCTIONS 1989-90

The Importance of Being Earnest, Oscar Wilde; (D) Mark Lamos; (S) Michael Yeargan; (C) Jess Goldstein; (L) Peter Kaczorowski
Stand-Up Tragedy, Bill Cain; (D) Ron Link; (S) Yael Pardess; (C) Carol Brolaski; (L) Robert W. Rosentel
The Illusion, Tony Kushner, from Pierre Corneille; (D) Mark Lamos; (S) John Conklin; (C) Martin Pakledinaz; (L) Pat Collins
Woyzeck, Georg Buchner; trans: Henry J. Schmidt; (D) Richard Foreman; (S) Richard Foreman; (C) Lindsay W. Davis; (L) Heather Carson
Daytrips, Jo Carson; (D) Michael Engler; (S) Loy Arcenas; (C) Catherine Zuber; (L) Pat Collins
The Miser, Moliere; adapt: Constance Congdon; (D) Mark Lamos; (S) John Arnone; (C) Martin Pakledinaz; (L) Pat Collins

PRODUCTIONS 1990-91

Our Country's Good, Timberlake Wertenbaker, from Thomas Keneally; (D) Mark Lamos; (S) Christopher Barreca; (C) Candice Donnelly; (L) Mimi Jordan Sherin
Marvin's Room, Scott McPherson; (D) David Petrarca; (S) Linda Buchanan; (C) Claudia Boddy; (L) Robert Christen
The Master Builder, Henrik Ibsen; trans: Gerry Bamman and Irene B. Berman; (D) Mark Lamos; (S) Marjorie Bradley Kellogg; (C) Jess Goldstein; (L) Pat Collins
The Snow Ball, A.R. Gurney, Jr.; (D) Jack O'Brien; (S) Douglas W. Schmidt; (C) Steven Rubin; (L) David F. Segal
Julius Caesar, William Shakespeare; (D) Mark Lamos; (S) Michael Yeargan; (C) Catherine Zuber; (L) Christopher Akerlind
From the Mississippi Delta, Dr. Endesha Ida Mae Holland; (D) Jonathan Wilson; (S) Eduardo Sicangco; (C) Eduardo Sicangco; (L) Allen Lee Hughes

Hartford Stage Company. Sam Waterston and Cynthia Nixon in *The Master Builder*. Photo: T. Charles Erickson.

Hippodrome State Theatre

MARY HAUSCH
Producing Director

MICHAEL CURRY
Business Manager

25 Southeast Second Place
Gainesville, FL 32601
(904) 373-5968 (bus.)
(904) 375-4477 (b.o.)

FOUNDED 1973
Mary Hausch, Marilyn Wall-Asse, Kerry McKenney, Bruce Cornwell, Gregory von Hausch, Orin Wechsberg

SEASON
Jan.-Dec.

FACILITIES
Mainstage
Seating Capacity: 266
Stage: thrust

Second Stage
Seating Capacity: 86
Stage: flexible

FINANCES
June 1, 1990-May 31, 1991
Expenses: $1,250,000

CONTRACTS
AEA LORT (D) and TYA

The Hippodrome State Theatre has been nationally recognized for its imaginative theatre that spans contemporary, classic and international boundaries. The Hippodrome was founded as an artistic cooperative in 1973. The collective artistic input, along with intensely individual visions and stylistic variety, creates the theatre's unique premieres, translations, original adaptations of screenplays and classical works. Internationally recognized playwrights, including Tennessee Williams, Adrian Mitchell, Eric Bentley, Lee Breuer, Mario Vargas Llosa and Brian Thomson, have all collaborated with the theatre's company to produce world premieres on the Hippodrome stage. Other programs include touring, an intern/conservatory program, an artistic residency program, and a Theatre for Young Audiences that has created 13 original plays and performed for more than one million children. The theatre's Improvisational Teen Theatre utilizes improvisational performances and discussion groups to address problems prevalent among teens, such as drug addiction, sexual abuse, suicide, pregnancy and AIDS.

—*Mary Hausch*

PRODUCTIONS 1989-90

Les Liaisons Dangereuses, Christopher Hampton, from Choderlos de Laclos; (D) Mary Hausch; (S) Carlos F. Asse; (C) Marilyn Wall-Asse; (L) Bob Robins
The Boys Next Door, Tom Griffin; (D) Carlos F. Asse; (S) Carlos F. Asse; (C) Marilyn Wall-Asse; (L) Bob Robins
The Mystery of Irma Vep, Charles Ludlam; (D) Mary Hausch; (S) Carlos F. Asse; (C) Marilyn Wall-Asse; (L) Bob Robins
Romance/Romance, book: Barry Harman; music: Keith Herrmann; (D) Carlos F. Asse; (S) Carlos F. Asse; (C) Marilyn Wall-Asse; (L) Bob Robins
The Road to Mecca, Athol Fugard; (D) Kerry McKenney Oliver-Smith; (S) Carlos F. Asse; (C) Marilyn Wall-Asse; (L) Bob Robins
Driving Miss Daisy, Alfred Uhry; (D) Mary Hausch; (S) Carlos F. Asse; (C) Marilyn Wall-Asse; (L) Bob Robins

Hippodrome State Theatre. Nell Page Sexton, Dan Jesse, Rachel Tench and Rusty Salling in *Rumors*. Photo: Randy Batista.

A Christmas Carol, book adapt and lyrics: Carlos F. Asse, from Charles Dickens; music: Jim Wren; (D) Carlos F. Asse; (S) Carlos F. Asse; (C) Marilyn Wall-Asse; (L) Bob Robins

PRODUCTIONS 1990-91

Steel Magnolias, Robert Harling; (D) Mary Hausch; (S) Carlos F. Asse; (C) Marilyn Wall-Asse; (L) Bob Robins

Evita, music: Andrew Lloyd Webber; lyrics: Tim Rice; (D) Carlos F. Asse; (S) Carlos F. Asse; (C) Marilyn Wall-Asse; (L) Bob Robins

Eleemosynary, Lee Blessing; (D) Mary Hausch; (S) Carlos F. Asse; (C) Marilyn Wall-Asse; (L) Bob Robins

The Heidi Chronicles, Wendy Wasserstein; (D) Mary Hausch; (S) Carlos F. Asse; (C) Marilyn Wall-Asse; (L) Bob Robins

Rumors, Neil Simon; (D) Carlos F. Asse; (S) Carlos F. Asse; (C) Marilyn Wall-Asse; (L) Bob Robins

Other People's Money, Jerry Sterner; (D) Mary Hausch; (S) Carlos F. Asse; (C) Marilyn Wall-Asse; (L) Bob Robins

A Christmas Carol, book adapt and lyrics: Carlos F. Asse, from Charles Dickens; music: Jim Wren; (D) Carlos F. Asse; (S) Carlos F. Asse; (C) Marilyn Wall-Asse; (L) Bob Robins

Honolulu Theatre for Youth

PAMELA STERLING
Artistic Director

JANE CAMPBELL
Managing Director

2846 Ualena St.
Honolulu, HI 96819
(808) 839-9885

FOUNDED 1955
Nancy Corbett

SEASON
July-May

FACILITIES
Castle High Theatre
Seating Capacity: 667
Stage: proscenium

Kaimuki High Theatre
Seating Capacity: 667
Stage: proscenium

McCoy Pavilion
Seating Capacity: 500
Stage: flexible

Richardson Theatre
Seating Capacity: 800
Stage: proscenium

FINANCES
June 1, 1990-May 31, 1991
Expenses: $1,084,000

Honolulu Theatre for Youth is dedicated to producing high-quality theatre for young audiences. It offers a broad spectrum of plays each season, from literary classics and childhood favorites to plays dealing with contemporary social issues and Pacific Rim cultures. HTY annually tours statewide with two major productions. Our education program provides materials, workshops and classes to teachers and students. Additionally, HTY actively encourages the development of new plays by commissioning works and sponsoring a young playwrights program through Very Special Arts Hawaii. HTY has provided international outreach programs and has toured to American Samoa, Micronesia and Australia. The ethnic mix of the HTY company is as diverse as the people of Hawaii: Nontraditional casting is the norm. The exploration of cultures, values and theatre forms is what HTY is all about.

—Pamela Sterling

PRODUCTIONS 1989-90

Ramayana, Edward Mast; (D) John Kauffman; (S) Joseph D. Dodd; (C) Clifford Jones; (L) Lloyd S. Riford, III

The Little Humpback Horse, adapt: Zinovi Korogodski; trans: Louis Zellikoff and Maria Lanina, from Pyotor Yershov; (D) Zinovi Korogodski; (S) Danila Korogodski; (C) Danila Korogodski; (L) Lloyd S. Riford, III

From Okuni to Danjuro: A Kabuki Retrospective, adapt: David Furumoto, from Okamuka Shiko; (D) David Furumoto; (S) Newton Koshi; (C) David Furumoto

Guns, book and lyrics: Doris Baizley and Harry Aguado; music: Harry Aguado; (D) John Kauffman; (S) Don Ranney, Jr.; (C) Susan Jozefiak; (L) Sandy Sandelin

Androcles and the Lion, Aurand Harris; (D) Karen Brilliande; (S) David Henderson; (C) Trudi Vetter; (L) Don Ranney, Jr.

The Original Absurd Revue for Children, Arne Zaslove; (D) Brian Clark; (C) Susan Jozefiak

Theatrefest '89:

Pulling Through, Sherry Molina; (D) Robert St. John; (S) Mike Dombroski; (L) Mike Dombroski

Your Majesty, Joyce Arita; (D) Daniel A. Kelin, II; (S) Mike Dombroski; (L) Mike Dombroski

Dance, Little Sister, Sharon Baker; (D) Cynthia See; (S) Mike Dombroski; (L) Mike Dombroski

PRODUCTIONS 1990-91

The Mask Messengers, Faustwork Mask Theater; (D) Rob Faust

The Odyssey, Gregory A. Falls and Kurt Beattie, from Homer; (D) Pamela Sterling; (S) Danila Korogodski; (C) Danila Korogodski; (L) Sandy Sandelin

Romeo and Juliet, adapt: Pamela Sterling, from William Shakespeare; (D) Pamela Sterling; (S) Paul Guncheon; (C) Casey Cameron Dinmore; (L) Sandy Sandelin

Honolulu Theatre for Youth. Ned Van Zandt and James Davenport in *Ramayana*. Photo: Robert St. John.

This Is Not a Pipe Dream, Barry Kornhauser; (D) Karen Brilliande; (S) Joseph D. Dodd; (C) Karen G. Wolfe; (L) Mike Dombroski
The Nose, adapt: Elizabeth Egloff, from Nikolai Gogol; (D) Pamela Sterling; (S) Alan Hunley; (C) Carol Rose Gackowski
Peter and the Wolf, adapt: Graham Whitehead, from Sergei Prokofiev; music: Sergei Prokofiev; (D) Graham Whitehead; (S) Tom Miller; (C) Vivien Frow; (L) Steve Tomlinson
Ginger and Pickles, book adapt: Pamela Sterling, from Beatrix Potter; music: Dan Davis; lyrics: Suzan Zeder; (D) David Furumoto; (S) Bob Campbell; (C) Susan Jozefiak; (L) Jo Scheder

Theatrefest '90:
Pictures, Honey Maltin; (D) Brian Shaughnessy; (L) Edwin Hollmann
Your World, Valerie Bush; (D) Cynthia See; (L) Edwin Hollmann
Broken Promises, Andrea Benson; (D) Jo Scheder; (L) Edwin Hollmann
Sand Dragons, Janet Allard; (D) Daniel A. Kelin, II; (L) Edwin Hollmann

Horse Cave Theatre

WARREN HAMMACK
Director

PAMELA WHITE
Associate Director

Box 215
Horse Cave, KY 42749
(502) 786-1200 (bus.)
(502) 786-2177 (b.o.)

FOUNDED 1977
Horse Cave citizens

SEASON
June-Nov.

FACILITIES
Seating Capacity: 347
Stage: thrust

FINANCES
Oct. 1, 1990-Sept. 30, 1991
Expenses: $432,685

CONTRACTS
AEA letter of agreement

Horse Cave Theatre is a professional resident theatre ensemble serving audiences in Kentucky. The theatre presents contemporary plays, new scripts and classics in rotating repertory, and seeks to encourage the development of theatre artists, with a particular commitment to Kentucky playwrights. Under the Kentucky Voices program, the theatre presents plays which combine the unique cultural resources of the region with its own professional resources. Believing that the spark of a live performance is a powerful teaching tool, the theatre provides a wide range of educational programs including workshops, a statewide touring program and, since 1979, a comprehensive outreach program wherein the plays of Shakespeare are presented at the theatre for students. Study guides, discussions and in-service training for teachers supplement the program.

—Warren Hammack

PRODUCTIONS 1990

One Husband Too Many, Georges Feydeau; adapt: Barnett Shaw; (D) Warren Hammack; (S) Sam Hunt; (C) Rebecca Shouse; (L) Gregory Etter
The Foreigner, Larry Shue; (D) Cynthia Bishop; (S) Eric Wegener; (C) Rebecca Shouse; (L) Gregory Etter
Desperate Fortune, Joseph Gray; (D) Walter Rhodes; (S) Sam Hunt; (C) Rebecca Shouse; (L) Gregory Etter
Macbeth, William Shakespeare; (D) Warren Hammack; (S) Sam Hunt; (C) Rebecca Shouse; (L) Gregory Etter
The Business of Murder, Richard Harris; (D) Liz Bussey; (S) Eric Wegener; (C) Rebecca Shouse; (L) Gregory Etter

PRODUCTIONS 1991

What Every Woman Knows, James M. Barrie; (D) Liz Bussey; (S) Sam Hunt; (C) Jane Pearl; (L) Jonathan Kitchen
Lettice & Lovage, Peter Shaffer; (D) Warren Hammack; (S) Sam Hunt; (C) Jane Pearl; (L) Jonathan Kitchen
A Streetcar Named Desire, Tennessee Williams; (D) Warren Hammack; (S) Sam Hunt; (C) Jane Pearl; (L) Jonathan Kitchen
A Midsummer Night's Dream, William Shakespeare; (D) Warren Hammack; (S) Sam Hunt; (C) Jane Pearl; (L) Jonathan Kitchen
Deathtrap, Ira Levin; (D) Kathryn Ballard; (S) Jonathan Kitchen; (C) Kimberley Barnhardt; (L) Jonathan Kitchen

Horse Cave Theatre. Steve Wise and Pamela White in *One Husband Too Many*. Photo: Warren Hammack.

Huntington Theatre Company

PETER ALTMAN
Producing Director

MICHAEL MASO
Managing Director

264 Huntington Ave.
Boston, MA 02115-4606
(617) 266-7900 (bus.)
(617) 266-0800 (b.o.)

FOUNDED 1982
Boston University

SEASON
Sept.-June

FACILITIES
Boston University Theatre
Seating Capacity: 855
Stage: proscenium

FINANCES
July 1, 1990-June 30, 1991
Expenses: $3,864,000

CONTRACTS
AEA LORT (B)

The Huntington Theatre Company's aim is to produce annual seasons of classic and superior contemporary plays that are acted, directed and designed at a standard of excellence comparable to that of the nation's leading professional companies. We continually seek to devote ourselves to the great masterpieces of dramatic literature; to respond to today's issues and emotions by presenting literate, trenchant contemporary plays new to Boston; and to be enterprising and cosmopolitan in choosing worthy writing from varied countries and periods. Because we honor the theatre's heritage, we strive to present classic works in their true spirit. In producing plays of any era or style, we enjoy and admire truthful situations, vivid characters, sound dramatic construction, eloquent language, imaginative staging with well-balanced casts and the finest possible level of craftsmanship. We believe that a flexible, allied family of professionals who share this vision will best extend, fulfill and serve our theatre's vision.

—Peter Altman

PRODUCTIONS 1989-90

Hyde Park, James Shirley; (D) Kyle Donnelly; (S) Kate Edmunds; (C) Lindsay W. Davis; (L) Rita Pietraszek
Boesman and Lena, Athol Fugard;

(D) Tazewell Thompson; (S) James Leonard Joy; (C) Amanda J. Klein; (L) Roger Meeker

O Pioneers!, adapt: Darrah Cloud, from Willa Cather; (D) Kevin Kuhlke; (S) John Wulp; (C) Ann Roth; (L) Brian Nason

The Merry Wives of Windsor, William Shakespeare; (D) Edward Gilbert; (S) John Falabella; (C) Mariann Verheyen; (L) Nicholas Cernovitch

The Lady from Maxim's, Georges Feydeau; adapt: Larry Carpenter; trans: Janice Orion; (D) Larry Carpenter; (S) John Falabella; (C) David Murin; (L) Marcia Madeira

PRODUCTIONS 1990-91

H.M.S. Pinafore, W.S. Gilbert and Arthur Sullivan; (D) Larry Carpenter; (S) James Leonard Joy; (C) Mariann Verheyen; (L) Stuart Duke

Two Trains Running, August Wilson; (D) Lloyd Richards; (S) Tony Fanning; (C) Chrisi Karvonides; (L) Geoff Korf

Aristocrats, Brian Friel; (D) Kyle Donnelly; (S) Kate Edmunds; (C) Erin Quigley; (L) Rita Pietraszek

Iphigenia, Euripides; trans: Witter Bynner (*Iphigenia in Taurus*); W.S. Merwin and George E. Dimock, Jr. (*Iphigenia at Aulis*); (D) Tazewell Thompson; (S) Donald Eastman; (C) Paul Tazewell; (L) Nancy Schertler

Mr. Dooley's America, Philip Dunne and Martin Blaine; (D) Vincent Dowling and John Love; (L) Eugene Warner

Travesties, Tom Stoppard; (D) Jacques Cartier; (S) James Leonard Joy; (C) John Falabella; (L) Roger Meeker

Frankie and Johnny in the Clair de Lune, Terrence McNally; (D) Leonard Foglia; (S) Robert D. Soule; (C) Marilyn Salvatore; (L) John F. Custer

Illinois Theatre Center

STEVE S. BILLIG
Artistic Director

ETEL BILLIG
Managing Director

400A Lakewood Blvd.
Park Forest, IL 60466
(708) 481-3693 (bus.)
(708) 481-3510 (b.o.)

FOUNDED 1976
Steve S. Billig, Etel Billig

SEASON
Sept.-May

FACILITIES
Seating Capacity: 187
Stage: thrust

FINANCES
Sept. 1, 1990-Aug. 31, 1991
Expenses: $250,000

CONTRACTS
AEA CAT

The Illinois Theatre Center was founded in 1976 with the belief that a vigorous artistic and cultural life should be part of all communities. It is through theatre that we hope to enrich the quality of life for all area residents. Through the world of theatre we want our audiences to appreciate man's infinite diversity of expression and the vast range of human invention. Along with our seven-play mainstage season, we have an active outreach program which provides special programming for the elderly, the handicapped and the economically disadvantaged. We also hold an annual free outdoor Classics Festival.

—*Steve S. Billig*

Huntington Theatre Company. Jonathan Earl Peck, Chuck Patterson, Al White and Ella Joyce in *Two Trains Running*. Photo: Richard Feldman.

Illinois Theatre Center. Nancy Nickel, Cathy Bieber and Greg Vinkler in *Othello*. Photo: Peter Le Grand.

PRODUCTIONS 1989-90

Lucky Stiff, book adapt and lyrics: Lynn Ahrens, from Michael Butterworth; music: Stephen Flaherty; (D) Steve S. Billig; (S) Archway Scenic; (C) Stephen E. Moore; (L) August Ziemann

Breaking the Code, Hugh Whitemore, from Andrew Hodges; (D) Paula Markovitz; (S) Jonathan Roark; (C) Pat Decker; (L) August Ziemann

Kismet, book: Luther Davis; lyrics: George Forrest; music: Robert Wright, based on classical themes by Alexander Borodin; (D) Steve S. Billig; (S) Archway Scenic; (C) Stephen E. Moore; (L) August Ziemann

Scrapbooks, Larry Gray; (D) Steve S. Billig; (S) Jonathan Roark; (C) Pat Decker; (L) August Ziemann

Othello, William Shakespeare; (D) Steve S. Billig; (S) Jonathan Roark; (C) Stephen E. Moore; (L) August Ziemann

Italian American Reconciliation, John Patrick Shanley; (D) Steve S. Billig; (S) Jonathan Roark; (C) Pat Decker; (L) August Ziemann

The Fantasticks, book adapt and lyrics: Tom Jones, from Edmond Rostand; music: Harvey Schmidt; (D) Steve S. Billig; (S) Archway Scenic; (C) Stephen E. Moore; (L) August Ziemann

PRODUCTIONS 1990-91

Flora the Red Menace, adapt: George Abbott, from Lester Atwell; book adapt: David Thompson; music: John Kander; lyrics: Fred Ebb; (D) Steve S. Billig; (S) Archway Scenic; (C) Stephen E. Moore; (L) August Ziemann

Exclusive Circles, Kendrew Lascelles; (D) Steve S. Billig; (S) Jonathan Roark; (C) Pat Decker; (L) August Ziemann

Dear World, book adapt: Jerome Lawrence and Robert E. Lee, from Jean Giradoux; music and lyrics: Jerry Herman; (D) Steve S. Billig; (S) Archway Scenic; (C) Stephen E. Moore; (L) August Ziemann

Naked Dancing, John Banach; (D) Etel Billig; (S) Jonathan Roark; (C) Pat Decker; (L) Jonathan Roark

Accomplice, Rupert Holmes; (D) Steve S. Billig; (S) Archway

Scenic; (C) Pat Decker; (L) Jonathan Roark

Winterset, Maxwell Anderson; (D) Steve S. Billig; (S) Jonathan Roark; (C) Pat Decker; (L) Jonathan Roark

Blues in the Night, conceived: Sheldon Epps; various composers and lyricists; (D) Steve S. Billig; (S) Wayne Adams; (C) Pat Decker; (L) Archway Design

Illusion Theater

MICHAEL ROBINS
Executive Producing Director

BONNIE MORRIS
Producing Director

528 Hennepin Ave., Suite 704
Minneapolis, MN 55403
(612) 339-4944 (bus.)
(612) 338-8371 (b.o.)

FOUNDED 1974
Michael Robins, Carole Harris Lipschulz, Bonnie Morris

SEASON
Feb.-Aug.

FACILITIES
Hennepin Center for the Arts
Seating Capacity: 220
Stage: thrust

FINANCES
Jan. 1, 1990-Dec. 31, 1990
Expenses: $936,386

CONTRACTS
AEA SPT

The Illusion Theater celebrates the power of the human spirit, creating theatre that can be a catalyst for change. We have produced more than 66 world premieres. We collaborate with a company of artists, writers, actors, directors and designers. We have an ongoing process of developing new material and are committed to having the plays created at Illusion produced at other theatres, supporting the writer in whatever needs to happen to "finish" the script. We've created plays with Jon Klein, David Feldshuh, Arthur Giron, Judy McGuire and Eric Anderson, to name just a few. We are also dedicated to the power of theatre to educate. We demonstrate this belief through our repertoire of plays dedicated to the prevention of sexual abuse, interpersonal violence, HIV/AIDS and the promotion of healthy sexuality. We tour throughout the country twice a year and produce a home season of five plays from February to August in our 220-seat theatre.

—Michael Robins

PRODUCTIONS 1990

No Place to Park, Eric Anderson; (D) Scott M. Rubsam; (S) Linda Cassone; (C) Katherine Maurer; (L) Frederic Desbois

Letters from Hell, Dane Stauffer; (D) George Sand; (S) James Salen; (C) Katherine Maurer; (L) Frederic Desbois

Duesenberg 55, Dane Stauffer; (D) Leslye Orr; (S) James Salen; (C) Katherine Maurer; (L) Frederic Desbois

Family, Cordelia Anderson, Bonnie Morris and Michael Robins; (D) Michael Robins; (S) Dean Holzman; (C) Katherine Maurer; (L) David Vogel

The Warrior Within, Buffy Sedlachek; (D) B. Rodney Marriott; (S) Nayna Ramey; (C) Rich Hamson; (L) Michael Murnane

Miss Evers' Boys, David Feldshuh; (D) D. Scott Glasser; (S) Dean Holzman; (C) Katherine Maurer; (L) Barry Browning

Women Who Drink, Leslye Orr; (D) Myron Johnson and Leslye Orr; (S) Leslye Orr; (C) Leslye Orr; (L) David Vogel

A Brother of Jackals, Alan Lindblad; (D) Alan Lindblad; (S) James Salen; (L) David Vogel

Bloodroot, Diane Elliot, Susan Delattre, Margie Fargnoli, Rebecca Frost and Erika Thorne; (D) Diane Elliot; (S) James Salen; (L) James Salen

Amazing Grace, Cordelia Anderson, Bonnie Morris and Michael Robins; (D) Michael Robins; (S) James Salen; (C) Katherine Maurer; (L) James Salen

Hope, Myron Johnson; (D) Myron Johnson; (S) Michael Murnane; (C) Lyle Jackson; (L) Michael Murnane

PRODUCTIONS 1991

I Don't Believe...We've Met, Leslye Orr; (D) Michael Robins; (S) James Salen; (C) Lyle Jackson; (L) Frederic Desbois

The Darren Cycle, Michael Sommers and Susan Haas; (D) Michael Sommers; (S) Michael Sommers and James Salen; (C) John Strauss; (L) David Vogel

Princess Power, Carolyn Goelzer; (D) Carolyn Goelzer; (S) James Salen; (C) John Strauss; (L) David Vogel

Oyster, Judy McGuire; (D) Judy McGuire; (S) James Salen; (C) John Strauss; (L) David Vogel

Objects in the Mirror Are Closer Than They Appear, Mark Cryer and Lester Purry; (D) Mark Cryer and Lester Purry; (S) James Salen; (C) John Strauss; (L) David Vogel

If We Never Meet Again, Josette Antomarchi, Beth Gilleland, Mary McDevitt and Sue Scott; (D) Wendy Knox; (S) James Salen; (C) John Strauss; (L) David Vogel

Miss Evers' Boys, David Feldshuh; (D) D. Scott Glasser and Michael Robins; (S) Dean Holzman; (C) Katherine Maurer and John Strauss; (L) Barry Browning

Honeymoon, Dane Stauffer; (D) Myron Johnson; (S) James Salen; (C) John Strauss; (L) Frederic Desbois

Illusion Theater. Nancy Marvy in *The Warrior Within*. Photo: John Montilino.

The Independent Eye

CONRAD BISHOP
Producing Director

LINDA BISHOP
Associate Producing Director

Box 8
Lancaster, PA 17603
(717) 393-9088

FOUNDED 1974
Conrad Bishop, Linda Bishop

SEASON
Variable

FACILITIES
Co-Motion Theatre
Seating Capacity: 100
Stage: proscenium

FINANCES
July 1, 1990-June 30, 1991
Expenses: $83,000

The Independent Eye is a progressive theatre ensemble devoted to new plays and new visions of classics. We look for startling, deeply felt stories, and we leapfrog through many styles to find the right language for each. We often start work without knowing whether it's to be funny, grisly, or both; we slosh our brimming jigger of hemlock and stain our best new sweater. For us, theatre is this art of juggling extremes to bring us into intense *presence*—to sit with the assembled tribe and feel the pain and promise of being human. Always, the core questions: Is the story's heart true? Surprising?

The Independent Eye. Elizabeth Fuller in *Beside Herself: Pocahontas to Patty Hearst*. Photo: C. Bishop.

What's our stake in telling it? Since 1974, the Eye has toured 34 states and produced nine resident seasons in Lancaster before returning, now, to our roots as a touring ensemble focused on long-term repertoire, co-production, and creation of video and radio drama.

—*Conrad Bishop*

PRODUCTIONS 1989-90

Mark Twain Revealed, adapt: Conrad Bishop, from Mark Twain; (D) Conrad Bishop; (S) Dan Gluibizzi; (L) Conrad Bishop

Mabel's Dreams, Conrad Bishop and Camilla Schade; (D) Conrad Bishop; (L) Peter Smith

Beside Herself: Pocahontas to Patty Hearst, Pamela White-Hadas; (D) Conrad Bishop; (S) Linda Cunningham; (C) P. Chelsea Harriman; (L) Conrad Bishop

Action News, Conrad Bishop and Elizabeth Fuller; (D) Conrad Bishop; (S) Conrad Bishop and Rick Mazzafro; (L) Conrad Bishop

PRODUCTIONS 1990-91

Rash Acts: Seven Snapshots of the Wall, Conrad Bishop and Elizabeth Fuller; (D) Conrad Bishop; (S) Conrad Bishop; (C) Nancy Whiting; (L) Conrad Bishop

Out Cry, Tennessee Williams; (D) Conrad Bishop; (S) Robert A. Nelson; (C) S.Q. Campbell; (L) Richard Latta

Beside Herself: Pocahontas to Patty Hearst, Pamela White Hadas; (D) Conrad Bishop; (S) Linda Cunningham; (C) P. Chelsea Harriman; (L) Conrad Bishop

Mark Twain Revealed, adapt: Conrad Bishop, from Mark Twain; (D) Conrad Bishop; (S) Dan Gluibizzi; (L) Conrad Bishop

Indiana Repertory Theatre

JANET ALLEN
Associate Artistic Director

VICTORIA NOLAN
Managing Director

140 West Washington St.
Indianapolis, IN 46204
(317) 635-5277 (bus.)
(317) 635-5252 (b.o.)

FOUNDED 1972
Edward Stern, Gregory Poggi, Benjamin Mordecai

SEASON
Oct.-May

FACILITIES
Mainstage
Seating Capacity: 607
Stage: proscenium

Upperstage
Seating Capacity: 269
Stage: proscenium

Cabaret
Seating Capacity: 150
Stage: thrust

FINANCES
July 1, 1990-June 30, 1991
Expenses: $2,985,000

CONTRACTS
AEA LORT (C) and TYA

As Indiana's only resident, professional theatre, the IRT's mission embraces a broad spectrum of activities, addressing an audience extending from those in whom an appreciation of theatre must be awakened, to those challenged only by the most innovative. In the Mainstage subscription series we dedicate our energies to creating a balanced bill of classic and contemporary plays by redefining the classics (both the well-known and the forgotten), exploring them stylistically and eliciting fresh perspectives on them, then juxtaposing them against an investigation of selected contemporary work that presents current trends in playwriting to our diverse audience. IRT's combined Educational Outreach Programs bring more than 35,000 students annually to the theatre: to matinees of our Mainstage productions; to a special high school program, "Classic Theatre for Youth"; and to "Junior Works," a project to which we have dedicated our Upperstage theatre, aiming to develop a young, multicultural company of professional actors to perform three plays annually for junior high school audiences. Our energies are turning with increasing vigor to this cultivation of tomorrow's audiences.

—*Janet Allen*

Note: During the 1989-90 and 1990-91 seasons, Tom Haas served as artistic director.

PRODUCTIONS 1989-90

The Rivals, Richard Brinsley Sheridan; (D) Tom Haas; (S) Ann Sheffield; (C) Gail Brassard; (L) Donald Holder

Black Coffee, Agatha Christie; (D) Tom Haas; (S) G.W. Mercier; (C) G.W. Mercier; (L) Donald Holder

The Nerd, Larry Shue; (D) Larry Arrick; (S) Bill Clarke; (C) Bobbi Owen; (L) Denny Clark

Benefactors, Michael Frayn; (D) Tom Haas; (S) Craig Clipper; (C) Kathy Jaremski; (L) Michael Lincoln

The Colored Museum, George C. Wolfe; (D) Ronald J. Himes; (S) Russell Metheny; (C) Gail Brassard; (L) Stuart Duke

Julius Caesar, William Shakespeare; (D) Tom Haas; (S) Ann Sheffield; (C) Ann Sheffield; (L) Michael Lincoln

The Gift of the Magi, book adapt, music and lyrics: Peter Ekstrom, from O. Henry; (D) Karen Azenberg; (S) Chuck Mullen;

Indiana Repertory Theatre. Michael Lipton, Donna Davis and Tom Bloom in *Hedda Gabler*. Photo: Tod Martens.

(C) Kathy Jaremski; (L) Joel Grynheim

PRODUCTIONS 1990-91

Cyrano de Bergerac, Edmond Rostand; trans: Brian Hooker; (D) Tom Haas; (S) Ann Sheffield; (C) Ellen McCartney; (L) Donald Holder

Sherlock's Last Case, Charles Marowitz; (D) Tom Haas; (S) Scott Chambliss; (C) Ellen McCartney; (L) Michael Lincoln

Speed-the-Plow, David Mamet; (D) Scott Wentworth; (S) David Birn; (C) Delmar L. Rinehart, Jr.; (L) Stuart Duke

Biloxi Blues, Neil Simon; (D) Karen Azenberg; (S) Russell Metheny; (C) Bobbi Owen; (L) James F. Ingalls

Hedda Gabler, Henrik Ibsen; adapt: Tom Haas; (D) Janet Allen and Scott Wentworth; (S) Ann Sheffield; (C) Ann Sheffield; (L) Michael Lincoln

Rough Crossing, Tom Stoppard; (D) Larry Arrick; (S) G.W. Mercier; (C) G.W. Mercier; (L) Donald Holder

A Dickens of a Christmas Carol, adapt: Janet Allen, from Charles Dickens; (D) Janet Allen; (S) Denny Clark; (C) Deborah Shippee; (L) Joel Grynheim

Young Abe Lincoln in Indiana, Dudley Saunders; (D) Michael Lipton; (S) Jeffrey D. Schneider; (C) Deborah Shippee; (L) Joel Grynheim

Tales from Olympus, Tom Evans; (D) Linda Atkinson; (S) Jennifer Q. Smith; (C) Jennifer Q. Smith; (L) Martha Mountain

INTAR Hispanic American Arts Center

MAX FERRA
Artistic Director

EVA BRUNE
Managing Director

Box 788
New York, NY 10108
(212) 695-6134 (bus.)
(212) 279-4200 (b.o.)

FOUNDED 1966
Max Ferra, Frank Robles, Elsa Ortiz Robles, Gladys Ortiz, Benjamin Lopez, Antonio Gonzalez-Jaen, Oscar Garcia

SEASON
Oct.-June

FACILITIES
INTAR on Theatre Row
Seating Capacity: 99
Stage: proscenium

INTAR Two
Seating Capacity: 95
Stage: proscenium

FINANCES
July 1, 1990-June 30, 1991
Expenses: $850,000

CONTRACTS
AEA Mini

INTAR Hispanic American Arts Center includes a theatre, a playwriting laboratory and a multicultural visual-arts gallery. Our theatre program is developmental in nature. In addition to our mainstage season, we present theatrical works-in-progress and a series of readings of new plays developed in our Hispanic Playwrights-in-Residence Laboratory. INTAR's aim is to see Hispanic voices take their place in the forefront of our nation's arts expression. We continue to respond to the ever-changing nature of this rich and vital American voice through commissioning, touring and interdisciplinary collaborations. Our mission today remains as focused as it was 25 years ago: to identify, develop and present the work of Hispanic-American theatre artists and multicultural visual artists, as well as to introduce outstanding works by internationally respected Latin artists to American audiences.

—*Max Ferra*

PRODUCTIONS 1989-90

Parting Gestures, Rafael Lima; (D) John Ferraro; (S) Loren Sherman; (C) Jennifer von Mayrhauser; (L) Jackie Manassee

Going to New England, Ana Maria Simo; (D) Maria Irene Fornes; (S) Maria Irene Fornes; (C) Maria Irene Fornes; (L) Stephen Quandt

The Body Builder's Book of Love, Fernando Arrabal; (D) Tom O'Horgan; (S) Christina Weppner; (C) Deborah Shaw; (L) Debra Dumas

INTAR Hispanic American Arts Center. Olga Merediz, Alina Troyana and Xonia Bengukla in *The Lady from Havana*. Photo: Carol Rosegg.

PRODUCTIONS 1990-91

The Lady from Havana, Luis Santeiro; (D) Max Ferra; (S) Campbell Baird; (C) Campbell Baird; (L) Debra Dumas

Blue Heat, John Jesurun; (D) John Jesurun; (S) John Jesurun; (C) John Jesurun; (L) Jeffrey Nash

The Have-little, Migdalia Cruz; (D) Nilo Cruz; (S) Donald Eastman; (C) Gabriel Berry; (L) Kenneth Posner

Intiman Theatre Company

ELIZABETH HUDDLE
Artistic Director

PETER DAVIS
Managing Director

Box 19760
Seattle, WA 98109-1760
(206) 626-0775 (bus.)
(206) 626-0782 (b.o.)

FOUNDED 1972
Margaret Booker

SEASON
May-Dec.

FACILITIES
Intiman Playhouse
Seating Capacity: 424
Stage: thrust

FINANCES
Jan. 1, 1990-Dec. 31, 1990
Expenses: $1,865,826

CONTRACTS
AEA LORT (C)

In keeping with its longstanding artistic vision, the Intiman Theatre Company is a theatre which focuses on the actor and the spoken word in an intimate setting. It is the mission of the Intiman Theatre Company to present to a diverse audience the great and enduring themes of world drama, both within our home at the Intiman Playhouse and through outreach into the community of greater Seattle and the Pacific Northwest.

—*Elizabeth Huddle*

PRODUCTIONS 1990

The Rivals, Richard Brinsley Sheridan; (D) Elizabeth Huddle; (S) Robert Dahlstrom; (C) Robert Wojewodski; (L) Rick Paulsen

The Three Sisters, Anton Chekhov; (D) Galina Volchek; (S) Peter Kirillov and Vyacheslav Zaitsev; (C) Vyacheslav Zaitsev; (L) Peter Kirillov and Vyacheslav Zaitsev

Into the Whirlwind, adapt: Alexander Getman, from Eugenia Ginzburg; (D) Galina Volchek; (S) Mikhail Frankel; (C) Mikhail Frankel; (L) Mikhail Frankel

Waiting for Godot, Samuel Beckett; (D) Susan Fenichell; (S) Scott Weldin; (C) Sarah Campbell; (L) Rick Paulsen

Aristocrats, Brian Friel; (D) Warner Shook; (S) Peggy

McDonald; (C) Frances Kenny; (L) Rick Paulsen
Arms and the Man, George Bernard Shaw; (D) Elizabeth Huddle; (S) Karen Gjelsteen; (C) Anne Thaxter Watson; (L) Jennifer Lupton

PRODUCTIONS 1991

The Kentucky Cycle, Robert Schenkkan; (D) Warner Shook; (S) Micheal Olich; (C) Frances Kenny; (L) Peter Maradudin
Misalliance, George Bernard Shaw; (D) Susan Fenichell; (S) Tim Saternow; (C) Sarah Campbell; (L) Rick Paulsen
A Streetcar Named Desire, Tennessee Williams; (D) Elizabeth Huddle; (S) Tim Saternow; (C) Sarah Campbell; (L) Rick Paulsen
The Grace of Mary Traverse, Timberlake Wertenbaker; (D) Susan Fenichell; (S) Tim Saternow; (C) David Zinn; (L) Mary Louise Geiger
A Midsummer Night's Dream, William Shakespeare; (D) Elizabeth Huddle; (S) Tim Saternow; (C) Paul Chi-Ming Louey; (L) Meg Fox

Intiman Theatre Company. John Aylward and Kurt Beattie in *Waiting for Godot*. Photo: Chris Bennion.

Irondale Ensemble Project

JIM NIESEN
Artistic Director

TERRY GREISS
Executive Director

782 West End Ave., Suite 74
New York, NY 10025
(212) 633-1292

FOUNDED 1983
Jim Niesen, Terry Greiss, Barbara MacKenzie-Wood

SEASON
Variable

FINANCES
July 1, 1990-June 30, 1991
Expenses: $325,000

CONTRACTS
AEA TYA and letter of agreement

Irondale Ensemble Project. *Peter Panic: Flying Underground*. Photo: Gerry Goodstein.

Irondale is an experimental company set up to challenge traditional assumptions about theatre—who makes it, how it gets made and how it can be used. Our long-term investigations have originated in the notion of a permanent group, beginning with how people from a variety of artistic backgrounds can come together to create a genuine ensemble capable of acting together and also of collaboratively creating original pieces. The majority of our work follows two closely related performance styles: the presentation of established texts in unorthodox and often irreverent productions; and the creation of new theatre works, usually by combining original material with a classic and blending multiple styles of performance, music, dance, design and scene work. In an attempt to further expand the boundaries of collaboration, Irondale maintains a permanent relationship with St. Petersburg Theater of Leningrad, and conducts extensive outreach programs in New York City schools, shelters and prisons.

—Jim Neisen

PRODUCTIONS 1989-90

Williams Plays: Beanstalk Country, adapt: Barbara Mackenzie-Wood, from Tennessee Williams; (D) Barbara Mackenzie-Wood; (S) Kennon Rothchild; (C) Elena Pellicciaro; (L) Kennon Rothchild
Peter Panic: Flying Underground, company-developed, from James M. Barrie and Abbie Hoffman; (D) Jim Niesen; (S) Kennon Rothchild; (C) Elena Pellicciaro; (L) Hillarie Blumenthal
Sacrifice, company-developed; (D) Annie-B Parson; (S) Kennon Rothchild; (C) Elena Pellicciaro; (L) David Moodey
Happy End, adapt and trans: Michael Feingold, from Bertolt Brecht; music: Kurt Weill; lyrics: Bertolt Brecht; (D) Jim Niesen; (S) Kennon Rothchild; (C) Elena Pellicciaro; (L) Hillarie Blumenthal

PRODUCTIONS 1990-91

Happy End, adapt and trans: Michael Feingold, from Bertolt Brecht; music: Kurt Weill; lyrics: Bertolt Brecht; (D) Jim Niesen; (S) Kennon Rothchild; (C) Elena Pellicciaro; (L) Hillarie Blumenthal
The Uncle Vanya Show, adapt: company, from Anton Chekhov; (D) Jim Niesen; (S) Kennon Rothchild; (C) Elena Pellicciaro; (L) Kennon Rothchild
St. Petersburg Vaudeville, adapt: Victor Kraslavski; (D) M. Chernozomov; (S) M. Nosova; (C) M. Nosova; (L) Hillarie Blumenthal
Ivanov, Anton Chekhov; adapt and trans: Eugene Lukoshkov; (D) Eugene Lukoshkov; (S) Kennon Rothchild; (C) Elena Pellicciaro; (L) Hillarie Blumenthal
Marriage Proposals, adapt and trans: Molly Hickok, from Anton Chekhov; (D) Molly Hickok; (S) Kennon Rothchild; (C) Elena Pellicciaro; (L) Hillarie Blumenthal
Peter Panic: Flying Underground, company-

developed, from James M. Barrie and Abbie Hoffman; (D) Jim Niesen; (S) Kennon Rothchild; (C) Elena Pellicciaro; (L) Hillarie Blumenthal

AIDS Show, company-developed; (D) Jim Niesen; (S) Kennon Rothchild; (C) Elena Pellicciaro

Sacrifice, company-developed; (D) Annie-B Parson; (S) Kennon Rothchild; (C) Elena Pellicciaro; (L) Hillarie Blumenthal

Jean Cocteau Repertory

ROBERT HUPP
Artistic Director

DAVID FISHELSON
Executive Director

Bouwerie Lane Theatre
330 Bowery
New York, NY 10012
(212) 677-0060

FOUNDED 1971
Eve Adamson

SEASON
Sept.-May

FACILITIES
Bouwerie Lane Theatre
Seating Capacity: 140
Stage: proscenium

FINANCES
July 1, 1990-June 30, 1991
Expenses: $400,000

The Cocteau is a resident company of artists performing in rotating repertory those works of world theatre which by their very nature demand to live on a stage. The company is committed to Jean Cocteau's "poetry of the theatre" in which all elements of production—performance, design, music—fuse into a whole that illuminates the heart of the play and elevates it into a "dramatic poem." Whether approaching a classic or a contemporary work of provocative content and structure, the Cocteau strives to create that unique production style appropriate to each play which will engage the audience intellectually and emotionally. Meeting this artistic challenge in rotating repertory requires a disciplined and flexible resident acting company, as well as bold and imaginative designers and directors. Towards that end, the Cocteau has developed and continued to nurture a growing community of repertory-oriented theatre artists.

—Robert Hupp

PRODUCTIONS 1989-90

The Importance of Being Earnest, Oscar Wilde; (D) Robert Perillo; (S) Giles Hogya; (C) Jonathan Bixby; (L) Giles Hogya

Travesties, Tom Stoppard; (D) Robert Hupp; (S) Giles Hogya; (C) Jonathan Bixby; (L) Giles Hogya

Life Is a Dream, Pedro Calderon de la Barca; trans: Roy Campbell; (D) Eve Adamson; (S) Sara Waterbury; (C) Jonathan Bixby; (L) Eve Adamson

A Man's a Man, Bertolt Brecht; trans: Eric Bentley; (D) Robert Hupp; (S) George Xenos; (C) Jonathan Bixby; (L) Craig Smith

The Prince of Homburg, Heinrich von Kleist; trans: Douglas Langworthy; (D) David Herskovits; (S) Tom Dale Keever; (C) Gregory Gale; (L) Trui Malten

The Stronger, August Strindberg; trans: Evert Sprinchorn; (D) Giles Hogya; (S) Giles Hogya; (C) Gregory Gale; (L) Giles Hogya

The Night of the Tribades, Per Olov Enquist; trans: Ross Schideler; (D) Giles Hogya; (S) Giles Hogya; (C) Gregory Gale; (L) Giles Hogya

PRODUCTIONS 1990-91

Misalliance, George Bernard Shaw; (D) Casey Kizziah; (S) Giles Hogya; (C) Jonathan Bixby; (L) Giles Hogya

The Infernal Machine, Jean Cocteau; trans: Albert Bermel; (D) Robert Hupp; (S) Robert Joel Schwartz; (C) Gregory Gale; (L) Craig Smith

When We Dead Awaken, Henrik Ibsen; trans: Rolf Fjelde; (D) Eve Adamson; (S) Sara Waterbury; (C) Jonathan Bixby; (L) Eve Adamson

Leonce and Lena and ***Woyzeck***, Georg Buchner; trans: Eric Bentley; (D) Robert Hupp; (S) George Xenos; (C) Jonathan Bixby; (L) Brian Aldous

Julius Caesar, William Shakespeare; (D) Eve Adamson; (S) Robert Joel Schwartz; (C) Martha Bromelmeier; (L) Eve Adamson

The Emigrants, Slawomir Mrozek; trans: Henry Beissel; (D) Jonathan Bank; (S) Jonathan Bank; (L) Craig Smith

Jean Cocteau Repertory. Keith Hamilton Cobb, Pascale Roger and Mark Waterman in *The Infernal Machine*. Photo: Gerry Goodstein.

Jewish Repertory Theatre

RAN AVNI
Artistic Director

344 East 14th St.
New York, NY 10003
(212) 674-7200 (bus.)
(212) 505-2667 (b.o.)

FOUNDED 1974
Ran Avni

SEASON
Oct.-June

FACILITIES
The Milton Weill Auditorium
Seating Capacity: 100
Stage: flexible

FINANCES
July 1, 1989-June 30, 1990
Expenses: $350,000

CONTRACTS
AEA Mini

The Jewish Repertory Theatre is now in its 18th season. JRT has revived such treasured classics as *Awake and Sing!, Green Fields* and *Incident at Vichy*; has rediscovered forgotten American works such as *Me and Molly, Unlikely Heroes, Success Story* and *Cantorial*; has shed new light on the plays of Chekhov, Pinter, Sartre and de Ghelderode; has produced a series of new musicals including *Vagabond Stars, Up from Paradise, Kuni-Lemi* (which won four Outer Critics Circle Awards, including Best Off Broadway Musical) *Pearls, The Special, The Shop on Main Street* and *Chu Chem*. The JRT Writers' Lab, led by associate director Edward M. Cohen, does readings, workshops and miniproductions aimed at developing the works of young writers. This program has resulted in JRT productions of *Taking Steam, Benya the King, 36, Crossing Delancy, Bitter Friends* and other plays which are now being produced throughout the country.

—Ran Avni

PRODUCTIONS 1989-90

The Witch, Abraham Goldfaden; adapt: Amielle Zemach; (D) Benjamin Zemach

The Return, Frederic Glover; (D) Michael Bloom

Dividends, Gary Richards; (D) Tony Giordano

New York 1937, Jose Yglesias; (D) Charles Maryan

What's Wrong With This Picture?, Donald Margulies; (D) Larry Arrick

PRODUCTIONS 1990-91

Spinoza, Dimitri Frenkel-Frank; trans: Martin Cleaver; (D) Robert Kalfin

Taking Spock, Richard Schotter; (D) Marilyn Chris

Jewish Repertory Theatre. Adam Heller, Michele Ragusa, Steve Sterner, Susan Friedman Schrott and Stuart Zagnit in *Encore!*. Photo: Carol Rosegg.

A Fierce Attachment, Vivian Gornick; adapt: Edward M. Cohen; (D) Edward M. Cohen
Modigliani, Dennis McIntyre; (D) Bryna Wortman
Encore!, company-developed; (D) Ran Avni

Jomandi Productions, Inc.

THOMAS W. JONES, II
Co-Artistic Director

MARSHA A. JACKSON
Co-Artistic Director/Managing Director

1444 Mayson St. NE
Atlanta, GA 30324
(404) 876-6346 (bus.)
(404) 873-1099 (b.o.)

FOUNDED 1978
Thomas W. Jones, II, Marsha A. Jackson

SEASON
Oct.-June

FACILITIES
14th Street Playhouse
Seating Capacity: 378-425
Stage: proscenium

FINANCES
July 1, 1990-June 30, 1991
Expenses: $750,000

CONTRACTS
AEA SPT

At Jomandi's philosophical and aesthetic center is the assertion of the African-American presence in a global community. That presence, while informed by tradition, concurrently acknowledges the present and future possiblilites. From this center evolves the design of our programs. Jomandi's upcoming season continues the development of an aesthetic within an ever-changing universe. The company's artistic voice is an articulation of the newest works from established and emerging playwrights. The commitment to tour productions nationally and internationally this year, while maintaining a schedule of productions in Atlanta, underscores the company's mission to fulfill the cultural needs of the widest possible community. As architects of the future, Jomandi will continue to redefine the means by which African-American artists examine the values of a new world culture. In this way, the company contributes to a future that encourages cultural pluralism and, specifically, an appreciation of the African-American presence, while capitalizing on the economic and development potentials of theatre in a world marketplace.

—Marsha Jackson, Thomas W. Jones, II

PRODUCTIONS 1989-90

Fraternity, Jeff Stetson; (D) Thomas W. Jones, II; (S) Art Johnson; (C) Goldie Dicks; (L) Jeff Guzik
Sisters, Marsha A. Jackson; (D) Thomas W. Jones, II; (S) John Harris; (C) Debi Barber; (L) John Harris
Do Lord Remember Me, James de Jongh; (D) Andrea Frye; (S) John Harris; (C) Goldie Dicks; (L) John Harris
Josephine Live!, book: Marsha A. Jackson; music: S. Renee Clark and Thomas W. Jones, II; lyrics: Marsha A. Jackson and Thomas W. Jones, II; (D) Thomas W. Jones, II; (S) Art Johnson; (C) Edouard; (L) Jeff Guzik
From the Mississippi Delta, Dr. Endesha Ida Mae Holland; (D) Edward G. Smith
The Wizard of Hip, Thomas W. Jones, II; (D) Kenny Leon; (S) Tony Loadholt; (C) Goldie Dicks; (L) Jeff Guzik

PRODUCTIONS 1990-91

And the Men Shall Also Gather, Jeff Stetson; (D) Thomas W. Jones, II; (S) Art Johnson; (C) Goldie Dicks; (L) Jeff Guzik
She'll Find Her Way Home, Valetta Anderson; (D) Andrea Frye; (S) Art Johnson; (C) Sharlene Roxx and Sheila Benning; (L) Rae Williams
21st Century Groove, Alonzo D. Lamont, Jr.; (D) Thomas W. Jones, II; (S) Tony Loadholt; (C) Goldie Dicks; (L) Rae Williams
House of Cold Funk, Rex Garvin; (D) Thomas W. Jones, II; (S) Tony Loadholt; (C) Goldie Dicks; (L) Paul Evans
The Wizard of Hip, Thomas W. Jones, II; (D) Kenny Leon; (S) Tony Loadholt; (C) Goldie Dicks; (L) Paul Evans
Queen of the Blues, book: Thomas W. Jones, II; various lyricists; (D) Thomas W. Jones, II; (S) John Harris; (C) Edouard; (L) John Harris

La Jolla Playhouse

DES McANUFF
Artistic Director

ALAN LEVEY
Managing Director

ROBERT BLACKER
Associate Director/Dramaturg

Box 12039
La Jolla, CA 92039
(619) 534-6760 (bus.)
(619) 534-3960 (b.o.)

FOUNDED 1947
Gregory Peck, Dorothy McGuire, Mel Ferrer

SEASON
May-Nov.

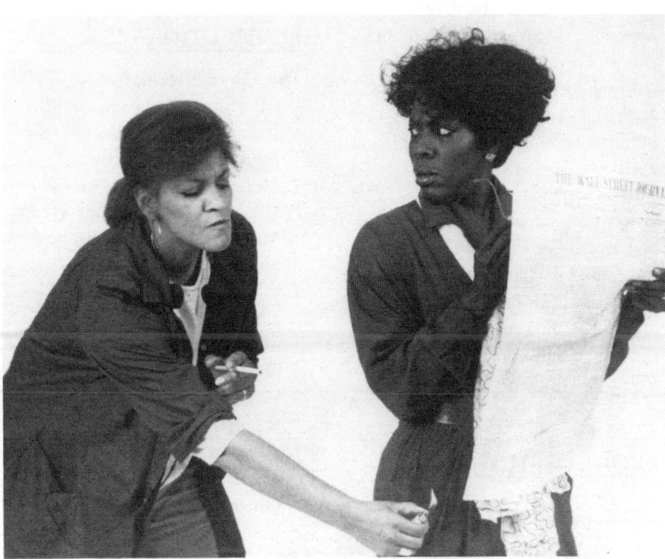

Jomandi Productions, Inc. Andrea Frye and Marsha Jackson in *Sisters*.

La Jolla Playhouse. Sterling Macer, Jr., Nancy Travis and Brock Peters in *My Children! My Africa!* Photo: Micha Langer.

FACILITIES
Mandell Weiss Theatre
Seating Capacity: 492
Stage: proscenium

Mandell Weiss Forum
Seating Capacity: 384
Stage: thrust

FINANCES
Nov. 1, 1989-Oct. 31, 1990
Expenses: $4,224,758

CONTRACTS
AEA LORT (B) and (C)

The La Jolla Playhouse provides a home in which theatre artists can gather, share ideas and extend themselves. At the heart of each project we produce is a director, playwright or performer who can impact the development of our art form and help define the course of American theatre. We encourage a variety of genres and styles, believing that the vitality of the American theatre is bound to our rich and diverse theatrical and cultural heritage. We produce new work and classics side by side, because we believe that they inform each other—that working on classics expands contemporary artists' ideas about theatre, and that new works keep classics honest by reminding us that they must be pertinent. This juxtaposition allows artists and audiences alike to examine contemporary issues in a historical context.

—Des McAnuff

PRODUCTIONS 1990

The Cherry Orchard, Anton Chekhov; trans: Elisaveta Lavrova; (D) Tom Moore; (S) Heidi Landesman; (C) Robert Blackman; (L) Peter Maradudin

Life During Wartime, Keith Reddin; (D) Les Waters; (S) Loy Arcenas; (C) David C. Woolard; (L) Stephen Strawbridge

A Funny Thing Happened on the Way to the Forum, book: Burt Shevelove and Larry Gelbart; music and lyrics: Stephen Sondheim; (D) Des McAnuff; (S) John Arnone; (C) Susan Hilferty; (L) Brenda Berry

Don Quixote de la Jolla, Eric Overmyer, from Miguel de Cervantes; (D) Stan Wojewodski, Jr.; (S) Neil Patel; (C) Christine Dougherty; (L) Stephen Strawbridge

My Children! My Africa!, Athol Fugard; (D) Athol Fugard; (S) Douglas Stein and Susan Hilferty; (C) Susan Hilferty; (L) Dennis Parichy

Twelfth Night, William Shakespeare; (D) Des McAnuff; (S) Neil Patel; (C) Christina Haatainen; (L) Chris Parry

PRODUCTIONS 1991

The Three Sisters, Anton Chekhov; trans: Jean-Claude van Itallie; (D) Des McAnuff; (S) John Arnone; (C) Patricia McGourty; (L) Peter Maradudin

Fortinbras, Lee Blessing; (D) Des McAnuff; (S) Robert Brill; (C) Susan Hilferty; (L) Chris Parry

The Regard of Flight and ***The Clown Bagatelles***, Bill Irwin with Nancy Harrington, M.C. O'Connor and Doug Skinner; (S) Vince Mountain; (L) Nancy Schertler

The Heliotrope Bouquet by Scott Joplin & Louis Chauvin, Eric Overmyer; (D) Stan Wojewodski, Jr.; (S) Christopher Barreca; (C) Catherine Zuber; (L) Richard Pilbrow

A Lesson from Aloes, Athol Fugard; (D) Athol Fugard; (S) Douglas Stein and Susan Hilferty; (C) Andrea Singer; (L) Dennis Parichy

Elmer Gantry, book adapt: John Bishop, from Sinclair Lewis; music: Mel Marvin; lyrics: Robert Satuloff and John Bishop; (D) Des McAnuff; (S) Heidi Landesman; (C) Susan Hilferty; (L) Chris Parry

Lamb's Players Theatre

ROBERT SMYTH
Producing Artistic Director

Box 26
National City, CA 91951
(619) 474-3385 (bus.)
(619) 474-4542 (b.o.)

FOUNDED 1978
Steve Terrell, Robert Smyth

SEASON
Jan.-Dec.

FACILITIES
Seating Capacity: 175
Stage: arena

Lyceum Space
Seating Capacity: 250
Stage: flexible

Theatre East
Seating Capacity: 1,000
Stage: proscenium

FINANCES
Jan. 1, 1990-Dec. 31, 1990
Expenses: $997,753

Lamb's Players Theatre is a year-round ensemble of artists—actors, designers, directors and playwrights—working in collaboration over an extended period of time, pushing each other toward their best work, seeking to integrate faith and art. While not a "religious" theatre, the company finds the basis of its artistic vision in the Judeo-Christian world view. In addition to our resident theatre we maintain a touring company which performs in schools and prisons nationwide.

—Robert Smyth

PRODUCTIONS 1990

Joseph and the Amazing Technicolor Dreamcoat, book and lyrics: Tim Rice; music: Andrew Lloyd Webber; (D) Robert Smyth; (S) Mike Buckley; (C) Veronica Smith; (L) Nathan Peirson

The Nerd, Larry Shue; (D) Robert

Lamb's Players Theatre. Gale West and Deborah Smyth in *An Ideal Husband*. Photo: Nate Peirson.

Smyth; (S) Mike Buckley; (C) Veronica Smith; (L) Nathan Peirson

An Ideal Husband, Oscar Wilde; (D) Kerry Meads; (S) Mike Buckley; (C) Jeanne Reith; (L) Alan Will

The Wind in the Willows, book adapt, music and lyrics: Douglas Post, from Kenneth Grahame; (D) Robert Smyth; (S) Christian Turner; (C) Jeanne Reith; (L) Mike Buckley

The Chalk Garden, Enid Bagnold; (D) Robert Smyth; (S) Mike Buckley; (C) Veronica Smith; (L) Nathan Peirson

Damien, Aldyth Morris; (D) David McFadzean; (S) David Thayer; (C) Gail Parrish; (L) David Thayer

Johnny Pye and the Foolkiller, book adapt and lyrics: Mark St. Germain, from Stephen Vincent Benet; music: Randy Courts; (D) Deborah Gilmour Smyth; (S) Mike Buckley; (C) Jeanne Reith; (L) Jerald Enos

Lamb's Players Festival of Christmas, Kerry Meads; (D) Robert Smyth; (S) Mike Buckley; (C) Veronica Smith; (L) Robert Smyth

PRODUCTIONS 1991

The Rivals, Richard Brinsley Sheridan; (D) Robert Smyth; (S) Mike Buckley; (C) Jeanne Reith; (L) C. Todd Brown

Cotton Patch Gospel, book adapt: Tom Key and Russell Treyz, from Clarence Jordan; music and lyrics: Harry Chapin; (D) Deborah Gilmour Smyth; (S) Mike Buckley; (C) Veronica Smith; (L) Nathan Peirson

The Boys Next Door, Tom Griffin; (D) Kerry Meads; (S) Mike Buckley; (C) Veronica Smith; (L) Nathan Peirson

The Trip to Bountiful, Horton Foote; (D) Robert Smyth; (S) Mike Buckley; (C) Veronica Smith; (L) Mike Buckley

Puff the Magic Dragon, Gilette Elvgren; (D) Kate McConnell; (S) O.P. Hadlock; (C) Mirian Laubert; (L) Brent Kelly

The Foreigner, Larry Shue; (D) Kerry Meads; (S) Mike Buckley; (C) Veronica Smith; (L) Nathan Peirson

Traveler in the Dark, Marsha Norman; (D) Deborah Gilmour Smyth

Quilters, book adapt: Molly Newman and Barbara Damashek, from Patricia Cooper and Norma Bradley Allen; music and lyrics: Barbara Damashek; (D) Robert Smyth

Lamb's Players Festival of Christmas, Kerry Meads; (D) Robert Smyth

The Gift of the Magi, book adapt and lyrics: Mark St. Germain, from O. Henry; music: Randy Courts; (D) Robert Smyth

L. A. Theatre Works

L.A. Theatre Works. *The Love of the Nightingale*. Photo: Michael LaMont.

SUSAN ALBERT LOEWENBERG
Producing Director

PEGGY SHANNON
Associate Producing Director

GALE COHEN
Business Manager

681 Venice Blvd.
Venice, CA 90291
(213) 827-0808

FOUNDED 1974
Susan Albert Loewenberg, Robert Greenwald, Jeremy Blahnik

SEASON
Variable

FINANCES
Oct. 1, 1989-Sept. 30, 1990
Expenses: $484,770

CONTRACTS
AEA LORT (D)

As producing director of L.A. Theatre Works my task has been to guide the evolution of the company—from an informally organized group of theatre artists exploring ways to make theatre in unorthodox settings such as prisons and community workshops, to a formal producing organization that develops and presents the work of playwrights from the U.S. and abroad. Our new L.A. Theatre Works Radio Company, an ensemble of 40 distinguished, classically trained actors who share our ideas about theatre, enlarges our artistic scope through innovative productions of both classic and contemporary plays for radio. Our commitment is to new work, new forms and the explication of a particular vision. As a post-Brechtian theatre that truly mirrors the "unease" of modern culture, we want our audience to experience the exhilaration of change, as opposed to the emotional release that comes from artifice. We support and nurture our theatrical vision through our Radio Theatre Series for New Plays and through collaborations involving conceptual directors, playwrights and designers.

—*Susan Albert Loewenberg*

PRODUCTIONS 1989-90

Wooman Lovely Wooman, What a Sex You Are!: A Look at the Women in Charles Dickens, conceived: Sonia Fraser and Miriam Margolyes; (D) Sonia Fraser; (S) Robert Israel; (C) Peter Mitchell; (L) Madie Greer

The Love of the Nightingale, Timberlake Wertenbaker; (D) Peter Mark Schifter; (S) Victoria Petrovich; (C) Catherine Meacham; (L) Michael Gilliam

PRODUCTIONS 1989-90

Radio Series For New Plays:

The Misanthrope, Moliere; adapt: Neil Bartlett; (D) Peggy Shannon

Behind the Veil, Lenore Bensinger; music: Fredric Myrow; lyrics: Martin Kibbee; (D) Peggy Shannon

The Key and ***Tone Clusters***, Joyce Carol Oates; (D) Gordon Hunt

American Dreams, Velina Hasu Houston; (D) Peggy Shannon

Phantasie, Sybille Pearson; (D) Darrell Larson

The White Plague, Karel Capek; trans: Michael Henry Heim; (D) Peggy Shannon

Top Secret: The Battle for the Pentagon Papers, Geoffrey Cowan and Leroy Aarons; (D) Tom Moore

Movements, Yvonne Farrow; (D) Judyann Elder

The Master and Margarita, adapt: Yuri Lyubimov, from Mikhail Bulgakov; (D) Colman de Kay

Heaven and Earth, Allan Havis; (D) Dan Bonnell

Cheap, Tom Topor, from Moliere; (D) Peggy Shannon

Undue Influence, Michael E. Wolfson; (D) Peggy Shannon

In the Moonlight Eddie, Jack Lo Giudice; (D) Dorothy Lyman

Questa, Stephanie Fleischmann; (D) Michael Bloom

An Evening with Raymond Carver, adapt: Harris Yulin

Final Passages, Robert Schenkkan; (D) Philip Killian

Oyakoshinju: Deathbond, Sachi Oyama; (D) Peggy Shannon

Lincoln Center Theater

ANDRE BISHOP
Artistic Director

BERNARD GERSTEN
Executive Producer

150 West 65th St.
New York, NY 10023
(212) 362-7600 (bus.)
(212) 239-6200 (b.o.)

FOUNDED 1985
Lincoln Center for the Performing Arts, Inc.

Lincoln Center Theater. Stockard Channing, Courtney B. Vance and John Cunningham in *Six Degrees of Separation*. Photo: Martha Swope.

SEASON
Jan.-Dec.

FACILITIES
Vivian Beaumont Theater
Seating Capacity: 1,100
Stage: thrust

Mitzi E. Newhouse Theater
Seating Capacity: 299
Stage: thrust

FINANCES
July 1, 1989-June 30, 1990
Expenses: $11,472,931

CONTRACTS
AEA LORT (A) and (C)

Note: During the 1989-90 and 1990-91 seasons, Gregory Mosher served as artistic director.

PRODUCTIONS 1989-90

Oh, Hell!: Bobby Gould in Hell, David Mamet; ***The Devil and Billy Markham***, Shel Silverstein; (D) Gregory Mosher; (S) John Lee Beatty; (C) Jane Greenwood; (L) Kevin Rigdon

The Tenth Man, Paddy Chayefsky; (D) Ulu Grosbard; (S) Santo Loquasto; (C) Jane Greenwood; (L) Dennis Parichy

Some Americans Abroad, Richard Nelson; (D) Roger Michell; (S) Alexandra Byrne; (C) Alexandra Byrne; (L) Rick Fisher

Six Degrees of Separation, John Guare; (D) Jerry Zaks; (S) Tony Walton; (C) William Ivey Long; (L) Paul Gallo

PRODUCTIONS 1990-91

Six Degrees of Separation, John Guare; (D) Jerry Zaks; (S) Tony Walton; (C) William Ivey Long; (L) Paul Gallo

Monster in a Box, Spalding Gray; (D) Renee Shafransky

Township Fever, book, music and lyrics: Mbongeni Ngema; (D) Mbongeni Ngema; (S) Sarah Roberts; (C) Sarah Roberts; (L) Mannie Manim

Mule Bone, book: Zora Neale Hurston and Langston Hughes; music: Taj Mahal; lyrics: Langston Hughes; (D) Michael Schultz; (S) Edward Burbridge; (C) Lewis Brown; (L) Allen Lee Hughes

The Fever, Wallace Shawn; (D) Wallace Shawn

Mr. Gogol and Mr. Preen, Elaine May; (D) Gregory Mosher; (S) John Lee Beatty; (C) Jane Greenwood; (L) Kevin Rigdon

The State Theater of Lithuania

Uncle Vanya , Anton Chekhov; (D) Eimuntas Nekrosius

The Square, Eimuntas Nekrosius; (D) Eimuntas Nekrosius

Live Oak Theatre

DON TONER
Producing Artistic Director

ANNA MORMAN
Administrative Director

311 Nueces
Austin, TX 78701
(512) 472-5143

FOUNDED 1982
Mac Williams, Jeanette Brown

SEASON
Jan.-Dec.

FACILITIES
Seating Capacity: 190
Stage: proscenium

FINANCES
Oct. 1, 1989-Sept. 30, 1990
Expenses: $248,612

CONTRACTS
AEA SPT

We believe that theatre provides communal nourishment of mind and spirit for better understanding of our world and fuller enjoyment of our lives. We are committed to providing the live-theatre experience to the broadest possible audience through professional productions of the best of the classic and contemporary plays with a special commitment to development and production of new works. The signing of a contract with Actors' Equity in 1989 reflects our desire to create a theatre where the creative life of the actor is supported and given opportunity to grow. Recognizing an additional responsibility to nurture emerging playwrights and to further the development and presentation of their work, we present at least one premiere production as part of our regular season. Live Oak Theatre has instituted a New Plays Award program which attracts more than 200 new scripts annually from across the country.

—Don Toner

PRODUCTIONS 1989-90

Sweet Bird of Youth, Tennessee Williams; (D) Don Toner; (S) Bil Pfuderer; (C) Peggy McKowen, Devon Painter and Dennis Kraft; (L) Don Toner

Irma la Douce, book adapt and lyrics: Monty Norman, Julian More and David Heneker, from Alexandre Freffort; music: Marguerite Monnot; (D) Bil

Live Oak Theatre. Janelle Buchanan and Jill Parker-Jones in *A Texas Romance*. Photo: Katie Kolodzey.

Pfuderer; (S) Bil Pfuderer; (C) Peggy McKowen; (L) Laura Sunkel Olden

The Immigrant, Mark Harelik; (D) Don Toner; (S) Gary van der Wege; (C) Dennis Kraft; (L) Ken Hudson

God's Favorite, Neil Simon; (D) Jim Fritzler; (S) Jim Fritzler; (C) Jim Fritzler; (L) Laura Sunkel Olden

Steel Magnolias, Robert Harling; (D) Don Toner; (S) Don Toner; (C) Dennis Kraft; (L) Laura Sunkel Olden

The Wonder Years, book: David Levy, Steve Liebman, Davie Holdbrive and Terry La Bolt; music and lyrics: David Levy; (D) Joe York; (S) Joe York; (C) Joe York; (L) Steven Truitt

PRODUCTIONS 1990-91

Driving Miss Daisy, Alfred Uhry; (D) Don Toner; (S) Don Toner; (C) Dennis Kraft; (L) Don Toner

Translations, Brian Friel; (D) Peter Sheridan; (S) Gary van der Wege; (C) coordinator: Nina Cockburn; (L) Steve Mallinson

The Lady's Not for Burning, Christopher Fry; (D) Don Toner; (S) Bob Brasfield; (C) Bil Pfuderer; (L) Steve Mallinson

Advice to the Players, Bruce Bonafede; (D) Tom Whitaker; (S) Bil Pfuderer; (C) coordinator: Nina Cockburn; (L) Steve Mallinson

A Texas Romance, Ellsworth Schave; (D) Don Toner; (S) Devon Painter; (C) Devon Painter; (L) Steve Mallinson

The Pirates of Penzance, W.S. Gilbert and Arthur Sullivan; (D) Bil Pfuderer; (S) Bil Pfuderer; (C) Bil Pfuderer; (L) Robert Whyburn

Talley's Folly, Lanford Wilson; (D) Don Toner; (S) Gary van der Wege; (C) Devon Painter; (L) Don Toner

Living Stage Theatre Company

ROBERT A. ALEXANDER
Director

CATHERINE IRWIN
Managing Director

6th and Maine Aves. SW
Washington, DC 20024
(202) 554-9066

FOUNDED 1966
Robert A. Alexander

SEASON
Sept.-June

FACILITIES
Living Stage Theatre
Seating Capacity: 124
Stage: flexible

FINANCES
July 1, 1990-June 30, 1991
Expenses: $650,000

CONTRACTS
AEA LORT (D)

The fundamental belief of Living Stage is that everyone is an artist. Living Stage enhances this artistry through improvised productions, combined with workshops, designed to actively engage the audience in the creative process. Living Stage inspires creativity and promotes a positive view of the self and the world. Living Stage's work focuses on children and special-needs audiences. In addition to performances and workshops, we offer training in the creative process for adults who work with children. Attendees include educators, artists, social activists and community organization workers. The training is offered through residencies—locally, nationally and internationally. We are most interested now in finding ways to show how the power of the artistic imagination can create positive change in our society. The future will include more work with adults to ensure that our philosophies and techniques will be utilized on a greater scale, along with public forums that provide an opportunity to explore solutions to societal problems such as racism, sexism, violence, drug abuse and poverty.

—Robert A. Alexander

PRODUCTIONS 1989-91

Note: All performances are company-developed from improvisations; (D) Robert A. Alexander.

Living Stage Theatre Company. Scott Fortune and a student improvising a scene about homelessness. Photo: Kelly Jerome.

Long Wharf Theatre

ARVIN BROWN
Artistic Director

M. EDGAR ROSENBLUM
Executive Director

222 Sargent Drive
New Haven, CT 06511
(203) 787-4284 (bus.)
(203) 787-4282 (b.o.)

FOUNDED 1965
Harlan Kleiman, Jon Jory

SEASON
Sept.-June

FACILITIES
Newton Schenck Stage
Seating Capacity: 487
Stage: thrust

Stage II
Seating Capacity: 199
Stage: flexible

FINANCES
July 1, 1990-June 30, 1991
Expenses: $4,440,000

CONTRACTS
AEA LORT (B) and (C)

Long Wharf Theatre is committed to plays that deal with character, incorporating those ethical, social, political, moral and aesthetic principles that help to define the human condition. We present classics and neglected works in a way that will open up our vision of the past, present and future; provide a forum for contemporary theatre voices by introducing new works of established and emerging playwrights; and foster creativity by supporting research and development of new plays and ideas. Long Wharf Theatre is dedicated to cultivating audiences that reflect the State of Connecticut and the diversity of our cities and our rural and suburban areas; serving as a forum for the examination of historical and current issues through humanities programs; and nurturing tomorrow's audiences through an arts-in-education initiative which enriches and enlightens the children of our community. We accomplish these goals within a supportive working environment for our staff and theatre artists.

—Arvin Brown

PRODUCTIONS 1989-90

A Flea in Her Ear, Georges Feydeau; trans: John Mortimer; (D) John Tillinger; (S) John Lee Beatty; (C) Jane Greenwood; (L) Marc B. Weiss

A Dance Lesson, David Wiltse; (D) Gordon Edelstein; (S) Hugh Landwehr; (C) David Murin; (L) Pat Collins

The Crucible, Arthur Miller; (D) Arvin Brown; (S) Michael Yeargan; (C) David Murin; (L) Ronald Wallace

Re: Joyce!, Maureen Lipman and James Roose-Evans, from Joyce Grenfell; (D) Alan Strachan; (S) John Lee Beatty; (C) Ben Frow; (L) Judy Rasmuson

Anna Christie, Eugene O'Neill; (D) Gordon Edelstein; (S) Hugh Landwehr; (C) Jess Goldstein;

(L) Arden Fingerhut

The Ruffian on the Stair, Joe Orton; (D) John Tillinger; (S) James Noone; (C) Jess Goldstein; (L) Craig Miller

The Lover, Harold Pinter; (D) John Tillinger; (S) James Noone; (C) Jess Goldstein; (L) Craig Miller

Is He Still Dead?, Donald Freed; (D) Charles Nelson Reilly; (S) Marjorie Bradley Kellogg; (C) Noel Taylor; (L) Marc B. Weiss

PRODUCTIONS 1990-91

The Voysey Inheritance, adapt: James Luse, from Harley Granville Barker; (D) Arvin Brown; (S) John Lee Beatty; (C) David Murin; (L) Arden Fingerhut

Generations of the Dead in the Abyss of Coney Island Madness, Michael Henry Brown; (D) L. Kenneth Richardson; (S) Donald Eastman; (C) Judy Dearing; (L) Anne Militello

Valued Friends, Stephen Jeffreys; (D) Robin Lefevre; (S) Sue Plummer; (C) Sue Plummer; (L) Marc B. Weiss

Betrayal, Harold Pinter; (D) John Tillinger; (S) John Lee Beatty; (C) Jane Greenwood; (L) Richard Nelson

The Baby Dance, Jane Anderson; (D) Jenny Sullivan; (S) Marjorie Bradley Kellogg; (C) David Murin; (L) Kirk Bookman

How Do You Like Your Meat?, Joyce Carol Oates; (D) Gordon Edelstein; (S) Hugh Landwehr; (C) David Murin; (L) Arden Fingerhut

Picnic, William Inge; (D) Arvin Brown; (S) Michael Yeargan; (C) Jess Goldstein; (L) Richard Nelson

Long Wharf Theatre. Linda Purl and Stephanie Zimbalist in *The Baby Dance*. Photo: T. Charles Erickson.

Los Angeles Theatre Center

BILL BUSHNELL
Artistic Director

DIANE WHITE
Producing Director

514 South Spring St.
Los Angeles, CA 90013
(213) 627-6500 (bus.)
(213) 627-5599 (b.o.)

FOUNDED 1985
Diane White, Bill Bushnell

SEASON
Jan.-Dec.

FACILITIES
Tom Bradley Theatre
Seating Capacity: 498
Stage: thrust

FINANCES
May 1, 1990-Apr. 30, 1991
Expenses: $6,699,555

CONTRACTS
AEA LORT (B), (C) and (D)

The Los Angeles Theatre Center's artistic mission springs from our own cares and concerns: to make theatre which, in its excellence, passion, truth and cultural diversity, reflects and improves the community and the world. The city of Los Angeles—a city of diverse cultures that personifies the social, ethnic and political future—is our inspiration. LATC's four stages and year-round programming serve as "a gathering place" where talented artists from various cultures can propagate brilliant artistic truth that is joyful, beautiful, passionate and entertaining, while reflecting the toughness and vitality of contemporary life for a multicultural audience. At the heart of LATC's philosophy is the belief that theatre is the synthesizer of all the arts, that all theatre is political in the universal sense, and that our role as artists is to agitate and disseminate our perception of the truth.

—Bill Bushnell, Diane White

Los Angeles Theatre Center. Tom Waits and Bill Pullman in *Demon Wine*. Photo: Chris Gulker.

PRODUCTIONS 1989-90

The Marriage of Bette and Boo, Christopher Durang; (D) Dennis Erdman; (S) John Iacovelli; (C) Marianna Elliott; (L) Casey Cowan

The Geography of Luck, Marlane Meyer; (D) David Schweizer; (S) John Iacovelli; (C) Gregory Poe; (L) Douglas D. Smith

Daytrips, Jo Carson; (D) Steven Kent; (S) Douglas D. Smith; (C) Donna Barrier; (L) Douglas D. Smith

Death of a Salesman, Arthur Miller; (D) Bill Bushnell; (S) Mark Wendland; (C) Marianna Elliott; (L) Casey Cowan

Once in Doubt, Raymond J. Barry; (D) David Saint; (S) Douglas D. Smith; (L) Douglas D. Smith

The Dance of Death, August Strindberg; trans: Michael Meyer; (D) Alan Mandell; (S) John Iacovelli; (C) Marianna Elliott; (L) Brian Gale

Piano, Anna Deavere Smith; (D) Bill Bushnell; (S) Timian Alsaker; (C) Marianna Elliott; (L) Todd A. Jared

Stevie Wants to Play the Blues, Eduardo Machado; music: Fredric Myrow; lyrics: Eduardo Machado and Fredric Myrow; (D) Simon Callow; (S) Timian Alsaker; (C) Timian Alsaker; (L) Douglas D. Smith

And Baby Makes Seven, Paula

Vogel; (D) Peggy Shannon; (S) D. Martyn Bookwalter; (C) Timian Alsaker and Donna Barrier; (L) Douglas D. Smith

The Illusion, Tony Kushner, from Pierre Corneille; (D) David Schweizer; (S) Douglas D. Smith; (C) Marianna Elliott; (L) Douglas D. Smith

Strong-Man's Weak Child, Israel Horovitz; (D) Israel Horovitz; (S) D. Martyn Bookwalter; (C) Ann Bruice; (L) D. Martyn Bookwalter

Viva Detroit, Derek Walcott; (D) Claude Purdy; (S) John Dexter; (C) Ann Bruice; (L) Douglas D. Smith

PRODUCTIONS 1990-91

The Wild Duck, Henrik Ibsen; trans: Gerry Bamman and Irene B. Berman; (D) Stein Winge; (S) Pavel Dobrusky; (C) Pavel Dobrusky; (L) Douglas D. Smith

The Mission, Richard Montoya, Ricardo Salinas and Herbert Siguenza; (D) Jose Luis Valenzuela; (S) Gronk; (C) Herbert Siguenza; (L) Jose Lopez

August 29, Violeta Calles; (D) Jose Luis Valenzuela; (S) Gronk and Douglas D. Smith; (C) Gronk; (L) Douglas D. Smith

The Crucible, Arthur Miller; (D) Bill Bushnell; (S) D. Martyn Bookwalter; (C) Timian Alsaker; (L) D. Martyn Bookwalter

The Joni Mitchell Project, conceived: Henry Edwards and David Schweizer; songs: Joni Mitchell; (D) David Schweizer; (S) Timian Alsaker; (C) Donna Barrier; (L) Timian Alsaker

Blues in the Night, conceived: Sheldon Epps; (D) Sheldon Epps; (S) Douglas D. Smith; (C) Marianna Elliott; (L) Douglas D. Smith

The Hip-Hop Waltz of Eurydice, Reza Abdoh; (D) Reza Abdoh; (S) Timian Alsaker; (C) Timian Alsaker; (L) Rand Ryan

Veins and Thumbtacks, Jonathan Marc Sherman; (D) David Saint; (S) David Gallo; (C) Marianna Elliott; (L) Kenneth Posner

My Children! My Africa!, Athol Fugard; (D) Athol Fugard; (S) Douglas Stein and Susan Hilferty; (C) Susan Hilferty; (L) Dennis Parichy

Absalom's Song, Selaelo Maredi; (D) Ann Bowen; (S) Timian Alsaker; (C) Timian Alsaker; (L) Douglas D. Smith

Life Is a Dream, Pedro Calderon de la Barca; trans: Edwin Honig, with addtl text from *The Tower*, by Hugo von Hofmannsthal; trans: Michael Hamburger; (D) Bill Bushnell and Sidney Montz; (S) Allison Koturbash; (C) Timian Alsaker; (L) Timian Alsaker

The Rabbit Foot, Leslie Lee; (D) Shabaka; (S) Douglas D. Smith; (C) Marianna Elliott; (L) Douglas D. Smith

Day of Hope, Birgir Sigurdsson; adapt: Patrick Tovatt; trans: Jill Brooke; (D) Bill Bushnell; (S) Timian Alsaker; (C) Marianna Elliott; (L) Donald D. Smith

Monster in a Box, Spalding Gray; (D) Renee Shafransky

Mabou Mines

LEE BREUER, RUTH MALECZECH, FREDERICK NEUMANN, TERRY O'REILLY
Artistic Directorate

JENNIFER GREENFIELD
Associate Producer

150 First Ave.
New York, NY 10009
(212) 473-0559

FOUNDED 1970
David Warrilow, Ruth Maleczech, Philip Glass, Lee Breuer, JoAnne Akalaitis

SEASON
Jan.-Dec.

FINANCES
July 1, 1989-June 30, 1990
Expenses: $760,000

CONTRACTS
AEA Guest Artist

Mabou Mines is an artistic collective based in New York City. The company has produced 40 works for theatre, film, video and radio during its 21-year history and has performed all over the U.S., and in Europe, Japan, South America, Israel and Australia. Combining the visual, aural, musical and sculptural arts with dramatic texts, and synthesizing film, video and live performances through the art of the actor, Mabou Mines has produced experimental theatre pieces that integrate aesthetic content with political substance. We have sought to make art that redefines the culture, punctures what is, pushes the limits of what's thinkable—to raise difficult issues in paradoxical ways and to challenge audiences with new ways of looking at our world. Twenty-one years is a long time to produce experimental works on the edge of an ever more conservative society. We feel strongly the need to continue working, to gather strength from the world community of artists and to share our vision with a hungry audience.

—*Ruth Maleczech*

PRODUCTIONS 1989-90

Cold Harbor, Dale Worsley; (D) Bill Raymond and Dale Worsley; (S) Linda Hartinian; (C) Greg Mehrten; (L) B. St. John Schofield

Mabou Mines' Lear, adapt: Lee Breuer, from William Shakespeare; (D) Lee Breuer; (S) Alison Yerxa; (C) Ghretta Hynd; (L) Arden Fingerhut and Lenore Doxsee

B. Beaver Animation, Lee Breuer; (D) Lee Breuer; (S) Tina Girouard, adapt by: Marcia Altieri; (C) Gabriel Berry; (L) David Tecson

PRODUCTIONS 1990-91

Through the Leaves, Franz Xaver Kroetz; trans: Roger Downey; (D) JoAnne Akalaitis; (S) Douglas Stein; (C) Teresa Snider-Stein; (L) Frances Aronson

The Bribe, Terry O'Reilly; music: John Zorn; (D) Ruth Maleczech; (C) Anne-Marie Wright

Worstward Ho, Samuel Beckett; (D) Frederick Neumann; (S) John Arnone; (C) Gabriel Berry; (L) Jennifer Tipton

Company, Samuel Beckett; (D) Frederick Neumann; (S) Gerald Marks; (L) Sabrina Hamilton

Mabou Mines. *B. Beaver Animation*. Photo: Georgina Bedrosian.

Madison Repertory Theatre. LeWan Alexander and Mark Corkins in *Blood Knot*. Photo: Zane Williams.

Madison Repertory Theatre

JOSEPH HANREDDY
Artistic Director

VICKI STEWART
Managing Director

211 State St.
Madison, WI 53703
(608) 256-0029 (bus.)
(608) 266-9055 (b.o.)

FOUNDED 1969
Katherine Waack, Vicki Stewart

SEASON
July-May

FACILITIES
Isthmus Playhouse
Seating Capacity: 335
Stage: thrust

FINANCES
July 1, 1990-June 30, 1991
Expenses: $550,000

CONTRACTS
AEA SPT

With exuberance and a probing curiosity, Madison Repertory Theatre approaches its 23rd season with the aim of finding and producing plays that are timely, passionate, original, theatrical, truthful and entertaining—plays that provide audiences with new visions, points of view and questions. With the play's text and the vision of the author as our guide, we endeavor to give each work a sharp, clear, exciting production—one that will stay with the audience long after the house lights come up. Our highest priorities continue to be: to improve our level of excellence in all aspects of production; to consistently challenge ourselves and our audience with our repertoire; and to attract the finest artists available by creating a generous, open, hospitable and creative atmosphere.

—Joseph Hanreddy

PRODUCTIONS 1989-90

The Boys Next Door, Tom Griffin; (D) Joseph Hanreddy; (S) Frank Schneeberger; (C) Mary Neuser and Catherine M. Mueller; (L) Thomas C. Hase

Blood Knot, Athol Fugard; (D) Joseph Hanreddy; (S) Frank Schneeberger; (C) Mary Neuser; (L) Thomas C. Hase

Holy Ghosts, Romulus Linney; (D) Joseph Hanreddy; (S) Frank Schneeberger; (C) Mary Neuser; (L) Thomas C. Hase

The Voice of the Prairie, John Olive; (D) Andrew J. Traister; (S) Frank Schneeberger; (C) Mary Neuser; (L) Thomas C. Hase

Ain't Misbehavin', conceived: Murray Horwitz and Richard Maltby, Jr.; music and lyrics: Fats Waller, et al; (D) Fred Weiss; (S) Frank Schneeberger; (C) Mary Neuser; (L) Thomas C. Hase

Burn This, Lanford Wilson; (D) Joseph Hanreddy; (S) Frank Schneeberger; (C) Mary Neuser; (L) Thomas C. Hase

PRODUCTIONS 1990-91

Quilters, book adapt: Molly Newman and Barbara Damashek, from Patricia Cooper and Norma Bradley Allen; music and lyrics: Barbara Damashek; (D) Larry Deckel; (S) Frank Schneeberger; (C) Rebecca Sandler Jallings, with Mary Neuser; (L) Thomas C. Hase

A...My Name Is Alice, conceived: Joan Micklin Silver and Julianne Boyd; various composers and lyricists; (D) Fred Weiss; (S) Frank Schneeberger; (C) Mary Neuser; (L) Thomas C. Hase

Taking Steps, Alan Ayckbourn; (D) Joseph Hanreddy; (S) Frank Schneeberger; (C) Mary Neuser and Anna Stevens; (L) Andrew Meyers

The Immigrant, Mark Harelik; (D) Doug Finlayson; (S) Frank Schneeberger; (C) Mary Waldhart; (L) Linda Essig

The Importance of Being Earnest, Oscar Wilde; (D) Joseph Hanreddy; (S) Frank Schneeberger; (C) Mary Waldhart and Anna Stevens; (L) Thomas C. Hase

Speed-the-Plow, David Mamet; (D) Joseph Hanreddy; (S) Frank Schneeberger; (C) Mary Waldhart; (L) Thomas C. Hase

All My Sons, Arthur Miller; (D) Joseph Hanreddy; (S) Frank Schneeberger; (C) Mary Waldhart; (L) Thomas C. Hase

Magic Theatre

HARVEY SEIFTER
General Director

Bldg. D, Fort Mason Center
San Francisco, CA 94123
(415) 441-8001 (bus.)
(415) 441-8822 (b.o.)

FOUNDED 1967
John Lion

SEASON
Jan.-Dec.

FACILITIES
Cowell Theatre
Seating Capacity: 399
Stage: proscenium

North Side
Seating Capacity: 165
Stage: thrust

South Side
Seating Capacity: 175
Stage: proscenium

FINANCES
Sept. 1, 1989-Aug. 31, 1990
Expenses: $1,200,000

CONTRACTS
AEA BAT

The Magic has always been a home for artistic innovation and risk-taking. The plays we produce are often characterized by poetic language, mythic imagery and nonlinear form. Three elements comprise the heart of the Magic's artistic agenda—a commitment to producing new plays that intellectually and aesthetically challenge and engage our audiences; an increased emphasis on the development of new plays through commissions, workshops, residencies and dramaturgical support; and a substantial focus on the evolution of a San Francisco-based, culturally and ethnically diverse artistic community of writers, directors, designers, composers and performers to collaborate on the in-house creation of new work.

—Harvey Seifter

Note: During the 1989-90 season, John Lion served as artistic director.

PRODUCTIONS 1989-90

The Film Society, Jon Robin Baitz; (D) Theodore Shank; (S) John

Wilson; (C) Kate Irvine; (L) Ellen Shireman

Spoils of War, Michael Weller; (D) John Lion; (S) Shevra Tait; (C) Fumiko Bielefeldt; (L) Kurt Landisman

Vegetal, Veronique Guillaud; (D) Veronique Guillaud; (S) Philippe Coutant; (L) Philippe Coutant

Once Removed, Eduardo Machado; (D) Jorge Cacheiro; (S) Ken Ellis; (C) Callie Floor; (L) Jeff Rowlings

Jacques & His Master, Milan Kundera; trans: Simon Callow; (D) Harvey Seifter; (S) John Wilson; (C) Fumiko Bielefeldt; (L) Kathy Pryzgoda

Vampire Dreams, Suzy McKee Charnas; (D) Michael Edwards; (S) Jeff Rowlings; (C) Callie Floor; (L) Maurice Vercoutere

The House of Yes, Wendy MacLeod; (D) Andrew Doe; (S) Jeff Rowlings; (C) Callie Floor; (L) Maurice Vercoutere

Dottie & the Boys, Lynne Kaufman; (D) Andrea Gordon; (S) Jeff Rowlings; (C) Callie Floor; (L) Maurice Vercoutere

Nebraska, Keith Reddin; (D) Kenn Watt; (S) Andy Stacklin; (C) Kate Irvine; (L) Dirk Epperson

Eastern Standard, Richard Greenberg; (D) Albert Takazauckas; (S) John Wilson; (C) Kate Irvine; (L) Kurt Landisman

Brave New Whirl, Paul Kwan and Arnold Iger; (D) Paul Kwan and Arnold Iger; (S) Paul Kwan and Arnold Iger; (C) Paul Kwan and Arnold Iger; (L) Jeff Rowlings

Space Between the Steps, Julie Regan; (D) Julie Regan

PRODUCTIONS 1990-91

Man of the Flesh, Octavio Solis; (D) Patrick Kelly; (S) Paul Porter; (C) Callie Floor; (L) Tom Kline

Mud, Maria Irene Fornes; (D) Mary Forcade; (S) John Mayne; (C) Laura Hazlett; (L) Jim Cave

Suspended Life, Veronique Guillaud; (D) Veronique Guillaud; (S) Jeff Hunt; (C) Veronique Guillaud; (L) Tony Avoid

East, Steven Berkoff; (D) Paul Hellyer; (S) Jeff Rowlings; (L) Jeff Rowlings

Temptation, Vaclav Havel; trans: Marie Winn; (D) Harvey Seifter; (S) John Wilson; (C) Fumiko Bielefeldt; (L) Tom Kline

The Red Address, David Ives; (D) Kenn Watt; (S) Jeff Rowlings; (C) Anne Tree Newson; (L) David Welle

Soiled Eyes of a Ghost, Erin Cressida Wilson; (D) Clay Snider; (S) Jeff Rowlings; (C) Laura Hazlett; (L) David Welle

The Last Frontier, David Barth; (D) R.A. White; (S) Jeff Rowlings; (C) Susan Doepner; (L) David Welle

The Swan, Elizabeth Egloff; (D) June Stein; (S) Jeff Rowlings; (C) Laura Hazlett; (L) Maurice Vercoutere

Mozart's Journey to Prague, James Keller; (D) Albert Takazauckas; (S) Barbara Mesney; (C) Sandra Woodall; (L) Kurt Landisman

Magic Theatre. John Robb, Wendy Vanden Heuvel and Greg Pace in *Mud*. Photo: Bob Hsiang.

Manhattan Theatre Club. Elain Graham, LaTanya Richardson and Marie Thomas in *The Talented Tenth*. Photo: Gerry Goodstein.

Manhattan Theatre Club

LYNNE MEADOW
Artistic Director

BARRY GROVE
Managing Director

453 West 16th St., 2nd Floor
New York, NY 10011
(212) 645-5590 (bus.)
(212) 581-7907 (b.o.)

FOUNDED 1970
Peregrine Whittlesey, A. Joseph Tandet, George Tabori, Gerard L. Spencer, Margaret Kennedy, A. E. Jeffcoat, Barbara Hirschl, William Gibson, Gene Frankel, Philip Barber

SEASON
Variable

FACILITIES
City Center Stage I
Seating Capacity: 299
Stage: proscenium

City Center Stage II
Seating Capacity: 150
Stage: flexible

FINANCES
July 1, 1989-June 30, 1990
Expenses: $4,365,965

CONTRACTS
AEA Off Broadway

Manhattan Theatre Club has a long tradition of developing and presenting important new works by American and international writers. We also produce earlier works we believe have not been fully interpreted or appreciated in the past, as well as New York premieres of plays that originated in American regional theatres. Many of the plays presented at MTC have gone on to be produced on Broadway, in London, in regional theatres nationwide and as major motion pictures. The flexibility of our two spaces enables us to offer greater visibility in a Stage I production, with production standards of the highest possible quality, as well as a more developmental environment in Stage II for new works by emerging and established playwrights, composers and lyricists. MTC's Writers in Performance series has, for nearly 22 years, presented an international array of writers of all genres whose works demonstrate the diversity and power of contemporary literature. Our subscription audience numbers close to 15,000. MTC is accessible to the broadest community through group discounts, free ticket distribution, sign-interpreted and audio-described performances, and an educational outreach program that combines in-class curriculum with exposure to live theatre for students at the intermediate and high school level.

—*Lynne Meadow*

PRODUCTIONS 1989-90

The Talented Tenth, Richard Wesley; (D) M. Neema Barnette;

(S) Charles McClennahan; (C) Alvin Perry; (L) Anne Militello
Wolf-Man, Elizabeth Egloff; (D) Thomas Allan Bullard; (S) James Youmans; (C) Jess Goldstein; (L) Phil Monat
The Art of Success, Nick Dear; (D) Adrian Noble; (S) Ultz; (C) Ultz; (L) Beverly Emmons
The American Plan, Richard Greenberg; (D) Evan Yionoulis; (S) James Youmans; (C) Jess Goldstein; (L) Donald Holder
Bad Habits, Terrence McNally; (D) Paul Benedict; (S) John Lee Beatty; (C) Jane Greenwood; (L) Peter Kaczorowski
The Piano Lesson, August Wilson; (D) Lloyd Richards; (S) E. David Cosier, Jr.; (C) Constanza Romero; (L) Christopher Akerlind
Mi Vida Loca, Eric Overmyer; (D) David Warren; (S) James Noone; (C) David C. Woolard; (L) Donald Holder
Prin, Andrew Davies; (D) John Tillinger; (S) John Lee Beatty; (C) Jane Greenwood; (L) Richard Nelson

PRODUCTIONS 1990-91

Abundance, Beth Henley; (D) Ron Lagomarsino; (S) Adrianne Lobel; (C) Robert Wojewodski; (L) Paulie Jenkins
The Wash, Philip Kan Gotanda; (D) Sharon Ott; (S) James Youmans; (C) Lydia Tanji; (L) Dan Kotlowitz
The American Plan, Richard Greenberg; (D) Evan Yionoulis; (S) James Youmans; (C) Jess Goldstein; (L) Donald Holder
Absent Friends, Alan Ayckbourn; (D) Lynne Meadow; (S) John Lee Beatty; (C) Jane Greenwood; (L) Ken Billington
Life During Wartime, Keith Reddin; (D) Les Waters; (S) James Noone; (C) David C. Woolard; (L) Michael R. Moody
Black Eagles, Leslie Lee; (D) Ricardo Khan; (S) Charles McClennahan; (C) Beth Ribblett; (L) Natasha Katz
The Stick Wife, Darrah Cloud; (D) David Warren; (S) James Youmans; (C) David C. Woolard; (L) Donald Holder
Lips Together, Teeth Apart, Terrence McNally; (D) John Tillinger; (S) John Lee Beatty; (C) Jane Greenwood; (L) Ken Billington

Marin Theatre Company

LEE SANKOWICH
Artistic Director

397 Miller Ave.
Mill Valley, CA 94941
(415) 388-5200 (bus.)
(415) 388-3200 (b.o.)

FOUNDED 1966
Sali Lieberman

SEASON
Sept.-May

FACILITIES
Mainstage
Seating Capacity: 250
Stage: proscenium

Sali Lieberman Studio Theatre
Seating Capacity: 99
Stage: flexible

FINANCES
July 1, 1990-June 30, 1991
Expenses: $840,953

CONTRACTS
AEA SPT

The Marin Theatre Company focuses its energies on using the theatre to its full potential as a unique medium with immediacy, affinity for illusion and distinctive ability to engage, stimulate, move, enlighten and entertain. We present American, English and world classics in fresh and creative ways to introduce important works lacking previous local exposure, and place strong emphasis on developing and premiering new works. We dedicate ourselves to supporting and compensating artists; to seeking, producing and casting plays that reflect a wide diversity of ethnic, social and cultural backgrounds; and to serving as a training ground for future actors, directors, designers, writers and technicians. Through the Marin Theatre Company School for Theatre Arts, our youth programs offer the opportunity for future artists and audiences to learn, perform and grow; and the school's home, the Sali Liberman Studio Theatre, will also be used to encourage the development of new talent and original works. The Marin Theatre Company seeks to be a creative, fertile environment with a national reputation for excellence.

—*Lee Sankowich*

Note: During the 1989-90 season, Will Marchetti served as artistic director.

PRODUCTIONS 1989-90

Modigliani, Dennis McIntyre; (D) Will Marchetti and Jeffrey Bihr; (S) Jeff Hunt; (C) Karin Simonson Kopischke; (L) Maurice Vercoutere
Loot, Joe Orton; (D) Simon Levy; (S) Andy Stacklin; (C) Laura Hazlett; (L) John Flanders
Glengarry Glen Ross, David Mamet; (D) Kenn Watt; (S) Andy Stacklin; (C) Karin Simonson Kopischke; (L) Tom Hansen
Becoming Memories, Arthur Giron; (D) Lee Sankowich; (S) Steve Coleman; (C) Karin Simonson Kopischke; (L) Kathy Pryzgoda
Room Service, John Murray and Allen Boretz; (D) James Dunn; (S) Ken Rowland; (C) Pat Polen; (L) Ellen Shireman

PRODUCTIONS 1990-91

Lemon Sky, Lanford Wilson; (D) Lee Sankowich; (S) Steve Coleman; (C) Karin Simonson Kopischke; (L) Novella Smith
Passion, Peter Nichols; (D) Kenn Watt; (S) Karl Rawicz; (C) Karin Simonson Kopischke; (L) Tom Hansen
Orphans, Lyle Kessler; (D) Robert Elross; (S) Will Combs; (C) Gail Russell; (L) Kurt Landisman
The Middle Ages, A.R. Gurney, Jr.; (D) Will Marchetti; (S) Jeff Hunt; (C) Karin Simonson Kopischke; (L) John Flanders
And a Nightingale Sang, C.P. Taylor; (D) Lee Sankowich; (S) Jeff Hunt; (C) Gail Russell; (L) Maurice Vercoutere

Marin Theatre Company. Leslie McCauley and Kenna Hunt in *The Middle Ages*. Photo: Joseph Greco.

Mark Taper Forum

GORDON DAVIDSON
Artistic Director/Producer

CHARLES DILLINGHAM
Managing Director

135 North Grand Ave.
Los Angeles, CA 90012
(213) 972-7353 (bus.)
(213) 972-7392 (b.o.)

FOUNDED 1967
Gordon Davidson

SEASON
Jan.-Dec.

FACILITIES
Mark Taper Forum
Seating Capacity: 752
Stage: thrust

Taper, Too
Seating Capacity: 99
Stage: flexible

Itchey Foot Cabaret
Seating Capacity: 99
Stage: flexible

FINANCES
July 1, 1990-June 30, 1991
Expenses: $9,931,000

CONTRACTS
AEA LORT (A) and (B)

Over the past 24 years the Mark Taper Forum has pursued a distinct and vigorous mission: to create, nurture and maintain a theatre that is socially and culturally aware; that continually examines and challenges the assumptions of our culture, community and society; and that expands the aesthetic boundaries of theatre as an art form. The Taper is committed to nurturing new voices and new forms for the American theatre; to enlightening, amazing, challenging and entertaining our audience by reflecting on our stages the rich multicultural heritage found in Los Angeles; and to encouraging tomorrow's audience through programming that addresses the concerns and challenges the imagination of young people. The future of the Mark Taper Forum lies in the pursuit of artistic excellence, aesthetic daring and community service. The challenge of these goals will continue to provide impetus to our broad-based programming as we move toward our second quarter-century.

—Gordon Davidson

PRODUCTIONS 1989-90

Our Country's Good, Timberlake Wertenbaker, from Thomas Keneally; (D) Max Stafford-Clark and Les Waters; (S) Peter Hartwell; (C) Peter Hartwell; (L) Kevin Rigdon

Mystery of the Rose Bouquet, Manuel Puig; adapt: Jeremy Lawrence; trans: Allan Baker; (D) Robert Allan Ackerman; (S) Kenny Miller; (C) Kenny Miller; (L) Arden Fingerhut

King Lear and ***A Midsummer Night's Dream***, William Shakespeare; (D) Kenneth Branagh; (S) Jenny Tiramani; (C) Jenny Tiramani; (L) Jon Linstrum

50/60 Vision, Edward Albee, Amiri Baraka, et al; (D) Michael Arabian, Peter C. Brosius, Daniel O'Connor, Carey Perloff and Ethan Silverman; (S) Yael Pardess; (C) Julie Weiss; (L) Paulie Jenkins

Aristocrats, Brian Friel; (D) Robert Egan; (S) Mark Wendland; (C) Dona Granata; (L) Kevin Rigdon

Miss Evers' Boys, David Feldshuh; (D) Irene Lewis; (S) Douglas Stein; (C) Catherine Zuber; (L) Pat Collins

PRODUCTIONS 1990-91

Hope of the Heart, adapt: Adrian Hall, from Robert Penn Warren; (D) Adrian Hall; (S) Eugene Lee; (C) Dona Granata; (L) Natasha Katz and Eugene Lee

The Lisbon Traviata, Terrence McNally; (D) John Tillinger; (S) Philipp Jung; (C) Jane Greenwood; (L) Ken Billington

The Wash, Philip Kan Gotanda; (D) Sharon Ott; (S) James Youmans; (C) Lydia Tanji; (L) Paulie Jenkins

Jelly's Last Jam, book: George C. Wolfe; music: Jelly Roll Morton; adapt and addtl composition: Luther Henderson; lyrics: Susan Birkenhead; (D) George C. Wolfe; (S) George Tsypin; (C) Toni-Leslie James; (L) James F. Ingalls

Julius Caesar, William Shakespeare; (D) Oskar Eustis; (S) Yael Pardess; (C) Jeffrey Struckman; (L) Tom Ruzika

Widows, adapt: Ariel Dorfman and Tony Kushner, from Ariel Dorfman; (D) Robert Egan; (S) Douglas Stein; (C) Dunya Ramicova; (L) Natasha Katz

Mark Taper Forum. Nance Williamson and Casey Biggs in *Hope of the Heart*. Photo: Jay Thompson.

McCarter Theatre Center for the Performing Arts

EMILY MANN
Artistic Director

JEFFREY WOODWARD
Managing Director

91 University Place
Princeton, NJ 08540
(609) 683-9100 (bus.)
(609) 683-8000 (b.o.)

FOUNDED 1972
Daniel Seltzer

SEASON
Oct.-June

FACILITIES
McCarter Theatre
Seating Capacity: 1,078
Stage: proscenium

FINANCES
July 1, 1990-June 30, 1991
Expenses: $5,031,213

CONTRACTS
AEA LORT (B+)

Each season, McCarter Theatre Center for the Performing Arts produces a four-play mainstage drama series augmented by a well-rounded program of scheduled events—music, dance and special programs—featuring artists of national and international repute. Our primary aspirations are: to foster major new works of the highest caliber that will enter the American repertoire; to present innovative interpretations of classic dramatic literature; to make possible unique collaborations among our foremost writers, actors, directors, designers and composers; and actively to sponsor work that is multiethnic and multicultural, work that brings all people together regardless of race, ethnicity, politics or creed. Integral to our mission is service to the community through broad-based outreach programming, a commitment to education, programs that support the elderly and people with disabilities, and a wide variety of ancillary activities including student matinees, postperformance discussions, an audio-description program, study guides, conferences and symposiums.

—Emily Mann

Note: During the 1989-90 season, Nagle Jackson served as artistic director.

PRODUCTIONS 1989-90

Smoke on the Mountain, Constance Ray; (D) Alan Bailey; (S) W. Joseph Stell; (C) Pamela Scofield; (L) Don Ehman

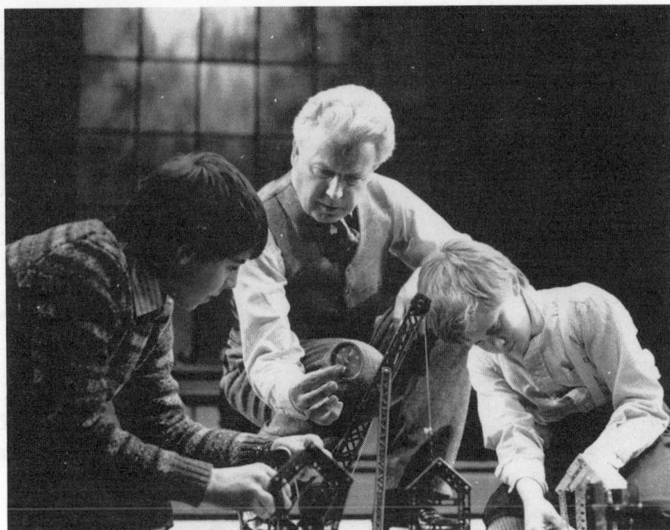

McCarter Theatre Center for the Performing Arts. Justin Tecce, Barry Boys and Davyd Stepper in *An Enemy of the People*. Photo: Randall Hagadorn.

The Importance of Being Earnest, Oscar Wilde; (D) Gavin Cameron-Webb; (S) Harry Fewer; (C) Gail Brassard; (L) F. Mitchell Dana

An Enemy of the People, Henrik Ibsen; trans: Rolf Fjelde; (D) Kjetl Bang-Hansen; (S) Stephan Olson; (C) Elizabeth Covey; (L) F. Mitchell Dana

A Tale of Two Cities, adapt: Nagle Jackson, from Charles Dickens; (D) Nagle Jackson; (S) Ralph Funicello; (C) Robert Fletcher; (L) Jane Reisman

Woman in Mind, Alan Ayckbourn; (D) Nagle Jackson; (S) Daniel Boylen; (C) Elizabeth Covey; (L) F. Mitchell Dana

PRODUCTIONS 1990-91

The Glass Menagerie, Tennessee Williams; (D) Emily Mann; (S) Ming Cho Lee; (C) Jennifer von Mayrhauser; (L) Robert Wierzel

Those the River Keeps, David Rabe; (D) David Rabe; (S) Loren Sherman; (C) Sharon Sprague; (L) Michael Lincoln

Betsey Brown, book adapt: Ntozake Shange and Emily Mann, from Ntozake Shange; music: Baikida Carroll; lyrics: Ntozake Shange, Emily Mann and Baikida Carroll; (D) Emily Mann; (S) David Mitchell; (C) Jennifer von Mayrhauser; (L) Pat Collins

The Film Society, Jon Robin Baitz; (D) Douglas Hughes; (S) Thomas Lynch; (C) Jess Goldstein; (L) Nancy Shertler

Meadow Brook Theatre

TERENCE KILBURN
Artistic Director

JAMES P. SPITTLE
Managing Director

Oakland University
Rochester, MI 48309-4401
(313) 370-3310 (bus.)
(313) 377-3300 (b.o.)

FOUNDED 1967
Oakland University, Woody Varner, Donald O'Dowd

SEASON
Oct.-May

FACILITIES
Seating Capacity: 608
Stage: proscenium

FINANCES
July 1, 1990-June 30, 1991
Expenses: $2,600,000

CONTRACTS
AEA LORT (B)

The 1990-91 season of Meadow Brook Theatre marked its 25th anniverary. At the time of its opening in 1966, no professional theatre existed in the area. Meadow Brook's primary artistic aim has been to provide its audience with the broadest possible spectrum of plays. Each season has consisted of eight plays chosen to represent the extraordinary variety and vitality that exists in the literature of the theatre. Almost 200 productions have been staged during 25 seasons. They have ranged from Shakespeare to Agatha Christie, Chekhov to Fugard, Kaufman and Hart to David Mamet, Wilder to Gurney, and have included many musicals such as *Guys and Dolls* and *Cabaret*. This variety is at the heart of Meadow Brook Theatre's continuing success as a meaningful artistic presence in Michigan.

—Terence Kilburn

PRODUCTIONS 1989-90

The Diary of a Scoundrel, Alexander Ostrovsky; adapt: Erik Brogger; (D) Terence Kilburn; (S) Peter W. Hicks; (C) Mary Lynn Bonnell; (L) Reid G. Johnson

The Boys Next Door, Tom Griffin; (D) John Ulmer; (S) Peter W. Hicks; (C) Mary Lynn Bonnell; (L) Reid G. Johnson

A Christmas Carol, adapt: Charles Nolte, from Charles Dickens; (D) Charles Nolte; (S) Peter W. Hicks; (C) Mary Lynn Bonnell; (L) Reid G. Johnson

Dial "M" for Murder, Frederick Knott; (D) Terence Kilburn; (S) Peter W. Hicks; (C) Mary Lynn Bonnell; (L) Reid G. Johnson

A Walk in the Woods, Lee Blessing; (D) Stephen Kanee; (S) C. Lance Brockman; (C) Mary Lynn Bonnell; (L) Jean A. Montgomery

The Great Sebastians, Howard Lindsay and Russel Crouse; (D) Terence Kilburn; (S) Peter W. Hicks; (C) Mary Lynn Bonnell; (L) Reid G. Johnson

The Immigrant, Mark Harelik; (D) Howard J. Millman; (S) Kevin Rupnik; (C) Peter W. Hicks and Barbara Jenks; (L) Reid G. Johnson

Dracula, adapt: Charles Nolte, from Bram Stoker; (D) Robert Spencer; (S) Peter W. Hicks; (C) Barbara Jenks; (L) Reid G. Johnson

PRODUCTIONS 1990-91

Cabaret, book: Joe Masteroff; music: John Kander; lyrics: Fred Ebb; (D) Carl Schurr; (S) Peter W. Hicks; (C) Peter W. Hicks; (L) Reid G. Johnson

The Mousetrap, Agatha Christie; (D) Terence Kilburn; (S) Peter W. Hicks; (C) Barbara Jenks; (L) Eric Stehl

A Christmas Carol, adapt: Charles Nolte, from Charles Dickens; (D) Charles Nolte; (S) Peter W. Hicks; (C) Barbara Jenks; (L) Reid G. Johnson

What I Did Last Summer, A.R. Gurney, Jr.; (D) Terence Kilburn; (S) Peter W. Hicks; (C) Barbara Jenks; (L) Reid G. Johnson

A Midsummer Night's Dream, William Shakespeare; (D) John Ulmer; (S) Peter W. Hicks; (C) Peter W. Hicks; (L) Reid G. Johnson

Barefoot in the Park, Neil Simon; (D) Terence Kilburn; (S) Peter W. Hicks; (C) Barbara Jenks; (L) George H. Sherlock

Sleuth, Anthony Shaffer; (D) Charles Nolte; (S) Peter W.

Meadow Brook Theatre. Alexander Webb and Arthur J. Beer in *Sleuth*.

Hicks; (C) Barbara Jenks; (L) Reid G. Johnson

Pump Boys and Dinettes, John Foley, Mark Hardwick, Debra Monk, Cass Morgan, John Schimmel and Jim Wann; (D) William S. Morris; (S) Peter W. Hicks; (C) Barbara Jenks; (L) Reid G. Johnson

Merrimack Repertory Theatre

DAVID G. KENT
Artistic Director

Box 228
Lowell, MA 01853
(508) 454-6324 (bus.)
(508) 454-3926 (b.o.)

FOUNDED 1979
Mark Kaufman, John Briggs

SEASON
Sept.-May

FACILITIES
Liberty Hall
Seating Capacity: 386
Stage: thrust

FINANCES
July 1, 1990-June 30, 1991
Expenses: $830,000

CONTRACTS
AEA LORT (D)

With new artistic leadership and the establishment of a resident company of actors and directors, MRT has expanded its artistic and stylistic reach. MRT's community of artists is committed to a stage language that is rich and exotic, to a stage poetry that is lyrical and musical, and to the plurality of views and attitudes found in our own multicultural region. MRT's artistic vision is rooted in a belief that the theatre is a mysterious and wonderful journey where there are no borders, only new frontiers. In pursuit of this vision MRT continues its evolution, serving the area with a new performance series, a new play series, and comprehensive educational, training and outreach programs. From freshly conceived approaches to Shakespeare and Chekhov to the diverse passions of O'Neill and Beckett, MRT recognizes that theatrical truth can help us experience meaning, and see ourselves and our desires in a creative, moral and original way.

—David G. Kent

Note: During the 1989-90 season, Daniel L. Schay served as producing director.

PRODUCTIONS 1989-90

The Anastasia Game, book: Guy Bolton and Jerome Chodorov; music and lyrics: George Forrest and Robert Wright; (D) Larry Carpenter; (S) John Falabella; (C) John Falabella; (L) Marcia Madeira

The Nerd, Larry Shue; (D) Michael Allosso; (S) Edwin Chapin; (C) Bradford Wood and Gregory Poplyk; (L) Dave Brown

A Christmas Carol, adapt: Larry Carpenter, from Charles Dickens; (D) Daniel L. Schay; (S) Alison Ford; (C) Kathleen Brown; (L) Dave Brown

Village Heroes, Jay O'Callahan; (D) Richard McElvain; (L) Dave Brown

Waiting for Godot, Samuel Beckett; (D) David G. Kent; (S) Gary English; (C) Gary English; (L) Dave Brown

The Mystery of Irma Vep, Charles Ludlam; (D) Paddy Swanson; (S) Leslie Taylor; (C) Craig Sonnenberg; (L) Dave Brown

The Immigrant, Mark Harelik; (D) Daniel L. Schay; (S) David Stern; (C) Craig Sonnenberg; (L) Dave Brown

PRODUCTIONS 1990-91

Ring Round the Moon, Jean Anouilh; trans: Christopher Fry; (D) Richard Rose; (S) Gary English; (C) Amanda Aldridge; (L) Kendall Smith

The Glass Menagerie, Tennessee Williams; (D) David G. Kent; (S) Alison Ford; (C) Gary English; (L) Sid Bennett

A Christmas Carol, adapt: Larry Carpenter, from Charles Dickens; (D) Richard McElvain; (S) Charles Morgan; (C) Kevin Pothier; (L) Dave Brown

Filumena, Eduardo De Filippo; trans: Keith Waterhouse and Willis Hall; (D) Steve McConnell; (S) Lewis Crickard; (C) Amanda Aldridge; (L) Jim Franklin

Lovers, Brian Friel; (D) Nora Hussey; (S) Jan Chambers; (C) Kevin Pothier; (L) Dave Brown

Merrimack Repertory Theatre. Sandra Shipley, Mary Klug, Frank Biancamano and Jay Alan Ginsberg in *Filumena*. Photo: Kevin Harkins.

An Enemy of the People, Henrik Ibsen; adapt: Arthur Miller; (D) David G. Kent; (S) Gary English; (C) Amanda Aldridge; (L) Mimi Jordan Sherin

Table Manners, Alan Ayckbourn; (D) Robert Walsh; (S) Charles Morgan; (C) Kevin Pothier; (L) Dave Brown

Mill Mountain Theatre

JERE LEE HODGIN
Executive/Artistic Director

Center in the Square
One Market Sq.
Roanoke, VA 24011
(703) 342-5730 (bus.)
(703) 342-5740 (b.o.)

FOUNDED 1964
Don Carter, Marta Byer

SEASON
Jan.-Dec.

FACILITIES
Mainstage
Seating Capacity: 411
Stage: proscenium

Theatre B
Seating Capacity: 125
Stage: flexible

FINANCES
Oct. 1, 1989-Sept. 30, 1990
Expenses: $1,007,435

CONTRACTS
AEA Guest Artist

I would venture to say that every regional theatre based in a nonmetropolitan area continually seeks to attain a balance between commercially viable, entertaining seasons and ones which provoke and engage both their audiences and creative artists. Mill Mountain Theatre is no exception. However, we see the development of both sides of our seemingly split personality as providing us with a unique freedom of expression. Our highly diverse program enables us to explore and take risks that a more narrowly defined personality would prohibit. Our educational outreach and enrichment programs, our Festival of New Works and our selection of material for both main and alternate stages all lead us to diversity. This diversity, which is demanded of us because of the region we serve, coincidentally encourages breadth of play selection, development of outreach programs that enliven and enrich, collaborations with other area arts organizations which challenge audiences, and the cultivation and creation of new works. The development of a strong artistic vision and mission in recent years has galvanized our program and promoted a healthy integrated personality.

—Jere Lee Hodgin

PRODUCTIONS 1989-90

The All Night Strut, Fran Charnas; various composers and lyricists; (D) Ernest Zulia; (S) John Sailer; (C) Jeff Fender; (L) John Sailer

My Fair Lady, book adapt and lyrics: Alan Jay Lerner, from George Bernard Shaw; music: Frederick Loewe; (D) Jere Lee Hodgin; (S) Robert Croghan;

(C) Robert Croghan; (L) John Sailer

The Dropper, Ron McLarty; (D) Ernest Zulia; (S) John Sailer; (C) Johann Stegmeir; (L) John Sailer

Zeke's Vision, Hank Bates; (D) Mary Best-Bova; (S) John Sailer; (C) Johann Stegmeir; (L) John Sailer

The Bug, Richard Strand; (D) Jere Lee Hodgin; (S) John Sailer; (C) Johann Stegmeir; (L) John Sailer

The Glass Menagerie, Tennessee Williams; (D) Mary Best-Bova; (S) John Sailer; (C) Jeff Fender; (L) John Sailer

The Road to Mecca, Athol Fugard; (D) Mary Best-Bova; (S) John Sailer; (C) Mimi Hodgin; (L) John Sailer

A Walk in the Woods, Lee Blessing; (D) Jere Lee Hodgin; (S) John Sailer; (C) Mimi Hodgin; (L) John Sailer

1776, book: Peter Stone; music and lyrics: Sherman Edwards; (D) Ernest Zulia; (S) John Sailer; (C) Richard E. Donnelly; (L) John Sailer

Magic to Do, book: Frank Bartolucci and Ernest Zulia; music and lyrics: Stephen Schwartz; (D) Ernest Zulia; (S) John Sailer; (C) Richard E. Donnelly; (L) John Sailer

You Can't Take It With You, George S. Kaufman and Moss Hart; (D) Jere Lee Hodgin; (S) John Sailer; (C) Richard E. Donnelly; (L) John Sailer

PRODUCTIONS 1990-91

Evita, music: Andrew Lloyd Webber; lyrics: Tim Rice; (D) Ernest Zulia; (S) John Sailer; (C) Jeff Fender; (L) John Sailer

A Christmas Carol, adapt: Jere Lee Hodgin, from Charles Dickens; (D) Jere Lee Hodgin; (S) John Sailer; (C) Kim Instenes; (L) John Sailer

Rooms of the King, Ron McLarty; (D) Ernest Zulia; (S) John Sailer; (C) Richie Smith; (L) John Sailer

I Don't Want to Die in China, Barbara Carlisle; (D) Mary Sutton; (S) John Sailer; (C) Richie Smith; (L) John Sailer

Miracle at Graceland, Dorothy Velasco; (D) Ernest Zulia; (S) John Sailer; (C) Richie Smith; (L) John Sailer

A Midsummer Night's Dream, William Shakespeare; (D) Jere Lee Hodgin; (S) Robert Croghan; (C) Robert Croghan; (L) John Sailer

The Boys Next Door, Tom Griffin; (D) Mary Best-Bova; (S) John Sailer; (C) Johann Stegmeir; (L) John Sailer

T Bone N Weasel, Jon Klein; (D) Ernest Zulia; (S) John Sailer; (C) Richie Smith; (L) John Sailer

Me and My Girl, book and lyrics: L. Arthur Rose and Douglas Fauber; music: Noel Gay; (D) Ernest Zulia; (S) John Sailer; (L) John Sailer

Tomfoolery, conceived: Cameron Mackintosh and Robin Ray; music and lyrics: Tom Lehrer; (D) Jere Lee Hodgin; (S) John Sailer; (L) John Sailer

Mill Mountain Theatre. Caroline Jones, Mark Lazore, Juan Fernandez and Melody Garrett in *The All Night Strut*.

Milwaukee Public Theatre. *The Cream City Semi-Circus!*. Photo: Francis Ford.

Milwaukee Public Theatre

Formerly FMT

MIKE MOYNIHAN
Artistic/Producing Director

BARBARA LEIGH
Co-Founder/Director

Box 07147
Milwaukee, WI 53207-0147
(414) 271-8484

FOUNDED 1973
Mike Moynihan, Barbara Leigh

SEASON
Variable

FINANCES
Jan. 1, 1990-Dec. 31, 1990
Expenses: $98,850

The primary environment we live in is made up of stories. Human beings are not able to gain understanding from direct experiences, so we have turned to stories as the main way of exploring our most basic questions: "Who are we? Where do we come from? How does the world work? What must we aspire to?" Our culture's mass storytelling structures—print, film, video—have largely been transformed into a marketing industry. To realize theatre's potential as a storytelling form that still reaches people in communal gathering places, Milwaukee Public Theatre focuses on three key elements: Access—to create theatre that is economically, intellectually and geographically accessible to everyone in the community interested in experiencing it; Diversity—to ensure that the wide variety of ethnic, racial, economic and minority sectors of our community have access to the creation of theatre; Imagination—to develop, focus and employ this most abundant but neglected resource to identify, address and solve our many societal problems. This is the purpose of Milwaukee Public Theatre.

—Mike Moynihan

PRODUCTIONS 1989-90

Seven Monsters, company-developed

Miss Margarida's Way, Roberto Athayde; (D) Mike Moynihan; (S) Mike Moynihan; (C) Rick Ney and Melinda Boyd; (L) Mike Moynihan

The Snow Queen, adapt from Hans Christian Andersen; (D) Mike Moynihan; (S) Mike Moynihan; (C) Melinda Boyd; (L) Mike Moynihan

The Survival Revival Revue!, conceived: Barbara Leigh; company-developed

The Big Little Show!, Melinda Boyd and Mike Moynihan; (D) Melinda Boyd and Mike Moynihan

The Cream City Semi-Circus!,

Mike Moynihan; (D) Rick Ney, Ron Anderson and Melinda Boyd; (S) Mike Moynihan; (L) Mike Moynihan

PRODUCTIONS 1990-91

The Snow Queen, adapt from Hans Christian Andersen; (D) Mike Moynihan; (S) Mike Moynihan; (C) Melinda Boyd; (L) Mike Moynihan

O Solo Mio Festival, festival of solo performance, various authors, directors

The EcoCircuZ!, Mike Moynihan; (D) Ron Anderson; (S) Mike Moynihan; (C) Melinda Boyd; (L) Mike Moynihan

Accidental Death of an Anarchist, Dario Fo; adapt: Richard Nelson; (D) Rick Ney; (S) Christian Pierce; (L) Christian Pierce

The Survival Revival Revue!, conceived: Barbara Leigh; company-developed

The Big Little Show!, Melinda Boyd and Mike Moynihan; (D) Melinda Boyd and Mike Moynihan

Milwaukee Repertory Theater

JOHN DILLON
Artistic Director

SARA O'CONNOR
Managing Director

108 East Wells St.
Milwaukee, WI 53202
(414) 224-1761 (bus.)
(414) 224-9490 (b.o.)

FOUNDED 1954
Mary John

SEASON
Sept.-May

FACILITIES
Powerhouse Theater
Seating Capacity: 720
Stage: thrust

Stiemke Theater
Seating Capacity: 198
Stage: flexible

Stackner Cabaret
Seating Capacity: 116
Stage: proscenium

Pabst Theater
Seating Capacity: 1,393
Stage: proscenium

FINANCES
July 1, 1990-June 30, 1991
Expenses: $3,825,000

CONTRACTS
AEA LORT (A), (C) and (D)

Virtually from its inception, the resident acting company has been at the core of Milwaukee Repertory Theater's identity. Over the years we've enlarged this multiracial troupe to include resident writers, directors, composers and dramaturgs. To challenge the company, we maintain an active program of exchange with theatres in Japan, Mexico, Ireland, Chile and Russia. And to deepen the bonds between the company and the community, we've commissioned works that explore the social and spiritual past and present of our region. Our acting interns work with company members in the Lab, our in-house research-and-development wing that seeks to develop new works and explore unusual acting styles, while innovative artists like Maria Irene Fornes, Tadashi Suzuki, Ping Chong and Daniel Stein help us try to keep our artistry on the cutting edge.

—John Dillon

PRODUCTIONS 1989-90

A Walk in the Woods, Lee Blessing; (D) John Dillon; (S) Steve Rubin; (C) Sam Fleming; (L) William H. Grant, III

Gone Hunting!, Georges Feydeau; trans: Sara O'Connor; (D) Kenneth Albers; (S) Victor Becker; (C) Charles Berliner; (L) Robert Jared

Fences, August Wilson; (D) Claude Purdy; (S) Vicki Smith; (C) Constanza Romero; (L) Don Darnutzer

McCarthy, Jeff Goldsmith; (D) Frank Condon; (S) Michael Devine; (C) Sam Fleming; (L) Doc Ballard

You Can't Take It With You, George S. Kaufman and Moss Hart; (D) John Dillon; (S) Joseph Varga; (C) Sam Fleming; (L) Robert Peterson

The Jeremiah, Diane Ney; (D) Mary B. Robinson; (S) Laura Maurer; (C) Michael Krass; (L) Ann G. Wrightson

The Mystery of Irma Vep, Charles Ludlam; (D) Howard Dallin; (S) John Story; (C) Sam Fleming; (L) Robert Zenoni

According to Coyote, John Kauffman; (D) John Kauffman; (S) Don Yanik; (C) coord: Dawna Gregory; (L) Chester Loeffler Bell

4 AM America, Ping Chong and company; (D) Ping Chong; (S) Ping Chong and Pat Doty; (C) Dawna Gregory; (L) Thomas C. Hase

The White Crow: Eichmann in Jerusalem, Donald Freed; (D) Kenneth Albers; (S) Kenneth Kloth; (C) Cecelia Mason; (L) Kenneth Kloth

A Christmas Carol, adapt: Amlin Gray, from Charles Dickens; music: John Tanner; (D) Kenneth Albers; (S) Stuart Wurtzel; (C) Carol Oditz; (L) Dan Kotlowitz

A Gershwin Serenade, devised: Larry Deckel; (D) Larry Deckel; (S) John Story; (C) coord: Dawna Gregory; (L) Chester Loeffler-Bell

Jukejointjammin', Robert Meiksins and Barbara Roberts; (D) Robert Meiksins; (S) John Story; (C) coord: Dawna Gregory; (L) Chester Loeffler-Bell

A Little Tomfoolery, conceived: Cameron Mackintosh and Robin Ray; music and lyrics: Tom Lehrer; (D) Larry Deckel; (S) John Story; (C) Dawna Gregory; (L) Chester Loeffler-Bell

At the Drop of Another Hat, Michael Flanders and Donald Swann; (D) Montgomery Davis; (S) John Story; (C) Dawna Gregory; (L) Chester Loeffler-Bell

Flywheel, Shyster, and Flywheel, adapt: Larry Deckel, from The Marx Brothers; (D) Larry Deckel; (S) John Story; (C) Dawna Gregory; (L) Chester Loeffler-Bell

PRODUCTIONS 1990-91

The Rivals, Richard Brinsley Sheridan; (D) Kenneth Albers; (S) Vicki Smith; (C) Sam Fleming; (L) William H. Grant, III

The Early Girl, Caroline Kava; (D) Libby Appel; (S) Michael C. Smith; (C) Constanza Romero; (L) Robert Peterson

4 AM America, conceived: Ping Chong; (D) Ping Chong; (S) Ping Chong and Pat Doty; (C) Dawna Gregory; (L) Thomas C. Hase

Inherit the Wind, Jerome Lawrence and Robert E. Lee; (D) Jeff Steitzer; (S) Scott Weldin; (C) Sam Fleming; (L) Peter Maradudin

Driving Miss Daisy, Alfred Uhry; (D) Kenny Leon; (S) Michael Olich; (C) Sam Fleming; (L) Ann G. Wrightson

Homebound, Tom Williams; (D) Kenneth Albers; (S) Constanza Romero; (C) Judy Dearing; (L) Dan Kotlowitz

Mud, Maria Irene Fornes; (D) Maria Irene Fornes; (S) John Story; (C) Cecelia Mason; (L) Kenneth Kloth

Going Forward Backward, conceived: Daniel Stein; (D) Daniel Stein; (S) John Story;

Milwaukee Repertory Theater. Linda Stephens and Adolphus Ward in *Driving Miss Daisy*. Photo: Mark Avery.

(C) Paule Stein; (L) Chester Loeffler-Bell

Windowspeak, Daniel Stein; (D) Daniel Stein, Fred Curchack and Christopher Gibson; (S) Paule Stein; (L) Eric Hager

Educating Rita, Willy Russell; (D) Joseph Hanreddy; (S) Kenneth Kloth; (C) Ellen M. Kozak; (L) Linda Essig

A Christmas Carol, adapt: Amlin Gray, from Charles Dickens; (D) Kenneth Albers; (S) Stuart Wurtzel; (C) Carol Oditz; (L) Robert Jared

Hoagy: The Life and Music of Hoagy Carmichael, Bruce Dettman and William C. Trichon; (D) Larry Deckel; (S) John Story; (C) Dawna Gregory; (L) Chester Loeffler-Bell

It's Bawdy, It's Brassy, It's Berserque...It's Burlesque, adapt: Kenneth Albers; (D) Kenneth Albers; (S) John Story; (C) Dawna Gregory; (L) Chester Loeffler-Bell

Tid-Bits, Louis Johnson; (D) Louis Johnson; (S) John Story; (C) coord: Dawna Gregory; (L) Chester Loeffler-Bell

A Little Tomfoolery, conceived: Cameron Mackintosh and Robin Ray; music and lyrics: Tom Lehrer; (D) Larry Deckel; (S) John Story; (C) Dawna Gregory; (L) Chester Loeffler-Bell

Hula Hoop Sha-Boop, John Leicht and Larry Deckel; music and lyrics: Larry Deckel and John Tanner; (D) Larry Deckel; (S) John Story; (C) Dawna Gregory; (L) Chester Loeffler-BellMissouri Repertory Theatre

Missouri Repertory Theatre

GEORGE KEATHLEY
Artistic Director

JAMES D. COSTIN
Executive Director

4949 Cherry St.
Kansas City, MO 64110
(816) 235-2727 (bus.)
(816) 235-2700 (b.o.)

FOUNDED 1964
Patricia McIlrath, James D. Costin

SEASON
Sept.-May

FACILITIES
Helen F. Spencer Theater
Seating Capacity: 730
Stage: flexible

Unicorn Theater
Seating Capacity: 170
Stage: thrust

FINANCES
July 1, 1990-June 30, 1991
Expenses: $3,703,907

CONTRACTS
AEA LORT (B)

Theatre has always been a medium through which we can see ourselves and therefore a medium through which we can influence behavior and alter perceptions. This influence is, I hope, in the upward direction of taste, of morality, of ideas. Since theatre both instructs and entertains, the material and style of production must be carefully chosen. The Missouri Repertory Theatre expends a great deal of energy in both these areas. New plays continue to be a high priority for us. To that end, we have a new Second Stage program offering six readings and two productions each season.

—George Keathley

PRODUCTIONS 1989-90

Jekyll!, James D. Costin, from Robert Louis Stevenson; (D) George Keathley; (S) John Ezell; (C) Vincent Scassellati; (L) Joseph Appelt

Absent Friends, Alan Ayckbourn; (D) Dennis Rosa; (S) James Leonard Joy; (C) Baker S. Smith; (L) Jackie Manassee

Woody Guthrie's American Song, conceived and adapt: Peter Glazer, from Woody Guthrie; (D) Peter Glazer; (S) Philipp Jung; (C) Baker S. Smith; (L) David Noling

A Christmas Carol, adapt: Barbara Field, from Charles Dickens; (D) Ross Freese; (S) John Ezell; (C) Baker S. Smith; (L) Joseph Appelt

Born Yesterday, Garson Kanin; (D) George Keathley; (S) James Leonard Joy; (C) Virgil Johnson; (L) Jeff Davis

Of Mice and Men, John Steinbeck; (D) George Keathley; (S) Harry Feiner; (C) Vincent Scassellati; (L) Jackie Manassee

Amadeus, Peter Schaffer; (D) Dennis Rosa; (S) John Ezell; (C) Vincent Scassellati; (L) Jackie Manassee

Missouri Repertory Theatre. Mark Robinson and K.T. Sullivan in *Born Yesterday*.

PRODUCTIONS 1990-91

Our Town, Thornton Wilder; (D) George Keathley; (S) John Ezell; (C) Vincent Scassellati; (L) Peggy Eisenhauer

A Moon for the Misbegotten, Eugene O'Neill; (D) William Woodman; (S) Joseph Nieminski; (C) Baker S. Smith; (L) Robert Christen

A Christmas Carol, adapt: Barbara Field, from Charles Dickens; (D) Ross Freese; (S) John Ezell; (C) Baker S. Smith; (L) Joseph Appelt

Billy Bishop Goes to War, John Gray and Eric Peterson; (D) Dennis Rosa; (S) E. David Cosier, Jr.; (C) Vincent Scassellati; (L) Jeff Davis

Fences, August Wilson; (D) Claude Purdy; (S) James Sandefur; (C) Martha Hally; (L) Phil Monat

Richard III, William Shakespeare; (D) George Keathley; (S) John Ezell; (C) Virgil Johnson; (L) Jackie Manassee

The Boys Next Door, Tom Griffin; (D) Mary G. Guaraldi; (S) Allen D. Cornell; (C) Michele Siler; (L) Rob Murphy

Mixed Blood Theatre Company

JACK REULER
Artistic Director

1501 South Fourth St.
Minneapolis, MN 55454
(612) 338-0937 (bus.)
(612) 338-6131 (b.o.)

FOUNDED 1976
Jack Reuler

SEASON
Sept.-June

FACILITIES
Mixed Blood Theatre
Seating Capacity: 200
Stage: flexible

McKnight Theatre (Ordway)
Seating Capacity: 315
Stage: proscenium

FINANCES
July 1, 1990-June 30, 1991
Expenses: $702,000

CONTRACTS
AEA Twin Cities Area

It is my contention that Mixed Blood Theatre Company

foreshadows the American regional theatre of the future: a well-paid, well-trained, multicultural staff of artists and administrators presenting flexible seasons that integrate original works with the tried-and-true rotating rep, with no subscription yet with accessible admission rates. I would like our new-play programming to remain strong, multifaceted and *production-oriented*. I am very proud that we are able to pay our actors salaries commensurate with their worth; that our touring programs promote cultural pluralism through more than 300 performances each year in 15 states; and that our training program is unique in America. Above all, our artistic quality and production values are at a zenith. For me theatre is a vehicle for artistry, entertainment, education and world change. Multiculturalism is more than a theory or a form of affirmative action: It is a way of life. I am confident that if we persevere, color-blind casting—currently misnamed "nontraditional" casting—will be tomorrow's tradition.

—*Jack Reuler*

PRODUCTIONS 1989-90

Only Kidding, Jim Geoghan; (D) Steve Pearson; (S) Robert Fuecker; (C) Anne Ruben; (L) Scott Peters
Speed-the-Plow, David Mamet; (D) Mike Kissin; (S) Robert Fuecker; (C) Anne Ruben; (L) Scott Peters
I Don't Have to Show You No Stinking Badges, Luis Valdez; (D) Jack Reuler; (S) Robert Fuecker; (C) Chris Cook; (L) Scott Peters
Wall of Water, Sherry Kramer; (D) Sharon Walton; (S) Robert Fuecker; (C) Chris Cook; (L) Scott Peters
According to Coyote, John Kauffman; (D) John Kauffman; (S) Don Yanik
Ali!, Graydon Royce and Geoffrey Ewing; (D) Dawn Renee Jones and Jack Reuler; (S) Robert Fuecker; (C) Anne Ruben; (L) Scott Peters

PRODUCTIONS 1990-91

Other People's Money, Jerry Sterner; (D) Mike Kissin; (S) Robert Fuecker; (C) Chris Cook; (L) Scott Peters
A...My Name Is Alice, Joan Micklin Silver and Julianne Boyd; various composers and lyricists; (D) Sharon Walton; (S) Robert Fuecker; (C) Anne Ruben; (L) Scott Peters
Throwing Bones, Michael Erickson; (D) Kent Stephens; (S) Robert Fuecker; (C) Chris Cook; (L) Barry Browning
La Nonna, Roberto M. Cossa; trans: Raul Moncada; (D) John Clark Donahue; (S) Robert Fuecker; (C) Chris Cook; (L) Scott Peters

Mixed Blood Theatre Company. Joe Minjares, Shawn Judge and Brent Hendon in *Throwing Bones*. Photo: Mike Paul.

Music-Theatre Group

LYN AUSTIN
Producing Director

DIANE WONDISFORD
Managing Director

29 Bethune St.
New York, NY 10014
(212) 924-3108

Music-Theatre Group. *Juan Darien*. Left photo: Richard M. Feldman. Right photo: Donna Gray.

FOUNDED 1971
Lyn Austin

SEASON
Variable

FINANCES
July 1, 1990-June 30, 1991
Expenses: $2,161,117

CONTRACTS
AEA LORT (B) and Off Broadway

Music-Theatre Group is a leading pioneer in the development of new works in which theatre, music, dance and the visual arts are combined to create new forms. Music-Theatre Group's work is deliberately eclectic and has been variously termed theatre with music, dance-theatre, opera and musical theatre. Most of the work is developed from an idea rather than a completed score or script. MTG brings together a carefully selected combination of director, composer, writer/lyricist and choreographer and places these artists in a supportive, collaborative environment. Long-term developmental periods and careful nurturing of the artists are key elements in the organization's artistic approach. We seek to create an atmosphere in which artists can set new sights and take risks, while receiving supporting insight and meaningful critical feedback. The work is fully produced in New York and often tours nationally and internationally.

—*Lyn Austin*

PRODUCTIONS 1989-90

Paradise for the Worried, book and lyrics: Holly Anderson; music: Stanley Silverman; (D) Diane Wondisford; (S) Victoria Petrovich; (C) Donna Zakowska; (L) Stan Pressner and Debra Dumas
Legacy, adapt: Paul Walker, from Breece D.J. Pancake; music: Jill Jaffe; (D) Paul Walker; (S) Carl Sprague; (C) Carl Sprague; (L) Debra Dumas
The Garden of Earthly Delights, conceived: Martha Clarke; music: Richard Peaslee; (D) Martha Clarke; (C) Jane Greenwood; (L) Paul Gallo
Juan Darien, adapt: Julie Taymor and Elliot Goldenthal, from Horacio Quiroga; music and lyrics: Elliot Goldenthal; (D) Julie Taymor; (S) G.W. Mercier and Julie Taymor; (C) G.W. Mercier and Julie Taymor; (L) Debra Dumas

PRODUCTIONS 1990-91

Juan Darien, adapt: Julie Taymor and Elliot Goldenthal, from Horacio Quiroga; music and lyrics: Elliot Goldenthal; (D) Julie Taymor; (S) G.W. Mercier and Julie Taymor; (C) G.W. Mercier and Julie Taymor; (L) Debra Dumas
Endangered Species, conceived: Martha Clarke; adapt: Robert Coe, from Walt Whitman; music: Richard Peaslee and Stanley Walden; (D) Martha Clarke; (S) Robert Israel; (C) Robert Israel; (L) Paul Gallo
Love & Science, libretto by: Richard Foreman; music: Stanley Silverman; (D) Richard Foreman; (S) Richard Foreman and Nancy Winters; (C) Donna Zakowska; (L) Heather Carson

National Jewish Theater. Barbara Faye Wallace and Chris Karchmar in *I Am a Camera*. Photo: Lisa Ebright.

National Jewish Theater

ARNOLD APRILL
Artistic Director

FRAN BRUMLIK
Managing Director

5050 West Church St.
Skokie, IL 60077
(708) 675-2200 (bus.)
(708) 675-5070 (b.o.)

FOUNDED 1986
Jewish Community Centers of Chicago

SEASON
Oct.-July

FACILITIES
Zollie and Elaine Frank Theater
Seating Capacity: 250
Stage: flexible

FINANCES
July 1, 1990-June 30, 1991
Expenses: $450,000

CONTRACTS
AEA CAT

National Jewish Theater's audiences are committed to seeing plays and musicals, performed in English, which deal with Jewish experience, placing a special emphasis on American Jewish experience. Our audiences are active and vocal, making their preferences clear by letter, phone and vociferous participation in our twice-a-week, well-attended, postshow discussions. Above all, they want variety in the season, which typically includes a serious "issue-oriented" drama, a Jewish classic (such as *The Dybbuk* or *The Golem*), a musical and a comedy. NJT has commissioned several adaptations and new scripts. The theatre consciously strives to present as full a range of theatrical forms and styles as possible, using the best professionals available in the Chicago theatre community. A network of fine theatre artists, including designers, playwrights, directors and actors, has gravitated to the theatre, creating the sense of an extended ensemble that contributes to the quality of our work.

—*Arnold Aprill*

Note: During the 1989-90 and 1990-91 seasons, Sheldon Patinkin served as artistic director.

PRODUCTIONS 1989-90

I Am a Camera, adapt: John Van Druten, from Christopher Isherwood; (D) Arnold Aprill; (S) Gary Baugh; (C) Jessica Hahn; (L) Mary Badger

Listen to My Song, Sheldon Patinkin; music: Kurt Weill; various lyricists; (D) Estelle Goodman and Sheldon Patinkin; (S) John Murbach; (C) Jessica Hahn; (L) Michael Rourke

First Is Supper, Shelley Berman; (D) Terry McCabe; (S) John Murbach; (C) Jessica Hahn; (L) Robert Shook

Cantorial, Ira Levin; (D) Jeff Ginsberg; (S) Jacqueline Penrod and Richard Penrod; (C) Jessica Hahn; (L) Robert Shook

PRODUCTIONS 1990-91

Bitter Friends, Gordon Rayfield; (D) Terry McCabe; (S) Jeff Bauer; (C) Kerry Fleming; (L) Robert Shook

Solomons' Choice, Marilynn Preston and Cheryl Lavin; (D) Michael Leavitt; (S) Mary Griswold; (C) John Paoletti; (L) Mary Badger

The Golem, Tom Mula; (D) Arnold Aprill; (S) Michael Merritt; (C) Frances Maggio; (L) Chris Phillips

The Sunshine Boys, Neil Simon; (D) Tom Gianal; (S) Jacqueline Penrod and Richard Penrod; (C) Jessica Hahn; (L) Robert Shook

Nebraska Theatre Caravan

CHARLES JONES
Founding Director

CAROLYN RUTHERFORD
Managing Director

6915 Cass St.
Omaha, NE 68132
(402) 553-4890 (bus.)
(402) 553-0800 (b.o.)

FOUNDED 1976
Charles Jones, Omaha Community Playhouse

SEASON
Sept.-May

FACILITIES
Omaha Community Playhouse
Seating Capacity: 600
Stage: proscenium

Fonda-McGuire Theatre
Seating Capacity: 250
Stage: flexible

FINANCES
July 1, 1990-June 30, 1991
Expenses: $870,910

CONTRACTS
AEA Guest Artist

The Nebraska Theatre Caravan is the professional touring wing of the Omaha Community Playhouse, the largest community theatre in the nation and the only community theatre to sponsor a national professional touring company. The original mission of the Caravan is to provide high-quality entertainment and educational opportunities to communities where distance, financial limitations or lack of appropriate resources have hindered or prevented such activities. However, we are finding that the company is now providing performances and workshops to cities of all sizes across the U.S. and Canada, as well as in our home state. The 15-member resident company now works together eight months each year. Our dream is to have year-round employment for the professional company that not only performs in our home theatre's Fonda-McGuire Series, but also tours nationally and internationally.

—*Charles Jones*

PRODUCTIONS 1989-90

Quilters, book adapt: Molly Newman and Barbara Damashek, from Patricia Cooper and Norma Bradley Allen; music and lyrics: Barbara Damashek; (D) Carolyn Rutherford; (S) Greg Scheer; (C) John Gergel; (L) Greg Scheer

Shakespeare, Shaw, Sandoz and Friends, Chris Kliesen, Frederick J. Rubeck and Matthew Kamprath; (D) Susan Baer Beck; (S) Greg Scheer; (C) John Gergel; (L) Greg Scheer

Conestoga Stories, book and lyrics: Susan Baer Beck; music: Jonathan D. Cole; (D) Susan Baer Beck; (S) Greg Scheer; (C) John Gergel; (L) Greg Scheer

The Pied Piper, book adapt and lyrics: Adrian Mitchell, from Robert Browning; music: Dominic Muldowney; (D) Richard L. Scott; (S) James

Nebraska Theatre Caravan. *Alice, a Curious Adventure*. Photo: Stuart Allen Scott.

Othuse; (C) Denise Ervin; (L) James Othuse

A Christmas Carol, adapt: Charles Jones, from Charles Dickens; (D) Carl Beck; (S) James Othuse; (C) Kathryn Wilson and Tom Crisp; (L) James Othuse

PRODUCTIONS 1990-91

110 in the Shade, book adapt: N. Richard Nash, from N. Richard Nash; music and lyrics: Tom Jones and Harvey Schmidt; (D) Charles Jones; (S) Steve Wheeldon; (C) Amy Schmidt; (L) Steve Wheeldon

Twelfth Night, William Shakespeare; (D) Susan Baer Beck; (S) Steve Wheeldon; (C) Amy Schmidt; (L) Steve Wheeldon

Alice, a Curious Adventure, book adapt: Susan Baer Beck, from Lewis Carroll; music: Jonathan D. Cole; lyrics: Susan Baer Beck and Jonathan D. Cole; (D) Susan Baer Beck; (S) Steve Wheeldon; (C) Denise Ervin; (L) Steve Wheeldon

A Christmas Carol, adapt: Charles Jones, from Charles Dickens; (D) Carl Beck; (S) James Othuse; (C) Kathryn Wilson and Tom Crisp; (L) James Othuse

New American Theater

J. R. SULLIVAN
Producing Director

SHARON L. HENSLEY
Managing Director

118 North Main St.
Rockford, IL 61101
(815) 963-9454 (bus.)
(815) 964-8023 (b.o.)

FOUNDED 1972
J. R. Sullivan

SEASON
Jan.-Dec.

FACILITIES
David W. Knapp Theater
Seating Capacity: 282
Stage: thrust

AMCORE Cellar Theater
Seating Capacity: 94
Stage: flexible

FINANCES
July 1, 1990-June 30, 1991
Expenses: $1,166,835

CONTRACTS
AEA SPT

New American Theater's mission is to produce classical, contemporary and new works in a manner consistent with the high standards of the contemporary American theatre: innovative productions that foster lasting audience and ensemble growth. When New American Theater was founded, its aim was the production of new plays. NAT is now poised to achieve the pursuit of this oft-stated mission with a modern, fully equipped mainstage thrust space designed to feature classic as well as contemporary plays, and a second stage providing workshop and performance space for new work. With a two-season planning process in place, NAT can now pursue workshops of new plays and transfer them to the main stage, while maintaining an ensemble. Energizing audiences with this mix of theatre has been central to NAT's concept of itself. With our new quarters offering workshops, classes, spaces for affiliate artists and attention to special populations within our community, the promise of consistent and high-quality new work seems on the threshold of fulfillment. To perform with dynamism and to perform with truth, while making every play a new play, remains New American Theater's greatest goal.

—J.R. Sullivan

PRODUCTIONS 1989-90

Noises Off, Michael Frayn; (D) Allan Carlsen; (S) James Wolk; (C) Jessica Hahn; (L) Peter Gottlieb

Precious Memories, Romulus Linney, from Anton Chekhov; (D) J.R. Sullivan; (S) E. Oliver Taylor; (C) Cecelia Mason; (L) Todd Hensley

A Christmas Carol, adapt: Amlin Gray, from Charles Dickens; (D) J.R. Sullivan; (S) James Wolk; (C) Jon R. Accardo; (L) Peter Gottlieb

The Boys Next Door, Tom Griffin; (D) Fontaine Syer; (S) Mary Griswold and John Paoletti; (C) John Paoletti and Mary Griswold; (L) Geoffrey Bushor

Our Town, Thornton Wilder; (D) J.R. Sullivan; (S) James Wolk; (C) Jon R. Accardo; (L) Peter Gottlieb

Wenceslas Square, Larry Shue; (D) J.R. Sullivan; (S) Michael S. Philippi; (C) Jon R. Accardo; (L) Thomas C. Hase

Born Yesterday, Garson Kanin; (D) Joseph Hanreddy; (S) Tamara Turchetta; (C) Jon R. Accardo; (L) Susan McElhaney

PRODUCTIONS 1990-91

Little Shop of Horrors, book and lyrics: Howard Ashman; music: Alan Menken; (D) Allan Carlsen; (S) Ray Recht; (C) Jessica Hahn; (L) Susan McElhaney

Arsenic and Old Lace, Joseph Kesselring; (D) Fontaine Syer; (S) Mary Griswold and John Paoletti; (C) John Paoletti and Mary Griswold; (L) Geoffrey Bushor

Our Country's Good, Timberlake Wertenbaker, from Thomas Keneally; (D) J.R. Sullivan; (S) Michael S. Philippi; (C) Laura

New American Theater. Catherine Davis and Mark Ulrich in *Born Yesterday*.

Cunningham; (L) Michael S. Philippi

A Christmas Carol, adapt: Amlin Gray, from Charles Dickens; (D) J.R. Sullivan; (S) Ray Recht; (C) Jon R. Accardo; (L) Peter Gottlieb

Fences, August Wilson; (D) Donald Douglas; (S) James Wolk; (C) Glenn Billings; (L) Susan McElhaney

The Sneeze, adapt and trans: Michael Frayn, from Anton Chekhov; (D) Allan Carlsen; (S) Mary Griswold and John Paoletti; (C) John Paoletti and Mary Griswold; (L) Geoffrey Bushor

You Never Can Tell, George Bernard Shaw; (D) J.R. Sullivan; (S) Bruce Bergner; (C) Jon R. Accardo; (L) Geoffrey Bushor

Marry Me a Little, conceived: Craig Lucas and Norman Rene; music and lyrics: Stephen Sondheim; (D) Allan Carlsen; (S) Bruce Bergner; (C) Jan Bacino; (L) Peter Gottlieb

New Dramatists

JOEL K. RUARK
Managing Director

424 West 44th St.
New York, NY 10036
(212) 757-6960

FOUNDED 1949
John Wharton, Richard Rodgers, Michaela O'Hara, Howard Lindsay, Moss Hart, Oscar Hammerstein, II, John Golden

SEASON
Sept.-May

FACILITIES
Mainstage
Seating Capacity: 90
Stage: flexible

Lindsay/Crouse Studio
Seating Capacity: 60
Stage: flexible

CONTRACTS
AEA letter of agreement

New Dramatists is entering its fifth decade, firmly establishing it as our country's oldest workshop for playwrights and, indeed, our country's oldest nonprofit service organization for the theatre. In all this time the mission remains the same: to serve both the artistic and the practical needs of our country's finest emerging playwrights. Our 40 member playwrights, a diverse, nationally based group, are chosen by a panel of their peers to serve seven-year terms. During this time they design their own program of working on developing their plays, with the advice and supervision of the artistic staff. In a sense each playwright is "artistic director" of her or his own workshop or reading; each is empowered, respected and assisted. At New Dramatists we believe in powerful playwrights: Our national theatre is still hooked on the word, and the word still belongs to the playwrights.

—Joel K. Ruark

PRODUCTIONS 1989-90

Casanova, Constance Congdon; (D) R.J. Cutler

Ascension Day, Michael Henry Brown; (D) Liz Diamond

Dreamhouse, Stuart Duckworth; (D) Amy Potozkin

Joy Solution, Stuart Duckworth; (D) Joan McGillis

The Closer, Willy Holtzman; (D) Liz Diamond

Gerald's Good Idea, Y York; (D) Mark Lutwak

State of the Art, Stuart Duckworth; (D) Josh Astracan

In the Eye of the Hurricane, Eduardo Machado; (D) James Hammerstein

Genuine Myth, Ben Siegler; (D) Jonathan Hogan

The Tower, Matthew Maguire; (D) Matthew Maguire

Terminal Hip, Mac Wellman; (D) Mac Wellman

Bait and Switch, Richard Dresser; (D) John Pynchon Holms

Crowbar, Mac Wellman; (D) Mac Wellman

77 M.L.K. Stop!, Don Glenn; (D) Kate Reed

Big, Fat and Ugly With a Moustache, Christopher Widney; (D) Scott Stohler

Indian Love Call, Paul D'Andrea; (D) Alma Becker

Martin Guerre, Laura Harrington; (D) Roger Ames

The Deadly Aim of the Straight and True, Michael Henry Brown; (D) Joel Bishoff

Slo-Pitch, Stuart Duckworth; (D) Liz Diamond

Marie-Antoine, Opus One, Lise Vialliancourt; trans: Jill MacDougal; (D) Liz Diamond

Three Johsons and a Mule, Ben Siegler

Related Retreats, Eduardo Machado

Not for Profit, Stuart Duckworth; (D) Kara Green

The Benefits of Doubt, Joe Sutton; (D) Josh Astracan

The Place to Be, Christopher Widney; (D) Stone Widney

Paint, Sean Eve; (D) Scott Stohler

Angels Still Falling, book and lyrics: Richard Blake; music: Peter Jagger; (D) John McGrath

Mood Indigo, Wendy MacLeod

Dreams of Home, Migdalia Cruz; (D) Liz Diamond

Sorrow of the Killer Gorilla, Heidi Herr; (D) John McGrath

Snowflakes, Y York; (D) Mark Lutwak

Wipeout, Nathaniel Nesmith

Sisters...A Legend, Stuart Duckworth; (D) Alma Becker

The Ninth World, Mac Wellman

Abnormaentatenkabinett, book and lyrics: Matthew Maguire; music: Michael Gordon

PRODUCTIONS 1990-91

The Global Generation, Antoine O'Flaherty; (D) Paul Walker

The Closer, Willy Holtzman; (D) Liz Diamond

Taking a Chance on Love, Matthew Maguire; (D) Josh Astracan

Big Deal, Stuart Duckworth; (D) Casey Childs

Static, Ben Siegler

Mary and Joseph, book and lyrics: Mark St. Germain; music: Randy Courts

The Devils, adapt: Elizabeth Egloff, from Fyodor Dostoevski; (D) Robert Woodruff

The Cenci, adapt: Elizabeth Egloff, from Percy Bysshe Shelley; (D) Robert Woodruff

Theresa, Dan Therriault

Beyond the Ruins, Marco Micone; (D) Liz Diamond

Sight Unseen, Donald Margulies

Camping with Henry and Tom, Mark St. Germain; (D) John Hickok

Malfi, Matthew Maguire; (D) Elana Greenfield

Once Removed, Eduardo Machado

Things That Break, Sherry Kramer

Chaos, book and lyrics: Matthew Maguire; music: Michael Gordon; (D) Anne Bogart

The Model Apartment, Donald Margulies

The Night Game, Willy Holtzman; (D) John Pynchon Holms

Flipping the Bird, Wendy MacLeod; (D) Lisa Peterson

The Opium War, Ana Maria Simo; (D) Linda Chapman

The Swan, Elizabeth Egloff; (D) June Stein

The Master and Margarita, book adapt: Sherry Kramer, from Mikhail Bulgakov; music: Margaret Pine; lyrics: Sherry Kramer and Margaret Pine; (D) Roger Ames

Experience of Dreams, Cary Wong; (D) Christina Kirk

Betty and the Kool Kat Club, book and lyrics: Phil Bosakowski; music: Catherine Stone; (D) Roger Ames

Hands of Orlac, book adapt and lyrics: Elizabeth Egloff, from Maurice Renard; music: Dan Schrier

Theresa, Dan Therriault

Bocon, Lisa Loomer

The Will, Paolo De Paola; (D) Paolo De Paola

Fabiola, Eduardo Machado; (D) Anne Bogart

The Snowflake Avalanche, Y York; (D) Mark Lutwak

Hearing Voices, Sheldon Rosen

Sisters...A Legend, Stuart Duckworth; (D) David Gannon

A Knife in the Heart, Susan Yankowitz; (D) Anne Bogart

The Hitch, Dan Therriault; (D) Marjorie Van Halteren

Temporary Life, Don Wollner

Show and Tell, Anthony Clarvoe; (D) Anne Bogart

When Night is Near, Willy Holtzman; (D) Liz Diamond

Play with Repeats, Martin Crimp; (D) Anne Bogart

Running for Blood No. 3, Migdalia Cruz; (D) Marjorie Van Halteren

New Federal Theatre

WOODIE KING, JR.
Producer

LINDA HERRING
Managing Director

466 Grand St.
New York, NY 10002
(212) 598-0400

FOUNDED 1970
Woodie King, Jr.

SEASON
Sept.-June

FINANCES
July 1, 1990-June 30, 1991
Expenses: $291,508

CONTRACTS
AEA letter of agreement

Growing out of the New York State Council on the Arts Ghetto Arts Program, the New Federal Theatre was officially founded by Woodie King Jr. at Henry Street Settlement. Now in its 21st season, the New Federal Theatre has carved a much admired special niche for itself in the New York and national theatre worlds. Specializing in minority drama, it has brought the joy of the living stage to the many minority audience members who live in the surrounding Lower East Side community and the greater metropolitan area. It has brought minority playwrights, actors and directors to national attention, and has sponsored a variety of ethnic theatre groups and events.

—Woodie King, Jr.

PRODUCTIONS 1989-90

Goree, Matsemela Manaka; (D) John Kani; (S) Matsemela Manaka; (C) Kate Manaka; (L) Siphiwe Khumalo

God's Trombones!, adapt: Woodie King, Jr. and Grenoldo Frazier, from James Weldon Johnson; (D) Woodie King, Jr.; (S) Llewellyn Harrison; (C) Judy Dearing; (L) William H. Grant, III

Survival, Fana Kekana, Selaelo Maredi, Mshengu Themba Ntinga and Seth Sibandi; (D) Jerry Mofokeng; (S) Craig Kennedy; (C) Ali Turns; (L) Richard Harmon

PRODUCTIONS 1990-91

The Wizard of Hip, Thomas W. Jones, II; (D) Kenny Leon; (S) Tony Loadholt; (L) Jeff Guzik

Jelly Belly, Charles Smith; (D) Dennis Zacek; (S) Richard Harmon; (C) Judy Dearing; (L) Richard Harmon

The Balm Yard, book adapt: Don Kinch; music and lyrics: Julius Williams; (D) Shauneille Perry; (S) Robert Joel Schwartz; (C) Judy Dearing; (L) Sandra Ross

New Federal Theatre. Kim Weston-Moran, Gary Dourdan and Roxie Roker in *The Balm Yard*. Photo: Bert Andrews.

New Jersey Shakespeare Festival

BONNIE J. MONTE
Artistic Director

MICHAEL STOTTS
General Manager

Drew University
Route 24
Madison, NJ 07940
(201) 408-3278 (bus.)
(201) 377-4487 (b.o.)

FOUNDED 1963
Paul Barry

SEASON
June-Sept.

FACILITIES
Bowne Theatre

New Jersey Shakespeare Festival. William Preston and Gordon Stanley in *The Tempest*. Photo: Richard Termine.

Seating Capacity: 238
Stage: thrust

FINANCES
Jan. 1, 1990-Dec. 31, 1990
Expenses: $761,380

CONTRACTS
AEA letter of agreement

The New Jersey Shakespeare Festival's mission is twofold. Dedicated to producing the plays of Shakespeare and other classic masterworks, NJSF is committed to the notion that through its longevity classical theatre can shed light on current concerns and issues, holding a mirror up to our lives and helping us understand personal dilemmas and those common to the human race. Classic works can also help us understand those who look and live differently, serving as a force for social and political change. Classics can accomplish these things as well as, and sometimes more effectively than, contemporary work because they have a history and a perspective. They show us where we've come from, what mankind is, what it will always be, and how we have changed and evolved. At their best, classics can show us where to go. We are interested in this work because it illuminates, not just because it exists. The second half of our mission is to nurture new talent and new audiences for the American stage, to strengthen and expand the venues for young professionals, and to do our part to revitalize the tradition of theatregoing in this country.

—Bonnie J. Monte

Note: During the 1989-90 season, Paul Barry served as artistic director.

PRODUCTIONS 1990

Romeo and Juliet, William Shakespeare; (D) Paul Barry; (S) James A. Bazewicz; (C) Ann Waugh; (L) Stephen Petrilli

Measure for Measure, William Shakespeare; (D) Paul Barry; (S) James A. Bazewicz; (C) Constance Hoffman; (L) Stephen Petrilli

King John, William Shakespeare; (D) Paul Barry; (S) James A. Bazewicz; (C) Ann Waugh; (L) Stephen Petrilli

A Life in the Theatre, David Mamet; (D) Paul Barry; (S) James A. Bazewicz; (C) Steven F. Graver; (L) Stephen Petrilli

Death of a Salesman, Arthur Miller; (D) Paul Barry; (S) Mark Evancho; (C) Julie Ables Chevan; (L) Stephen Petrilli

PRODUCTIONS 1991

The Tempest, William Shakespeare; (D) Bonnie J. Monte; (S) Michael Ganio; (C) B. Christine McDowell; (L) Bruce Auerbach

The Skin of Our Teeth, Thornton Wilder; (D) Kay Matschullat; (S) Christine Jones; (C) David Burke; (L) Michael Giannitti

A Midsummer Night's Dream, William Shakespeare; (D) Dylan Baker; (S) James Sandefur; (C) Cynthia Dumont; (L) Phil Monat

Dark of the Moon, Howard Richardson and William Berney; (D) Jimmy Bohr; (S) Rob Odorisio; (C) B. Christine McDowell; (L) Bill Berner

Twelfth Night, William Shakespeare; (D) Bonnie J. Monte; (S) Charles McCarry; (C) Hwa Parks; (L) Steven Rosen

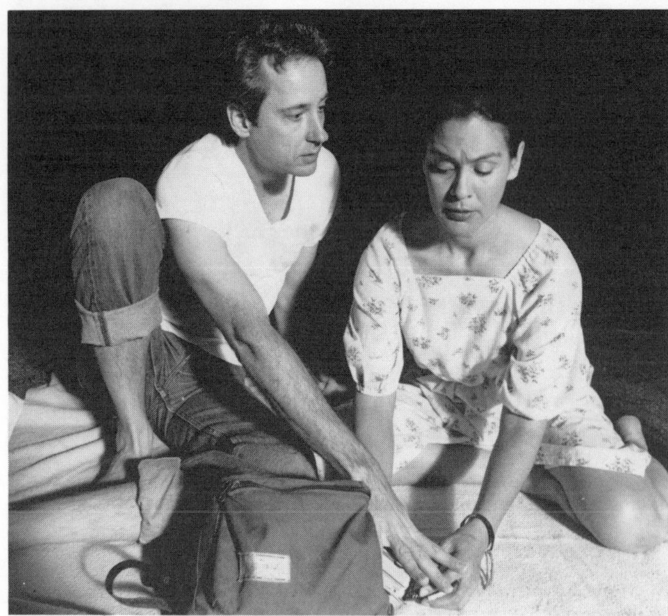

New Mexico Repertory Theatre. David A. Kimball and Raquel Salinas in *¿De Donde?* Photo: Murrae Haynes.

New Mexico Repertory Theatre

ROSARIO PROVENZA
Interim Artistic Director

STANLEY WEINSTEIN
Executive Director

Box 9279
Santa Fe, NM 87504-9279
(505) 983-2382 (bus.)
(505) 984-2226 (b.o.)

Box 789
Albuquerque, NM 87103-0789
(505) 243-4577 (bus.)
243-4500 (b.o.)

FOUNDED 1983
Andrew Shea, Steven Schwartz-Hartley, Clayton Karkosh

SEASON
Oct.-May

FACILITIES
Santa Fe Armory for the Arts
Seating Capacity: 340
Stage: thrust

***KiMo Theatre*, Albuquerque**
Seating Capacity: 755
Stage: proscenium

FINANCES
July 1, 1990-June 30, 1991
Expenses: $1,150,000

CONTRACTS
AEA LORT (D)

Theatre, by its nature and examinations, is multidimensional and diverse. We celebrate the storytelling ritual among our fellow beings. The aim of New Mexico Repertory Theatre is to nurture this gathering of storytellers and listeners. In residence both in Albuquerque, an emerging city of 500,000, and in Santa Fe, the cultural center of the Southwest, the theatre has developed extensive outreach, education and humanities programs. New Mexico's only professional company, NMRT is committed to a broad and eclectic repertoire.

—*Rosario Provenza*

Note: During the 1989-90 and 1990-91 seasons, Andrew Shea served as artistic director.

PRODUCTIONS 1989-90

The Rocky Horror Show, book, music and lyrics: Richard O'Brien; (D) Andrew Shea and Bill Evans; (S) Rosario Provenza; (C) Rusty Smith; (L) Mary Louise Geiger

Alfred Stieglitz Loves O'Keeffe, Lanie Robertson; (D) Libby Appel; (S) Michael C. Smith; (C) Elizabeth Novak; (L) Robert Peterson

Nero's Last Folly, Leo Bassi; (D) Leo Bassi; (S) John Malolepsy; (L) Robert Wierzel

Stumps, Mark Medoff; (D) Andrew Shea; (S) Jim Billings; (C) Catherine Zuber; (L) Jim Billings

Fences, August Wilson; (D) Seret Scott; (S) John Malolepsy; (C) Deborah Shaw; (L) John Malolepsy

PRODUCTIONS 1990-91

Man and Superman, George Bernard Shaw; (D) Andrew Shea; (S) Rosario Provenza; (C) Connie Singer; (L) Robert Wierzel

Other People's Money, Jerry Sterner; (D) Susan Fenichell; (S) Bill Clarke; (C) Sarah Campbell; (L) Mary Louise Geiger

The Heidi Chronicles, Wendy Wasserstein; (D) Phil Killian; (S) Michael C. Smith; (C) Claremarie Verheyen; (L) Robert Peterson

Othello, William Shakespeare; (D) Jim Holmes; (S) Tom Umfrid; (C) Dean Mogle; (L) Danianne Mizzy

¿De Donde?, Mary Gallagher; (D) Jules Aaron; (S) Rosario Provenza; (C) Constanza Romero; (L) Robert Wierzel

The Great Divide, William Vaughn Moody; (D) Andrew Shea; (S) John Malolepsy; (C) Sarah Campbell; (L) John Malolepsy

New Repertory Theatre, Inc.

LARRY LANE
Artistic Director

ERNEST E. FULTON
Managing Director

Box 418
Newton Highlands, MA 02161
(617) 332-1646

FOUNDED 1984
Larry Lane, Kathryn Lubar, Nora Singer, Richard Fairbanks, Donna Glick

New Repertory Theatre, Inc. Ricardo Pitts-Wiley and Monique McIntyre in *Fences*. Photo: Richard Feldman.

SEASON
Sept.-May

FACILITIES
New Repertory Theatre
Seating Capacity: 150
Stage: thrust

FINANCES
Aug. 1, 1990-July 31, 1991
Expenses: $342,746

CONTRACTS
AEA SPT

We believe that audiences come to the theatre to be stirred, moved and exposed, to share in the mysterious contact between actor and actor, actor and audience. In our small, 150-seat thrust-stage theatre, such contact is very direct. Detail is magnified. Actors can work small and still cast a spell. For this reason, we seek to produce with meticulous care, with a sense of quality and concern for detail. Our interest in contact extends also to our connection with the community through many postshow discussions, classes, forums and workshops that explore the plays we produce—their themes, their relevance and the feelings they engender. In a culture in which a sense of "community" seems increasingly absent, we believe that theatre should be a gathering point in which we seek out and explore what is difficult, consoling and challenging...together.

—Larry Lane

PRODUCTIONS 1989-90

Alphabetical Order, Michael Frayn; (D) Jayme Koszyn; (S) Eric Levenson; (C) Mirjana Mladinov; (L) Eric Levenson
The Promise, Aleksei Arbuzov; trans: Ariadne Nicolaeff; (D) Larry Lane; (S) Peter B. Portnov; (C) Leslie Held; (L) Peter B. Portnov
The Night of the Iguana, Tennessee Williams; (D) Larry Lane; (S) Ed Howe; (C) Jane Alois Stein; (L) Steven Rosen
Educating Rita, Willy Russell; (D) Pat Dougan; (S) Eric Levenson; (C) Dana Woods; (L) Eric Levenson

PRODUCTIONS 1990-91

Candida, George Bernard Shaw; (D) Larry Lane; (S) L. Stacy Eddy; (C) Janet Bobcean; (L) L. Stacy Eddy
Fences, August Wilson; (D) Clinton Turner Davis; (S) Eric Levenson; (C) Marcia Belton; (L) Steven Rosen
The Plough and the Stars, Sean O'Casey; (D) Larry Lane; (S) Eric Levenson; (C) Jennifer Lansdale; (L) Eric Levenson
The Gin Game, D.L. Coburn; (D) Munson Hicks; (S) Bobby Summerlin; (C) Lesley Taylor; (L) Geoffrey Cunningham

New Stage Theatre

JANE REID-PETTY
Producing Artistic Director

JOE K. LEDFORD
Managing Director

Box 4792
Jackson, MS 39296-4792
(601) 948-3533 (bus.)
(601) 948-3531 (b.o.)

FOUNDED 1966
Jane Reid-Petty

SEASON
Jan.-Dec.

FACILITIES
Meyer Crystal Auditorium
Seating Capacity: 364
Stage: proscenium

Jimmy Hewes Room
Seating Capacity: 100
Stage: flexible

FINANCES
July 1, 1990-June 30, 1991
Expenses: $648,000

CONTRACTS
AEA letter of agreement

We create an environment where the artist can do his or her best work. Everybody at New Stage talks about plays, and exploration is not limited to rehearsal and production meetings. Mississippi audiences are bred on the rich literary heritage of the state, and our emphasis on new playwrights evolves from this heritage. Our special programming of the Eudora Welty New Plays Series, for example, encourages writers both locally and nationally. Our educational programming features a Teaching Shakespeare Institute in collaboration with the Folger Library. Our statewide touring program spotlights scenes from Shakespeare and Mississippi fiction writers. Minority involvement is a priority, and our commitment to this principle is reflected in the composition of our intern company, our acting company and the group of Mississippi teachers who participated in the 1991 New Stage/Folger Library Shakespeare Institute.

—Jane Reid-Petty

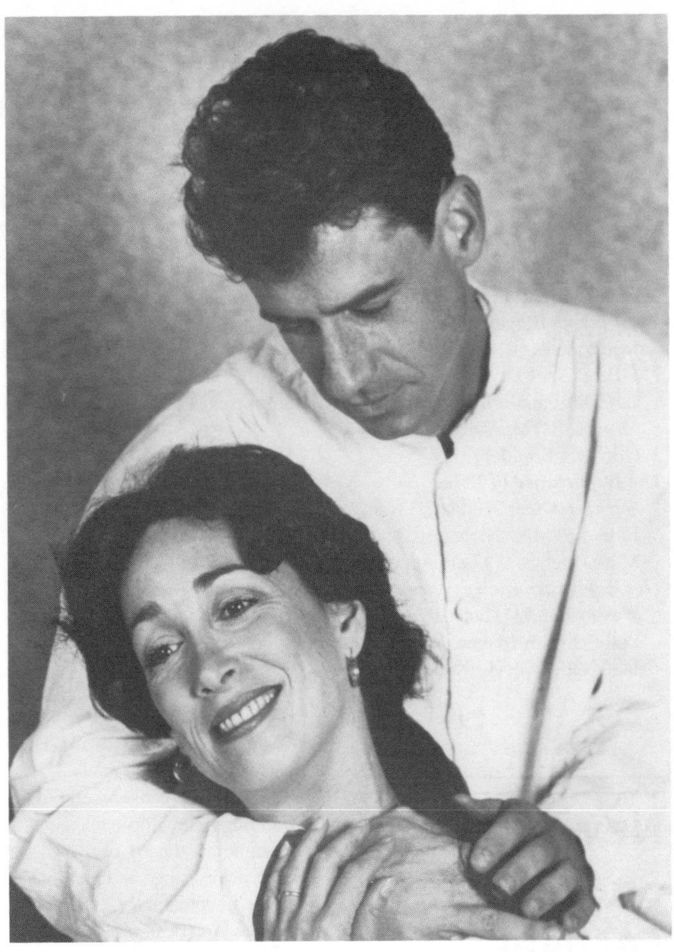

New Stage Theatre. David Breitbarth and Amy Brooks-Jackson in *The Immigrant*. Photo: Scott Boyd.

PRODUCTIONS 1989-90

Noises Off, Michael Frayn; (D) Terence Lamude; (S) Janet Gray; (C) Janet Gray; (L) Ann G. Wrightson
Painting Churches, Tina Howe; (D) Jane Reid-Petty; (S) Roger Farkash; (C) Janet Gray; (L) Roger Farkash
Jerry's Girls, conceived: Jerry Herman and Larry Alford; music and lyrics: Jerry Herman; (D) Annie Chadwick; (S) Richard Crowell; (C) Rosemary Bengele; (L) Richard Crowell
Long Day's Journey Into Night, Eugene O'Neill; (D) Tom Irwin; (S) Janet Gray; (C) Janet Gray; (L) Bill Kickbush
Androcles and the Lion, adapt: Aurand Harris; (D) Russell Luke; (S) Janet Gray; (C) Janet Gray; (L) Ken Hudson
Fallen Angels, Noel Coward; (D) Stephen Hollis; (S) Larry Kadlec; (C) Janet Gray; (L) Ken Hudson
Steel Magnolias, Robert Harling; (D) Ivan Rider; (S) Jimmy Robertson and Marvin "Sonny" White; (C) Janet Gray; (L) Ken Hudson

PRODUCTIONS 1990-91

Oh, Mr. Faulkner, Do You Write?, John Maxwell and Tom Dupree; (D) William Partlan; (S) Jimmy Robertson and Marvin "Sonny" White; (L) Tina Charney
Oil City Symphony, Mike Craver, Mark Hardwick, Debra Monk and Mary Murfitt; (D) Terry Sneed; (S) Richard Crowell; (C) Lisa Slaybach; (L) Richard Crowell
The Immigrant, Mark Harelik;

(D) Ivan Rider; (S) Roger Farkash; (C) Mark Hughes; (L) Roger Farkash

A Christmas Carol, adapt: Ivan Rider, from Charles Dickens; (D) Ivan Rider; (S) Jimmy Robertson and Marvin "Sonny" White; (C) Janet Gray; (L) Ken Lewis

The Snow Queen, adapt: Artie Olaison, from Hans Christian Andersen; (D) Francine Thomas; (S) Edwin Higginbotham; (C) Jean Mucha; (L) Nick Wurzel

The Boys Next Door, Tom Griffin; (D) Cliff Fannin Baker; (S) Mike Nichols; (C) Marilyn Powers; (L) Crickette Brendel

The Importance of Being Earnest, Oscar Wilde; (D) Ivan Rider; (S) Mike Nichols; (C) Mark Hughes; (L) Lani Apperson

The Heidi Chronicles, Wendy Wasserstein; (D) Jane Reid-Petty; (S) Roy Magee, III; (C) Lani Apperson; (L) Nick Wurzel

New York Shakespeare Festival

JOANNE AKALAITIS
Artistic Director

JASON STEVEN COHEN
Managing Director

ROSEMARIE TICHLER
Artistic Associate

425 Lafayette St.
New York, NY 10003
(212) 598-7100 (bus.)
(212) 598-7150 (b.o.)

FOUNDED 1954
Joseph Papp

SEASON
Jan.-Dec.

FACILITIES
Newman Theater
Seating Capacity: 299
Stage: proscenium

Martinson Hall
Seating Capacity: 190
Stage: flexible

LuEsther Hall
Seating Capacity: 150
Stage: flexible

Little Theater
Seating Capacity: 99
Stage: flexible

Susan Stein Shiva Theater
Seating Capacity: 100
Stage: flexible

Anspacher Theater
Seating Capacity: 275
Stage: 3/4 arena

***Delacorte Theater*, Central Park**
Seating Capacity: 1,932
Stage: thrust

FINANCES
Sept. 1, 1990-Aug. 31, 1991
Expenses: $15,000,000

CONTRACTS
AEA LORT (B) and Off Broadway

Since 1954, the New York Shakespeare Festival has operated in the belief that a theatre with the highest professional standards can attract, and should be made available to, a broadly based public. From this guiding principle a contemporary theatre of extraordinary range and quality has emerged, rooted in the classics but with new American plays as its primary focus. Each summer for the past 35 years, NYSF has presented free outdoor productions of the classics throughout New York City, and for the past 30 years, at the Delacorte Theater in Central Park. NYSF's permanent home is the Public Theater, the landmark Astor Library building. There, a repertoire of new American plays and a generation of American actors, directors and designers have been developed through the Festival's working process. Programs fully integrated into the NYSF's activities include Playwriting in the Schools, Festival Latino and Film at the Public. The Festival recently embarked on a six-year marathon of Shakespeare's entire works—36 plays with the foremost American actors in the leading roles. In 1990-91 an innovative approach to producing plays at the Public Theater was introduced with creation of a coalition of talented artists (David Greenspan, Michael Greif, George C. Wolfe and JoAnne Akalaitis) responsible for the season's productions.

—*Joseph Papp*

Note: During the 1989-90 and 1990-91 seasons, Joseph Papp served as producer.

New York Shakespeare Festival. Tracey Ullman and Morgan Freeman in *The Taming of the Shrew*. Photo: Martha Swope.

PRODUCTIONS 1989-90

The Secret Rapture, David Hare; (D) David Hare; (S) Santo Loquasto; (C) Jane Greenwood; (L) Richard Nelson

Up Against It, book adapt: Tom Ross, from Joe Orton; music and lyrics: Todd Rundgren; (D) Kenneth Elliott; (S) B.T. Whitehill; (C) John Glaser; (L) Vivian Leone

Romance in Hard Times, book, music and lyrics: William Finn; (D) David Warren; (S) James Youmans; (C) David C. Woolard; (L) Peter Kaczorowski

Kate's Diary, Kathleen Tolan; (D) David Greenspan; (S) William Kennon; (C) Elsa Ward; (L) David Bergstein

Kingfish, Marlane Meyer; (D) David Schweizer; (S) Bob Prevenca; (C) Susan Nininger; (L) Robert Wierzel

Macbeth, William Shakespeare; (D) Richard Jordan; (S) John Conklin; (C) Jeanne Button; (L) Brian Gale

One of the Guys, Marilyn Suzanne Miller; (D) Arthur Penn; (S) Loren Sherman; (C) Ruth Moreley; (L) Richard Nelson

Jonah, book adapt, music and lyrics: Elizabeth Swados, from Robert Nathan; (D) Elizabeth Swados; (S) Michael Downs; (C) Judy Dearing; (L) Beverly Emmons

A Mom's Life, Kathryn Grody; (D) Timothy Near; (S) James Youmans; (C) Holly Vose; (L) Phil Monat

Hamlet, William Shakespeare; (D) Kevin Kline; (S) Robin Wagner; (C) Martin Pakledinaz; (L) Jules Fisher

Spunk, adapt: George C. Wolfe, from Zora Neale Hurston; (D) George C. Wolfe; (S) Loy Arcenas; (C) Toni-Leslie James; (L) Donald Holder

Ice Cream with Hot Fudge, Caryl Churchill; (D) Les Waters; (S) Annie Smart; (C) Annie Smart; (L) Stephen Strawbridge

The Taming of the Shrew, William Shakespeare; (D) A.J. Antoon; (S) John Lee Beatty; (C) Lindsay W. Davis; (L) Peter Kaczorowski

Richard III, William Shakespeare; (D) Robin Phillips; (S) Elis Y. Lam; (C) Elis Y. Lam; (L) Louise Guinand

PRODUCTIONS 1990-91

Machinal, Sophie Treadwell; (D) Michael Greif; (S) David Gallo; (C) Sharon Lynch; (L) Kenneth Posner

Gonza the Lancer, Chikamatsu Monzaemon; trans: Donald Keene; (D) David Greenspan; (S) William Kennon; (C) Elsa Ward; (L) David Bergstein

The Caucasian Chalk Circle, Bertolt Brecht; adapt: Thulani Davis; trans: William Spiegelberger; (D) George C. Wolfe; (S) Loy Arcenas; (C) Toni-Leslie James; (L) Donald Holder

The Big Funk, John Patrick Shanley; (D) John Patrick Shanley; (S) Nancy Winters; (C) Lindsay Davis; (L) Arden Fingerhut

A Bright Room Called Day, Tony Kushner; (D) Michael Greif; (S) John Arnone; (C) Walker

Hicklin; (L) Frances Aronson

Dead Mother; or Shirley Not All in Vain, David Greenspan; (D) David Greenspan; (S) William Kennon; (C) Elsa Ward; (L) David Bergstein

Henry IV, Parts 1 and 2, William Shakespeare; (D) JoAnne Akalaitis; (S) George Tsypin; (C) Gabriel Berry; (L) Jennifer Tipton

The Way of the World, William Congreve; (D) David Greenspan; (S) William Kennon; (C) Elsa Ward; (L) David Bergstein

Casanova, Constance Congdon; (D) Michael Greif; (S) John Arnone; (C) Gabriel Berry; (L) Frances Aronson

Othello, William Shakespeare; (D) Joe Dowling; (S) Frank Conway; (C) Jane Greenwood; (L) Richard Nelson

New York State Theatre Institute

Formerly Empire State Institute for the Performing Arts

PATRICIA B. SNYDER
Producing Director

RENEE HARITON
Acting Managing Director

1400 Washington Ave.
PAC 266
Albany, NY 12222
(518) 442-5399 (bus.)
(518) 442-5373 (b.o.)

FOUNDED 1976
Patricia B. Snyder, Empire State Youth Theatre Institute (State University of New York), Governor Nelson A. Rockefeller Empire State Plaza Performing Arts Center Corporation

SEASON
Sept.-June

FACILITIES
Kitty Carlisle Hart Theatre
Seating Capacity: 900
Stage: flexible

Lewis A. Swyer Theatre
Seating Capacity: 450
Stage: thrust

FINANCES
July 1, 1990-June 30, 1991
Expenses: $2,490,000

CONTRACTS
AEA TYA

Known until 1990 as the Empire State Institute for the Performing Arts (ESIPA), the newly named New York State Theatre Institute has undergone numerous peripheral changes which have left the central mission of its 15-year history unaltered. As have some other regional theatres, the NYS Theatre Institute has become a professional program of a university, the State University of New York at Albany. However, its productions continue to be performed in downtown Albany's famous arts center, known as "the Egg." Since its founding in 1976, the Theatre Institute continues its dedication to cultural exchange and the nurturing of tomorrow's theatre today through the development of new works and the introduction of young audiences to theatre. By enriching the lives of our youthful and family audiences through an active blending of quality theatre and education, the institute strives to reveal and reaffirm the wonder of the human spirit.

—Patricia B. Snyder

Note: During the 1990-91 season, Ed Lange served as acting artistic director.

PRODUCTIONS 1989-90

Knockabout Boy, book: W.A. Frankonis; music: George Harris; lyrics: George Harris and W.A. Frankonis; (D) John Briggs; (S) Victor Becker; (C) Brent Griffin; (L) Victor En Yu Tan

The Sleeping Beauty, book adapt: Richard Shaw and company, from The Brothers Grimm; music and lyrics: George Harris; (D) Joseph Balfior and Adrienne Posner; (S) Marsha Louis Eck; (C) Patrizia von Brandenstein; (L) Lloyd S. Riford, III

Better Days, Richard Dresser; (D) Ed. Lange; (S) Victor Becker; (C) Brent Griffin; (L) Victor En Yu Tan

Arsenic and Old Lace, Joseph Kesselring; (D) Terence Lamude; (S) Victor A. Becker; (C) Karen Kammer; (L) Ann G. Wrightson

The Snow Queen, book adapt and lyrics: Adrian Mitchell, from Hans Christian Andersen; music: Richard Peaslee; (D) Richard Williams; (S) Sally Jacobs; (C) Gregg Barnes; (L) F. Mitchell Dana

PRODUCTIONS 1990-91

Spider's Web, Agatha Christie; (D) Ed. Lange; (S) Richard Finkelstein; (C) Karen Kammer; (L) Richard Finkelstein

Narnia, book adapt: Jules Tasca, from C.S. Lewis; music: Thomas Tierney; lyrics: Ted Drachman; (D) Shela Xoregos; (S) Stuart Wurtzel; (C) Patrizia von Brandenstein; (L) John McLain

Slow Dance on the Killing Ground, William Hanley; (D) Ed. Lange; (S) Victor A. Becker; (C) Brent Griffin; (L) Victor En Yu Tan

Othello, William Shakespeare; (D) Tina Packer; (S) Victor A. Becker; (C) Jay Herring; (L) Lenore Doxsee

Vasilisa the Fair, Sofia Prokofieva and Irina Tokmakova; adapt: Adrian Mitchell; trans: Sabina Modzhalevskaya and Harlow Robinson; (D) Patricia DiBenedetto Snyder and Adrienne Posner; (S) Richard Finkelstein; (C) Brent Griffin; (L) John McLain

New York State Theatre Institute. Richard Barrows, Betsy Normile, John Romeo, Joel Aroeste and Marlene Goudreau in *Spider's Web*. Photo: Tim Raab.

New York Theatre Workshop

JAMES C. NICOLA
Artistic Director

NANCY KASSAK DIEKMANN
Managing Director

220 West 42nd St.
18th Floor, New York, NY 10036
(212) 302-7737

FOUNDED 1979
Stephen Graham

SEASON
Oct.-June

FACILITIES
Perry Street Theatre
Seating Capacity: 99
Stage: flexible

FINANCES
July 1, 1990-June 30, 1991
Expenses: $786,000

CONTRACTS
AEA Mini

New York Theatre Workshop maintains its commitment to producing works of artistic merit that provide society with a perspective on our history and on the events and institutions that shape our lives. Each season we present four to six fully mounted productions of literate, unconventional plays. These new works are primarily developed from continuing relationships with writers and directors. We seek out artists who can combine an interest in the exploration of theatrical forms with intelligent and substantial content, and who can maintain the highest standards of quality. In addition to the New Works Series, we present the New Directors Series, which provides opportunities for the most promising directors of the next generation, and "O Solo Mio," an annual festival of solo performance art. Our Mondays at Three Program provides a forum for presentation of and comment on work in progress, and discussion of current social and artistic issues, thereby creating a sense of community amongst artists and staff.

—James C. Nicola

PRODUCTIONS 1989-90

My Children! My Africa!, Athol Fugard; (D) Athol Fugard; (S) Susan Hilferty; (C) Susan Hilferty; (L) Dennis Parichy

A Forest in Arden, adapt: Christopher Grabowski, from William Shakespeare; (D) Christopher Grabowski; (S) Tom Kamm; (C) Claudia Brown; (L) Pat Dignan

The Nature of Things, David Cale, Roy Nathanson, Marc Ribot and E.J. Rodriguez; (D) Bill Barnes; (L) Anne Militello

The Waves, book adapt: David Bucknam and Lisa Peterson, from Virginia Woolf; music and lyrics: David Bucknam; (D) Lisa Peterson; (S) Randy Benjamin; (C) Michael Krass; (L) Brian MacDevitt

PRODUCTIONS 1990-91

Love and Anger, George F. Walker; (D) James C. Nicola and Christopher Grabowski; (S) James A. Schuette; (C) Gabriel Berry; (L) Christopher Akerlind

Light Shining in Buckinghamshire, Caryl Churchill; (D) Lisa Peterson; (S) Bill Clarke; (C) Michael Krass; (L) Brian MacDevitt

Artificial Reality, Jeffrey Essmann; (D) David Warren; (S) George Xenos; (C) David C. Woolard; (L) Pat Dignan

Eve's Diary and ***The Story of the Tiger***, Dario Fo; trans: Ron Jenkins; (D) Christopher Ashley; (S) George Xenos; (C) David C. Woolard; (L) Pat Dignan

New York Theatre Workshop. Courtney Vance and Lisa Fugard in *My Children! My Africa!* Photo: Gerry Goodstein.

Northlight Theatre. Jacqueline Kim and William Dick in *Mrs. Warren's Profession*. Photo: Mark Avery.

Northlight Theatre

RUSSELL VANDENBROUCKE
Artistic Director

600 Davis St.
Evanston, IL 60201
(708) 869-7732 (bus.)
(708) 869-7278 (b.o.)

FOUNDED 1974
Gregory Kandel

SEASON
Sept.-May

FACILITIES
Coronet Theatre
Seating Capacity: 377
Stage: proscenium

FINANCES
July 1, 1990-June 30, 1991
Expenses: $1,300,000

CONTRACTS
AEA LORT (D)

Now in its 17th season, Northlight Theatre has emerged as a nationally respected theatre with a reputation for ambitious programming and high-quality productions. We are the third largest not-for-profit theatre in Chicago and a vital player in its culture. At the heart of Northlight's artistic identity is the twin belief that the writer's voice is the center of the theatre and that every production provides an opportunity to understand the world we live in, not simply to escape it. Our international repertoire includes new plays, adaptations and incisive interpretations of the classics. The theatre also develops new works through workshops, staged readings and commissions. Each year more than 225 performances are seen by an audience of 65,000. Many patrons discover theatre through Northlight's extensive outreach programs, which provide special access for students, older adults, veterans and people with disabilities. The theatre also sponsors STAR, a program designed to serve student audiences through ongoing relationships with teachers.

—Russell Vandenbroucke

PRODUCTIONS 1989-90

The Butter and Egg Man, George S. Kaufman; (D) Doug Finlayson; (S) Gary Baugh; (C) Jessica Hahn; (L) Ken Bowen

84, Charing Cross Road, adapt: James Roose-Evans, from Helene Hanff; (D) Russell Vandenbroucke; (S) Michael Merritt; (C) Nan Zabriskie; (L) Linda Essig

From the Mississippi Delta, Dr. Endesha Ida Mae Holland; (D) Jonathan Wilson; (S) Michael S. Philippi; (C) Jeffrey Kelly; (L) Chris Phillips

Mrs. Warren's Profession, George Bernard Shaw; (D) Richard E.T. White; (S) Linda Buchanan; (C) Jessica Hahn; (L) Michael S. Philippi

Born in the RSA, Barney Simon and original cast; (D) Barney Simon; (S) Michael S. Philippi; (C) Susan Hilferty; (L) Michael S. Philippi

PRODUCTIONS 1990-91

Eleanor: In Her Own Words, adapt: Russell Vandenbroucke, from Eleanor Roosevelt; (D) Russell Vandenbroucke; (S) James Maronek; (C) Gayland Spaulding; (L) Rita Pietraszek
Pick Up Ax, Anthony Clarvoe; (D) Richard E.T. White; (S) Linda Buchanan; (C) Renee Liepins; (L) Michael S. Philippi
Uncommon Ground, Jeremy Lawrence; (D) Gwen Arner; (S) Michael S. Philippi; (C) Jessica Hahn; (L) Linda Essig
An Enemy of the People, Henrik Ibsen; adapt: Russell Vandenbroucke; trans: Jerry Turner; (D) Kyle Donnelly; (S) Michael Merritt; (C) Gayland Spaulding; (L) Robert Christen
Woody Guthrie's American Song, conceived and adapt: Peter Glazer, from Woody Guthrie; (D) Peter Glazer; (S) Philipp Jung; (C) Baker S. Smith; (L) David Noling

Oakland Ensemble Theatre

SHARON WALTON
Producing Director

KIM EUELL
Managing Director

1615 Broadway, Suite 800
Oakland, CA 94612
(415) 763-7774

FOUNDED 1974
Ron Stacker Thompson

SEASON
Sept.-June

FACILITIES
The Alice Arts Center
Seating Capacity: 500
Stage: flexible

FINANCES
July 1, 1990-June 30, 1991
Expenses: $494,139

CONTRACTS
AEA BAT

The Oakland Ensemble Theatre is committed to providing insightful and engaging works of contemporary theatre, shaped by the sensitivities and sensibilities of African Americans. Through this African-American voice, we speak to a culturally and ethnically diverse American audience. To carry out this mission fully, our goals include the development of new audiences, especially people of color, and the nurturing in them of the idea that theatre is an indispensable part of life, and that attending the theatre is a necessary component of one's entertainment options. We also wish to produce and present types of work that show how African-American theatre is as integral to American culture as all other forms of expression. Equally important is the ability to provide a venue in which theatre artists, especially those who are African-American, can gain professional experience and further hone their skills.

—Sharon Walton

Note: During the 1989-90 season, Benny Sato Ambush served as producing director.

Oakland Ensemble Theatre. Oscar Brown, Jr. and Oscar Brown III in *It's About Time*. Photo: Bob Hsiang.

PRODUCTIONS 1989-90

Fraternity, Jeff Stetson; (D) Clinton Turner Davis; (S) Ken Ellis and Jeff Boyle; (C) Callie Floor; (L) Stephanie Johnson
It's About Time, book, music and lyrics: Oscar Brown, Jr. and Oscar Brown, III; (D) Oscar Brown, Jr. and Oscar Brown, III; (S) Jeff Boyle; (L) Jeff Boyle
MLK: We Are the Dream, Al Eaton; (D) Benny Sato Ambush; (S) Pamela S. Peniston; (L) Jeff Boyle
From the Mississippi Delta, Dr. Endesha Ida Mae Holland; (D) LaTanya Richardson; (S) Steven Perry; (C) Judy Dearing; (L) William H. Grant, III

PRODUCTIONS 1990-91

The Gospel at Colonus, adapt: Lee Breuer, from Sophocles; music: Bob Telson; (D) Lee Breuer; (S) Alison Yerxa; (C) Ghretta Hynd; (L) Derek Duarte
Yonder Comes Day, Marijo; (D) Keryl McCord; (S) Matthew Antaky; (C) Marijo; (L) Matthew Antaky
Sisters, Marsha A. Jackson; (D) Sharon Walton; (S) Pamela S. Peniston; (C) Callie Floor; (L) Stephanie Johnson

Odyssey Theatre Ensemble

RON SOSSI
Artistic Director

LINDA HOEGER-THOMPSON
Managing Director

2055 South Sepulveda Blvd.
Los Angeles, CA 90025
(320) 477-2055

FOUNDED 1969
Ron Sossi

SEASON
Jan.-Dec.

FACILITIES
Odyssey 1
Seating Capacity: 99
Stage: thrust

Odyssey 2
Seating Capacity: 99
Stage: thrust

Odyssey 3
Seating Capacity: 99
Stage: arena

FINANCES
July 1, 1990-June 30, 1991
Expenses: $520,000

CONTRACTS
AEA 99-seat Theatre Plan

The Odyssey Theatre Ensemble's prime *raison d'etre* is the production of exploration-oriented projects drawn from contemporary, classical and original sources, with a strong leaning toward international and multicultural work. Almost every Odyssey production is, in some important sense, an adventure in form—an attempt to push outward the boundaries of theatrical possibility. Year by year, more Odyssey-evolved work moves out into the larger theatre world. OTE's long-running world premiere production of Steven Berkoff's *Kvetch* opened Off Broadway; *The Chicago Conspiracy Trial* by Ron Sossi and Frank Condon received an ACE award for its production on HBO and recently opened at Chicago's Remains Theatre; Odyssey's *Tracers* has enjoyed long runs throughout the U.S. and Europe; and OTE-developed *McCarthy* moved on to the Milwaukee Repertory Theater. Its innovation-oriented nine-play and lab seasons, its resident Hispanic Unit (LAAFO) and its ever-burgeoning literary program rank the Odyssey as one of the West Coast's leading experimental and process-oriented theatres.

—Ron Sossi

PRODUCTIONS 1989-90

Disability: A Comedy, Ron Whyte; (D) Frank Condon; (S) Christa Bartels; (C) Martha Ferrara; (L) Doc Ballard
Faith Healer, Brian Friel; (D) Jack Rowe; (S) Russell Pyle; (C) Ritchie M. Spencer; (L) Russell Pyle
Accidental Death of an

Odyssey Theatre Ensemble. *Mojave*. Photo: Jan Deen.

Anarchist, Dario Fo; trans: Richard Nelson; (D) Ron Sossi; (S) Jeff Klarin; (C) Betty Berberian; (L) David Carlton
Nightclub Cantata, conceived: Elizabeth Swados; music: Elizabeth Swados; various lyricists; (D) Bill Castellino; (S) Lorraine Heitzman; (C) Lyndall L. Otto; (L) Craig E. Lathrop
It's a Girl!, book and lyrics: John Burrows; music: Andy Whitfield; (D) Robin Saex; (S) Craig E. Lathrop; (C) Neal San Teguns; (L) Kathi O'Donohue
East, Steven Berkoff; (D) Barry Philips; (S) Nancy Dunn Eisenman; (C) Lindsay Stewart; (L) Doc Ballard
The Crackwalker, Judith Thomson; (D) Colman de Kay; (S) Alan Jones; (C) Lili Dove; (L) Lynne Peryon and Doc Ballard
Salt Lake City Skyline, Thomas Babe; (D) Frank Condon; (S) Bob Heller; (C) Lynda Peto; (L) Bob Heller

PRODUCTIONS 1990-91

Struggling Truths, Peter Mellencamp; (D) Ron Sossi; (S) Don Llewellyn; (C) Neal San Teguns; (L) J. Kent Inasy
Acapulco, Steven Berkoff; (D) Steven Berkoff; (S) Craig E. Lathrop; (C) Lynda Peto; (L) Doc Ballard
Diary of a Madman, adapt: Ismail Kanater, from Nikolai Gogol; (D) Ismail Kanater; (C) Linda Hoeger-Thompson; (L) Lynne Peryon
Cirque Du L.A.: Working Without Annette, The Glorious Players; (D) Debbie Devine; (S) Victoria Carpenter; (C) Martha Ferrara; (L) Doc Ballard
Rameau's Nephew, Shelley Berc and Andrei Belgrader, from Denis Diderot; (D) Andrei Belgrader; (S) Anita Stewart; (C) Candice Donnelly; (L) Doc Ballard
Tea, Velina Hasu Houston; (D) Julianne Boyd; (S) Craig E. Lathrop; (C) Bella Arguetty; (L) J. Kent Inasy
A Macbeth, adapt: Charles Marowitz, from William Shakespeare; (D) Charles Marowitz; (S) Geryd Pojawa; (C) Dean Harris and Judith Bartnick; (L) Lynne Peryon
Mojave, Bradley Rand Smith; (D) Charles Otte; (S) Charles Otte; (C) Susan Lyall; (L) Charles Otte
Absurd Person Singular, Alan Ayckbourn; (D) Ron Sossi; (S) Paul William Hawker; (C) Ruth A. Brown; (L) Eileen Cooley
Hospitality, Allan Havis; (D) Steven Albrezzi; (S) James Leonard Joy; (C) Todd Roehrman; (L) Craig Pierce
Accelerando, Lisa Loomer; (D) Jody McAuliffe and Ron Sossi; (D) Vincent Jefferds; (C) Jenny T. Jefferds; (L) Mitchell S. Levine

The Old Creamery Theatre Company

THOMAS P. JOHNSON
Producing Director

MERRITT OLSEN
Associate Producing Director

Box 160
Garrison, IA 52229-0160
(319) 477-3925 (bus.)
(800) 332-5200 Garrison (b.o.)
(800) 352-6262 Amana (b.o.)

FOUNDED 1971
David Berendes, Rita Davies, Mick Denniston, Judy Johnson, Thomas P. Johnson, Steve Koch, Merritt Olsen, Ann Olson, David Olson, Erica Zaffarano

SEASON
May-Dec.

FACILITIES
Garrison Main Stage
Seating Capacity: 260
Stage: thrust

Brenton Stage
Seating Capacity: 150
Stage: flexible

Amana Stage
Seating Capacity: 270
Stage: proscenium

FINANCES
Jan. 1, 1990-Dec. 31, 1990
Expenses: $725,000

CONTRACTS
AEA SPT

Founded in 1971 by Thomas P. Johnson, the Old Creamery Theatre Company's purpose was to provide a wide range of high-quality theatre to audiences in Iowa and throughout the Midwest. This mission still holds true today. The Creamery performs 30 weeks out of the year at locations both in Garrison and at the Amana Colonies Visitors Center. In addition, an aggressive touring schedule allows shows to be presented to schools and community groups. As a result, last year more than 70,000 school children were able to experience live theatre. The only Equity theatre in its state, the Creamery's impact on rural Iowa has been significant, influencing the growth of community theatre, secondary drama departments and creative dramatics activities on the elementary school level. Seeking to continue this growth, the Creamery offers internships to developing artists in both performance and technical theatre.

—Thomas P. Johnson

PRODUCTIONS 1990

Same Time, Next Year, Bernard Slade; (D) Thomas P. Johnson
Run for Your Wife!, Ray Cooney; (D) Debra Wicks; (S) Thomas P. Johnson (C) Marquetta Senters; (L) Steve Weiss
Joseph and the Amazing Technicolor Dreamcoat, book

The Old Creamery Theatre Company. Ed Sarna and Lynnae Lehfeldt in *Run For Your Wife!* Photo: David Pedersen.

and lyrics: Tim Rice; music: Andrew Lloyd Webber; (D) Thomas P. Johnson; (S) George Dowker; (C) Julie McLaughlin; (L) George Dowker

Nunsense, Dan Goggin; book, music and lyrics: Dan Goggin; (D) Jan Czechowski; (C) Julie McLaughlin; (L) Marc Eby

Oil City Symphony, Mike Craver, Mark Hardwick, Debra Monk and Mary Murfitt

Come Blow Your Horn, Neil Simon; (D) Merritt Olsen; (S) Jan Czechowski; (C) Julie McLaughlin; (L) Jan Czechowski

Paradise Hotel, Georges Feydeau; adapt: Thomas P. Johnson; (D) Thomas P. Johnson; (S) Jan Czechowski; (C) Julie McLaughlin; (L) Jan Czechowski

Twelfth Night, William Shakespeare; adapt: Thomas P. Johnson and Roger Kern; (D) Breton Frazier; (S) Jan Czechowski; (C) Julie McLaughlin; (L) Jan Czechowski

One Flew Over the Cuckoo's Nest, Dale Wasserman, from Ken Kesey; (D) Roald J. Himes; (S) Thomas P. Johnson; (C) Amy Svoboda; (L) Mark C. Ax and Marc Eby

PRODUCTIONS 1991

I Do! I Do!, book adapt and music: Tom Jones, from Jan de Hartog; lyrics: Harvey Schmidt; (D) Blaine Stephens; (C) Julie McLaughlin; (L) Richard Burk

The Apple Tree, Mark Twain, Frank R. Stockton and Jules Feiffer; music: Jerry Bock; lyrics: Sheldon Harnick; (D) David Madison; (S) Richard Burk; (C) Kristy Limberg; (L) Richard Burk

The Foreigner, Larry Shue; (D) David Madison; (S) Thomas P. Johnson; (C) Mary Graham; (L) Allen Joseph Coleman

A Christmas Carol, Charles Dickens; (D) Merritt Olsen; (C) Julie McLaughlin

Spoon River Anthology, Edgar Lee Masters; conceived and adapt: Charles Aidman; (D) Thomas P. Johnson; (S) Richard Burk; (C) Julie McLaughlin; (L) Richard Burk

John Brown's Body, Stephen Vincent Benet; (D) Mark Light; (S) Richard Burk; (C) Julie McLaughlin; (L) Richard Burk

Arms and the Man, George Bernard Shaw; (D) Merritt Olsen; (S) Richard Burk; (C) Julie McLaughlin; (L) Richard Burk

First Ladies of the Stage, company-developed; (D) Anne Oberbroeckling; (S) Thomas P. Johnson; (C) Kristy Limberg; (L) Allen Joseph Coleman

Social Security, Andrew Bergman; (D) Debra Wicks; (S) Tim Flavin; (C) Julie McLaughlin

Old Globe Theatre

JACK O'BRIEN
Artistic Director

CRAIG NOEL
Executive Director

TOM HALL
Managing Director

Box 2171
San Diego, CA 92112
(619) 231-1941 (bus.)
(619) 239-2255 (b.o.)

FOUNDED 1937
Community members

SEASON
Jan.-Oct.

FACILITIES
Old Globe Theatre
Seating Capacity: 581
Stage: flexible

Lowell Davies Festival Theatre
Seating Capacity: 612
Stage: thrust

Cassius Carter Centre Stage
Seating Capacity: 225
Stage: arena

FINANCES
Nov. 1, 1990-Oct. 31, 1991
Expenses: $8,456,293

CONTRACTS
AEA LORT (B), (B+) and (C)

I believe the network of regional theatres is in transition, moving toward its inevitable emergence as the American National Theatre. The Old Globe Theatre, a bastion of craft, skill and technique, has kept the classical tradition flourishing in Southern California for 54 years. From the vantage point of this tradition, we offer remarkable venues to writers and artists who formerly flocked to New York for exposure and artistic freedom. Across this country, over the last decade or so, our ability to articulate the classics has shrunk in direct proportion to the influence of film and television, but the Globe still offers an opportunity to actors, directors and designers to stretch their talents and add to their skills in a healthy, competitive market alongside the literature that has sustained theatre for hundreds of years. Currently, the influx of major American writers premiering their newest works at this theatre shows the healthy relationship between the classics and new American plays. By juxtaposing the contemporary and the classical we offer audiences the most vigorous, comprehensive theatre experience possible, and we have a wonderful time doing it.

—Jack O'Brien

Old Globe Theatre. Pippa Pearthree and Charley Lang in *As You Like It*. Photo: Will Gullette.

PRODUCTIONS 1990

La Nonna, Roberto M. Cossa; trans: Raul Moncada; (D) Lillian Garrett-Groag; (S) Robert Brill; (C) Robert Wojewodski; (L) John B. Forbes

Uncle Vanya, Anton Chekhov; trans: Michael Henry Heim; (D) Jack O'Brien; (S) Hugh Landwehr; (C) Robert Wojewodski; (L) Peter Maradudin

Rebel Armies Deep Into Chad, Mark Lee; (D) Adrian Hall; (S) Kent Dorsey; (C) Christina Haatainen; (L) Chris Parry

Jake's Women, Neil Simon; (D) Ron Link; (S) Tony Straiges; (C) Joseph G. Aulisi; (L) Tharon Musser

Lady Day at Emerson's Bar and Grill, Lanie Robertson; (D) Will Roberson; (S) Robert Brill; (C) Lewis Brown; (L) David F. Segal

And a Nightingale Sang, C.P. Taylor; (D) Craig Noel; (S) Kent Dorsey; (C) Lewis Brown; (L) Peter Maradudin

As You Like It, William Shakespeare; (D) Julianne Boyd; (S) David Jenkins; (C) Robert Wojewodski; (L) Peter Maradudin

Cobb, Lee Blessing; (D) Lloyd Richards; (S) Rob Greenberg; (C) Joel O. Thayer; (L) Ashley York Kennedy
White Man Dancing, Stephen Metcalfe; (D) Thomas Allan Bullard; (S) Kent Dorsey; (C) Robert Wojewodski; (L) Kent Dorsey
Our Town, Thornton Wilder; (D) Edward Payson Call; (S) Ralph Funicello; (C) Lewis Brown; (L) Peter Maradudin
Hamlet, William Shakespeare; (D) Jack O'Brien; (S) Ralph Funicello; (C) Lewis Brown; (L) Peter Maradudin
Heartbeats, conceived: Amanda McBroom and Bill Castellino; music: Amanda McBroom, Jerry Sternbach, Michele Brourman and Tom Snow; lyrics: Amanda McBroom; (D) Bill Castellino; (S) Kent Dorsey; (C) Christina Haatainen; (L) Kent Dorsey

PRODUCTIONS 1991

Other People's Money, Jerry Sterner; (D) Milton Katselas; (S) Cliff Faulkner; (C) Shigeru Yaji; (L) Barth Ballard
The White Rose, Lillian Garrett; (D) Craig Noel; (S) Ralph Funicello; (C) Steven Rubin; (L) David F. Segal
Sun Bearing Down, Larry Ketron; (D) Stephen Metcalfe; (S) Robert Brill; (C) Robert Wojewodski; (L) Ashley York Kennedy
Two Trains Running, August Wilson; (D) Lloyd Richards; (S) Tony Fanning; (C) Chrisi Karvonides; (L) Geoff Korf
Remembrance, Graham Reid; (D) Andrew J. Traister; (S) Nick Reid; (C) Lewis Brown; (L) John B. Forbes
The Snow Ball, A.R. Gurney, Jr.; (D) Jack O'Brien; (S) Douglas W. Schmidt; (C) Steven Rubin; (L) David F. Segal
The Merchant of Venice, William Shakespeare; (D) Jack O'Brien; (S) Ralph Funicello; (C) Lewis Brown; (L) Peter Maradudin
Necessities, Velina Hasu Houston; (D) Julianne Boyd; (S) Cliff Faulkner; (C) Shigeru Yaji; (L) Ashley York Kennedy
Forever Plaid, Stuart Ross; (D) Stuart Ross; (S) Neil Peter Jampolis; (C) Debra Stein; (L) Jane Reisman
The Tempest, William Shakespeare; (D) Adrian Hall; (S) Ralph Funicello; (C) Lewis Brown; (L) Peter Maradudin
The Show-Off, George Kelly; (D) Jack O'Brien; (S) Cliff Faulkner; (C) Robert Wojewodski; (L) Robert Wojewodski
La Fiaca, Ricardo Talesnik; trans: Raul Moncada; (D) Lillian Garrett

Omaha Magic Theatre

JO ANN SCHMIDMAN
Producing Artistic Director

2309 Hanscom Blvd.
Omaha, NE 68105
(402) 346-1227

FOUNDED 1968
Jo Ann Schmidman

SEASON
Jan.-Dec.

FACILITIES
Mainstage
Seating Capacity: 93
Stage: flexible

FINANCES
June 1, 1990-May 31, 1991
Expenses: $261,852

Living Sculpture. Breathing Words. Fresh Committed Performance. New Music. Resounding Installations. Large Scale Projections. These words describe our work. Our theatre is a mix of words, visual image, performers, directorial concept and new music pulsing together into audience consciousness. Now entering its 24th year, the Omaha Magic Theatre is one of America's longest-lived alternative theatres. We produce visually charged, aurally intense, vital, engaging and entertaining performance experiences. We work to impact, impassion and provide an active forum for nurturing audiences in this otherwise passive world. We publish our work and tour, and six of our creations are currently being produced by other theatres.

—Jo Ann Schmidman

Omaha Magic Theatre. Jo Ann Schmidman, Robert N. Gilmer and Sora Kimberlain in *Body Leaks*. Photo: Megan Terry.

PRODUCTIONS 1989-90

Lucy Loves Me, Migdalia Cruz; (D) Jo Ann Schmidman; (S) Sora Kimberlain; (C) Megan Terry; (L) Jim Schumacher
Fat, book, music and lyrics: Terra Daugirda Pressler; (D) Jo Ann Schmidman; (S) Sora Kimberlain; (C) Megan Terry; (L) Jim Schumacher
Angel Face, Laura Harrington; (D) Jo Ann Schmidman; (S) Sora Kimberlain; (C) Hollie McClay; (L) Jim Schumacher
Tales of the Lost Formicans, Constance Congdon; (D) Deborah E. Leech; (S) Diane Degan; (C) Jude Barrier; (L) Jim Schumacher
Body Leaks, book and lyrics: Megan Terry, Jo Ann Schmidman and Sora Kimberlain; music: Marianne de Pury, Luigi Waites and Megan Terry; (D) Jo Ann Schmidman; (S) Sora Kimberlain; (C) Kenda Slavin and Robert N. Gilmer; (L) Jo Ann Schmidman
Headlights, book and lyrics: Megan Terry; music: Frank Fong, Rex Gray, Rick Hiatt, Lori Loree, Mark Nelson and Luigi Waites; (D) Jo Ann Schmidman; (S) Sora Kimberlain and Bill Farmer; (C) Kenda Slavin; (L) Jo Ann Schmidman

PRODUCTIONS 1990-91

Body Leaks, book and lyrics: Megan Terry, Jo Ann Schmidman and Sora Kimberlain; music: Marianne de Pury, Luigi Waites and Megan Terry; (D) Jo Ann Schmidman; (S) Sora Kimberlain; (C) Kenda Slavin and Robert N. Gilmer; (L) Jo Ann Schmidman
Heads, Murray Mednick; (D) Jonathan Warman; (S) Diane Degan; (C) Hollie McClay; (L) Jonathan Warman
Lawyers, Micah Hackler and George Sewell; (D) Amy Harmon; (S) Roger Reeves; (C) Jeanne Garreans; (L) Marci Keegan
Animals Have Rights, Too, book: Ann Carroll; music and lyrics: Jeanette McDonald; (D) Ann Carroll; (L) Steve Sheehan

Ontological-Hysteric Theater

RICHARD FOREMAN
Artistic Director

PAUL SCHIFF BERMAN
Administrative Director

c/o Performing Artservices
105 Hudson St., Room 200
New York, NY 10013
(212) 941-8911

FOUNDED 1968
Richard Foreman

SEASON
Jan.-Dec.

FINANCES
July 1, 1990-June 30, 1991
Expenses: $125,000

Since 1968 I have evolved my own idiosyncratic theatre language, which is nevertheless applicable to many different moods, subjects and settings. I attempt to stretch the employment of that language further each year, which in itself seems self-evident. But, more important, I try to build into my plays secret reflections upon the inevitable failure involved in pursuing such a goal.

—Richard Foreman

PRODUCTIONS 1990

Lava, Richard Foreman; (D) Richard Foreman; (S) Richard Foreman; (C) Richard Foreman; (L) Heather Carson

Love & Science, libretto: Richard Foreman; music: Stanley Silverman; (D) Richard Foreman; (S) Richard Foreman; (C) Donna Zakowska; (L) Heather Carson

Eddie Goes to Poetry City, Part 1, Richard Foreman; (D) Richard Foreman; (S) Richard Foreman

PRODUCTIONS 1991

Eddie Goes to Poetry City, Part 2, Richard Foreman; (D) Richard Foreman; (S) Richard Foreman; (C) Donna Zakowska; (L) Heather Carson

Ontological-Hysteric Theater. Matthew Courting, Neil Bradles, Kyle de Camp and Peter Davis in *Lava*. Photo: Suzanne Tobias.

The Open Eye: New Stagings

AMIE BROCKWAY
Artistic Director

ADRIENNE J. BROCKWAY
Production/Business Manager

270 West 89th St.
New York, NY 10024
(212) 769-4141 (bus.)
(212) 769-4143 (b.o.)

FOUNDED 1972
Jean Erdman, Joseph Campbell

SEASON
Oct.-June

The Open Eye: New Stagings. Roger Howarth and Debra Whitfield in *On the Move*. Photo: Scott Humbert.

FACILITIES
Seating Capacity: 115
Stage: proscenium

FINANCES
July 1, 1990-June 30, 1991
Expenses: $255,503

CONTRACTS
AEA TYA and letter of agreement

The Open Eye: New Stagings draws on the creative power of the theatre arts—music, dance, drama and comedy—to mount innovative productions, many based on ancient myths and folklore, that appeal to people of all cultures and ages. Our commitment to the city's youth is seen in special programs that help foster a strong sense of community and emphasize the power of diverse cultures. Through timely original works and classics (or plays by important writers from the past), we seek to bring people together, communicate our shared heritage and provide a fresh perspective on universal human experience.

—Amie Brockway

PRODUCTIONS 1989-90

Souvenirs of Old New York, conceived: Amie Brockway; (D) Amie Brockway; (S) Adrienne J. Brockway; (C) Adrienne J. Brockway; (L) Donald A. Gingrasso

The Contrast, Royall Tyler; (D) Russell Treyz; (S) Bob Phillips; (C) Jane Trapnell; (L) Spencer Mosse

A Woman Called Truth, Sandra Fenichel Asher; (D) Ernest Johns; (S) Adrienne J. Brockway; (C) Adrienne J. Brockway; (L) Donald A. Gingrasso

On the Move, Tony Howarth; (D) Kim T. Sharp; (S) Adrienne J. Brockway; (C) Leslie McGovern; (L) Donald A. Gingrasso

Eye on Directors Festival:

Amelia Again, Michele Lowe; (D) Gail Noppe

El Amor Brujo, adapt: James Furlong, from Manuel de Falla; (D) James Furlong

The Exception and the Rule, Bertolt Brecht; trans: Eric Bentley; (D) Rachel Kranz

Killer, John Rawlins; (D) Ernest Johns

Love's the Best Doctor, Moliere; (D) Sharone Stacy

Brand, Henrik Ibsen; trans: Geoffrey Hill; (D) Nedim Saban

The Young Hack and His Girl, Clifford Odets; (D) Edward Griffith

The Gift of Stones, Jim Crace; (D) Kim T. Sharp

Measure for Measure, William Shakespeare; (D) Olivia Honegger

A Turn of the Screw, adapt: Nick Olcott, from Henry James; (D) Melody Owens

Gardinias 'N Blum, Nicholas A. Patricca; (D) Amie Brockway

PRODUCTIONS 1990-91

A Place Beyond the Clouds, Sandra Biano; (D) Sharone Stacy; (S) Adrienne J. Brockway; (C) Adrienne J. Brockway; (L) Adrienne J. Brockway

A Woman Called Truth, Sandra Fenichel Asher; (D) Ernest Johns; (S) Adrienne J. Brockway; (C) Adrienne J. Brockway; (L) Adrienne J. Brockway

Eagle or Sun, adapt: Amie Brockway, from Sabina Berman; trans: Isabel Saez; (D) Amie Brockway; (S) Adrienne J. Brockway; (C) Adrienne J. Brockway; (L) Adrienne J. Brockway

Eye on Directors Festival:

The Jet of Blood, Antonin Artaud; (D) Ernie Barbarash

Nobody Was Supposed to Survive: The MOVE Massacre, adapt: Patricia R. Floyd, from Alice Walker; (D) Patricia R. Floyd

Such Sweet Thunder: Shakespeare Suite, adapt: James Furlong, from William Shakespeare; (D) James Furlong

Phaedra, Jean Racine; trans: Margaret Rawlings; (D) Lisa Brailoff

A Dream Deferred, Celeste A. Frazier; (D) Joan Kane

Here We Are, Dorothy Parker; (D) Susan Jacobson

The Incredible Shrinking Family, Alice Elliot; (D) Kim T. Sharp

Naim, A.B. Yehoshua; adapt: Nola Chilton; (D) Marc Weiner

Don Surrealism, Elena Penga; (D) Sherry Teitelbaum

Leonce and Lena, Georg Buchner; trans: Hedwig Rappolt; (D) Brian Leahy Doyle

Oregon Shakespeare Festival

HENRY WORONICZ
Artistic Director

WILLIAM W. PATTON
Executive Director

DENNIS BIGELOW
Producer, OSF Portland

Box 158
Ashland, OR 97520
(503) 482-2111 (bus.)
(503) 482-4331 (b.o.)

Box 9008
Portland, OR 97207
(503) 248-6309 (bus.)
(503) 274-6588 (b.o.)

FOUNDED 1935
Angus Bowmer

SEASON
Nov.-Apr.

FACILITIES
Angus Bowmer Theatre
Seating Capacity: 600
Stage: modified thrust

Black Swan
Seating Capacity: 140
Stage: flexible

Elizabethan Theatre
Seating Capacity: 1200
Stage: outdoor

Intermediate Theatre, Portland
Seating Capacity: 885
Stage: proscenium

FINANCES
Nov. 1, 1989-Oct. 30, 1990
Expenses: $9,863,615

CONTRACTS
AEA LORT (B)

The Oregon Shakespeare Festival operates four theatres in two cities: Ashland and Portland. Most members of the Ashland company work on long-term (10-month) contracts in rotating repertory. The Portland company creates a season of five plays running consecutively from November to April. In all our theatres we produce plays of high literary stature—ancient and modern, classic and contemporary—that have special resonances in our time. Style is dictated primarily by respect for the text, but also by the talent and sensibilities of the artists and the taste and experience of the audience. We serve a large, broad-based audience of disparate backgrounds and interests, but are dedicated uncompromisingly to quality both of text and production. We intend to be bold, innovative and demanding, but we also seek clarity, accessibility and vividness. Shakespeare's work has a special place in our repertoire, not as an icon but as representative of a constantly renewable freshness and dramatic power. We aim, in all our work, for the same combination of continuity and immediacy found in the classics.

—Henry Woronicz

Oregon Shakespeare Festival. Dennis Robertson and Robert Nadir in *The Recruiting Officer*. Photo: Rick Adams.

PRODUCTIONS 1989-90

The Seagull, Anton Chekhov; trans: Michael Frayn; (D) Libby Appel; (S) Anne Gibson; (C) Jeannie Davidson; (L) Robert Peterson

Holiday, Philip Barry; (D) Philip Killian; (S) Joel Fontaine; (C) Deborah Dryden; (L) Stephen Strawbridge

Burn This, Lanford Wilson; (D) Dennis Bigelow; (S) William Bloodgood; (C) Michael Olich; (L) Jim Sale

Six Characters in Search of an Author, Luigi Pirandello; trans: Robert Cornthwaite; (D) Dennis Bigelow; (S) Michael C. Smith; (C) David Kay Mickelsen; (L) Robert W. Rosentel

Noises Off, Michael Frayn; (D) Allen Nause; (S) Scott Weldin; (C) Debra Bruneaux; (L) Peter Maradudin

Peer Gynt, Henrik Ibsen; trans: Jerry Turner; (D) Jerry Turner; (S) William Bloodgood; (C) Jeannie Davidson; (L) Robert Peterson

The House of Blue Leaves, John Guare; (D) Sandy McCallim; (S) John Dexter; (C) Michael Olich; (L) Jim Sale

The Merry Wives of Windsor, William Shakespeare; (D) Pat Patton; (S) Vicki Smith; (C) Claudia Everett; (L) Jim Sale

The Voice of the Prairie, John Olive; (D) Cynthia White; (S) Richard L. Hay; (C) Frances Kenny; (L) Jim Sale

The Second Man, S.N. Behrman; (D) Henry Woronicz; (S) William Bloodgood; (C) Michael Olich; (L) Robert Peterson

God's Country, Steven Dietz; (D) Michael Kevin; (S) William Bloodgood; (C) Jeannie Davidson; (L) Robert Peterson

The Comedy of Errors, William Shakespeare; (D) Tom Ramirez; (S) Michael Miller; (C) Barbara Bush; (L) Jim Sale

Henry V, William Shakespeare; (D) James Edmondson; (S) Richard L. Hay; (C) Deborah M. Dryden; (L) Jim Sale

The Winter's Tale, William Shakespeare; (D) Libby Appel; (S) William Bloodgood; (C) Jeannie Davidson; (L) Jim Sale

At Long Last Leo, Mark Stein; (D) Kirk Boyd; (S) William Bloodgood; (C) Robert Peterson; (L) Debra Bruneaux

Aristocrats, Brian Friel; (D) Philip Killian; (S) Richard L. Hay; (C) David Kay Mickelsen; (L) Robert Peterson

PRODUCTIONS 1990-91

M. Butterfly, David Henry Hwang; (D) Philip Killian; (S) William Bloodgood; (C) Deborah M. Dryden; (L) Robert Peterson

The Recruiting Officer, George Farquhar; (D) Dennis Bigelow; (S) Richard L. Hay; (C) Michael Olich; (L) Jim Sale

Our Country's Good, Timberlake Wertenbaker, from Thomas Keneally; (D) Dennis Bigelow; (S) Richard L. Hay; (C) Michael Olich; (L) Jim Sale

Glengarry Glen Ross, David Mamet; (D) Philip Killian; (S) Cliff Faulkner; (C) Debra Bruneaux; (L) Peter Maradudin

The Tempest, William Shakespeare; (D) Dennis

Bigelow; (S) Michael C. Smith; (C) David Kay Mickelsen; (L) Robert W. Rosentel

The Merchant of Venice, William Shakespeare; (D) Libby Appel; (S) William Bloodgood; (C) Deborah M. Dryden; (L) Robert Peterson

Our Town, Thornton Wilder; (D) James Edmondson; (S) William Bloodgood; (C) Claudia Everett; (L) Robert Peterson

Major Barbara, George Bernard Shaw; (D) Jerry Turner; (S) Richard L. Hay; (C) Jeannie Davidson; (L) Jim Sale

Woman in Mind, Alan Ayckbourn; (D) Cynthia White; (S) Carolyn Leslie Ross; (C) Frances Kenny; (L) Jim Sale

Some Americans Abroad, Richard Nelson; (D) Jeff Steitzer; (S) Vicki Smith; (C) Michael Olich; (L) Jim Sale

Other People's Money, Jerry Sterner; (D) Henry Woronicz; (S) William Bloodgood; (C) Michael Olich; (L) Jim Sale

The Taming of the Shrew, William Shakespeare; (D) Sandy McCallim; (S) Michael Ganio; (C) David Kay Mickelsen; (L) Robert Peterson

Henry VI, Part 1, William Shakespeare; (D) Pat Patton; (S) Richard L. Hay; (C) Barbara Bush; (L) Robert Peterson

Julius Caesar, William Shakespeare; (D) Michael Kevin; (S) William Bloodgood; (C) Sarah Nash Gates; (L) Robert Peterson

Two Rooms, Lee Blessing; (D) Kirk Boyd; (S) William Bloodgood; (C) Carole Wheeldon; (L) Michael Holcombe

Organic Theater Company

RICHARD FIRE
Producing Artistic Director

JEFF NEAL
General Manager

3319 North Clark St.
Chicago, IL 60657
(312) 327-2427 (bus.)
(312) 327-5588 (b.o.)

FOUNDED 1969
Carolyn Purdy-Gordon, Stuart Gordon

SEASON
Jan.-Dec.

FACILITIES
Greenhouse Lab
Seating Capacity: 90
Stage: proscenium

Greenhouse South Hall
Seating Capacity: 70
Stage: flexible

Mainstage
Seating Capacity: 400
Stage: thrust

FINANCES
July 1, 1990-June 30, 1991
Expenses: $977,000

CONTRACTS
AEA CAT

The Organic Theatre Company is dedicated to the development and production of new work and original adaptations. We believe that theatre is for everyone and theatre must be fun. This does not mean that everything we do will please every taste or that we play everything for laughs. It does mean that we seek to reflect the diversity of human experience and deliver the thrill of emotion. We have no hard-and-fast aesthetic. We seek scripts and ideas with which the writer is passionately involved. Readings and workshops nourish new work. It's risky. Not all projects reach production and not every production succeeds, but the journey of discovery is the greatest adventure that theatre can provide. It is to this process that the Organic Theatre is devoted.

—Richard Fire

PRODUCTIONS 1989-90

Bleacher Bums '89, company-developed, updated by: Richard Fire; (D) Joe Mantegna; (S) John Paoletti and Mary Griswold; (C) Mary Griswold and John Paoletti; (L) Geoffrey Bushor

Do the White Thing, Aaron Freeman and Rob Kolson; (D) Bob Curry and Nate Herman; (S) Jimmy Bickerstaff; (L) Jimmy Bickerstaff

You Hold My Heart Between Your Teeth, Blair Thomas; (D) Blair Thomas; (S) Blair Thomas and company

Organic Theater Company. Josette Dicarlo and Lindsay Porter in *Erotica: Little Birds*. Photo: Sue Hostetler.

Galena Rose, Jim Post; (D) Jim Post; (S) Stacey Post; (L) Stacey Post

Kerouac: The Essence of Jack, Vincent Balestri; (D) Vincent Balestri; (S) Reda Tipton; (L) Reda Tipton

Physical Vision, Lynn Book; (D) Jill Daley; (S) Brian Dobrich, Jody Tucci, Eric Leonardson, Dennis Moore and Jolanta Czarnacka; (L) Lou Mazolli

The Cookie Crumb Club, Jim Post; (D) Jim Post

PRODUCTIONS 1990-91

Do the White Thing, Aaron Freeman and Rob Kolson; (D) Bob Curry and Nate Herman; (S) Jimmy Bickerstaff; (L) Jimmy Bickerstaff

American Enterprise, Jeffrey Sweet; (D) Wesley Savick; (S) Richard Penrod and Jacqueline Penrod; (C) Yslan Hicks; (L) Kevin Snow

M: The Murderer, adapt: Bob Meyer and Jack Clark, from Fritz Lang; (D) Bob Meyer; (S) Randy Buescher; (L) Randy Buescher

Erotica: Little Birds, adapt: Karen Goodman, from Anais Nin; (D) Karen Goodman; (S) Kevin Hackett; (C) Gayle Whitehead; (L) Kevin Hackett

Pan Asian Repertory Theatre

TISA CHANG
Artistic/Producing Director

RUSSELL MURPHY
Business Manager

47 Great Jones St.
New York, NY 10012
(212) 505-5655 (bus.)
(212) 245-2660 (b.o.)

FOUNDED 1977
Tisa Chang

SEASON
Oct.-May

FACILITIES
Playhouse 46
Seating Capacity: 151
Stage: arena

FINANCES
Sept. 1, 1990-Aug. 31, 1991
Expenses: $480,000

CONTRACTS
AEA letter of agreement

Pan Asian Rep is the New York theatre of Asian-American actors

Pan Asian Repertory Theatre. Dennis Dun, Stan Egi and Ann Tsuji in *FOB*. Photo: Corky Lee.

and directors, promoting the works of Asian-American playwrights and Asian masterworks translated into English. As a natural step in artistic maturation the company designated a resident ensemble in 1987, in order to sharpen artistic excellence by working on long-term dream projects, new commissions and adaptations from classical Asian sources. New initiatives include educational outreach and exploration into music-theatre. *Cambodia Agonistes*, scheduled for spring 1992, is the culmination of three years of research in developing an original music-theatre piece, a response to the recent holocaust in Kampuchea as seen through the "eyes" of a Cambodian dancer. Because we value our relationship with our community, which is ever-increasing in diversity and numbers, and because our work so often reflects its stories, Pan Asian Rep has limitless opportunities for artistic inspiration and nourishment for years to come.

—*Tisa Chang*

PRODUCTIONS 1989-90

The Song of Shim Chung, Terence Cranendonk and Du-Yee Chang; (D) Du-Yee Chang; (S) Atsushi Moriyashi; (C) James Livingston; (L) Victor En Yu Tan

And the Soul Shall Dance, Wakako Yamauchi; (D) Kati Kuroda; (S) Robert Klingelhoefer; (C) Toni-Leslie James; (L) Tina Charney

Rosie's Cafe, R.A. Shiomi; (D) Raul Aranas; (S) Bob Phillips; (C) Eiko Yamaguchi; (L) Victor En Yu Tan

FOB, David Henry Hwang; (D) David Henry Hwang; (S) Alex Polner; (C) Eiko Yamaguchi; (L) Victor En Yu Tan

PRODUCTIONS 1990-91

Lucky Come Hawaii, Jon Shirota; (D) Ron Nakahara; (S) Robert Klingelhoefer; (C) Maggie Raywood; (L) Victor En Yu Tan

And the Soul Shall Dance, Wakako Yamauchi; (D) Kati Kuroda; (S) Robert Klingelhoefer; (C) Toni-Leslie James; (L) Tina Charney

Letters to a Student Revolutionary, Elizabeth Wong; (D) Ernest Abuba; (S) Kyung Won Chang; (C) Maggie Raywood; (L) Anne Somogye

PCPA Theaterfest

JACK SHOUSE
Managing Artistic Director

JUDY FROST
Business Manager

Box 1700
Santa Maria, CA 93456
(805) 928-7731 (bus.)
(805) 922-8313 (b.o.)

FOUNDED 1964
Donovan Marley

SEASON
Jan.-Dec.

FACILITIES
Marian Theatre
Seating Capacity: 508
Stage: thrust

Interim Theatre
Seating Capacity: 175
Stage: flexible

Festival Theatre
Seating Capacity: 772
Stage: thrust

Backstage Theatre
Seating Capacity: 132
Stage: flexible

FINANCES
Oct. 1, 1989-Sept. 30, 1990
Expenses: $2,687,429

CONTRACTS
AEA U/RTA

We, as theatre artists, performers and craftsmen, share our product with our audience in an attempt to entertain and create a heightened awareness of the human condition, and to promote a better understanding of what our roles are as individuals and contributors to society. This collaboration is the essence of the theatre. It is the artist who initiates the creative process and the audience who responds, thus maintaining a cycle of realization and growth for both. At PCPA Theaterfest we create an environment for those artists dedicated to taking that creative initiative. We strive to protect and nurture a theatrical process we feel is vital to our development as individuals and our growth as a civilization. As a performing company and conservatory, we commit ourselves to serving the community and our professional staff and students by producing an even wider variety of theatrical works of excellence, while preserving our tradition of offering the classics of world theatre, new plays, contemporary plays and the new and classic in American musical theatre.

—*Jack Shouse*

PRODUCTIONS 1989-90

Peter Pan, James M. Barrie; (D) Paul Barnes; (S) Jack Shouse; (C) Judith A. Ryerson; (L) Michael A. Peterson

The Elephant Man, Bernard Pomerance; (D) Roger DeLaurier; (S) John Dexter; (C) Judith A. Ryerson; (L) Michael A. Peterson

PCPA Theaterfest. Joel Goldes and Karen Barbour in *Loot*. Photo: Tom Smith.

Little Shop of Horrors, book adapt and lyrics: Howard Ashman, from Charles Griffith; music: Alan Menken; (D) Tom Gardner; (S) Greg Timm; (C) Judith A. Ryerson; (L) Kevin J. Ugar
The Crucible, Arthur Miller; (D) James Edmondson; (S) John Dexter; (C) Judith A. Ryerson; (L) Michael A. Peterson
Billy Bishop Goes to War, John Gray and Eric Peterson; (D) Jonathan Gillard Daly; (S) Alan Hines; (C) Joseph M. Kowalski; (L) Kevin J. Ugar
Mass Appeal, Bill C. Davis; (D) Frederic Barbour; (S) Everett Chase; (C) Joseph M. Kowalski; (L) Kevin J. Ugar
Christmas Is..., book, music and lyrics: Brad Carroll and Jeremy Mann; (D) Brad Carroll and Jeremy Mann; (S) Everett Chase; (C) Joseph M. Kowalski; (L) David R. White
Yours, Anne, book adapt and lyrics: Enid Futterman, from Anne Frank; music: Michael Cohen; (D) Paul Barnes; (S) Tim Hogan; (C) Gabriel Espinosa; (L) Thomas G. Gaffney
Much Ado About Nothing, William Shakespeare; (D) Paul Barnes; (S) Michael Ganio; (C) Judith A. Ryerson; (L) Michael A. Peterson
The Importance of Being Earnest, Oscar Wilde; (D) Jonathan Gillard Daly; (S) Everett Chase; (C) Judith A. Ryerson; (L) John Martin
A Chorus Line, book: James Kirkwood and Nicholas Dante; music: Marvin Hamlisch; lyrics: Edward Kleban; (D) Michael Barnard; (S) Everett Chase; (C) Michael Ganio; (L) Michael A. Peterson
Guys and Dolls, book adapt: Jo Swerling and Abe Burrows, from Damon Runyon; music and lyrics: Frank Loesser; (D) Brad Carroll; (S) Thomas Buderwitz; (C) Dorothy L. Marshall; (L) Jerald Enos
Ghosts, Henrik Ibsen; trans: Jerry Turner; (D) Roger DeLaurier; (S) D. Martyn Bookwalter; (C) Dorothy L. Marshall; (L) Jerald R. Enos

PRODUCTIONS 1990-91

Joseph and the Amazing Technicolor Dreamcoat, book and lyrics: Tim Rice; music: Andrew Lloyd Webber; (D) Brad Carroll; (S) Everett Chase; (C) Judith A. Ryerson; (L) Michael A. Peterson
Baby, book: Sybille Pearson; music: David Shire; lyrics: Richard Maltby, Jr.; (D) Brad Carroll; (S) Norm Spencer; (C) Judith A. Ryerson; (L) Michael A. Peterson
Pygmalion, George Bernard Shaw; (D) Roger DeLaurier; (S) Everett Chase; (C) Judith A. Ryerson; (L) Michael A. Peterson
The Diviners, Jim Leonard, Jr.; (D) Paul Barnes; (S) Norm Spencer; (C) Gabriel Espinosa; (L) David Lee Cuthbert
Loot, Joe Orton; (D) Frederic Barbour; (S) Greg Timm; (C) Gabriel Espinosa; (L) David Lee Cuthbert
The Belle of Amherst, William Luce; (D) Roger DeLaurier; (S) Abby Hogan; (C) Judith A. Ryerson
The Normal Heart, Larry Kramer; (D) James Edmondson; (S) Norm Spencer; (C) Abby Hogan; (L) David Lee Cuthbert
A Walk in the Woods, Lee Blessing; (D) Kirk Boyd; (S) Jack Shouse; (C) Gabriel Espinosa; (L) Theodore Michael Dolas

Pegasus Players

ARLENE J. CREWDSON
Artistic Director

DAVID DILLON
Producing Director

1145 West Wilson
Chicago, IL 60640
(312) 878-9761 (bus.)
(312) 271-2638 (b.o.)

FOUNDED 1978
Arlene J. Crewdson

SEASON
Jan.-Dec.

FACILITIES
O'Rourke Center for the Performing Arts
Seating Capacity: 250
Stage: proscenium

Edgewater Presbyterian Church
Seating Capacity: 119
Stage: thrust

FINANCES
Sept. 1, 1990-Aug. 31, 1991
Expenses: $574,739

Pegasus Players. Larry Yando and Harry J. Lennix in *Kiss of the Spider Woman*. Photo: Jennifer Girard.

Pegasus Players is a non-Equity theatre company located in Chicago's Uptown area. Our mission is twofold: to produce the highest quality artistic work, and to provide exemplary theatre, entertainment and arts education at no charge to groups who have little or no access to the arts. The primary motivation for selecting works for mainstage production is that they address issues which reflect humanity's tribute to the lasting values of the spirit. Because of the diverse audiences Pegasus reaches, the works selected also are chosen to include a broad spectrum of theatrical history and dramatic forms. Pegasus has built a reputation for mounting challenging works—plays that have previously been commercial failures, or have problematic subject matter, large casts or demanding technical requirements. Our multifaceted outreach program provides performing arts events and theatre education for Chicago's underserved and disadvantaged communities, from the very young to the very elderly.

—*Arlene J. Crewdson*

PRODUCTIONS 1989-90

Kiss of the Spider Woman, adapt and trans: Allan Baker, from Manuel Puig; (D) Eric Simonson; (S) Walter Martishus; (C) Jeffrey Kelly; (L) Peter Gottlieb
A History of the American Film, Christopher Durang; (D) Roy Hine; (S) Roy Hine; (C) Jeffrey Kelly; (L) Todd Hensley
Fraternity, Jeff Stetson; (D) Jonathan Wilson; (S) Russ Borski; (C) Jeffrey Kelly; (L) Peter Gottlieb
The Death of Carmen, trans: Francesca Zambello and Carlo Palca; (D) Victoria Bussert; (S) Russ Borski; (C) Jeffrey Kelly; (L) Russ Borski

Young Playwrights Festival:
Seeing It Her Way, Nilwona Nowlin; (D) Gary Griffin; (S) Stewart Dawson; (C) Jeffrey Kelly; (L) Todd Hensley
Friends to the End, Marvin Scott; (D) Gary Griffin; (S) Stewart Dawson; (C) Jeffrey Kelly; (L) Todd Hensley
Off Highway 21, Christi Rankin; (D) Christine Sumption; (S) Stewart Dawson; (C) Jeffrey Kelly; (L) Todd Hensley
Pipedreams, students of Jobs For Youth; (D) Edward Wilkerson; (S) Stewart Dawson; (C) Jeffrey Kelly; (L) Todd Hensley

PRODUCTIONS 1990-91

Into the Woods, book: James Lapine; music and lyrics: Stephen Sondheim; (D) Victoria Bussert; (S) Russ Borski; (C) Jeffrey Kelly, adapt from Patricia Zipprodt and Ann Hould-Ward; (L) Russ Borski
Broadway Bound, Neil Simon; (D) Michael Leavitt; (S) Laura Cowell Kinter; (C) Jeffrey Kelly; (L) John R. Lederle
Cane, adapt: Charles Smith, from Jean Toomer; (D) Dennis Zacek; (S) James Darienne; (C) Claudia Boddy; (L) Michael Bourke
Sylvia's Real Good Advice, book adapt: Nicole Hollander, Arnold Aprill and Tom Mula, from Nicole Hollander; music: Steve Rashid; lyrics: Nicole Hollander, Arnold Aprill, Cheri Coons, Tom Mula and Steve Rashid; (D) David H. Bell; (S) Tom Ryan; (C) Claudia Boddy; (L) Diane Ferry Williams

Young Playwrights Festival
Absolution, Luis Perez; (D) Gary Griffin; (S) Allan Donahue; (C) Jeffrey Kelly; (L) Tom Fleming
The Chevy Odyssey, Clarence Lang; (D) Christine Sumption; (S) Allan Donahue; (C) Jeffrey Kelly; (L) Tom Fleming
Black Ink on a Black Page, Shanton Russell; (D) Don Mayo; (S) Allan Donahue; (C) Jeffrey Kelly; (L) Tom Fleming
Empty Spaces, students of Sullivan House West; (D) Catherine Slade; (S) Allan Donahue; (C) Jeffrey Kelly; (L) Tom Fleming

Pennsylvania Stage Company

PETER WRENN-MELECK
Producing Artistic Director

MARIE MAZZINI
Company Manager

837 Linden St.
Allentown, PA 18101
(215) 434-6110 (bus.)
(215) 433-3394 (b.o.)

FOUNDED 1977
Anna Rodale

SEASON
Oct.-June

FACILITIES
J. I. Rodale Theater
Seating Capacity: 274
Stage: proscenium

FINANCES
July 1, 1990-June 30, 1991
Expenses: $1,226,473

CONTRACTS
AEA LORT (D)

Pennsylvania Stage Company is dedicated to creating relevant, innovative, artistically viable productions ranging from American and worldwide classics to contemporary works. We produce plays that serve our artists and our audience by illuminating the human condition—our love of self, our love of others, our hopes and desperations. In addition to producing a seven-play season, PSC is committed to serving eastern Pennsylvania and western New Jersey as a cultural and educational resource through a variety of outreach programs. "Stage Two" provides the opportunity to develop new works by emerging playwrights with actors and directors. Our "Visiting Artists in the Schools" program, featuring two touring productions, reaches more than 20,000 students annually, and nearly 200 adults and children enroll in our community theatre school. As the region's only Equity theatre, Pennsylvania Stage Company provides a stimulating and supportive environment for national, regional and local artists.

—Peter Wrenn-Meleck

PRODUCTIONS 1989-90

Wait Until Dark, Frederick Knott; (D) Stephen Rothman; (S) Sarah Baptist; (C) Kathleen Egan; (L) Donald Holder
Oil City Symphony, Mike Carver, Mark Hardwick, Debra Monk and Mary Murfitt; (D) Maureen Heffernan; (S) Sarah Baptist; (C) Kathleen Egan; (L) Donald Holder
A Shayna Maidel, Barbara Lebow; (D) Charles Richter; (S) Rob Odorisio; (C) Anna Ungar Herman; (L) Curtis Dretsch
Educating Rita, Willy Russell; (D) Stephen Rothman; (S) Bennet Averyt; (C) Barbara Forbes; (L) Bennet Averyt
The Glass Menagerie, Tennessee Williams; (D) Scott Edmiston; (S) Curtis Dretsch; (C) Kathleen Egan; (L) Curtis Dretsch
Talley's Folly, Lanford Wilson; (D) Charlie Hensley; (S) Curtis Dretsch; (C) Kathleen Egan; (L) Curtis Dretsch
Noises Off, Michael Frayn; (D) Maureen Heffernan; (S) Ray Recht; (C) Patricia Adshead; (L) Donald Holder

PRODUCTIONS 1990-91

The Penultimate Problem of Sherlock Holmes, John Nassivera; (D) Charlie Hensley; (S) Curtis Dretsch; (C) Gail Brassard; (L) Curtis Dretsch
Nunsense, book, music and lyrics: Dan Goggin; (D) Maureen Heffernan; (S) Sarah Baptist; (C) Kathleen Egan; (L) Spencer Mosse
Speed-the-Plow, David Mamet; (D) Scott Edmiston; (S) Rob Odorisio; (C) Barbra Kravitz; (L) Curtis Dretsch
Kuru, Josh Manheimer; (D) Peter Wrenn-Meleck; (S) Bennet Averyt; (C) David Brooks; (L) Bennet Averyt
A Walk in the Woods, Lee Blessing; (D) Charles Richter; (S) Sarah Baptist; (C) Kathleen Egan; (L) Curtis Dretsch
The Rainmaker, N. Richard Nash; (D) Scott Edmiston; (S) Rob Odorisio; (C) Kathleen Egan; (L) Mark Evancho
Driving Miss Daisy, Alfred Uhry; (D) Gavin Cameron-Webb; (S) Sarah Baptist; (C) Charlotte M. Yetman; (L) Harry Feiner

Pennsylvania Stage Company. Tia Speros, Kathy Robinson and Lynn Eldredge in *Nunsense*. Photo: Gregory M. Fota.

The Penumbra Theatre Company

LOU BELLAMY
Artistic Director

CLAUDIA WALLACE-GARDNER
Managing Director

The Martin Luther King Bldg.
270 North Kent St.
St. Paul, MN 55102-1794
(612) 224-4601

FOUNDED 1976
Lou Bellamy

SEASON
Jan.-Dec.

FACILITIES
Hallie Q. Brown Theater
Seating Capacity: 260
Stage: modified thrust

FINANCES
July 1, 1990-June 30, 1991
Expenses: $350,000

CONTRACTS
AEA SPT

Penumbra Theatre Company's mission is to create productions that are artistically excellent, thought-provoking, relevant and entertaining. Penumbra's goals are: to increase public awareness of the significant contributions that African Americans have made in creating a diversified American theatrical tradition; to encourage a culturally diverse and all-inclusive America by using theatre to teach, criticize, comment and provide a model; to use theatre to create an American mythology that includes African Americans and other people of color in every thread of the fabric of our society; to redefine and expand the consciousness of our audiences and our theatrical communities to include a sympathetic and realistic portrayal of people of color; to encourage the staging of plays that address the African-American experience; and to continue to establish a black performing arts community. Mainstage productions, tours, lectures and conferences contribute to these ends.

—Lou Bellamy

The Penumbra Theatre Company. James A. Williams and Marvette Knight in *Who Causes the Darkness*. Photo: R. DuShaine.

PRODUCTIONS 1989-90

Tambourines to Glory, Langston Hughes; (D) Lewis Whitlock, III; (S) Sean D. Zein; (C) Deidrea Whitlock; (L) Mike Wangen
Les Blancs, Lorraine Hansberry; (D) Horace Bond; (S) Gregory Ray; (C) Deidrea Whitlock; (L) Mike Wangen
Black Nativity, Langston Hughes; (D) Lewis Whitlock, III; (S) James P. Taylor; (C) Deidrea Whitlock; (L) Mike Wangen
Who Causes the Darkness, Marion Isaac McClinton; (D) Terry Bellamy; (S) Gregory Ray; (C) Deidrea Whitlock; (L) Mike Wangen
Unfinished Women Cry in No Man's Land While a Bird Dies in a Gilded Cage, Aishah Rahman; (D) Marion Isaac McClinton; (S) Gregory Ray; (C) Deidrea Whitlock; (L) Mike Wangen
Fences, August Wilson; (D) Claude Purdy; (S) W.J.E. Hammer; (C) Wayne E. Murphey; (L) Mike Wangen

PRODUCTIONS 1990-91

Don't Bother Me, I Can't Cope, conceived: Vinnette Carroll; book, music and lyrics: Micki Grant; (D) Lewis Whitlock, III; (S) Michael Burden; (C) Jennifer Anderson; (L) Mike Wangen
Playboy of the West Indies, Mustapha Matura; (D) Horace Bond; (S) Kenneth F. Evans; (C) Terry Antonich; (L) Mike Wangen
Black Nativity, Langston Hughes; (D) Lewis Whitlock, III and Rev. Carl Lewis; (S) James P. Taylor; (C) Deidrea Whitlock; (L) Mike Wangen
Pill Hill, Samuel L. Kelley; (D) Terry Bellamy; (S) Kenneth F. Evans; (C) Terry Antonich; (L) Mike Wangen
Spell #7, Ntozake Shange; (D) Beverly Smith-Dawson; (S) Kenneth F. Evans; (C) Terry Antonich; (L) Mike Wangen
Joe Turner's Come and Gone, August Wilson; (D) Claude Purdy; (S) W.J.E. Hammer; (C) Ainslie G. Bruneau; (L) Mike Wangen

The People's Light and Theatre Company

DANNY S. FRUCHTER
Producing Director

GREGORY T. ROWE
General Manager

39 Conestoga Road
Malvern, PA 19355-1798
(215) 647-1900 (bus.)
(215) 644-3500 (b.o.)

FOUNDED 1974
Ken Marini, Richard L. Keeler, Danny S. Fruchter, Margaret E. Fruchter

SEASON
Variable

FACILITIES
Main Stage
Seating Capacity: 325-400
Stage: flexible

Steinbright Stage
Seating Capacity: 160-220
Stage: flexible

FINANCES
Feb. 1, 1990-Jan. 31, 1991
Expenses: $1,918,183

CONTRACTS
AEA LORT (D)

At People's Light we present work unique to our resident ensemble through a multiyear phased development process. Phased development relies on actors, directors, designers and writers to conceive, train, rehearse, reconsider and revise over sufficient time to bring our best ideas to the stage, rather than our first ideas. We have planned our promotion and marketing strategies, our educational outreach program and our management structures to follow the lead of our artistic programming rather than to drive it. In 1990 the artistic company spent 60 percent of its 44-week season developing and training for work to be presented in future seasons. Concentration on major large-scale work, and extraordinary dedication to outreach and diversity, describe our artistic commitment. We are committed to serving our art so completely that we feel we can do it properly only by dedicating a serious chunk of our lives to it—it takes years of working together to make social art. And that vision is defining our immediate future.

—*Danny S. Fruchter*

PRODUCTIONS 1990

The Last Good Moment of Lily Baker, Russell Davis; (D) Abigail Adams; (S) James F. Pyne, Jr.; (C) P. Chelsea Harriman; (L) James F. Pyne, Jr.
The Devil and All His Works, Ernest Joselovitz; (D) Michael Nash; (S) James F. Pyne, Jr.; (C) P. Chelsea Harriman; (L) James F. Pyne, Jr. and Deborah Peretz
Our Town, Thornton Wilder; (D) Danny S. Fruchter; (S) James F. Pyne, Jr.; (C) coord: Shirley Horwith; (L) James F. Pyne, Jr. and Deborah Peretz
Jazz Is...Too, book: Miche Braden and Harold McKinney; various composers and lyricists; (D) Deborah Teller; (L) James F. Pyne, Jr. and Deborah Peretz
Billy Bishop Goes to War, John Gray and Eric Peterson; (D) Louis Rackoff; (S) Richard L. Smith; (C) Tony French; (L) William Savage
As You Like It, William Shakespeare; music: Adam Grant and Daniel Olmstead; (D) Aaron Posner; (S) Tina Krovetz; (C) Jilline Ringle; (L) Whitney Quesenbery

The People's Light and Theatre Company. Tom Teti and Elizabeth Meeker in *Sister Carrie*. Photo: Gerry Goodstein.

PRODUCTIONS 1991

Sister Carrie, adapt: Lou Lippa, from Theodore Dreiser; (D) Ken Marini; (S) James F. Pyne, Jr.; (C) Lindsay W. Davis; (L) James Leitner

Achilles, A Kabuki Play, Karen Sunde; (D) Shozo Sato; (S) Shozo Sato; (C) Shozo Sato; (L) James F. Pyne, Jr.

A Christmas Carol, adapt: Peter DeLaurier, from Charles Dickens; (D) Peter DeLaurier; (S) James F. Pyne, Jr.

Banjo Dancing, Stephen Wade; (D) Milton Kramer

Short Stuff Festival:

Private Wars, James McLure; (D) Abigail Adams

Russian Strip, Drury Pifer; (D) Peter DeLaurier

American Welcome, Brian Friel; (D) Ceal Phelan

Rupert's Birthday, Ken Jenkins; (D) Danny S. Fruchter

What Leona Figured Out, David J. Hill; (D) Tom Teti

From the Ashes, Robert Smythe and Mum Puppettheatre

Anton, Himself and Masha Too, Karen Sunde; (D) Abigail Adams

A Boy, a Dog, & a Dinosaur! and ***Earth For Sale***, Mum Puppettheatre and Stone Soup

The Old Lady Shows Her Medals, James M. Barrie; (D) Tom Teti

Chinamen, Michael Frayn; (D) Mark Abram

A Betrothal, Lanford Wilson; (D) Stephen Novelli

One for the Road, Harold Pinter; (D) Peter DeLaurier

Minnesota, George Sand; (D) Paul Meshejian

Trifles, Susan Glaspell; (D) Paul Meshejian

Periwinkle National Theatre for Young Audiences

SUNNA RASCH
Executive Director

KATHY SHARPE
Business Manager

19 Clinton Ave.
Monticello, NY 12701
(914) 794-1666

FOUNDED 1963
Sunna Rasch

SEASON
Jan.-Dec. touring

FINANCES
Aug. 1, 1990-July 31, 1991
Expenses: $460,000

The premise—and promise—of Periwinkle National Theatre is to develop theatre programs that have relevance for young people while exposing them to theatre on a high artistic level. Each theatre production is developed for a specific audience, ranging from college and high school audiences to audiences at each of the public school levels, from middle school to primary grades. The bond that unites all productions is the underlying theme of feelings, which is in keeping with the Periwinkle credo: *Before you can unlock a mind, you have to first open a heart.* Periwinkle's productions can stand alone as theatre, but they go further, because we believe that theatre is a vital educational tool as well. Thus, Periwinkle is dedicated to pursuing the arts in education through dynamic programs that tour schools throughout the United States as well as abroad. Our productions stimulate thinking and motivate creative expression. All programs are developed with an eye to having audience members always leave the theatre auditorium a little different from the way they were when they walked in.

—*Sunna Rasch*

PRODUCTIONS 1989-90

Halfway There, company-developed; (D) Michael Dacunto; (S) Michael Daughtry; (C) Megan Hartley; (L) Craig Kennedy

The Frog Prince, book adapt, music and lyrics: Scott Laughead, from The Brothers Grimm; (D) Scott Laughead; (S) Michael Daughtry; (C) Megan Hartley

The Fabulous Dream of Andrew H. Lupone, book, music and lyrics: Scott Laughead; (D) Scott Laughead; (S) Michael Daughtry; (C) Megan Hartley

PRODUCTIONS 1990-91

Halfway There, company-developed; (D) Michael Dacunto and Chris Briante; (S) Michael Daughtry; (C) Megan Hartley; (L) Jim Ghisalbert and Tom Kline

The Magic Word, book: Sunna Rasch; music and lyrics: Scott Laughead; (D) Scott Laughead; (S) Michael Daughtry; (C) David Zyla

The Mad Poet Strikes—Again!, Sunna Rasch; (D) Scott Laughead; (S) David Zyla; (C) David Zyla

Hooray For Me!, book: Scott Laughead; music and lyrics: Grenoldo Frazier; (D) Scott Laughead; (S) Michael Daughtry; (C) Megan Hartley

Periwinkle National Theatre for Young Audiences. Don Close, Jocelyn Benford, Jack Cavan, Donna Lyn Carfi and Tyrone Fermin in *Halfway There*.

Perseverance Theatre

MOLLY D. SMITH
Artistic Director

LYNETTE A. TURNER
Producing Director

914 Third St.
Douglas, AK 99824
(907) 364-2151 (bus.)
(907) 364-2421 (b.o.)

FOUNDED 1979
Molly D. Smith, Kay Smith, Joe Ross, Bill C. Ray, Susie Fowler, Jack Cannon, Kate Bowns

SEASON
Jan.-Dec.

FACILITIES
Mainstage
Seating Capacity: 150
Stage: flexible

Phoenix Stage
Seating Capacity: 50
Stage: flexible

Voices Stage
Seating Capacity: 175
Stage: flexible

FINANCES
July 1, 1990-June 30, 1991
Expenses: $975,740

Perservance Theatre is located in Juneau, the capital of Alaska, a community of 28,000 that is inaccessible by road. Alaska's rich cultural heritage and its environmental and social background contribute profoundly to the artistic direction and scope of Perservance Theatre. The complex personality of the state encompasses many kinds of people: winners and losers, people out to get rich quick, Aleuts, Tlingits, Filipinos, Eskimos, whites, oil tycoons and environmentalists looking for the "last frontier." Our major artistic goal is to wrestle with this spirit, this uniquely Alaskan experience and, using a company of multitalented artists with differing performance traditions from around the state, develop a voice for it. We produce a full season of classical and contemporary theatre on our main stage (including at least one new play by an Alaskan playwright) as well as productions on our Phoenix and Voices stages. We also tour the state and offer extensive training programs.

—*Molly D. Smith*

PRODUCTIONS 1989-90

The Odyssey, Bill C. Ray, Dennis Remick and Nancy Schaufelberger, with Dave Hunsaker and Ken Melville, from Homer; (D) Molly D. Smith; (S) Pavel Dobrusky, with various assistants

Pieces of Eight, book and lyrics: Dave Hunsaker; music: Dave Hunsaker and T.D. Eckles; (D) Betsy Scott; (S) Dan DeRoux; (C) Marta Ann Lastufka; (L) P. Dudley Riggs

The Snow Queen, adapt: Darrah Cloud, from Hans Christian Andersen; (D) Molly D. Smith; (S) Bill Hudson; (C) Marta Ann Lastufka; (L) Jim Sale

Born Yesterday, Garson Kanin; (D) Steve Pearson; (S) Duke Russell; (C) Marilyn Wright; (L) P. Dudley Riggs

Signs of Life, Debbie Baley; (D) Christopher Hanna; (S) Dan DeRoux; (C) Barbara Casement; (L) Arthur Rotch

Moo, Sally Clark; (D) Annabel Lund; (S) Jane Terzis; (C) Nadine Siminelli; (L) Pat Gorman

On the Verge, Eric Overmyer; (D) Tim Wilson; (S) Moe Schwartz; (C) Vikki Benner; (L) Marvin Borgmier

The Lady Lou Revue, book adapt and lyrics: Gordon Duffey, from Robert Service; music: Alan Chapman; (D) Kate Bowns; (S) Arthur Rotch; (C) Barbara Casement; (L) Arthur Rotch

PRODUCTIONS 1990-91

Wonderland, company-developed, from Lewis Carroll; (D) Molly D. Smith; (S) Pavel Dobrusky; (C) Pavel Dobrusky; (L) Pavel Dobrusky

An Enemy of the People, Henrik Ibsen; (D) Ronald J. Himes; (S) Dan DeRoux; (C) Marilyn Wright; (L) Vikki Benner

Democracy, John Murrell; (D) Molly D. Smith; (S) Arthur Rotch; (C) Marta Ann Lastufka; (L) Arthur Rotch

Hay Fever, Noel Coward; (D) Patricia Van Kirk; (S) Dan DeRoux; (C) Barbara Casement; (L) P. Dudley Riggs

Judevine, David Budbill; (D) Tim Wilson; (S) Renate Hampke; (C) Vikki Benner; (L) Arthur Rotch

The Baltimore Waltz, Paula Vogel; (D) Annie Stokes-Hutchinson; (S) Bill Hudson; (C) Barbara Casement and Kari Minnick; (L) John E. Miller

In Two Worlds, Earl Atchak; (D) Kate Bowns and Jamieson McLean; (S) Bill Hudson and Clarissa Hudson; (C) Bill Hudson and Clarissa Hudson; (L) Arthur Rotch

The Lady Lou Revue, book adapt and lyrics: Gordon Duffey, from Robert Service; music: Alan Chapman; (D) Mike Peterson; (S) Arthur Rotch; (C) Barbara Casement; (L) John E. Miller

Perseverance Theatre. Jim Stowell and Peter T. Ruocco in *Democracy*. Photo: Mark Daughhetee.

Philadelphia Drama Guild. Walter Jones, Seret Scott and Lou Ferguson in *Boesman and Lena*. Photo: Ken Kauffman.

Philadelphia Drama Guild

MARY B. ROBINSON
Artistic Director

DANIEL L. SCHAY
Managing Director

Robert Morris Bldg.
100 North 17th St.
Philadelphia, PA 19103
(215) 563-7530 (bus.)
(215) 563-6791 (b.o.)

FOUNDED 1956
Sidney S. Bloom

SEASON
Oct.-May

FACILITIES
Zellerbach Theatre
Seating Capacity: 944
Stage: thrust

FINANCES
June 1, 1990-May 31, 1991
Expenses: $2,500,500

CONTRACTS
AEA LORT (B+)

The Philadelphia Drama Guild is dedicated to creating an environment that recognizes the worth of each individual artist, and to gradually building a core group of diverse theatre artists who will work with us in developing projects for the future. We are also committed to intensifying and deepening our relationship with our audience, and to actively seeking out new, more diverse and younger audiences. The ultimate aim of all theatre is connection, but when the connection is too easily made it does not have much lasting impact. I believe in a theatre that opens us to new worlds, that connects us tangibly to the past, to people in cultures other than our own, to new ideas and new forms of communication.

—*Mary B. Robinson*

Note: During the 1989-90 season, Gregory Poggi served as producing director.

PRODUCTIONS 1989-90

Clouds, Michael Frayn; (D) Charles Karchmer; (S) Rosario Provenza; (C) Deborah Shaw; (L) Jeff Davis

The Glass Menagerie, Tennessee Williams; (D) Allen R. Belknap; (S) David Potts; (C) Mimi Maxmen; (L) Dennis Parichy

The Importance of Being Earnest, Oscar Wilde; (D) Gavin Cameron-Webb; (S) Harry Feiner; (C) Gail Brassard; (L) James Leitner

Fences, August Wilson; (D) Edmund J. Cambridge; (S) Daniel Boylen; (C) Frankie Fehr; (L) William H. Grant, III

A Walk in the Woods, Lee Blessing; (D) Alex Dmitriev; (S) Charles McCarry; (C) Holly Hynes; (L) Jerold Forsyth

PRODUCTIONS 1990-91

Boesman and Lena, Athol Fugard; (D) Mary B. Robinson; (S) Charles McClennahan; (C) Suzanne Jackson; (L) Dennis Parichy

Mrs. Warren's Profession, George Bernard Shaw; (D) Gloria Muzio; (S) David Jenkins; (C) Jess Goldstein; (L) Jackie Manassee

A Normal Life, Erik Brogger; (D) Mary B. Robinson; (S) Kent Dorsey; (C) Mimi Maxmen; (L) Kent Dorsey

A Midsummer Night's Dream, William Shakespeare; (D) Mary B. Robinson; (S) Allen Moyer; (C) Michael Krass; (L) Dennis Parichy

Tales of the Lost Formicans, Constance Congdon; (D) Greg Leaming; (S) Robert Odorisio; (C) Michael Krass; (L) Ken Tabachnick

Philadelphia Festival Theatre for New Plays

CAROL ROCAMORA
Artistic/Producing Director

THEA R. LAMMERS
Managing Director

3900 Chestnut St.
Philadelphia, PA 19104-3105
(215) 222-5000 (bus.)
(215) 898-6791 (b.o.)

FOUNDED 1981
Carol Rocamora

SEASON
Oct.-June

FACILITIES
Harold Prince Theatre
Seating Capacity: 211-233
Stage: flexible

FINANCES
July 1, 1990-June 30, 1991
Expenses: $883,275

CONTRACTS
AEA LORT (D)

The Philadelphia Festival Theatre for New Plays is one of the few independent, nonprofit professional theatres in the country dedicated exclusively to the production of new plays by American playwrights. The theatre's mission is twofold: to foster a commitment to new play development and production for the local and national theatre audience, and to make a lasting contribution to American dramatic literature by discovering new plays by established and new writers. In its first 10 years the theatre has produced 70 world premieres from more than 12,000 script submissions. Three-quarters of these premieres have gone on to additional productions or publication. Playwrights' residencies, Curtain Call discussions for playwrights, directors, actors and audiences, new play development seminars, and the Play-Offs reading series are among the programs offered by PFT.

—Carol Rocamora

PRODUCTIONS 1989-90

Squirrels, David Mamet; (D) W.H. Macy; (S) James Wolk; (C) Pamela Scofield; (L) Curt Senie

The Belmont Avenue Social Club, Bruce Graham; (D) James J. Christy; (S) James Wolk; (C) Vickie Esposito; (L) Curt Senie

The Inuit, Bill Bozzone; (D) Rob Barron; (S) Philip Graneto; (C) Vickie Esposito; (L) Curt Senie

Sins of the Father, Chaim Potok; (D) Carol Rocamora; (S) Philip Graneto; (C) Vickie Esposito; (L) Curt Senie

PRODUCTIONS 1990-91

The Three Sisters, Anton Chekhov; adapt: David Mamet; trans: Vlada Chernomordik; (D) W.H. Macy; (S) James Wolk; (C) Laura Cunningham; (L) Howard Werner

Top of the World, Bruce Graham; (D) James Christy; (S) James Wolk; (C) Vickie Esposito; (L) Curt Senie

Moonshadow, Richard Hellesen; (D) Carol Rocamora; (S) James Wolk; (C) Vickie Esposito; (L) Curt Senie

The Wizards of Quiz, Steve Feffer; (D) William Partlan; (S) Philip Graneto; (C) Vickie Esposito; (L) Curt Senie

Philadelphia Festival Theatre for New Plays. Stephen Mailer, Josh Reid Gordon in *Moonshadow*. Photo: Stan Sadowski.

The Philadelphia Theatre Company

SARA GARONZIK
Producing Artistic Director

ADA COPPOCK
General Manager

21 South 5th St.
The Bourse Building, Suite 550
Philadelphia, PA 19106
(215) 592-8333

FOUNDED 1974
Robert Headley, Jean Harrison

SEASON
Oct.-June

FACILITIES
Plays and Players Theater
Seating Capacity: 324
Stage: proscenium

TUCC Stage III
Seating Capacity: 100
Stage: proscenium

FINANCES
Sept. 1, 1990-Aug. 31, 1991
Expenses: $600,000

CONTRACTS
AEA letter of agreement

The Philadelphia Theatre Company retains a strong commitment to celebrating the vision and variety of the American playwright, producing the emerging as well as the established contemporary voice. This mission permits not only world and regional premieres but the "second look" so critical for writers whose work has had a previous viewing. Superior acting and clear, inventive directing are our aesthetic cornerstones, and we create an enlightened and supportive environment where actors and directors can achieve their best work. Our mission also permits the achievement of great visual and thematic diversity, although we are clearly an urban theatre with a strong social and humanitarian conscience. Since 1986, our Stages program has grown into a full-time laboratory where playwrights and their collaborators can thoroughly explore developing work away from deadline pressure. From Stages has sprung the Mentor Project, which pairs nationally recognized master writers with their younger counterparts. It was our recent privilege to have playwright Arthur Kopit as our first "mentor."

—Sara Garonzik

PRODUCTIONS 1989-90

The Middle of Nowhere, book: Tracy Friedman; music and lyrics: Randy Newman; (D) Tracy Friedman; (S) Loren Sherman; (C) Vickie Esposito; (L) James Leitner

Tea, Velina Hasu Houston; (D) Julianne Boyd; (S) Daniel Boylen; (C) C.L. Hundley; (L) Victor En Yu Tan

Stages New Play Festival 1990:
The Line That Picked Up 1000 Babes, Eric Berlin; (D) Lynn M.

The Philadelphia Theatre Company. *Pill Hill*. Photo: Mark Garvin.

Thomson
Observatory Conditions, Kate Snodgrass; (D) Lynn M. Thomson
Deep Under, Doug Grissom; (D) Lynn M. Thomson

PRODUCTIONS 1990-91

Speed-the-Plow, David Mamet; (D) Lynn M. Thomson; (S) James Sandefur; (C) Vickie Esposito; (L) James Leitner
The Cocktail Hour, A.R. Gurney, Jr.; (D) Christopher Ashley; (S) Paul Wonsek; (C) Candice Donnelly; (L) James Leitner
Pill Hill, Samuel L. Kelley; (D) Oz Scott; (S) Paul Wonsek; (C) Judy Dearing; (L) James Leitner

Stages New Play Festival 1991:
The Old Lady's Guide to Survival, Mayo Simon; (D) Lynn M. Thomson
Driving Lessons, Jason Katims; (D) Lynn M. Thomson
Julie Johnson, Wendy Hammond; (D) Lynn M. Thomson

Ping Chong and Company

PING CHONG
Artistic Director

BRUCE ALLARDICE
Managing Director

47 Great Jones St.
New York, NY 10012
(212) 529-1557

FOUNDED 1975
Ping Chong

SEASON
Variable

FINANCES
July 1, 1990-June 30, 1991
Expenses: $265,500

Ping Chong and Company was founded to explore the meaning of "contemporary theatre" on a national and international level. Our mission is to question the syntax of the American theatre and to enrich it with an Asian sensibility. To survive, the theatre must reconcile its primal purpose, that is, as a forum for poetry and metaphysical exploration, with technical and perceptual changes brought on by the communications revolution. In recent years, the company has expanded the range of its works to include video and visual arts installations in an effort to develop expressive works of art for contemporary multicultural audiences.

—Ping Chong

PRODUCTIONS 1989-90

Angels of Swedenborg, Ping Chong; (D) Ping Chong and John Fleming; (S) Ping Chong; (C) Mel Carpenter; (L) Tina Charney and Michael Chybowski
Brightness, Ping Chong and Louise Smith; (D) Ping Chong; (S) Ping Chong and Matthew Yokobosky; (C) Matthew Yokobosky; (L) Howard Thies
Kind Ness, Ping Chong and company; (D) Ping Chong; (S) Ping Chong; (C) Mel Carpenter; (L) Howard Thies
4 AM America, Ping Chong and company; (D) Ping Chong; (S) Ping Chong and Pat Doty; (C) Dawna Gregory; (L) Thomas C. Hase
Deshima, Ping Chong; (D) Ping Chong; (S) Ping Chong; (C) Adrienne Henriet; (L) Johan Vonk

PRODUCTIONS 1990-91

Elephant Memories, Ping Chong and company; (D) Ping Chong; (S) Ping Chong and Matthew Yokobosky; (C) Matthew Yokobosky; (L) Thomas C. Hase
4 AM America, Ping Chong and company; (D) Ping Chong; (S) Ping Chong and Pat Doty; (C) Dawna Gregory; (L) Thomas C. Hase
Nosferatu, Ping Chong and company; (D) Ping Chong; (S) Ping Chong and Miguel Lopez-Castillo; (C) Carol Ann Pelletier; (L) Howard Thies
Kind Ness, Ping Chong and company; (D) Ping Chong; (S) Ping Chong; (C) Mel Carpenter; (L) Howard Thies

Pioneer Theatre Company

CHARLES MOREY
Artistic Director

CHRISTOPHER LINO
Managing Director

Pioneer Memorial Theatre
University of Utah
Salt Lake City, UT 84112
(801) 581-6356 (bus.)
(801) 581-6961 (b.o.)

FOUNDED 1962
C. Lowell Lees, University of Utah, local citizens

SEASON
Sept.-May

FACILITIES
Lees Main Stage
Seating Capacity: 1,000
Stage: proscenium

FINANCES
July 1, 1990-June 30, 1991
Expenses: $2,000,000

CONTRACTS
AEA LORT (B) and U/RTA

The Pioneer Theatre Company is the resident professional theatre of the University of Utah. PTC has the largest subscription audience of

Ping Chong and Company. Louise Smith and Roger Babb in *Nosferatu*. Photo: Carol Rosegg.

Pioneer Theatre Company. Warren Kelley, Samuel Maupin, Richard Mathews and Anne Stewart Mark in *A Penny for a Song*. Photo: Robert Clayton.

any arts organization in Utah and draws theatregoers from four western states. The company's mission is twofold: first, to provide the community with an ongoing resident theatre of the highest professional standards; and, second, to serve as an educational and cultural resource to the university community and a training ground for aspiring professionals. Central to this dual purpose is the assumption that the educational mission cannot be fulfilled without first satisfying the primary concern for artistic excellence. As befits PTC's position as the largest professional theatre in the region and a division of a major research university, the company produces a broad and eclectic repertoire focused upon the classics of world literature augmented by contemporary work of distinction.

—*Charles Morey*

PRODUCTIONS 1989-90

West Side Story, book: Arthur Laurents; music: Leonard Bernstein; lyrics: Stephen Sondheim; (D) Paul Lazarus; (S) George Maxwell; (C) K.L. Alberts; (L) Peter L. Willardson

The Three Musketeers, adapt: Charles Morey, from Alexandre Dumas pere; (D) Charles Morey; (S) Ariel Ballif; (C) David C. Paulin; (L) Peter L. Willardson

Blithe Spirit, Noel Coward; (D) Charles Morey; (S) Peter Harrison; (C) Linda Sarver; (L) Karl E. Haas

Broadway Bound, Neil Simon; (D) Tom Markus; (S) Eric Fielding; (C) K.L. Alberts; (L) Karl E. Haas

The Comedy of Errors, William Shakespeare; (D) Charles Morey; (S) George Maxwell; (C) Elizabeth Novak; (L) Peter L. Willardson

Saint Joan, George Bernard Shaw; (D) Allen R. Belknap; (S) Peter Harrison; (C) David C. Paulin; (L) Richard Winkler

Big River, book adapt: William Hauptman, from Mark Twain; music and lyrics: Roger Miller; (D) Charles Morey; (S) Ariel Ballif; (C) Linda Sarver; (L) Peter L. Willardson

PRODUCTIONS 1990-91

Ain't Misbehavin', conceived: Murray Horwitz and Richard Maltby, Jr.; music and lyrics: Fats Waller, et al; (D) Patti D'Beck; (S) George Maxwell; (C) David C. Paulin; (L) Peter L. Willardson

Dracula, adapt: Charles Morey, from Bram Stoker; (D) Charles Morey; (S) Peter Harrison; (C) David C. Paulin; (L) Peter L. Willardson

The Miser, Moliere; trans: Miles Malleson; (D) Tom Markus; (S) Ariel Ballif; (C) Linda Sarver; (L) Ann G. Wrightson

A Penny for a Song, John Whiting; (D) Charles Morey; (S) George Maxwell; (C) K.L. Alberts; (L) Kendall Smith

Driving Miss Daisy, Alfred Uhry; (D) Dan Bonnell; (S) Ariel Ballif; (C) Linda Sarver; (L) Peter L. Willardson

Peer Gynt, Henrik Ibsen; trans: William Archer; (D) Charles Morey; (S) George Maxwell; (C) David C. Paulin; (L) Richard Winkler

Sunday in the Park with George, book: James Lapine; music and lyrics: Stephen Sondheim; (D) Allen R. Belknap; (S) Allen R. Belknap; (C) David C. Paulin; (L) Peter L. Willardson

Pittsburgh Public Theater

WILLIAM T. GARDNER
Producing Director

DAN FALLON
Managing Director

Allegheny Square
Pittsburgh, PA 15212-5349
(412) 323-8200 (bus.)
(412) 321-9800 (b.o.)

FOUNDED 1975
Joan Apt, Margaret Rieck, Ben Shaktman

SEASON
Sept.-July

FACILITIES
Seating Capacity: 452
Stage: flexible

FINANCES
Sept. 1, 1990-Aug. 31, 1991
Expenses: $3,963,432

CONTRACTS
AEA LORT (B)

The Pittsburgh Public Theater aims to present the finest plays in the American and world repertoire to the widest possible audience in a city noted for its cultural diversity. The 1989-90 and 1990-91 seasons represent the Public's increasing commitment to developing new audiences and new works. Highlights from these seasons include the local presentation of Pittsburgh native August Wilson's *Joe Turner's Come and Gone* with Roscoe Lee Browne, and the premieres of the musical *Eleanor* by Jonathan Bolt, Thomas Tierney and John Forster, the Kesselring Prize-winning comedy *The Lay of the Land* by Mel Shapiro and the powerful family drama *A Sunbeam* by John Henry Redwood. The Public's outreach programs include performances for student, senior-citizen and handicapped constituencies; professional internships; programs in schools; and a developing professional affiliation with a number of local educational institutions.

—*William T. Gardner*

PRODUCTIONS 1989-90

Joe Turner's Come and Gone, August Wilson; (D) Claude Purdy; (S) James Sandefur; (C) Mary Mease Warren; (L) Phil Monat

George Washington Slept Here, George S. Kaufman and Moss Hart; (D) Kip Niven; (S) Ray Recht; (C) Martha Hally; (L) Jackie Manassee

Reckless, Craig Lucas; (D) Maureen Heffernan; (S) Ray Recht; (C) Michael J. Cesario; (L) Phil Monat

Les Liaisons Dangereuses, Christopher Hampton, from Choderlos de Laclos; (D) Robin

Pittsburgh Public Theater. Mary Alice and Paul Bates in *A Sunbeam*. Photo: Ric Evans.

Phillips; (S) Cletus Anderson; (C) David Murin; (L) Louise Guinand

Burn This, Lanford Wilson; (D) Lee Sankowich; (S) Anne Mundell; (C) Martha Hally; (L) Phil Monat

Eleanor, book: Jonathan Bolt; music: Thomas Tierney; lyrics: John Forster; (D) Mel Shapiro; (S) Karl Eigsti; (C) Laura Crow; (L) Roger Morgan

PRODUCTIONS 1990-91

The Night of the Iguana, Tennessee Williams; (D) Claude Purdy; (S) James Sandefur; (C) Martha Hally; (L) Phil Monat

Our Town, Thornton Wilder; (D) Robert Allan Ackerman; (S) David Sackeroff; (C) Robert Wojewodski; (L) Brian MacDevitt

Speed-the-Plow, David Mamet; (D) Mel Shapiro; (S) Karl Eigsti; (C) Karl Eigsti; (L) Andrew David Ostrowski

My Children! My Africa!, Athol Fugard; (D) Peter Bennett; (S) Gary English; (C) Jeffrey Ullman; (L) Brian MacDevitt

The Lay of the Land, Mel Shapiro; (D) Lee Grant; (S) Karl Eigsti; (C) Laura Crow; (L) Dennis Parichy

A Sunbeam, John Henry Redwood; (D) Claude Purdy; (S) James Sandefur; (C) Felix E. Cochren; (L) Phil Monat

Players Theatre Columbus

ED GRACZYK
Artistic Director

ROBERT W. TOLAN
Managing Director

Box 18185
Columbus, OH 43218-0185
(614) 644-5300 (bus.)
(614) 644-8425 (b.o.)

FOUNDED 1923
Agnes Jeffrey Shedd

SEASON
Oct.-May

FACILITIES
Capitol Theatre
Seating Capacity: 750
Stage: flexible

Studio I
Seating Capacity: 250
Stage: flexible

Studio II
Seating Capacity: 100
Stage: flexible

FINANCES
July 1, 1990-June 30, 1991
Expenses: $2,545,000

CONTRACTS
AEA LORT (D), SPT and letter of agreement

The mission of Players Theatre Columbus is to create a true regional theatre for adult and young audiences alike that examines the nature of the human experience and its implications for contemporary life. The theatre's artistic vision places a strong emphasis on the creation and development of accessible new work that reflects the concerns, conflicts and values of the people of the region. Modern American and European classics augment this commitment to new work, ensuring our audiences of diverse exposure to the finest dramatic literature in all its forms. Being designated the managing tenant for the three-theatre complex in the Vern Riffe Center for Government and the Arts has enabled Players Theatre Columbus to continue its phenomenal growth and extend its reach to the people of central Ohio and beyond.

—Ed Graczyk

PRODUCTIONS 1989-90

Fences, August Wilson; (D) L. Kenneth Richardson; (S) James Sandefur; (C) Lauren K. Lambie; (L) Danianne Mizzy

The Merry Wives of Windsor, Texas, book adapt: John L. Haber, from William Shakespeare; music and lyrics: Jack Herrick, Tommy Thompson, Bland Simpson, Jim Wann and John Foley; (D) Edward Stern; (S) Kevin Rupnik; (C) Candice Donnelly; (L) Robert Wierzel

A Country Christmas Carol, book adapt: Ed Graczyk, from Charles Dickens; music: David Tolley; lyrics: Ed Graczyk, Steven C. Anderson and David Tolley; (D) Ed Graczyk; (S) Anne Mundell; (C) Ruth Boyd; (L) Mary Louise Geiger

Players Theatre Columbus. Allyn Burrows, Michelle Horman, Wynn Harmon and Larry Hansen in *The Nerd*. Photo: Greg Sailor.

The Foreigner, Larry Shue; (D) Martin L. Platt; (S) Lowell Detweiler; (C) Lauren K. Lambie; (L) Karen Spahn

Precious Memories, Romulus Linney, from Anton Chekhov; (D) Edward Morgan; (S) Bill Clarke; (C) Lauren K. Lambie; (L) Robert Wierzel

Beehive, Larry Gallagher; (D) David Holdgrive; (S) Nancy Thun; (C) Bill Clarke; (L) Tom Sturge

Woman in Mind, Alan Ayckbourn; (D) Mark Brokaw; (S) Bill Clarke; (C) Lauren K. Lambie; (L) Mary Louise Geiger

PRODUCTIONS 1990-91

The Mousetrap, Agatha Christie; (D) Edward Morgan; (S) Bill Clarke; (C) Lauren K. Lambie; (L) Robert Wierzel

Driving Miss Daisy, Alfred Uhry; (D) Luke Yankee; (S) Joseph Varga; (C) Lauren K. Lambie; (L) Brackley Frayer

A Country Christmas Carol, book adapt: Ed Graczyk, from Charles Dickens; music: David Tolley; lyrics: John Dempsey; (D) Ed Graczyk; (S) Ed Graczyk; (C) Ruth Boyd; (L) Betsy Adams

Shakin' the Mess Outta Misery, Shay Youngblood; (D) Glenda Dickerson; (S) Felix E. Cochran; (C) Felix E. Cochran; (L) Mary Louise Geiger

The Nerd, Larry Shue; (D) Maureen Heffernan; (S) Gary Eckhart; (C) Lauren K. Lambie; (L) Peter M. Reader

Dames at Sea, book and lyrics: George Haimsohn and Robin Miller; music: Jim Wise; (D) Randy Skinner; (S) Bill Clarke; (L) Betsy Adams

Playhouse on the Square

JACKIE NICHOLS
Executive Producer

ELIZABETH HOWARD
Administrative Director

51 South Cooper St.
Memphis, TN 38104
(901) 725-0776 (bus.)
(901) 726-4498 (b.o.)

FOUNDED 1968
Jackie Nichols

SEASON
Jan.-Dec.

FACILITIES
Playhouse on the Square
Seating Capacity: 260
Stage: proscenium

Circuit Playhouse
Seating Capacity: 140
Stage: proscenium

FINANCES
July 1, 1989-June 30, 1990
Expenses: $625,987

Playhouse on the Square, the only professional company in the Memphis/Mid-South area, serves a broad constituency in a diverse ethnic and cultural community approaching one million people. We produce a varied season and are committed to providing long-term employment to a core acting company and artistic staff. The resident company concept therefore requires us to seek out versatile individuals to support the seasons selected, individuals who are committed to ensemble growth. This philosophy provides artists the opportunity to work and expand their skills with productions for which they may not normally be considered. The manageable size of our organization and our dedication to our principles help us maintain our goals in a society that embraces specialization and lack of personal long-term commitment. We also have well-established and highly effective theatre for youth and outreach programs dedicated to the audience of the future.

—*Jackie Nichols*

PRODUCTIONS 1989-90

Anything Goes, book: Guy Bolton, P.G. Wodehouse, Howard Lindsay and Russel Crouse; music and lyrics: Cole Porter; (D) Ken Zimmerman; (S) Michael Dempsey and Gail Wood; (C) Elizabeth Garat; (L) John Rankin

The Boys Next Door, Tom Griffin; (D) Ken Zimmerman; (S) John Rankin; (C) Elizabeth Garat; (L) John Rankin

West Memphis Mojo, Martin Jones; (D) Sharon Reives; (S) Kim Potter; (C) Elizabeth Garat; (L) Chuck Britt

Annie, book: Thomas Meehan; music: Charles Strouse; lyrics: Martin Charnin; (D) Ken Zimmerman; (S) Michael Dempsey; (C) Elizabeth Garat and Elizabeth Wheat; (L) John Rankin

Working, adapt: Stephen Schwartz and Nina Faso, from Studs Terkel; various composers and lyricists; (D) Lois Mytas; (S) Kathy Haaga; (C) Elizabeth Garat; (L) John Rankin

The Lion, the Witch and the Wardrobe, book adapt: Jules Tasca, from C.S. Lewis; music: Thomas Tierney; lyrics: Ted Drachman; (D) Jay Kinney; (S) Jackie Nichols; (C) Elizabeth Garat and Elizabeth Wheat; (L) John Rankin

To Serve and Protect, William Stackhouse; (D) Ken Zimmerman; (S) Chuck Britt; (L) Chuck Britt

Twelfth Night, William Shakespeare; (D) Kate Davis; (S) John Rankin; (C) Elizabeth Garat; (L) John Rankin

A Flea in Her Ear, Georges Feydeau; trans: Barnett Shaw; (D) Ken Zimmerman; (S) Chuck Britt; (C) Elizabeth Garat; (L) John Rankin

Charlotte's Web, adapt: Joseph Robinette, from E.B. White; (D) Jay Kinney; (S) John Rankin; (C) Elizabeth Garat; (L) Chuck Britt

Burn This, Lanford Wilson; (D) Jerry Chipman; (S) Steve Pair; (C) Angela Seymour; (L) Chuck Britt

Jacques Brel Is Alive and Well and Living in Paris, book: Eric Blau and Mort Shuman; music and lyrics: Jacques Brel; (D) Sidney Lynch; (S) Mike Hayes and Billy Riley; (L) Steve Forsyth

Tuesday/Wednesday, Larry Gray; (D) Buck Clark; (S) Michael Schagger; (C) Elizabeth Wheat; (L) David Wilk

Nunsense, book, music and lyrics: Dan Goggin; (D) Ken Zimmerman; (S) Michael Nichols; (C) Elizabeth Wheat; (L) John Rankin

Playhouse on the Square. Gabrielle Mason, Wally Dressen, Colleen Sudduth, Michael Detroit and Curtis Jackson in *Working*. Photo: Saul Brown.

PRODUCTIONS 1990-91

Damn Yankees, book: George Abbott and Douglas Wallop; music: Jerry Ross; lyrics: Richard Adler; (D) Ken Zimmerman; (S) Kathy Haaga; (C) Brenda Seawright; (L) John Rankin

Driving Miss Daisy, Alfred Uhry; (D) Ken Zimmerman; (S) Lois Mytas; (C) Elizabeth Wheat; (L) John Rankin

Eleemosynary, Lee Blessing; (D) Brian Mott; (S) Brentley Elzey and L.D. Beghtol; (L) Steve Forsyth

Sherlock's Last Case, Charles Marowitz; (D) Cecelia Pickle; (S) Chuck Britt; (C) Elizabeth Wheat; (L) Chuck Britt

Annie, book: Thomas Meehan; music: Charles Strouse; lyrics: Martin Charnin; (D) Ken Zimmerman; (S) Michael Dempsey; (C) Elizabeth Garat and Elizabeth Wheat; (L) John Rankin

The Lion, the Witch and the Wardrobe, book adapt: Jules Tasca, from C.S. Lewis; music: Thomas Tierney; lyrics: Ted Drachman; (D) Jay Kinney; (S) Jackie Nichols; (C) Elizabeth Garat and Elizabeth Wheat; (L) John Rankin

La Ronde, Arthur Schnitzler; adapt: John Barton; trans: Sue Davies; (D) Tom Prewitt; (S) Brentley Elzey and L.D. Beghtol; (C) Elizabeth Wheat; (L) Steve Forsyth

Our Town, Thornton Wilder; (D) Ken Zimmerman; (S) John Rankin; (C) Elizabeth Wheat; (L) John Rankin

Greater Tuna, Jaston Williams, Joe Sears and Ed Howard; (D) Ken Zimmerman; (S) Chuck Britt; (C) Elizabeth Wheat; (L) John Rankin

Two Rooms, Lee Blessing; (D) Sidney Lynch; (S) Michael Walker; (L) Steve Forsyth

Privates on Parade, book and lyrics: Peter Nichols; music: Denis King; (D) John Tolley; (S) Chuck Britt; (C) L.D. Beghtol; (L) David Wilk

Eastern Standard, Richard Greenberg; (D) Scott Maitland; (S) Chuck Britt; (C) Donna Blackard; (L) Chuck Britt

The Rocky Horror Show, book, lyrics and music: Richard O'Brien; (D) Ken McCullough; (S) Mary Kay LeFaber; (C) Elizabeth Garat; (L) John Rankin

The Rear Column, Simon Gray; (D) Buck Clark; (S) Terry Twyman; (C) Pat Bogan; (L) Chuck Britt

PlayMakers Repertory Company

DAVID HAMMOND
Artistic Director

MILLY S. BARRANGER
Executive Producer

REGINA LICKTEIG
Managing Director

CB# 3235 Graham Memorial Bldg. 052A
Chapel Hill, NC 27599-3235
(919) 962-1122 (bus.)
(919) 962-PLAY (b.o.)

FOUNDED 1976
Arthur L. Housman

SEASON
Sept.-May

FACILITIES
Paul Green Theatre
Seating Capacity: 499
Stage: thrust

PlayMakers Theatre
Seating Capacity: 285
Stage: proscenium

FINANCES
July 1, 1990-June 30, 1991
Expenses: $1,100,012

CONTRACTS
AEA LORT (D)

PlayMakers Repertory Company. Tobias Andersen and Pilar Herrera in *Nothing Sacred*. Photo: Kevin Keister.

PlayMakers Repertory Company is dedicated to the actor as the center of the performance event. We are committed to the revelation of each play through the varying processes used by the actor in meeting the demands of the text, rather than through scenographic metaphors or directorially imposed thematic statements. Our repertoire is eclectic, and we hope that audiences are unable to anticipate our production "style" from play to play. We aspire to bring classic and standard works the sense of excitement and discovery too often reserved only for new scripts, and we approach new texts with the discipline, skill and theatrical perceptions of a classically trained company. The interaction of our professional company with students in our training program is a vital aspect of our work: Our students carry the results of our efforts to other stages throughout the country.

—David Hammond

PRODUCTIONS 1989-90

The Cherry Orchard, Anton Chekhov; trans: Jean-Claude van Itallie; (D) David Hammond; (S) Bill Clarke; (C) Bill Clarke; (L) Robert Wierzel

Old Times, Harold Pinter; (D) Kathryn Long; (S) McKay Coble; (C) Jeff Fender; (L) Mary Louise Geiger

The Nutcracker: A Play, adapt: David Hammond, from E.T.A. Hoffmann; (D) David Hammond; (S) Bill Clarke; (C) McKay Coble; (L) Marcus Dilliard

Love's Labour's Lost, William Shakespeare; (D) Charles Newell; (S) Anita Stewart; (C) Anita Stewart; (L) Marcus Dilliard

True West, Sam Shepard; (D) Martin L. Platt; (S) Russell Parkman; (C) Anita Stewart; (L) Robert Wierzel

The Rivals, Richard Brinsley Sheridan; (D) David Hammond; (S) McKay Coble; (C) Anita Stewart; (L) Marcus Dilliard

PRODUCTIONS 1990-91

You Never Can Tell, George Bernard Shaw; (D) David Hammond; (S) Bill Clarke; (C) Bill Clarke; (L) Mary Louise Geiger

Nothing Sacred, George F. Walker; (D) Eugene Lesser; (S) Russell Parkman; (C) McKay Coble; (L) Marcus Dilliard

The Nutcracker: A Play, adapt: David Hammond, from E.T.A. Hoffmann; (D) David Hammond; (S) Bill Clarke; (C) McKay Coble; (L) Marcus Dilliard

The Miser, Moliere; trans: Sara O'Connor; (D) William Woodman; (S) Anita Stewart; (C) Mary Louise Geiger; (L) Anita Stewart

Scenes from American Life, A. R. Gurney, Jr.; (D) Bill Gile; (S) McKay Coble; (C) McKay Coble; (L) Ashley York Kennedy

Pericles, William Shakespeare; (D) David Hammond; (S) Bill Clarke; (C) Bill Clarke; (L) Robert Wierzel

The Playwrights' Center

DAVID MOORE, JR.
Executive Director

BETH SCHOEPPLER
Managing Director

2301 Franklin Ave. E
Minneapolis, MN 55406
(612) 332-7481

FOUNDED 1971
Gregg Almquist, Erik Brogger, Thomas G. Dunn, Barbara Field, Jon Jackoway, John Olive

SEASON
Jan.-Dec.

FACILITIES
Playwrights' Center
Seating Capacity: 175
Stage: flexible

Rarig Center (Playlabs)
Seating Capacity: 300
Stage: thrust

FINANCES
July 1, 1990-June 30, 1991
Expenses: $473,867

CONTRACTS
AEA letter of agreement

The Playwrights' Center fuels the contemporary theatre, providing services that support the development and public appreciation of playwrights and playwriting. Year-round programs, suited to the diversity of crafts and values, and designed to accelerate artistic growth at all stages of the playwright's career, deliver professional assistance to hundreds of dramatists working in Minnesota and across the country. These programs include a Playwrights Lab that funds and administers public readings, nonperformance workshops, special projects and collaborations with visiting artists; the award of $115,000 each year to 18 American and Minnesota playwrights in Jerome and McKnight Fellowships, Advancement Grants, Jones Commissions and stipends; a Playlabs summer conference; a national, tiered playwright membership program offering information and related services; a Young Playwrights Lab and Summer Conference; quarterly classes; Playwright-in-the-School Residencies; and Playworks touring performances to underserved communities across this state.

—David Moore, Jr.

PRODUCTIONS 1990

Wait, There's More, Eric Anderson; (D) John D. Richardson

Girl Bar, Phyllis Nagy; (D) Christine Sumption

Fireline, Mark Rosenwinkel; (D) Claude Purdy

Young Richard, Charles Smith; (D) Clinton Turner Davis

PRODUCTIONS 1991

Dream of a Common Language, Heather McDonald; (D) Kent Stephens

Show and Tell, Anthony Clarvoe; (D) William Partlan

Motorcade, Bill Corbett; (D) Kent Stephens

Shelter, Caridad Svich; (D) William Partlan

On the Bum, Neal Bell; (D) Amy Gonzalez

Playwrights Horizons. *Once on This Island*. Photo: Martha Swope.

Playwrights Horizons

DON SCARDINO
Artistic Director

PAUL S. DANIELS
Executive Director

416 West 42nd St.
New York, NY 10036
(212) 564-1235 (bus.)
(212) 279-4200 (b.o.)

FOUNDED 1971
Robert Moss

SEASON
Variable

FACILITIES
Mainstage
Seating Capacity: 145
Stage: proscenium

Studio Theatre
Seating Capacity: 72
Stage: flexible

FINANCES
Sept. 1, 1989-Aug. 31, 1990
Expenses: $4,733,661

CONTRACTS
AEA Off Broadway

Playwrights Horizons is dedicated to the support and development of contemporary American playwrights, composers and lyricists and to the production of their work.
—*Don Scardino*

Note: During the 1989-90 and 1990-91 seasons, Andre Bishop served as artistic director.

PRODUCTIONS 1989-90

Hyde in Hollywood, Peter Parnell; (D) Gerald Gutierrez; (S) Douglas Stein; (C) Ann Hould-Ward; (L) Frances Aronson

When She Danced, Martin Sherman; (D) Tim Luscombe; (S) Steven Rubin; (C) Jess Goldstein; (L) Nancy Schertler

Once on This Island, book and lyrics: Lynn Ahrens; music: Stephen Flaherty; (D) Graciela Daniele; (S) Loy Arcenas; (C) Judy Dearing; (L) Allen Lee Hughes

Falsettoland, book: William Finn and James Lapine; music and lyrics: William Finn; (D) James Lapine; (S) Douglas Stein; (C) Franne Lee; (L) Nancy Schertler

Subfertile, Tom Mardirosian; (D) John Ferraro; (S) Rick Dennis; (C) Abigail Murray; (L) Brian MacDevitt

Miriam's Flowers, Migdalia Cruz; (D) Roberta Levitow; (S) Tom Kamm; (C) Mary Myers; (L) Kenneth Posner

PRODUCTIONS 1990-91

Subfertile, Tom Mardirosian; (D) John Ferraro; (S) Rick Dennis; (C) Abigail Murray; (L) Brian MacDevitt

Assassins, book: John Weidman; music and lyrics: Stephen Sondheim; (D) Jerry Zaks; (S) Loren Sherman; (C) William Ivey Long; (L) Paul Gallo

The Substance of Fire, Jon Robin Baitz; (D) Daniel Sullivan; (S) John Lee Beatty; (C) Jess Goldstein; (L) Arden Fingerhut

The Old Boy, A.R. Gurney, Jr.; (D) John Rubinstein; (S) Nancy Winters; (C) Jane Greenwood; (L) Nancy Schertler

Portland Repertory Theater

GEOFFREY SHERMAN
Artistic Director

NANCY D. WELCH
Executive Director

Two World Trade Center
25 Southwest Salmon St.
Portland, OR 97204-3233
(503) 224-4491

FOUNDED 1980
Mark Allen, Nancy D. Welch

SEASON
Oct.-June

FACILITIES
World Trade Center
Seating Capacity: 230
Stage: proscenium

FINANCES
Sept. 1, 1990-Aug. 31, 1991
Expenses: $860,000

CONTRACTS
AEA SPT

The Portland Repertory Theater is the oldest professional theatre company in the city. We are committed to the presentation of the finest and most innovative of both American and international drama and are presently engaged in a thorough examination of our artistic policy in order to expand the nature and quantity of our work. To achieve this goal we intend to increase the level of compensation for all artists involved with the theatre; to establish a second performance space of considerable flexibility to facilitate the production of new work by both emerging and established playwrights; to vigorously encourage new actors, directors and designers; and to promote exchanges of work with other companies—locally, nationally and internationally. In reflecting the complexity of our existence, theatre can be a wondrous celebration of humanity. From the first words produced by the playwright to each and every performance, we believe there should be evolution—continual flux and movement brought about by

Portland Repertory Theater. *A Shayna Maidel*. Photo: Owen Carey.

the presence of an ever-changing group of people we call our audience.

—Geoffrey Sherman

Note: During the 1989-90 season, Brenda Hubbard served as artistic director. During the 1990-91 season, Mark Allen served as interim artistic director.

PRODUCTIONS 1989-90

A Walk in the Woods, Lee Blessing; (D) Nikki Appino; (S) Lawrence Larsen; (C) Susan Bonde; (L) Meg Fox

Bus Stop, William Inge; (D) Brenda Hubbard; (S) Lawrence Larsen; (C) Susan Bonde; (L) Roberta Russell

Blithe Spirit, Noel Coward; (D) Cynthia White; (S) John Gerth; (C) Susan Bonde; (L) Patty Mathieu

Les Liaisons Dangereuses, Christopher Hampton, from Choderlos de Laclos; (D) Brenda Hubbard; (S) Karen Gjelsteen; (C) Susan Bonde; (L) Rogue Conn

A Shayna Maidel, Barbara Lebow; (D) Penny Metropulos; (S) Joel Fontaine; (C) Susan Bonde; (L) Lawrence Larsen

What the Butler Saw, Joe Orton; (D) Brenda Hubbard; (S) John Gerth; (C) Susan Bonde; (L) Roberta Russell

PRODUCTIONS 1990-91

Hard Times, adapt: Stephen Jeffreys, from Charles Dickens; (D) Pat Patton; (S) Norm Spenser; (C) Gene Davis Buck; (L) Blake Gage

The Cocktail Hour, A.R. Gurney, Jr.; (D) Penny Metropulos; (S) Lawrence Larsen; (C) Terri Lewis; (L) Roberta Russell

Driving Miss Daisy, Alfred Uhry; (D) Clayton Corzatte; (S) Roberta Russell; (C) Debra Bruneaux; (L) Lawrence Larsen

The Boys Next Door, Tom Griffin; (D) Brenda Hubbard; (S) John Gerth; (C) Terri Lewis; (L) Lawrence Larsen

Other People's Money, Jerry Sterner; (D) Brenda Hubbard; (S) Jim Weisman; (C) Terri Lewis; (L) Gary Cotter

Shirley Valentine, Willy Russell; (D) Jeff Lee; (S) Jim Weisman; (C) Terri Lewis; (L) Lawrence Larsen

Portland Stage Company

RICHARD HAMBURGER
Artistic Director

CAROLINE TURNER
Managing Director

Box 1458
Portland, ME 04104
(207) 774-1043 (bus.)
(207) 774-0465 (b.o.)

FOUNDED 1974
Ted Davis

SEASON
Oct.-Apr.

FACILITIES
Portland Performing Arts Center
Seating Capacity: 290
Stage: proscenium

FINANCES
June 1, 1990-May 31, 1991
Expenses: $1,137,650

CONTRACTS
AEA LORT (D)

Our common purpose at Portland Stage Company is to nurture the imaginative worlds of gifted writers, actors, directors, designers and composers. Hand in hand with this dedication to artistic growth and experimentation is our desire that Portland Stage serve as a vital center in the community: a place where people of diverse backgrounds and ages come together to learn not only from the plays but from each other. Portland Stage is committed to reaching out both to the artists who are working to bring a play to living expression and to the audience, without whom that expression is bankrupt. Our mainstage season forms the spiritual spine of the theatre. We search for plays, both classic and contemporary, that use language and imagery to examine human anxiety, aspiration and behavior from fresh, startling and often humorous perspectives. Believing that theatre can be a catalyst for psychological and social change, we surround each production with a constellation of programs designed to provoke questions and to place the play in social, political and literary contexts: humanities lectures, discussions and essays, student matinees and the annual A Little Festival of the Unexpected.

—Richard Hamburger

Portland Stage Company. Geraldine Librandi in *Wolf at the Door*. Photo: David A. Rodgers.

PRODUCTIONS 1989-90

Joe Egg, Peter Nichols; (D) Pamela Berlin; (S) Michael Ganio; (C) Deborah Shaw; (L) David Noling

Accidental Death of an Anarchist, Dario Fo; adapt: Richard Nelson; (D) William Foeller; (S) Ray Kluga; (C) Claudia Brown; (L) Christopher Akerlind

Sizwe Bansi Is Dead and ***The Island***, Athol Fugard, John Kani and Winston Ntshona; (D) Liz Diamond; (S) Anita Stewart; (C) Sally J. Lesser; (L) Pat Dignan

Twelfth Night, William Shakespeare; (D) Richard Hamburger; (S) Christopher Barecca; (C) Claudia Brown; (L) Karl E. Haas

Driving Miss Daisy, Alfred Uhry; (D) Paul Moser; (S) Derek McLane; (C) Connie Singer; (L) David Noling

Little Egypt, Lynn Siefert; (D) Richard Hamburger; (S) Russell Parkman; (C) Candice Donnelly; (L) Stuart Duke

Terminal Hip, Mac Wellman; (D) Mac Wellman

A Play of Not and Now, adapt: Cheryl Faver, from Gertrude Stein; (D) Cheryl Faver

1000 Avant-Garde Plays, Kenneth Koch; (D) Kenneth Koch

PRODUCTIONS 1990-91

Loot, Joe Orton; (D) Steve Stettler; (S) Michael Ganio; (C) Martha Hally; (L) Stuart Duke

A Man's a Man, Bertolt Brecht; trans: Gerhard Nellhaus; (D) Liz Diamond; (S) Bill Stabile and Richard Cordtz; (C) Sally J. Lesser; (L) Beverly Emmons

Miss Julie, August Strindberg; trans: Harry G. Carlson; (D) Richard Hamburger; (S) Anita Stewart; (C) Martha Hally; (L) Christopher Akerlind

Lady Day at Emerson's Bar and Grill, Lanie Robertson; (D) Victoria Bussert; (S) Russ Borski; (C) Susan Brown; (L) Mary Jo Dondlinger

Mirandolina, Carlo Goldoni; adapt: Melissa Cooper; (D) Evan Yionoulis; (S) James Youmans; (C) Teresa Snider-Stein; (L) Donald Holder

Wolf at the Door, Erik Ehn; (D) Richard Hamburger; (S) Christopher Barecca; (C) Susan Brown; (L) Christopher Akerlind

Remains Theatre

LARRY SLOAN
Artistic Director

R. P. SEKON
Producing Director

1800 North Clybourn
Chicago, IL 60614
(312) 335-9595 (bus.)
(312) 335-9800 (b.o.)

FOUNDED 1979
Jim Roach, Earl Pastko, David Alan Novak, D. W. Moffett, Lindsay McGee

SEASON
Variable

FACILITIES
Remains Theatre
Seating Capacity: 250
Stage: thrust

FINANCES
July 1, 1990-June 30, 1991
Expenses: $924,679

CONTRACTS
AEA CAT

Some things you should know about Remains Theatre: 1) We're an ensemble of 10-odd actors and a staff, all die-hard Bulls fans except for one Celtic fan who has learned to be quiet about it. 2) After 11 years without a theatre of our own, we moved into a mall in the summer of 1990. We have 250 seats and a bar next to a lingerie shop and a miniature golf course. 3) Stars come and see our plays and we leave them alone. 4) When we moved into our little mall we reduced our ticket prices substantially to make the theatre accessible to as wide an audience as possible. We produce a season of eclectic works without subscriptions, plus many concerts, late-night shows and other special events. 5) Fourteen of our productions have been world or American premieres. (Can you name six of them?) 6) "In a dark time, the eye begins to see." —Theodore Roethke. 7) Come and see our work when you're in Chicago.

—Larry Sloan

Note: During the 1989-90 season, Amy Morton and William L. Petersen served as artistic directors.

PRODUCTIONS 1989-90

Our Country's Good, Timberlake Wertenbaker, from Thomas Keneally; (D) Amy Morton; (S) Jeff Bauer; (C) Laura Cunningham; (L) Rita Pietraszek

PRODUCTIONS 1990-91

The Making of Ashenden, adapt: Larry Sloan, from Stanley Elkin; (D) Larry Sloan; (S) Steve Pickering; (C) Frances Maggio; (L) Kevin Snow

Jack, David Greenspan; (D) Mary Zimmerman; (S) Steve Pickering; (C) Frances Maggio; (L) Kevin Snow

Rameau's Nephew, adapt: Andrei Belgrader and Shelley Berc, from Denis Diderot; (D) Neel Keller; (S) Steve Pickering; (C) Frances Maggio; (L) Kevin Snow

The Plucky and Spunky Show, Susan Nussbaum and Mike Ervin; (D) Jeff Michalski; (S) David Csiscko; (C) Frances Maggio; (L) Kevin Snow

American Buffalo, David Mamet; (D) Mike Nussbaum; (S) Kevin Snow; (C) Laura Cunningham; (L) Kevin Snow

Remains Theatre. Amy Morton, Glenda Starr Kelley and Martha Lavey in *Jack*. Photo: Steve Leonard.

Repertorio Español

RENE BUCH
Artistic Director

GILBERTO ZALDIVAR
Producer

138 East 27th St.
New York, NY 10016
(212) 889-2850

FOUNDED 1968
Gilberto Zaldivar, Rene Buch

SEASON
Jan.-Dec.

FACILITIES
Gramercy Arts Theatre
Seating Capacity: 140
Stage: proscenium

Equitable Tower Auditorium
Seating Capacity: 485
Stage: proscenium

FINANCES
Sept. 1, 1989-Aug. 31, 1990
Expenses: $1,400,000

The Repertorio Español has three components, all acclaimed for their artistic achievements and their service to the Hispanic community in the U.S. The dramatic ensemble is a true repertory company presenting more than 12 productions a year, from the classics of Spain's Golden Age to the great 20th-century plays of Latin America and Spain, and new plays by emerging Hispanic-American playwrights. The musical company, since 1981, has introduced zarzuelas and Spanish operettas, as well as anthologies of music from Mexico, Puerto Rico, Spain and Cuba. Dance is represented by Pilar Rioja, the Spanish dancer, who has been an invited artist since 1973. Besides giving year-round performances at the historic Gramercy Arts Theatre, the company performs at the Equitable Tower and on tour throughout the U.S. Its services for students are acclaimed as some of the most effective by the New York City Cultural Affairs commissioner. Recent highlights include the inauguration of an infrared simulcast system offering audiences English translations, and a series of productions directed by three of Latin America's most respected and innovative directors.

—Rene Buch

PRODUCTIONS 1989-90

El Huesped, Pedro Juan Soto; (D) Beatriz Cordoba; (S) Robert Weber Federico; (C) Robert Weber Federico; (L) Robert Weber Federico

El Eterno Femenino, Rosario Castellanos; (D) Beatriz Cordoba; (S) Robert Weber Federico; (C) Robert Weber Federico; (L) Robert Weber Federico

Nelson 2 Rodrigues: Family Album and ***All Nudity Will Be Punished***, Nelson Rodrigues; adapt: Antunes Filho; trans: Antunes Filho; (D) Antunes Filho; (S) J.C. Serroni; (C) J.C. Serroni; (L) J.C. Serroni

La Casa de Bernarda Alba, Federico Garcia Lorca; (D) Rene Buch; (S) Robert Weber Federico; (C) Robert Weber Federico; (L) Robert Weber Federico

La Nonna, Roberto M. Cossa; (D) Braulio Villar; (S) Robert Weber Federico; (C) Robert Weber Federico; (L) Robert Weber Federico

Padre Gomez y Santa Cecilia, Gloria Gonzalez; (D) Rene Buch; (S) Robert Weber Federico; (C) Robert Weber Federico; (L) Robert Weber Federico

Revoltillo, Eduardo Machado; (D) Rene Buch; (S) Robert Weber Federico; (C) Robert Weber Federico; (L) Robert Weber Federico

Don Juan Tenorio, Jose Zorrilla; (D) Rene Buch; (S) Robert Weber Federico; (C) Robert Weber Federico; (L) Robert Weber Federico

El Burlador de Sevilla, Tirso de Molina; (D) Rene Buch; (S) Robert Weber Federico; (C) Robert Weber Federico; (L) Robert Weber Federico

Cafe Con Leche, Gloria Gonzalez; (D) Rene Buch; (S) Robert Weber Federico; (C) Robert Weber Federico; (L) Robert Weber Federico

Los Jibaros Progresistas, book and lyrics: Ramon Mendez Quinones; music: Manuel B. Gonzalez; (D) Rene Buch; (S) Robert Weber Federico; (C) Robert Weber Federico; (L) Robert Weber Federico

La Viuda Alegre, book, music and lyrics: Franz Lehar; trans: Rene Buch; (D) Rene Buch; (S) Robert Weber Federico; (C) Robert Weber Federico; (L) Robert Weber Federico

Mexico Romantico, various composers; (D) Rene Buch; (S) Robert Weber Federico; (C) Robert Weber Federico; (L) Robert Weber Federico

La Generala Alegre, book and lyrics: Perrin & Palacios; music: Amadeo Vives; (D) Rene Buch; (S) Robert Weber Federico; (C) Robert Weber Federico; (L) Robert Weber Federico

Repertorio Español. Gregorio Rangel and Brenda Feliciano in *El Consul*. Photo: Gerry Goodstein.

Puerto Rico: Encanto y Cancion, various composers; (D) Rene Buch; (S) Robert Weber Federico; (C) Robert Weber Federico; (L) Robert Weber Federico

Habana: Antologia Musical, various composers; (D) Rene Buch; (S) Robert Weber Federico; (C) Robert Weber Federico; (L) Robert Weber Federico

PRODUCTIONS 1990-91

Botanica, Dolores Prida; (D) Manuel Martin; (S) Randy Barcelo; (C) Robert Weber Federico; (L) Robert Weber Federico

Cafe Con Leche, Gloria Gonzalez; (D) Rene Buch; (S) Robert Weber Federico; (C) Robert Weber Federico; (L) Robert Weber Federico

El Abanderado, Luis Alberto Heiremans; (D) Guillermo Semler; (S) Jose Luis Plaza; (C) Jose Luis Plaza; (L) Guillermo Semler

El Alcalde de Zalamea, Pedro Calderon de la Barca; (D) Rene Buch; (S) Robert Weber Federico; (C) Robert Weber Federico; (L) Robert Weber Federico

El Eterno Femenino, Rosario Castellanos; (D) Beatriz Cordoba; (S) Robert Weber Federico; (C) Robert Weber Federico; (L) Robert Weber Federico

El Huesped, Pedro Juan Soto; (D) Beatriz Cordoba; (S) Robert Weber Federico; (C) Robert Weber Federico; (L) Robert Weber Federico

Esperando la Carroza, Jacobo Langser; (D) Braulio Villar; (S) Robert Weber Federico; (C) Robert Weber Federico; (L) Robert Weber Federico

La Casa de Bernarda Alba, Federico Garcia Lorca; (D) Rene Buch; (S) Robert Weber Federico; (C) Robert Weber Federico; (L) Robert Weber Federico

La Nonna, Roberto M. Cossa; (D) Braulio Villar; (S) Robert Weber Federico; (C) Robert Weber Federico; (L) Robert Weber Federico

El Beso de la Mujer Arana, Manuel Puig; (D) Beatriz Cordoba; (S) Robert Weber Federico; (C) Robert Weber Federico; (L) Robert Weber Federico

Habana: Antologia Musical, various composers; (D) Rene Buch; (S) Robert Weber Federico; (C) Robert Weber Federico; (L) Robert Weber Federico

Mexico Romantico, various composers; (D) Rene Buch; (S) Robert Weber Federico; (C) Robert Weber Federico; (L) Robert Weber Federico

Puerto Rico: Encanto y Cancion, various composers; (D) Rene Buch; (S) Robert Weber Federico; (C) Robert Weber Federico; (L) Robert Weber Federico

La Viuda Alegre, book, music and lyrics: Franz Lehar; trans: Rene Buch; (D) Rene Buch; (S) Robert Weber Federico; (C) Robert Weber Federico; (L) Robert Weber Federico

Los Jibaros Progresistas, book and lyrics: Ramon Mendez Quinones; music: Manuel B. Gonzalez; (D) Rene Buch; (S) Robert Weber Federico; (C) Robert Weber Federico; (L) Robert Weber Federico

El Consul, book, music and lyrics: Gian Carlo Menotti; trans: Pablo Zinger; (D) Rene Buch; (S) Robert Weber Federico; (C) Robert Weber Federico; (L) Robert Weber Federico

The Repertory Theatre of St. Louis

STEVEN WOOLF
Artistic Director

MARK D. BERNSTEIN
Managing Director

Box 191730
St. Louis, MO 63119
(314) 968-7340 (bus.)
(314) 968-4925 (b.o.)

FOUNDED 1966
Webster College

SEASON
Sept.-Apr.

FACILITIES
Mainstage
Seating Capacity: 733
Stage: thrust

Studio
Seating Capacity: 125
Stage: flexible

Lab Space
Seating Capacity: 75
Stage: flexible

FINANCES
June 1, 1990-May 31, 1991
Expenses: $3,648,000

CONTRACTS
AEA LORT (C1) and (D), and TYA

The Repertory Theatre of St. Louis. Keith Jochim in *Henry IV, Part 1*. Photo: Judy Andrews.

Celebrating 25 seasons of partnership with community, audiences, artists, technicians and administrators, the Repertory Theatre of St. Louis has become an integral part of the artistic life of its region. An eclectic mix of styles creates a widely varied season: mainstage selections offer work from many sources, giving a wide view of theatre literature to our largest audience; our Studio Theatre explores the new, the old seen in new ways, poetry, music and sometimes season-long themes; the Imaginary Theatre Company, our touring component, plays throughout Missouri and surrounding states, using literature and specially comissioned scripts as its basis for introducing theatre to younger audiences; the Lab series focuses on playwrights, giving them a full rehearsal period and a professional cast and director to work on a new script. Through these activities and others, the Rep seeks to develop audiences who become strong advocates for live performance.

—*Steven Woolf*

PRODUCTIONS 1989-90

The Merry Wives of Windsor, Texas, book adapt: John L. Haber, from William Shakespeare; music and lyrics: Jack Herrick, Tommy Thompson, Bland Simpson, Jim Wann and John Foley; (D) Edward Stern; (S) Kevin Rupnik; (C) Candice Donnelly; (L) Peter E. Sargent

A Walk in the Woods, Lee Blessing; (D) Timothy Near; (S) Joel Fontaine; (C) Holly Poe Durbin; (L) Peter Maradudin

The Matchmaker, Thornton Wilder; (D) Susan Gregg; (S) Anne Gibson; (C) Dorothy L. Marshall; (L) Max De Volder

Precious Memories, Romulus Linney, from Anton Chekhov; (D) John Dillon; (S) Carolyn Leslie Ross; (C) John Carver Sullivan; (L) Allen Lee Hughes

Fences, August Wilson; (D) Harold Scott; (S) Peter Harrison; (C) Celia Bryant; (L) Max De Volder

Hay Fever, Noel Coward; (D) Donald Ewer; (S) John Ezell; (C) Dorothy L. Marshall; (L) Peter E. Sargent

Tomfoolery, conceived: Cameron Mackintosh and Robin Ray; music and lyrics: Tom Lehrer; (D) Pamela Hunt; (S) John Roslevich, Jr.; (C) Dorothy L. Marshall; (L) Max De Volder

Dog Logic, Tom Strelich; (D) Steven Woolf; (S) Jim Burwinkel; (C) Elizabeth Eisloeffel; (L) Mark Wilson

Rain. Some Fish. No Elephants., Y York; (D) James Abar; (S) Richard Tollkuhn; (C) John Carver Sullivan; (L) Glenn Dunn

Hansel and Gretel, adapt: Susie Bradley, from The Brothers Grimm; (D) Jeffery Matthews; (S) Kim Wilson; (C) Norma West

A Holiday Garland of Tales, Kim Allen Bozark, Susan May Greenberg, Tim Hendrixson and Sandra Vago; (D) Jeffery Matthews; (S) Kim Wilson; (C) Norma West

Scene of the Crime, Jeffery Matthews; (D) Jeffery Matthews; (S) Kim Wilson; (C) Norma West

The Last Song of John Proffit, Tommy Thompson; (D) Susan Gregg

The Education of Paul Bunyan, Barbara Field; (D) Susan Gregg

PRODUCTIONS 1990-91

Our Country's Good, Timberlake Wertenbaker, from Thomas Keneally; (D) Edward Stern; (S) Andrew Jackness; (C) Candice Donnelly; (L) Peter Kaczorowski

The Heidi Chronicles, Wendy Wasserstein; (D) Jim O'Connor; (S) Michael S. Philippi; (C) Dorothy L. Marshall; (L) Peter E. Sargent

A Day in Hollywood/A Night in the Ukraine, book and lyrics: Dick Vosburgh; music: Frank Lazarus; (D) Pamela Hunt; (S) John Roslevich, Jr.; (C) Dorothy L. Marshall; (L) Peter E. Sargent

Terra Nova, Ted Tally; (D) Steven Woolf; (S) Carolyn Leslie Ross; (C) John Carver Sullivan; (L) Max De Volder

Henry IV, Part 1, William Shakespeare; (D) Martin L. Platt; (S) John Ezell; (C) Alan Armstrong; (L) Peter Maradudin

Driving Miss Daisy, Alfred Uhry; (S) Susan Gregg; (S) Joel Fontaine; (C) Holly Poe Durbin; (L) Max De Volder

The Last Song of John Proffit, Tommy Thompson; (D) Susan Gregg; (S) Dale F. Jordan; (C) Carole Tucker; (L) Dale F. Jordan

From the Mississippi Delta, Dr. Endesha Ida Mae Holland; (D) Edward G. Smith; (S) Jim Burwinkel; (C) Arthur Ridley; (C) Glenn Dunn

Daytrips, Jo Carson; (D) Tom Martin; (S) William F. Schmiel; (C) Elizabeth Eisloeffel; (L) Joseph W. Clapper

Alice in Wonderland, adapt: Susie Bradley, from Lewis Carroll; (D) Jeffery Matthews; (S) Nicholas Kryah; (C) J. Bruce Summers

A Holiday Garland of Tales, adapt: Kim Allen Bozark; (D) Tom Martin; (S) Kathy Lewis; (C) Norma West

A Thousand Cranes, Kathryn Schultz Miller; (D) Jeffery Matthews; (S) Nicholas Kryah; (C) Holly Poe Durbin

An American Tune, Stephen Burns Kessler; (D) Susan Gregg

River Arts Repertory

LAWRENCE SACHAROW
Artistic Director

ALBERT IHDE
Producing Director

Box 1166
Woodstock, NY 12498
(914) 679-5899 (bus.)
(914) 679-2100 (b.o.)

FOUNDED 1979
Lawrence Sacharow, Mrs. Lawrence Webster

SEASON
May-Dec.

FACILITIES
Bearsville Theatre
Seating Capacity: 230
Stage: proscenium

Bearsville Studio Theatre
Seating Capacity: 80
Stage: flexible

FINANCES
Apr. 1, 1990-Mar. 31, 1991
Expenses: $450,000

CONTRACTS
AEA SPT

The mission of River Arts is to foster new play development, present innovative productions of the classics and build a community of artists committed to exploring the universality of the human spirit. Completing its 12th season, River Arts is more than a theatre: It is a multidimensional organization that also sponsors an outreach program touring a play about substance abuse; a film institute providing ongoing workshops in screenwriting, acting and directing; and an international writers program. The international program brings together artists for collaborative work that celebrates unique cultural, political and spiritual sources while searching out our common humanity. In 1989 River Arts presented a Jewish-Palestinian Festival of performances, workshops and seminars, and in 1990 a Soviet

River Arts Repertory. Susan Greenhill and Stephen McHattie in *Velvet Elvis*. Photo: Marianne Courville.

Theatre Festival. We have premiered or developed new works by Alan Bolt, Constance Congdon, Michael Cristofer, Janusz Glowacki, Irene Fornes, Len Jenkin, Richard Nelson, Anton Shammas, Joshua Sobol, Eric Overmyer, Jean-Claude van Itallie, Derek Walcott and Mac Wellman.

—Lawrence Sacharow

PRODUCTIONS 1990

The Lady and the Clarinet, Michael Cristofer; (D) Liz Diamond; (S) Tom Kamm; (C) Marianne Powell-Parker; (L) Michael Chybowski

Velvet Elvis, Matthew Carnahan; (D) Joanne Woodward; (S) Andrew Jackness; (C) Marianne Powell-Parker; (L) Michael Chybowski

Viva Detroit, Derek Walcott; (D) Lawrence Sacharow; (S) Tom Kamm; (C) Marianne Powell-Parker; (L) Michael Chybowski

Jazzman, Vitali Pavlov; trans: Ulla Backlund; (D) Vitali Pavlov; (L) Peter Waldron

PRODUCTIONS 1991

Marry Me a Little , conceived: Craig Lucas and Norman Rene; music and lyrics: Stephen Sondheim; (D) Wesley Fata; (S) Joe Ferris; (C) Arionne Medici; (L) Peter Waldron

A Mom's Life, Kathryn Grody; (S) Kathryn Grody; (C) Kathryn Grody; (L) Peter Waldron

Talley's Folly, Lanford Wilson; (D) Lawrence Sacharow; (S) James Noone; (C) Arionne Medici; (L) Peter Waldron

Ghosts, Henrik Ibsen; adapt: Michael Cristofer; (D) Michael Cristofer; (S) James Noone; (C) Arionne Medici; (L) Peter Waldron

Riverside Theatre

ALLEN D. CORNELL
Artistic Director

IDA SPADA
Business Manager

Box 3788
Vero Beach, FL 32963
(407) 231-5860 (bus.)
(407) 231-6990 (b.o.)

FOUNDED 1985
Vero Beach Community Theatre Trust

SEASON
Oct.-May

FACILITIES
Riverside Theatre
Seating Capacity: 633
Stage: proscenium

FINANCES
June 1, 1990-May 31, 1991
Expenses: $822,927

CONTRACTS
AEA letter of agreement

Our theatre exists because its community has been involved since day one of its existence. We are a reflection of this unique Floridian place, this time, this society. Our artists are very much like the professional guides who venture forth on the river here to expose the uninitiated to the profundity of ultramarine shadows along mangrove-lined shores. They are the navigators who bridge the inlet between the art of nature and the nature of art. Our place is called the Treasure Coast. Gold escudos are found on these shores. We believe theatre, too, is like a prodigious strongbox and that we as artists hold the key to the bounty within. The programs we produce are an eclectic mixture of the past and present. They are designed to reaffirm the commitment of the initiated and enlist the uninitiated. We are fortunate to live and work in an extraordinarily beautiful place. Our theatre is a celebration of this good fortune.

—Allen D. Cornell

PRODUCTIONS 1989-90

I Do! I Do!, book and lyrics: Tom Jones; music: Harvey Schmidt; (D) Katrina Ploof; (S) Allen D. Cornell; (C) Chris Carpenter; (L) Allen D. Cornell

I'm Not Rappaport, Herb Gardner; (D) Mary G. Guaraldi; (S) Allen D. Cornell; (C) Tonya Hively; (L) Allen D. Cornell

Some Enchanted Evening, music and lyrics: Richard Rodgers and Oscar Hammerstein, II; (D) Brian Spitler; (S) Allen D. Cornell; (C) Tonya Hively; (L) Allen D. Cornell

The 1940's Radio Hour, book: Walton Jones; various composers and lyricists; (D) Michael Kint; (S) Allen D. Cornell; (C) Tonya Hively; (L) Allen D. Cornell

Fallen Angels, Noel Coward; (D) Allen D. Cornell; (S) Allen D. Cornell; (C) Chris Carpenter; (L) Allen D. Cornell

Nunsense, book, music and lyrics: Dan Goggin; (D) Steven Smeltzer; (S) Allen D. Cornell; (C) Chris Carpenter; (L) Allen D. Cornell

Riverside Theatre. David Staller and Sherry Skinker in *Angel Street*. Photo: Egan Rassmusson.

PRODUCTIONS 1990-91

Angel Street, Patrick Hamilton; (D) Peter Bennett; (S) Allen D. Cornell; (C) Chris Carpenter; (L) Allen D. Cornell

Steel Magnolias, Robert Harling; (D) Michael Kint; (S) Jeffrey Dean; (C) Chris Carpenter; (L) Allen D. Cornell

Driving Miss Daisy, Alfred Uhry; (D) Peter Bennett; (S) Jeffrey Dean; (C) Chris Carpenter; (L) John Wilson

Guys and Dolls, book adapt: Jo Swerling and Abe Burrows, from Damon Runyon; music and lyrics: Frank Loesser; (D) Katrina Ploof; (S) Allen D. Cornell and John Wilson; (C) Chris Carpenter; (L) Allen D. Cornell and John Wilson

Fences, August Wilson; (D) C. Rosalind Bell; (S) Allen D. Cornell; (C) Julie Geiger; (L) Allen D. Cornell

Side by Side by Sondheim, book: Ned Sherrin; music and lyrics: Stephen Sondheim; (D) Brian Spitler; (S) Allen D. Cornell; (C) Chris Carpenter; (L) Allen D. Cornell

The Road Company

ROBERT H. LEONARD
Artistic Director

NANCY FISCHMAN
Development Director

Box 5278 EKS
Johnson City, TN 37603
(615) 926-7726

FOUNDED 1975
Robert H. Leonard

SEASON
Sept.-June

FACILITIES
The Down Home
Seating Capacity: 150
Stage: flexible

FINANCES
July 1, 1990-June 30, 1991
Expenses: $152,423

I believe theatre is a community event. The Road Company is a working environment for artists who want to apply their skills to the investigation and expression of our community in upper east Tennessee. The ensemble works on the premise that theatre is a compact between the artists and the audience—artistically and organizationally. The successful

The Road Company. *Changes*. Photo: Sue Beyer.

theatre event happens when the audience joins the imagination of the production during performance. This belief assumes the enjoyment of theatre is active not passive. It also assumes a long-term relationship between the ensemble and the community. These concepts do not define or restrict subject matter, form or style. These are matters of constant investigation. What subjects are actually of concern? To whom? What style or form is effective within the framework of content and audience aesthetic? These issues and the artistic growth of the ensemble constitute the basis of our dramaturgy. We tour our own works to communities all over Tennessee and the nation.

—*Robert H. Leonard*

PRODUCTIONS 1989-90

Echoes & Postcards, company-developed; (D) Robert H. Leonard; (S) Robert H. Leonard; (C) the ensemble; (L) Robert H. Leonard

Cancell'd Destiny, Pat Arnow, Steve Giles and Christine Murdock; (D) Robert H. Leonard; (S) Beate Czogalla; (L) Beate Czogalla

Audience, Unveiling and Protest, Vaclav Havel; (D) Shawn M. Gulyas; (S) Cheri d'Emu Vasek; (C) Cheri d'Emu Vasek; (L) Light Impressions

The Voice of the Prairie, John Olive; (D) Robert H. Leonard; (S) Cheri d'Emu Vasek; (C) Cheri d'Emu Vasek; (L) Light Impressions

PRODUCTIONS 1990-91

Changes, company-developed; (D) Robert H. Leonard; (S) Cheri d'Emu Vasek; (C) Debbie McClintock; (L) Robert H. Leonard

A Preacher with a Horse to Ride, Jo Carson; (D) David Johnson; (S) Randy Ingram; (C) Cheri d'Emu Vasek; (L) Lee-Zen M. Chen

Descent to the Goddess, Amy Appleyard, Emily Green, Sheila A. Malone, Ellen Norris Spencer and Ginger West; (D) Emily Green; (S) Emily Green; (C) the ensemble; (L) Amy Appleyard

Echoes & Postcards, company-developed; (D) Robert H. Leonard; (S) Robert H. Leonard; (C) the ensemble; (L) Robert H. Leonard

Roadside Theater

DUDLEY COCKE
Director

DONNA PORTERFIELD
Administrative Director

306 Madison St.
Whitesburg, KY 41858
(606) 633-0108

FOUNDED 1974
Appalshop, Inc.

SEASON
Jan.-Dec.

FACILITIES
Appalshop Theater
Seating Capacity: 175
Stage: thrust

FINANCES
Oct. 1, 1990-Sept. 30, 1991
Expenses: $400,000

Roadside is an ensemble of actors, musicians, designers, writers, directors and managers, most of whom grew up in the Appalachian mountains. Appalachia is the subject of the theatre's original plays, and the company has developed its theatrical style from its local heritage of storytelling, mountain music and oral history. In making indigenous theatre and creating a body of native dramatic literature, Roadside sees itself as continuing its region's cultural tradition. Roadside's hometown has 1,200 people; coal mining is the main occupation. The theatre tours nationally year-round, often performing for rural and working-class audiences, and conducting residencies that examine and celebrate local life. Roadside is an integral part of the multimedia organization Appalshop, which also produces work about Appalachia through the media of film, television, radio, photography, music and sound recording, and visual art.

—*Dudley Cocke*

PRODUCTIONS 1989-90

South of the Mountain, Ron Short; (D) Dudley Cocke; (L) Ron Short

Pretty Polly, Ron Short; (D) Ron Short and Dudley Cocke; (L) Ron Short

Leaving Egypt, Ron Short; (D) Dudley Cocke; (L) Ron Short

Mountain Tales & Music, company-developed; (D) the company; (L) Ben Mays

Red Fox and Second Hangin', Don Baker and Dudley Cocke; (D) Don Baker, Michael Posnick and Dudley Cocke; (L) Don Baker

PRODUCTIONS 1990-91

South of the Mountain, Ron Short; (D) Dudley Cocke; (L) Ron Short

Pretty Polly, Ron Short; (D) Ron Short and Dudley Cocke; (L) Ron Short

Leaving Egypt, Ron Short; (D) Dudley Cocke; (L) Ron Short

Mountain Tales & Music, company-developed; (D) Dudley Cocke; (L) Ben Mays

Red Fox and Second Hangin', Don Baker and Dudley Cocke; (D) Michael Posnick, Dudley Cocke and Don Baker; (L) Don Baker

Junebug Jack, company-developed; (D) Dudley Cocke and Steven Kent; (L) Ben Mays

From Belfast to Dayton, Ron Short; (D) Dudley Cocke; (L) Ben Mays

Pine Mountain Trilogy, Ron Short; (D) Dudley Cocke; (L) Ben Mays

Roadside Theater. Kim Cole, Ron Short and Tommy Bledsoe in *Leaving Egypt*. Photo: Dan Carraco.

Roundabout Theatre Company. *The Crucible*. Photo: Martha Swope.

Roundabout Theatre Company

TODD HAIMES
Producing Director

ELLEN RICHARD
General Manager

1514 Broadway
New York, NY 10036
(212) 719-9393 (bus.)
(212) 869-8400 (b.o.)

FOUNDED 1965
Gene Feist, Elizabeth Owens

SEASON
Oct.-Sept.

FACILITIES
Criterion Theatre Center
Seating Capacity: 499
Stage: thrust

Susan Bloch Theatre
Seating Capacity: 152
Stage: arena

FINANCES
Sept. 1, 1990-Aug. 31, 1991
Expenses: $3,800,000

CONTRACTS
AEA LORT (B)

Celebrating its 25th anniversary with the largest subscription audience in New York City, Roundabout Theatre Company continues its dedication to producing the highest quality revivals of classic theatre. Roundabout's rich and eclectic repertoire ranges from the tragedies of Shakespeare to the satires of Shaw to the social dramas of Miller. By combining the finest actors, directors and designers to work on these plays, the company strives to preserve our cultural heritage for a broad-based audience. Roundabout is particularly proud of its educational programs. Through internships, staged readings, open seminars, student matinees and postperformance discussions, Roundabout provides a deeper understanding of theatre to a growing audience. The 26th season will open at the company's new home at the Criterion Theatre Center in the heart of Broadway, which will further enhance Roundabout's ability to offer the stimulating and diversified seasons that have become its trademark.

—Todd Haimes

PRODUCTIONS 1989-90

The Tempest, William Shakespeare; (D) Jude Kelly; (S) Franco Colavecchia; (C) Lindsay W. Davis; (L) Dennis Parichy
The Doctor's Dilemma, George Bernard Shaw; (D) Larry Carpenter; (S) Campbell Baird; (C) John Falabella; (L) Jason Kantrowitz
The Crucible, Arthur Miller; (D) Gerald Freedman; (S) Christopher Barreca; (C) Jeanne Button; (L) Mary Jo Dondlinger
Price of Fame, Charles Grodin; (D) Gloria Muzio; (S) David Jenkins; (C) Jess Goldstein; (L) Tharon Musser
Light Up the Sky, Moss Hart; (D) Larry Carpenter; (S) Andrew Jackness; (C) Martin Pakledinaz; (L) Dennis Parichy

PRODUCTIONS 1990-91

King Lear, William Shakespeare; (D) Gerald Freedman; (S) John Ezell; (C) Robert Wojewodski; (L) Thomas R. Skelton
The Country Girl, Clifford Odets; (D) Kenneth Frankel; (S) Hugh Landwehr; (C) David Murin; (L) Stephen Strawbridge
Pygmalion, George Bernard Shaw; (D) Paul Weidner; (S) John Conklin; (C) Martin Pakledinaz; (L) Natasha Katz
The Subject Was Roses, Frank D. Gilroy; (D) Jack Hofsiss; (S) David Jenkins; (C) Michael Krass; (L) Beverly Emmons
The Matchmaker, Thornton Wilder; (D) Lonny Price; (S) Russell Metheny; (C) Gail Brassard; (L) Stewart Duke

Round House Theatre

JERRY WHIDDON
Artistic Director

TONY ELLIOT
Producing Associate

12210 Bushey Drive
Silver Spring, MD 20902
(301) 217-6770 (bus.)
(301) 217-3300 (b.o.)

FOUNDED 1978
June Allen, Montgomery County Department of Recreation

SEASON
Sept.-June

FACILITIES
Round House Theatre
Seating Capacity: 218
Stage: thrust

FINANCES
July 1, 1990-June 30, 1991
Expenses: $773,850

CONTRACTS
AEA SPT

In an increasingly urbanized world, we constantly yearn for ways to nurture a sense of community, for when we feel truly part of the "tribe," we are more confident that issues will be addressed and solutions found, and then celebrations can be truly joyous. Theatre can be a powerful agent of community bonding when audiences are willing to share the adventure of new voices and new ways of looking at ourselves. Theatre imbues us with purpose. We welcome the commitment to making our art accessible through classes, through performances in schools and through our mainstage productions. It is through all these programs that we at the Round

Round House Theatre. Loretta Toscano and Michael Wells in *Italian American Reconciliation*. Photo: Geri Olson.

House reacquaint ourselves with the actor's impulse. Why theatre is "needed" becomes simply and wonderfully obvious. That joy comes full circle in the darkened room where a member of the tribe tells a story.

—*Jerry Whiddon*

PRODUCTIONS 1989-90

Of Mice and Men, John Steinbeck; (D) Edward Morgan; (S) Jane Williams Flank; (C) Rosemary Pardee-Holz; (L) Joseph B. Musumeci, Jr.
Italian American Reconciliation, John Patrick Shanley; (D) James Petosa; (S) Joseph B. Musumeci, Jr.; (C) Rosemary Pardee-Holz; (L) Joseph Ronald Higdon
Emerald City, David Williamson; (D) Gillian Drake; (S) Jane Williams Flank; (C) Rosemary Pardee-Holz; (L) Joseph Ronald Higdon
Not About Heroes, Stephen MacDonald; (D) Tony Elliot; (S) Joseph B. Musumeci, Jr.; (C) Rosemary Pardee-Holz; (L) Jane Williams Flank
T Bone N Weasel, Jon Klein; (D) Jeff Davis; (S) Jane Williams Flank; (C) Rosemary Pardee-Holz; (L) Joseph Ronald Higdon

PRODUCTIONS 1990-91

Rebel Armies Deep Into Chad, Mark Lee; (D) Mary Hall Surface; (S) Jane Williams Flank; (C) Rosemary Pardee-Holz; (L) Joseph B. Musumeci, Jr.
The Diary of Anne Frank, adapt: Frances Goodrich and Albert Hackett, from Anne Frank; (D) James Petosa; (S) Jane Williams Flank; (C) Rosemary Pardee-Holz; (L) Neil McFadden
Odd Jobs, Frank Moher; (D) Jeff Davis; (S) Joseph B. Musumeci, Jr.; (C) Rosemary Pardee-Holz; (L) Thomas F. Donahue
Love and Anger, George F. Walker; (D) Daniel F. De Raey; (S) James Kronzer; (C) Rosemary Pardee-Holz; (L) Joseph B. Musumeci, Jr.
The Illusion, Tony Kushner, from Pierre Corneille; (D) Edward Morgan; (S) Joseph B. Musumeci, Jr.; (C) Rosemary Pardee-Holz; (L) Daniel MacLean Wagner

Sacramento Theatre Company

MARK CUDDY
Artistic Director

JAY DRURY
Managing Director

1419 H St.
Sacramento, CA 95814
(916) 446-7501 (bus.)
(916) 443-6722 (b.o.)

FOUNDED 1942
Eleanor McClatchy

SEASON
Sept.-May

FACILITIES
McClatchy Mainstage
Seating Capacity: 301
Stage: proscenium

Stage Two
Seating Capacity: 86
Stage: flexible

FINANCES
July 1, 1990-June 30, 1991
Expenses: $1,200,000

CONTRACTS
AEA letter of agreement

The Sacramento Theatre Company is a resident theatre company working toward LORT status. This brings with it several responsibilities including: responding to the city's sociopolitical makeup, taking subscribers on journeys through their hearts and minds, and making contributions to the American theatre both artistically and administratively. We are building a trust with our audience that secures our future and allows them the ownership that they deserve. Our task is to select plays of dramatic stature and present them vividly, clearly and boldly, making demands of ourselves and our audience. We strive to create a cathartic experience which will enhance a sense of community within the theatre. The theatre can be a focal point for the exchange of ideas and emotion among members of a shared community. Above all, we want the Sacramento Theatre Company to be a sane place to work and an adventurous place to visit.

—*Mark Cuddy*

PRODUCTIONS 1989-90

Broadway Bound, Neil Simon; (D) Mark Cuddy; (S) William Bloodgood and Norm Spencer; (C) Phyllis Kress; (L) Kathryn Burleson
Fences, August Wilson; (D) Stanley E. Williams; (S) Ken Ellis; (C) Susan D. Anderson; (L) Maurice Vercoutere
A Christmas Carol, book adapt: Richard Hellesen, from Charles Dickens; music and lyrics: David de Berry; (D) Tim Ocel; (S) Ralph Fetterly; (C) Roxanne Femling; (L) Kathryn Burleson
Much Ado About Nothing, William Shakespeare; (D) Tim Ocel; (S) Bruce Hill and Jenny Guthrie; (C) Pat Polen; (L) Kathryn Burleson
The Cherry Orchard, Anton Chekhov; (D) Barbara Damashek; (S) Jeff Hunt; (C) B. Modern; (L) Maurice Vercoutere
Three Men on a Horse, John Cecil Holm and George Abbott; (D) Andrew J. Traister; (S) Everett Chase; (C) Mary Nigro; (L) Kathryn Burleson
A Cappella, book, music and lyrics: David de Berry; (D) David de Berry; (S) properties: Jenifer Hovell
Hurry Up Please It's Time, Joyce Lander; (D) Charles Slater; (S) properties: Jenifer Hovell
In the Belly of the Beast: Letters from Prison, adapt: Adrian Hall and Robert Woodruff, from Jack Henry Abbott; (D) Tim Ocel and Mark Cuddy; (S) properties: Jenifer Hovell
A Woman Alone and ***Tomorrow's News Today***, Dario Fo and Franca Rame; (D) Vincent Murphy; (S) properties: Jenifer Hovell
Honeymoon Near Lava Lands, Carolyn Brooks-Holden; (D) Charles Slater; (S) properties: Jenifer Hovell
The Island, Athol Fugard, John Kani and Winston Ntshona; (D) Mark Cuddy; (S) properties: Jenifer Hovell

PRODUCTIONS 1990-91

Driving Miss Daisy, Alfred Uhry; (D) Mark Cuddy; (S) Jeff Hunt; (C) Roxanne Femling; (L) Kathryn Burleson
Heartbreak House, George Bernard Shaw; (D) Mark Cuddy; (S) Nicholas Dorr; (C) Jeffrey Struckman; (L) Maurice Vercoutere
A Christmas Carol, book adapt: Richard Hellesen, from Charles Dickens; music and lyrics: David de Berry; (D) Tim Ocel; (S) Ralph Fetterly; (C) Roxanne Femling; (L) Kathryn Burleson
Joe Turner's Come and Gone, August Wilson; (D) Luther James; (S) Pamela S. Peniston; (C) Cassandra Carpenter; (L) Kathryn Burleson
The Good Person of Setzuan, Bertolt Brecht; trans: Ralph

Sacramento Theatre Company. David de Berry and George Maguire in *The Mystery of Irma Vep*. Photo: J. Kenneth Wagner.

Manheim; (D) Tim Ocel; (S) Mark Hopkins; (C) B. Modern; (L) Maurice Vercoutere
The Mystery of Irma Vep, Charles Ludlam; (D) Mark Cuddy; (S) Nicholas Dorr; (C) B. Modern; (L) Kathryn Burleson
Gold's Fool, Richard Hellesen; (D) Charles Slater; (S) Sean Timberlake; (L) Robert Young
Dog Logic, Tom Strelich; (D) Charles Slater; (S) Sean Timberlake
Red Channels, Jennifer Martin and Leslie Mildener; (D) Tim Ocel; (S) Sean Timberlake; (C) Roxanne Femling; (L) Robert Young
Sizwe Bansi Is Dead, Athol Fugard, John Kani and Winston Ntshona; (D) Bob Devin Jones and Mark Cuddy; (S) Mark Hopkins; (C) Victoria Tana Birenbaum; (L) Mark Hopkins
Wartime Recipes, Evelyn E. Smith; (D) Charles Slater; (S) Sean Timberlake; (L) Robert Young
Stuffed, Frank X. Hogan; (D) Charles Slater; (S) Sean Timberlake; (C) Robert Young

The Salt Lake Acting Company

EDWARD J. GRYSKA
Producing Artistic Director

VICTORIA M. PANELLA
Managing Director

168 West 500 North
Salt Lake City, UT 84103
(801) 363-0526 (bus.)
(801) 363-0525 (b.o.)

FOUNDED 1970
Edward J. Gryska

SEASON
Sept.-Aug.

FACILITIES
The Salt Lake Acting Company
Seating Capacity: 150-220
Stage: thrust

FINANCES
Sept. 1, 1990-Aug. 31, 1991
Expenses: $697,336

The Salt Lake Acting Company presents a unique and innovative repertoire of plays including world and regional premieres and award-winning contemporary plays. For the past 20 years, the Salt Lake Acting Company has supported new works and new playwrights, particularly Utah writers, and is proud to have delivered new works and new writers to the forefront of an international theatre community. The Salt Lake Acting Company is committed to producing theatre of the highest artistic integrity. It serves the needs of a responsive audience and continues, in its 21st season, to make a significant contribution to the world of professional theatre.

—*Edward J. Gryska*

PRODUCTIONS 1989-90

La Cage Aux Folles, book adapt: Harvey Fierstein, from Jean Poiret; music and lyrics: Jerry Herman; (D) Edward J. Gryska; (S) Cory Dangerfield; (C) Susan Crotts; (L) Megan McCormick
Saturday's Voyeur, Nancy Borgenicht and Edward J. Gryska, from Nancy Borgenicht and Michael Buttars; (D) Edward J. Gryska; (S) Cory Dangerfield; (C) Sylvia D. Flem; (L) Megan McCormick
Women and Wallace, Jonathan Marc Sherman; (D) Nancy Borgenicht; (S) George Maxwell; (C) Catherine Zublin; (L) Megan McCormick
The Ghostman, Wendy Hammond; (D) Edward J. Gryska; (S) Cory Dangerfield; (C) Sylvia D. Flem; (L) Megan McCormick
The Road to Mecca, Athol Fugard; (D) Kenneth Washington; (S) Cory Dangerfield; (C) Barbara Smith; (L) Megan McCormick
The Voice of the Prairie, John Olive; (D) Anne Cullimore Decker; (S) Ladd Lambert; (C) Catherine Zublin; (L) Megan McCormick

PRODUCTIONS 1990-91

M. Butterfly, David Henry Hwang; (D) Edward J. Gryska; (S) Cory Dangerfield; (C) Barb Nelson; (L) Megan McCormick
White Man Dancing, Stephen Metcalfe; (D) Nancy Borgenicht; (S) Eddie Coe; (C) Valerie Kittel; (L) Megan McCormick
White Money, Julie Jensen; (D) Robert Graham Small; (S) Cory Dangerfield; (C) Christine Murdoch Becz; (L) Megan McCormick

The Salt Lake Acting Company. Patsy Stephen and Tony Larimer in *The Road to Mecca*. Photo: Jess Allen.

The Heidi Chronicles, Wendy Wasserstein; (D) Edward J. Gryska; (S) Cory Dangerfield; (C) Christine Murdoch Becz; (L) Megan McCormick
Saturday's Voyeur, Nancy Borgenicht; (D) Edward J. Gryska; (S) Cory Dangerfield; (L) Megan McCormick

San Diego Repertory Theatre

DOUGLAS JACOBS
Artistic Director

SAM WOODHOUSE
Producing Director

ADRIAN W. STEWART
Managing Director

79 Horton Plaza
San Diego, CA 92101
(619) 231-3586 (bus.)
(619) 235-8025 (b.o.)

FOUNDED 1976
Sam Woodhouse, Douglas Jacobs

SEASON
May-Dec.

FACILITIES
Lyceum Stage
Seating Capacity: 500
Stage: flexible

Lyceum Space
Seating Capacity: 250
Stage: flexible

Sixth Avenue Playhouse
Seating Capacity: 190
Stage: thrust

FINANCES
Jan. 1, 1990-Dec. 31, 1990
Expenses: $2,100,000

CONTRACTS
AEA letter of agreement

Based on the conviction that theatre continually reinvents itself through an ongoing blending of all the arts, the San Diego Repertory Theatre operates its three theatres as a multidisciplinary, multicultural arts complex. We produce our own season for nine months of the year; during the other three months we book, present or rent our theatre to other artists. Our eclectic programming is based on the belief that the arts should reflect the diversity of the world around and within us, and that the theatre is a uniquely appropriate place to

San Diego Repertory Theatre. Tom Oleniazc and Jon Matthews in *Loot*. Photo: Ken Jacques.

explore the boundaries and borders of life and art. Our seasons emphasize contemporary plays, seldom-seen classics and revivals of well-known classics. We are committed to ensemble development, nontraditional casting and lifelong training for professionals; and to explorations of music, dance, visual arts and poetry, in order to expand and deepen the range of theatrical expression.

—*Douglas Jacobs*

PRODUCTIONS 1989-90

The Marriage of Bette and Boo, Christopher Durang; (D) Walter Schoen; (S) George Suhayda; (C) Nancy Jo Smith; (L) John B. Forbes

Orinoco!, Emilio Carballido; trans: Margaret Sayers Peden; (D) Jorge Huerta; (S) D. Martyn Bookwalter; (C) David Kay Mickelsen; (L) Peter Nordyke

The Scandalous Adventures of Sir Toby Trollope, Ron House and Allan Shearman; (D) Stephen Rothman; (S) Fred M. Duer and Alan K. Okazaki; (C) David Kay Mickelsen; (L) John B. Forbes

Are You Lonesome Tonight?, Alan Bleasdale; (D) George Ferencz; (S) Victoria Petrovich; (C) Sally J. Lesser; (L) Brenda Berry

Albanian Soft Shoe, Mac Wellman; (D) Douglas Jacobs and Michael Roth; (S) Jill Moon; (C) Clare Henkel; (L) Brenda Berry

Slingshot, Nikolai Kolyada; trans: Susan Larsen; (D) Roman Viktyuk; (S) Vladimir Boyer; (C) Sally Cleveland; (L) Brenda Berry

A Christmas Carol, adapt: Douglas Jacobs, from Charles Dickens; (D) Walter Schoen; (S) Thomas Buderwitz; (C) Catherine Meacham; (L) John B. Forbes

Animal Nation, Steve Friedman; (D) Jael Weisman and Sam Woodhouse; (S) Victoria Petrovich; (C) Nancy Jo Smith; (L) Peter Nordyke

PRODUCTIONS 1990-91

Latins Anonymous, Armando Molina, Diane Rodriguez, Luisa Leschin and Rick Najera; (D) Miguel Delgado and Jose Cruz Gonzalez; (S) Victoria Petrovich; (C) Patssi Valdez and Jim Reva; (L) Brenda Berry

Loot, Joe Orton; (D) Walter Schoen; (S) Thomas Buderwitz; (C) Emelle Holmes; (L) Diane Boomer

A Lovely Sunday for Creve Coeur, Tennessee Williams; (D) Douglas Jacobs; (S) Neil Patel; (C) Mary Gibson; (L) Brenda Berry

Burn This, Lanford Wilson; (D) Sam Woodhouse; (S) Robert Brill; (C) Christine Dougherty; (L) Ashley York Kennedy

Cymbeline, William Shakespeare; (D) Douglas Jacobs; (S) Brenda Berry; (C) Catherine Meacham Hunt; (L) Brenda Berry

Man of the Flesh/El Ladron de Corazones, Octavio Solis; trans: Octavio Solis; (D) Sam Woodhouse and Jorge Huerta; (S) Victoria Petrovich; (C) Victoria Petrovich; (L) Brenda Berry

The Life and Life of Bumpy Johnson, book and lyrics: Amiri Baraka; music: Max Roach; (D) George Ferencz; (S) Bill Stabile; (C) Sally J. Lesser; (L) Ashley York Kennedy

San Jose Repertory Theatre

TIMOTHY NEAR
Artistic Director

SHANNON LESKIN
Managing Director

Box 2399
San Jose, CA 95109-2399
(408) 291-2266 (bus.)
(408) 291-2255 (b.o.)

FOUNDED 1980
James P. Reber

SEASON
Oct.-June

FACILITIES
The Montgomery Theatre
Seating Capacity: 535
Stage: proscenium

FINANCES
July 1, 1990-June 30, 1991
Expenses: $2,165,000

CONTRACTS
AEA LORT (C) and TYA

San Jose Repertory Theatre performs in the Montgomery Theatre in downtown San Jose, a city that is fast becoming the cultural center of the Santa Clara Valley. The theatre gives focus to this culturally diverse and widespread community by producing seasons of visually exciting, challenging and evocative plays selected from both classical and contemporary periods, including an original touring show created specifically for the young people of the multicultural Santa Clara Valley. As well as striving to reflect and enhance its own community, the Rep works to contribute on a national level to the essential growth of live theatre in the United States, developing new plays and encouraging artists to take an innovative approach to existing work. The Rep provides a creative and nurturing environment that

San Jose Repertory Theatre. Sean Runnette, Will Marchetti and Tony Soper in *Pick Up Ax*. Photo: Shari Cohen.

offers unique theatre experiences for artists and audiences alike.

—Timothy Near

PRODUCTIONS 1989-90

Fences, August Wilson; (D) Kenny Leon; (S) Jeffrey Struckman; (C) Cassandra Carpenter; (L) Robert Peterson

A Day in Hollywood/A Night in the Ukraine, book and lyrics: Dick Vosburgh; music: Frank Lazarus; (D) Pamela Hunt; (S) Richard R. Goodwin; (C) Jeffrey Struckman; (L) Pamela Gray Bones

The Caretaker, Harold Pinter; (D) Timothy Near; (S) John Wilson; (C) B. Modern; (L) Timothy Wessling

The School For Wives, Moliere; trans: Richard Wilbur; (D) John C. Fletcher; (S) Jeffrey Struckman; (C) Beaver Bauer; (L) Michael A. Peterson

Dracula, John L. Balderston and Hamilton Dean, from Bram Stoker; (D) John McCluggage; (S) Barbara Mesney; (C) Jeffrey Struckman; (L) Brenda Berry

The Geography of Luck, Marlane Meyer; (D) Timothy Near; (S) Jeffrey Struckman; (C) Cassandra Carpenter; (L) Derek Duarte

PRODUCTIONS 1990-91

Oedipus the King, Sophocles; trans: Stephen Berg and Diskin Clay; (D) Timothy Near; (S) Joel Fontaine; (C) Warren Travis; (L) Peter Maradudin

Closer than Ever, conceived: Steven Scott Smith; music: David Shire; lyrics: Richard Maltby, Jr.; (D) Marcia Milgrom Dodge; (S) Philipp Jung; (C) Michael Krass; (L) Kent Dorsey

The Glass Menagerie, Tennessee Williams; (D) John McCluggage; (S) John Wilson; (C) Jeffrey Struckman; (L) Derek Duarte

Pick Up Ax, Anthony Clarvoe; (D) John McCluggage; (S) Tom Kamm; (C) Deborah Weber Krahenbuhl; (L) Jerald Enos

Fire in the Rain/Singer in the Storm, Holly Near; (D) Timothy Near; (S) Kate Edmunds; (C) Sigrid Insull; (L) Robert Peterson

The Mousetrap, Agatha Christie; (D) Edward Stern; (S) Jeffrey Struckman; (C) Warren Travis; (L) Derek Duarte

Seattle Children's Theatre

LINDA HARTZELL
Artistic Director

THOMAS PECHAR
Managing Director

305 Harrison St.
Seattle, WA 98109
(206) 443-0807 (bus.)
(206) 633-4567 (b.o.)

FOUNDED 1975
Seattle City Parks Department, Jenifer McClauchlan Carlson, Molly Welch Reed

SEASON
Sept.-June

FACILITIES
The PONCHO Theatre
Seating Capacity: 280
Stage: proscenium

FINANCES
July 1, 1990-June 30, 1991
Expenses: $1,700,000

CONTRACTS
AEA TYA

Seattle Children's Theatre, which has a national reputation for producing innovative, thought-provoking professional theatre for young audiences and their families, will be embarking on its 17th year during the 1991-92 season. SCT has commissioned more than 40 new works for young audiences since its founding in 1975, and its plays have been produced by theatres across the country. In addition to its mainstage season, SCT offers a wide variety of programs to make the theatre accessible to as many children and their families as possible. These include providing classroom workshops, study guides and postplay discussions to further enhance the educational experience of the main stage. In addition, SCT brings mainstage and educational plays to schools through its regional touring program. As part of its mission, SCT is committed to providing education and training for young people. The theatre offers year-round classes in acting and theatre skills for grades K-12, which are taught by professional artists. Professional theatre makes a lasting impression on today's youth. Creative discovery inspired by a sophisticated, entertaining theatre experience is my vision of Seattle Children's Theatre.

—Linda Hartzell

Seattle Children's Theatre. *The Magic Mrs. Piggle-Wiggle*. Photo: Fred Andrews.

PRODUCTIONS 1989-90

Rip Van Winkle and The Legend of Sleepy Hollow, adapt: Bruce Hurlbut, from Washington Irving; (D) Rita Giomi; (S) Patti Henry; (C) Anne Thaxter Watson; (L) Rogue Conn

The Magic Mrs. Piggle-Wiggle, book adapt: Jeff Church and Chad Henry, from Betty MacDonald; music and lyrics: Chad Henry; (D) Linda Hartzell; (S) Patti Henry; (C) Sarah Campbell; (L) Patty Mathieu

Amelia Earhart: Flights of Fancy, Will Huddleston; (D) Rex E. Allen; (S) Silas Morse; (C) Paul Chi-Ming Louey; (L) Rogue Conn

Apollo: To The Moon, Mary Hall Surface; (D) Mary Hall Surface; (S) Kevin Reese; (C) Kevin Reese; (L) Rogue Conn

Jungalbook, Edward Mast, from Rudyard Kipling; (D) Linda Hartzell; (S) Jennifer Lupton; (C) Michael Murphy; (L) Jennifer Lupton

Tuck Everlasting, adapt: Jeff Church and Amy Tepel, from Natalie Babbitt; (D) John Schwab; (S) Robert Gardiner; (C) Josie Gardner; (L) Rogue Conn

PRODUCTIONS 1990-91

Captain Fantasto, adapt and trans: Roger Downey, from Volker Ludwig and Henning Spangenberg; (D) Linda Hartzell; (S) Jennifer Lupton; (C) Paul Chi-Ming Louey; (L) Rogue Conn

The Reluctant Dragon, adapt: Mary Hall Surface, from Kenneth Grahame; (D) Rex E. Allen; (S) Shelley Henze Schermer; (C) Paul Chi-Ming Louey; (L) Rogue Conn

The Council, William S. Yellow Robe, Jr.; (D) Diane Schenker; (S) Peggy McDonald; (C) Paul Chi-Ming Louey; (L) Rogue Conn

The Magic Mrs. Piggle-Wiggle, book adapt: Jeff Church and Chad Henry, from Betty MacDonald; music and lyrics: Chad Henry; (D) Linda Hartzell; (S) Patti Henry; (C) Sarah Campbell; (L) Patty Mathieu

Anne of Green Gables, adapt: R.N. Sandberg, from L.M. Montgomery; (D) Rita Giomi; (S) Robert Gardiner; (C) Sarah Campbell; (L) Jennifer Lupton

There's a Boy in the Girls' Bathroom, Louis Sachar; (D) Linda Hartzell; (S) Tim Saternow; (C) Mark Mitchell; (L) Darren McCroom

Seattle Group Theatre. Anthony Lee and John Gilbert in *Incommunicado*. Photo: John Stamets.

Seattle Group Theatre

RUBEN SIERRA
Founding Artistic Director

PAUL O'CONNELL
Producing Director

3940 Brooklyn Ave. NE
Seattle, WA 98105
(206) 685-4969 (bus.)
(206) 543-4327 (b.o.)

FOUNDED 1978
Gilbert Wong, Ruben Sierra, Scott Caldwell

SEASON
Sept.-June

FACILITIES
Ethnic Theatre
Seating Capacity: 195
Stage: modified thrust

FINANCES
July 1, 1989-June 30, 1990
Expenses: $583,950

CONTRACTS
AEA SPT and TYA

The Seattle Group Theatre believes that theatre should be an experience of social, educational and artistic relevance. We seek to provide the best opportunities for all artists to voice, through their art, their dreams, their hopes and their despairs. We want our audience to laugh, to cry—but ultimately we want them to think. We want to serve as a negotiator and a catalyst for playwrights, actors, directors; to open our doors to artists so that they in turn can reach our audience and share that humanity which makes theatre great. We have created programs that go into the elementary and high schools, addressing students' need for art and literature. We are in the seventh year of our Multicultural Playwrights' Festival, in which we focus solely on new scripts by American ethnic playwrights. We do one to three world premieres during our season by both new and established playwrights. We have toured nationally with such shows as *I am Celso*, created from the poems of Leo Romero, and *Nappy Edges*, a one-woman show by Tawnya Pettiford-Waites. Finally, we are a theatre that attempts to transform and transcend circumstances, limitations and obstacles—theatre that reflects all of America!

—Ruben Sierra

PRODUCTIONS 1989-90

Growing Up Queer in America, Chris Cinque; (D) Chris Cinque; (S) Rex Carleton; (C) Chris Cinque; (L) Elisa River Stacy

The Boys Next Door, Tom Griffin; (D) Ruben Sierra; (S) David Henderson; (C) Kathleen Maki; (L) Darren McCroom

Voices of Christmas, company-developed; (D) Ruben Sierra; (S) Robert Dahlstrom; (C) Barbara Conroy; (L) Jim Verderey

For Colored Girls Who Have Considered Suicide/When the Rainbow Is Enuf, Ntozake Shange; (D) Trazana Beverley; (S) Janet Snyder; (C) Barbara Conroy; (L) Collier Woods

Winnetou's Snake Oil Show, company-developed; (D) Lisa Mayo; (S) the ensemble; (C) the ensemble; (L) Rex Carleton

A...My Name Is Alice, conceived: Joan Micklin Silver and Julianne Boyd; (D) Christine Sumption; (S) Yuri Degtjar; (C) Josie Gardner; (L) Rex Carleton

PRODUCTIONS 1990-91

Incommunicado, Tom Dulack; (D) Bill Ontiveros; (S) Yuri Degtjar; (C) Kathleen Maki; (L) Kyle Iddings

Heart of the World, Martha Boesing, Albert Greenberg and Helen Stoltzfus; (D) Martha Boesing; (S) Allan Droyan; (C) the ensemble; (L) David Welle

Voices of Christmas, company-developed; (D) Ruben Sierra; (S) Yuri Degtjar; (C) Kathleen Maki; (L) Darren McCroom

Fraternity, Jeff Stetson; (D) Marion Isaac McClinton; (S) Rex Carleton; (C) Kathleen Maki; (L) Darren McCroom

It's a Girl!, book and lyrics: John Burrows; music: Andy Whitfield; (D) Bill Ontiveros; (S) Rex Carleton; (C) Marienne O'Brien; (L) Kyle Iddings

Latins Anonymous, Armando Molina, Diane Rodriguez, Luisa Leschin and Rick Najera; (D) Luisa Leschin; (S) Rex Carleton; (C) Gabriela Fernandez; (L) Darren McCroom

The Independence of Eddie Rose, William S. Yellow Robe, Jr.; (D) Tim Bond; (S) Yuri Degtjar; (C) Kathleen Maki; (L) Darren McCroom

Seattle Repertory Theatre

DANIEL SULLIVAN
Artistic Director

BENJAMIN MOORE
Managing Director

DOUGLAS HUGHES
Associate Artistic Director

155 Mercer St.
Seattle, WA 98109
(206) 443-2210 (bus.)
(206) 443-2222 (b.o.)

FOUNDED 1963
Bagley Wright

SEASON
Oct.-May

FACILITIES
Bagley Wright Theatre (Mainstage)
Seating Capacity: 856
Stage: proscenium

PONCHO Forum (Stage 2)
Seating Capacity: 133
Stage: flexible

FINANCES
July 1, 1989-June 30, 1990
Expenses: $5,301,307

CONTRACTS
AEA LORT (B+) and (D)

The Seattle Repertory Theatre continues to support a resident acting company, offering long-term employment to members who are cast across a season of six mainstage and three Stage 2 productions. Both the main stage and Stage 2 offer work ranging from the classics to world premieres. Each year we seek to collaborate with other nonprofit theatres to present a special production on the main stage, thus providing extra time for the resident company to prepare subsequent productions. A strong commitment to new work is reflected in workshop productions of four new scripts every spring. Building the resources of a resident acting company and developing new plays remain parallel artistic priorities. Outreach programs include workshops and performances in the schools and a regional tour of one or two mainstage productions to a dozen western state venues.

—Daniel Sullivan

PRODUCTIONS 1989-90

The Heidi Chronicles, Wendy Wasserstein; (D) Daniel Sullivan; (S) Thomas Lynch; (C) Rose Pederson; (L) Pat Collins

A Flea in Her Ear, Georges Feydeau; adapt: Frank Galati; trans: Abbott Chrisman; (D) Michael Maggio; (S) John Lee Beatty; (C) Kaye Nottbusch; (L) Craig Miller

Feast of Fools, Geoff Hoyle; (D) consultant: Anthony Taccone;

(S) Scott Weldin; (L) Neil Peter Jampolis

The Playboy of the Western World, John Millington Synge; (D) Douglas Hughes; (S) Marjorie Bradley Kellogg; (C) Michael Olich; (L) Craig Miller

The Cherry Orchard, Anton Chekhov; trans: Jean-Claude van Itallie; (D) Daniel Sullivan; (S) Ralph Funicello; (C) Ann Hould-Ward; (L) Pat Collins

Sunday in the Park with George, book: James Lapine; music and lyrics: Stephen Sondheim; (D) Laird Williamson; (S) Richard Seger; (C) Andrew V. Yelusich; (L) Pat Collins

Measure for Measure, William Shakespeare; (D) Douglas Hughes; (S) Hugh Landwehr; (C) Michael Olich; (L) Peter Maradudin

Robbers, Lyle Kessler; (D) Daniel Sullivan; (S) Ralph Funicello; (C) Rose Pederson; (L) Paulie Jenkins

Woody Guthrie's American Song, conceived and adapt: Peter Glazer, from Woody Guthrie; (D) Peter Glazer; (S) Philipp Jung; (C) Deborah Shaw; (L) David Noling

PRODUCTIONS 1990-91

Much Ado About Nothing, William Shakespeare; (D) Stan Wojewodski, Jr.; (S) Derek McLane; (C) Catherine Zuber; (L) Stephen Strawbridge

The House of Blue Leaves, John Guare; (D) Douglas Hughes; (S) Tim Saternow; (C) Rose Pederson; (L) Pat Collins

Two Trains Running, August Wilson; (D) Lloyd Richards; (S) Tony Fanning; (C) Chrisi Karvonides; (L) Geoff Korf

Six Characters in Search of an Author, Luigi Pirandello; trans: Robert Cornthwaite; (D) Liviu Ciulei; (S) Liviu Ciulei; (C) Smaranda Branescu; (L) Allen Lee Hughes

The Miser, Moliere; trans: Douglas Hughes; (D) Douglas Hughes; (S) Hugh Landwehr; (C) Catherine Zuber; (L) Peter Maradudin

Conversations with My Father, Herb Gardner; (D) Daniel Sullivan; (S) Tony Walton; (C) Robert Wojewodski; (L) Pat Collins

Long Day's Journey Into Night, Eugene O'Neill; (D) Michael Engler; (S) Andrew Jackness; (C) Rose Pederson; (L) Peter Maradudin

Home and Away, Kevin Kling; (D) Kenneth Washington; (S) Tim Saternow; (L) Marcus Dilliard

Elliot Loves, Jules Feiffer; (D) John Ferraro; (S) Rick Dennis; (C) Rose Pederson; (L) Richard Moore

Seattle Repertory Theatre. Judd Hirsch in *Conversations with My Father*. Photo: Chris Bennion.

Second Stage Theatre. Richard Thomas and Dianne Wiest in *Square One*. Photo: Susan Cook.

Second Stage Theatre

ROBYN GOODMAN
CAROLE ROTHMAN
Artistic Directors

MICHAEL VARGAS
General Manager

Box 1807, Ansonia Station
New York, NY 10023
(212) 787-8302 (bus.)
(212) 873-6103 (b.o.)

FOUNDED 1979
Robyn Goodman, Carole Rothman

SEASON
Oct.-Aug.

FACILITIES
McGinn/Cazale Theatre
Seating Capacity: 108
Stage: proscenium

FINANCES
July 1, 1990-June 30, 1991
Expenses: $1,179,615

CONTRACTS
AEA letter of agreement

Second Stage Theatre was founded in July, 1979 to produce American plays that we felt deserved a second chance. These include plays that were ahead of their time, not accessible to a wide audience or obscured by inferior productions. This "second staging" not only rescued some great works from obscurity, but launched the careers of many actors, directors and playwrights. As relationships developed, artists wanted to bring their original concepts to the theatre. So in 1982 we expanded our misson to include presenting new plays by our developing corps of writers. These plays include *Painting Churches* and *Coastal Disturbances* by Tina Howe, and *Spoils of War* by Michael Weller. Throughout our 12 seasons Second Stage has been honored with 18 Obie awards, 2 Clarence Derwent Awards, 4 Theatre World Awards, 4 Outer Critics Circle Awards and 4 Tony nominations.

—*Robyn Goodman, Carole Rothman*

PRODUCTIONS 1989-90

Baba Goya, Steve Tesich; (D) Harris Yulin; (S) Tom Kamm; (C) Candice Donnelly; (L) Mal Sturchio

Square One, Steve Tesich; (D) Jerry Zaks; (S) Tony Walton; (C) Ann Roth; (L) Paul Gallo

What a Man Weighs, Sherry Kramer; (D) Carole Rothman; (S) Andrew Jackness; (C) Susan Hilferty; (L) Dennis Parichy

Jersey City, Wendy Hammond; (D) Risa Bramon; (S) James Youmans; (C) Sharon Sprague; (L) Anne Militello

PRODUCTIONS 1990-91

Lake No Bottom, Michael Weller; (D) Carole Rothman; (S) Adrianne Lobel; (C) Jess Goldstein; (L) Kevin Rigdon
Earth and Sky, Douglas Post; (D) Andre Ernotte; (S) William Barclay; (C) Deborah Shaw; (L) Phil Monat
The Good Times Are Killing Me, Lynda Barry; (D) Mark Brokaw; (S) Rusty Smith; (C) Ellen McCartney; (L) Donald Holder
Home and Away, Kevin Kling; (D) David Esbjornson; (L) Frances Aronson

Seven Stages

DEL HAMILTON
Artistic Director

LISA MOUNT
Managing Director

1105 Euclid Ave. NE
Atlanta, GA 30307
(404) 522-0911 (bus.)
(404) 523-7647 (b.o.)

FOUNDED 1979
Faye Allen, Del Hamilton

SEASON
Jan.-Dec.

FACILITIES
Mainstage Theater
Seating Capacity: 250
Stage: flexible

Back Door Theater
Seating Capacity: 100
Stage: flexible

FINANCES
Jan. 1, 1990-Dec. 31, 1990
Expenses: $245,000

CONTRACTS
AEA SPT

Seven Stages produces mostly new plays in a lengthy developmental process involving artists as collaborators. We have produced more than 50 premieres by American and foreign playwrights. Occasionally we produce a classic or modern classic. The content of the plays focuses on spiritual, social and political issues of concern to our audiences and artists. We also present national and international theatre artists and companies in residencies. Our cross-cultural workshop program initiates projects that usually involve artists in several disciplines.

—Del Hamilton

PRODUCTIONS 1989-90

The Park, Botho Strauss; trans: Christopher Martin and Daniel Woker; (D) Christopher Martin; (S) Christopher Martin and Roy Magee, III; (C) Barbara Bush; (L) Christopher Martin
The Lizard of Tarsus, Jim Grimsley; (D) Jim Grimsley; (S) Roy Magee and Bill Georgia; (C) Barbara Mahoney and Patsy Mills; (L) Eric Jennings
Junebug Volume III, John O'Neal, Nayo Watkins and Q.R. Hand, Jr.; (D) Steven Kent; (L) Eric Jennings
Yardbird's Vamp, Robert Earl Price; music: Fuasi Abdul Khaliq; (D) Del Hamilton; (C) Barbara Mahoney and Patsy Mills; (L) Eric Jennings
Haiti...A Dream, Karen Sunde; (D) Robert Earl Price; (L) Eric Jennings

PRODUCTIONS 1990-91

The Orange Earth, Adam Small; (D) Adam Small and Del Hamilton; (L) Eric Jennings
Mr. Universe, Jim Grimsley; (D) Del Hamilton; (S) Leslie Taylor; (C) Barbara Mahoney and Patsy Mills; (L) Eric Jennings
Belle Ives, Jim Grimsley; (D) Jim Peck; (S) Leslie Taylor; (C) Barbara Mahoney and Patsy Mills; (L) Eric Jennings
Daytrips, Jo Carson; (D) Steven Kent; (S) Douglas D. Smith; (C) Buffy Aguero; (L) Eric Jennings
Carmen Kittel, Georg Seidel; trans: Frank Heibert; (D) Lore Stefanek; (S) Martin Kraemer; (C) Martin Kraemer; (L) Martin Kraemer

Seven Stages. Del Hamilton and Felicia Hernandez in *The Park*. Photo: Jonathan Burnett.

Shakespeare Repertory

BARBARA GAINES
Artistic Director

CRISS HENDERSON
Managing Director

2140 Lincoln Park W, #1001
Chicago, IL 60614
(312) 281-2101 (bus.)
(312) 281-1878 (b.o.)

FOUNDED 1987
Kathleen Buckley, Barbara Gaines, Susan Geffen, Camilla Hawk, Liz Jacobs, Tom Joyce

SEASON
Oct.-Apr.

FACILITIES
Ruth Page Theatre
Seating Capacity: 278
Stage: thrust

Royal George Theatre
Seating Capacity: 438
Stage: proscenium

FINANCES
July 1, 1990-June 30, 1991
Expenses: $586,000

CONTRACTS
AEA CAT and TYA

Shakespeare Repertory is known for its productions of the less-often produced plays—*Troilus and Cressida* in 1987, *Antony and Cleopatra* in 1988, and *Cymbeline*, which won the Joseph Jefferson Award for best production of the 1989-90 season. None of these plays had ever been produced in Chicago, and all of them are now considered "favorites." And I think that's the point. Every play Shakespeare wrote has the potential to become a hit. His relevance to our lives is apparent. He *is* our lives. That *Cymbeline* and *King John* (1991) became "hits" after 400 years is a testament to our audience's hunger for the great range of knowledge and human sympathy in every line he wrote. I see Shakespeare Rep becoming a center for the study and performance of Shakespeare: a place where great directors from around the world would work with our artists, sharing their cultures with ours. Our first guest director will arrive from Czechoslovakia for the 1991-92 season. We hope this will be the first of many brilliant talents to enrich our community.

—Barbara Gaines

PRODUCTIONS 1989-90

Cymbeline, William Shakespeare; (D) Barbara Gaines; (S) Michael Merritt; (L) Robert Shook
Shakespeare's Greatest Hits, adapt: Barbara Gaines, from William Shakespeare; (D) Barbara Gaines; (C) Nanette Acosta

PRODUCTIONS 1990-91

Shakespeare's Greatest Hits, adapt: Barbara Gaines, from William Shakespeare; (D) Barbara Gaines; (C) Nanette Acosta
King John, William Shakespeare; (D) Barbara Gaines; (S) Michael Merritt; (C) Nan Cibula-Jenkins; (L) Robert Shook
Much Ado About Nothing, William Shakespeare; (D) Barbara Gaines; (S) Michael Merritt; (C) Nan Cibula-Jenkins; (L) Robert Shook

Shakespeare Repertory. Karl Maschek and Greg Vinkler in *King John*. Photo: Jennifer Girard.

The Shakespeare Theatre at the Folger

MICHAEL KAHN
Artistic Director

JESSICA L. ANDREWS
Managing Director

301 East Capitol St. SE
Washington, DC 20003
(202) 547-3230 (bus.)
(202) 546-4000 (b.o.)

FOUNDED 1969
O.B. Hardison, Richmond Crinkley, Folger Shakespeare Library

SEASON
Sept.-June

FACILITIES
Folger Theatre
Seating Capacity: 243
Stage: modified proscenium

FINANCES
July 1, 1990-June 30, 1991
Expenses: $4,300,000

CONTRACTS
AEA LORT (C)

The central issue of the Shakespeare Theatre at the Folger is the development of an American classical style for the 1990s and beyond. Our true challenge is to connect the technical demands made on the classical actor (vocal range, articulation of the text, etc.) and the necessary emotional life (including the larger-than-real-life feelings that Shakespearean characters experience in connecting themselves to the cosmos) to the full use of the actor's intellectual powers and a highly physical acting style. Our other concerns include the need to merge multigenerational artists in all areas of the theatre in a true collaboration; to continue our policy of multicultural casting and staffing in artistic and administrative leadership positions; to expand our educational and outreach programs, including two weeks of free Shakespeare at Carter Barron Amphitheatre; to address major social issues as the plays illuminate them; and to connect productively with the complex community in which we work and live.

—Michael Kahn

PRODUCTIONS 1989-90

Twelfth Night, William Shakespeare; (D) Michael Kahn; (S) Derek McLane; (C) Martin Pakledinaz; (L) Nancy Schertler

The Tempest, William Shakespeare; (D) Richard E.T. White; (S) Kent Dorsey; (C) Barbara Bush; (L) Peter Maradudin

Mary Stuart, Friedrich von Schiller; trans: Robert David MacDonald; (D) Sarah Pia Anderson; (S) Donald Eastman; (C) Martin Pakledinaz; (L) Frances Aronson

The Merry Wives of Windsor, William Shakespeare; (D) Michael Kahn; (S) Derek McLane; (C) Catherine Zuber; (L) John McLain

PRODUCTIONS 1990-91

Richard III, William Shakespeare; (D) Michael Kahn; (S) Derek McLane; (C) Merrily Murray-Walsh; (L) Howell Binkley

Othello, William Shakespeare; (D) Harold Scott; (S) John Ezell; (C) Daniel L. Lawson; (L) Nancy Schertler

Fuente Ovejuna, Lope de Vega; trans: Adrian Mitchell; (D) Rene Buch; (S) Robert Weber Federico; (C) Robert Weber Federico; (L) Robert Weber Federico

King Lear, William Shakespeare; (D) Michael Kahn; (S) Derek McLane; (C) Martin Pakledinaz; (L) Howell Binkle

Snowmass/ Aspen Repertory Theatre

GORDON REINHART
Artistic Director

MARCI MAULLAR
Managing Director

Box 6275
Snowmass Village, CO 81615
(913) 923-2618

The Shakespeare Theatre at the Folger. Kelly McGillis and Philip Goodwin in *Twelfth Night*. Photo: Joan Marcus.

Snowmass/Aspen Repertory Theatre. Roger Bechtel and George Holmes in *Sleuth*. Photo: Portia Fehr.

FOUNDED 1984
Ruth Kevan, Michael T. Yeager

SEASON
June-Sept.

FACILITIES
Snowmass Performing Arts Center Theatre
Seating Capacity: 253
Stage: proscenium

FINANCES
Oct. 1, 1989-Sept. 30, 1990
Expenses: $215,000

CONTRACTS
AEA LORT (D)

The Rep is a place where theatre artists come to work. It is a place where the public comes to witness and participate in that work. The Rep, as an organization, works to provide a supportive environment that both enables and encourages artist and audience to reach for their greatest potential. It is this relationship between the actor and the spectator in the moment of performance that we wish to promote because we know that in this connection lies the magic of theatre. All artistic and managerial decisions are approached with this goal in mind. Play selection, for example, is not based on any political mandate or any considerations of genre or style—we select plays from the whole range of dramatic literature with the sole aim of challenging, inspiring and entertaining our artists and their audience.

—Gordon Reinhart

PRODUCTIONS 1990

Barefoot in the Park, Neil Simon; (D) Gordon Reinhart; (S) Loren Brame; (C) Dana M. Pinkston; (L) Loren Brame
Speed-the-Plow, David Mamet; (D) Gordon Reinhart; (S) Loren Brame; (C) Dana M. Pinkston; (L) Loren Brame
Sleuth, Anthony Shaffer; (D) Gordon Reinhart; (S) Loren Brame; (C) Dana M. Pinkston; (L) Thomas Cochran
Huck Finn, adapt: Doeri A. Welch, from Mark Twain; (D) Doeri A. Welch; (S) Loren Brame; (C) Dana M. Pinkston; (L) Loren Brame

PRODUCTIONS 1991

The Mystery of Irma Vep, Charles Ludlam; (D) Gordon Reinhart; (S) Loren Brame; (C) Deb Brunsen; (L) Loren Brame
A...My Name Is Alice, conceived: Joan Micklin Silver and Julianne Boyd; (D) Gordon Reinhart; (S) Loren Brame; (C) Deb Brunsen; (L) Loren Brame
Billy Bishop Goes to War, John Gray and Eric Peterson; (D) Gordon Reinhart; (S) Loren Brame; (C) Dana M. Pinkston; (L) Loren Brame
The Young King Arthur, Charlotte McFarland; (D) Charlotte McFarland; (S) Dana M. Pinkston; (C) Dana M. Pinkston; (L) Dylan Costa

Society Hill Playhouse

JAY KOGAN
Artistic Director

DEEN KOGAN
Managing Director

507 South 8th St.
Philadelphia, PA 19147
(215) 923-0211 (bus.)
(215) 923-0210 (b.o.)

FOUNDED 1959
Deen Kogan, Jay Kogan

SEASON
Jan.-Dec.

FACILITIES
Mainstage
Seating Capacity: 223
Stage: proscenium

Second Space
Seating Capacity: 99
Stage: flexible

FINANCES
July 1, 1990-June 30, 1991
Expenses: $430,362

CONTRACTS
AEA SPT

The primary goal of Society Hill Playhouse was and is to present great contemporary plays to Philadelphians who might not otherwise see them. For years we produced the Philadelphia premieres of such playwrights as Brecht, Genet, Sartre, Frisch and Beckett. England's Arden, Wesker and Pinter first played here. American playwrights like Arthur Kopit and LeRoi Jones were first seen in Philadelphia at this theatre. During the years, many experiments pursued by other theatres of the world were also pursued by us in Philadelphia: public script-in-hand readings, playwrights' workshops, one-act play marathons, street theatre, youth theatre. As an arts institute functioning as much more than just a presenter of plays, our interaction with Philadelphians, not just as spectators but in every aspect of making theatre, produced an expanding commitment and role in the community, affecting many people. Our continued dedication to our original goals still leads us into new paths of community involvement.

—Jay Kogan

PRODUCTIONS 1989-90

Sisters In Crime, adapt: Susan Turlish, from Gillian Roberts and Mickey Friedman; (D) Susan Turlish; (S) Ray Neil; (L) Robin Miller
The Maids, Jean Genet; (D) Jay

Society Hill Playhouse. Michael Toner in *Beginning to End*. Photo: Ray Buffington.

Kogan; (S) Elizabeth Costello; (L) Stephen Keever

Noel Coward at the Cafe de Paris, adapt: Will Stutts, from Noel Coward; (D) Adelle S. Rubin; (S) Robin Jaffe; (L) Stephen Keever

Beginning to End, adapt: Michael P. Toner, from Samuel Beckett; (D) Veit Schaeffer; (S) Elizabeth Costello; (L) Robin Miller

Old Times, Harold Pinter; (D) Don Auspitz; (S) Elizabeth Costello; (L) Robin Miller

Nunsense, book, music and lyrics: Dan Goggin; (D) Dan Goggin; (S) Barry Aytell; (L) Morris Cooperman

PRODUCTIONS 1990-91

Alberta K. Johnson Among Others, Joee Hall-Hoxter; (D) Susan Turlish; (S) Ray Buffington; (C) Enid Reid Wickes; (L) Neil Tomlinson

The Unknown Soldier, Michael P. Toner; (D) Susan Turlish; (S) Ray Buffington; (C) Enid Reid Wickes; (L) Neil Tomlinson

Pump Boys and Dinettes, John Foley, Mark Hardwick, Debra Monk, Cass Morgan, John Schimmel and Jim Wann; (D) John Foley; (S) Miguel Lopez-Castillo; (C) Enid Reid Wickes; (L) Robin Miller

Nunsense, book, music and lyrics: Dan Goggin; (D) Dan Goggin; (S) Ray Buffington; (L) Neil Tomlinson

Ten Percent Revue, book, music and lyrics: Tom Wilson Weinberg; (D) Deen Kogan; (S) Barry Marron; (C) Barry Marron; (L) Neil Tomlinson

Source Theatre Company

PAT MURPHY SHEEHY
Producing Artistic Director

KEITH PARKER
Literary Manager

1835 14th St. NW
Washington, DC 20009
(202) 232-8012 (bus.)
(202) 462-1073 (b.o.)

FOUNDED 1977
Bart Whiteman

SEASON
Jan.-Dec.

FACILITIES
Source Theatre Company
Seating Capacity: 107
Stage: thrust

FINANCES
Sept. 1, 1990-Aug. 31, 1991
Expenses: $253,364

CONTRACTS
AEA SPT

Celebrating its 15th season, Source Theatre Company continues its vital role in expanding opportunities for the creative work of Washington theatre artists. Through an innovative season of contemporary plays and reexaminations of the classics, we explore issues relevant to our culturally diverse community in the nation's capital. Our annual Washington Theatre Festival, which produces more than 60 new plays at various venues throughout the city each summer, inspires and anchors our commitment to the development of new work and new artists. A pioneer in the establishment of a viable alternative theatre district on 14th Street, Source has proved the springboard for the careers of some of Washington's finest professional talents, including its actors, directors, designers and playwrights. Through classes, a Late Night play series, the SourceWorks reading program, Mystery Events, touring and a vital community outreach, we continue to be an energetic center that celebrates the joy of the creative experience.

—*Pat Murphy Sheehy*

PRODUCTIONS 1989-90

Don Juan of Seville, Tirso de Molina; adapt and trans: Lynne Alvarez; (D) Joe Banno; (S) Thomas J. Donahue; (C) Rosa Leland; (L) Jeff Guzik

Titanic, Christopher Durang; (D) Jim Stone; (S) Thomas J. Donahue; (C) Susan Barreca and Dathan Manning; (L) Jeff Guzik

The Voice of the Prairie, John Olive; (D) Edward Morgan; (S) Edward Morgan and Eric Schaeffer; (C) Tracey White; (L) Jennifer Garrett

Bluesman, Bruce Clarke; (D) Edward Morgan; (S) Elizabeth Jenkins; (C) Christina Rosendaul; (L) Jennifer Garrett

Source Theatre Company. Elizabeth Pierotti, Cynthia Webb, Kara Russell, Lisa DeMont and Deidre Boddie-Henderson in *The Well of Horniness*. Photo: Ron Franklin.

Three Tits, Ellen K. Anderson; (D) Michael McFadden; (S) Elizabeth Jenkins; (C) Luba I. McFadden; (L) Ruth Yamamoto

Dumb Stuff, Terryl Paiste; (D) Elizabeth Robelen; (S) Elizabeth Jenkins; (C) Luba I. McFadden; (L) Ruth Yamamoto

Mother's Day, Barbara McConagha; (D) Jim Stone; (S) Elizabeth Jenkins; (C) Luba I. McFadden; (L) Ruth Yamamoto

Being Frank, Sara Scopp; (D) Richard Schooch; (S) Elizabeth Jenkins; (C) Luba I. McFadden; (L) Ruth Yamamoto

Bamsville, Raymond Embrack; (D) Kenneth Daugherty; (S) Elizabeth Jenkins; (C) Luba I. McFadden; (L) Ruth Yamamoto

Women and Wallace, Jonathan Marc Sherman; (D) Randye Hoeflich; (S) Joseph B. Musumeci, Jr.; (C) Luba I. McFadden; (L) Jennifer Garrett

The Well of Horniness, Holly Hughes; (D) Connie Lane; (S) Amy Austin; (C) Timothy White; (L) Ruth Yamamoto

PRODUCTIONS 1990-91

The Meeting, Jeff Stetson; (D) Jennifer Nelson; (S) Thomas J. Donahue; (C) Luba I. McFadden; (L) Jennifer Garrett

Murder in Memoriam, Sara Scopp; (D) Karen Berman; (S) Thomas J. Donahue; (C) Karen Berman; (L) Jennifer Garrett

Children With Stones, book, music and lyrics: Roy Barber; (D) Janet Wallis; (S) Elizabeth Jenkins; (C) Janet Wallis; (L) David R. Zemmels

Avenue of the Americas, Martin Blank; (D) Joe Banno; (S) Elizabeth Jenkins; (C) Joe Banno; (L) David R. Zemmels

Eastern Standard, Richard Greenberg; (D) Joe Banno; (S) Tom Meyer; (C) Thomas W. Mallen; (L) Jennifer Garrett

intimacies, Michael Kearns; (D) Kelly Hill; (S) Tom Meyer; (L) Aaron Carmichael

Abingdon Square, Maria Irene Fornes; (D) Elizabeth Robelen; (S) Elizabeth Jenkins; (C) John A. Robelen, III; (L) Elizabeth Jenkins

Mud, Maria Irene Fornes; (D) Pat Murphy Sheehy; (S) Elizabeth Jenkins; (C) Randye Hoeflich; (L) Elizabeth Jenkins

Psycho Beach Party, Charles Busch; (D) Jerry Manning; (S) Tony Cisek; (C) Hugh Hanson; (L) Christopher V. Lewton

South Coast Repertory

DAVID EMMES
Producing Artistic Director

MARTIN BENSON
Artistic Director

South Coast Repertory. Elizabeth McGovern and Dana Ivey in *When I Was a Girl I Used to Scream and Shout*. Photo: Ron Stone.

Box 2197
655 Town Center Drive
Costa Mesa, CA 92628-2197
(714) 957-2602 (bus.)
(714) 957-4033 (b.o.)

FOUNDED 1964
David Emmes, Martin Benson

SEASON
Sept.-July

FACILITIES
Mainstage
Seating Capacity: 507
Stage: modified thrust

Second Stage
Seating Capacity: 161
Stage: thrust

SCR Amphitheatre
Seating Capacity: 200
Stage: flexible

FINANCES
Sept. 1, 1990-Aug. 31, 1991
Expenses: $5,700,000

CONTRACTS
AEA LORT (B) and (D), and TYA

South Coast Repertory commits itself to exploring the most important human and social issues of our time and to testing the bounds of theatre's possibilities. While valuing all elements of theatrical production, we give primacy to the text and its creators. Through premiere productions and an array of developmental programs, we serve, nurture and establish long-term relationships with America's most promising playwrights. Around our core company of actors we have built a large and dynamic ensemble of artists, constantly infusing their work with the fresh perspective of artists new to our collaboration. We devote our financial resources to making theatre a viable and rewarding profession for all our artists. While striving to advance the art of theatre, we also serve our community with a variety of educational, multicultural and outreach programs designed to support our artistic mission.

—*Martin Benson*

PRODUCTIONS 1989-90

A Chorus of Disapproval, Alan Ayckbourn; (D) David Emmes; (S) Michael Devine; (C) Tom Ruzika; (L) Susan Denison Geller

Breaking the Code, Hugh Whitemore; (D) Martin Benson; (S) Cliff Faulkner; (C) Peter Maradudin; (L) Walker Hicklin

A Christmas Carol, adapt: Jerry Patch, from Charles Dickens; (D) John-David Keller; (S) Cliff Faulkner; (C) Tom Ruzika and Donna Ruzika; (L) Dwight Richard Odle

Search and Destroy, Howard Korder; (D) David Chambers; (S) Christopher Barreca; (C) Chris Parry; (L) Dunya Ramicova

A Midsummer Night's Dream, William Shakespeare; (D) Paul Marcus; (S) Cliff Faulkner; (C) Paulie Jenkins; (L) Shigeru Yaji

Once in Arden, Richard Hellesen; (D) Martin Benson; (S) Michael Devine; (C) Tom Ruzika; (L) Dwight Richard Odle

Speed-the-Plow, David Mamet; (D) Mary B. Robinson; (S) Ralph Funicello; (C) Paulie Jenkins; (L) Ann Bruice

Frankie and Johnny in the Clair de Lune, Terrence McNally; (D) Warner Shook; (S) John Iacovelli; (C) Brian Gale; (L) Ann Bruice

When I Was a Girl I Used to Scream and Shout, Sharman McDonald; (D) Simon Stokes; (S) Cliff Faulkner; (C) Paulie Jenkins; (L) Shigeru Yaji

Holy Days, Sally Nemeth; (D) Martin Benson; (S) John Iacovelli; (C) Tom Ruzika; (L) Ann Bruice

Emerald City, David Williamson; (D) David Emmes; (S) Michael Devine; (C) Peter Maradudin; (L) Karen J. Weller

Man of the Flesh, Octavio Solis; (D) Jose Cruz Gonzalez; (S) Cliff Faulkner; (C) Tom Ruzika; (L) Shigeru Yaji

The Ramp, Shem Bitterman; (D) Steven Albrezzi; (S) Cliff Faulkner; (C) Tom Ruzika; (L) Shigeru Yaji

PRODUCTIONS 1990-91

Man and Superman, George Bernard Shaw; (D) Martin Benson; (S) Cliff Faulkner; (C) Paulie Jenkins; (L) Shigeru Yaji

The Secret Rapture, David Hare; (D) David Emmes; (S) Robert Jones; (C) Tom Ruzika; (L) Robert Jones

A Christmas Carol, adapt: Jerry Patch, from Charles Dickens; (D) John-David Keller; (S) Cliff Faulkner; (C) Tom Ruzika and Donna Ruzika; (L) Dwight Richard Odle

Pirates, Mark Lee; (D) Martin Benson; (S) Marjorie Bradley Kellogg; (C) Tom Ruzika; (L) Walker Hicklin

You Can't Take It With You, Moss Hart and George S. Kaufman; (D) Warner Shook; (S) Michael Devine; (C) Peter Maradudin; (L) Ann Bruice

El Dorado, Milcha Sanchez-Scott; (D) Peter C. Brosius; (S) Loy Arcenas; (C) Peter Maradudin; (L) Lydia Tanji

Happy End, adapt and trans: Michael Feingold; book and lyrics: Bertolt Brecht; music: Kurt Weill; (D) Barbara Damashek; (S) Ralph Funicello; (C) Paulie Jenkins; (L) Shigeru Yaji

Pick Up Ax, Anthony Clarvoe; (D) David Esbjornson; (S) John Iacovelli; (C) Brian Gale; (L) Ann Bruice

Alekhine's Defense, Robert Daseler; (D) Eli Simon; (S) Cliff Faulkner; (C) Peter Maradudin; (L) Sylvia Vega-Vasquez

Kiss of the Spider Woman, Manuel Puig; trans: Allan Baker; (D) David Chambers; (S) Ralph Funicello; (C) Tom Ruzika

The Russian Teacher, Alexander Burafsky; adapt: Keith Reddin; (D) David Emmes; (S) Cliff Faulkner; (C) Brenda Berry; (L) Dwight Richard Odle

Moonshadow, Richard Hellesen; (D) Martin Benson; (S) Cliff Faulkner; (C) Paulie Jenkins; (L) Ann Bruice

Stage One: The Louisville Children's Theatre

MOSES GOLDBERG
Producing Director

G. JANE JARRETT
Managing Director

425 West Market St.
Louisville, KY 40202
(502) 589-5946 (bus.)
(502) 584-7777 or
(800) 283-7777 (b.o.)

FOUNDED 1946
Sara Spencer, Ming Dick

SEASON
Oct.-May

FACILITIES
Kentucky Center for the Arts
Bomhard Theater
Seating Capacity: 626
Stage: thrust

Kentucky Center for the Arts
Large Rehearsal Hall
Seating Capacity: 250
Stage: arena

FINANCES
June 1, 1990-May 31, 1991
Expenses: $1,197,630

CONTRACTS
AEA TYA

Stage One: The Louisville Children's Theatre provides theatre experiences for young people and families. Choosing plays for specific age groups, we attempt to develop the aesthetic sensitivity of our audience members, step by step, until they emerge from our program as committed adult theatregoers. We play to both school groups and weekend family audiences. Stage One is also committed to developing professionalism in theatre for young audiences, including upgrading artist compensation to the level of adult theatres our size. We perform an eclectic repertoire, including traditional children's plays, company-created pieces, commissioned plays, plays translated from other cultures and carefully selected works from the adult repertoire. Stage One operates in the belief that the classics (both ancient and modern) of folk and children's literature concern archetypal human relationships and are worthy of serious artistic exploration.

—*Moses Goldberg*

PRODUCTIONS 1989-90

Vasilisa, The Russian Cinderella, Moses Goldberg; (D) Susan Hazen; (S) Brenda K. Kiefer; (C) Polly Byers; (L) Chuck Schmidt

The Glass Menagerie, Tennessee Williams; (D) Moses Goldberg; (S) Brenda K. Kiefer; (C) Polly Byers; (L) Chuck Schmidt

The Adventures of a Bear Called Paddington, Alfred Bradley and Michael Bond; (D) Tom Schreier; (S) F. Elaine Williams; (C) Polly Byers; (L) Chuck Schmidt

The Best Christmas Pageant Ever, adapt: Barbara Robinson; (D) J. Daniel Herring; (S) Ken Terrill; (C) Mary Bruns; (L) Chuck Schmidt

Hansel and Gretel, Moses Goldberg, from The Brothers Grimm; (D) Tom Schreier; (S) Brenda K. Kiefer; (C) Polly Byers

Snow White and the Seven Dwarfs, Gail Fairbank, from The Brothers Grimm; (D) Moses Goldberg; (S) Randal R. Cochran; (C) Polly Byers

Frankenstein, adapt: Nick DiMartino, from Mary Shelley; (D) Kyle Donnelly; (S) Curtis C. Trout; (C) Polly Byers; (L) Chuck Schmidt

The Secret Garden, adapt: Laura Amy Schlitz, from Frances Hodgson Burnett; (D) Moses Goldberg; (S) Brenda K. Kiefer; (C) Polly Byers; (L) Justin C. Reiter

Japanese Fairy Tales, Robin Hall; (D) Ron Nakahara; (S) Brenda K. Kiefer; (C) Polly Byers; (L) Chuck Schmidt

Stage One: The Louisville Children's Theatre. Art Burns and Thomas Richter in *Young King Arthur*. Photo: Richard Trigg.

Stages Repertory Theatre. Karen D. Anderson and Ginnie Randall in *Shakin' the Mess Outta Misery*.

PRODUCTIONS 1990-91

Bridge to Terabithia, book: Katherine Paterson and Stephanie S. Tolan, from Katherine Paterson; music and lyrics: Steve Liebman; (D) Tom Schreier; (S) John Saari; (C) Polly Byers; (L) Chuck Schmidt

The Story of Babar, the Little Elephant, adapt: Thomas W. Olson, from Jean de Brunhoff; (D) Moses Goldberg; (S) John Saari; (C) Polly Byers; (L) Chuck Schmidt

Little Red Riding Hood and ***The Three Little Pigs***, book and lyrics: Moses Goldberg; music: Ewel Cornett; (D) Tom Schreier; (S) Chuck Schmidt; (C) Polly Byers

The Best Christmas Pageant Ever, adapt: Barbara Robinson; (D) J. Daniel Herring; (S) Ken Terrill; (C) Polly Byers; (L) Chuck Schmidt

The Miracle Worker, William Gibson; (D) Moses Goldberg; (S) Brenda K. Kiefer; (C) Polly Byers; (L) Chuck Schmidt

Nuthin' But Trouble, Theatre Beyond Words; (D) Harro Maskow; (S) David Satterthwaite; (C) Elizabeth Severin

Young King Arthur, Laura Amy Schlitz; (D) Moses Goldberg; (S) Ken Terrill; (C) Polly Byers; (L) Chuck Schmidt

James and the Giant Peach, from Roald Dahl; (D) J. Daniel Herring; (S) Ken Terrill; (C) Polly Byers; (L) Chuck Schmidt

Stages Repertory Theatre

PETER BENNETT
Artistic Director

3201 Allen Parkway, Suite 101
Houston, TX 77019
(713) 527-0220 (bus.)
(713) 527-8243 (b.o.)

FOUNDED 1978
Ted Swindley

SEASON
Jan.-Dec.

FACILITIES
Thrust
Seating Capacity: 191
Stage: thrust

Arena
Seating Capacity: 208
Stage: arena

FINANCES
Sept. 1, 1990-Aug. 31, 1991
Expenses: $850,000

CONTRACTS
AEA SPT

Providing an alternative to mainstream theatre, Stages devotes its repertoire to provocative contemporary plays and reinterpretations of classics. It is especially committed to new works by both developing and established playwrights, and to plays by women and minority authors. This commitment extends beyond the play and production to the long-term development of writers, actors and other theatre artists. The company's highly successful EarlyStages series consists of professional productions of plays for children and young audiences.

—Peter Bennett

Note: During the 1989-90 season, Ted Swindley served as artistic director. During the 1990-91 season, Jack Stehlin served as artistic director and Jim Bernhard served as acting artistic director.

PRODUCTIONS 1989-90

The World of Beauty, Alex Finlayson; (D) Ted Swindley; (C) Norma Catlin; (L) Tenna Matthews

Rock and Betty Dance, Joe Turner Cantu; (D) Ted Swindley; (S) Tenna Matthews; (C) Norma Catlin; (L) Tenna Matthews

Reckless, Craig Lucas; (D) Joe Turner Cantu; (S) Harold Hynick; (C) Lisa A. Vollrath; (L) Tenna Matthews

The Night of the Iguana, Tennessee Williams; (D) Ted Swindley; (S) Gerald Enos; (C) Lisa A. Vollrath; (L) Tenna Matthews

Little Shop of Horrors, book and lyrics: Howard Ashman; music: Alan Menken; (D) Jack Lampert; (S) Joe Carpenter; (C) Lisa A. Vollrath; (L) Tenna Matthews

Torch Song Trilogy, Harvey Fierstein; (D) Joe Turner Cantu; (S) Harold Hynick; (L) Tenna Matthews

PRODUCTIONS 1990-91

Driving Miss Daisy, Alfred Uhry; (D) Jack Stehlin; (S) Jay Michael Jagim; (C) Nanette Griffin; (L) Jonathan Belcher

The Gift of the Magi, adapt: Peter Ekstrom, from O. Henry; (D) Jack Lampert; (S) Jonathan Belcher and Greg Roach; (C) Nanette Griffin; (L) Jonathan Belcher

The Cocktail Hour, A.R. Gurney, Jr.; (D) Richard Ziman; (S) Paul Blumenthal; (C) Nanette Griffin; (L) Jonathan Belcher, Karen Bull

Shakin' the Mess Outta Misery, Shay Youngblood; (D) Brenda Redmond; (S) Jonathan Belcher; (C) Patrick Collins; (L) Jonathan Belcher

Miss Julie, August Strindberg; (D) Edwin Wilson; (S) Jay Michael Jagim; (C) Nanette Griffin; (L) Jonathan Belcher

Closer Than Ever, conceived: Steven Scott Smith; music: David Shire; lyrics: Richard Maltby, Jr.; (D) Jack Lampert; (S) Arch Andrus; (C) Patrick Collins; (L) Jonathan Belcher

Talking Pictures, Horton Foote; (D) Peter Masterson; (S) Jay Michael Jagim; (C) Nanette Griffin; (L) Jerry Ford

Stage West

JERRY RUSSELL
Artistic/Managing Director

JAMES COVAULT
Associate Director

Box 2587
Fort Worth, TX 76113
(817) 332-6265 (bus.)
(817) 332-6238 (b.o.)

FOUNDED 1979
Jerry Russell

SEASON
Jan.-Dec.

FACILITIES
Stage West
Seating Capacity: 150
Stage: thrust

FINANCES
Oct. 1, 1989-Sept. 30, 1990
Expenses: $422,251

CONTRACTS
AEA SPT

Stage West has established the first professional theatre that Fort Worth has ever known. From a beginning with no outside support and only the commitment of our founders, we have grown to more than 1,500 subscribers and to the second highest annual attendance among the city's performing arts groups, and have gained an enviable reputation in the Dallas-Fort Worth area. Our play-selection philosophy is broad-based, with each season containing a mix of contemporary and period pieces, musicals, classical adaptations and original works. We are committed to producing one new work each season. Future objectives include the building of a new 350-seat theatre, the redevelopment of our experimental performing space, and advancement to LORT contract status with Actors' Equity Association. To date, budgets have allowed only local casting. The next five years should see an expansion in our casting policies, and possibly a small resident company.

—Jerry Russell

PRODUCTIONS 1989-90

What the Butler Saw, Joe Orton; (D) Jerry Russell; (S) Dale Domm; (C) James Covault; (L) Michael O'Brien

Blithe Spirit, Noel Coward; (D) James Covault; (S) Nelson Robinson; (C) James Covault; (L) Michael O'Brien

The Boys Next Door, Tom Griffin; (D) Jerry Russell; (S) James Covault; (C) James Covault; (L) Michael O'Brien

King Lear, William Shakespeare; (D) James Covault; (S) Dale Domm; (C) James Covault and Suzi McLaughlin; (L) Michael O'Brien

Back to Back, Al Brown; (D) Jerry Russell; (S) Dale Domm; (C) James Covault; (L) Michael O'Brien

A...My Name Is Alice, conceived: Joan Micklin Silver and Julianne Boyd; (D) Jerry Russell and Buckley Sachs; (S) James Covault; (C) James Covault; (L) Michael O'Brien

Away, Michael Gow; (D) James Covault; (S) Nelson Robinson; (C) James Covault and Suzi McLaughlin; (L) Michael O'Brien

A Walk in the Woods, Lee Blessing; (D) Nicolas Sandys; (S) Nelson Robinson; (C) James Covault; (L) Michael O'Brien

PRODUCTIONS 1990-91

Sisterly Feelings, Alan Ayckbourn; (D) James Covault; (S) Dale Domm; (C) James Covault; (L) Michael O'Brien

Romance/Romance, book and lyrics: Barry Harman; music: Keith Herrmann; (D) Jerry Russell; (S) James Covault; (C) James Covault; (L) Michael O'Brien

Driving Miss Daisy, Alfred Uhry; (D) Jerry Russell; (S) James Covault; (C) James Covault; (L) Michael O'Brien

Twelfth Night, William Shakespeare; (D) James Covault; (S) Nelson Robinson; (C) Bruce Coleman; (L) Michael O'Brien

Serious Money, Caryl Churchill; (D) Jerry Russell; (S) Nelson Robinson; (C) James Covault; (L) Michael O'Brien

Closer Than Ever, conceived: Steven Scott Smith; music: David Shire; lyrics: Richard Maltby, Jr.; (D) Jerry Russell; (S) Dale Domm; (C) James Covault; (L) Michael O'Brien

Once in Arden, Richard Hellesen; (D) James Covault; (S) Dale Domm; (C) Bruce Coleman; (L) Michael O'Brien

The Philadelphia Story, Philip Barry; (D) James Covault; (S) Nelson Robinson; (C) James Covault and Bruce Coleman; (L) Michael O'Brien

Stage West. Nick Sandys and Elizabeth Rouse in *Twelfth Night*. Photo: Buddy Myers.

StageWest

ERIC HILL
Artistic Director

MARTHA RICHARDS
Managing Director

One Columbus Center
Springfield, MA 01103
(413) 781-4470 (bus.)
(413) 781-2340 (b.o.)

FOUNDED 1967
Stephen E. Hays

SEASON
Oct.-May

FACILITIES
S. Prestly Blake Theatre
Seating Capacity: 447
Stage: thrust

Winifred Arms Studio Theatre
Seating Capacity: 99
Stage: flexible

FINANCES
July 1, 1990-June 30, 1991
Expenses: $1,760,600

CONTRACTS
AEA LORT (C) and (D)

StageWest's artistic identity is reflected in its commitment to a company of artists whose ongoing collaboration in a varied and expanded repertoire forms the central condition of our work. The goals of the theatre are to develop and cultivate the artists; to present a full range of theatrical works to the broadest possible audience; to promote opportunities for creative individuals of all cultural backgrounds to exercise their artistic and technical skills; to train and develop young talent; and to continue to collaborate with other theatre companies. Ongoing classes for students and special projects in research and development continue through the season. An intern acting company works alongside the Equity company all season, and daily classes in the Suzuki method of actor training are offered to every company member throughout the season.

—Eric Hill

PRODUCTIONS 1989-90

Educating Rita, Willy Russell; (D) John Tyson; (S) Keith Henery; (C) Kristin Yungkurth; (L) Clifford E. Berek

A Christmas Carol, adapt: John Tyson, from Charles Dickens; (D) Eric Hill and John Tyson; (S) Keith Henery; (C) Kristin Yungkurth; (L) Clifford E. Berek

Watch on the Rhine, Lillian Hellman; (D) Eric Hill; (S) Keith Henery; (C) Kristin Yungkurth; (L) Jeff Hill

The Boys Next Door, Tom Griffin; (D) Eric Hill; (S) Keith Henery; (C) Kristin Yungkurth; (L) Robert Jared

Fences, August Wilson; (D) Clinton Turner Davis; (S) Charles McClennahan; (C) Alvin Perry; (L) Jeff Hill

Betrayal, Harold Pinter; (D) John Tyson; (S) Keith Henery; (C) Kristin Yungkurth; (L) Clifford E. Berek

The Mystery of Irma Vep, Charles Ludlam; (D) David Eppel; (S) Keith Henery; (C) Kristin Yungkurth; (L) Victor En Yu Tan

The Tempest, William Shakespeare; adapt: John Tyson; (D) John Tyson; (S) Sarah Sullivan; (C) Andrew Carson; (L) Clifford E. Berek

Hamlet, William Shakespeare; adapt: Eric Hill; (D) Eric Hill; (S) Keith Henery, Sarah Sullivan and Michelle M. Klemaszewski; (C) Andrew Carson; (L) David A. Strang

PRODUCTIONS 1990-91

Night Must Fall, Emlyn Williams; (D) John Tyson; (S) Keith Henery; (C) Kristin Yungkurth; (L) Jeff Hill

Holiday, Philip Barry; (D) Eric Hill; (S) Keith Henery; (C) Kristin Yungkurth; (L) Jeff Hill

Visions of an Ancient Dreamer, adapt: Eric Hill, from Euripides; (D) Eric Hill; (S) Sarah Sullivan and Keith Henery; (C) Randy Brown; (L) David A. Strang

Sweet 'N' Hot in Harlem, conceived: Robert Elliot Cohen; music: Harold Arlen; various lyricists; (D) Clinton Turner Davis; (S) Keith Henery; (C) Kristin Yungkurth; (L) William H. Grant, III

The Field of Blue Children and Suddenly Last Summer, Tennessee Williams; (D) Eric Hill; (S) Keith Henery; (C) Kristin Yungkurth; (L) David A. Strang

The Immigrant, Mark Harelik; (D) Eric Hill; (S) Keith Henery; (C) Kristin Yungkurth; (L) Jeff Hill

StageWest. *Hamlet.*

Steppenwolf Theatre Company

RANDALL ARNEY
Artistic Director

STEPHEN B. EICH
Managing Director

1650 N. Halsted St.
Chicago, IL 60614
(312) 335-1888 (bus.)
(312) 335-1650 (b.o.)

FOUNDED 1976
Terry Kinney, Jeff Perry, Gary Sinise

SEASON
Jan.-Dec.

FACILITIES
Steppenwolf Mainstage
Seating Capacity: 510
Stage: proscenium

FINANCES
Sept. 1, 1990-Aug. 31, 1991
Expenses: $3,153,679

CONTRACTS
AEA CAT

Steppenwolf Theatre Company is comprised of actors, directors, designers, administrative and production staffs, and a board of directors who work closely together towards a cooperative and common artistic vision. With a 23-member ensemble of actor-directors and a wide-ranging repertoire, Steppenwolf aims to provide exceptional theatre through a collective approach conducive to artistic growth and thus challenging to audience and actor alike. Each artist's commitment to the ensemble approach testifies to its worth: Seven of the nine original members remain with the group after 16 years. The company achieves a rare combination: Talented individuals put the group effort first and thereby simultaneously develop their own individual potential. Steppenwolf is committed to maintaining a permanent resident company in Chicago and to promoting the goals of the ensemble by the presentation of its works to new audiences. With the completion of its new permanent home in the spring of 1991, these future commitments are ensured.

—Randall Arney

PRODUCTIONS 1989-90

The Homecoming, Harold Pinter; (D) Jeff Perry; (S) Kevin Rigdon; (C) Erin Quigley; (L) Kevin Rigdon

The Geography of Luck, Marlane Meyer; (D) Randall Arney; (S) Kevin Rigdon; (C) Erin Quigley; (L) Kevin Rigdon

Reckless, Craig Lucas; (D) Terry Kinney; (S) Kevin Rigdon; (C) Laura Cunningham; (L) Kevin Rigdon

Love Letters, A.R. Gurney, Jr.; (D) Randall Arney and Stephen B.

Steppenwolf Theatre Company. Joan Allen and Boyd Gaines in *Reckless*. Photo: Michael Brosilow.

Eich; (S) Kevin Rigdon; (L) Kevin Rigdon

Wrong Turn at Lungfish, Garry Marshall and Lowell Ganz; (D) Garry Marshall; (S) Michael Merritt; (C) Erin Quigley; (L) Kevin Rigdon

PRODUCTIONS 1990-91

The Secret Rapture, David Hare; (D) Eric Simonson; (S) Linda Buchanan; (C) Erin Quigley; (L) Peter Gottlieb

Harvey, Mary Chase; (D) Austin Pendleton; (S) Kevin Rigdon; (C) Erin Quigley; (L) Kevin Rigdon

Another Time, Ronald Harwood; (D) Ronald Harwood; (S) Kevin Rigdon; (C) Erin Quigley; (L) Kevin Rigdon

Curse of the Starving Class, Sam Shepard; (D) Randall Arney; (S) Kevin Rigdon; (C) Erin Quigley; (L) Kevin Rigdon

Earthly Possessions, adapt: Frank Galati, from Anne Tyler; (D) Frank Galati; (S) Robert Christen; (C) Erin Quigley; (L) Kevin Rigdon

St. Louis Black Repertory Company

RONALD J. HIMES
Producing Director

DONNA ADAMS
General Manager

634 North Grand Blvd., Suite 10-F
St. Louis, MO 63103
(314) 534-3807

FOUNDED 1976
Ronald J. Himes

SEASON
Sept.-May

FACILITIES
23rd Street Theatre
Seating Capacity: 200
Stage: proscenium

FINANCES
July 1, 1990-June 30, 1991
Expenses: $450,000

CONTRACTS
AEA SPT

St. Louis Black Repertory Company was founded to heighten the social, cultural and educational awareness of the community–and to create an ongoing arts program for that community. As the company has expanded so have our programs: We now produce six mainstage shows; we have an extensive educational component that includes four to six touring shows, workshops and residencies, and a professional intern program. We have also presented dance, music and film series. Our main stage has strong commitment to producing the works of black American and Third World writers in an environment that supports not only the development of the work, but also the actors, directors and designers involved. Thus the majority of our productions are area and regional premieres, aimed at artistic rather than commercial success.

—*Ronald J. Himes*

PRODUCTIONS 1989-90

Seones, book: John Reeger; music and lyrics: Julie Shannon; (D) Ronald J. Himes; (S) John Roslevich, Jr.; (C) John Carver Sullivan; (L) Mark Wilson

Jelly Belly, Charles Smith; (D) Debra Wicks; (S) Mel Dickerson; (C) Chris Anthony; (L) Richard Barrett

The Meeting, Jeff Scetson; (D) Stephen McKinley Henderson and Ron O.J. Parson; (S) Jim Burwinkel; (C) Chris Anthony; (L) Jim Burwinkel

Oedipus the King, adapt: Berj Clay, from Sophocles; (D) Ben Halley, Jr.; (S) Frank Bradley; (C) Laurie Trevethan; (L) Kathy Perkins

Lady Day at Emerson's Bar and Grill, Lanie Robertson; (D) Ronald J. Himes; (S) John Roslevich, Jr.; (C) J. Bruce Summers; (L) David Kunz

Joe Turner's Come and Gone, August Wilson; (D) Edward G. Smith; (S) David Sill; (C) Barbara Vaughan; (L) Kathy Perkins

PRODUCTIONS 1990-91

Three Ways Home, Casey Kurtti; (D) Ronald J. Himes; (S) Jim Burwinkel; (C) Antonitta Barnes; (L) Glenn Dunn

I Don't Have to Show You No Stinking Badges, Luis Valdez; (D) Michael Ramirez; (S) Miles R. Vesich; (C) Laurie Trevethan; (L) Kathy Perkins

Ceremonies in Dark Old Men, Lonne Elder, III; (D) Lorna Littleway; (S) Frank Bradley; (C) Laurie Trevethan; (L) Glenn Dunn

Wet Carpets, Marian Warrington; (D) Debra Wicks; (S) James Walker; (C) Antonitta Barnes; (L) Sue Grenberg, Christine Smith

Young Richard, Charles Smith; (D) Ronald J. Himes; (S) Jim Burwinkel; (C) John Carver Sullivan; (L) Chris Abernathy

One Mo' Time, book: Vernel Bagneris; (D) Fontaine Syer; (S) John Roslevich, Jr.; (C) J. Bruce Summers; (L) Kathy Perkins

St. Louis Black Repertory Company. Regina Frye, Crystal Henry and Kathy Taylor Harper in *Wet Carpets*.

The Street Theater. J. Michael Reeds, Emmett Smith, Kathryn Markey and Angela Bullock in *Alex Underground*. Photo: Kraft/General Food Corp.

The Street Theater

GRAY SMITH
Executive Director

228 Fisher Ave., Room 226
White Plains, NY 10606-2702
(914) 761-3307

FOUNDED 1970
Gray Smith

SEASON
Sept.-June

FINANCES
June 1, 1990-May 31, 1991
Expenses: $245,000

CONTRACTS
AEA TYA

All Street Theater audience members—whether in parks, blocked-off streets, day camps, schools or other institutions—are viewed as potential actors. If they see themselves on stage our work is validated; if not, we have more work to do. We try to eliminate spectacle and to provide little support for "spectators"; whenever possible our performances lead to their performances—of pieces developed with our directors through training and collaboration. Some of these pieces go on tours, usually within the school districts where they originate. All of our work is original, growing either out of actor-director collaboration or the development of commissioned scripts. Most members of our audience are also "originals": They are eager to challenge, celebrate and renew our capacity to tell their story.

—Gray Smith

PRODUCTIONS 1989-90

Me and You, company-developed; (D) Sara Rubin
Turned Around Tales, company-developed; (D) Sara Rubin

PRODUCTIONS 1990-91

Alex Underground, Vincent J. Cardinal; (D) Vincent J. Cardinal
Me and You, company-developed; (D) Vincent J. Cardinal
Turned Around Tales, company-developed; (D) Katherine Markey and Joe Giardina

Studio Arena Theatre

GAVIN CAMERON-WEBB
Artistic Director

RAYMOND BONNARD
Executive Director

710 Main St.
Buffalo, NY 14202-1990
(716) 856-8025 (bus.)
(716) 856-5650 (b.o.)

FOUNDED 1965
Neal DuBrock

SEASON
Sept.-June

FACILITIES
Mainstage
Seating Capacity: 637
Stage: thrust

FINANCES
July 1, 1990-June 30, 1991
Expenses: $3,201,000

CONTRACTS
AEA LORT (B)

Studio Arena Theatre takes joy in its efforts to create a "popular" theatre of integrity and ambition. We conceive of our work as entertainment adventurously enlarged through the insight of the artist, rather than as art narrowly defined and self-righteously distinct from entertainment. Our work is eclectic because our taste is so and because we can afford no self-imposed limitations in the pursuit of our goal, beyond a determination to choose work which excites us and which we believe will also engage our remarkably large and varied audience. We aspire to the creation of an outstanding regional theatre, dedicated to the audience that has chosen us, in the belief that this is the most effective way of making a contribution of more than regional significance to the art form as a whole.

—David Frank

Note: During the 1989-90 and 1990-91 seasons, David Frank served as artistic director.

PRODUCTIONS 1989-90

You Can't Take It With You, George S. Kaufman and Moss Hart; (D) David Frank; (S) Hugh Landwehr; (C) Mary Ann Powell; (L) Peter Kaczorowski
Joe Turner's Come and Gone, August Wilson; (D) Edward G. Smith; (S) Charles

Studio Arena Theatre. Donald Berman in *Birdsend*. Photo: Irene Haupt

McClennahan; (C) Judy Dearing; (L) Allen Lee Hughes

Galileo, book and lyrics: Keith Levenson and Alexa Junge; music: Jeanine Levenson; (D) David Frank and Keith Levenson; (S) David Jenkins; (C) Julie Weiss; (L) Peter Kaczorowski

Speed-the-Plow, David Mamet; (D) Kathryn Long; (S) Victor Becker; (C) Timothy Averill; (L) Pat Collins

A Moon for the Misbegotten, Eugene O'Neill; (D) Vincent Dowling; (S) Wendy Shea; (C) Wendy Shea; (L) Brian Nason

Beyond Therapy and ***Laughing Wild***, Christopher Durang; (D) Ross Wasserman; (S) Philipp Jung; (C) Ellen V. McCartney; (L) Michael Chybowski

Last Love, Tom Cole; (D) Tony Giordano; (S) Kent Dorsey; (C) Christine Dougherty; (L) Kent Dorsey

PRODUCTIONS 1990-91

A Flea in Her Ear, Georges Feydeau; adapt: David Frank; trans: Abbott Chrisman; (D) David Frank; (S) Philipp Jung; (C) Philipp Jung; (L) Michael Chybowski

Jane Eyre, book and lyrics: Ted Davis, from Charlotte Bronte; music: David Clark; (D) Ted Davis; (S) Bob Barnett; (C) Pamela Scofield; (L) F. Mitchell Dana

A Christmas Carol, adapt: Amlin Gray, from Charles Dickens; (D) David Frank; (S) Paul Wonsek; (C) Mary Ann Powell; (L) Paul Wonsek

Birdsend, Keith Huff; (D) Kathryn Long; (S) Tom Kamm; (C) David C. Woolard; (L) Peter Kaczorowski

Driving Miss Daisy, Alfred Uhry; (D) William Gregg; (S) James Fenhagen; (C) Susan E. Mickey; (L) F. Mitchell Dana

The Caucasian Chalk Circle, Bertolt Brecht; trans: Ralph Manheim; music: Don Rebic; (D) Kathryn Long; (S) Anne Servanton; (C) Candice Donnelly; (L) Nancy Schertler

Children, A.R. Gurney, Jr.; (D) Paul Sparer; (S) John Lee Beatty; (C) Mary Ann Powell; (L) Dennis Parichy

The Studio Theatre

JOY ZINOMAN
Artistic/Managing Director

KEITH ALAN BAKER
Associate Managing Director/Artistic Director, Secondstage

1333 P Street NW
Washington, DC 20005
(202) 232-7267 (bus.)
(202) 332-3300 (b.o.)

FOUNDED 1978
Joy Zinoman

SEASON
Jan.-Dec.

FACILITIES
Mainstage
Seating Capacity: 200
Stage: thrust

Secondstage
Seating Capacity: 50
Stage: flexible

FINANCES
Sept. 1, 1990-Aug. 31, 1991
Expenses: $1,027,500

CONTRACTS
AEA SPT

The Studio Theatre is a vital and vibrant artistic force, a leader of Washington's professional theatre movement. Since its founding, the Studio has produced more than 70 productions, gaining a national reputation for innovative and challenging work. The Studio Theatre offers a wide range of works, primarily area premieres, emphasizing what is best in contemporary theatre today and the latest from such performance artists as David Cale, Paul Zaloom and Tom Jones, II. The theatre's developmental Secondstage offers opportunities for emerging directors, designers and actors. The Studio Theatre Acting Conservatory is the region's largest and most comprehensive training program. As the downtown anchor of the newly created 14th Street Arts Corridor, the Studio maintains a commitment to the cultural revival of this historic arts and entertainment area and the revitalization of this dynamic urban community. The Studio's primary focus is producing bold material which maintains the essence of our work—a highly energetic, eclectic, urban theatre dedicated to performance, intimacy and high production values.

—Joy Zinoman

The Studio Theatre. Richard Thompson and Barry Mann in *Principia Scriptoriae*. Photo: Joan Marcus.

PRODUCTIONS 1989-90

The Common Pursuit, Simon Gray; (D) Rob Barron; (S) Russell Metheny; (C) Gail Brassard; (L) Daniel MacLean Wagner

Principia Scriptoriae, Richard Nelson; (D) James Petosa; (S) Russell Metheny; (C) Gail Brassard; (L) Daniel MacLean Wagner

The Gifts of the Magi, book adapt: Mark St. Germain, from O. Henry; music: Randy Courts; lyrics: Randy Courts and Mark St. Germain; (D) Rob Bowman; (S) Dan Conway; (C) Ric Thomas Rice; (L) Daniel MacLean Wagner

West Memphis Mojo, Martin Jones; (D) Edward G. Smith; (S) James Kronzer; (C) William Pucilowsky; (L) David R. Zemmels

Made in Bangkok, Anthony Minghella; (D) Joy Zinoman; (S) Michael Layton; (C) Mary Ann Powell; (L) Daniel MacLean Wagner

Frankie and Johnny in the Clair de Lune, Terrence McNally; (D) Joy Zinoman and Michael Russotto; (S) James Kronzer; (C) Ric Thomas Rice; (L) Daniel MacLean Wagner

Bouncers, John Godber; (D) Michael Russotto; (S) James Kronzer; (C) Janice Benning; (L) Gil Thompson

Laughing Wild, Christopher Durang; (D) Maynard Marshall; (S) Steve Thorpe; (C) Janice Benning; (L) Steve Thorpe

All Men Are Whores, David Mamet; (D) Keith Alan Baker; (S) David R. Zemmels; (C) Sandra Smoker-Duraes; (L) David R. Zemmels

PRODUCTIONS 1990-91

In Perpetuity Throughout the Universe, Eric Overmyer; (D) Ron Nakahara; (S) Russell Metheny; (C) Helen Qizhi Huang; (L) Daniel MacLean Wagner

The Puppetmaster of Lodz, Gilles Segal; trans: Sara O'Connor; (D) Joy Zinoman; (S) Russell Metheny; (C) Ric Thomas Rice; (L) Daniel MacLean Wagner

My Civilization, Paul Zaloom; (D) Donny Osman; (L) William Shipley Schaffner

Unchanging Love, Romulus Linney, from Anton Chekhov; (D) Edward Morgan; (S) James Kronzer; (C) Helen Qizhi Huang; (L) David R. Zemmels

A Tale of Two Cities, adapt: Everett Quinton, from Charles Dickens; (D) John Going;

(S) Dan Conway; (C) Don Newcomb; (L) Daniel MacLean Wagner

spell #7, Ntozake Shange; (D) Ronald J. Himes; (S) Russell Metheny; (C) Ric Thomas Rice; (L) Michael Giannitti

Drinking in America, Eric Bogosian; (D) Maynard Marshall; (S) Chris Ellis; (C) T. Hutchinson; (L) Chris Ellis

Road, Jim Cartwright; (D) Keith Alan Baker; (S) James Kronzer; (C) Sandra Smoker-Duraes; (L) David R. Zemmels

Oil City Symphony, Mike Craver, Mark Hardwick, Debra Monk and Mary Murfitt; (D) R.L. Rowsey; (S) James Kronzer; (C) Sandra Smoker-Duraes; (L) David R. Zemmels

Syracuse Stage

ARTHUR STORCH
Producing Artistic Director

JAMES A. CLARK
Managing Director

820 East Genesee St.
Syracuse, NY 13210
(315) 443-4008 (bus.)
(315) 443-3275 (b.o.)

FOUNDED 1974
Arthur Storch

SEASON
Jan.-Dec.

FACILITIES
John D. Archbold Theatre
Seating Capacity: 510
Stage: proscenium

Daniel C. Sutton Pavilion
Seating Capacity: 100
Stage: flexible

FINANCES
July 1, 1990-June 30, 1991
Expenses: $2,500,000

CONTRACTS
AEA LORT (C)

The principal purpose of Syracuse Stage is to present central New York State residents with a variety of plays selected from the world's dramatic literature as well as American and foreign contemporary playwriting; each season, the theatre strives to present at least one new play. Commitment to the actor in all aspects of his or her stay in Syracuse is a cornerstone of this theatre's policy, and giving the actor the supportive environment to encourage the highest degree of creativity is our goal. Because of the relationship between Syracuse Stage and the Syracuse University drama department, both headed by the same person, there is a mutual commitment to excellence and creativity.

—*Arthur Storch*

Syracuse Stage. Michael John McGann, Edward Conery, Bill Ullman and Allison Briner in *Rough Crossing*. Photo: Lawrence Mason, Jr.

PRODUCTIONS 1989-90

Oil City Symphony, Mike Craver, Mark Hardwick, Debra Monk and Mary Murfitt; (D) Larry Forde; (S) Jeffrey Schissler; (C) Maria Marrero; (L) Natasha Katz

The Rose Tattoo, Tennessee Williams; (D) John Gulley; (S) Debra Booth; (C) Maria Marrero; (L) Harry Feiner

A Walk in the Woods, Lee Blessing; (D) Arthur Storch; (S) David Potts; (C) Jennifer von Mayrhauser; (L) Marc B. Weiss

The Taming of the Shrew, William Shakespeare; (D) Larry Carpenter; (S) John Falabella; (C) Marcia Madeira; (L) Marcia Madeira

Finding Donis Anne, Hal Corley; (D) Arthur Storch; (S) John Doepp; (C) Pamela Scofield; (L) Phil Monat

Speed-the-Plow, David Mamet; (D) Kathryn Long; (S) Victor Becker; (C) Timothy Averill; (L) Pat Collins

Dangerous Corner, J.B. Priestley; (D) Arthur Storch; (S) Timothy Averill; (C) Nanzi Adzima; (L) Phil Monat

PRODUCTIONS 1990-91

Closer Than Ever, conceived: Steven Scott Smith; music: David Shire; lyrics: Richard Maltby, Jr.; (D) William Roudebush; (S) Michael Miller; (C) Maria Marrero; (L) Michael Newton-Brown

The Three Sisters, Anton Chekhov; trans: Michael Henry Heim; (D) John Going; (S) James Wolk; (C) Pamela Scofield; (L) Phil Monat

The Cocktail Hour, A.R. Gurney, Jr.; (D) William Woodman; (S) Gary May; (C) Maria Marrero; (L) Harry Feiner

As You Like It, William Shakespeare; (D) Libby Appel; (S) Michael Miller; (C) Nanzi Adzima; (L) Phil Monat

The Mystery of Irma Vep, Charles Ludlam; (D) Robert Fuhrmann; (S) Dan Conway; (C) Don Newcomb; (L) Phil Monat

Fences, August Wilson; (D) Claude Purdy; (S) James Sandefur; (C) Martha Hally; (L) Phil Monat

Rough Crossing, Tom Stoppard; (D) Arthur Storch; (S) Timothy Averill; (C) Timothy Averill; (L) Kerro Knox 3

Tacoma Actors Guild

BRUCE K. SEVY
Artistic Director

KATE HAAS
Managing Director

1323 South Yakima Ave.
Tacoma, WA 98405
(206) 272-3107 (bus.)
(206) 272-2145 (b.o.)

FOUNDED 1978
Rick Tutor, William Becvar

SEASON
Oct.-May

FACILITIES
Seating Capacity: 299
Stage: proscenium

FINANCES
July 1, 1990-June 30, 1991
Expenses: $817,489

CONTRACTS
AEA letter of agreement

Tacoma Actors Guild continually strives to achieve the highest standards of excellence in the theatre it presents. Desiring to be neither elitist in outlook, nor ruled strictly by box-office pressures, TAG seeks to engage the community it serves in a dynamic partnership by constantly exploring challenging, entertaining works selected from the entire breadth of dramatic literature. Also TAG sees the development of new works which contribute to the growth and development of American theatre as part of its greater artistic misson. In our efforts to become a true regional theatre center, we are committed to developing programs which will broaden our audience and reflect the diversity of the region. We plan to expand programs like our student performance series and summer conservatory, and to develop other programs which provide theatre-related forums for community outreach. Long-range goals include theatre for young audiences and a second stage for the presentation of adventurous programming and cabaret.

—*Bruce K. Sevy*

PRODUCTIONS 1989-90

Brighton Beach Memoirs, Neil Simon; (D) Bruce K. Sevy; (S) Bill Forrester; (C) Ron Erickson; (L) Michael Wellborn

Expectations, Dean Corrin; (D) William Becvar; (S) Jeffrey A. Frkonja; (C) Marienne O'Brien; (L) Robert A. Jones

Corpse!, Gerald Moon; (D) Steven Williford; (S) Bill Forrester; (C) Ron Erickson; (L) Phil Schermer

First Night, Jack Neary; (D) Bruce K. Sevy; (S) David Henderson; (C) Marienne O'Brien; (L) Robert A. Jones

The Dining Room, A.R. Gurney, Jr.; (D) Bruce K. Sevy; (S) Shelley Henze Schermer; (C) Frances Kenny; (L) Robert A. Jones

The Nerd, Larry Shue; (D) Bill Ontiveros; (S) Barbara Mesney; (C) Marienne O'Brien; (L) Robert A. Jones

PRODUCTIONS 1990-91

Little Shop of Horrors, book and lyrics: Howard Ashman, from Charles Griffith; music: Alan Menken; (D) Bruce K. Sevy; (S) Bill Forrester; (C) Marienne O'Brien; (L) Robert A. Jones

The Immigrant, Mark Harelik; (D) Randal Myler; (S) Bill Forrester; (C) Ron Erickson; (L) Peter Allen

A Christmas Carol, adapt: Chad Henry, from Charles Dickens; (D) Bruce K. Sevy; (S) Carey Wong; (C) Marienne O'Brien; (L) Michael Wellborn

Dear Liar, Jerome Kilty; (D) Bruce K. Sevy; (S) Jeffrey A. Frkonja; (C) Marienne O'Brien; (L) Robert A. Jones

Ain't Misbehavin', conceived: Murray Horwitz and Richard Maltby, Jr.; music and lyrics: Fats Waller, et al; (D) Tony B. White; (S) David Henderson; (C) Frances Kenny; (L) Phil Schermer

Broadway Bound, Neil Simon; (D) Bruce K. Sevy; (S) Bill Forrester; (C) Ron Erickson; (L) Robert A. Jones

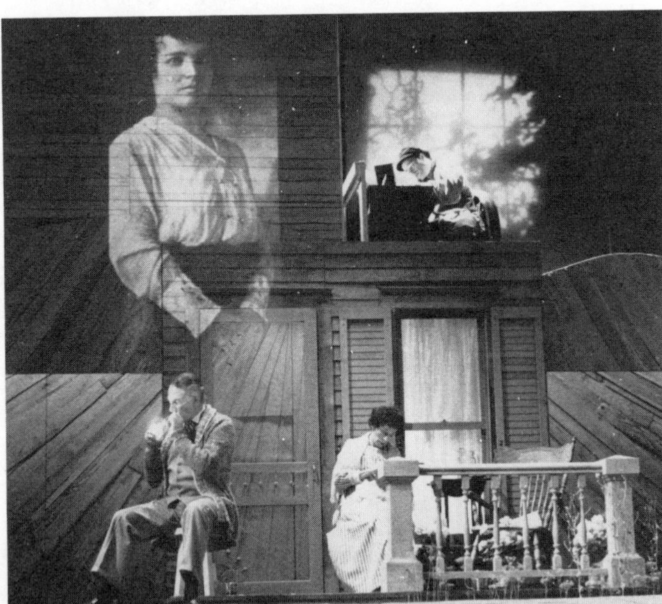

Tacoma Actors Guild. Ben Bottoms, Paul Roland and Dee Maaske in *The Immigrant*. Photo: Sherry Bockwinkel.

Tennessee Repertory Theatre

MAC PIRKLE
Artistic Director

BRIAN J. LACZKO
Managing Director

427 Chestnut St.
Nashville, TN 37203
(615) 244-4878 (bus.)
(615) 741-7777 (b.o.)

Tennessee Repertory Theatre. Chris Harrod in *A House Divided*. Photo: Rhea Rippey.

FOUNDED 1985
Mac Pirkle, Martha Rivers Ingram

SEASON
Sept.-June

FACILITIES
Polk Theatre
Seating Capacity: 1,054
Stage: modified thrust

FINANCES
July 1, 1989-June 30, 1990
Expenses: $1,472,000

CONTRACTS
AEA LORT (C)

Tennesse Rep was founded with the simple mission of establishing a high-quality professional theatre in Nashville. We accomplished this in the same manner as any other theatre—through hard work, good friends and creative problem-solving. Our mainstage programming parallels our audience's tastes as we learn each other's boundaries. Having spent our first five years establishing a significant professional theatre for the community, our mission is now expanding to include our not so "hidden agenda" of exploring and developing new American musicals. Our Music Theatre Laboratory includes readings, workshops and mainstage performances. Our goal is to become a center in the southern United States for new music-theatre. We are located in the midst of an incredibly creative music industry, with songwriters gathered much as they were in Tin Pan Alley during the early part of this century. Give us a call and come on down for a visit.

—Mac Pirkle

PRODUCTIONS 1989-90

Ain't Misbehavin', conceived: Murray Horwitz and Richard Maltby, Jr.; music and lyrics: Fats Waller, et al; (D) Eric Riley; (S) Rick Stetson; (C) Kate Knies; (L) Jeffrey A. Hall

Romeo and Juliet, William Shakespeare; (D) David Shookhoff; (S) Bennet Averyt; (C) Cindy Russell; (L) Scott Leathers

Christmas Memories, book: Mac Pirkle; music and lyrics: Stan Tucker, et al; (D) Mac Pirkle; (S) Brian J. Laczko and Sam Craig; (C) Jennifer S. Orth; (L) Brian J. Laczko

My Fair Lady, book and lyrics: Alan Jay Lerner; music: Frederick Lowe; (D) John Going; (S) Jeffrey A. Hall; (C) Marianne Powell-Parker; (L) Christopher Wilson

Steel Magnolias, Robert Harling; (D) Steven Kent; (S) Craig Spain; (C) Cindy Russell; (L) Jonathan Hutchins

PRODUCTIONS 1990-91

A Chorus Line, book: James Kirkwood and Nicholas Dante; music: Marvin Hamlisch; lyrics: Edward Kleban; (D) Mac Pirkle; (S) Craig Spain; (C) Kate Knies; (L) Jonathan Hutchins

Crimes of the Heart, Beth Henley;

(D) Don Jones; (S) Craig Spain; (C) Fred Crane; (L) Scott Leathers

A Christmas Carol, adapt: Don Jones, from Charles Dickens; (D) Mary Jane Harvill; (S) Bennet Averyt; (C) Cindy Russell; (L) Bennet Averyt

A House Divided, book: Mac Pirkle; music: Mike Reid; lyrics: Mike Reid and Mac Pirkle; (D) Mac Pirkle; (S) Craig Spain; (C) Martha H. Cooper; (L) Brian J. Laczko

Our Town, Thornton Wilder; (D) John Briggs; (S) Craig Spain; (C) Martha H. Cooper; (L) Jonathan Hutchins

Some Sweet Day, book: Don Jones and Mac Pirkle; music and lyrics: Si Kahn; from: Don Jones, Donna Kelsey, John O'Neal, Katherine Pearson and Mac Pirkle; (D) Steven Kent; (S) Brian J. Laczko; (C) Jennifer S. Orth; (L) Brian J. Laczko

The Theater at Monmouth

RICHARD SEWELL
Artistic Director

BETSY SWEET
General Manager

Box 385
Monmouth, ME 04259
(207) 933-2952 (bus.)
(207) 933-9999 (b.o.)

FOUNDED 1970
Richard Sewell, Robert Joyce

SEASON
June-Sept.

FACILITIES
Cumston Hall
Seating Capacity: 275
Stage: thrust

FINANCES
Oct. 1, 1989-Sept. 30, 1990
Expenses: $200,000

CONTRACTS
AEA SPT

The Theater at Monmouth's rolling repertory season is mounted in a jewel box of a historic opera house, Cumston Hall. Using the plays of Shakespeare as our criterion and centerpiece, we draw from the whole range of classical—and some modern—literature. Our quest is always for actors comfortable with a wide scope of style and type, and scripts that respect the excitement and power of language.

—Richard Sewell

Note: During the 1989-90 and 1990-91 seasons, Ted Davis served as artistic director.

PRODUCTIONS 1989-90

The Merchant of Venice, William Shakespeare; (D) Ted Davis; (S) Wayne Merritt; (C) Jane Snider; (L) Wayne Merritt

Light Up the Sky, Moss Hart; (D) John Ahlin; (S) Wayne Merritt; (C) Jane Snider; (L) Wayne Merritt

The Cherry Orchard, adapt: David Mamet, from Anton Chekhov; (D) Ted Davis; (S) Wayne Merritt; (C) Laura Wortham; (L) Wayne Merritt

Brave New World, adapt: Ted Davis, from Aldous Huxley; (D) Timothy Wheeler; (S) Wayne Merritt; (C) Laura Wortham; (L) Wayne Merritt

PRODUCTIONS 1990-91

The Liar, Pierre Corneille; adapt and trans: Ranjit Bolt; (D) Christopher Rock; (S) Christopher Rock; (C) Elisabeth Tobey; (L) John Ervin

The Comedy of Errors, William Shakespeare; (D) Richard Sewell; (S) James Thurston; (C) Richard Sewell; (L) Randy Emory

Our Country's Good, Timberlake Wertenbaker, from Thomas Keneally; (D) Christopher Rock; (S) Christopher Rock; (C) Elisabeth Tobey; (L) John Ervin

King Lear, William Shakespeare; (D) Christopher Rock; (S) Christopher Rock; (C) Elisabeth Tobey; (L) Randy Emory

The Theater at Monmouth. James L. Walker, Marilyn Mays and Timothy Wheeler in *The Cherry Orchard*. Photo: Maura Smith.

The Theatre Club of the Palm Beaches

LOUIS TYRRELL
Producing Director

NANCY BARNETT
Company Manager

262 South Ocean Blvd.
Manalapan, FL 33462
(407) 585-3403 (bus.)
(407) 585-3433 (b.o.)

FOUNDED 1987
Louis Tyrrell

SEASON
Oct.-Apr.

FACILITIES
Theatre Club Mainstage
(Lois Pope Theatre)
Seating Capacity: 250
Stage: thrust

Broward Performing Arts Center
(Intimate Theatre)
Seating Capacity: 593
Stage: proscenium

Kravis Center of Performing Arts
(Outdoor Theatre)
Seating Capacity: 1,000
Stage: flexible

FINANCES
July 1, 1990-June 30, 1991
Expenses: $645,000

CONTRACTS
AEA SPT

The Theatre Club of the Palm Beaches is dedicated to locating and nurturing the finest new works in the American theatre, and bringing them to an ever-expanding South Florida audience. We hope to challenge our audience with contemporary literature of the theatre that deals with issues, ideas and innovative use of language, structure and style. By presenting high-quality, thought-provoking plays, the Theatre Club has experienced tremendous growth during our first four seasons, expanding our subscriber base to 4,400. We also develop and encourage a new generation of theatregoers through our educational outreach program, the Learning Stage. Annually, more than 50,000 children experience company-created works that focus on relevant issues; performance is combined with workshops and curriculum study materials for a comprehensive arts/education experience. As the South Florida population explodes, the Theatre Club will continue to fill the growing needs of our diverse and demanding audience.

—Louis Tyrrell

PRODUCTIONS 1989-90

The Immigrant, Mark Harelik; (D) J. Barry Lewis; (S) Stephen Placido, Jr.; (C) Christine E. Field; (L) Pamela A. Mara

The Floating Palace, Charles R. Johnson; (D) Charles R. Johnson; (S) Stephen Placido, Jr.; (C) Mark Pirolo; (L) Pamela A. Mara

Not About Heroes, Stephen Macdonald; (D) J. Barry Lewis; (S) Stephen Placido, Jr.; (C) Mark Pirolo; (L) Pamela A. Mara

The Theatre Club of the Palm Beaches. Judith Townsend and Frederick Walters in *The Stick Wife*. Photo: Lydia Hersloff.

The Stick Wife, Darrah Cloud; (D) John Briggs; (S) Stephen Placido, Jr.; (C) Christine E. Field; (L) Suzanne Clement Jones
The Voice of the Prairie, John Olive; (D) Lynnette Barkley; (S) Stephen Placido, Jr.; (C) Mark Pirolo; (L) Pamela A. Mara

PRODUCTIONS 1990-91

Vital Signs, Jane Martin; (D) Lynnette Barkley; (S) Stephen Placido, Jr.; (L) Pamela A. Mara
Two Rooms, Lee Blessing; (D) Jeanne Blake; (S) Stephen Placido, Jr.; (L) Pamela A. Mara
Shy of Dallas, Charles L. Green; (D) John Briggs; (S) Stephen Placido, Jr.; (L) Stuart Reiter
The Tattler, Terri Wagener; (D) J. Barry Lewis; (S) Stephen Placido, Jr.; (C) Jack Pinkley; (L) Pamela A. Mara

Theatre de la Jeune Lune

BARBRA BERLOVITZ DESBOIS, VINCENT GRACIEUX, ROBERT ROSEN, DOMINIQUE SERRAND
Artistic Directors

KIT WAICKMAN
Business Director

Box 582176
Minneapolis, MN 55458-2176
(612) 332-3968 (bus.)
(612) 333-6200 (b.o.)

FOUNDED 1978
Dominique Serrand, Vincent Gracieux, Barbra Berlovitz Debois

SEASON
Sept.-July

FACILITIES
Theatre de la Jeune Lune
Seating Capacity: 550
Stage: flexible

Hennepin Center for the Arts
Seating Capacity: 385
Stage: thrust

Southern Theatre
Seating Capacity: 220
Stage: proscenium

Minneapolis Theatre Garage
Seating Capacity: 160
Stage: thrust

FINANCES
Aug. 1, 1990-July 31, 1991
Expenses: $600,000

Theatre de la Jeune Lune is a theatre of actors. What is important to us is what the actor puts on the stage when the curtain goes up—what happens in front of the audience. With that end result in mind, we enter into each production. There isn't a play we won't do. We could be interested in a classic, a modern work or an original new play. What we do with it is a different matter. We strive to make the play "ours," to bring across, as our audience would agree, our style. Our heart, passions and emotions open the paths to ideas. We create exactly what we want to, within our obvious financial restrictions. Every production is different and each play must be attacked from a new angle with our experience of the past. Pushing ourselves into new areas every year, we want to continue bringing exciting, eventful and important theatre to our community.

—Dominique Serrand

PRODUCTIONS 1989-90

The Force of Habit, Thomas Bernhard; trans: Neville Plaice and Stephen Plaice; (D) Barbra Berlovitz-Desbois; (S) Michael Sommers; (C) Felicity Jones; (L) Frederic Desbois
Cyrano, Edmond Rostand; trans: Christopher Fry; (D) John Clark Donahue; (S) Marvin Carpentier and Delbert Ball; (C) Ricia Birturk; (L) Richard Borgen
Some People's Kids, company-developed; (D) the company; (S) Vincent Gracieux and Dominique Serrand; (C) Margot Curran; (L) Frederic Desbois

PRODUCTIONS 1990-91

Il Campiello, Carlo Goldoni; adapt: Felicity Jones, Robert Rosen and Julie Siege; trans: Ron Martinez; (D) Vincent Gracieux; (S) Dominique Serrand; (C) Margot Curran; (L) Robert Rosen
Puntila and His Chauffeur Matti, Bertolt Brecht; adapt: Paul Walsh; trans: Erica Christ; (D) Barbra Berlovitz-Desbois; (S) Michael Sommers; (C) Matthew LeFebvre; (L) Frederic Desbois
Crusoe, Friday, and the Island of Hope, adapt: Felicity Jones, Steven Epp, Dominique Serrand and the company, from Daniel Defoe and Michael Tournier; (D) Dominique Serrand; (S) Vincent Gracieux; (C) Barbra Berlovitz-Desbois; (L) Robert Rosen

Theatre for a New Audience

JEFFREY HOROWITZ
Artistic/Producing Director

220 East 4th St., 4th Floor
New York, NY 10009
(212) 505-8345 (bus.)
(212) 228-6621 (b.o.)

FOUNDED 1979
Jeffrey Horowitz

SEASON
Jan.-May

FACILITIES
St. Clement's
Seating Capacity: 151
Stage: proscenium

Theatre de la Jeune Lune. Dominique Serrand in *Il Campiello*. Photo: Michal Daniel.

Theatre for a New Audience. Jeff Sugarman in *A Midsummer Night's Dream*. Photo: Gerry Goodstein.

FINANCES
Sept. 1, 1990-Aug. 31, 1991
Expenses: $682,000

CONTRACTS
AEA TYA and letter of agreement

Theatre for a New Audience is committed to an interplay between the classic and the contemporary. On the one hand, it keeps the art and wisdom of the past fresh and vital. On the other, it stimulates today's artists to contribute to that living repertoire with works that convey the form and pressure of our own era. Our mission is to advance and promote excellence in both the classic and contemporary theatre. We explore Shakespeare in at least one production annually, and commission new plays by dramatists whose styles draw not only on the masterworks of the past, but on the multicultural heritage of our own setting. The company's productions play for both general audiences and elementary, junior high and high school students from diverse backgrounds. Theatre for a New Audience also presents schools with arts education programs that promote literacy and creativity.

—Jeffrey Horowitz

PRODUCTIONS 1989-90

A Midsummer Night's Dream, William Shakespeare; (D) Jeffrey Horowitz; (S) Julie Taymor; (C) Julie Taymor
Othello, William Shakespeare; (D) William Gaskill; (S) Annie Smart; (C) Annie Smart; (L) Frances Aronson
The Red Sneaks, book, music and lyrics: Elizabeth Swados; (D) Elizabeth Swados; (S) G.W. Mercier; (C) G.W. Mercier; (L) Mary Louise Geiger

PRODUCTIONS 1990-91

The Mud Angel, Darrah Cloud; (D) Kevin Kuhlke; (S) Clay Snider; (C) Marina Draghici; (L) Mary Louise Geiger
Romeo and Juliet, William Shakespeare; (D) Bill Alexander; (S) Fotini Dimou; (C) Fotini Dimou; (L) Frances Aronson

Theater for the New City

CRYSTAL FIELD
Artistic Director

GEORGE BARTENIEFF
Executive Director

155 First Ave.
New York, NY 10003
(212) 475-3302 (bus.)
(212) 254-1109 (b.o.)

FOUNDED 1971
Larry Kornfield, Crystal Field, George Bartenieff, Theo Barnes

SEASON
Jan.-Dec.

FACILITIES
Johnson Theater
Seating Capacity: 99-240
Stage: flexible

Theater II
Seating Capacity: 99
Stage: proscenium

Theater III
Seating Capacity: 74
Stage: flexible

FINANCES
July 1, 1990-June 30, 1991
Expenses: $447,055

CONTRACTS
AEA letter of agreement

Theater for the New City, now in its 20th season, is a center dedicated to the discovery of relevant new writing and the nurturing of new playwrights. TNC has presented 600 new American plays to more than 750,000 audience members, including the premieres of works by playwrights like Sam Shepard, Maria Irene Fornes, Harvey Fierstein and Romulus Linney, and has also presented many of America's most important theatre companies and artists. TNC's commitment to new artists, lesser-known writers and young performers is evidenced by our Emerging Playwrights Program, our Street Theatre Performers Workshop and our extensive new play commissioning program. Each year, TNC provides 30,000 free admissions to members of 90 community, senior citizen and youth groups, and creates a free street-theatre traveling festival bringing outdoor performances to New York City's five boroughs. In 1986, after performing in rented spaces, TNC purchased a new home that is being converted into a community-based cultural and performance art center.

—Crystal Field, George Bartenieff

PRODUCTIONS 1989-90

Rookie of the Year, Crystal Field and Christopher Cherney; (D) Crystal Field
Anulah, Let Them Eat Cake, Karen Williams and Tom Andrews; (D) Karen Williams and Tom Andrews
Large Number of Small Rooms, Kevin G. Floreno; (D) Kevin G. Floreno
Macbeth in Hell, Steve Lott; (D) Steve Lott
Lycanthrope, John McLaughlin; (D) Tom Gladwell
Antigona Hurtado Esguerra, Nelly Vivas; (D) Nelly Vivas
Sour Springs, John Jiler; (D) Stefano LoVerso
Body Game, Roger Durling; (D) Eduardo Machado
Watchman, Bina Sharif; (D) Bina Sharif
Monster Time, Stephen DiLauro; (D) Willem Brugman
The Trojan Women, Robert Patrick; (D) Robert Patrick
Thin Air, Glyn Vincent; (D) Glyn Vincent
Three Poets, Romulus Linney; (D) Romulus Linney
When the Colored Band Goes Marching, John Patterson; (D) John Patterson
Home Family God Country Flag, Joanne Schultz; (D) Joanne Schultz
Flight of the Endangered, Beth Skinner and Ed Herbst; (D) Beth Skinner and Ed Herbst
Get Hur, Ray Dobbins; (D) Bette Bourne
The Foundation, Antonio Buero-Vallejo; (D) James Houghton
Smothering Coals, Kay M. Osborne; (D) Rome Neal
Stealth, Margo Lee Sherman; (D) Sandy Clarke and Robert Landau
Carrion Sisters & The Vulgar Mother, Heidi Herr; (D) John McGrath
Better People, Karen Malpede; (D) Karen Malpede
Political Wife, Bill Talen; (D) David Ford
'Til the Eagle Hollers, James Purdy; (D) John Uecker
Coyolxuahqui: ***Woman Without Borders***, Vira Colorado and

Hortensia Colorado
Dose Center, Michael Brodsky; (D) David Herskovits
Two Centuries, Mario Fratti and Penelope Bradford; (D) Eve Collyer
A Feature Film, Bob Morris
Spiderwoman Theatre: ***Reverberations***, company-developed; (D) Muriel Miguel
Love of the Operetta, Jiri Schubert and Ron Havern; (D) Jiri Schubert
Related Retreats, Eduardo Machado; (D) Eduardo Machado
White Boys Can't Rap, Larry Myers; (D) Michael McKenzie Wills
The Radiant City, Theodora Skipitares; (D) Theodora Skipitares
Signs, Gabrielle N. Lane, and ***Passion Without Reason***, Neil Harris; (D) Rome Neal
Music Rescue Service, Sidney Goldfarb; (D) Roger Babb
The Talking Band: ***On the Road to Holeness***, Chris Mealey; (D) Chris Mealey
Ingenuous, Bob Borsodi; (D) Bob Borsodi
Future Tense, Walter Corwin; (D) H. Shap Pamplin

PRODUCTIONS 1990-91

The Census Taker, Crystal Field; (D) Crystal Field
Bitch, Dyke, Faghag, Whore, Penny Arcade; (D) Penny Arcade
Jimi—Slight Return, Jerome P. Bates; (D) Rome Neal
Waiters for Godot—A One Act Play Festival
Mystic Arts Fair
If It's Not One Thing, It's Another, Terry King; (D) Terry King
And Then Some, C. Meade, D. Kelley, Scott Lilly and J. Villegas; (D) Scott Lilly
12 by 12, various authors; (D) Alan Roy
Hot Peaches: ***Hot Peaches and Friends***, company-developed; (D) Jimmy Camicia
Two One Acts, Jack Brown; (D) Jack Brown
Kings Must Dance, (D) Daisy Von Scheler Mayer
The Witch-Way? Travel Agency, Wycherly Sisters; (D) Wycherly Sisters
The Blue Fairy, Crystal Field; (D) Crystal Field
Rock & Roll Extravaganza, (D) George Bellici
Fire, Bina Sharif; (D) Bina Sharif
Stop the War—A Festival for Peace in the Middle East
The Bunny & Dorris Show, Sebastian Stuart; music: Tom Judson; (D) Sebastian Stuart
Felicia, Patricia Cobey; (D) Robert Bresnick
Wise Guise, C. Meade, D. Kelley, S. Lilly and J. Villegas; (D) Scott Lilly
Charlotte in Wonderland, Steve Lott; (D) John Jiler
The Talking Band: ***Fata Morgana***, Paul Zimet; (D) Paul Zimet
Huipil, Vira Colorado and Hortensia Colorado
Valentine to Carole Lombard, Larry Myers; (D) Chris Mealey
The Harris Sisters Salute the Andrews Sisters, (D) Robert Dahdah
Mary Jemison, Toby Armour; (D) Muriel Miguel
Mrs. President, Phoebe Legere; (D) Phoebe Legere

Theater for the New City. Adrienne Thompson and Scott Sowers in *Three Poets*. Photo: Jonathan Slaff.

Theatre in the Square

MICHAEL HORNE
Producing Artistic Director

PALMER D. WELLS
Managing Director

11 Whitlock Ave.
Marietta, GA 30064
(404) 425-5873 (bus.)
(404) 422-8369 (b.o.)

FOUNDED 1982
Michael Horne, Palmer D. Wells

SEASON
Jan.-Dec.

FACILITIES
Main Stage
Seating Capacity: 169
Stage: proscenium

Alley Stage
Seating Capacity: 60
Stage: flexible

FINANCES
July 1, 1990-June 30, 1991
Expenses: $530,840

CONTRACTS
AEA SPT

As the only year-round professional theatre in Georgia outside the Atlanta city limits, we face certain pressures, a few advantages and some vital responsibilities. We expose many people to their first and only live theatre. Among their numbers are young people, some of whom will decide to choose careers in the arts or at least include the arts as part of their adult lives. So, aside from fulfilling our own artistic sensibilities, we strive to educate and stimulate audiences. Our mission is to: 1) program shows which appeal to our instincts because of strong writing, subject matter, suitability to our space and/or audience or the opportunity to showcase regional talent; 2) build a loyal audience who will hunger for diverse work; 3) acquire the resources to grow and diversify; 4) nurture talent and develop materials indigenous to the Southeast. We pride ourselves on varied work—from classics to new works—and run the gamut of comedies, dramas and musicals. We enjoy the challenge of making our smaller size work for us rather than limit us, often exchanging epic proportions for epic emotions.

—Michael Horne

PRODUCTIONS 1989-90

The Boys Next Door, Tom Griffin; (D) Dan Bonnell; (S) Robert Lott; (C) Margaret Waterbury; (L) Liz Lee
Going to See the Elephant, Karen Hensel, Patti Johns, Elana Kent, Sylvia Meredith, Elizabeth Lloyd Shaw and Laura Toffenetti; (D) Michael Horne; (S) Robert Lott; (C) Therra C. Gwynn; (L) Liz Lee
The 1940's Radio Hour, Walton Jones; (D) Jack Mason; (S) Robert Lott; (C) Carl Curnutt; (L) Liz Lee
The Bug, Richard Strand; (D) Greg Abbott; (S) Robert Lott; (C) Michael Horne; (L) Liz Lee
Aftershocks, Doug Haverty; (D) Francis Trotter; (S) Robert Lott; (C) Gaye Markley; (L) Liz Lee
Zion!, Beverly Trader; (D) Tom Jones; (S) Robert Lott; (C) Judy Winograd; (L) Liz Lee

PRODUCTIONS 1990-91

All Over This Land, conceived: Phillip DePoy and Michael Horne; (D) Michael Horne; (S) Robert Lott; (C) Michael Horne; (L) Liz Lee
Elizabeth the Queen, Maxwell Anderson; (D) Michael Horne; (S) Robert Lott and Jeroy Hannah; (C) Michael Reynolds; (L) Liz Lee
Eleemosynary, Lee Blessing; (D) Bill Hardy; (S) Robert Lott; (C) Michael Reynolds; (L) Liz Lee
The 1940's Radio Hour, Walton Jones; (D) Scott Green; (S) Robert Lott; (C) Tina Hightower; (L) Liz Lee
The Dining Room, A.R. Gurney, Jr.; (D) Piet Kretsch; (S) Robert Lott; (C) Michael Reynolds; (L) Liz Lee
Fallen Angels, Noel Coward; (D) Frank Miller; (S) Jeroy Hannah;

Theatre in the Square. Yetta Yevitt and Nicole Torre in *Going to See the Elephant*. Photo: Palmer Wells.

(C) Stanley Poole; (L) Liz Lee

The Night Hank Williams Died, Larry King; (D) Michael Horne; (S) Dex Edwards; (C) Joanna Schmink; (L) Liz Lee

Theatre IV

BRUCE MILLER
Artistic Director

PHILIP WHITEWAY
Managing Director

7 1/2 West Marshall St.
Richmond, VA 23220
(804) 783-1688 (bus.)
(804) 344-8040 (b.o.)

FOUNDED 1975
Bruce Miller, Philip Whiteway

SEASON
Jan.-Dec.

FACILITIES
Empire Theatre
Seating Capacity: 604
Stage: proscenium

Little Theatre
Seating Capacity: 79
Stage: proscenium

FINANCES
July 1, 1990-June 30, 1991
Expenses: $1,278,360

CONTRACTS
AEA SPT

Theatre IV presents an eclectic mix of plays and musicals for adults, and an ambitious roster of original plays for children, teens and their families. As our company has grown, we have added more mainstream plays to our season (*The Rainmaker, When We Are Married*), while continuing to produce contemporary plays which challenge our central Virginia audience (*The Normal Heart, Frankie and Johnny in the Clair de Lune*). Most of our budget is devoted to youth productions which tour extensively; we present more than 1,500 performances a year from San Juan to Chicago. Our original plays *Hugs and Kisses, Runners, Walking the Line* and *Dancing in the Dark* deal honestly and effectively with the issues of child sexual abuse, runaways, teenage suicide, substance abuse and teenage pregnancy/sexual responsibility. Our new homes—the grand Empire Theatre and the intimate Little Theatre—first opened in 1911 and are the oldest extant theatres in our state.

—*Bruce Miller*

PRODUCTIONS 1989-90

Is There Life After High School?, book: Jeffrey Kindley; music and lyrics: Craig Carnelia; (D) John Glenn; (S) Terrie Powers; (C) Thomas W. Hammond; (L) Bruce Rennie

The Golden Goose, book: Ford Flannagan; music: K Strong and Michael Strong; lyrics: Ford Flannagan and K Strong; (D) John Glenn; (S) Terrie Powers; (C) Catherine Szari

Hugs and Kisses, book: Bruce Miller and Terry Bliss; music: Richard Giersch; lyrics: Bruce Miller; (D) Denise Simone; (S) Terrie Powers; (C) John Glenn

The Magic of Hans Christian Andersen, Terry Snyder, from Hans Christian Andersen; (D) John Glenn; (S) Terry Snyder; (C) John Glenn

The Bremen Town Band, book adapt and lyrics: Douglas Jones, from The Brothers Grimm; music: Ron Barnett; (D) John Glenn; (S) Terrie Powers; (C) Thomas W. Hammond

Tales of the Indian Drum, Marilyn Mattys; (D) Russell Wilson; (S) Terrie Powers; (C) Thomas W. Hammond

Sherlock's Last Case, Charles Marowitz; (D) Nancy Cates; (S) Barry Fitzgerald; (C) Thomas W. Hammond; (L) Jefferson Lindquist

The Snow Queen, book adapt and lyrics: Douglas Jones, from Hans Christian Andersen; music: Ron Barnett; (D) John Glenn; (S) Terrie Powers; (C) Thomas W. Hammond

The Mistletoe Moose, Bruce Miller; (D) Bruce Miller; (S) Terrie Powers; (C) John Glenn

Christmas Around the World, book and lyrics: Bruce Miller; music: Richard Giersch; (D) Russell Wilson; (S) Terrie Powers; (C) John Glenn

The Schumacher and the Elves, book adapt and lyrics: Bruce Miller, from The Brothers Grimm; music: Richard Giersch; (D) Denise Simone; (S) Terrie Powers; (C) John Glenn

Harriet Tubman and the Underground Railroad, book and lyrics: Douglas Jones; music: Ron Barnett; (D) John Glenn; (S) Terrie Powers; (C) Nancy Allen

The Boys Next Door, Tom Griffin; (D) Jack Welsh; (S) Bruce Miller; (C) Nancy Allen; (L) Dana Thomas

Bull Run to Appomattox, Ford

Theatre IV. Timothy T. Swift, Robert Throckmorton, Phillip J. Whiteway and Debra Wagoner in *The Wizard of Oz*.

Flannagan; (D) Russell Wilson; (S) Terrie Powers; (C) John Glenn

The Tortoise and the Hare, book adapt and lyrics: Douglas Jones, from Aesop; music: Ron Barnett; (D) John Glenn; (S) Terrie Powers; (C) John Glenn

The Town Mouse and the Country Mouse, book adapt and lyrics: Douglas Jones, from Aesop; music: Ron Barnett; (D) John Glenn; (S) Terrie Powers; (C) Thomas W. Hammond

Walking the Line, Bruce Miller; (D) Denise Simone; (S) Terrie Powers; (C) John Glenn

Shake Hands with Shakespeare, adapt: Denise Simone, from William Shakespeare; (D) Denise Simone; (S) Terrie Powers; (C) John Glenn

The Ugly Duckling, book adapt: Bruce Miller, from Hans Christian Andersen; music and lyrics: Richard Giersch; (D) Bruce Miller; (S) Terrie Powers; (C) Thomas W. Hammond

Four Part Harmony, book: Marcus Fisk; music and lyrics: Douglas Minerd; (D) John Glenn; (S) Terrie Powers; (C) John Glenn; (L) Bruce Rennie

PRODUCTIONS 1990-91

The Tortoise and the Hare, book adapt and lyrics: Douglas Jones, from Aesop; music: Ron Barnett; (D) John Glenn; (S) Terrie Powers; (C) John Glenn

The Frog Prince, book adapt and lyrics: Douglas Jones, from The Brothers Grimm; music: Ron Barnett; (D) John Glenn; (S) Terrie Powers; (C) Thomas W. Hammond

James Madison and the Bill of Rights, Bruce Miller; (D) Bruce Miller; (S) Terrie Powers; (C) Thomas W. Hammond

Beauty and the Beast, book adapt and lyrics: Douglas Jones, from Mme. Le Prince de Beaumont; music: Ron Barnett; (D) K Strong; (S) Terrie Powers; (C) Thomas W. Hammond

Hugs and Kisses, book: Bruce Miller and Terry Bliss; music: Richard Giersch; lyrics: Bruce Miller; (D) Denise Simone; (S) Terrie Powers; (C) John Glenn

The Steadfast Tin Soldier, book adapt and lyrics: Douglas Jones, from Hans Christian Andersen; music: Ron Barnett; (D) John Glenn; (S) Terrie Powers; (C) Thomas W. Hammond

Christmas Around the World, book: Bruce Miller and Richard Giersch; music: Ron Barnett; lyrics: Bruce Miller; (D) Bruce Miller; (S) Terrie Powers; (C) John Glenn

The Snow Queen, book adapt and lyrics: Douglas Jones, from Hans Christian Andersen; music: Ron Barnett; (D) K Strong; (S) Terrie Powers; (C) Thomas W. Hammond

Santa's Enchanted Workshop, book, music and lyrics: Richard Giersch; (D) Denise Simone; (S) Fred Brumbach; (C) Joan U. Brumbach

Booker T., book: John Glenn and Lenny Brisendine; music and lyrics: Ron Barnett; (D) Bruce Miller; (S) Terrie Powers; (C) Thomas W. Hammond

Snow White and the Seven Dwarfs, book adapt: Bruce Miller and Ford Flannagan, from The Brothers Grimm; music: Ron Barnett; lyrics: Bruce Miller; (D) John Glenn; (S) Terrie Powers; (C) Thomas W. Hammond

Freedom's Song, K Strong; (D) K Strong; (S) Terrie Powers; (C) John Glenn

The Ugly Duckling, book adapt: Bruce Miller and Richard Giersch, from Hans Christian Andersen; music: Richard Giersch; lyrics: Bruce Miller; (D) John Glenn; (S) Terrie Powers; (C) Thomas W. Hammond

Walking the Line, Bruce Miller; (D) Denise Simone; (S) Terrie Powers; (C) John Glenn

Wonderful World, book and lyrics: Denise Simone; music: Ron Barnett; (D) John Glenn; (S) Terrie Powers; (C) Thomas W. Hammond

Runners, Bruce Miller; (D) K Strong; (S) Terrie Powers; (C) John Glenn

The Wizard of Oz, book adapt: John Kane, from L. Frank Baum; music and lyrics: Harold Arlen and E.Y. Harburg; (D) Bruce Miller; (S) Brad Boynton; (C) Thomas W. Hammond; (L) Fred Brumbach

Quilters, book adapt: Molly Newman and Barbara Damashek, from Patricia Cooper and Norma Bradley Allen; music and lyrics: Barbara Damashek; (D) John Glenn; (S) Terrie Powers; (C) Elizabeth Weiss Hopper; (L) Jefferson Lindquist

Theatre Rhinoceros

ADELE PRANDINI
Artistic Director

JUDITH GHIDINELLI
Finance Director

2926 16th St.
San Francisco, CA 94103
(415) 552-4100 (bus.)
(415) 861-5079 (b.o.)

FOUNDED 1977
Allan B. Estes, Jr.

SEASON
Sept.-June

FACILITIES
Mainstage
Seating Capacity: 112
Stage: proscenium

Studio
Seating Capacity: 57
Stage: flexible

Theatre Rhinoceros develops and produces plays that examine contemporary issues and social concerns from a lesbian and gay perspective, and presents this work both in the gay and lesbian community and in the wider society with which it interacts. Theatre Rhinoceros is dedicated to providing a professional environment where lesbian and gay theatre artists from diverse backgrounds and cultures can train to develop new skills and polish existing skills. Theatre Rhinoceros is committed to presenting high-quality theatre which is both challenging and entertaining while maintaining a gay and lesbian visibility within the mainstream culture.

—Adele Prandini

Note: During the 1989-90 season, Kenneth R. Dixon served as artistic director.

PRODUCTIONS 1989-90

Friedrich, William Andrew Jones; (D) Adele Prandini; (S) Clay James; (C) Nina Capriola; (L) Joe Williams

Lust and Pity, Hilary Sloin; (D) Rebecca Patterson; (S) Pamela S. Peniston; (C) Val Von; (L) Stephanie Johnson

The Boys in the Band, Mart Crowley; (D) Kenneth R. Dixon; (S) David Newell; (C) Mark Jones; (L) Stephanie Johnson

Gertrude Stein and a Companion, Win Wells; (D) Iris Landsberg; (S) Pamela S. Peniston; (C) Val Von; (L) Joelle Chartier-Serban

Dirty Dreams of a Clean Cut Kid, music: Paul Katz; lyrics: Henry Mach; (D) Allen F. Sawyer and John Karr; (S) Edward Gottesman; (C) Dana Peter Porras; (L) Jane Hall

Secrets, Rebecca Ranson; (D) Donna Davis; (S) Clay James; (C) Kathrin Farley; (L) Stephanie Johnson

Pavane, Richard Wiltshire;

Theatre Rhinoceros. Justin Bond, Jeff Thompson and Greg Schuh in *Friedrich*. Photo: Jill Posener.

(D) Steve Omlid; (S) Bill Schmidt; (C) Nina Capriola; (L) Nancy York
Dolores Street, Theresa Carilli; (D) Nina Capriola; (S) Robert D. Cook; (C) Cindy Cho; (L) Michael Halton

PRODUCTIONS 1990-91

Roy, Joel Ensana; (D) Ed Decker; (S) Clay James; (C) Val Von; (L) Carol Majewski
Picture Me, Margery Kreitman; (D) Amy Mueller; (S) Laurie Polster; (C) Jean Frederickson; (L) Wendy Gilmore
Earl, Ollie, Austin & Ralph, Glenn Rawls; (D) Dyke Garrison; (S) Michael Berg; (C) Michael Berg; (L) Stephanie Johnson
Cradle and All, book and lyrics: Ellen Cooper; music: Joan Simcoe; (D) Maggie Wheels; (S) Pamela S. Peniston; (C) C.E. Haynes; (L) Jeff Nellis
Drag Queen in Outer Space, Sky Gilbert; (D) Iris Landsberg; (S) Alan Greenspan; (C) Ralph Sauer; (L) Will Summons

TheatreVirginia

WILLIAM GREGG
Artistic Director

2800 Grove Ave.
Richmond, VA 23221
(804) 367-0840 (bus.)
(804) 367-0831 (b.o.)

FOUNDED 1954
Virginia Museum of Fine Arts

SEASON
Oct.-May

FACILITIES
Mainstage
Seating Capacity: 494
Stage: proscenium

Second Stage
Seating Capacity: 239
Stage: proscenium

FINANCES
July 1, 1990-June 30, 1991
Expenses: $1,800,000

CONTRACTS
AEA LORT (C) and (D)

TheatreVirginia continues to develop and produce the works of provocative new playwrights while maintaining a balance of programming with the classics. This blend makes for vitally exciting and innovative theatre. We hope to develop a broad audience with a true appreciation for the art by implementing high-quality production techniques and dynamic, challenging staging; engaging the best local and national talent available; creating an environment where all theatre artists, administrators and craftspeople can be challenged to collaborate effectively; and serving as a cultural resource to enrich the community, state and region. We have enhanced the theatre's accessibility for the physically challenged, and expanded statewide education and outreach efforts through internships and apprenticeships, as well as through our Shakespeare in the Schools, Read Me a Song, Sing Me a Story and Visiting Professional programs.

—William Gregg

Note: During the 1989-90 and 1990-91 seasons, Terry Burgler served as executive artistic director.

PRODUCTIONS 1989-90

Sweeney Todd, book adapt: Hugh Wheeler, from Christopher Bond; music and lyrics: Stephen Sondheim; (D) Terry Burgler; (S) Charles Caldwell; (C) Charles Caldwell; (L) Terry Cermak
Guys and Dolls, book adapt: Jo Swerling and Abe Burrows, from Damon Runyon; music and lyrics: Frank Loesser; (D) Terry Burgler; (S) David Crank; (C) Marjorie McCown; (L) Terry Cermak
Tartuffe, Moliere; trans: Richard Wilbur; (D) Terry Burgler; (S) Charles Caldwell; (C) Charles Caldwell; (L) Jeff Stroman
Fences, August Wilson; (D) Terry Burgler; (S) Charles Caldwell; (C) Sue Griffin; (L) Terry Cermak
Steel Magnolias, Robert Harling; (D) Nancy Cates; (S) Charles Caldwell; (C) Rosemary Ingham; (L) Jeff Stroman
Oh, Mr. Faulkner, Do You Write?, John Maxwell and Tom Dupree; (D) William Partlan; (S) Jimmy Robertson; (C) Martha Wood; (L) Terry Cermak
Scratchy Glass, Doug Grissom; (D) Terry Burgler; (S) Chris Harrison; (C) Lynette Cram; (L) Terry Cermak
Year of Pilgrimage, Doug Grissom; (D) Nancy Cates; (S) Chris Harrison; (C) Lynette Cram; (L) Terry Cermak
Motherwit, adapt: Katherine Clark and Terry Burgler, from Katherine Clark and Onnie Lee Logan; (D) Terry Burgler; (S) Chris Harrison; (C) Lynette Cram; (L) Terry Cermak
Pump Boys and Dinettes, John Foley, Mark Hardwick, Debra Monk, Cass Morgan, John Schimmel and Jim Wann; (D) Terry Burgler; (S) David Crank; (C) Sue Griffin; (L) Terry Cermak

TheatreVirginia. Allen Fitzpatrick and Irene Ziegler in *The Night of the Iguana*. Photo: Eric Dobbs.

PRODUCTIONS 1990-91

Driving Miss Daisy, Alfred Uhry; (D) Nancy Cates; (S) Alan Williamson; (C) Lynette Cram; (L) Jeff Stroman
South Pacific, book adapt: Oscar Hammerstein, II and Joshua Logan, from James Michener; music: Richard Rodgers; lyrics: Oscar Hammerstein, II; (D) Terry Burgler; (S) Ron Keller; (C) Thomas W. Hammond; (L) Jeff Stroman
She Stoops to Conquer, Oliver Goldsmith; (D) Terry Burgler; (S) Joseph Varga; (C) Susan Tsu; (L) Jeff Stroman
The Night of the Iguana, Tennessee Williams; (D) Terry Burgler; (S) Ron Keller; (C) David Crank; (L) Jeff Stroman
A Walk in the Woods, Lee Blessing; (D) William Gregg; (S) Sandy Bates; (C) Sue Griffin; (L) John Carter Hailey
Apple Dreams, Tom Ziegler; (D) Terry Burgler; (S) Alan Williamson; (C) Sue Griffin; (L) Jeff Stroman
Pump Boys and Dinettes, John Foley, Mark Hardwick, Debra Monk, Cass Morgan, John Schimmel and Jim Wann; (D) Terry Burgler; (S) David Crank; (C) Sue Griffin; (L) Terry Cermak

TheatreWorks

ROBERT KELLEY
Artistic Director

RANDY ADAMS
Managing Director

1305 Middlefield Road
Palo Alto, CA 94301
(415) 323-8311 (bus.)
(415) 329-2623 or 903-6000 (b.o.)

FOUNDED 1970
Robert Kelley

SEASON
Jan.-Dec.

FACILITIES
Mountain View Center for the Performing Arts
Seating Capacity: 625
Stage: proscenium

Lucie Stern Theatre
Seating Capacity: 425
Stage: proscenium

Cubberley Stage II
Seating Capacity: 110
Stage: flexible

FINANCES
June 1, 1990-May 31, 1991
Expenses: $1,400,000

CONTRACTS
AEA Guest Artist

TheatreWorks explores and celebrates the human spirit through contemporary plays, musicals of literary merit, new works in development and innovative reinterpretations of the classics, offering audiences in the San Francisco Bay Area a regional theatre of exceptional diversity. We are a theatre for all races and ages, a longtime leader in nontraditional casting and programming. Our mainstage season is selected to expand the social and artistic horizons of a large audience. Stage II offers world and regional premieres in intimate spaces, and our recently launched Playwrights Forum develops and reads eight new plays annually, many by our regional writers. As we celebrate 22 years this season, we have focused our financial and artistic efforts on the growth and support of a multiracial company, creating a community that will be a model of diversity and commitment for the larger community we serve.

—Robert Kelley

PRODUCTIONS 1989-90

Candide, book: Hugh Wheeler, from Voltaire; music: Leonard Bernstein; lyrics: Richard Wilbur; (D) Robert Kelley; (S) Joe Ragey; (C) Marcia Frederick; (L) John G. Rathman

A Walk in the Woods, Lee Blessing; (D) Ginger Drake; (S) Michael Puff; (C) Pamela Ritchey; (L) John G. Rathman

The Tempest, William Shakespeare; (D) Robert Kelley; (S) Bruce McLeod; (C) Fumiko Bielefeldt; (L) John G. Rathman

Broadway Bound, Neil Simon; (D) Virginia Abascal; (S) Keith Snider; (C) Jill C. Bowers; (L) Dan Wadleigh

Oliver, book adapt, music and lyrics: Lionel Bart, from Charles Dickens; (D) Robert Kelley; (S) Michael Puff; (C) Cassandra Carpenter; (L) Bruce McLeod

Tea, Velina Hasu Houston; (D) Yuriko Doi; (S) Joe Ragey; (C) Pamela Ritchey; (L) Stephanie Johnson

Big River, book adapt: William Hauptman, from Mark Twain; music and lyrics: Roger Miller; (D) Robert Kelley; (S) Keith Snider; (C) Fumiko Bielefeldt; (L) John G. Rathman

I'm Not Rappaport, Herb Gardner; (D) Ric Prindle; (S) Dean Tison; (C) Jill C. Bowers; (L) John G. Rathman

The Voice of the Prairie, John Olive; (D) Leslie Martinson; (S) Joe Ragey; (C) Sherrol A. Simard; (L) Barry Griffith

Fraulein Dora, Carol Lashof; (D) Kathleen Woods; (S) Keith Snider; (C) Allison Connor; (L) Bruce McLeod

No Way to Treat a Lady, book, music and lyrics: Douglas J. Cohen; (D) Randal K. West; (S) W. Truett Roberts; (C) Pamela Ritchey; (L) Lee J. Keylon

Our Lady of the Desert, Lynne Kaufman; (D) Leslie Martinson; (S) Joe Ragey; (C) Pamela Ritchey; (L) Barry Griffith

PRODUCTIONS 1990-91

Galileo, book and lyrics: Keith Levenson and Alexa Junge; music: Jeanine Levenson; (D) Robert Kelley; (S) Joe Ragey; (C) Fumiko Bielefeldt; (L) John G. Rathman

My Children! My Africa!, Athol Fugard; (D) Clinton Turner Davis; (S) John G. Rathman; (C) Jill C. Bowers; (L) Bruce McLeod

The Miser, Moliere; trans: Albert Bermel; (D) Robert Kelley; (S) David Jon Hoffman; (C) Jeffrey Struckman; (L) John G. Rathman

Emerald City, David Williamson; (D) Dennis Martin; (S) Bruce McLeod; (C) Susan Archibald Grote; (L) Stephanie Johnson

Into the Woods, book: James Lapine; music and lyrics: Stephen Sondheim; (D) Robert Kelley; (S) Michael Puff; (C) Jill C. Bowers; (L) John G. Rathman

Steel Magnolias, Robert Harling; (D) George Ward; (S) David Jon Hoffman; (C) Pamela Lampkin; (L) Stephanie Johnson

Rashomon, Fay Kanin and Michael Kanin, from Ryunosuke Akutagawa; (D) Yuriko Doi; (S) Jeffrey Struckman; (C) Fumiko Bielefeldt; (L) Maurice Vercoutere

Go Down Garvey, book, music and lyrics: Danny Duncan; (D) Tony Haney; (S) Joe Ragey; (C) Pamela Lampkin; (L) Barbara DuBois

Lady Day at Emerson's Bar and Grill, Lanie Robertson; (D) Tony Haney; (S) Joe Ragey; (C) Susan Archibald Grote; (L) Bruce McLeod

Brilliant Traces, Cindy Lou Johnson; (D) Leslie Martinson; (S) W. Truett Roberts; (C) Sherrol A. Simard; (L) Dan Wadleigh

¿De Donde?, Mary Gallagher; (D) David Nagey Gassner; (S) Paul Vallerga; (C) Sherrol A. Simard; (L) Brett Waggoner

Vital Signs, Jane Martin; (D) Christina Yao; (S) Bruce McLeod; (C) Kristin Lewis; (L) Bruce McLeod

TheatreWorks. *Go Down Garvey*. Photo: WPG Enterprises.

Theatreworks/USA

JAY HARNICK
Artistic Director

CHARLES HULL
Managing Director

890 Broadway, 7th Floor
New York, NY 10003
(212) 677-5959 (bus.)
(212) 420-8202 (b.o.)

FOUNDED 1961
Jay Harnick, Robert K. Adams

SEASON
Jan.-Dec.

FACILITIES
Promenade Theatre
Seating Capacity: 400
Stage: thrust

Town Hall
Seating Capacity: 1,500
Stage: proscenium

FINANCES
July 1, 1990-June 30, 1991
Expenses: $3,780,000

CONTRACTS
AEA TYA

After 30 seasons of creating theatre for young and family audiences, Theatreworks/USA continues to be inspired by the belief that young people deserve theatre endowed with the richness of content demanded by the most discerning adult audience. To that end, we have commissioned an ever-expanding collection of original works from established playwrights, composers and lyricists. Our creative roster includes Ossie Davis, Charles Strouse, Alice Childress, Joe Raposo, Thomas Babe, Mary Rodgers, Saul Levitt, John Forster, Leslie Lee, Lynn Ahrens, Stephen Flaherty, Jonathan Bolt, Marta Kauffman, David Crane, Michael Skloff, John Allen and Douglas J. Cohen. We are also dedicated to the development of fresh voices for the American theatre and encourage emerging playwrights to develop projects about issues that concern them and affect the young audiences they seek to address. We currently give more than a thousand performances annually in a touring radius encompassing 49 of the 50 states.

—Jay Harnick

PRODUCTIONS 1989-90

The Play's the Thing, book: Thomas Edward West; music: Robert Waldman; lyrics: Thomas Edward West and Robert Waldman; (D) R.J. Cutler; (S) James Youmans; (C) Heidi Hollman

Footprints on the Moon, book and

Theatreworks/USA. Tom Gallop, James Barbour, Peter-Michael Marino, Tonye Patano and Elizabeth Silon in *Class Clown*.

lyrics: Arthur Perlman; music: Jeffrey Lunden; (D) Stuart Ross; (S) Richard Block; (C) Bruce Goodrich

Freedom Train, book: Marvin Gordon; music arranged by: Garrett Morris and Ron Burton; (D) Michael-David Gordon; (S) Hal Tine; (C) Linda Geley

The Secret Garden, book adapt: Linda B. Kline and Robert Jess Roth, from Frances Hodgson Burnett; music: Kim Oler; lyrics: Alison Hubbard; (D) Barbara Pasternack; (S) Stanley A. Meyer; (C) Deborah Rooney

The Velveteen Rabbit, book adapt and lyrics: James Still, from Margery Williams; music: Jimmy Roberts; (D) Stuart Ross; (S) Richard Block; (C) Debra Stein

A Charles Dickens Christmas, book: Robert Owens Scott; music: Douglas J. Cohen; lyrics: Thomas Toce; (D) Bruce Colville; (S) Robert Edmunds; (C) Heidi Hollman

Harriet the Spy, book: James Still, from Louise Fitzhugh; music: Kim Oler; lyrics: Alison Hubbard; (D) Thomas Edward West; (S) Vaughn Patterson; (C) Julie Doyle

Play to Win, book: Carles Cleveland and James de Jongh; music: Jimi Foster; lyrics: Carles Cleveland, James de Jongh and Jimi Foster; (D) Ken Nixon; (S) Tom Barnes; (C) Linda Geley

Jekyll & Hyde, book adapt and lyrics: David Crane and Marta Kauffman, from Robert Louis Stevenson; music: Michael Skloff; (D) Jay Harnick; (S) Vaughn Patterson; (C) Anne-Marie Wright

PRODUCTIONS 1990-91

Footprints on the Moon, book and lyrics: Arthur Perlman; music: Jeffrey Lunden; (D) Ruth Kramer; (S) Richard Block; (C) Bruce Goodrich

Harold and the Purple Crayon, book adapt: Jane Merlin Shepard, from Crockett Johnson; music: Jon Ehrlich; lyrics: Robin Pogrebin and Jon Ehrlich; (D) Tony Phelan; (S) Rick Dennis; (C) Michael Krass

Harriet the Spy, book adapt: James Still, from Louise Fitzhugh; music: Kim Oler; lyrics: Alison Hubbard; (D) Thomas Edward West; (S) Vaughn Patterson; (C) Julie Doyle

Jekyll & Hyde, book adapt and lyrics: David Crane and Marta Kauffman, from Robert Louis Stevenson; music: Michael Skloff; (D) Jay Harnick; (S) Vaughn Patterson; (C) Anne-Marie Wright

Play to Win, book: James de Jongh and Carles Cleveland; music: Jimi Foster; lyrics: Jimi Foster, James de Jongh and Carles Cleveland; (D) Bruce Butler; (S) Tom Barnes; (C) Linda Geley

Rapunzel, book adapt and lyrics: David Crane and Marta Kauffman, from The Brothers Grimm; music: Michael Skloff; (D) John Brady; (S) Mavis Smith; (C) Joel Vig

The Velveteen Rabbit, book adapt and lyrics: James Still, from Margery Williams; music: Jimmy Roberts; (D) Larry Raben; (S) Richard Block; (C) Debra Stein

A Charles Dickens Christmas, book: Robert Owens Scott; music: Douglas J. Cohen; lyrics: Thomas Toce; (D) Bruce Colville; (S) Robert Edmunds; (C) Heidi Hollman

Class Clown, book: Thomas Edward West; music: Kim Oler; lyrics: Alison Hubbard; (D) Steve Kaplan; (S) Vaughn Patterson; (C) Sharon Lynch

Theatre X

WESLEY SAVICK
JOHN SCHNEIDER
Co-Artistic Directors

PAMELA PERCY
Managing Director

Box 92206
Milwaukee, WI 53202
(414) 278-0555

FOUNDED 1969
Conrad Bishop, Linda Bishop, Ron Gural

SEASON
Sept.-June

FACILITIES
MKE
Seating Capacity: 79
Stage: flexible

FINANCES
Sept. 1, 1990-Aug. 31, 1991
Expenses: $135,000

The "X" in Theatre X, as conceived in 1969, represents the algebraic symbol for "the unknown factor." The motion-picture rating system, implemented years later, has complicated the associations of this symbol. The enigmatic implications of the "X" appropriately describe an aesthetic sensibility which seeks to represent an ever-changing present, to create a truly contemporary and illuminating theatre art. Theatre X's work is characterized by a combination of pseudo-naturalism and an equally self-conscious theatricality involving artifices derived from theatre history, mass culture and the ongoing fruits of interdisciplinary collaborations. It strives to say what is not said in a culture where content decays as words and images multiply.

Theatre X's artistic mission, above all else, is to encourage and provoke the process of thinking for its audiences as well as for itself.

—Wesley Savick, John Schneider

PRODUCTIONS 1989-90

Margery Kempe: The Desire of the Moth for the Star, Deborah Clifton, Flora Coker and Wesley Savick; (D) Wesley Savick; (S) Robert Kushner; (C) Ellen M. Kozak; (L) Andrew Meyers

An Interest in Strangers, John Schneider; (D) Wesley Savick

Success, John Kishline; (D) Mark Anderson; (S) John Starmer; (L) John Starmer

PRODUCTIONS 1990-91

Instinct, book and lyrics: John Schneider; music: Connie Graver; (D) Wesley Savick;

Theatre X. John Schneider and Claire Morkin in *Instinct*. Photo: Fred Fischer.

(S) Scott Schanke; (C) Carrie Skoczek; (L) Andrew Meyers

Margery Kempe: The Desire of the Moth for the Star, Deborah Clifton, Flora Coker and Wesley Savick; (D) Wesley Savick; (S) Robert Kushner; (C) Ellen M. Kozak; (L) Andrew Meyers

Sincerity Forever, Mac Wellman; (D) John Schneider; (S) John Starmer; (C) Carrie Skoczek; (L) John Starmer

The Strength and Indifference of the Snow: The Writings of George F. Kennan, company-developed, from George F. Kennan; (D) Wesley Savick and John Schneider; (S) John Starmer; (C) the company; (L) John Starmer

Theatrical Outfit

PHILLIP DEPOY
Producing Artistic Director

ROBERT HILL
General Manager

Box 7098
Atlanta, GA 30309
(404) 872-0665

FOUNDED 1976
David Head, Sharon Levy

SEASON
Jan.-Dec.

FACILITIES
Mainstage
Seating Capacity: 200
Stage: flexible

FINANCES
July 1, 1990-June 30, 1991
Expenses: $360,000

CONTRACTS
AEA SPT

Theatrical Outfit's mission is to present unique, mostly original works with music for Georgia audiences, with the expectation of national exposure. Many of these new works are musicals; most are interdisciplinary, collaborative efforts with artists from every artistic discipline. Our intimate 200-seat theatre allows for flexibility in audience/performer relationships, and most productions break "the fourth wall." Each show is designed with touring potential, and our curriculum-based School Theatre from the Outfit is designed to be placed in educational institutions statewide. Our Great Writers Series produces one show each season commissioned by the Outfit and based on literature by recognized "great writers," again with national curriculum guidelines in mind. The Outfit also reaches out to other theatres and arts organizations to present co-productions in an effort to vivify, excite, entertain and enlighten the entire human community.

—Phillip DePoy

Note: During the 1989-90 and 1990-91 seasons, Eddie Levi Lee served as artistic director.

PRODUCTIONS 1989-90

Oedipus Rex, book adapt: Phillip DePoy, Eddie Levi Lee and Rebecca Wackler, from Sophocles; music: Phillip DePoy; lyrics: Eddie Levi Lee and Phillip DePoy; (D) Eddie Levi Lee; (S) Jeroy Hannah; (C) Stephanie Kaskel; (L) Hal McCoy

Appalachian Christmas, Phillip DePoy and Eddie Levi Lee; book: Phillip DePoy and Eddie Levi Lee; music and lyrics: Phillip DePoy; (D) Rebecca Wackler; (S) Ken Murray; (L) Hal McCoy

Baby with the Bathwater, Christopher Durang; (D) Eddie Levi Lee; (S) Robert Lott; (C) Stephanie Kaskel; (L) Jeff Nealer

Crossing Delancey, Susan Sandler; (D) Piet R. Knetsch; (S) Dex Edwards; (C) Stephanie Kaskel; (L) Liz Lee

The Mystery of Irma Vep, Charles Ludlam; (D) Eddie Levi Lee; (S) Bruce Starr and Michael Allen; (C) Stephanie Kaskel; (L) Hal McCoy

PRODUCTIONS 1990-91

Steambath, Bruce Jay Friedman; (D) Eddie Levi Lee; (S) Dex Edwards; (C) Stephanie Kaskel; (L) Hal McCoy

Appalachian Christmas, Phillip DePoy and Eddie Levi Lee; book: Phillip DePoy and Eddie Levi Lee; music and lyrics: Phillip DePoy; (D) Rebecca Wackler; (S) Bruce Starr; (L) Hal McCoy

Poe Festival, Phillip DePoy and Jim Grimsley, from Edgar Allan Poe; (D) Bill Yates and Pamela O'Connor; (S) John Ludwig and Stephanie Kaskel; (C) Stephanie Kaskel; (L) Liz Lee

Mandragola, Phillip DePoy and Eddie Levi Lee; book adapt: Phillip DePoy and Eddie Levi Lee, from Machiavelli; music: Phillip DePoy; lyrics: Phillip DePoy and Eddie Levi Lee; (D) Eddie Levi Lee; (S) Rochelle Barker; (C) Therra C. Gwynn; (L) R. Scott Preston

Odd Night in an Odd Place, Phillip DePoy and Eddie Levi Lee; book: Phillip DePoy and Eddie Levi Lee; music and lyrics: Phillip DePoy; (D) Jim Brooks; (S) Michael Allen; (C) Steven Joslin; (L) Hal McCoy

Theatrical Outfit. V. Joy Trimble, Scott DePoy, Eric Stenson and Signe Albertson in *Mandragola*.

Three Rivers Shakespeare Festival

ATTILIO FAVORINI
Producing Director

1617 CL
University of Pittsburgh
Pittsburgh, PA 15260
(412) 624-1953 (bus.)
(412) 624-7529 (b.o.)

FOUNDED 1980
Attilio Favorini

SEASON
May-Aug.

FACILITIES
Stephen Foster Memorial
Seating Capacity: 560
Stage: proscenium

The Pit
Seating Capacity: 115
Stage: flexible

FINANCES
Sept. 30, 1989-Oct. 1, 1990
Expenses: $584,890

CONTRACTS
AEA U/RTA

The mission of Three Rivers Shakespeare Festival is to produce the works generally categorized as "the classics" of world drama, as well as contemporary plays of classical aspiration and scope. In practice, this means we do Shakespeare mostly, but also Ben Johnson, Rostand's *Cyrano*, Shakespeare offshoots and the occasional new adaptation of Feydeau. The U/RTA contract under which we operate permits us to mix Equity actors and student performers, allowing us to fulfill a training mission as well. We also have an ambitious outreach program, which presents Shakespeare adaptations in schools and museums to children as young as kindergarten age. Our approach to the plays is eclectic. Transpositions of time and place are common, as is nontraditional and cross-gender casting. More recently, we have become interested in multicultural performance. In 1992 we will employ a European guest director and also produce a Noh-inspired *Hamlet*-offshoot (*Ophelia*), centered on a Japanese Master Artist.

—*Attilio Favorini*

PRODUCTIONS 1989-90

The Tempest, William Shakespeare; (D) Gillette Elvgren; (S) Henry Heymann; (C) Henry Heymann; (L) William O'Donnell
Richard II, William Shakespeare; (D) W. Stephen Coleman; (S) Robert Cothran; (C) Bill Black; (L) William O'Donnell
As You Like It, William Shakespeare; (D) James J. Christy; (S) Anne Mundell; (C) Lorraine Venberg; (L) William O'Donnell
The Merry Wives of Windsor, William Shakespeare; (D) Jay Scott Chipman; (S) Diane Melchitzky; (L) Jean-Pierre Nutini
Tartuffe, Moliere; (D) David Skeele; (S) Diane Melchitzky; (L) Jean-Pierre Nutini

PRODUCTIONS 1990-91

Othello, William Shakespeare; (D) W. Stephen Coleman; (S) Ellen Seeling; (C) Henry Heymann; (L) William O'Donnell
A Horse of a Different Color, Georges Feydeau; adapt: Ralph G. Allen; (D) Ralph G. Allen; (S) Robert Cothran; (C) Lorraine Venberg; (L) William O'Donnell
The Comedy of Errors, William Shakespeare; (D) James J. Christy; (S) Charles McCarry; (C) Diane Collins; (L) William O'Donnell
Good Night Desdemona (Good Morning Juliet), Ann-Marie MacDonald; (D) Peter Harrigan; (S) Diane Melchitzky; (C) Peter Harrigan and Pidge Meade; (L) Jean-Pierre Nutini
Cymbeline, William Shakespeare; (D) Jay Scott Chipman; (S) Diane Melchitzky; (C) Jay Scott Chipman and Pidge Meade; (L) Jean-Pierre Nutini

Three Rivers Shakespeare Festival. Jonathan Cantor and Mary Stout in *A Horse of a Different Color*. Photo: Sue Ellen Fitzsimmons.

Touchstone Theatre

BRIDGET GEORGE
Producing Director

GARY WEBSTER
Executive Director

321 East 4th St.
Bethlehem, PA 18015
(215) 867-1689

FOUNDED 1981
William George, Bridget George

SEASON
Jan.-Dec.

Touchstone Theatre. *Changes*. Photo: B. Stanley.

FACILITIES
Touchstone Theatre
Seating Capacity: 72
Stage: flexible

FINANCES
Sept. 1, 1990-Aug. 31, 1991
Expenses: $306,878

Touchstone is a theatre home where our resident acting ensemble and visiting artists can generate and develop innovative work in an ongoing dialogue with diverse audiences, and foster international and intercultural collaborations. Our repertoire has a consistently distinctive spirit, yet it utilizes a broad range of styles. Our work has grown from love of the rich beauty found in abstract drama and from a history of 15 years of performing street theatre in Pennsylvania—a form of drama that naturally emphasizes a more visual and presentational style. In one sense, Touchstone is modern folk theatre. We take our role in the community very seriously. The ensemble immerses itself in the tide of Bethlehem's diverse cultural spirit (48 different nationalities represented)—its day-to-day fears, joys, aspirations—and responds with a theatre of inner discovery, hope and revelation. Selected ensemble creations, premiered at Touchstone, join our national touring repertoire.

—*Bridget George*

Note: During the 1989-90 season, William George served as producing director.

PRODUCTIONS 1989-90

The Road Company: ***Echoes & Postcards***, company-developed; (D) Robert H. Leonard
Windowspeak, Daniel Stein; (D) Daniel Stein, with Fred Curchack and Christopher Gibson; (S) Paule Stein; (L) Eric Hager
How Far to Bethlehem?, Bridget George; (D) Jennie Gilrain; (S) Richard Kendrick; (C) Polly Kendrick; (L) Vicki Neal
Figures of Speech: Anerca, company-developed; (D) Philip Arnoult; (L) Stoney Cook
The Luftkugel Association: DaVinci and the New Cadillac, Andre Baer, Ledlie Borgerhoff and Jim Calder; (D) Andre Baer, Ledlie Borgerhoff and Jim Calder
Twelfth Night, adapt: Gary Webster and Eric Beatty, from William Shakespeare; (D) Francoise Marty; (S) Francoise Marty and Tim Frey
Rumpelstiltskin, adapt: Sara Zielinska; (D) Mark McKenna; (S) Jennie Gilrain; (C) Jennie Gilrain

PRODUCTIONS 1990-91

Changes, company-developed; (D) Robert H. Leonard
The Secret Obscenity of Every Day Life, Marco Antonio de la Parra; trans: Charles Philip Thomas; (D) Maria Elena Devauchelle
Contrabass, Patrick Suskind; trans:

Michael Hoffman; (D) Hector Nogeura

The Canterbury Tales, trans: Nevill Coghill; book: Susan Chase, from Geoffrey Chaucer; music and lyrics: Dave Fry; (D) Susan Chase; (S) Neil Hever; (C) Annie-Laurie Wheat

Sandglass Theatre: ***Invitations to Heaven***, Eric Bass, Richard Edelman and Alan Bern; (D) Richard Edelman

The Independent Eye: ***Beside Herself: Pocahontas to Patty Hearst***, adapt: Elizabeth Fuller, from Pamela White-Hadas; (D) Conrad Bishop; (S) Linda Cunningham; (C) P. Chelsea Harriman; (L) Conrad Bishop

Under Milk Wood, Dylan Thomas; (D) Gerard Stropnicky; (S) Sarah Baptist; (C) Kathleen Egan; (L) Tom Sturge

Rootabaga Stories, adapt: William George, from Carl Sandburg; (D) Madelaine Ramsey; (S) Rosemary Geseck; (C) Rosemary Geseck

Trinity Repertory Company

RICHARD JENKINS
Artistic Director

DENNIS E. CONWAY
General Manager

201 Washington St.
Providence, RI 02903
(401) 521-1100 (bus.)
(401) 351-4242 (b.o.)

FOUNDED 1963
Adrian Hall

SEASON
Jan.-Dec.

FACILITIES
Upstairs Theatre
Seating Capacity: 650+
Stage: thrust

Downstairs Theatre
Seating Capacity: 297
Stage: flexible

FINANCES
July 1, 1990-June 30, 1991
Expenses: $3,100,000

CONTRACTS
AEA LORT (B) and (C)

Concluding our 27th season, Trinity Repertory Company has earned recognition for its dedication to a resident company of artists, its vigorous ensemble style of production, its long commitment to the development of original works and adaptations, its daring and innovative treatment of world classics and its fresh approach to traditional material. From the beginning Trinity Rep's two goals have been to provide permanent employment to its resident artists and to engage its audience as participants, rather than spectators, in the theatre experience. The first aim has been supported since we became the first theatre in American history to receive an Ongoing Ensemble grant from the National Endowment for the Arts, enabling us to provide yearly financial security to our artists. The second aim continues to be met with more than 20,000 subscribers supporting the company's invigorating theatrical output. Trinity Rep's award-winning humanities program, with essay booklets and postperformance discussions, and the Project Discovery program continue to develop and enhance the audience's theatre experience.

—Richard Jenkins

Note: During the 1989-90 season, Anne Bogart served as artistic director.

Trinity Repertory Company. Gustave Johnson and Janice Duclos in *The Lower Depths*. Photo: Mark Morelli.

PRODUCTIONS 1989-90

No Plays, No Poetry..., Anne Bogart, from Bertolt Brecht; (D) Anne Bogart

Summerfolk, Maxim Gorky; adapt: Anne Bogart; trans: John Tillinger and Edward Gilbert; (D) Anne Bogart; (S) Victoria Petrovich; (C) William Lane; (L) Rob Murphy

Italian American Reconciliation, John Patrick Shanley; (D) David Wheeler; (S) Rob Murphy; (C) William Lane; (L) John Murphy, Jr.

A Christmas Carol, adapt: Tina Landau and Jeff Halpern, from Charles Dickens; (D) Tina Landau; (S) Jon Hutman; (C) Catherine Zuber; (L) John Murphy, Jr.

And What of the Night?, Maria Irene Fornes; (D) Maria Irene Fornes; (S) John Murphy, Jr.; (C) William Lane; (L) Anne Militello

Julius Caesar, William Shakespeare; (D) Oskar Eustis; (S) Rob Murphy; (C) William Lane; (L) Rob Murphy

The Obscene Bird of Night, Jose Donoso; adapt: Darrah Cloud; (D) Molly D. Smith; (S) John Murphy, Jr.; (C) William Lane; (L) Rob Murphy

Baal, Bertolt Brecht; (D) Robert Woodruff; (S) Douglas Stein; (C) Susan Hilferty; (L) Rob Murphy

Amateurs, Tom Griffin; (D) David Wheeler; (S) Rob Murphy; (C) William Lane; (L) Rob Murphy

On the Town, book and lyrics: Betty Comden and Adolph Green; music: Leonard Bernstein; (D) Anne Bogart and Jeff Halpern; (S) Rob Murphy; (C) Marilyn Salvatore; (L) Carol Mullins

Rebecca, adapt: Tina Landau, from Daphne Du Maurier; (D) Tina Landau; (S) Rob Murphy; (C) William Lane; (L) Rob Murphy

PRODUCTIONS 1990-91

Golden Boy, Clifford Odets; (D) Richard Jenkins; (S) Eugene Lee; (C) William Lane; (L) Eugene Lee

Juno and the Paycock, Sean O'Casey; (D) David Wheeler; (S) Robert D. Soule; (C) William Lane; (L) John F. Custer

A Christmas Carol, adapt: Adrian Hall and Richard Cumming, from Charles Dickens; (D) Adrian Hall; (S) Eugene Lee; (C) William Lane; (L) Eugene Lee

Frankie and Johnny in the Clair de Lune, Terrence McNally; (D) Leonard Foglia; (S) Robert D. Soule; (C) Marilyn Salvatore; (L) John F. Custer

The School for Wives, Moliere; trans: Richard Wilbur; (D) Richard Jenkins; (S) Eugene Lee; (C) William Lane; (L) Natasha Katz

The Water Principle, Eliza Anderson; (D) Judith Swift; (S) David A. Rotondo; (C) Marilyn Salvatore; (L) Jeff Clark

Reckless, Craig Lucas; (D) Leonard Foglia; (S) Robert D. Soule; (C) William Lane; (L) Michael Giannitti

The Lower Depths, Maxim Gorky; trans: Alex Szogyi; (D) Richard Jenkins; (S) Eugene Lee; (C) William Lane; (L) Natasha Katz

The Stick Wife, Darrah Cloud; (D) Lee Shallat; (S) Robert D. Soule; (C) William Lane; (L) John F. Custer

Other People's Money, Jerry Sterner; (D) Richard Jenkins; (S) David A. Rotondo; (C) William Lane; (L) Michael Giannitti

Unicorn Theatre

CYNTHIA LEVIN
Producing Artistic Director

3820 Main St.
Kansas City, MO 64111
(816) 531-3033 (bus.)
(816) 531-7529 (b.o.)

FOUNDED 1973
Liz Gordon, Ronald Dennis, James Cairns

SEASON
Jan.-Dec.

FACILITIES
Unicorn Theatre
Seating Capacity: 150
Stage: thrust

FINANCES
July 1, 1990-June 30, 1991
Expenses: $280,405

CONTRACTS
AEA SPT

The Unicorn Theatre is dedicated to exploring the issues that confront and affect our lives. Racism, terrorism, sexual persecution, mental illness and the AIDS crisis are topics on which the Unicorn has focused in recent productions, reinforcing our commitment to the idea that theatre is a provocative tool used to inspire emotional response, intellectual discussion and even argument within the community. It is the power to incite that keeps us moving forward, testing our artistic boundaries and functioning outside the commercial mainstream. By producing lesser-known plays and playwrights and premiering one previously unproduced play each season, we hope to nurture emerging voices in the American theatre. The strong sense of collaboration felt by the local actors, designers and directors who work here is reflected in the productions themselves. Our audiences' overwhelming response to the plays we produce confirms the need for this type of theatre in Kansas City.

—*Cynthia Levin*

PRODUCTIONS 1989-90

Burn This, Lanford Wilson; (D) Cynthia Levin; (S) Atif Rome; (C) Cheryl Benge; (L) Art Kent
Savage in Limbo, John Patrick Shanley; (D) Cynthia Levin; (S) Atif Rome; (C) Wendy Hardy; (L) Art Kent
Expiring Minds Want to Know or Six Women with Brain Death, Cheryl Benge, Christy Brandt, Rosanna E. Coppedge, Valerie Fagan, Ross Freese, Mark Houston, Sandee Johnson and Peggy Pharr Wilson; (D) Cynthia Levin; (S) Art Kent; (C) Mary Traylor; (L) Art Kent
Ten Below, Shem Bitterman; (D) Beth Leonard; (S) Mimi Hedges; (C) Cheryl Benge; (L) Jay Wilson
Breaking the Code, Hugh Whitemore, from Andrew Hodges; (D) Carol Blitgen; (S) Atif Rome; (C) Mary Traylor; (L) Art Kent
Beirut, Alan Bowne; (D) Cynthia Levin; (S) Art Kent; (C) Cheryl Benge; (L) Art Kent
The Rocky Horror Show, book, music and lyrics: Richard O'Brien; (D) Fred Goodson; (S) Art Kent; (C) Mary Traylor; (L) Randy Winder

PRODUCTIONS 1990-91

Waiting for Godot, Samuel Beckett; (D) Raymond E. Smith; (S) Atif Rome; (C) Kate Crowley; (L) Jay Wilson
Frankie and Johnny in the Clair de Lune, Terrence McNally; (D) Cynthia Levin; (S) Atif Rome; (C) Cheryl Benge; (L) Ruth E. Cain
Living in Exile, adapt: Jon Lipsky, from Homer; (D) Mary G. Guaraldi; (S) Gary Mosby; (C) Rebecca S. Larson; (L) Rob Murphy
Eleemosynary, Lee Blessing; (D) Cynthia Levin; (S) Med Hornecker; (C) Rebecca S. Larson; (L) Art Kent
Reckless, Craig Lucas; (D) Richard Alan Nicholas; (S) Atif Rome; (C) Mary Traylor; (L) Rob Murphy
Speed-the-Plow, David Mamet; (D) Carol Blitgen; (S) Atif Rome; (C) Mary Traylor; (L) Ruth E. Cain

Unicorn Theatre. Geoffrey Beauchamp and Mark Robbins in *Speed-the-Plow*. Photo: Bud Simpson.

Victory Gardens Theater

DENNIS ZACEK
Artistic Director

JOHN P. WALKER
Managing Director

MARCELLE McVAY
Development Director

2257 North Lincoln Ave.
Chicago, IL 60614
(312) 549-5788 (bus.)
(312) 871-3000 (b.o.)

FOUNDED 1974
David Rasche, June Pyskacek, Cecil O'Neal, Mac McGinnes, Roberta Maguire, Stuart Gordon, Cordis Fejer, Warren Casey

SEASON
Sept.-July

FACILITIES
Mainstage
Seating Capacity: 195
Stage: thrust

Studio
Seating Capacity: 60
Stage: proscenium

FINANCES
July 1, 1990-June 30, 1991
Expenses: $1,101,163

CONTRACTS
AEA CAT

Victory Gardens Theater is a not-for-profit professional developmental theatre unique in the city for its commitment to the Chicago artist, with a special emphasis on the playwright. The theatre features a number of basic programs all geared toward connecting playwright and audience. The mainstage series consists of five diverse multiethnic productions, many of which are world premieres. The studio series presents three productions focusing on new work suited to a smaller space. The free Readers Theater series presents works-in-progress on a bimonthly basis. A recently established playwright development fund supports residencies and workshops for Chicago playwrights throughout the year. The training center offers classes in all aspects of theatre and serves more than a thousand students a year. The touring program usually features an abbreviated version of one of the mainstage shows, which is seen by more than 10,000 high school students annually. A number of areas interact to produce the same result—developmental theatre.

—*Dennis Zacek*

PRODUCTIONS 1989-90

Three Ways Home, Casey Kurtti; (D) Sandy Shinner; (S) Linda L. Lane; (C) Glenn Billings; (L) Ellen E. Jones
Beau Jest, James Sherman; (D) Dennis Zacek; (S) Stephen Packard; (C) Jessica Hahn; (L) Larry Schoeneman

Victory Gardens Theater. Daniel Oreskes and Celeste Williams in *Pecong*. Photo: Jennifer Girard.

Diesel Moon, Robert Auletta; (D) James Bohnen; (S) Chuck Drury; (C) Mark-Anthony Summers; (L) Ellen E. Jones
Pecong, Steve Carter; (D) Dennis Zacek; (S) James Dardenne; (C) Claudia Boddy; (L) Robert Shook
The Angels of Warsaw, Marisha Chamberlain; (D) Sandy Shinner; (S) Jeff Bauer; (C) Claudia Boddy; (L) Rita Pietraszek
Scarred Ground, Thomas Cadwaleder Jones; (D) Philip Euling; (S) Linda L. Lane; (C) Lynne Palmer; (L) Ann M. Greenstein
Dear Elena Sergaevna, Lyudmilla Razumovskaya; (D) Svetlana Vragova; (S) Nikita Tkachuk; (C) Nikita Tkachuk; (L) Nikita Tkachuk
Nightside, Philip Reed; (D) Dennis Zacek; (S) Chuck Drury; (C) Glenn Billings; (L) Larry Schoeneman

PRODUCTIONS 1990-91

T Bone N Weasel, Jon Klein; (D) Dennis Zacek; (S) James Dardenne; (C) Claudia Boddy; (L) Todd Hensley
Phantasie, Sybille Pearson; (D) Judy O'Malley; (S) Mark E. Netherland; (C) Daryl A. Stone; (L) Ellen E. Jones
Cane, adapt: Charles Smith, from Jean Toomer; (D) Dennis Zacek; (S) James Dardenne; (C) Claudia Boddy; (L) Michael Rourke
Still Waters, Claudia Allen; (D) Sandy Shinner; (S) Jeff Bauer; (C) Margaret Morettini; (L) Rita Pietraszek
Scorched Earth, John Logan; (D) Dennis Zacek; (S) Chuck Drury; (C) Marsha Kowal; (L) Robert Shook

Vineyard Theatre

DOUGLAS AIBEL
Artistic Director

BARBARA ZINN KRIEGER
Executive Director

JON NAKAGAWA
Managing Director

108 East 15th St.
New York, NY 10003
(212) 353-3366 (bus.)
(212) 353-3874 (b.o.)

FOUNDED 1981
Barbara Zinn Krieger

SEASON
Variable

FACILITIES
Vineyard Theatre at 26th St.
Seating Capacity: 71
Stage: thrust

Dimson Theatre
Seating Capacity: 120
Stage: flexible

FINANCES
Sept. 1, 1990-Aug. 31, 1991
Expenses: $550,000

CONTRACTS
AEA letter of agreement

The Vineyard Theatre, a multiart chamber theatre now entering its second decade, produces new plays and musicals, music-theatre collaborations and revivals of works that have previously failed in the commercial arena. While the range of our programming is eclectic, we've been consistently drawn to writers with a distinctively poetic style and an affinity for adventurous theatrical forms. We hope to produce work that provides our audience with an experience that is at once emotional and visceral, and that gives our artists a true opportunity to collaborate and experiment with their material. Because the company sponsors several music programs, including early music and jazz, we've also attempted to explore different ways in which music can enhance and enrich a dramatic text. The recent opening of our new theatre at Union Square has been the realization of a dream for us, and we look forward to many new creative opportunities there.

—Douglas Aibel

PRODUCTIONS 1989-90

The House of Horror, Paul Zaloom; (D) Paul Zaloom
Feast Here Tonight, book and lyrics: Ken Jenkins and Daniel Jenkins; music: Daniel Jenkins; (D) Gloria Muzio; (S) William Barclay; (C) Jess Goldstein; (L) Phil Monat
Moving Targets, Joe Pintauro; (D) Andre Ernotte; (S) William Barclay; (C) Juliet Polcsa; (L) Phil Monat
Hannah...1939, book, music and lyrics: Bob Merrill; (D) Douglas Aibel; (S) G.W. Mercier; (C) James Scott; (L) Phil Monat
Soulful Scream of a Chosen Son, Ned Eisenberg; (D) June Stein; (S) Stephan Olson; (C) Muriel Stockdale; (L) Phil Monat

PRODUCTIONS 1990-91

Nightingale, Elizabeth Diggs; (D) John Rubinstein; (S) William Barclay; (C) James Scott; (L) Phil Monat
Bodoni County, book and lyrics: Frank Gagliano; music: Claibe

Vineyard Theatre. Lori Wilner, Patti Perkins and Leah Hocking in *Hannah...1939*. Photo: Carol Rosegg.

Richardson; (D) Andre Ernotte; (S) William Barclay; (C) Muriel Stockdale; (L) Robert Jared

The Don Juan and the Non Don Juan, book and lyrics: James Milton and David Goldstein; music: Neil Radisch; (D) Evan Yionoulis; (S) William Barclay; (C) Teresa Snider-Stein; (L) Robert Jared

Food and Shelter, Jane Anderson; (D) Andre Ernotte; (S) Ann Sheffield; (C) Muriel Stockdale; (L) Donald Holder

Virginia Stage Company

Box 3770
Norfolk, VA 23514
(804) 627-6988 (bus.)
(804) 627-1234 (b.o.)

FOUNDED 1979
Community members

SEASON
Oct.-Mar.

FACILITIES
Wells Theatre
Seating Capacity: 677
Stage: proscenium

Second Stage
Seating Capacity: 100
Stage: flexible

FINANCES
July 1, 1990-June 30, 1991
Expenses: $1,372,155

CONTRACTS
AEA LORT (C)

As Virginia Stage Company enters its 13th season it is making a new effort to understand, respond to and communicate with the region it serves. A change in artistic leadership will naturally mean a newly articulated dramaturgical stance which will be developed within the institution's continued commitment to professional standards. The Wells Theatre, VSC's beautifully restored proscenium house, has emerged as one of Norfolk's most prized cultural resources, and establishes the framework for the kind and quality of work produced. A new affiliation with the Governor's Magnet School for the Arts means the development of a long-awaited second stage which can be used by the company as an alternative space. An overwhelming community response to a recent emergency appeal has shown that VSC has built a broad base of support over the years, which will see it through its current economic difficulties and allow it to restore and expand both its efforts and its reach during the coming decade.

Note: During the 1989-90 and 1990-91 seasons, Charles Towers served as artistic director. At press time, the positions of artistic director and managing director were open.

PRODUCTIONS 1989-90

The Road to Mecca, Athol Fugard; (D) Jody McAuliffe; (S) Andrew Jackness; (C) Candice Cain; (L) Nancy Schertler

The Secret Garden, book adapt and lyrics: Marsha Norman, from Frances Hodgson Burnett; music: Lucy Simon; (D) R.J. Cutler; (S) Heidi Landesman; (C) Martin Pakledinaz; (L) Roger Morgan

T Bone N Weasel, Jon Klein; (D) Christopher Hanna; (S) Donald Eastman; (C) Candice Cain; (L) Nancy Schertler

Speed-the-Plow, David Mamet; (D) Charles Towers; (S) Bill Clarke; (C) Candice Cain; (L) Jackie Manassee

Fences, August Wilson; (D) Tazewell Thompson; (S) Donald Eastman; (C) C.L. Hundley; (L) Anne Militello

Fairy Tales of New York, J.P. Donleavy; (D) Charles Towers; (S) Bill Clarke; (C) Candice Cain; (L) Spencer Mosse

PRODUCTIONS 1990-91

Wedding Band, Alice Childress; (D) Charles Towers; (S) Donald Eastman; (C) Candice Cain; (L) Nancy Schertler

The Rainmaker, N. Richard Nash; (D) Christopher Hanna; (S) Michael Miller; (C) Candice Cain; (L) Dan Kotlowitz

Waiting for Godot, Samuel Beckett; (D) Charles Towers; (S) Pavel Dobrusky; (C) Candice Cain; (L) Pavel Dobrusky

Otherwise Engaged, Simon Gray; (D) Jody McAuliffe; (S) Lawrence Casey; (C) Candice Cain; (L) Jackie Manassee

Virginia Stage Company. Kelly Walters and LeLand Gantt in *T Bone N Weasel*. Photo: Mark Atkinson.

Billy Bishop Goes to War, John Gray and Eric Peterson; (D) Dennis Rosa; (S) E. David Cosier, Jr.; (C) Vincent Scassellati; (L) Jeff Davis

White River Theatre Festival

STEPHEN LEGAWIEC
Artistic Director

STEVEN B. LEON
Managing Director

Box 336
White River Junction, VT 05001
(802) 296-2033 (bus.)
(802) 296-2505 (b.o.)

FOUNDED 1988
Stephen Legawiec, Steven B. Leon

SEASON
June-Dec.

FACILITIES
Briggs Opera House
Seating Capacity: 246
Stage: thrust

FINANCES
May 1, 1990-Apr. 30, 1991
Expenses: $286,400

CONTRACTS
AEA SPT

The White River Theatre Festival is the only year-round professional theatre in Vermont. The company is dedicated to presenting a variety of dramatic genres from contemporary, classic and world literature. It has devoted itself to creating theatre pieces which not only entertain but challenge the audience. Its mission is to contribute to the body of world theatre by developing new plays, by offering fresh interpretations of classic plays and by exploring new theatrical conventions.

—Stephen Legawiec

PRODUCTIONS 1990

The School for Wives, Moliere; trans: Donald M. Frame; (D) Stephen Legawiec; (S) Stephen Legawiec; (C) Stephen Legawiec; (L) Steven B. Leon

Born Yesterday, Garson Kanin; (D) Steven B. Leon; (S) Stephen Legawiec; (C) Stephen Legawiec; (L) Steven B. Leon

Journal of the Plague Year, Stephen Legawiec, from Daniel Defoe; (D) Stephen Legawiec; (S) Stephen Legawiec; (C) Stephen Legawiec; (L) Steven B. Leon

Our Town, Thornton Wilder; (D) Michael Friedman; (S) Bob Raiselis; (C) Michael Friedman; (L) Steven B. Leon

Romeo and Juliet, William Shakespeare; (D) Aleksandra Wolska; (S) Stephen Legawiec; (C) Aleksandra Wolska; (L) Steven B. Leon

Give 'em Hell, Harry, Samuel Gallu; (D) Steven B. Leon; (S) Steven B. Leon; (C) Steven B. Leon; (L) Steven B. Leon

The Warrior Queen, book, music and lyrics: Stephen Legawiec;

(D) Stephen Legawiec; (S) Bob Raiselis; (C) Rachel Kurland; (L) Steven B. Leon

Educating Rita, Willy Russell; (D) Sidney Friedman; (S) Bob Raiselis; (C) Stephen Legawiec; (L) Steven B. Leon

Deathtrap, Ira Levin; (D) Steven B. Leon; (S) Bob Raiselis; (C) Steven B. Leon; (L) Steven B. Leon

PRODUCTIONS 1991

Play It Again, Sam, Woody Allen; (D) Steven B. Leon; (S) Bob Raiselis; (C) Steven B. Leon; (L) Steven B. Leon

Speed-the-Plow, David Mamet; (D) Sidney Friedman; (S) Stephen Legawiec; (C) Stephen Legawiec; (L) Steven B. Leon

Jungle of the Cities, Bertolt Brecht; trans: Anselm Hollo; (D) Stephen Legawiec; (S) Stephen Legawiec; (C) Stephen Legawiec; (L) Steven B. Leon

The Alchemist, Ben Jonson; (D) Stephen Legawiec; (S) Bob Raiselis; (C) Stephen Legawiec; (L) Steven B. Leon

Kate Chopin, Stephen Legawiec; (D) Mara Sabinson; (S) Stephen Legawiec; (C) Mara Sabinson; (L) Steven B. Leon

True West, Sam Shepard; (D) Steven B. Leon; (S) Stephen Legawiec; (C) Stephen Legawiec; (L) Steven B. Leon

Private Lives, Noel Coward; (D) Michael Friedman; (S) Bob Raiselis; (L) Steven B. Leon

K2, Patrick Meyers; (D) Steven B. Leon; (S) Stephen Legawiec; (C) Stephen Legawiec; (L) Steven B. Leon

The Mystery of Irma Vep, Charles Ludlam; (D) Steven B. Leon; (S) Ray Rue; (C) Adrian Cedeno; (L) Steven B. Leon

White River Theatre Festival. Nicolette Vajtay and Julia Pearlstein in *Romeo and Juliet*. Photo: Steven Leon.

Williamstown Theatre Festival

PETER HUNT
Artistic/Executive Director

WILLIAM STEWART
Managing Director

Williamstown Theatre Festival. David Huddleston, James Whitmore and Robert Ousley in *Inherit the Wind*. Photo: Richard Feldman.

Box 517
Williamstown, MA 01267
(413) 458-3200 (bus.)
(413) 597-3400 (b.o.)

FOUNDED 1955
Nikos Psacharopoulos, Trustees of the Williamstown Theatre Festival

SEASON
June-Aug.

FACILITIES
Adams Memorial Theatre
Seating Capacity: 521
Stage: proscenium

The Other Stage
Seating Capacity: 96
Stage: thrust

FINANCES
Dec. 1, 1989-Nov. 30, 1990
Expenses: $1,517,284

CONTRACTS
AEA CORST (X) and letter of agreement

The Williamstown Theatre Festival is devoted to the growth of the individual artist. Through productions of classics and epic works on its main stage, new works focusing on the playwright at its Other Stage and adaptations of world literature in its Free Theatre, WTF offers its extended family of actors, directors, designers and writers an array of theatrical challenges rarely available elsewhere. As an educational institution concerned with the future of the theatre, WTF champions intensive programs for interns and apprentices. These involve training and opportunities for constant interaction between talented students and gifted professionals, and the results are both revitalizing and inspirational. WTF dedicates itself to being a haven—a place where artists have done, and will continue to do, their best work.

—*Peter Hunt*

PRODUCTIONS 1990

A Funny Thing Happened on the Way to the Forum, book: Burt Shevelove and Larry Gelbart; music and lyrics: Stephen Sondheim; (D) Peter Hunt; (S) Robert T. Williams; (C) Jess Goldstein; (L) Rui Rita

Harvey, Mary Chase; (D) William Francisco; (S) Hugh Landwehr; (C) David Murin; (L) Rui Rita

The Persecution and Assassination of Jean-Paul Marat as Performed by the Inmates of the Asylum of Charenton under the Direction of the Marquis de Sade, Peter Weiss; adapt: Adrian Mitchell; trans: Geoffrey Skelton; (D) Paul Weidner; (S) Robert Darling; (C) Kenneth Mooney; (L) Thomas R. Skelton

Death Takes a Holiday, Alberto Cassella; adapt: Walter Ferris; (D) Peter Hunt; (S) Hugh Landwehr; (C) David Murin; (L) Arden Fingerhut

A Moon for the Misbegotten, Eugene O'Neill; (D) Kevin Dowling; (S) Jane Musky; (C) Rita B. Watson; (L) Rui Rita

No Orchids for Miss Blandish, adapt: Robert David MacDonald, from James Hadley Chase; (D) Rosey Hay; (S) Craig Clipper; (C) Eric Hansen; (L) Christina Giannelli
The Baby Dance, Jane Anderson; (D) Jenny Sullivan; (S) Dutch Fritz, adapt from: Deborah Raymond and Dorian Vernacchio; (L) Betsy Finston
Carthaginians, Frank McGuinness; (D) Rosey Hay; (S) Barbara Cohig; (C) Steffani Compton; (L) Betsy Finston
The Adventures of Huckleberry Finn, adapt: Steve Lawson, from Mark Twain; (D) Kevin Kelley; (S) Michael Dempsey; (C) Rita B. Watson

PRODUCTIONS 1991

1776, book: Peter Stone; music and lyrics: Sherman Edwards; (D) Peter Hunt; (S) John Doepp, adapt from: Jo Mielziner; (C) Jeanne Button; (L) Peter Hunt
Picnic, William Inge; (D) Kevin Dowling; (S) John Doepp; (C) Therese A. Bruck; (L) Rui Rita
Inherit the Wind, Jerome Lawrence and Robert E. Lee; (D) Peter Hunt; (S) Hugh Landwehr; (C) Jess Goldstein; (L) Thomas R. Skelton
Speed-the-Plow, David Mamet; (D) John Badham; (S) Robert Darling; (C) Rita B. Watson; (L) Rui Rita
Booth Is Back, Austin Pendleton; (D) Arvin Brown; (S) John Lee Beatty; (C) Jess Goldstein; (L) Rui Rita
Defying Gravity, Jane Anderson; (D) Jenny Sullivan; (S) Hugh Landwehr; (C) David Murin; (L) Arden Fingerhut
Ad Wars, Vince McKewin; (D) Gordon Hunt; (S) Emily Beck; (C) Robin J. Orloff; (L) Betsy Finston
Man in His Underwear, Jay Tarses; (D) Paul Benedict; (S) Barbara Cohig; (C) Deborah A. Brothers; (L) Betsy Finston
Straight Arrows, Colleen Dodson; (D) John Monteith; (S) Jana Bialon; (L) Betsy Finston
Stand-up Opera, B.J. Ward; (D) Gordon Hunt; (S) Sherri Adler; (L) Betsy Finston
The Moonstone, adapt: Steve Lawson, from Wilkie Collins; (D) Neel Keller; (S) Barbara Cohig; (C) Therese A. Bruck; (L) Benjamin Pearcy

The Wilma Theater

BLANKA ZIZKA
JIRI ZIZKA
Artistic/Producing Directors

W. COURTENAY WILSON
Managing Director

2030 Sansom St.
Philadephia, PA 19103
(215) 963-0249 (bus.)
(215) 963-0345 (b.o.)

FOUNDED 1973
Liz Stout, Linda Griffith

SEASON
Sept.-June

FACILITIES
The Wilma Theater
Seating Capacity: 106
Stage: proscenium

FINANCES
Sept. 1, 1990-Aug. 31, 1991
Expenses: $974,660

CONTRACTS
AEA letter of agreement

The Wilma Theater presents theatre as an art form that engages both audience and artists in an adventure of aesthetic and philosophical reflection on the complexities of contemporary life. We believe that a fine performance of a great play is one of the most rewarding experiences our culture provides. The Wilma relies on the selection of powerful, compelling scripts, to which mixed media add another dimension, allowing each production to evolve beyond the confines of verbal communication into the world of metaphor and poetic vision. Our productions are a synthesis of many artistic disciplines—visual arts, music, choreography, writing, acting; our challenge lies in finding new connections among these disciplines to illuminate the dramatic essence of the script. Our staging utilizes a succession of impermanent images, cinematic and three-dimensional, to heighten the inner emotional realities of the characters and create a unique scenic rhythm that captures our age of constant speed, surprise and visual stimulation.

—Blanka Zizka, Jiri Zizka

PRODUCTIONS 1989-90

The Road to Mecca, Athol Fugard; (D) Kent Paul; (S) Tim Saternow; (C) Tim Saternow; (L) Jerold Forsyth
On the Verge, Eric Overmyer; (D) Jiri Zizka; (S) Andrei Efremoff; (C) Hiroshi Iwasaki; (L) Jerold Forsyth
Alfred & Victoria: A Life, Donald Freed; (D) Blanka Zizka; (S) Andrei Efremoff; (C) Maxine Hartswick; (L) Jerold Forsyth
Santiago, Manuel Pereiras Garcia; (D) Robert Fuhrmann; (S) Kevin Joseph Roach; (C) Maxine Hartswick; (L) Jerold Forsyth

PRODUCTIONS 1990-91

The Puppetmaster of Lodz, Gilles Segal; trans: Sara O'Connor; (D) Paul Berman; (S) Andrei Efremoff; (C) Maxine Hartswick; (L) Jerold Forsyth
The President, Thomas Bernhard; trans: Gitta Honegger; (D) Blanka Zizka; (S) Andrei Efremoff; (C) Maxine Hartswick; (L) Jerold Forsyth
Loot, Joe Orton; (D) Jiri Zizka; (S) Anne C. Patterson; (C) Hiroshi Iwasaki; (L) Jerold Forsyth
Three Poets, Romulus Linney; (D) Blanka Zizka; (S) Anne C. Patterson; (C) Anne C. Patterson; (L) Jerold Forsyth

Wisdom Bridge Theatre

JEFFREY ORTMANN
Producing Director

1559 West Howard St.
Chicago, IL 60626
(312) 743-0486 (bus.)
(312) 743-6000 (b.o.)

FOUNDED 1974
David Beaird

SEASON
Sept.-July

The Wilma Theater. Derek Meader and Bonnie Burgess in *Three Poets*. Photo: Arturo Castillo.

FACILITIES
Wisdom Bridge Theatre
Seating Capacity: 196
Stage: proscenium

FINANCES
Aug. 1, 1989-July 31, 1990
Expenses: $1,314,545

CONTRACTS
AEA CAT

Wisdom Bridge Theatre is located on the northernmost edge of Chicago in a second-story loft space. The theatre was named after a painting entitled "The Wisdom Bridge," subtitled "The Bridge to Wisdom lies in the continual asking of questions." The work of the theatre focuses on plays which ask large questions about society, art and the political system, by producing both new works and innovative interpretations of classics. In addition to WBT's main emphasis on producing plays on Howard Street, the theatre also plays a significant role in the community in which it is located. WBT has a nationally recognized outreach program that works with local primary and secondary schools, senior centers, social service agencies, restaurants, the neighborhood (economic) development corporation and community groups. WBT has also toured productions nationally and abroad.

—Jeffrey Ortmann

PRODUCTIONS 1989-90

Lady Day at Emerson's Bar and Grill, Lanie Robertson; (D) Arnold Mittelman; (S) Rob Hamilton; (L) Kevin Rigdon

Forever Plaid, Stuart Ross; (D) Jeffrey Ortmann; (S) Kevin Rigdon; (C) Renee Liepins; (L) Kevin Rigdon

The Peace of Brest-Litovsk, Mikhail Shatrov; (D) Robert Sturua; (S) George Meskhishvili; (C) Marina Chernyakhovskaya; (L) Vladimir Amelin

Soft Remembrance, Sol Saks; (D) Arnie Saks; (S) Michael S. Philippi; (C) Lynn Sandberg; (L) Michael S. Philippi

PRODUCTIONS 1990-91

Straight Arrows, Colleen Dodson; (D) Tom Mula; (S) John Murbach; (L) Michael Rourke

Only Kidding, Jim Geoghan; (D) Terry McCabe; (S) James M. Yates; (C) Sara Davidson; (L) David Gipson

The Great Gatsby, adapt: John Carlile, from F. Scott Fitzgerald; (D) John Carlile; (S) John Murbach; (C) Claudia Boddy; (L) Peter Gottlieb

Rollin' with Stevens and Stewart, adapt: Ronald "Smokey" Stevens and Jaye Stewart, from various authors; (D) Ronald "Smokey" Stevens and Jaye Stewart; (S) John Murbach; (C) Claudia Boddy; (L) Tom Fleming

Wisdom Bridge Theatre. Eddie Jemison, Bob Kohut and Gus Buktenica in *Only Kidding*. Photo: Roger Lewin.

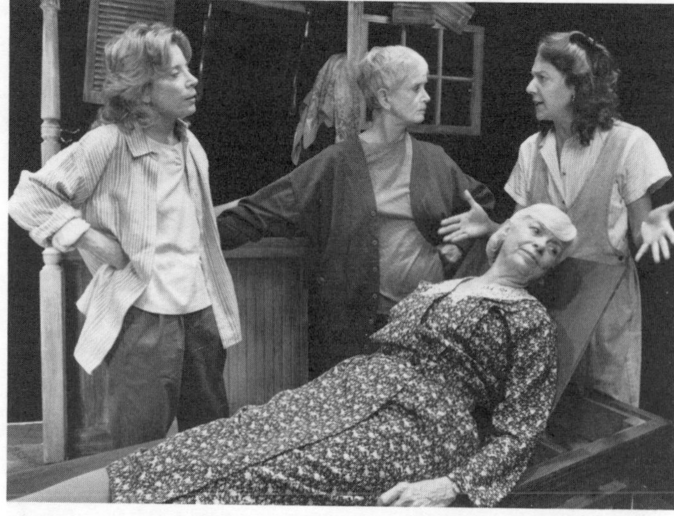

The Women's Project and Productions. Linda Atkinson, Barbara Barrie, Beth Dixon and Helen Stenborg in *Daytrips*. Photo: Martha Holmes.

The Women's Project and Productions

JULIA MILES
Artistic Director

7 West 63rd St.
New York, NY 10023
(212) 873-3040 (bus.)
(212) 873-3767 (b.o.)

FOUNDED 1978
Julia Miles

SEASON
Oct.-May

FACILITIES
Judith Anderson
Seating Capacity: 99
Stage: proscenium

FINANCES
July 1, 1990-June 30, 1991
Expenses: $620,029

CONTRACTS
AEA Mini

I founded the Women's Project with one goal—to bring women to the forefront of the American theatre. Through a variety of innovative programs, including high-quality professional productions, Next Stage work-in-progress productions, rehearsed readings, the Directors' Forum, Departures, Southern Exposure and an active advocacy program, the Women's Project creates a supportive environment in which women can experiment, exchange ideas and see their work expertly brought to the stage. The Women's Project currently has 300 member artists, has produced 58 new plays, has edited four play anthologies and has helped to develop literally hundreds of new plays by women. The Women's Project exists to foster and give equal acceptance to women of all cultures who choose theatre as their means of communicating and interpreting the world—for, by their choice, these women artists contribute to the theatre and to society.

—Julia Miles

PRODUCTIONS 1989-90

Mill Fire, Sally Nemeth; (D) David Petrarca; (S) Linda Buchanan; (C) Robert Christen; (L) Laura Cunningham

Violent Peace, Lavonne Mueller; (D) Bryna Wortman; (S) James Noone; (C) Mimi Maxmen; (L) Victor En Yu Tan

Tales of the Lost Formicans, Constance Congdon; (D) Gordon Edelstein; (S) James Youmans; (C) Danielle Hollywood; (L) Anne Militello

The House That Goes On Forever, Gretchen Cryer; songs: Gretchen Cryer, John Dumke and Nancy Ford; (D) Andre Ernotte

Dream of a Common Language, Heather McDonald; (D) Liz Diamond

PRODUCTIONS 1990-91

Daytrips, Jo Carson; (D) Billie Allen; (S) James Noone; (C) Barbara Beccio; (L) Anne Militello

The Encanto File and other short plays, Rosa Lowinger, Marlane Meyer, Sally Nemeth, Mary Sue Price and Caridad Svich; (D) Melia Bensussen, Melanie Joseph and Susana Tubert; (S) Mark Fitzgibbons; (C) Barbara Beccio; (L) Franklin Meissner, Jr.

Night Sky, Susan Yankowitz; (D) Joseph Chaikin; (S) George Xenos; (C) Mary Brecht; (L) Beverly Emmons

Maggie and Misha, Gail Sheehy; (D) Julianne Boyd; (S) James Noone; (L) Andria Fiegel

The Wooster Group

ELIZABETH LECOMPTE, WILLEM DAFOE, SPALDING GRAY, JIM CLAYBURGH, PEYTON SMITH, KATE VALK, RON VAWTER
Artistic Directors

CYNTHIA HEDSTROM
Producing Director

Box 654, Canal St. Station
New York, NY 10013
(212) 966-9796 (bus.)
(212) 966-3651 (b.o.)

FOUNDED 1975

SEASON
Variable

FACILITIES
The Performing Garage
Seating Capacity: 200
Stage: flexible

FINANCES
July 1, 1989-June 30, 1990
Expenses: $591,000

The Wooster Group has worked together for more than 15 years producing original theatre and media pieces. Wooster Group productions are composed by the Group and directed by Elizabeth LeCompte. The Group's theatre works join an ongoing repertoire and are periodically revived in conjunction with new work. All the work is created and produced at the group's permanent theatre space, the Performing Garage, a space that is collectively owned and operated by the group. The company's season is flexible, and the group regularly tours throughout Europe and the United States.

—The Wooster Group

PRODUCTIONS 1989-90

Frank Dell's The Temptation of Saint Antony, company-developed, from Gustave Flaubert, et al; (D) Elizabeth LeCompte; (S) Jim Clayburgh

Brace Up!, adapt: the company, from Anton Chekhov; trans: Paul Schmidt; (D) Elizabeth LeCompte

PRODUCTIONS 1990-91

Brace Up!, adapt: the company, from Anton Chekhov; trans: Paul Schmidt; (D) Elizabeth LeCompte

The Wooster Group. Willem Dafoe, Kate Valk and Jeff Webster in *Brace Up!* Photo: Mary Gearhart.

Worcester Foothills Theatre Company

MARC P. SMITH
Executive Producer/Artistic Director

GREG DEJARNETT
General Manager

074 Worcester Center
100 Front St.
Worcester, MA 01608
(508) 754-3314 (bus.)
(508) 754-4018 (b.o.)

FOUNDED 1974
Marc P. Smith

SEASON
Oct.-May

FACILITIES
Foothills Theatre
Seating Capacity: 349
Stage: proscenium

FINANCES
June 1, 1990-May 31, 1991
Expenses: $980,200

CONTRACTS
AEA letter of agreement

I think of artistic success when I see people from all parts of our diverse community gather together in our theatre. To me, they are doing something much more than "seeing" a play. They are *considering* all the elements that go into any production: the ideas, the plot, the characters, the sets, costumes, lights, props, sound, etc. More and more of our audience members have become "repeat business," and they are becoming educated in the complexities of this very human endeavor we call theatre. As this happens they realize their own importance as an audience that participates in creating a dynamic dialogue between a community and its artists. Of course, people then talk to others about what they've experienced. How many more people are then affected by what happens in our theatre? This multiplication will only happen over a period of time if people care. And that brings us round robin. I think of artistic success as presenting a program of what a community truly cares about.

—Marc P. Smith

PRODUCTIONS 1989-90

The Nerd, Larry Shue; (D) Michael Allosso; (S) Edwin Chapin; (C) Bradford Wood and Gregory Poplyk; (L) Karen Perlow

Mass Appeal, Bill C. Davis; (D) Thomas Ouellette; (S) Don Ricklin and Catherine Gruetzke; (C) Bradford Wood and Gregory Poplyk; (L) Karen Perlow

Viva Vaudeville, adapt: Marc P. Smith; various lyricists; (D) Marc P. Smith; (S) Edwin Chapin; (C) Bradford Wood and Gregory Poplyk; (L) Karen Perlow

Ten Little Indians, Agatha Christie; (D) Jack Magune; (S) Edwin Chapin; (C) Bradford Wood and Gregory Poplyk; (L) Karen Perlow

Children of a Lesser God, Mark Medoff; (D) James C. Nicola; (S) Edwin Chapin; (C) Bradford Wood and Gregory Poplyk; (L) Karen Perlow

Crossing Delancey, Susan Sandler; (D) Howard Rossen; (S) Lino Toyos; (C) Bradford Wood and Gregory Poplyk; (L) Karen Perlow

Little Shop of Horrors, book and lyrics: Howard Ashman; music: Alan Menken; (D) Harland Meltzer; (S) Edwin Chapin; (C) Bradford Wood and Gregory Poplyk; (L) Karen Perlow

PRODUCTIONS 1990-91

Ain't Misbehavin', conceived: Murray Horwitz and Richard Maltby, Jr.; music and lyrics: Fats Waller, et al; (D) Doug Landrum; (S) Edwin Chapin; (C) Kent Streed; (L) Karen Perlow

The Importance of Being Earnest, Oscar Wilde; (D) Howard Rossen; (S) Edwin Chapin; (C) Kent Streed; (L) Karen Perlow

My Three Angels, Samuel Spewack and Bella Spewack; (D) Thomas Ouellette; (S) Edwin Chapin; (C) Kent Streed; (L) Karen Perlow

Driving Miss Daisy, Alfred Uhry; (D) Jack Magune; (S) Edwin Chapin; (C) Kent Streed; (L) Karen Perlow

Rashomon, Fay Kanin and Michael Kanin; (D) Marc P. Smith; (S) Edwin Chapin; (C) Kent Streed; (L) Karen Perlow

Worcester Foothills Theatre Company. Frank T. Wells in *Mass Appeal.* Photo: Patrick O'Connor.

The Dining Room, A.R. Gurney, Jr.; (D) Michael G. Dell'Orto; (S) Edwin Chapin; (C) Kent Streed; (L) Karen Perlow

A Day in Hollywood/A Night in the Ukraine, book and lyrics: Dick Vosburgh; music: Frank Lazarus; (D) Jim L'Ecuyer; (S) Edwin Chapin; (C) Kent Streed; (L) Karen Perlow

Yale Repertory Theatre

STAN WOJEWODSKI, JR.
Artistic Director

BENJAMIN MORDECAI
Managing Director

Box 1903A Yale Station
222 York St.
New Haven, CT 06520
(203) 432-1515 (bus.)
(203) 432-1234 (b.o.)

FOUNDED 1966
Robert Brustein

SEASON
Oct.-May

FACILITIES
Yale Repertory Theatre
Seating Capacity: 489
Stage: thrust

University Theatre
Seating Capacity: 656
Stage: proscenium

FINANCES
July 1, 1989-June 30, 1990
Expenses: $3,118,520

CONTRACTS
AEA LORT (C)

As the new artistic director/dean of the Yale Repertory Theatre/Yale School of Drama, I will seek a seamless horizon in which the rhythm of artistry becomes the dominant influence on cycles of planning and production. This requires a theatre always teeming with ideas, the ripest and readiest of which can then be born to the public view as their own internal logic dictates. Such a vision mandates that the institution become, in fact, a patron of the individual artist. In the consortium of theatre and school at Yale, we have a tangible head start toward the realization of this ideal. The classical repertoire is juxtaposed, as stimulus and target for aspiration, with new writing for the stage to provide an environment in which theatre professionals and conservatory students become engaged in the exchange of ideas vital to the creation of new works of art.

—Stan Wojewodski, Jr.

Note: During the 1989-90 and 1990-91 seasons, Lloyd Richards served as artistic director.

PRODUCTIONS 1989-90

The Solid Gold Cadillac, George S. Kaufman and Howard Teichmann; (D) Gitta Honegger; (S) Ed Check; (C) James A. Schuette; (L) Jennifer Tipton

Miss Julie, August Strindberg; trans: Elizabeth Sprigge; (D) Dennis Scott; (S) Michael Yeargan; (C) Nephelie Andonyadis; (L) Ashley York Kennedy

Summer and Smoke, Tennessee Williams; (D) James Simpson; (S) Sarah Lambert; (C) Melina Root; (L) Scott Zielinski

Daylight in Exile, James D'Entremont; (D) Amy Saltz; (S) Barbra Kravitz; (C) Suzanne Jackson; (L) Ashley York Kennedy

Rust and Ruin, William Snowden; (D) Walton Jones; (S) Michael Loui; (C) Helen C. Ju; (L) Robert F. Campbell

Pill Hill, Samuel L. Kelley; (D) Walter Dallas; (S) Nephelie Andonyadis; (C) Chrisi Karvonides; (L) Ashley York Kennedy

Dinosaurs, Doug Wright; (D) Rob Barron; (S) Ed Check; (C) Tony Fanning; (L) Mark McCullough

Troilus and Cressida, William Shakespeare; (D) Andrei Belgrader; (S) Anita Stewart; (C) Constanza Romero; (L) Christopher Akerlind

Two Trains Running, August Wilson; (D) Lloyd Richards; (S) Tony Fanning; (C) Chrisi Karvonides; (L) Geoff Korf

Pygmalion, George Bernard Shaw; (D) Douglas C. Wager; (S) Michael Yeargan; (C) Barbra Kravitz; (L) Mark McCullough

PRODUCTIONS 1990-91

Ivanov, Anton Chekhov; adapt: Oleg Yefremov; trans: Robert W. Corrigan; (D) Oleg Yefremov; (S) David Borovsky; (C) Jess Goldstein; (L) Geoff Korf

Largo Desolato, Vaclav Havel; trans: Tom Stoppard; (D) Gitta Honegger; (S) Allison Koturbash;

Yale Repertory Theatre. Jan Triska in *Largo Desolato*. Photo: Gerry Goodstein.

(C) Elizabeth Hope Clancy; (L) Mark McCullough

Search and Destroy, Howard Korder; (D) David Chambers; (S) Christopher Barreca; (C) Dunya Ramicova; (L) Chris Parry

Bricklayers, Elvira J. DiPaolo; (D) Walter Dallas; (S) Michael Yeargan; (C) Susan Branch; (L) Mark McCullough

Ties That Bind, Walter Allen Bennett, Jr.; (D) Jordan Corngold; (S) Debra Booth; (C) Jess Goldstein; (L) Karen TenEyck

Ohio State Murders, Adrienne Kennedy; (D) Gerald Freedman; (S) Tom Broecker; (C) Tom Broecker; (L) Mark McCullough

The Size of the World, Charles Evered; (D) Walton Jones; (S) Elizabeth Hope Clancy; (C) Helen C. Ju; (L) Rick Martin

Underground, Joshua Sobol; adapt: Ron Jenkins; (D) Adrian Hall; (S) Andrew W. Boughton; (C) Azan Kung; (L) Glen Fasman

Scapin, Moliere; adapt and trans: Shelley Berc and Andrei Belgrader; (D) Andrei Belgrader; (S) Karen TenEyck; (C) B. Christine McDowell; (L) Rick Martin

A Moon for the Misbegotten, Eugene O'Neill; (D) Lloyd Richards; (S) Debra Booth; (C) Helen C. Ju; (L) Jennifer Tipton

Young Playwrights Festival

NANCY QUINN
Producing Director

SHERI GOLDHIRSCH
Managing Director

321 West 44th St.
#906, New York, NY 10036
(212) 307-1140

FOUNDED 1982
Stephen Sondheim, Ruth Goetz, Jules Feiffer, Eve Merriam, Murray Horwitz, Mary Rodgers, Richard Wesley

SEASON
Sept.-Oct.

FACILITIES
Playwrights Horizons Mainstage
Seating Capacity: 147
Stage: proscenium

FINANCES
Oct. 1, 1989-Sept. 30, 1990
Expenses: $615,377

CONTRACTS
AEA Off Broadway

The Young Playwrights Festival develops new generations of talented writers for the theatre by involving them as active participants in professional productions of their plays. YPF alumni have already made a major contribution to the theatre; 86 percent of the playwrights who participated in the festival's first nine seasons (all under the age of 19 when we produced their plays) have continued to write successfully for the theatre as well as for film and television. YPF has been the recipient of the Jujamcyn award, an Obie award, the Alliance for the Arts Schools and Culture award, the Margo Jones award and seven Oppenheimer-Newsday playwriting awards. YPF is committed to making the arts an integral part of basic education through in-school playwriting workshops, teacher training institutes, school tours and student matinees. We believe that talent has no age, no color, no gender, and that theatre must reflect and honor the diversity of the world we live in.

—*Nancy Quinn*

PRODUCTIONS 1989-90

Painted Rain, Janet Allard; (D) Mary B. Robinson; (S) Allen Moyer; (C) Jess Goldstein; (L) Karl E. Haas

Finnegan's Funeral Parlor and Ice Cream Shoppe, Robert Kerr; (D) Thomas Babe; (S) Allen Moyer; (C) Jess Goldstein; (L) Karl E. Haas

Twice Shy, Debra Neff; (D) Mark Brokaw; (S) Allen Moyer; (C) Jess Goldstein; (L) Karl E. Haas

Peter Breaks Through, Alejandro Membreno; (D) Thomas Babe; (S) Allen Moyer; (C) Jess Goldstein; (L) Karl E. Haas

PRODUCTIONS 1990-91

Mutterschaft, Gregory Clayman; (D) Michael Mayer; (S) Allen Moyer; (C) Claudia Stephens; (L) Pat Dignan

Believing, Allison Birch; (D) Clinton Turner Davis; (S) Allen Moyer; (C) Claudia Stephens; (L) Pat Dignan

Psychoneurotic Phantasies, Gilbert David Feke; (D) Gloria Muzio; (S) Allen Moyer; (C) Claudia Stephens; (L) Pat Dignan

Hey Little Walter, Carla D. Alleyne; (D) Mark Brokaw; (S) Allen Moyer; (C) Claudia Stephens; (L) Pat Dignan

Young Playwrights Festival. Kimble Joyner and Christopher Shaw in *Painted Rain*. Photo: Tess Steinkolk.

THEATRE CHRONOLOGY

The following is a chronological list of founding dates for the theatres included in this book. Years refer to dates of the first public performance or, in a few cases, the company's formal incorporation.

1915
The Cleveland Play House

1923
Players Theatre Columbus

1925
Goodman Theatre

1928
Berkshire Theatre Festival

1933
Barter Theatre

1935
Oregon Shakespeare Festival

1937
Old Globe Theatre

1942
Sacramento Theatre Company

1946
Stage One: The Louisville Children's Theatre

1947
Alley Theatre
La Jolla Playhouse

1949
Emmy Gifford Children's Theater
New Dramatists

1950
Arena Stage

1954
Milwaukee Repertory Theater
New York Shakespeare Festival
TheatreVirginia

1955
Court Theatre
Honolulu Theatre for Youth
Williamstown Theatre Festival

1956
Academy Theatre
Philadelphia Drama Guild

1957
Detroit Repertory Theatre

1959
Dallas Theater Center
Society Hill Playhouse

1960
Asolo Center for the Performing Arts
Cincinnati Playhouse in the Park

1961
The Children's Theatre Company
Theatreworks/USA

1962
Great Lakes Theater Festival
Pioneer Theatre Company

1963
The American Place Theatre
The Arkansas Arts Center Children's Theatre
Center Stage
Fulton Opera House
Goodspeed Opera House
The Guthrie Theater
New Jersey Shakespeare Festival
Periwinkle National Theatre for Young Audiences
Seattle Repertory Theatre
Trinity Repertory Company

1964
Actors Theatre of Louisville
Hartford Stage Company
Mill Mountain Theatre
Missouri Repertory Theatre
PCPA Theaterfest
South Coast Repertory

1965
A Contemporary Theatre
American Conservatory Theater
Cumberland County Playhouse
East West Players
El Teatro Campesino
Long Wharf Theatre
Roundabout Theatre Company
Studio Arena Theatre

1966
The Body Politic Theatre
INTAR Hispanic American Arts Center
Living Stage Theatre Company
Marin Theatre Company
New Stage Theatre
The Repertory Theatre of St. Louis
Yale Repertory Theatre

1967
Arizona Theatre Company
CSC Repertory Ltd.-The Classic Stage Company
Magic Theatre
Mark Taper Forum
Meadow Brook Theatre
StageWest

1968
Alliance Theatre Company
Berkeley Repertory Theatre
Ford's Theatre
Omaha Magic Theatre
Ontological-Hysteric Theater
Playhouse on the Square
Repertorio Español

1969
Circle Repertory Company
Free Street Theater
Madison Repertory Theatre
Odyssey Theatre Ensemble
Organic Theater Company
The Shakespeare Theatre at the Folger
Theatre X

1970
American Theatre Company
BoarsHead: Michigan Public Theater
The Empty Space Theatre
Mabou Mines
Manhattan Theatre Club
New Federal Theatre
The Salt Lake Acting Company
The Street Theater
The Theater at Monmouth
TheatreWorks

1971
Baltimore Theatre Project
The Cricket Theatre
Dell'Arte Players Company
Ensemble Studio Theatre
Jean Cocteau Repertory
Music-Theatre Group
The Old Creamery Theatre Company
The Playwrights' Center
Playwrights Horizons
Theater for the New City

1972
The Acting Company
Alabama Shakespeare Festival
Eureka Theatre Company
GeVa Theatre
Indiana Repertory Theatre
Intiman Theatre Company
McCarter Theatre Center for the Performing Arts
New American Theater
The Open Eye: New Stagings

1973
Bilingual Foundation of the Arts
City Theatre Company
Florida Studio Theatre
Hippodrome State Theatre
Milwaukee Public Theatre
Unicorn Theatre
The Wilma Theater

1974
California Shakespeare Festival
The CAST Theatre
Clarence Brown Theatre Company
George Street Playhouse
Germinal Stage Denver
Illusion Theater
The Independent Eye
Jewish Repertory Theatre
L. A. Theatre Works
Northlight Theatre
Oakland Ensemble Theatre
The People's Light and Theatre Company
The Philadelphia Theatre Company
Portland Stage Company
Roadside Theater
Syracuse Stage
Victory Gardens Theater
Wisdom Bridge Theatre
Worcester Foothills Theatre Company

1975
American Stage Festival
Attic Theatre
Caldwell Theatre Company
Ping Chong and Company
Pittsburgh Public Theater
The Road Company
Seattle Children's Theatre
Theatre IV
The Wooster Group

1976
American Theatre Works
Arkansas Repertory Theatre
ArtReach Touring Theatre
California Theatre Center
Illinois Theatre Center
Mixed Blood Theatre Company
Nebraska Theatre Caravan
New York State Theatre Institute
The Penumbra Theatre Company
PlayMakers Repertory Company
San Diego Repertory Theatre
Steppenwolf Theatre Company
St. Louis Black Repertory Company
Theatrical Outfit

1977
Childsplay, Inc.
Horse Cave Theatre
Pan Asian Repertory Theatre
Pennsylvania Stage Company
Source Theatre Company
Theatre Rhinoceros

1978
A Traveling Jewish Theatre
Bloomsburg Theatre Ensemble
Crossroads Theatre Company
Great American History Theatre
Jomandi Productions, Inc.
Lamb's Players Theatre
Pegasus Players
Round House Theatre
Seattle Group Theatre
Stages Repertory Theatre
The Studio Theatre
Tacoma Actors Guild
Theatre de la Jeune Lune
The Women's Project and Productions

1979
American Repertory Theatre
American Stage
Child's Play Touring Theatre
The Coterie
Delaware Theatre Company
Gloucester Stage Company
Grove Shakespeare Festival
Merrimack Repertory Theatre
New York Theatre Workshop
Perseverance Theatre
Remains Theatre
River Arts Repertory
Second Stage Theatre
Seven Stages
Stage West
Theatre for a New Audience
Virginia Stage Company

1980
The Bathhouse Theatre
Capital Repertory Company
Denver Center Theatre Company
Portland Repertory Theater
San Jose Repertory Theatre
Three Rivers Shakespeare Festival

1981
Philadelphia Festival Theatre for New Plays
Touchstone Theatre
Vineyard Theatre

1982
Blackfriars Theatre
Huntington Theatre Company
Live Oak Theatre
Theatre in the Square
Young Playwrights Festival

1983
Irondale Ensemble Project
New Mexico Repertory Theatre

1984
Boston Post Road Stage Company
Center Theater
New Repertory Theatre, Inc.
Snowmass/Aspen Repertory Theatre

1985
Lincoln Center Theater
Los Angeles Theatre Center
Riverside Theatre
Tennessee Repertory Theatre

1986
Cornerstone Theater Company
National Jewish Theater

1987
Bristol Riverside Theatre
First Stage Milwaukee
Shakespeare Repertory
The Theatre Club of the Palm Beaches

1988
Arden Theatre Company
White River Theatre Festival

REGIONAL INDEX

NORTH CAROLINA

OHIO

OKLAHOMA

OREGON

PENNSYLVANIA

RHODE ISLAND

TENNESSEE

TEXAS

UTAH

VERMONT

VIRGINIA

WASHINGTON

WISCONSIN

INDEX OF NAMES

A

B

C

D

E

F

G

H

I

J

K

L

N

O

P

Q

R

S

T

U

V

W

INDEX OF TITLES

C

D

N

O

P

Q

R

S

T

U

ABOUT TCG

Theatre Communications Group is the national organization for the nonprofit professional theatre. Since its founding in 1961, TCG has developed a unique and comprehensive support system that addresses the artistic and management concerns of theatres, as well as institutionally based and freelance artists nationwide.

TCG provides a national forum and communications network for a field that is as aesthetically diverse as it is geographically widespread. Its goals are to foster the cross-fertilization of ideas among the individuals and institutions comprising the profession; to improve the artistic and administrative capabilities of the field; to enhance the visibility and demonstrate the achievements of American theatres and theatre artists by increasing public awareness of the theatre's role in society; and to encourage the development of a mutually supportive network of professional companies and artists that collectively represent our "national theatre."

TCG's centralized services and programs facilitate the work of thousands of actors, artistic and managing directors, playwrights, literary managers, directors, designers, trustees and administrative personnel, as well as a constituency of more than 300 theatre institutions across the country that present performances to a combined annual attendance of nearly 19 million people.

THEATRE COMMUNICATIONS GROUP, INC.

Peter Zeisler, Executive Director
Lindy Zesch, Deputy Director
Karen Byers, Managing Director

Board of Directors